Prentice Hall Series in Accounting
CHARLES T. HORNGREN, Editor

KU-661-686

AUDITING: AN INTEGRATED APPROACH 4/E
Arens/Loebbecke

KOHLER'S DICTIONARY FOR ACCOUNTANTS, 6/E
Cooper/ljiri

INTERMEDIATE ACCOUNTING, 2/E
Danos/Imhoff

FINANCIAL STATEMENT ANALYSIS, 2/E
Foster

FINANCIAL ACCOUNTING: PRINCIPLES AND ISSUES, 3/E
Granof

COST ACCOUNTING: A MANAGERIAL EMPHASIS, 6/E
Horngren/Foster

ACCOUNTING
Horngren/Harrison

INTRODUCTION TO FINANCIAL ACCOUNTING, Third Revised Edition
Horngren/Sundem

INTRODUCTION TO MANAGEMENT ACCOUNTING, 7/E
Horngren/Sundem

CPA PROBLEMS AND APPROACHES TO SOLUTIONS, Volume 1, 5/E
Horngren/Leer

ADVANCED MANAGEMENT ACCOUNTING, 2/E
Kaplan/Atkinson

GOVERNMENT AND NONPROFIT ACCOUNTING THEORY & PRACTICE, 3/E
Freeman/Shoulders/Lynn

A NEW INTRODUCTION TO FINANCIAL ACCOUNTING, 2/E
May/Mueller/Williams

AUDITING PRINCIPLES, 5/E
Stettler

BUDGETING, 5/E
Welsch

second edition

Advanced Management Accounting

ROBERT S. KAPLAN
Harvard University
Carnegie Mellon University

ANTHONY A. ATKINSON
University of Waterloo

 Prentice-Hall International, Inc.

This edition may be sold only in those countries to which it is consigned by Prentice-Hall International. It is not to be re-exported and it is not for sale in the U.S.A., Mexico, or Canada.

to our wives

Ellen and Anne

 © 1989, 1982 by Prentice-Hall, Inc.
A Division of Simon & Schuster
Englewood Cliffs, NJ 07632

All rights reserved. No part of this book may be reproduced, in any form or by any means, without permission in writing from the publisher.

No cases in this book may be reproduced, stored in a retrieval system, or transmitted, in any form or by any means, electronic, mechanical, photocopying, recording, or otherwise, without the prior written permission of the copyright holder. Cases in this book whose copyright is held by the President and Fellows of Harvard College are published herein by express permission. Permissions requests to use individual Harvard copyrighted cases should be directed to the Permissions Manager, Harvard Business School Publishing Division, Boston, MA 02163.

Case material of the Harvard Graduate School of Business Administration is made possible by the cooperation of business firms and other organizations which may wish to remain anonymous by having names, quantities, and other identifying details disguised while maintaining basic relationships. Cases are prepared as the basis for class discussion rather than to illustrate either effective or ineffective handling of an administrative situation.

Printed in the United States of America
10 9 8 7 6 5 4 3 2 1

ISBN 0-13-011636-X

Prentice-Hall International (UK) Limited, *London*
Prentice-Hall of Australia Pty. Limited, *Sydney*
Prentice-Hall Canada Inc., *Toronto*
Prentice-Hall Hispanoamericana, S.A., *Mexico*
Prentice-Hall of India Private Limited, *New Delhi*
Prentice-Hall of Japan, Inc., *Tokyo*
Simon & Schuster Asia Pte. Ltd., *Singapore*
Editora Prentice-Hall do Brasil, Ltda., *Rio de Janeiro*
Prentice-Hall, Inc., *Englewood Cliffs, New Jersey*

CONTENTS

9 Sales, Profitability, and Productivity Variances 321

10 Measuring Quality 372

11 New Technology for Manufacturing Operations: JIT and CIM 412

12 Justifying Investments in New Technology 473

13 Decentralization 522

PREFACE

The enormous changes during the past ten years in manufacturing, service operations, and the technology of information processing have dramatically affected the environment of management accounting systems. Also, recent research has introduced new measuring and reporting concepts that, in turn, have created an expanded role for management accountants in organizations. These developments required that much new material be introduced into the Second Edition of this book and that some of the material retained from the First Edition be re-oriented to the realities of contemporary practice. Material from the First Edition that we now view as less important for management accounting practice was deleted. Thus, the Second Edition, while not a complete departure from the First, still reflects much more change than would normally be expected from a revision.

The major additions to the Second Edition begin with the introductory chapter where we incorporate the work of Professors H. Thomas Johnson of Portland State University and Alfred D. Chandler of the Harvard Business School on the origins of management accounting. These scholars taught us that the cost accounting role—to allocate periodic production costs between cost of goods sold and inventory—developed 100 years after management accounting practices had emerged to coordinate and control transactions within complex, hierarchical organizations. Thus, Chapter 1 has been completely rewritten to describe the rich historical role for management accounting in the development of large industrial and service enterprises.

In Chapters 2 through 5, we have swapped the order from the First Edition of chapters on cost-volume-profit analysis with those on statistical estimation of cost behavior. We felt that students should first understand the motivation behind identifying fixed and variable costs before having to worry about estimating them. Two major changes have occurred in our treatment of cost-volume-profit analysis. The first, and more obvious change, introduces a major section on the use of spreadsheet languages, such as Lotus® 1-2-3, for short-term financial forecasting. Personal computers, which were just making their appearance at the time of publication of the First Edition, are now widespread. We have provided an extended example in Chapter 2 of how short-run financial models can be created and analyzed with spreadsheet languages running on personal computers. In fact, spreadsheets are used in several chapters, and many of the end-of-chapter problems are available on the course diskette that accompanies the Second Edition. We assume that students using the text will have access to a personal computer with software that can run spreadsheet languages, regression analysis, and linear programming models.

The second change in the cost-volume-profit analysis material is perhaps less obvious. Recent research questions the traditional role of short-run variable costs and contribution margin analysis for decisions such as make-buy, product introduction and abandonment, and acceptance of incremental orders. We believe that short-run variable costs remain useful for forecasting the near-term effects of volume fluctuations once decisions are made on product availability and mix. This role for forecasting short-run (weekly and monthly) income and cash flows, but not for decision-making on products, is the focus of Chapter 2.

Chapter 3, on linear programming for decision making on product mix, also assumes that the firm already has made decisions on the products it is willing to produce and sell, and that capacity already exists for these products. Given decisions to support certain products and to maintain existing capacity resources in the near term, the linear programming model selects a product mix that maximizes short-run contribution margin. In another philosophical break from the First Edition, we have eliminated mathematical notation to the maximum extent possible. The revised chapter also contains an extended example to help students learn how to formulate a reasonably complex joint product model. The problem helps to illustrate issues and problems in the presence of joint costs. The chapter closes with some cautionary advice on the limitations of LP models for global optimization of the firm's product mix problems.

Chapters 4 and 5 on regression analysis are relatively minor variations from the corresponding chapters in the First Edition. The major addition is a systematic approach for testing the validity of the regression assumptions from actual data. The major deletion is material on estimating learning curves. We now believe that learning curves are complex phenomena and that it would be misleading to suggest to students that future costs can be extrapolated, with any accuracy, based on the pattern of past cost reduction with cumulated experience. Both Chapters 4 and 5 contain almost entirely new problem material.

Chapter 6, on using cost information for pricing decisions, draws heavily from the First Edition. New material on activity-based-costing is incorporated in this chapter to show how full product costs, correctly calculated, are relevant for long-run product decisions such as pricing, make-buy, introduction, and abandonment. Some readers may wonder why the recent research in activity-based-costing is not featured more extensively in the Second Edition. After considerable thought, we decided to keep the underlying tone of *Advanced Management Accounting* oriented to the short-run financial forecasting, and operational and management control perspective of the First Edition. A full treatment of strategic analysis with activity-based product costs will require a new and separate book. Thus Chapter 6 introduces strategic cost analysis but defers to other courses and other books a comprehensive treatment of product costing.

Chapters 7 and 8, on service department and joint costs, are similar to the First Edition treatments of these subjects. The chapter on assigning service department (or, in general, support department) costs provides more explicit guidance than the First Edition on the important distinction between *attributing* costs, when a causal cost driver is known and measured, and *allocating* costs, when a measure of resource consumption is either not measurable or too costly to measure. The joint cost chapter is also more explicit than the previous edition on the limited role for joint cost allocation for decision making.

Chapter 9 extends the sales mix and sales volume variance analysis from the First Edition to incorporate productivity measurement. The heightened interest in having management accounting data motivate and evaluate the continuing improvement activities of operating managers makes it essential that we establish a linkage between traditional accounting variance analysis and productivity measurement. Such a linkage is provided in Chapter 9. The analysis again shows the value of spreadsheet languages for performing important managerial accounting functions.

Chapters 10–12 are entirely new chapters in the Second Edition. They are designed to introduce students to the new operating environment for manufacturing and service organizations, and to describe the role for financial and operating measures of performance in these environments. These chapters also indicate how traditional cost accounting measurements, applied without sensitivity to the new operations management environment, can be highly dysfunctional to the firm's operating strategy.

Chapter 10 introduces the Total Quality Control philosophy. The notions of a zero defects goal coupled with a measurement system recording defects in Parts Per Million are introduced. Also included is new material on measuring the cost of quality.

Chapter 11 develops the role for Just-In-Time (JIT) production and delivery systems. JIT is viewed not simply as an inventory control technique but as a method, a philosophy, for eliminating delays in production. The JIT approach featured here emphasizes the shift in thinking in many advanced manufacturing companies from managing costs to managing time. The chapter also features the impact of shifting operations from a direct labor to a highly automated environment with its discussion of Computer-Integrated-Manufacturing (CIM) technology. Measurement issues that arise in both JIT and CIM environments are introduced, though the emphasis is on measures to support operating managers rather than the detailed journal entries needed for inventory valuation purposes. This emphasis is consistent with the book's focus on management accounting not cost accounting issues.

Chapter 12 discusses the practical problems that arise when traditional capital budgeting analysis is used to justify investments in new technology. Common pitfalls that have occurred in practice are discussed and remedies offered to overcome them.

Chapters 13 to 17, on management control in decentralized operations, follow the treatment of the First Edition with relatively minor changes. Analytic material with limited application to practice, such as mathematical programming for transfer pricing and the use of present value depreciation for ROI calculations, have been dropped entirely. Consistent with our goal of deleting mathematical notation whenever possible, the formal treatment of agency theory in Chapter 17 is presented qualitatively rather than mathematically. New material from recent field studies on transfer pricing and a description of the Matsushita internal capital allocation system, has been incorporated but readers familiar with the First Edition will not find major changes in these five management control chapters.

In order to accommodate the three new chapters (10–12) on quality, JIT, and new technology, significant cuts in material used in the First Edition had to be made. The brunt of these cuts fell on the formal treatment of decision making under uncertainty. While this material has attracted extensive interest among academics for the past two decades, we believe that our students and the organizations that will eventually employ them are better served by the material added rather than the material deleted.

Thus, in summary the Second Edition has a different philosophical emphasis from the First Edition. The First Edition attempted to present management accounting research in a way that might make it relevant for practice. Its goal was to focus on "the firm's planning and control decisions that require a more sophisticated approach than the rule-of-thumb procedures advocated for traditional cost accounting problems." The Second Edition retains analytic material but only material that has already proved its worth in practice—such as spreadsheet models for short-term financial forecasting, linear programming for optimizing product mix decisions, and regression analysis of cost behavior. Rather than speculate, as in the First Edition, about the applicability of analytic models for management accounting practice, we have, in the Second Edition, worked from issues and problems that have already arisen in practice and then developed the relevant management accounting treatments. We believe that each chapter, with the possible exception of Chapter 17, contains material that can be immediately applied to contemporary organizations.

The emphasis on the practices of actual organizations is reinforced by much greater use of case material in the Second Edition. The cases attempt to illustrate how the concepts in each chapter can be applied not just in somewhat mechanical and idealized situations, but in the context of the real problems faced by actual organizations. There may be no simple answers to these cases but their analysis should prepare students to understand and be able to apply the relevant concepts in the organizations that employ them after leaving an academic setting.

Some of the cases are quite long since they imbed the decision on measurement and control issues in the context of an actual production setting, organizational structure, and company strategy. In fact, some of the cases are virtually chapters in their own right as they describe the details of a Total Quality Program (Signetics), a Cost of Quality system (Texas Instruments), a Just-in-Time program (G.E. Thermocouple), a Flexible Manufacturing System (Ingersoll Milling), a capital budgeting system (MRC), formal annual planning and budgeting systems (Laitier, Empire Glass, Continental Can), an extensive inflation-adjusted return-on-investment system (American Standard, and management compensation systems (Analog Devices, Natomas North America, and Wertheimer-Betz). Thus, the cases provide extensive descriptions of the actual applications of concepts discussed in the chapters.

Course Organization

This book can be used in a flexible manner. By spending up to one week on each chapter, it can easily fill a 15-week, 45-session course. Each chapter contains a significant amount of new material that can be reviewed and discussed for at least one class session. Problems and cases at the end of each chapter can easily occupy two additional sessions for each chapter. Instructors working with a 30-session course (2 classes per week for 15 weeks, or 3 classes per week for a quarter (10 weeks) can spend two sessions on each chapter. For shorter courses, say 15 to 20 sessions, the book could be used in two different courses: cost measurement, decision making and operational control material in Chapters 2 through 12 can constitute one course; management control material, Chapters 13 through 17, with extensive use of the cases and perhaps outside reading material can constitute a second course.

Outside readings can supplement the textual material. We have included many references to articles in the popular business press and in professional and academic journals that provide more detailed and comprehensive treatment of some of the subjects raised in the text. Students may be interested in several of the management accounting field studies described in William J. Bruns, Jr. and Robert S. Kaplan (eds), *Accounting & Management: Field Study Perspectives* (Boston, Harvard Business School Press, 1987), or in the historical evolution of management accounting, up through the present time, described in H. Thomas Johnson and Robert S. Kaplan, *Relevance Lost: The Rise and Fall of Management Accounting* (Boston, Harvard Business School Press, 1987). A conceptual framework for the design of new cost management systems appears in Callie Berliner and James A. Brimson (eds), *Cost Management for Today's Advanced Manufacturing: The CAM-I Conceptual Design* (Boston, Harvard Business School Press, 1988). The proceedings of recent conferences on innovations in cost management systems provide yet another source of supplementary reading material: *Cost Accounting for the 90s: The Challenge of Technological Change* (Montvale, NJ: National Association of Accountants, 1986) and Robert Capettini and Donald K. Clancy (eds), *Cost Accounting, Robotics, and the New Manufacturing Environment* (Sarasota, FL: American Accounting Association, 1987).

Acknowledgments

We have benefited from the assistance of many individuals and institutions. Some of the new material appearing in this book was originally developed in collaborative research with Tom Johnson of Portland State University, Robin Cooper of Harvard Business School and Rajiv Banker and Srikant Datar of Carnegie Mellon University. Several of our colleagues, especially George Foster and Charles Horngren of Stanford University, Germain Boer of Vanderbilt University, and Tom Johnson of Portland State University, provided helpful reviews of preliminary drafts of Chapters 1 through 12 that led to significant improvements of these chapters.

We are fortunate to have been able to include excellent cases prepared by many individuals. We are grateful to Harvard Business School Professors Julie Hertenstein, Ken Merchant, Robin Cooper, Bill Bruns, John Dearden, Bob Anthony, Earl Sasser, Warren McFarlan, Bob Hayes, Steve Wheelwright, David Garvin, Tom Piper, David Hawkins, John Kotter, and Bill Sahlman for allowing us to use cases they authored. We acknowledge in addition the case contributions by John Shank of Dartmouth, Charles Horngren of Stanford, Jim Reece of Michigan, Ed Deakin of Texas, Neil Churchill and Les Livingstone of Babson College, Ed Barrett of Southern Methodist, and Felix Kollaritsch of Ohio State. Both Harvard Business School and Stanford University provided institutional permission for use of their copyrighted cases. We would also like to thank the Certified General Accountants' Association of Canada for permission to use material originally developed for their Management Accounting 2 Course. The contributions of all these individuals and institutions permitted us to include a diversity of educational material that should enrich the students' learning experiences.

The enthusiasm of Julie Warner, formerly at Prentice Hall, motivated us to undertake the project, and Esther Koehn, production editor, was invaluable in handling the complex details of bringing the book to print.

Finally, we acknowledge the great assistance and support of our families who allowed us to pursue this project, despite an already crowded and over-loaded work schedule, which further limited our availability outside of normal work hours.

Robert S. Kaplan
Anthony A. Atkinson

chapter 1

INTRODUCTION: PAST AND PRESENT OF MANAGEMENT ACCOUNTING

Management accounting systems provide information to assist managers in their planning and control activities. Management accounting activities include collecting, classifying, processing, analyzing, and reporting information to managers. Unlike the financial accounting information prepared for external constituencies, such as investors, creditors, suppliers, and tax and regulatory authorities, management accounting information should be designed to help decision making **within** the firm. Therefore, the scope of management accounting extends beyond traditional measures of the costs and revenues from the transactions that have already occurred to include also information on sales backlogs, unit quantities, prices, demands on capacity resources, and extensive performance measures based on physical or nonfinancial measures.

Since the information to aid internal planning and control activities is not constrained by external reporting requirements, the management accounting system can use data that are less objective and less verifiable than the data used in the financial accounting system. Greater use can be made of forecasts and estimates, as well as measures of opportunity costs from transactions not taken. Ultimately, the test of a management accounting system is whether it motivates and assists managers in attaining their organizational objectives in a timely, efficient, and effective manner.

Origins of Cost Management Systems[1]

Prior to the nineteenth century, organizations conducted virtually all their transactions with other independent entities to perform individual func-

---

[1] The following discussion summarizes material in H. Thomas Johnson and Robert S. Kaplan, *Relevance Lost: The Rise and Fall of Management Accounting* (Boston: Harvard Business School Press, 1987); and Robert S. Kaplan, "The Evolution of Management Accounting," *Accounting Review* (July 1984). The development of managerial capitalism in the United States is documented in Alfred D. Chandler, *The Visible Hand* (Cambridge, MA: Harvard University Press, 1977). Chandler's work provides an enormously valuable historical perspective on the development of the U.S. corporate organization that has great implications for the practice and theory of management accounting.

tions in the manufacturing process. When the bulk of transactions are carried out with entities external to the firm, and few long-term investments were made within the firm, the financial accounting system—the official recorder of such transactions—provides sufficient information to assess the efficiency and profitability of the enterprise.

The origins of modern management accounting can be traced to the emergence of managed, hierarchical enterprises in the early nineteenth century, such as armories and textile mills. These enterprises were formed to conduct an entire multistage production process within a single organization. The organizations took advantage of the economies of scale from relatively capital intensive processes to hire groups of workers who manufactured the firm's output. Frequently, the manufacturing facility or factory was located next to a readily available energy source, such as rapidly running water, geographically separated from the urban home office of the owners. Information was needed to replace information formerly available from market transactions so that the efficiency of internal production processes could be measured as products moved internally from stage to stage. Also, the home office wanted an information system to motivate the managers at the remote factory site, and to judge the efficiency of the managers and workers at the factory. Thus, for a textile mill, internal measures were developed on cost per yard or cost per pound in the separate processes of carding, spinning, weaving, and blanching fabrics.

Perhaps the largest force for developing management accounting systems came from the emergence and rapid growth of the railroads in the mid-nineteenth century. Railroads were the largest and most complex organizations yet created by human beings, with operations having to be conducted and coordinated over vast geographical distances. Fortunately, the telegraph was invented at roughly the same time, and it provided the capability for rapid, inexpensive communication across these vast distances. Innovative railroad managers developed sophisticated approaches to handle the financial transactions required by their extensive operations. New measures such as cost per gross ton mile, cost per passenger mile, and the operating ratio—the ratio of operating expenses to revenues— were developed to help managers evaluate the efficiency of their operating processes.

Many of the innovative management accounting ideas developed by railroad managers were subsequently adopted and extended by the managers of companies in the steel industry. Andrew Carnegie, in particular, was known for having an obsession with knowing his costs and with continually attempting to improve his cost structure relative to competitors:

> Each department listed the amount and cost of materials and labor used on each order as it passed through the subunit. Such information [was used to prepare] monthly statements and, in time, even daily ones

providing data on the costs of ore, limestone, coal, coke, pig iron, spiegel, molds, refractories, repairs, fuel and labor for each ton of rails produced. . . .

These cost sheets were Carnegie's primary instrument of control. Costs were Carnegie's obsession . . . He was forever asking [department heads] the reasons for changes in unit costs. Carnegie concentrated . . . on the cost side of the operating ratio, comparing current costs of each operating unit with those of previous months and, where possible, with those of other enterprises. . . . Indeed, one reason Carnegie joined the Bessemer pool . . . was to have the opportunity to get a look at the cost figures of his competitors. These controls were effective . . . The minutest detail of cost of materials and labor in every department appeared from day to day and week to week in the accounts; and soon every man about the place was made to realize it. The men felt and often remarked that the eyes of the company were always on them through the books.

In addition to using the cost sheets to evaluate the performance of department managers, foremen and men, Carnegie [and his general managers] relied on them to check the quality and mix of raw materials. They used them to evaluate improvements in process and in product and to make decisions on developing by-products. In pricing, particularly nonstandardized items like bridges, cost-sheets were invaluable.[2]

Large merchandisers, such as Sears-Roebuck, Marshall Field, and Woolworth, developed in the late nineteenth century to take advantage of the economies of scale from mass distribution of consumer products. These enterprises also needed measures to assess the efficiency of their internal operations. Traditional manufacturing measures, such as cost per pound or cost per mile, were not relevant for the purchasing, stocking, and selling activities of retail organizations. Instead, these companies used measures such as gross margin (sales revenues less purchases and operating costs) and the stock-turn ratio (the ratio of sales to inventory level) to measure the profitability and speed with which purchased merchandise became converted to sales.

In all these examples—textile mills, railroads, steel mills, and retail distributors—we see managers developing measures to motivate and assess the efficiency of internal operating processes. There was little concern with measuring the costs of different products or even the periodic "profit" of the enterprise. These organizations had only to process their relatively homogeneous products efficiently: convert raw materials into a single final product such as cloth or steel, move passengers or freight, or resell purchased goods. If the basic activity were performed efficiently, the managers believed that the enterprise would be profitable. The measures developed were specific to the type of product and process of the organization but

_____

[2] Chandler, *Visible Hand*, pp. 267–68.

had one common characteristic—they measured the efficiency by which input resources were converted to finished products or sales revenue. Even though the production processes of these organizations were quite complex, involving multiple stages of conversion and processing, the organizations had a narrow product focus that enabled them to use simple summaries of output. Textile mills produced yards of fabric, railroads produced gross-ton miles of freight moved, steel mills produced tons of steel, and retailers produced, simply, revenue dollars. Therefore, product costs could be obtained with the same measures used to motivate and evaluate efficient operating processes.

The Scientific Management Movement

Complex metal-machining companies, emerging in the mid-nineteenth century, introduced a new set of challenges for management accounting systems. Metal-forming and metal-cutting shops produced a wide variety of finished products, and the different products consumed resources at widely different rates. Because of the dispersion in demands that the various output products made on the firm's capital, labor, and support resources, simple measures of cost per pound or cost per unit of output were not adequate to summarize the efficiency of the conversion processes. While an early version of job-order costing could capture actual material and labor costs, such costs would not include the cost of capital resources used to bend, form, and cut the metal, and no standards or even historical trends existed to determine whether the costs actually incurred represented efficient operations.

This void was addressed by a group of mechanical engineers who founded the **scientific management** movement. Frederick Taylor is the best known of this group, but many other individuals played an active role in developing this important new field. The scientific management engineers studied work processes closely in order to redesign material and work flow, and decompose complex processes into a sequence of simpler and more controllable processes. The goal was to simplify the work, make the workers more efficient, and be able to monitor the workers' efforts. Detailed and accurate standards for material and labor usage were developed to control work and to pay workers on a "scientifically determined" piecework basis.

Frederick Taylor was primarily interested in worker efficiency, and he relied heavily on quantity standards for the amount of labor and material that should be used under ideal conditions. Others were more interested in evaluating the commercial (financial) success of the enterprise, not just maximizing the efficiency of individual workers. These engineers and accountants extended the quantity standards of the scientific management engineers to include, as well, a labor cost per hour and a material cost per unit so that labor and material cost standards could be developed for production processes. In this way, the standard material and labor cost of products could be predicted and subsequently compared with the costs actually incurred. By the first decade of the twentieth century, sophisticated systems to record and analyze the variances of actual from standard costs had already been articulated.

Prior to metal-working shops and the scientific management movement, management accounting systems had focused on directly measured costs, such as material and labor, that could easily be traced to the output product. While overhead and capital costs existed in all organizations, the narrow product lines of early manufacturing corporations created little demand to attempt to assign indirect costs to output products. Managers focused on the efficiency with which direct labor and material were consumed in the conversion operations, and they assumed that adequate profits would be produced if such efficiencies were achieved. Also, with focused single-product, processlike organizations, it was easy to get summary measures of total cost per unit of output.

The metal-working shops, however, had both high product diversity and relatively high indirect or support costs. Their engineers and managers searched for ways to assign overhead costs to products, especially when bidding on new jobs. Because information collection and processing costs were quite high a century ago, and overhead costs were still less important than direct material and labor costs, it was not deemed worthwhile to invest large amounts of energy and resources to accurately measure and assign indirect and support department costs to products. Simple rules were adopted, such as marking up direct labor hours or dollars by a percentage that reflected the ratio of indirect and support department expenses (i.e., the overhead costs) to anticipated direct labor quantities. This procedure was inexpensive because direct labor was already being measured both to monitor the efficiency of individual workers and to pay them. Thus, the practice of applying overhead to products based on their direct labor content had its origins in the labor-intense production processes of a century ago.

This shortcut, or approximation, of attributing the consumption of overhead resources to the quantity of direct labor in a product was criticized even at the time:

> We find that as against $100 direct wages on order, we have an indirect expenditure of $59, or in other terms, our shop establishment charges are 59 percent of direct wages in that shop for the period in question. This is, of course, very simple. It is also as usually worked out very inexact. It is true that as regards the output of the shop as a whole a fair idea is obtained of the general cost of the work. . . . And in the case of a shop with machines all of a size and kind, performing practically identical operations by means of a fairly average wages rate, it is not alarmingly incorrect.
>
> If, however, we apply this method to a shop in which large and

small machines, highly paid and cheap labor, heavy castings and small parts, are all in operation together, then the result, unless measures are taken to supplement it, is no longer trustworthy.[3]

Attempts, however, to use machine hours, multiple labor rates, or material quantities as alternative bases for allocating overhead proved unsuccessful, probably because of the added expense of measuring all these new bases. Machines did not have to be paid for their work, so that the only reason for measuring and recording machine hours would have been for a more accurate assignment of overhead costs to products. Apparently the benefits of more accurate overhead allocations must have been well below the cost of such supplementary measurement, since the practice did not persist in discrete part production processes. The assignment of overhead costs to products based on machine time, however, had been extensively used in process industries—such as chemicals, glass, and petroleum—where labor costs were relatively small and processing times had to be measured in order to control the physical conversion process.

Management Control for Diversified Organizations

Further innovations in management accounting systems occurred in the early decades of the twentieth century to support the growth of multiactivity, diversified corporations. The DuPont Powder Company, established in 1903 as a combination of previously separate family-run or independent companies, provided the prototype for this new organizational form. The managers of the new DuPont Company faced the problem of coordinating the diverse activities of a vertically integrated manufacturing and marketing organization and of deciding on the most profitable allocation of capital to a variety of different activities. DuPont was one of the first entities to have to decide which of several diverse operations should be expanded, not just the appropriate scale of operation for processing a single type of product.

Several important operating and budgeting activities were devised by the senior managers of DuPont to coordinate the activities of and allocate resources to their many operating groups. But the most important and enduring management accounting innovation was the return-on-investment (ROI) measure. ROI provided an overall measure of the commercial success of each operating unit and of the entire organization. Senior managers used the ROI measure to help direct the allocation of capital to the most profitable divisions. Donaldson Brown, the chief financial officer, showed how the ROI formula could be decomposed into a product of two efficiency measures—the operating ratio (net income divided by sales) and

---

[3] Alexander Hamilton Church, *The Proper Distribution of Expense Burden* (New York: The Engineering Magazine Co., 1908), pp. 28–29.

stock turn (sales divided by assets)—developed and used by nineteenth-century single-activity enterprises. Each of these ratios could be decomposed further (see the discussion in Chapter 15) into the income, expense, asset, and liability accounts under the responsibility of local decentralized managers.

Use of the ROI measure was expanded in the 1920s as the multidivisional form of organization evolved in the DuPont and General Motors corporations. (The developments in these two organizations were not independent of each other. Pierre Du Pont rescued General Motors from imminent bankruptcy in 1919, and Donaldson Brown became GM's chief financial officer, serving under the newly promoted president—Alfred Sloan.) The decentralized multidivisional corporation developed to capture economies of scope—the gains from sharing common organizational functions across a broad spectrum of related products. But the enormous diversity in the product markets served by these giant corporations demanded new systems and measures to coordinate dispersed and decentralized activities. Division managers became responsible for the profitability and return on capital employed of their divisions and had authority to generate capital requests. Corporate-level departments of marketing, purchasing, and finance could not possibly have all the requisite information to function effectively or efficiently in all the markets served by their organizations. Decentralization was necessary, and central managers' functions shifted to running an efficient internal capital and labor market for the organization, and to coordinate, motivate, and evaluate the performance of their divisional managers. The ROI measure played a vital role in permitting the internal markets for managers and capital to function. An impressive array of budgeting and forecasting procedures were also developed to plan and coordinate divisional operations.[4]

In retrospect, the one-hundred-year period of 1825–1925 saw the emergence and growth of both giant, successful industrial enterprises and an impressive array of management accounting practices. These two phenomena were not independent of each other. In fact, organizations of the size of DuPont, General Motors, or United States Steel were unlikely to have survived without extensive management accounting systems to provide information on the efficiency and effectiveness of their decentralized operations. Technology innovation in transportation (the railroad), communication (telegraph, telephone), and basic processes (for steel, aluminum, metal cutting and forming, machine tools, chemicals, and the internal combustion engine, among many others) created a demand for large enterprises to capture the potential gains from economies of scale and scope.[5]

---

[4] These developments are described in Chapters 4 and 5 of Johnson and Kaplan, *Relevance Lost*. One particularly impressive achievement, the GM pricing formula based on ROI control, is described in a problem at the end of Chapter 7.

[5] This theme has been developed in Chandler *The Visible Hand*.

But these gains would not have been realized had there not been simultaneous innovation in measurement systems. These systems communicated corporate goals clearly to decentralized managers and provided feedback on the efficiency of operations managed within the hierarchy of these corporations. Such information was especially valuable for organizations that integrated vertically back to raw materials acquisition and forward into direct delivery to consumers of their products.

From Cost Management to Cost Accounting

The next sixty years, from 1925 to 1985, were not nearly as productive in the development of management accounting procedures. The exact reasons for the slowdown, even halt, of management accounting innovation are still being debated. But at least part of the reason appears to lie in the demand for product cost information for financial accounting reports. The early part of the twentieth century also saw increased emphasis on the financial accounting function due to the use of capital markets for providing funds for large corporations. Increasingly, the owners and creditors of the firm provided capital but little or no day-to-day supervision to their corporation. Elaborate systems of financial accounting were developed to generate information about companies to investors and creditors, and to monitor the performance of the managers hired to run the corporations. Regulations established by the stock exchanges where the shares of publicly held corporations were traded, by the auditors of the corporations through their professional organization—the American Institute of Certified Public Accountants—and, after the legislation of the early 1930s, by the Securities and Exchange Commission, created demands for periodic, audited financial statements prepared according to an explicit and implicit set of rules (known as Generally Accepted Accounting Principles, or GAAP). In addition, the passage of the corporate income tax and development of regulatory principles based on "net income," as measured by accountants, contributed to a greatly increased emphasis on published financial statements.

To allocate periodic production costs between goods sold and goods still on hand (i.e., inventory) auditors developed the field of cost accounting. The auditors' goals for simplicity, objectivity, and verifiability led them to prefer a system where inventory could be valued using numbers already existing in the double-entry ledgers of original transactions. Auditors attached costs to products by flowing original-transaction costs into work-in-process, finished goods inventory accounts, and the cost-of-goods-sold figure for the income statement. The cost-attaching procedures were executed in an efficient manner. Indirect or support department costs were aggregated into large, plant-wide cost pools and allocated to products using simple and available measures of activity—typically direct-labor hours. Nonmanufacturing costs, such as marketing, selling, distribution, general administration, and financing, were not allocated to products, since GAAP procedures considered them **period costs,** not **product costs.**

Cost accounting procedures were adequate for their intended goal: to produce systematic, objective, and aggregate statements on the profitability of a company's operations and its financial position. The cost allocations to individual products were not intended to indicate causality; the allocated costs did not have to bear any relation to the cost of indirect and support resources demanded by individual products. Thus, individual product costs could be highly inaccurate as an estimate of the resources consumed by each product, yet still produce accurate-enough information for inventory values and cost of goods sold at the aggregate level reported on the financial statements.

In principle, there was no particular reason why the greatly increased demand for published, objective, audited financial statements, and the increased regulations on the procedures used to prepare these statements, should have had any impact on the development of management accounting systems. Companies could have continued to refine their internal measurement techniques to provide independent and more accurate estimates of individual product costs and timely information on operating performance. Separate financial and management accounting staffs have persisted in companies located in German-speaking countries (Germany, Austria, and eastern Switzerland). For many companies in these countries, financial and cost systems are run independently of each other, with a reconciliation module provided to articulate between the two sets of statements at the end of the year when financial statements are prepared. But U.S. companies must have decided, sixty and seventy years ago, that the benefits of keeping two sets of books—one for external parties and one for internal management decisions—were too costly relative to the benefits.

The high cost of information collection, processing, and reporting coupled with the relatively low distortion for companies with homogeneous product lines led companies to attempt to manage their internal operations with the same information used to report to external constituencies. Thus, product costs were computed based on aggregate, average allocations of manufacturing overhead, and control procedures used monthly variances computed from general ledger financial accounts.

Recent Developments

The User-Decision-Making Approach

Academic accountants, during the 1930s, 1940s, and 1950s, observing the extensive use of arbitrary full-cost allocations—for pricing, incremental orders, and product discontinuance—wrote extensively on the value of using more relevant information for these decisions. Many accountants discovered that product costs that had been constructed for financial reporting purposes were used seriously by executives for product profitability, pricing, product mix, and management control decisions. The accountants attempted to dissuade the use of fully allocated product costs for such decisions by devising alternative cost accounting procedures that would be more relevant and helpful for particular decisions. Direct costing was advocated for many internal decision-making and control procedures.

This user-decision-making approach was extended in the 1960s and 1970s by academics who introduced formal analytic models of managerial decisions. These models were motivated by advances in the fields of operations research, mathematical economics, and statistics to improve managerial planning and control decisions. Much of the material in the first half of this book, particularly in Chapters 2 through 8, reflects this analytic approach to management accounting.

The Information-Economics Approach

The user-decision model approach was extended, starting in the late 1960s, by a new school of management accounting thinking that has come to be known as the **information-economics approach.** This new approach viewed management accounting systems as representative of information systems in general. Paralleling developments in statistical decision theory and the economics of uncertainty, the information-economics approach treated information as a commodity that could be acquired and sold much like other economic commodities (such as bread or automobiles). If information is an economic commodity, we should not talk about a "need" for information without regard to the cost of acquiring and producing it. We do not talk about a "need" for bread or a "need" for automobiles. We analyze the cost of these goods and their value to consumers when deciding whether and how much of each should be acquired. The information-economics approach attempts to measure the **demand** for information, a demand based on the **value** of the information and the **cost** of supplying it, including the perhaps higher cost for more accurate or more timely information.[6]

The value of the information is derived from an explicit model of

1. The environment faced by the decision maker
2. All possible actions that can be taken by the decision maker
3. All possible outcomes from each course of action and their likelihood of occurrence as jointly determined by the action taken and the environment or state of nature that occurred

---

[6] For extensive treatments of the information-economics approach, the interested reader should refer to Joel Demski, *Information Analysis*, 2nd ed. (Reading, MA: Addison-Wesley, 1980); and Robert P. Magee, *Advanced Managerial Accounting* (New York: Harper & Row, 1986).

4. The role of the information system in signaling the state of the environment and the outcomes of the decisions; this includes knowing
   (a) All possible signals from the system
   (b) The a priori probability of receiving each of these signals
   (c) The probabilistic nature of the information system (in effect, the conditional probability of each signal as a function of each possible state of the environment)
   (d) The effects of each signal on the beliefs of the decision maker (a calculation that assumes that the decision maker uses a Bayesian revision process with the signal from the information system)
5. The cost of the information system (not a trivial calculation, since there could initially be a heavy investment for developing and installing the system but with a relatively low cost per signal once installed)
6. The risk attitude or preferences of the decision maker, usually represented by an explicitly assumed utility function

The intuitive message from the information-economics approach is the need to compare the benefits and costs of any proposed initiative for new information. Decision models and sophisticated control procedures should be used only in contexts where the benefits are expected to exceed the costs. Unfortunately, we do not now have, nor are we likely to obtain in the near future, techniques for explicitly measuring the benefits (and perhaps the costs as well) from improved information for decision making. Therefore, the benefit-cost calculation must be based on a subjective, intuitive evaluation. Fortunately, though, the cost of information technology has been dropping so rapidly in recent years that techniques and procedures that might have been considered much too expensive in the past are now easily within reach of even the smallest organizations. Thus, introducing more rather than less information for improved planning and control will likely be the correct decision because of the greatly reduced cost for information collection, processing, and display.

The Principal-Agent Approach

Recent developments in the theory of the firm and of economic equilibrium with private information (a situation in which not all the owners or managers are equally informed about all aspects of a decision-making situation) have led to new insights into the central role of accounting information when designing contracts between owners and managers, and between senior managers and subordinate managers. This contracting literature is often referred to as **principal-agent analysis.** The principal could be the set of owners (shareholders), and the agent would be the chief executive of the company who has been hired to run the company for the owners. Alternatively, the principal could be the central management group that hires agents (divisional managers) to manage decentralized units. The principal-agent literature attempts to determine how to devise both an incentive scheme and a supporting information system so that the agents are motivated to act in the best interests of the principal.[7]

The problem of optimal organizational design is not new. People have been writing about decentralization and delegation of authority and responsibility for years. Accountants have addressed many of the relevant issues in management control of decentralized operations even before the emergence of the principal-agent approach. The more recent principal-agent literature has added formal economic reasoning to help guide the design of incentive, evaluation, and compensation systems. The recent principal-agent literature is featured prominently in our discussions of management control systems in Chapters 13 to 17.

Influence of New Production Technology

During the decade of the 1980s, major new challenges emerged for management accounting. Companies rediscovered the critical role that manufacturing plays in creating a competitive advantage for their organizations. Examples of the new emphasis on manufacturing operations could be found in the commitment to quality for manufacturing processes and in product design, in the reduction of inventory levels and manufacturing lead times (as represented by just-in-time production and distribution systems), and by the introduction of computer-controlled manufacturing operations (the CIM, or computer-integrated-manufacturing environment). All of the manufacturing innovations stressed continuing improvement activities; the need to constantly improve operating processes from the levels achieved in prior years.

These new (or, in some cases, rediscovered) manufacturing technologies frequently stand in stark contrast to the stable manufacturing environment of mass production of standardized products that has been the basis for management and cost accounting thinking for the past sixty years. It has not been unusual for companies to find that their traditional cost accounting measures have inhibited the introduction of innovative manufacturing technologies. For example, measures of individual worker efficiency or machine utilization conflict with factory goals to improve quality and reduce inventory levels. Attempting to absorb factory overhead into products by producing items well in advance of when they are needed does absorb fixed manufacturing overhead into inventory and does create increases in reported period income (because of favorable volume variances), but the practice undermines the company's efforts to

---

[7] Basic references for this literature include Kenneth Arrow, "Control in Large Organizations," *Management Science* (April 1964); and Michael Jensen and William H. Meckling, "Theory of the Firm: Managerial Behavior, Agency Costs and Ownership Structure," *Journal of Financial Economics* (October 1976), pp. 305–60.

reduce inventory levels, eliminate manufacturing defects, speed up throughput times, and improve customer responsiveness.

Management accounting systems must support, not inhibit, the drive for manufacturing excellence. Measurement systems must evolve to support efforts to increase quality and productivity, move to just-in-time and computer-integrated-manufacturing production systems, and help justify investment in new technologies. These issues are discussed in Chapters 9 through 12.

Management Accounting for Service Companies

Our discussion may, at a superficial level, appear to focus exclusively on manufacturing rather than service organizations. Discussions on inventory and manufacturing processes might seem of little relevance to managers in financial service, transportation, health-care, and telecommunications companies. The extensive use of manufacturing terms should not cause readers interested in service industries to ignore the underlying and fundamental messages in this chapter and in the remainder of the book. The distinctions between manufacturing and service industries are not critical for the design of effective management accounting systems. About the only substantive difference between manufacturing and service companies arises from the financial accounting demand on manufacturing companies to allocate periodic production costs to items produced but not yet sold.

All service industries have products that they produce and deliver to customers; the product may be only a little more difficult to define than it is in a manufacturing organization. The products of service organizations have costs that must be understood and analyzed for a wide variety of planning and control decisions. Certainly, issues on planning and estimating cost variability and making product-pricing decisions are important for all service companies. Understanding the role of support department and joint costs is perhaps even more important for service companies than for manufacturing ones. And measuring productivity, improving quality, and making critical investments in information technology will be highly relevant for service organizations as well. Even the discussion apparently about inventory management (just-in-time [JIT] systems) can and should be applied to service organizations once JIT is understood, not as a technique to reduce inventory, but as a discipline to reduce product lead times and improve customer responsiveness.

Summary

Management accounting systems play a vital role in helping the managers of complex, hierarchical organizations to plan and control their operations. A superb management accounting system may not guarantee competitive success, particularly if companies do not have good products, efficient operating processes, or effective marketing and sales activities. But an ineffective management accounting system, producing delayed, distorted, or too highly aggregated information, can easily undermine the efforts of companies with excellent research and development, production, and marketing activities. The challenge is to develop management accounting practices that support the basic managerial tasks of organizing, planning, and controlling operations to achieve excellence throughout the organization. The management accounting system cannot be viewed as a system designed by accountants for accountants. The one-hundred-year history from 1825 to 1925 provides evidence on the necessity for parallel development of new management accounting practices to support the company's innovations in production, marketing, and organizational design.

This book takes a user-decision-oriented approach to the design of management accounting procedures and systems. The "user" is assumed to be a manager or executive who will be making decisions and controlling operations **within** the organization. The book also emphasizes the challenges and opportunities from new information technology and the new technology of production processes. Students who complete the book should be rewarded with an increased understanding of how management accounting information can facilitate critical planning and control activities in all organizations.

PROBLEMS

Problem 1-1   (G. Shillinglaw)

Artech Products Company manufactured computer systems. Its manufacturing facilities were located in a single large factory, which was divided by partitions into separate departments. One such department was the "clean room," which was kept as free of dust and other air contaminants as possible; another was the metal shop, where bars and sheets of metal were received, stored, and cut, drilled, and shaped for use elsewhere in the factory.

The factory employed a large number of "knowledge workers"; direct labor accounted for less than 10 percent of total factory cost in 1986. Job order costing was used, with overhead initially accumulated in seven large pools, as follows:

Problem based on Robert S. Kaplan, "Accounting Lag: The Obsolescence of Cost Accounting Systems," *California Management Review* (Winter 1986), pp. 174–77.

- Manufacturing engineering
- Quality engineering
- Depreciation
- General employee benefits
- Manufacturing support services
- Site services
- Financial services

The costs in each pool were allocated to production departments by broad-based allocation rates (e.g., depreciation and site services costs were allocated by a rate based on the number of square feet of space the departments occupy). The overhead costs allocated to each department were then apportioned to products by means of departmental overhead rates based on direct labor hours. The rate in one department rose from $90 a direct labor hour in 1983 to $140 an hour in 1986; similar increases occurred in the other departments.

Artech management's primary strategy was twofold: (1) develop and nurture new products and (2) automate and simplify manufacturing processes to reduce direct labor costs. One new product, introduced in 1980, had the following history in its first four years:

	1980	1981	1982	1983
Quantity produced (000)	3	11	58	100
Yield (%)	3.2	3.8	6.7	75
Labor hours per unit	4.0	2.4	1.6	1.2
Average cost per unit	$152	$102	$95	$100

Despite the dramatic improvements in direct labor and material efficiency, the average cost of this product remained relatively flat between 1981 and 1983. Unit costs began to rise after 1983, however, and management was seeking alternative suppliers of low-tech components whose average costs would be lower because these suppliers wouldn't have to pay $140 or more to support each direct labor hour.

Management was also concerned because the clean room was being used at close to its full-time capacity, and some of this usage was for products that didn't really require clean space.

Required:

1. Determine (a) the problems Artech may have been encountering due to weaknesses in its product costing system, (b) the nature of these weaknesses, and (c) corrective cost-effective steps that could be taken.

2. Which of the corrective steps recommended in your answer to requirement 1, if any, would you recommend if you were told that the sole objective of the product costing system was to provide unit cost data for measuring the costs of inventories and the cost of goods sold?

Problem 1–2 *Great Lakes Diversified Corporation: The Detroit Plant*

> As you know, each of our plants must stand on its own in terms of profitability. Over the past 10 years, the picture at the Detroit plant has not been a good one and, recently, the losses suffered have been substantial.
>
> *Bob Jerel, November 1971, talking to members of the Detroit plant feasibility study team*

Robert M. Jerel, vice president and one of two general plants managers in the Heavy Equipment Division of the Automotive Supplier Group of the Great Lakes Diversified Corporation, knew only too well that the Detroit plant was a problem. As division controller, his previous position, he had for several years watched the plant perform at a level well below division expectations. In addition, he sensed that the plant had lost its spirit. Over the years, products with growth potential had been transferred to new plants and with them had gone investment dollars and management talent. "For the past 20 years," a plant engineer said, "people have been expecting the plant to close." Several months earlier, Jerel had appointed a team to study the issue of what to do with the plant.

Jerel had just received the sales forecast for the Detroit plant, dated 5 November 1971. Sales were expected to remain in the $17–20 million range, and the analysis concluded that "at best a break-even or loss operation is expected for at least five years if the operation is left as is." Jerel noted, "On the first cut, it looks like we cannot achieve an acceptable level of profitability at Detroit even if we raise prices by 20% and cut hourly wages by 50%." With the Detroit facility now his direct responsibility, Jerel felt it important to address the problem. He did not believe that the existing plant was viable in the long run; in the shorter run, however, he saw three major alternatives:

1. Close the plant as soon as possible.
2. Operate the plant for another one to four years with minimal investment.
3. Invest moderately in plant tooling in an attempt to develop a viable operation for the next 5- to 10-year period.

He knew that the decision would be difficult. "We must," he noted, "consider the company's responsibilities to the employees and to the many customers; and we must look beyond the Detroit plant to the needs of

This case was prepared by David C. Rikert, associate fellow, under the supervision of Professor W. Earl Sasser.

Copyright © 1979 by the President and Fellows of Harvard College. Harvard Business School case 679–121 the division and the corporation. In the end, however, the decision may well boil down to what we think we can do with the people we have available."

Heavy Equipment Division

The Heavy Equipment Division (HED) was a large axle and brake manufacturer. (See *Exhibit 1* for a corporation organization chart and *Exhibit 2* for recent corporate financial results.) The Great Lakes Diversified Corporation's 1970 annual report stated:

> During 1970, Heavy Equipment Division continued to lead the original equipment field through the marketing of improved products. These included tandem axles for heavy-duty vehicles, both on- and off-highway; a new family of front-driving axles for 4- and 6-wheel drive smaller trucks; a new line of nondriving front axles; and an improved hydraulic brake for the truck market.
>
> Improved products were also introduced in the off-highway market for construction, agricultural, and mining equipment. Among these was a series of planetary axles for large loaders.
>
> The Heavy Equipment Division continues to manufacture drive train and suspension components for several U.S. Army vehicles.

HED was headquartered in Pontiac (north of Detroit). In 1971 the division had nine plant on-stream and a tenth under construction (see *Exhibit 3* for plant data). For a number of years, the division had been moving toward plant specialization by product line. "The reason for this," Jerel explained, "was to minimize fixed investment in machine tools by tooling for a product line in only one location." Manufacturing at HED was organized by three major product categories: on-highway axles (mainly trucks), off-highway axles (construction, mining, and agricultural equipment), and brakes.

The on-highway axles were produced in six different plants. The simple nondriven front axles were all produced in Lebanon, Pennsylvania. The more complex rear axles were produced in the remaining five plants. The Detroit plant produced most of the "low runners" (low-volume axles including prototypes and replacements); the plant both manufactured axle components and assembled the final products.[1] The Tiffin, Ohio, plant was a feeder plant for the medium-volume Fremont, Ohio, plant and the high-volume Maysville, Kentucky, plant. The Tiffin plant manufactured components that were common to the axles produced in both plants. The Fremont and Maysville plants manufactured components that were unique

---

[1] *Volume* refers to the annual number of units assembled per model. See *Exhibit 3* for data by plant.

EXHIBIT 1
Organization Chart

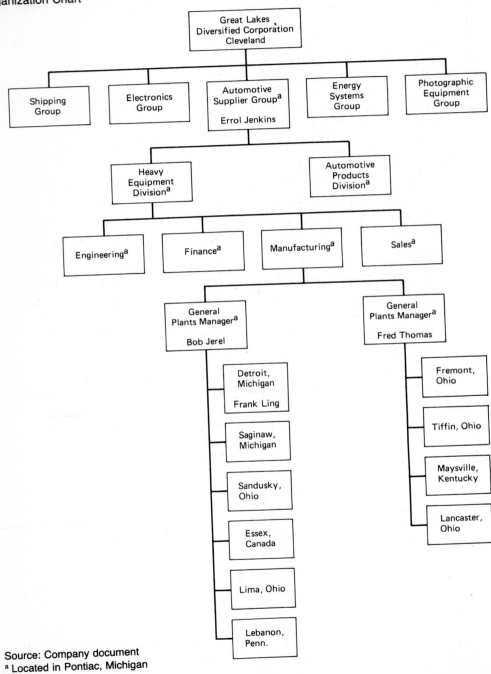

Source: Company document
[a] Located in Pontiac, Michigan

EXHIBIT 2
Corporate Financial Data by Groups ($ millions)

Groups	1971		1970		1969		1968	
	Sales	Income	Sales	Income	Sales	Income	Sales	Income
Automotive Supplier	$ 533[a]	$28.0	$ 494	$26.0	$ 555	$32.0	$ 488	$30.5
Energy Systems	367	7.7	420	5.2	381	0.1	398	2.0
Electronics	551	13.6	571	8.1	552	0.7	575	8.3
Shipping	294	4.9	444	10.4	699	12.5	908	20.9
Photographic Equipment	153	7.1	162	6.2	155	6.4	146	7.7
Other	313	7.3	320	8.8	325	13.2	288	11.8
Total	$2,211	$68.6	$2,411	$64.7	$2,667	$64.9	$2,803	$81.2

Source: Company documents
[a] In 1971 the Heavy Equipment Division accounted for $367 million of the Automotive Supplier Group's total sales of $533 million.

to their particular product lines and assembled the axles. With the completion of the Lancaster, Ohio, plant, the task of assembling the higher-volume models in the Fremont mix would be transferred to Lancaster. Tiffin would remain a feeder plant providing Fremont, Maysville, and Lancaster with common components. Fremont would continue both to manufacture components for use at Fremont and Lancaster, and to assemble lower-volume models. Bob Jerel explained the Lancaster decision:

> A key in our business is the technology of gear machining. Fremont is a very high technology plant, our strongest in the gear machining area. We needed to expand that machining capacity, but felt that the Fremont plant was already as large a plant as we wanted. So we decided that it would be less expensive to build an assembly plant nearby Fremont and let Fremont focus mainly on machining than it would be to build a new, integrated plant to do both.

The off-highway axles were produced in three plants. Detroit manufactured the components for and assembled the lowest-volume models. The Saginaw, Michigan, plant specialized in component manufacturing and assembly of the lower-to-moderate volume off-highway axles. The higher-volume off-highway axles were manufactured and assembled at Lima, Ohio.

Brakes were produced in only two plants. The Sandusky, Ohio, plant manufactured components and assembled brakes for the U.S. market; the plant in Essex, Canada, served the Canadian market.

The on-highway rear axle plants of Tiffin, Fremont, Maysville, and Lancaster were the responsibility of general plants manager Fred Thomas. The two off-highway and two brake plants were the responsibility of Bob

EXHIBIT 3
Heavy Equipment Division Plants (data as of November 1971)

Plant	Primary Product	Fiscal 1971 Sales ($ millions)	Return[a]	Production Workers	Plant Area (000 sq. ft.)	Plant Capacity ($ millions)	Annual Number of Units Assembled per Model	
							Range	Average
Sandusky, Ohio	Brakes	$ 33.4	54%	555	275	$ 50	na	na
Detroit, Michigan	Axles	17.4	(7%)	458	941	25	1–1,000	200
Lima, Ohio	Off-highway axles	6.0	(12%)	161	200	12	500–1,500	900
Lebanon, Pennsylvania	Front axles	36.0	37%	650	522	45	na	na
Saginaw, Michigan	Off-highway axles	47.0	28%	986	510	50	1–1,000	400
Essex, Canada	Brakes	11.3	28%	128	150	15	na	na
Tiffin, Ohio	Axle components	45.0	30%	720	556	60	na	na
Lancaster, Ohio[b]	Rear axles (assembly only)			300[c]	300[c]	53[c]	2,000–5,000[c]	3,000[c]
Fremont, Ohio	Rear axles (machining, some assembly)	110.0	56%	2,200	760	125	400–2,500	1,000
Maysville, Kentucky	High-volume rear axles	55.0	16%	1,150	530	75	5,000–30,000	10,000

a Pretax plant profit/investment
b This plant under construction
c Estimated

Jerel as were the hybrid Detroit plant and the front axle plant at Lebanon. Each of the plants was a profit center. Plant managers were evaluated on a variety of measures, but return on assets employed was a major concern.

Bob Jerel, 41, had joined the Heavy Equipment Division in 1968 as division controller. He had previously held positions within the financial function at Chrysler. He had been promoted to his present position in March 1971.

Jerel had known and worked with Fred Thomas since 1968:

> Fred and I work well together, and I think this is important. Our objective is for the division as a whole to perform at the highest possible level. Fred and I often have to balance the needs and wants of one plant against the needs of the division as a whole. For example, Fremont developed an improved process for a particular rear axle. They can make it much more cheaply than Detroit can, but the volume isn't high enough to give them the return they want. However, we as a division are better off manufacturing that product at Fremont.

Division Concerns

Jerel had recently received the division sales forecast for the next five fiscal years:

	Sales ($ millions)
1972	$424
1973	460
1974	504
1975	551
1976	604

He knew, however, that Great Lakes Diversified Corporation's sales had been declining for three years, led by the precipitous decline in the shipping business. He was aware of increasing pressure on divisions such as Heavy Equipment to perform well, and of a related, tightened scrutiny of investment proposals.

Within Fred Thomas's area of responsibility, the Maysville plant was finally beginning to perform reasonably well. The first part had been machined there in 1968. The plant had lost money in 1968 and 1969 and had shown a small profit in 1970. Thomas stated that "sufficient management quality and depth was the single most difficult challenge in the Maysville startup, and now we have Lancaster coming on-stream."

Within Jerel's area of responsibility, the Lima, Saginaw, and Detroit plants presented problems in 1971. The Lima plant had become a problem area the previous four years. It had been built for a sale level of $12 million; however, volume had declined to about $5 million in 1970, with 70% of

FIGURE A

Saginaw Plant: Forecasted Sales, Fiscal 1971–1976 ($ millions)

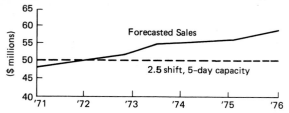

the loss accounted for by one customer. In October 1970 virtually the entire management team had been eliminated; since then, the plant had operated essentially as a department for Saginaw. Jerel was considering three options for the Lima plant:

1. Close the plant and transfer the machining capacity to Saginaw or Detroit.
2. Sell the plant and machinery to the major customer.
3. Keep the plant open and transfer in products from Saginaw.

In addition, the Saginaw plant was approaching capacity constraints, as shown in *Figure A*.

The Detroit Plant

The Detroit plant, built in 1914, was the headquarters plant, the local plant near division headquarters. Almost all products of the division had roots that could be traced to Detroit. Over the years, as the market for a new product grew, production was transferred to a new plant specifically built or acquired for it.

In 1947 brakes had been transferred from Detroit to Sandusky. One of the higher-volume on-highway rear axles was moved to Tiffin in 1948. When Tiffin was dedicated to component manufacture, that line was transferred to Fremont. Some on-highway products had developed into very high-volume standardized products used by several original equipment manufacturers and eventually were switched from Fremont to Maysville. Other products, customized for particular customers, developed moderate volume and were candidates to be switched from assembly at Fremont to assembly at Lancaster.

The Detroit plant had thus been left with a residue of low-volume parts, and, unlike other plants in the division, with two product lines: 60% of sales were on-highway axles, 40% off-highway axles. In addition, it re-

EXHIBIT 4
Detroit Plant Financial Results

	1971	1970	1969	1968
Historical ($ millions)				
Sales	$17.4	$20.2	$21.0	$17.8
PBT	(0.5)	(0.7)	(1.4)	(1.1)
1971 ($ thousands)				
Sales				$17,360
Direct labor			$1,369	
Materials			8,275	
Variable overhead			2,916	
			$12,560	
Gross profit				4,800
Other plant overhead				5,322
Plant profit (loss) before taxes				($522)

Source: Company document.

tained primary responsibility for "service" (replacement) parts.[2] Detroit plant customers ranged from large manufacturers to small operators totally dependent upon the company for their axles. (See *Exhibit 4* for Detroit plant financial statement.)

The Detroit plant manager was 58-year-old Frank Ling. He was a long-time Great Lakes employee who had started his career as a supervisor at the Detroit plant. Ling had left Detroit to accompany a product transfer to Tiffin and had moved later to Fremont. He had returned to Detroit as plant manager in the late sixties. A prolonged illness had kept him away from work for a significant part of 1971.

Based upon his experience as division controller, Jerel knew that several factors (most resulting from the pattern of transferring growth/high-volume products out of the plant) had contributed to the poor performance of the Detroit plant.

Investment. The plants to which Detroit transferred growth/high-volume products were usually very successful. Their managers became heroes within a division that treated plants as profit centers. Over time, available investment dollars flowed to the newer plants; the Detroit plant could not compete effectively for these funds because capital was seldom allocated to the low-volume, and often dying, products that remained there. The condition of the machine tools—the heart of the plant—reflected the lack of investment. (See *Exhibit 5* for investment and depreciation trends at the Detroit plant.)

---

[2] The division was committed to providing replacement parts for all of its products, including out-of-production models.

EXHIBIT 5
Investment and Depreciation Trends: The Detroit Plant, 1960–1970

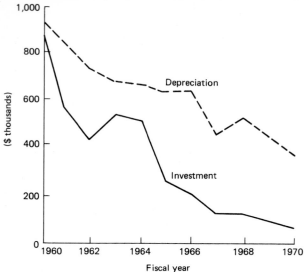

Machine Tools. These tools were large (often 10 feet long by 6 feet wide by 10 feet high) machines that removed metal from rough forgings and castings to produce the exact shape and size specified for the finished parts. A variety of machine types was used—drilling, boring, grinding, milling, turning. Each had jigs in which parts were positioned precisely and securely, and cutters to remove the metal; on some, the cutters rotated (milling, drilling), while on others, the part rotated (turning). Throughout the operation, the part and the cutters were continuously sprayed with oil for lubricating, cooling, and waste metal removal purposes. While the plant did have four numerically controlled machines (modern tools that ran automatically), many of the tools were "antiques," including some still driven by wide leather belts from an overhead power shaft. Many tended to be relatively specialized and set-up times could easily run 10 times the running time for a lot of parts.

The machines were scattered throughout the plant: "While the products and the processes have changed over time, the machine locations have tended to remain the same, leading to increased handling costs and lower operator utilization," Ling explained.

The average age of the machine tools at the Detroit axle plant was 33.1 years; at the Heavy Equipment Division, 15.9 years.

The Plant. The plant was a collection of over 40 multi-level buildings dating from 1914 to 1960. A 1970 report had stated: "The plant has degenerated to the point that major improvements will be mandatory in a few years. The electrical system is inadequate. The water system is constantly springing leaks. Column spacing and ceiling heights compromise storage and machine layouts. A major improvement has been made to the fire sprinkler system, but it is still below our insurance underwriters' standards."

An engineer noted that "the plant is really quite dirty and unorganized. Machine tool operations are, of course, not clean, but there is no excuse for the piles of shavings and scrap all over, and for the accumulation of grime that pervades even the office area."

Labor. The plant was unionized by the United Automobile, Aerospace, and Agriculture Implement Workers of America (UAW), which had a National Agreement with Great Lakes Diversified (covering all plants in the division). Labor relations were described as good. Machine operators were skilled workers, with expertise both in set-up procedures and in monitoring machines during runs. The plant had a history of long-service employment: in 1971 the work force included 28 employees with more than 30 years' service. . . .

Overhead. The Detroit plant overhead was significantly higher than that of other division plants. In part, this was due to the increasing maintenance costs associated with the old facility and machines. A significant additional factor, however, was the past-service pension funding expense. The Detroit plant was in the process of funding the pensions of workers who had already retired (of which, with the long-service history of the plant, there were many). In 1971 the expense was $648,000; funding would continue, in increasing amounts, until 1980. However, Ling noted, "Many of these retired employees had worked on products that had later been transferred to other plants, yet the pension expense remained with the Detroit plant."

Bob Jerel concurred:

> If we decide to transfer more work out of Detroit, we should offer our senior employees the opportunity to transfer to another one of our plants or to elect early retirement. We owe it to these people who really have helped build up the division over the years. It has been management's decision to transfer high-volume profitable products out of Detroit to the other plants.
>
> We are not contractually obligated to offer job security benefits to our younger employees. However, the trend is for unions to bargain for job security clauses. To date, these clauses have been used mainly as bargaining chips that have been given up in actual negotiations. Recently, however, unions have begun to press for this item. If we wait too much longer in closing Detroit, we may have contractual obligations to provide job security for all our employees. Right now our only obligation for job security is a moral one.

The Feasibility Study

Jerel had requested a feasibility study in August to identify and evaluate alternatives for Detroit. The report was due for completion in mid-February 1972; while he did not know all the details of the study, he was aware of the several issues being raised and alternatives studied. Jerel reflected:

> One thing that intrigues me is that there has been talk of shutting down the plant for years—but it never seems to happen. A major consideration, of course, has been the employees. I expect the termination costs would approach $3 million. And this has been a bleak fall in the city of Detroit—the media now greets word of another plant closing with phrases such as "another Detroit company bit the dust today." A further consideration is our customers. I worry that discontinuing products might be viewed as arbitrary and drive some customers to seek alternative sources for products they now purchase from other plants in the division. We also don't want to give competitors any openings in the heavy-axle market.
>
> Our study team has taken a first-cut look at our product line. They've concluded that the axles can be put in three general groups: on-highway axles that are economically worth continuing to produce; off-highway axles that are worth continuing; and both on- and off-highway axles that are not economically justified. [See *Exhibit 6* for the study team's preliminary estimates about these groups.]
>
> And so the questions are: Do we close Detroit? If so, do we transfer the better products? Or build a new, low-volume plant for the division? What would we do with Detroit employees? And with the customers of any products we dropped?
>
> If we don't close Detroit now, which might be a necessary action if the investment climate is sufficiently tight, do we operate it just for the short run or try to get another 10 years out of it? What could we do to make it more profitable?

Required:

1. Evaluate the profitability of the Detroit plant and the role it plays for the Heavy Equipment Division.
2. How should Jerel evaluate the alternatives proposed for the Detroit plant?

EXHIBIT 6
Working Paper Estimates from Study Group

1. 1971 financial results for the three product groupings at Detroit ($000):

	Group 1	Group 2	Group 3	Total
Sales	$6,944	$4,629	$5,787	$17,360
Direct labor	296	258	815	1,369
Materials	3,195	2,170	2,910	8,275
Variable overhead	630	551	1,735	2,916
Fixed overhead	2,129	1,419	1,774	5,322
Plant profit (loss)	694	231	(1,447)	(522)

Where:
Group 1: About two-thirds of the on-highway axles that look like they could economically be continued
Group 2: About two-thirds of the off-highway axles that look like they could economically be continued
Group 3: The remainder, both on- and off-highway, that cannot economically be continued

2. Estimates about Group 1:
We could probably increase their prices by 10%. If we transferred them, they'd go to Fremont; we estimate a direct labor savings there of 5% due to the better machines and more skilled work force, and a materials savings of 2% due to lowered scrap and higher-volume purchasing. The variable overhead rate in Fremont is currently 197% (of direct labor $). Additional tooling for the Detroit products would cost about $8.5 million, and incremental fixed costs at Fremont are estimated to be about $600K per year.

3. Estimates about Group 2:
We don't think any price increase is possible. If we transferred these axles, they'd go to Saginaw; we estimate a direct labor savings there of 6% due to the better machines and very productive work force, and a materials savings of about 1%. The variable overhead rate there is currently 191%. Additional tooling for the Detroit products would cost about $5.5 million, and incremental fixed costs at Saginaw are estimated to be about $420K per year.

4. Comments on Group 3:
There doesn't seem to be much hope for economic production of these axles; their volume is just too low. If we drop them, what do we do for our customers?

5. The Detroit Plant:
If we close it, we could realize about $2 million on the sale of the plant and a few of the tools (most aren't worth moving). We'd incur the employee termination costs of about $3 million, and we still have that $8–10 million pension expense that has to be paid.

If we keep the plant open at a minimal level (1–4 years), we'll probably have to invest about $200,000/year on tooling and the plant. For about $1 million/year in tools (primarily general purpose), we could probably keep the plant going for another 5 to 10 years.

6. A New Plant:
If we were to build a new low-volume plant for the division, we could probably save about $1.5 million/year, based on the Detroit sales forecast and the assumption that there's not more than $3 million in really low-volume stuff now out in the other plants. We'd have to invest about $18.5 million in the plant and tools, and launching costs would probably run to $3 million.

chapter 2

COST-VOLUME-PROFIT ANALYSIS

Many managerial decisions require a careful analysis of the behavior of costs and profits as a function of the expected volume of sales. In the short run (less than a year), most of the costs and prices of a firm's products will, in general, be determined. The principal uncertainty is not the cost or price of a product but the quantity that will be sold. Thus, the short-run profitability of a product line will be most sensitive to the volume of sales. Cost-volume-profit (C-V-P) analysis highlights the effect of changes in sales volume on the organization's profitability.

Traditionally, C-V-P analysis has been applied to simple, single-product situations. This has permitted the approach to be applied with a minimum of algebra and to be presented in graphical form. Recent advances in computer software have made powerful financial modeling languages available that permit complex multiple-product situations to be modeled, analyzed, and displayed. After reviewing the basics of C-V-P analysis—definitions of fixed and variable costs, the basic C-V-P equation, and breakeven analysis—we will illustrate the use of financial modeling languages for planning.

Fixed and Variable Costs

C-V-P analysis requires a separation between fixed and variable costs. Therefore, before proceeding with the analysis, we must first define these two cost categories.

Fixed costs are those costs unaffected by variations in activity level in a given period. They are expected to be constant throughout the period independent of the level of output produced or inputs consumed. Of course, whether a cost is fixed or variable will depend both on what factor is selected to predict cost variation and on the time period over which the cost is expected to vary. Fixed costs can be thought of as short-run, perhaps annual, capacity costs; they represent the cost of resources required to perform a planned level of activities.

We can distinguish between two types of fixed costs: committed costs and discretionary costs. *Committed costs* are the costs of long-term capacity resources. They include depreciation, property taxes, and the salaries of senior supervisory personnel. The acquisition of many of these resources, primarily plant and equipment, is usually controlled by the capital-budgeting or resource allocation process.

Committed costs can be predicted fairly easily because either the expenditures have already been incurred or they represent a contractual commitment (such as a rental or lease payment). These costs are not controllable or avoidable in the short run. Effective control of these costs requires postimplementation audits of capital-budgeting projects to compare each project's planned and realized outcomes.

Discretionary costs arise from decisions made during the periodic, usually annual, budgeting process. Advertising, research and development, factory support, and maintenance are examples of such discretionary costs. Once authorized, these costs are generally controllable by the periodic reporting system that compares actual with budgeted expenditures. Because of the difficulty of measuring the outputs or benefits from discretionary cost expenditures, little effort is usually made to evaluate discretionary costs on a formal cost-benefit basis. The authorizations are made based on the informed judgment of experienced, senior-level managers.

Variable costs (sometimes called "engineered costs") fluctuate in response to changes in the underlying activity level of the firm or in response to changes in the scale of activity. Materials, some components of labor (both direct and supervisory), overhead, and marketing costs are typical examples of short-term variable costs. Some short-run variable costs, such as direct materials and direct labor costs, will increase proportionately with the level of output. Other short-term variable costs, such as the salaries of intermediate-level supervisory personnel, may vary in steps, such as when an extra shift is added or subtracted, or in some other disproportionate fashion, with the level of output.

Relevant Time Period

Notions of fixed and variable must always be made relative to a specific time period. Over a sufficiently long period ranging up to several years or decades, all costs will be variable. During such a long period of time, equipment can become obsolete and need not be replaced, buildings and land can be sold, and even the top management of a division can be transferred or released in response to declining demand. Over long periods of time, contractions in activity can be accompanied by a contraction in virtually all categories of costs. And large expansions in activity will eventually cause all cost components to increase, especially when the increase in activity is accomplished by increasing the diversity and complexity in the product line and in marketing channels.

For example, university administrators occasionally think that most of their costs are "fixed," so that large sources of new revenues can be earned by expanding the number of tuition-paying students. They usually learn that expanding the number of students soon leads to demands for more support services (admission, placement, counseling, advising, athletic facilities, financial aid, financial administration), more teaching assistants, certainly more space, more academic administrators, and eventually more faculty if the quality of the delivered product is not to deteriorate substantially. Academic administrators should assume that almost all their costs are variable instead of assuming that large amounts of them are fixed.

For a sufficiently short time period—a day, an hour, a minute—virtually all costs will be fixed. Material has been acquired, utilities are turned on, and the firm is already committed to paying its employees. For this brief time period, variations in activity will not be associated with much cost variation. Within the two extremes of quite long and quite short time periods, there will be a time interval that corresponds to our usual notions of fixed and variable costs. This interval will typically be shorter than a year, since many costs that appear fixed with respect to short-term fluctuations in activity are authorized during the annual budgeting cycle. For statistical analysis, time periods of a week, a month, or a quarter should be kept in mind.

The Simple Model

Consider a single-product firm. To avoid inventory valuation issues, we keep the analysis simple by assuming that production equals sales. We further assume that the selling price of a product is given and is independent of the amount of the product we sell. Finally, we assume that costs can be uniquely divided between fixed costs and variable costs over the relevant range of analysis, although the model can be extended to situations where revenues and costs are nonlinear functions of production and sales.

C-V-P analysis works from the general profit equation:

$$\text{Profit} = \text{Sales} - \text{Variable costs} - \text{Fixed costs}$$
$$= \text{Units sold} * \text{Price per unit} - \text{Units sold}$$
$$* \text{Variable cost per unit} - \text{Fixed costs}$$

We define the following notation:

$x =$ units produced and sold

$p =$ price per unit

$v =$ variable cost per unit

$f =$ fixed costs

so that we can write,

$$\text{Profit} = px - vx - f = (p - v)x - f,$$

the basic C-V-P equation.

The difference between the price and the variable cost per unit $(p - v)$ is referred to as the **contribution margin per unit.** The product of the contribution margin per unit and the number of units sold, $(p - v)x$, is generally referred to as the **contribution margin.**

A quantity of special interest from the basic C-V-P equation is the **breakeven point** (BEP), defined as the level of output at which the contribution margin just covers the fixed costs, that is, the output level at which profits are zero. The BEP can easily be determined from our basic C-V-P equation by setting the left-hand side (profits) equal to 0 and substituting BEP for x:

$$0 = (p - v)\text{BEP} - f$$
$$(p - v)\text{BEP} = f$$
$$\text{BEP} = f/(p - v)$$

The last equation is referred to as the **breakeven equation.**

To express the BEP in revenue rather than units sold, we multiply both sides of the BEP equation by price per unit, p, and obtain

$$p * \text{BEP} = p * f/(p - v)$$

or

$$\text{BEP}_r = f/[(p - v)/p]$$

where BEP_r is the breakeven point in terms of dollar sales, and the quantity, $(p - v)/p$, is referred to as the **contribution margin ratio.**

The equations reveal that the breakeven point increases if either fixed costs, f, or variable costs, v, increase, and it decreases if the price per unit, p, increases. The breakeven volume provides a useful summary statistic of the three parameters—price, variable costs, and fixed cost—in the C-V-P equation and thereby gives managers a simple number by which to judge whether a given activity in a product line will be profitable.

There is nothing particularly significant about just breaking even. Apparently, though, many managers consider a $2,000 increase in profits that transforms a $1,000 loss into a $1,000 gain much more valuable than a $2,000 increase that raises profits from $8,000 to $10,000 (or decreases a $6,000 loss to a $4,000 loss). Even though the firm has $2,000 more cash in all three situations, the $2,000 increment in the first case enables the manager to avoid the stigma of showing a loss and hence may be considered more valuable.

The basic C-V-P analysis can be illustrated with a simple example.

SAN ANTONIO DISKETTES

San Antonio Diskettes (SAD) manufactures $5\frac{1}{4}$-inch diskettes that are used in the computer industry. SAD faces the following price and cost structure:

Average price per diskette	$ 0.80
Variable manufacturing costs per unit	0.25
Variable selling and shipping costs per unit	0.05
Fixed manufacturing costs (annual)	4,000,000
Fixed selling and administration costs (annual)	2,000,000

Management has the following questions about the upcoming year:

1. What is the anticipated level of profit if diskette sales are 15,000,000 units?
2. At what level of unit sales will SAD break even?
3. A special one-time order has been received to manufacture 1,000,000 diskettes under a private-brand label. Capacity is available, and the order will not affect SAD's other sales. Special ordering and shipping costs of $150,000 will be incurred. The variable manufacturing costs will remain at $0.25 per diskette, and no variable selling and shipping costs will be required. What is the minimum price per diskette that SAD can accept and still break even on this special order?

These questions can be answered by a straightforward application of the basic C-V-P equation.

Part 1

The expected profit is given by:

$$
\begin{aligned}
\text{Profit} &= (p - v)x - f \\
&= [(0.80 - 0.25 - 0.05) * 15,000,000] \\
&\quad - (4,000,000 + 2,000,000) \\
&= \$1,500,000
\end{aligned}
$$

Part 2

The breakeven point, in unit sales, is given by:

$$\text{BEP} = f/(p - v)$$
$$= (4{,}000{,}000 + 2{,}000{,}000)/(0.80 - 0.25 - 0.05)$$
$$= 12{,}000{,}000 \text{ diskettes}$$

Part 3

The breakeven point on the special order can be found by applying the BEP equation:

$$(p - v)x = f$$
$$(p - 0.25) * 1{,}000{,}000 = 150{,}000$$
$$p - 0.25 = 0.15$$
$$p = \$0.40$$

Of course, this last calculation assumes that no additional hidden costs arise from accepting the special order, such as increased scheduling expense, extra demands on a bottleneck resource, or more confusion in the factory because of the higher volume of activity required.

Although this basic C-V-P analysis is primitive, it does demonstrate how a good understanding of cost and revenue behavior is necessary for managerial decision making. It also provides the basis for a more extensive financial model to handle multiproduct situations, as the following example illustrates.

PARRY SOUND DISKETTES

Parry Sound Diskettes (PSD) manufactures and sells a line of diskettes for microcomputers. Three models are produced: Economy, Standard, and Premium. Unit cost and revenue data, as well as fixed costs, for PSD are as follows.

	Economy		*Standard*		*Premium*	
Selling price		$10		$15		$25
Variable costs:						
Direct materials	2		3		5	
Direct labor	2		4		6	
Overhead	1		2		3	
Selling	2	7	2	11	2	16
Contribution margin		$ 3		$ 4		$ 9
Product % of total sales		10%		50%		40%
Fixed manufacturing costs			$200,000			
Advertising			$100,000			
Fixed administrative costs			$100,000			
Total expected sales						
(all products)			80,000 (units)			
Capacity (total all products)			100,000 (units)			

You have been asked by management to prepare a report analyzing each of the following issues:

a. What is the projected profit given the initial data?

b. Management is considering increasing the advertising budget by $100,000 to increase total unit sales from 80,000 to 100,000. The mix of products would remain the same. Is the advertising campaign desirable?

c. Management is considering altering the manufacturing budget so that more effort will be placed on selling the Premium model. The advertising budget could be increased by $150,000. While this would not increase the total unit sales, this campaign would result in the mix of Economy, Standard, and Premium model being 5%, 30%, and 65%. Is this change desirable?

d. Management is considering increasing the selling commissions paid to the sales force. The marketing manager believes that if the selling commission of each product is increased by 2%, the total level of sales will rise to 90,000 units. Is the change desirable?

e. Management is considering altering the production process. By installing new manufacturing equipment, the direct materials, direct labor, and variable overhead costs can be reduced to 75% of their current levels for all products. Fixed manufacturing costs would rise by $200,000, reflecting depreciation on the new equipment. What is the minimum level of total sales for which this change would be desirable?

It is quite easy to answer these questions (independently of each other) once the behavior of costs is understood. By assumption only the revenue and the variable costs will change with changes in volume. The fixed costs remain constant over the relevant range. As a result, we can simulate the effects of different decisions on the profitability of the firm. Recall the basic profit equation:

$$\text{Profit} = (\text{Price} - \text{Variable costs}) * \text{Units sold} - \text{Fixed costs}$$
$$= \text{Contribution margin} - \text{Fixed costs}$$

In multiproduct situations, we sum the contribution margin provided by each product to obtain the overall contribution margin for the firm.

a.
$$\text{Profit} = 3 * (0.1 * 80,000) + 4 * (0.5 * 80,000)$$
$$+ 9 * (0.4 * 80,000) - 400,000$$
$$= (5.9 * 80,000) - 400,000$$
$$= \$72,000$$

where $5.90 is the weighted-average contribution margin per diskette sold (at the assumed product mix).

b.
$$\text{Profit} = (5.9 * 100,000) - 500,000$$
$$= \$90,000$$

This alternative causes profits to increase from the initial level of $72,000 to $90,000, a desirable option.

c.
$$\text{Profit} = 3 * (0.05 * 80{,}000) + 4 * (0.3 * 80{,}000)$$
$$+ 9 * (0.65 * 80{,}000) - 550{,}000$$
$$= (7.2 * 80{,}000) - 550{,}000$$
$$= \$26{,}000$$

This alternative causes profits to decrease from the initial level of $72,000 to $26,000. Thus, the change is undesirable.

d.
$$\text{Profit} = (3 - 0.02 * 10) * (0.1 * 90{,}000)$$
$$+ (4 - 0.02 * 15) * (0.5 * 90{,}000)$$
$$+ (9 - 0.02 * 25) * (0.4 * 90{,}000) - 400{,}000$$
$$= (5.53 * 90{,}000) - 400{,}000$$
$$= \$97{,}700$$

This alternative causes profits to increase from the initial level of $72,000 to $97,700. Thus, the change is desirable.

e. Let the level of unit sales be x. Find x such that

$$\text{Profit} = (3 + 0.25 * 5) * (0.1 * x) + (4 + 0.25 * 9) * (0.5 * x)$$
$$+ (9 + 0.25 * 14) * (0.4 * x) - 600{,}000$$
$$= 72{,}000$$

$$(8.55 * x) - 600{,}000 = 72{,}000$$

$$8.55 * x = 672{,}000$$

$$x = 78{,}596 \text{ units}$$

Thus, if the total anticipated sales are more than 78,596 units, the new equipment would be desirable. If the anticipated sales are less than 78,596 units, the change would not be desirable.

The analysis of this problem was rendered almost trivial with the C-V-P framework as long as we had confidence in our estimates of fixed and variable costs. In Chapters 4 and 5, we will examine the process of estimating such cost-volume relationships.

Even the three-product C-V-P model may seem somewhat transparent and perhaps too simplistic for practical problems. As long as we can develop a reasonably good model of cost-volume relationships, C-V-P analysis can be applied to complex multiple-product situations. In general, cost estimation is the difficult part of the analysis, and not the modeling of extensive numbers of products. Once we understand the behavior of costs, we can insert the cost information into an electronic worksheet and the computational task becomes trivial.

C-V-P analysis will be most realistic when applied to forecasting short-term costs and profits with the existing product line. The short-term qualification implies that fluctuations in output mix and volume will not affect discretionary fixed costs, particularly indirect manufacturing costs such as setups, inspections, material handling, scheduling, and expediting. This assumption will be violated if companies adjust spending on such categories as advertising, promotion, distribution, maintenance, training and education, research and development, and travel and entertainment in response to near-term fluctuations in sales activity. In this case, costs we may have classified as fixed will, in fact, vary with changes in output mix and volume.

The assumptions of the C-V-P analysis may also be violated if companies start to offer new products in their product line based on apparent short-term contribution margins. Because many discretionary costs appear to be fixed with respect to changes in output volume and mix, managers are tempted to increase profits through product proliferation: accepting special orders for products and introducing new variants of products.

The C-V-P approach reinforces the tendency to product proliferation by showing how profits will apparently rise as sales volume increases and "fixed costs" remain constant. This line of thinking, however, is misleading and dangerous. Most of the discretionary "fixed costs" exist to handle the diversity and complexity currently in the product line. They will remain "fixed" only if diversity and complexity are not increased further. If companies, based on short-term contribution-margin analysis, make a series of incremental decisions to offer new products and variants, their discretionary "fixed costs" will soon increase. The increase will be caused by needed additions to indirect labor and support staff to handle the greater number of vendor negotiations, production schedule changes, purchases, receipts, inspections, material movements, setups, and so on, that accompany the proliferation in the product line. Thus, the C-V-P analysis should be restricted to situations in which product proliferation will not occur and discretionary fixed costs will therefore remain fixed relative to the assumed changes in output.[1] With this limitation to C-V-P analysis explicitly acknowledged, we can now demonstrate the use of computer models for financial forecasting in more complex situations.

Financial Models

Casual readers of the popular business press might believe that financial modeling had just recently been invented, shortly after software such as

---

[1] The increase in discretionary fixed costs from product proliferation is described in Robin Cooper and Robert S. Kaplan, "How Cost Accounting Systematically Distorts Product Costs," in *Accounting & Management: Field Study Perspectives*, ed. William H. Bruns, Jr., and Robert S. Kaplan (Boston: Harvard Business School Press, 1987), Chap. 8.

LOTUS 1-2-3 became available on personal computers. In fact, financial models have been around for a long time. A pro forma income statement, and indeed, even a set of financial statements, are examples of financial models.

A model is a representation of a relevant part of reality. A model allows us to experiment with different situations in order to predict the effects of alternative courses of action. For example, automobile models are used in wind-tunnel tests to determine the aerodynamic properties of alternative designs.

A financial model attempts to represent, with financial measures, an organizational entity, usually a firm or a division within a firm. The model allows the analyst to examine the effect of alternative actions on the entity's financial statements and financial condition.

Financial models have three important attributes:

1. Financial models and what-if forecasting can be complex, since all inter-relationships among units and effects of decisions should be considered.
2. Financial models should be as flexible as possible to allow many options to be explored.
3. The potential value of the modeling exercise will depend strongly on the validity of the relationships assumed within the model.

These points should be kept in mind, since many people feel that good hardware and software are sufficient for effective model building. This is not true. Human ingenuity and creativity remain the most important ingredients of model building. In fact, several observers have predicted that easy access to microcomputers and user-friendly planning languages will produce large-scale fiascoes as individuals who have neither the training nor the insight to produce accurate models use available software and hardware to create invalid financial models.

A Financial Modeling and What-If Forecasting Exercise

This section requires the use of LOTUS 1-2-3 or a worksheet package that can read LOTUS 1-2-3 files. Students without access to such software should skip this section.

We will provide a simple example (by practical standards, a very simple example) to illustrate some basic building blocks in financial modeling.

SACKVILLE ENTERPRISES

Sackville Enterprises, a new firm, produces and sells potato harvesters. In September 1988, Frank Morgan, the president and major share-holder of Sackville Enterprises, approached his bank for an operating loan to cover working capital needs for the upcoming year. Jacob Marley, the bank manager, requested a pro forma projection of the firm's operating cash flows for the upcoming year. The projection will help determine whether the loan can be repaid during the firm's operating cycle.

On the basis of market studies, Frank estimates the annual demand for his harvesters to be 180 units. Sales are expected in the following pattern: May, 10%; June, 30%; July, 40%; August, 20%. Each potato harvester sells for $16,000. All sales are made on credit with collections arriving in the following pattern: 70% in the month following the month of sale, 20% in the second month following the month of sale, 8% in the third month following the month of sale, and 2% uncollectible. Customers who pay in the month following the month of sale receive a 5% discount.

To smooth the production process and to maintain a core of skilled workers, Frank uses a uniform production schedule of 15 harvesters manufactured each month. The practical capacity of the existing plant is 20 harvesters per month.

On January 1 of next year, Frank expects to have 60 harvesters in inventory. Completed harvesters are stored nearby in sheds and barns. The storage charge per harvester per month is $50. This charge is payable at the end of each month, based on the number of harvesters stored during that month (computed as the average of opening and ending inventory).

The annual fixed manufacturing costs are:

Labor	$ 300,000
Supervisory salaries	100,000
Depreciation	200,000
Taxes	200,000
Other	200,000
Total	$1,000,000

Labor, supervisory salaries, and other fixed manufacturing costs are incurred in a uniform pattern over the year. Depreciation is recognized annually, and taxes are paid in equal installments on June 30 and December 31 of each year.

Variable manufacturing costs per unit are:

Direct materials	$5,000
Variable overhead	500

Material and variable overhead items are acquired as needed during the production process. These items are acquired on a cash basis, since the company's suppliers are not yet prepared to extend credit terms.

Fixed selling and administrative costs amount to $300,000 per year. Of these costs, $180,000 is incurred uniformly over the year. The balance of the fixed selling and administrative costs, relating primarily to promotional expenditures, occur uniformly over the months of April, May, June, and July.

Variable selling and administrative costs consist of two components: shipping costs and selling costs. The shipping costs amount to $300 per unit sold. The selling costs are 6% of the sales price. Both selling and shipping costs are paid in the month in which they are incurred.

The cash balance in the firm on January 1 is projected as $50,000. The firm wishes to maintain, for its own purposes, a minimum cash balance of $50,000.

The company employs the following accounting practices:

1. The estimated uncollectible portion of any month's sales is charged to cost of goods sold in the month in which the sale occurs.

2. The amount of accounts receivable created by any sale is the revenue from the sale, net of the estimated amount of the prompt payment discount.

3. Direct costing is used to value inventory for financial statement purposes.

The bank has indicated its willingness to extend an operating loan to Sackville Enterprises under the following conditions:

1. The minimum cash balance to be maintained during any month is to equal one-half of the current loan outstanding. All loans are made, and repaid, in any amount on the first day of each month.

2. Interest is payable on the first day of each month at the rate of 1.45% of the balance of the loan outstanding during the preceding month.

Required:

Consider each question below separately

Part 1. Prepare a cash flow budget for twelve months beginning January 1989 that would indicate the nature and extent of any financing required over this period.

Part 2. Frank is thinking about raising the price of the harvester. If the price is raised to $18,000, he expects that demand will fall to 150 harvesters. Is the price increase desirable?

Part 3. Frank may discontinue the use of credit sales. Insisting on cash payment is expected to reduce sales to 160 harvesters. In this change desirable?

Part 4. Another bank has offered to meet Sackville's operating loan requirements. The conditions would be the same as those offered by Sackville Enterprise's current bank except that the compensating cash balance would be 30%, not the 50% required by Frank's current banker. To compensate for the higher level of risk implied by the lower compensating balance, the new bank will require Sackville Enterprises to pay monthly interest at the rate of 1.6% of the balance of the loan outstanding. Evaluated on purely an economic basis, is a change in banks worthwhile?

This problem has been set up on a worksheet file and has been provided on the course diskette as **SACKVILLE.** Get LOTUS 1-2-3, or software capable of reading LOTUS 1-2-3 files, active on your computer and load the Sackville worksheet. When the worksheet is loaded, note that cells A1 through D20 describe the contents of the worksheet and their location.

This problem has been laid out with data for the problem in the B column (the data labels are in column A). The data have been put in one place so that (1) they can easily be found and (2) what-if changes can quickly be made.[2]

The data are stored in column B, the data column, in disaggregated form to preserve the flexibility of the analysis. Although the worksheet will inevitably require some structure, if you keep the primitive data in a form that permits changes to be made easily, you will enhance the flexibility of the financial model. For example, instead of entering the fraction of annual sales occurring each month, you could compute monthly sales directly (by hand or using a calculator) and insert each figure into the appropriate monthly columns. Such a direct data entry would be silly for two reasons: (1) first you would be doing a calculation that the worksheet could do, without error, for you (if the formula is entered properly), and (2) if annual sales or the monthly distribution of sales were to change, then each of the twelve monthly sales numbers would have to be manually recalculated and reentered. A simple, but effective, rule of thumb is to permit or require only basic data entry. No aggregated or computed data should be entered directly into the worksheet.

The same type of flexibility is incorporated into the collections portion of the worksheet. Inevitably some flexibility must be lost. The worksheet contains rows for three-month, two-month, one-month, and current collections. Obviously, if a new credit policy is implemented wherein collections after four months are expected, the worksheet will have to be amended.

The working portion of the worksheet (cell F1 through cell S73) divides into four basic sections:

1. The production schedule (cells F1 through S24)
2. The projected net cash flow statement section (cells F26 through S47)
3. The financing data section (cells F49 through S61)
4. The income statement section (cells F63 through S73)

The worksheet is laid out so that each schedule provides data to the schedule beneath it (except for the interest calculation schedule, which

---

[2] The data have been put in the leftmost columns of the worksheet for convenience. You may prefer to put the data elsewhere when you build your own models. Another popular location is above or below the pro forma statement display area of the worksheet. In this location, however, the column width required for the data labels affects the width of the display area columns.

uses loan balance information from the financing schedule). Moreover, only the January column (of the January through December columns) was entered manually. The /**copy** command was used to create the other columns from the January column. Because this is a small worksheet, the production, cash flow, and income statement schedules can be placed in a single worksheet. In practice, these schedules may be placed in separate worksheets with data passed from one worksheet to another using the /**File,Combine** command.

The production schedule (F1 through S24) has a traditional format. The monthly sales and production figures are used in the cash flow section to compute the collection and disbursement patterns.

The monthly projection of net cash flow from operations (cells F26 through S47) provides the data critical for calculating the need for bank financing, the highlight of the report that Frank has been asked to prepare. The projected net cash flow statement is divided into two components: cash receipts and cash disbursements. The cash inflows are aligned by the month in which the sale occurred. The cash disbursements section is straightforward, since all purchases are paid in cash. In practice, this section could be complicated by a payment schedule for accounts payable with discounts for prompt payment.

The financing section of the worksheet takes the opening balances of cash and loan, determines whether a loan needs to be made or repaid, and computes the ending balance of the loan and cash accounts. Up to this point of the worksheet, simple formulas have been used. The calculation of the loan required or loan repaid amounts for each month requires more complex commands.

The Loan Made and Loan Repaid Calculations: An Illustration of the Use of Logical Operators in a Worksheet

Handling the loan calculations would be easy if the bank did not require a compensating balance or if the company did not simultaneously impose a minimum cash balance. The combination of a required compensating balance and a minimum cash balance makes the model moderately complicated.

We start by examining the loan required calculation using cell G55 as an example. The loan required calculation is recursive. The ending balance of cash determines the loan that will be required in order to finance operations. But to compute the required minimum cash balance, the ending balance of the loan must be known. The relationship is recursive, since the loan balance determines the cash balance and the cash balance determines the loan required. Therefore, the two values have to be determined simultaneously.

When you do a recursive calculation by hand, it is deceptively easy.

For example, you would probably just increase or decrease the ending balance of the loan until the loan and required cash balances met the stated criteria. Along the way, you would probably develop heuristics, or rules of thumb, to make the calculations go faster. But when we program a formula to make the calculation, we have to know in advance how to handle any contingency that might arise. This is one of the challenges of financial modeling—clear, logical thinking.

You should study the formulas for the loan made and the loan repaid amounts that appear in cells G55 and G56. The formulas represent only one way of modeling these functions. Perhaps you can think of simpler or more elegant solutions to determine the minimum cash balance and loan requirements. The loan formulas presented in the worksheet reflect the following basic thinking:

If net cash flow is zero, we neither borrow money nor repay a loan. We continue with the loan and cash balances that existed at the start of the period.

We never have to borrow more money when the net cash flow is positive. (This would imply that the opening cash balance was less than required, a prohibited situation.) Therefore, if the net cash flow is positive, we can attempt to repay part of any outstanding loan. More definitely, if a loan exists, we will repay some of the loan if net cash flow is positive. (If not, the opening balance of cash was too low, a situation we would not have permitted.)

Finally, if the net cash flow is negative, we never repay any loan. If we did, the opening balance of cash would have been more than required, a situation we would not permit because taking out a loan, when excess cash exists, has no benefit in our model. Therefore, if the net cash flow is negative, we must determine whether a loan is required.

With these overall guidelines in mind, you can study the loan increase and loan repayment cells in more detail.

Income Statement

The Income Statement that appears in cells F63 through S73 follows the format

Net income = Sum of increases in asset accounts

– Sum of increases in liability accounts

Note that the accounts receivable change is computed by subtracting current collections from current *net* sales and that inventory is valued using *direct costing* (no fixed overhead is applied to the products). The Net Income figure will be required to evaluate the profitability of alternative decisions. The Net Income in the baseline case is $53,360.

The Net Income figure computed in cell S72 is replicated in cell B24.

The replication permits easy access to the income figure associated with proposed new settings of the decision parameters so that the decision maker can readily see the effects of contemplated changes. Another way to highlight a key figure, such as Net Income, is to use the **WINDOWS** option.

What-If Forecasting

Once the worksheet has been laid out for the initial problem, we can answer the questions asked by Sackville's manager.

Part 1 The projected cash flow statement indicates that an operating loan will be required during the months January through June. The amount of the loan required will reach a maximum of $2,034,532 in June. This loan pattern satisfies the bank's requirement that the loan be liquidated for at least some months during the year.

You can undertake your own experiments with this worksheet. For example, by varying the overall units sold figure, you can show that, under currently assumed conditions, the breakeven level of sales is about 174 units.

Part 2 Let us turn to the what-if questions that Frank is considering. To answer the question in part 2, we have to insert the new price of $18,000 and the new sales level of 150 in cells B27 and B26, respectively. You will see that the new level of income is $79,312, indicating that this decision provides an improvement over the initial projected level of profit.

Even this simple variation shows the power and attractiveness of financial modeling languages. We made two changes, waited a few seconds, and received our answer. It would be neither practical nor feasible to consider many alternatives without a computer-based worksheet. Consequently, the availability of electronic worksheets has opened new opportunities for managerial analysis.

Part 3 Retrieve the initial solution for Sackville Enterprises. This time we change the total sales cell, B26, and the cells that specify the collections pattern (cells B43 through B47). In this case, collections equal current sales. With these contemplated changes, the projected Net Income becomes $85,146, an improvement over the initial situation.[3]

Part 4 Again, retrieve the initial solution. Change the monthly interest rate in cell B74 to 1.6% and the compensating balance requirement in cell B75

---

[3] You can save yourself some time when making several changes, such as those required for part 3, by suspending LOTUS 1-2-3's automatic recalculation until all changes have been entered. Consult your manual for the description of the **/Worksheet,Global,Recalculation,Manual** option. Once LOTUS 1-2-3's automatic recalculation feature has been disabled, the recalculation, after all changes have been entered, is accomplished by pressing the **CALC** (F9) key.

to 30%. You will see that the projected Net Income with this alternative is $78,469, an improvement over the initial value of Net Income. Think about how many manual calculations would have been required to obtain this answer, and you can begin to appreciate the power of computer-based financial worksheets. Also, we have illustrated the financial modeling process with an extremely simple one-product example. In general, we could build a model to handle multiple products and then explore the consequences from changes in the volume and mix of sales. Such a model would truly provide the capability for multiproduct C-V-P analysis.

Financial Simulation

Our worksheet model allowed us to determine the effects of certain decisions on the organization's profits and finances. We refer to such an exercise as *what-if forecasting*, since the worksheet allows us to answer what-if questions relating to changing decision parameters.

Even though the worksheet enables us to *simulate* the effects of changing decisions on the operation of the firm, a true *simulation* analysis usually connotes a different type of exercise in which the decisions are held constant but the outcomes are allowed to vary depending on different realizations of a key parameter, such as sales. For example, if we repeated the model for Sackville Enterprises over, say, one hundred years of sales data, we would have simulated the effects of a particular decision policy over a broad range of sales outcomes. Thus, simulation analysis estimates the range of outcomes from a given set of decisions. In contrast, the "what-if" analysis compares the marginal effect of one decision with that of another decision or set of decisions, holding all other parameters constant.

A Simulation Exercise

Classical simulation analysis, also called Monte Carlo analysis because of its extensive use of random numbers and repeated trials, can be illustrated with the following problem.

ROBERVAL NOVELTIES

Roberval Novelties produces an inexpensive watch. The selling price for this watch is $15 and quarterly sales vary between 10,000 and 20,000 units, with all values between the lower and upper limit considered equally likely (a uniform distribution).

Production costs for the watch depend on the number of watches produced. The following table summarizes the variable production cost per watch for different levels of quarterly production:

Level of Production	Variable Cost per Unit
0–14,000	$5.00
14,001–16,000	8.00
16,000–17,000	9.00

Production cannot exceed 17,000 units per month.

The total fixed costs associated with the watch production are $60,000 per quarter.

The inventory at the start of the current quarter is 1,000 watches. The company estimates that the out-of-pocket inventory holding cost is $2 per watch per quarter. The inventory holding cost is computed by multiplying the average inventory held during the quarter by the $2 holding cost. The average inventory is computed using the opening and closing balances of inventory.

Each quarter, production must be planned before the sales for that quarter are known but after the sales for the preceding quarter are known.

The company is interested in determining an inventory policy to effectively balance among stockout costs, excessive inventory holding costs, and excess production costs.

A worksheet for this problem is stored on the course diskette under the name **Roberval.** Get LOTUS 1-2-3 active on your computer and load this worksheet.

You should take some time to look around this worksheet and verify that it has been set up properly. Cells A23 through A29 contain a LOTUS 1-2-3 **macro** that simulates the effects of the current inventory policy on average quarterly Net Income. Macros are very useful features that allow a series of steps in the worksheet to be executed automatically.

The initial production plan produces 15,000 watches per quarter, the expected quarterly demand. Enter a number, such as 100, in cell B19 to indicate the number of years you would like the simulation exercise to use. Then press the **alt** and the **s** keys simultaneously. This command invokes the macro that is stored beginning in cell A23 and, with the value in cell B19 set at 100, takes the firm through a one-hundred-year simulation using the current inventory policy. Each year, the random number generator generates new sales levels for each quarter. The Average Quarterly Net Income is the average net income that has been recorded since the start of the simulation. You can keep track of what year is currently being simulated by observing the value in cell E19. While the simulation is ongoing, you will lose control of the keyboard and you will see **WAIT** displayed at the top-right corner of the screen (in the status indicator box). This tells you that a macro is currently being executed. When the macro stops executing, the status indicator box will signal **READY** and you have now regained control of the keyboard.

The simulation permits you to study the effects of alternative policies on a key performance indicator, such as average quarterly income. You might try an alternative production/inventory policy, such as letting production be 15,000 plus a buffer stock of, say, 2,000 units less opening inventory to see the impact on average quarterly net income.

Simulation provides a picture of the potential effect of a decision in a complex situation. It might occur to you: Why not just use average sales and a formula to predict the average quarterly net income of different policies? The reason is that the environment is often too complex to allow the effects of a decision to be summarized by a single outcome based on the expected value. The simulation indicates a range of possible outcomes that may result from a given decision rule. Especially when the cost or production function is nonlinear or discontinuous, as with Roberval Novelties, it will be difficult to predict the effect of random outcomes in a key variable, such as sales or production quantities, without a simulation model. The response function is too complex to be modeled analytically.

For the simulation to be valid, the random variable used in the simulation must capture the underlying uncertainty in the process. In this case, quarterly sales are supposed to be uniformly distributed between 10,000 and 20,000 units. If the random number generator generates a sequence of numbers that deviates from this distribution, a potential for misleading outcomes exists.

Moreover, the random number generator may produce different sequences of numbers each time you go through the simulation. In this case, the random numbers that represent demand will vary in different simulations, which may hinder comparability across successive runs. The user should check whether such a problem exists in the random number generator being used. It can be overcome by running very large numbers of trials that will minimize the effects of different realizations from the random number generator.

Summary

We began this chapter by developing the basic C-V-P equation and applying it to simple situations. Concepts of contribution margin and breakeven analysis were explored, and limitations to static C-V-P analysis were identified.

We then developed an alternative approach to model the firm. Computer-based worksheets allow managers to forecast the financial consequences from alternative courses of action. Simulation, allowing the effects of a particular policy to be studied under a distribution of outcomes, provides a further enhancement of worksheets.

We have only been able to scratch the surface of the potential of worksheets in this chapter. It is important to bear in mind that worksheets are merely tools that can never replace thoughtful reflection or careful evaluation. Indeed, if anything, the availability of worksheets will provide management with more challenges by relieving the analyst from the drudgery of calculation and providing more time to think, model, and plan, as well as to explore a much wider range of alternatives than were heretofore possible.

PROBLEMS

2–1   Breakeven Analysis on a Decision to Purchase New Equipment

Trenton Bat Company (TBC) manufactures a popular baseball bat that is prized by both professional and amateur players. The current variable cost of manufacturing the bat is $10 per unit. The cost of operating the lathe that produces the bat is about $200,000 per year. This cost includes maintenance and physical obsolescence.

TBC is now evaluating the possibility of purchasing a new lathe to manufacture the bat. By using a digital control unit, the lathe replaces the mechanical patterns currently used to manufacture lathes and relies instead on direct laser sensing by a computer within the lathe to compare the current size of the wood stock being turned on the lathe with a pattern stored in the computer's memory. Although the new machine would not increase the capacity of the bat-making operation, which is 500,000 bats per year, it would reduce the variable cost of producing the bats to $9 per unit, and the cost of operating the new lathe would be about $500,000 per year.

If the current level of production and sales of this bat is 400,000 units, should the new lathe be purchased? Ignore the effect of income taxes in answering this question.

2–2   Cost-Volume-Profit Analysis and Pricing in the Airline Industry* (Edward Deakin)

Trans Western Airlines is considering a proposal to initiate air service between Phoenix, Arizona and Las Vegas, Nevada. The route would be designed primarily to serve the recreation and tourist travelers that frequently travel between the two cities. By offering low-cost tourist fares,

---

* Copyright 1982 by CIPT Co. Reproduced with permission.

the airline hopes to persuade persons who now travel by other modes of transportation to switch and fly Trans Western on this route.

In addition, the airline expects to attract business travelers during the hours of 7 A.M. to 6 P.M. on Mondays through Fridays. The fare price schedule or tariff would be designed to charge a higher fare during business-travel hours so that tourist demand would be reduced during those hours. The company believes that a business fare of $75 one way during business hours and a fare of $40 for all other hours would result in the passenger load being equal during business-travel and tourist-travel hours.

To operate the route, the airline would need two 120-passenger jet aircraft. The aircraft would be leased at an annual cost of $3,800,000 each. Other fixed costs for ground service would amount to $1,500,000 per year.

Operation of each aircraft requires a flight crew whose salaries are based primarily on the hours of flying time. The costs of the flight crew are approximately $400 per hour of flying time.

Fuel costs are also a function of flying time. These costs are estimated at $500 per hour of flying time. Flying time between Phoenix and Las Vegas is estimated at 45 minutes each way.

The costs associated with processing each passenger amount to $3. This includes ticket processing, agent commissions, and variable costs of baggage handling. Food and beverage service cost $7.80 per passenger and will be offered at no charge on flights during business hours. The cost of this service on non-business hour flights is expected to be recovered through charges levied for alcoholic beverages.

Required:

1. If five business flights and three tourist flights are offered each way every weekday, and ten tourist flights are offered each way every Saturday and Sunday, what is the average number of passengers that must be carried on each flight to break even?
2. What is the breakeven load factor or percentage of available seats occupied on a route?
3. If Trans Western Airlines operates the Phoenix–Las Vegas route, its aircraft on that route will be idle between midnight and 6 A.M. The airline is considering offering a "Red Die" special, which would leave Phoenix daily at midnight and return by 6 A.M. The marketing division estimates that if the fare were no more than $20, at least 60 new passengers could be attracted to each "Red Die" flight. Operating costs would be at the same rate for this flight, but advertising costs of $1,225 per week would be required for promotion of the service. No food or beverage costs would be borne by the company. Management wishes to know the minimum fare that would be required to break

even on the "Red Die" special assuming the marketing division's passenger estimates are correct.

2–3 Multiple-Product Cost-Volume-Profit Analysis (CMA, adapted)

Hewtex Electronics manufactures two products, tape recorders and electronic calculators, and sells them nationally to wholesalers and retailers. The Hewtex management is very pleased with the company's performance for the current fiscal year. Projected sales through December 31, 1989 indicate that 70,000 tape recorders and 140,000 electronic calculators will be sold this year. The projected earnings statement, which appears below, shows that Hewtex will exceed its earnings goal of 9% on sales after taxes.

The tape recorder business has been fairly stable for the last few years, and the company does not intend to change the tape recorder price. However, the competition among manufacturers of electronic calculators has been increasing. Hewtex's calculators have been very popular with consumers. In order to sustain this interest in its calculators and to meet the price reductions expected from competitors, management has decided to reduce the wholesale price of its calculator from $22.50 to $20.00 per unit effective January 1, 1990. At the same time, the company plans to spend an additional $57,000 on advertising during fiscal year 1990. As a consequence of these actions, management estimates that 80% of its total revenue will be derived from calculator sales as compared to 75% in 1989. As in prior years, the sales mix is assumed to be the same at all volume levels.

The total fixed overhead costs will not change in 1990, nor will the variable overhead cost rates (applied on a direct labor hour base). However, the cost of materials and direct labor is expected to change. The cost of solid state electronic components will be cheaper in 1990. Hewtex estimates that material costs will drop 10% for the tape recorders and 20% for the calculators in 1990. However, direct labor costs for both products will increase 10% in the coming year.

Required:

1. How many tape recorder and electronic calculator units did Hewtex Electronics have to sell in 1989 to break even?
2. What volume of sales is required if Hewtex Electronics is to earn a profit in 1990 equal to 9% on sales after taxes?
3. Derive the equation describing the level of profits in 1990 as a function of the number of tape recorders and electronic calculators sold. Plot the breakeven line and the line representing a profit of 9% of sales after taxes.

HEWTEX ELECTRONICS
Projected Earnings Statement
For the Year Ended December 31, 1989

	Tape Recorders		Electronic Calculators		Total
	Total Amount (000 omitted)	Per Unit	Total Amount (000 omitted)	Per Unit	(000 omitted)
Sales	$1,050	$15.00	$3,150	$22.50	$4,200.0
Production costs:					
Materials	$ 280	$ 4.00	$ 630	$ 4.50	$ 910.0
Direct labor	140	2.00	420	3.00	560.0
Variable overhead	140	2.00	280	2.00	420.0
Fixed overhead	70	1.00	210	1.50	280.0
Total production costs	$ 630	$ 9.00	$1,540	$11.00	$2,170.0
Gross margin	$ 420	$ 6.00	$1,610	$11.50	$2,030.0
Fixed selling and administrative					1,040.0
Net income before income taxes					990.0
Income taxes (55%)					544.5
Net income					$ 445.5

2–4 Working Capital Management—The Management of Accounts Receivable

Lockport Produce is a wholesale produce company whose customers are mainly small grocery stores. Recently, Gail MacDonald, the general manager and owner of Lockport Produce, has become concerned about the firm's level of accounts receivable.

Because Lockport Produce handles a variety of produce, sales are stable throughout the year, averaging $1,000,000 per month, 90% of which are credit sales. Credit sales are billed immediately to customers upon delivery. The average collection period for credit sales is 40 days, and bad debts usually amount to 4% of credit sales. The average markup over variable costs is 50%.

Lockport Produce has been very successful and has grown rapidly in the six years since its inception. Because Gail has resisted issuing further equity capital, funds for working capital purposes have often been tight and the firm has had to borrow constantly from the bank, both for operating and for intermediate financing purposes. The firm's average cost of debt has been 14%.

Gail is now considering some alternatives to reduce the firm's level of accounts receivable.

Consider each of the following questions separately

1. By hiring an accounts receivable clerk to manage collections, Gail figures that the average collection period for credit sales can be reduced to 30 days. If the clerk's salary would be $20,000 per year, would hiring the clerk be a good idea?
2. If credit sales are eliminated, monthly sales will fall to $970,000. Assuming that the administrative cost savings from eliminating credit sales would be negligible, would eliminating credit sales be a good idea?

2–5 Multiple-Product and Multiple-Decision Cost-Volume-Profit Analysis

Rich Gogan, a promoter, is considering the possibility of booking the Wild World of Wrestling (WWW) in the Oxford Futuredome. Currently, due to intense television exposure, the WWW is enjoying great popularity. Rich figures that the possibility of earning money, which would be donated to the building drive to replace the roof on the local curling arena, is pretty good.

The Oxford Futuredome is a domed arena that will seat 60,000 fans as a wrestling or boxing venue. Rich figures that there would be three types of seating: ringside, reserved, and rush. The distribution and the ticket prices for these seats are expected to be as follows:

Seat Type	% Total Capacity	% Total Ticket Sales	Price
Ringside	10%	10%	$50
Reserved	70	70	25
Rush	20	20	10

At these prices, total ticket sales are expected to be 45,000.

The costs associated with such a promotion are high. The rent for the Futuredome is $100,000. The cost of hiring the private security personnel will be $30,000. In addition, a city ordinance requires that police be in attendance. The number of police required depends on the number of customers, and the police cost will be about $1 per customer. The cost of hiring ushers for the event will be $20,000. Clean-up and the repair of property damage caused by the fans is expected to cost $80,000 plus about $2 per fan. Insurance and other incidental costs will be $10,000.

The promotional fee for the event will be $10,000. The basic fee for the wrestlers who will appear on the card is $400,000. In addition, the wrestlers demand, and get, 10% of the gross receipts. The restaurant, snack bars, and vendors are controlled by the owners of the Futuredome. Futuredome management requires a flat fee of $100,000 to provide food services for the evening plus 25% (15% for the owners, 10% for the vendors) of the total food sales. The lessor, in this case Rich, must also pay the variable cost of the food provided, which averages $3 per fan. The average sales are $8 per fan. Finally, total sales taxes are 8% on any sales, food, or tickets. (All the prices provided above include taxes.)

Required:

Consider each case below separately.

1. What is the expected profit from this promotion?
2. Given the anticipated prices and distribution of sales, how many tickets, in total, must be sold for the promotion to break even?
3. An alternative, and more expensive, seating plan will increase the rent for the event to $150,000. Under this seating plan, the distribution of seats, and sales, would be ringside, 15%; reserved, 70%; and rush, 15%. Is the upgrade to the more expensive seating plan worthwhile?
4. If the food prices were cut so that the average revenue from each customer was $6, the total ticket sales would rise to 48,000. Is this price cut worthwhile?
5. Cutting all ticket prices by 10% is expected to increase total ticket sales by 10%. Is this change worthwhile?
6. One of the main attractions of the event would be a feature match between the Mighty Hercules, the current WWW heavyweight champion, and his archrival, Warren the Weasel. Hercules and Warren could be brought in a few days before the event in order to appear on local television and in some shopping centers. The total cost of the promotion would be $50,000 and would increase ticket sales by 10%. Is the promotion worthwhile?
7. One possibility is to organize a lottery for the available tickets. Under this scheme, all tickets to the event would sell for $20, and the names of the customers to be assigned the seats would be drawn randomly by a computer. The additional cost of this alternative would be $50,000, which includes the cost of promoting the lottery, as well as the fee to be paid to the accounting firm that would supervise the lottery. If the lottery were used, all 60,000 seats to the event would probably be sold. Is the lottery worthwhile?

2–6   *Nonlinear Cost Structure and Breakeven Analysis*

Bill Alexander is president of the Mason Company, a small producer of valves in a highly competitive market. A recent drop in the price of the valves has caused him great concern, since the price is now below the Mason Company's standard cost. Standard cost was determined from operating at 80% of the maximum capacity of 10,000 valves per month. The company does not normally operate above this level (of 8,000 valves per month), since the higher production requires overtime work that significantly increases variable costs.

The fixed costs of the Mason Company are $40,000 per month, and variable costs are $15 per valve for production levels up to 8,000 valves per month. Consequently, the standard cost of the valve is set at $20, based on operating at the desired level of 80% of capacity. Normally the price of the valve ranges from $21 to $23, allowing a small but adequate return on the Mason Company's modest investment in machinery and facilities.

For production above the standard volume, unit variable costs for the additional units increase by

- 15% above the normal variable cost for volume between 80% and 85% of capacity
- 20% above the normal variable cost for volume between 85% and 90% of capacity
- 30% above the normal variable cost for volume between 90% and 100% of capacity

Recently the price of valves has dropped about 10% to $19 per valve. Bill feels that he is now in a no-win situation, since he is losing money on every valve he is selling. While he sees some opportunities for increasing his sales volume above the current level of 8,000 units per month, he believes this would only make matters worse, since he feels that he is losing money at current volumes and the variable costs on the additional units produced will be even greater.

Required:

1. Comment on Bill's analysis of the price-cost squeeze in which he now finds himself. At what point would you recommend that he actually turn down orders at $19 per valve?
2. Assuming the price returns to its previous level of $21, at what volumes will the Mason Company operate profitably?

2–7 *Choosing the Scale of Operations with Declining Marginal Revenue*

Penticton Oil Products Limited (POPL) operates a small oil refinery that refines crude oil produced in the immediate geographical vicinity of the refinery. POPL processes the crude oil in batches. Each batch of crude oil refined produces five different products. The number of units of each product produced, per batch of crude oil processed, is as follows:

Product Number	Units Produced per Batch
1	100
2	50
3	10
4	20
5	40

The marketing manager has indicated that the price received for each product is a function of the number of units sold. The marketing manager has provided the following schedule of estimated market prices for the upcoming month for each of the five products where, in each case, x is the number of units of that product sold during the month:

Product Number	Estimated Market Price per Unit
1	$(150—0.01x)$
2	$(80 —0.006x)$
3	$(400—0.02x)$
4	$(600—0.05x)$
5	$(250—0.015x)$

For example, if 1,000 units of product 3 were sold, the price per unit that would be received would be $380 (computed as $400 - 0.02 * 1,000$).

In addition, the marketing manager has stated that, apart from any price considerations, an upper limit exists on the number of units of each product that can be sold during the upcoming month. These limits are:

Product Number	Maximum Sales Units
1	5,000
2	4,000
3	550
4	1,500
5	2,500

The cost of **each batch** of crude oil that is processed through the refinery is estimated as $15,000 for the cost of the crude oil and $7,000 for the out-of-pocket cost of refining.

Finally, the production manager has advised you that a disposal cost must be paid for any products that are produced and not sold. The disposal cost per unit for each of the products is:

Product Number	Disposal Cost per Unit
1	$10
2	5
3	20
4	50
5	15

Required:

1. How many batches of crude oil should the refinery process this month?
2. The president of POPL is concerned that, at the current market prices, some of the products may not be covering their costs. How would you respond to the president?

2–8 Choosing the Scale of Operations with Sales Constraints

Grande Cache Office Products Limited (GCOP) produces a line of ten products that are distributed to stationery supply retailers for resale in the office products industry. The selling price, variable costs, and estimated maximum sales for each of the ten products are as follows:

Product	Price	Variable Costs	Maximum Sales
1	$ 7.65	$ 3.07	125,000
2	11.72	5.39	75,000
3	4.41	1.21	350,000
4	15.12	10.32	95,000
5	19.65	11.75	105,000
6	8.54	3.76	450,000
7	15.97	9.90	80,000
8	13.96	7.96	200,000
9	5.86	1.87	600,000
10	10.78	6.97	120,000

The planning committee, consisting of the vice-president of marketing and the vice-president of production, has devised five alternative operating plans for the upcoming year. The **potential** production levels and the total fixed manufacturing and selling costs for each of the five alternatives are given below (the potential production levels are given in the column corresponding to each plan, and the total fixed costs are given at the bottom of the column corresponding to each plan).

Product	1	Plan Number (Maximum Possible Production) 2	3	4	5
1	119,000	154,000	170,000	68,000	105,000
2	85,000	110,000	51,000	85,000	75,000
3	289,000	374,000	323,000	255,000	255,000
4	68,000	88,000	51,000	102,000	60,000
5	102,000	132,000	34,000	136,000	90,000
6	374,000	484,000	408,000	323,000	330,000
7	34,000	44,000	17,000	68,000	30,000
8	204,000	264,000	153,000	255,000	180,000
9	323,000	418,000	357,000	289,000	285,000
10	102,000	132,000	136,000	119,000	90,000
Fixed costs	$4,000,000	$6,000,000	$3,000,000	$5,000,000	$3,500,000

The maximum sales potential for each product is independent of the plan number chosen.

Required:

1. Compute the net income associated with each of the five plans.
2. The corporate controller has made the following comments:

> I feel that you are making a mistake by ignoring the fixed cost per unit of production. By not allocating the fixed marketing and production costs to the individual products, you do not know if all these products are profitable. The fixed-cost allocation may point out some products that are unprofitable.

> Why not allocate the fixed production and marketing costs associated with each plan to the individual products in proportion to the production of each product? You can then eliminate those products whose price is less than the resulting full cost. Only by considering the full cost of each product will you make the proper decisions.

> Furthermore, you have ignored the general and administrative expenses. These costs are fixed and amount to $2,500,000, irrespective of which plan you choose. You have to find a way of allocating these costs to the products in order to evaluate overall profitability. You should allocate these costs to the individual products in proportion to the relative profitability of each product.

   On behalf of the planning committee, draft a reply to the company controller.
3. The marketing staff believes that if $100,000 is spent promoting Grande Cache Office Products Limited's corporate image, the maximum sales potential for all products will increase by 15%. Assuming that this belief is correct, should the promotion be undertaken?

2–9 Cash Flow Projection and What-If Financial Analysis

This question requires access to worksheet software and should not be attempted unless such software is available.

Burks Traps is a small firm specializing in the manufacture of lobster traps. Although production occurs year-round, sales occur primarily in the months of May through September.

Since the business is seasonal, the company has required short-term operating loans from its bank in order to meet the working capital demands of its peak sales season. These loans, on which monthly interest of 1.5% is payable, are made by the bank on the conditions that (1) the loan is liquidated for at least part of each year, and (2) the firm maintains a cash balance of at least 25% of the current loan balance. On the first day of each month, interest is to be paid on the loan amount outstanding during the preceding month. Loans are made, and repaid, in any amount on the first day of each month.

The company's president, Frank Maxwell, has hired you to undertake a study of the firm's operating loan requirements for the upcoming year.

Sales of lobster traps have increased steadily over the last five years. During October, November, and December of the past year, unit sales were as planned and equaled 1,350, 900, and 450 units, respectively. This year, Frank expects that sales could be anywhere between 24,000 and 32,000 units, with any point on this interval equally likely.

Monthly sales, as a percentage of annual sales, have had the following pattern over the last five years:

January	3%	April	8%	July	15%	October	6%
February	5%	May	12%	August	13%	November	4%
March	5%	June	16%	September	11%	December	2%

Frank believes that this pattern of sales will repeat itself in the upcoming year.

The primary raw materials used in manufacturing lobster traps are wood and netting. The standard cost card for the lobster trap is as follows:

Materials:	
Wood	$1.25
Netting	.85
Direct labor (0.5 hours @ $7.00)	3.50
Manufacturing overhead (0.5 hours @ $8.00)	4.00
Manufacturing cost per unit	$9.60

The predetermined rate of $8 per direct labor-hour used to apply manufacturing overhead to production includes $6 for fixed manufacturing overhead and $2 for variable manufacturing overhead. The $6 rate for fixed overhead was computed by dividing budgeting fixed manufacturing overhead of $60,000 by the normal activity level of 10,000 direct labor-hours per year.

The budgeted amounts for fixed manufacturing overhead include:

Factory rent	$30,000
Supervisor's salary	18,000
Maintenance	6,000
Depreciation on equipment	6,000

Direct materials are paid for in the month following their acquisition. Direct labor costs are paid for on a current basis.

The variable overhead items, which amount to $2 per direct labor-hour worked, consist mainly of power and incidental carpentry supplies such as sandpaper, glue, and replacement parts for the power tools used in the factory. These items are acquired in the month in which they are used and are purchased for cash from a local hardware distributor.

The factory rent and supervisor's salary are paid monthly and in equal amounts. The maintenance expenses are incurred in two equal amounts in February and August. The depreciation on the equipment is recognized annually in the month of December.

The firm's manufacturing policy is to have on hand, at the start of each month, an inventory level that equals that month's expected sales. This production policy has resulted in highly variable production rates. As a result, workers are only paid for hours worked. They expect to work more hours during the peak periods than during the slack periods.

Other expenses are classified as selling and administrative. These expenses amount to $85,000 in a normal year and include:

Clerical salaries	$30,000
Shipping costs ($0.50 per unit)	10,000
Sales commissions (10% of selling price)	30,000
Other office expenses	15,000

The clerical salaries and other office expenses are incurred and paid in equal monthly amounts. Shipping costs and sales commissions are paid in the month following the month in which they are incurred.

The only other cost is a storage cost paid to a warehouse for storing the completed lobster traps. The storage charge, which is payable at the end of each month, is $0.50 multiplied by the average number of units in storage during the month. The average is computed using the opening and closing inventory levels.

The selling price per lobster trap is $15. All sales are credit sales. The usual pattern of collections has been as follows:

20% in the month of sale
60% in the month following the month of sale
10% in the second month following the month of sale
8% in the third month following the month of sale
2% uncollected

The opening balance of cash this year is $5,000, which is the minimum balance of cash the firm wishes to maintain. Production during December was 840 units, and the inventory level at December 31 is 840 units.

The company uses the following accounting practices for accounts receivable and inventory:

a. The estimated uncollectible portion of any month's sales is charged to cost of goods sold in the month in which the sale occurs.

b. The company uses direct costing to value inventory for financial statement purposes.

Required:

Consider each question below separately.

1. Prepare a statement forecasting the firm's cash monthly flows for the upcoming year. Indicate clearly when financing will be required and when it will be repaid.

2. Frank is considering abandoning credit sales and instituting a cash-only policy. This policy is expected to decrease sales by 10%. Is this policy desirable?

3. Frank has just returned from a seminar that discussed just-in-time inventory techniques, and he wants to see whether he can cut month-end inventories to zero. This policy is expected to result in occasional stockouts, and Frank figures that the lost sales resulting from these stockouts will amount to 5% of current sales. Should the new inventory policy be adopted?

4. The same seminar has made Frank think about improving product quality. By increasing the materials cost by 15%, he figures that he can increase sales by 10% at the current price. Is this quality change worthwhile?

5. If Frank cuts his selling price by $2 per unit, sales will increase by 20%. Is the price cut worthwhile?

6. Another bank is vying for Frank's business. The bank will require a minimum cash balance of 75% of the outstanding loan but will only charge interest at the rate of 1.35% per month. Should Frank switch banks?

7. The workers have proposed to Frank that a new production policy be instituted wherein all production will occur in equal monthly amounts over the three-month period between February and April. The workers are enthusiastic about this plan, since it allows them to work at other jobs during the summer.

   The workers' enthusiasm for the new policy will cause them to be more productive, so that only 0.4 direct labor-hours will be required per unit. Factory rent will be reduced to $12,000 per year, and maintenance will be reduced to $2,000 per year. Both of these costs would be paid in equal monthly amounts over the production period. All other costs, as well as their associated payment patterns, would remain the same as they are under the current production plan. Should this new policy be implemented?

2–10 *Cash Flow Projection and the Evaluation of a Capital Project*

(From Jack McGrath, "Spreadsheets: Breakeven Analysis," CFO, May 1987, pp. 83–89.) The CFO worksheet on the course diskette was provided in the McGrath article. The following instructions were provided with the worksheet.

The formula for unit contribution assumes that variable cost is a percentage of selling price. If such is not the case, you should change B1 to the dollar value of variable cost, and change the formula at F1 to +B2–B1.

You have to supply a value for unit sales that will serve as the basis for periodic growth . . . this value is Seed Sales at cell B3.

The template assumes that at first sales grow by 1.5 percent per month (cell B6). Then, at some time in the future, the growth rate will fall to 0.5 percent per month (cell B7). These rates are variable . . . they can readily be changed to fit your experience. If you make them the same, sales will grow steadily. If B7 is greater than B6, you define an accelerating trend; if B7 is negative, you define a decline in unit sales . . . the transition (point) from one rate to another is entered in cell B8. If no such transition takes place, set the value to 0.

[There is] a set of calculations in cells F7 through F11 that is designed to allow you to isolate a single month . . . the calculations make it easier to home in on the month in which breakeven takes place.

The initial formula for receipts assumes that the lag between sales and receipts is one period . . . you should change this value to reflect your actual receivables lag.

Similarly, the formulas in row 19 assume that your production and distribution cycle is such that, by the time products are sold, their variable costs will have been paid.

. . . you can examine the effect of delaying the project for one or more periods by changing the value in B9. You may also wish to change the receivables lag or the payables lead by changing the formulas in C18 and B19.

With these instructions in mind, adapt and use this worksheet to address the following problem.

SALEM ELECTRICAL

The Salem Electrical Company is a small company that has developed a revolutionary starter for automobiles. The selling price of this starter would be $50, and the variable costs for producing, shipping, and selling the starter are $10 per unit.

The initial outlay cost associated with the project would be $12,000,000, and the monthly fixed costs would amount to $100,000.

Production would begin in month 1 and sales would begin in month 2. The production in each month would equal sales in the following month. All fixed and variable production costs would be paid as incurred. Sales would occur uniformly throughout each month, and all sales would be on credit. Of these sales, 25% would be collected in the month of sale, 65% would be collected in the second month following the month of sale, 8% in the second month following the month of sale, and 2% would never be collected.

Because of limitations on production, sales in month 2 are expected to amount to 12,000 units, and sales are expected to increase at the rate of 1% per month for the next 24 months. Salem Electrical expects that after 24 months of growth, its large competitors will have perfected substitute products and Salem's sales will decline at the rate of 2% per month. Salem plans to discontinue sale of the starters after month 60.

Salem faces a marginal tax rate of 40% and will use straight-line depreciation to depreciate the initial $12,000,000 investment for both tax and financial accounting purposes. Salem makes tax installment payments, and will recognize the depreciation on the initial investment, at the end of each quarter beginning in month 3. You should assume that all cash flows take place on the last day of each month and that the last tax payment on cash flows resulting from this project will take place in month 62.

Salem has enough other business such that any initial losses recorded by the new product could be used to offset other business income. Also, assume for convenience that Salem uses a cash basis for tax accounting.

Salem requires an after-tax return of 15% on this type of investment. Is the project desirable? (In fact, you should determine that the actual rate of return on this project is 17.7%. The worksheet provided to you is **not** currently equipped to compute net present values, nor is the worksheet equipped to handle a cash flow analysis beyond twelve months.)

In addition, you should project the cash flows associated with this project over its lifetime for the company's treasurer.

chapter 3

LINEAR-PROGRAMMING MODELS FOR PLANNING

In the preceding chapter, we forecasted profitability as a function of the volume and mix of product sales. We used the basic C-V-P framework to explore the implications of changes in sales volume on overall profitability. All the analysis was conducted in the absence of any production constraints. We implicitly assumed that increases in demand could always be satisfied by increased production.

In practice, bottlenecks will usually arise to constrain the amount of product the firm can deliver. Introducing bottleneck constraints changes the perspective of C-V-P analysis in fundamental ways. Without production constraints, managers and salespeople would be correct to focus their efforts on increasing the output of high-contribution-margin products. But if production constraints exist, the high-contribution-margin products may no longer be the most profitable. Only by explicitly modeling the nature of the production process and its constraints will we be able to determine the most profitable products to produce and sell.

Single Production Constraint

A particularly simple and instructive situation arises when only one resource constrains production; this resource would truly be the bottleneck resource. For example, if all the firm's products must be processed through a single machine, then the firm's output will be limited by the available hours on this machine. Let us assume a simple situation where only two products are produced with the following characteristics:

	Product 1	Product 2
Selling price	$10	$15
Variable cost	4	7
Contribution margin	$ 6	$ 8
Machine time per unit	3 hours	6 hours

Looking solely at contribution margin, product 2 appears to be the more profitable, generating $2 more contribution margin than product 1 for each extra unit produced and sold. Indeed, if there were no constraints on production or if current production were far from capacity, the firm would clearly prefer to sell more of product 2 than of product 1 (assuming such a 1-to-1 trade-off existed). But assume that we could sell as much of either product as we wanted (without being allowed to raise price to ration demand). In this case, it would be incorrect to produce any of product 2. Profits are maximized by using the bottleneck machine to produce only product 1 and to produce zero of product 2.

This claim is easy to verify. Assume that 24,000 hours of machine time are available. If we concentrated on product 2, we could produce 24,000/6 = 4,000 units, generating a contribution of $32,000 toward fixed overhead and profits. But if we concentrated production and sales solely on product 1, we could produce 24,000/3 = 8,000 units, generating a total contribution of $48,000, an increase of 50% over the best we could do when we produced only product 2. You can check that any feasible production schedule that includes positive amounts of product 2 will yield less contribution than the $48,000 we earn by concentrating solely on product 1. A feasible schedule would have total machine-hours less than or equal to 24,000 hours. Numerically, we require that

$$3*(\text{quantity of product 1}) + 6*(\text{quantity of product 2}) \leq 24,000.$$

At first glance, it may seem surprising that the product with the lower contribution margin per unit turns out to be the most profitable one to produce. But this apparent paradox is easily resolved once we recognize that, in the presence of a scarce production resource, the correct criterion for ranking product profitability is **contribution margin per unit consumed of the scarce (bottleneck) resource,** not contribution margin per unit. In our example, product 1 generates $2 contribution margin per machine-hour ($6 contribution margin/3 machine-hours), whereas product 2 generates only $1.33 contribution per machine-hour ($8 contribution margin/6 machine-hours). The $2 per hour margin for product 1 is 50% higher than the $1.33 margin for product 2. This ratio explains why contribution margin ($48,000) is 50% higher when product 1 is produced rather than product 2 (which yields only $32,000). When we are constrained by the number of machine-hours available, we maximize profits by concentrating production on the products that have the highest contribution margin per machine-hour, in this case product 1.

Multiple Production Constraints

In general, more than one resource will constrain the amount that can be produced. For this situation, we can no longer obtain a ranking of product profitability simply by using the ratio of contribution margin per unit of scarce resource. The ranking of products across the different constraining resources will generally differ. For example, with our simple situation, assume that only 12,000 hours of supervisory time are available and that both products require 2 hours of supervision time for each unit produced. For the supervisory resource, product 1 has $3 of contribution margin per hour of supervision used and product 2 has $4, thereby reversing the profitability rankings when machine-time was the only constraining resource.

When multiple constraining resources exist, simple profitability rankings among products are no longer possible. Fortunately, we can use linear programming to determine an optimal product mix in the presence of constraining resources. For our two-product numerical example, we can formulate the linear program as follows:

$$\text{Maximize: } 6x_1 + 8x_2$$
$$\text{Subject to: } 3x_1 + 6x_2 \leq 24{,}000$$
$$2x_1 + 2x_2 \leq 12{,}000$$
$$x_1 , x_2 \quad \geq 0$$

where

$$x_1 = \text{quantity of product 1 produced}$$
$$x_2 = \text{quantity of product 2 produced}$$

The optimal solution to this program is $x_1 = 4{,}000$ and $x_2 = 2{,}000$ for a total contribution margin of $40,000 (see Exhibit 3-1). The addition of the supervision time constraint has reduced the maximum contribution from $48,000 to $40,000. The reduction in contribution margin is not surprising. As we add more constraints to a problem, the contribution margin will decrease (unless the new constraints are not binding). We can never be better off by increasing the number of constraints we place on our productive opportunities.

Also, unlike the situation when only one constraining resource existed, both products are produced in the optimal solution. This is not an accident. In general, as many different products will be produced as there are constraining resources.

In summary, extending the simple, single-product C-V-P analysis to multiple products with multiple constraints on production requires a linear programming formulation to determine a production plan that maximizes contribution margin from the product mix. The linear programming approach highlights the important point that the most profitable products are those that have maximum contribution margin per unit of scarce resource consumed. While simple profitability rankings are not possible if multiple constraining resources exist, the linear programming solution maximizes total contribution margin subject to the described constraints.

EXHIBIT 3-1
Linear Programming
Graphical Solutions for Two-Variable Problem

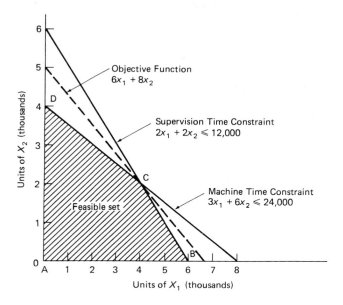

	Extreme Points of Feasible Set		
Point	*Units of x_1*	*Units of x_2*	*Total Contributions Margin*
A	0	0	0
B	6,000	0	$36,000
C	4,000	2,000	$40,000 (optimal solution)
D	0	4,000	$32,000

Linear Programming and Production Planning

Linear programming (LP) models for product and resource planning are most beneficial when the firm has considerable discretion in the product mix it produces on its capacity-constraining resources. LP has been extensively used for short-term planning by processlike industries, including paper, petroleum, steel, and chemicals. For example:

A large integrated paper products firm uses a comprehensive LP model to schedule the cutting of logs, to determine the distribution and processing of these logs among its sawmills, paper mills, and plywood mills, and to plan the cutting and sales of excess logs not processed through its mills.

A large integrated oil company uses LP to schedule the operating of its railroad tanker car fleet including the delivery of products to customers and the hauling and locating of empty tank cars. A separate LP model helps to determine the mix of products produced in its refineries.

This chapter is not intended to develop the theory and interpretation of linear programming models. That task is properly left to Operations Management and Operations Research courses. On the other hand, a simple, but not trivial, planning model will help to illustrate the accounting implications of linear programming planning models. In this section, we will show how to

a. Formulate operations planning problems as linear programs
b. Develop a structured approach to determine the constraints of an operations planning problem
c. Investigate the accounting implications of such planning models

The following extended example will be used to illustrate the relevant concepts.

RIMOUSKI CHEMICAL WORKS

Rimouski Chemical Works (RCW) produces industrial chemicals. In the Solvents Division, two operations, each using one machine, produce a variety of products in batches of fixed proportions.

In the first operation, 100 kiloliters of chemical A are combined with 50 kiloliters of chemical B to produce: 20 kiloliters of chemical C, 90 kiloliters of chemical D, and 40 kiloliters of chemical E. This batch size and the output proportions cannot be varied. Each batch requires 10 labor-hours (relating to preparing and cleaning the machines) and 3 machine-hours (relating to blending the product).

Chemical A has a purchase price of $80 per kiloliter, and chemical B can be manufactured internally (see below) or purhased externally for $100 per kiloliter.

Chemical C is a waste byproduct that costs $50 per kiloliter to be disposed. Chemical D is used as an intermediate product in the second operation. Chemical E can be sold for $100 per kiloliter.

In the second operation, batches of 70 kiloliters of chemical D are processed to produce 60 kiloliters of chemical F and 10 kiloliters of chemical B. This batch size and the output proportions cannot be varied. Each batch requires 15 labor-hours and 5 machine-hours.

Chemical F is sold externally for $250 per kiloliter, and chemical B can be used in the first operation or sold externally for a net realizable value of $75 per kiloliter.

Processing Operations in Rimouski Chemical Works

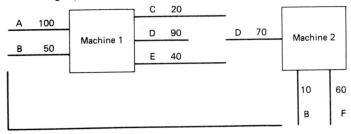

Because of the volatility of the market, production plans are revised each week. The availability of labor- and machine-hours this week are:

Machine-hours:	
Operation 1	75
Operation 2	80
Labor-hours:	
Total available for both operations	350

The labor force consists of two types of workers: (1) those who are part of the permanent work force and are never laid off, irrespective of whether work is available, and (2) temporary workers who are hired as required. All the workers are paid the same hourly rate of $10 per hour, but the permanent workers are guaranteed payment for a forty-hour week, whereas the temporary workers are paid only for the hours actually worked. Of the 350 worker-hours available for this week, 275 relate to permanent workers and 75 relate to temporary workers.

A cost study has determined that variable factory overhead equals $8 per direct labor-hour worked, plus $300 per hour worked on machine 1 or machine 2.

This week, the marketing department has contracted to supply 300 kiloliters of chemical E at the current market price. Moreover, the marketing manager indicates that the maximum amounts of chemical D, chemical E, chemical F, and chemical B that can be sold this week are 100, 400, 800, 350 kiloliters, respectively. (The maximum demand for chemical E excludes the contracted sales of 300 kiloliters.)

What is the optimal production plan to maximize short-run contribution margin for the upcoming week?

To solve this problem, we first have to specify what the firm wants to accomplish (the objective function) and identify the factors (the constraints) that operate to limit the attainment of management's objectives. Then, jointly considering the objective function and the constraints, an optimal production plan can be chosen by using a computerized linear programming package.

Defining the Objective Function

In this case, we wish to maximize the short-run contribution margin. But for this production process, we are unable to determine the variable cost, and therefore the contribution margin, of individual products.

Rimouski Chemical Works is an example of a joint-product situation (to be discussed in more detail in Chapter 8) in which the total cost of producing individual products cannot be unambiguously determined. An oil refiner cannot determine the total cost of a liter of aviation fuel, nor can a butcher determine the total cost of a steak. For Rimouski, none of the costs for the individual products can be computed. Fortunately, we do not have to compute individual product costs in order to develop the objective function for the linear program. Moreover, if we attempt to determine an optimal production plan based on allocating the joint costs to individual products, we are likely to obtain an inferior solution.

In formulating the objective function, we include any variable with which a cost or a revenue can be directly associated. Only directly attributable costs or revenues should be associated with objective function variables.

In this problem, we can directly associate a cost or a revenue with two types of variables: (1) variables that create products and costs and (2) variables that generate revenues. In the joint-product case, the variables creating costs and products are usually the levels of operations (such as the number of barrels of crude oil refined or the number of cows processed). In this case, the cost variables are the number of batches processed by machines 1 and 2. We look to the levels of activity of the operations (the batches) as the cost objectives rather than to the individual joint products because of the impossibility of directly assigning costs to the individual products.

We define a variable, x_1, to represent the level of operation of Department 1 (or, equivalently, machine 1). The costs that can be directly associated with the number of batches of chemicals that are processed by machine 1 include:

100 kiloliters of chemical A @ $80		$8,000
10 labor-hours @ $8		80
3 machine-hours @ $300		900
Total		$8,980

Note that the cost of chemical B and the cost of labor were excluded from this calculation. These costs were excluded because they cannot be directly attributed to the level of machine 1 operations. The cost of chemical B was excluded because we can determine neither the cost of the intermediate product B nor the quantity of B that will be purchased externally versus produced internally. For labor, we do not know whether we will be using permanent labor (which has a variable cost of $0 because these workers are paid whether products are produced or not) or temporary labor (which has a variable cost of $10 per hour). Evidently we will have to find alternative ways of including these costs in the model.

For machine 2, we let x_2 represent the number of batches processed. The cost per batch processed by machine 2 includes:

15 labor-hours @ $8	$ 120
5 machine-hours @ $300	1,500
Total	$1,620

The two variables, x_1 and x_2, accumulate the directly attributable production costs of any production plan that we undertake.

Following the diagram of the production process for RCW, we next wish to determine the cost of the activity "disposal of chemical C." Let x_3 equal the number of kiloliters of chemical C disposed. Since the disposal cost per kiloliter of chemical C is $50, x_3's objective function coefficient is -50.

Next in the diagram we find chemical D. Since this chemical is an intermediate product, we cannot associate either a cost or a revenue with it. Hence no variable needs to be defined for this product in the objective function.

Chemical E, the only salable product produced by machine 1, does generate a revenue of $100 per liter, so this product must appear in the objective function. We define x_4 to be the number of kiloliters of chemical E sold, and the objective function coefficient of x_4 equals $100. Chemical E is a joint product that does not have any directly attributable costs. All the costs of producing chemical E have been included in the cost of processing batches through machine 1 (i.e., these costs have been associated with the x_1 coefficient). We will see later how to tie the costs of machine 1 batches to the revenues of the products that machine 1 produces.

Chemical F sells for $250 per kiloliter. Letting x_6 represent the number of kiloliters of chemical F sold, the objective function coefficient for x_6 will be 250. Similarly, chemical B sells for $75 per kiloliter. If we let x_7 equal the number of kiloliters of chemical B sold, then x_7's objective function coefficient will be 75.

We still have some loose ends to tie up. There are two elements of variable cost that we have not yet considered. The first relates to the number of kiloliters of chemical B purchased externally. We will refer to this variable as x_5, and its objective function coefficient will be -100. The second variable, x_8, represents the number of hours of temporary labor used. Its objective function coefficient will be -10, since the rate for temporary labor is $10 per hour.

At this point, we have defined all the decision variables that affect costs and revenues. Our objective function, to be maximized, has become:

$$-8{,}980x_1 - 1{,}620x_2 - 50x_3 + 100x_4 - 100x_5 + 250x_6 + 75x_7 - 10x_8$$

Defining the Constraints

In general, three types of constraints arise in linear programming problems:

a. Resource constraints, which define the availability of the input factors of production, such as materials, labor, and machine time

b. Marketing constraints, which define the minimum and maximum levels of sales that are possible during the planning period

c. Balance constraints, which define the production and availability of products in the production system

Resource Constraints Four resource constraints exist for the production process; two for labor and one for each machine (department). The first resource constraint is defined by the availability of the two types of labor:

Labor-Hours Constraint: $10x_1 + 15x_2 \leq 275 + x_8$

The labor used in the operation of machine 1 $(10x_1)$ plus the labor used in the operation of machine 2 $(15x_2)$ cannot exceed the amount of time available from permanent worker (275 hours) plus the amount of part-time worker labor-hours acquired (x_8).

Temporary Worker-Hours Constraint: $x_8 \leq 75$

The amount of temporary labor acquired cannot exceed the available pool of 75 hours. The cost of temporary hours used is accumulated separately, via the coefficient of x_8, in the objective function, since (1) this cost cannot be directly associated with any individual process or product (in effect, this cost must be treated as an indirect overhead cost), and (2) we will not know how many, if any, of these labor-hours will be used until the problem has been solved.

Machine 1 Hours Constraint: $3x_1 \leq 75$

The amount of machine time used on machine 1 (Department 1) cannot exceed the available time of 75 hours. The usage of machine time is associated with batches of production (x_1), not with units of individual products.

Machine 2 Hours Constraint: $5x_2 \leq 80$

The amount of machine time used on machine 2 (Department 2) cannot exceed the available time of 80 hours.

Marketing Constraints We have four marketing constraints: one for the minimum sales of chemical E to ensure that the firm meets its contractual commitments, and three that set maximum limits on the amount of chemicals E, F, and B that can be sold.

- **Minimum Sales—Chemical E:** $x_4 \geq 300$
- **Maximum Sales—Chemical E:** $x_4 \leq 700$
- **Maximum Sales—Chemical F:** $x_6 \leq 800$
- **Maximum Sales—Chemical B:** $x_7 \leq 350$

Balance Constraints The final set of constraints, the balance constraints, plays a unique role in formulating RCW's production-planning model. Until this point, we have not linked the variables that create costs with the variables that create revenues. If we were to solve the LP formulated so far, the solution would make the cost variables (x_1 and x_2) both 0 and make the revenue variables (x_4, x_6, and x_7) as large as the marketing and resource constraints allow. The balance constraints are needed to link the cost variables (input batches) with the revenue variables (the output products) so that a feasible production plan can be calculated. There should be one balance constraint for each product (both final and intermediate). The general form of a balance constraint is

$$\text{Uses of a product} = \text{Availability of a product}$$

or, more specifically,

$$\text{Sales} + \text{Internal use as intermediate product} + \text{Ending inventory}$$
$$= \text{Production} + \text{Opening inventory} + \text{Purchases}$$

If ending inventory has no value and excess units can be disposed of at no cost, then the balance equation can be rewritten[1] as

$$\text{Sales} + \text{Internal use as intermediate product} \leq \text{Production}$$
$$+ \text{Purchases}$$

---

[1] Because of the way that some linear programming software handles equality constraints, it is preferable to rewrite an equality constraint as a "less than or equal to" constraint (or a "greater than or equal to" constraint) whenever possible.

We can now write the balance constraint for each of the intermediate and final products.

Balance Constraint—Chemical B: $50x_1 + x_7 \leq 10x_2 + x_5$

The total of chemical B used in the batches processed by machine 1 $(50x_1)$ plus the amount of chemical B sold (x_7) must be less than the amount of chemical B produced by machine 2 $(10x_2)$ plus the amount of chemical B purchased externally (x_5).

Balance Constraint—Chemical C: $x_3 = 20x_1$

The amount of chemical C disposed of (x_3) must equal the amount of chemical C produced by machine 1 $(20x_1)$.[2]

Balance Constraint—Chemical D: $70x_2 \leq 90x_1$

The amount of chemical D used in the batches processed on machine 2 $(70x_2)$ must be less than the amount of chemical D produced by machine 1 $(90x_1)$.

Balance Constraint—Chemical E: $x_4 \leq 40x_1$

The amount of chemical E sold (x_4) must be less than the amount of chemical E produced by machine 1 $(40x_1)$.

Balance Constraint—Chemical F: $x_6 \leq 60x_2$

The amount of chemical F sold (x_6) must be less than the amount of chemical F produced by machine 2 $(60x_2)$.

Complete Model

We can now write the objective function and the constraints for RCW as follows:

Maximize
$$-8980x_1 - 1620x_2 - 50x_3 + 100x_4 - 100x_5 + 250x_6 + 75x_7 - 10x_8$$
Subject to
   Less than constraints:
Resources
(1)	labor-hours constraint:	$10x_1 + 15x_2 - x_8 \leq 275$
(2)	temporary-hours constraint:	$x_8 \leq 75$
(3)	machine 1 hours constraint:	$3x_1 \leq 75$

---
[2] This constraint is formulated as an equality constraint to force disposal to occur. Alternatively, we could rewrite it as a "greater than or equal to" constraint: $x_3 \geq 20\,x_1$.

(4)   machine 2 hours constraint: $5x_2 \le 80$

Marketing

(5)   maximum sales of chemical E: $x_4 \le 700$

(6)   maximum sales of chemical F: $x_6 \le 800$

(7)   maximum sales of chemical B: $x_7 \le 350$

Product Balance

(8)   chemical B: $50x_1$ $-10x_2 - x_5 + x_7 \le 0$

(9)   chemical D: $-90x_1 + 70x_2 \le 0$

(10)   chemical E: $-40x_1 + x_4 \le 0$

(11)   chemical F: $-60x_2 + x_6 \le 0$

Equal to constraints:

(12)   chemical C balance: $-20x_1 + x_3 = 0$

Greater than or equal to constraints:

(13)   minimum sales of chemical E: $x_4 \le 300$

In addition, each decision variable must be constrained to be greater than or equal to zero.

We use this formulation with LPROG, the linear programming package provided for this text, to determine the optimal solution for this problem.[3] LPROG yields the following solution (any variable not explicitly mentioned below has a value equal to zero in the optimal solution):

x_1	batches on machine 1	10.37
x_2	batches on machine 2	13.33
x_3	kiloliters of chemical C disposed	207.41
x_4	kiloliters of chemical E sold	414.82
x_5	kiloliters of chemical B bought	385.19
x_6	kiloliters of chemical F sold	800
x_8	hours of temporary labor used	28.70

Slack and surplus variables[4] are:

x_{10}	unused temporary labor-hours	46.30
x_{11}	unused machine 1 hours	43.89

---

[3] The LPROG data and solution files for this problem are available in the course diskette under the names RCWDATA and RCWRES, respectively.

[4] LPROG adds its own variables to represent slack, surplus, or artificial variables in the constraints. Slack variables 9 through 19 are associated with the Less Than Or Equal To constraints (1)–(11), artificial variable 20 is associated with the Equal To constraint (12), and surplus variable 21 is associated with the Greater Than Or Equal To constraint (13).

x_{12}	unused machine 2 hours	13.33
x_{13}	unused potential for E sales	285.18
x_{15}	unused potential for B sales	350
x_{21}	B sales in excess of contract	114.82

Two critical factors are currently limiting further increases in overall contribution margin: the maximum level of sales for chemical F (constraint [6]), and the availability of permanent force labor-hours (in constraint [1]). The solution prefers permanent to temporary workers, since we have not assigned any cost to the use of permanent workers. We considered the cost of permanent workers to be fixed and hence not relevant for the short-run operational plan.

The production plan implied by the optimal solution is:

1. Produce 10.37 batches of chemicals on machine 1. This activity uses 103.7 labor-hours, 31.11 machine 1 hours, 1,037 kiloliters of chemical A (purchased externally), 133.33 kiloliters of chemical B produced by machine 2, and 385.19 kiloliters of chemical B purchased externally. This activity yields: (i) 207.41 kiloliters of chemical C that must be disposed of, (ii) 933.33 kiloliters of chemical D to be used by machine 2, and (iii) 414.82 kiloliters of chemical E, which are sold.

2. Produce 13.33 batches of chemicals on machine 2. This activity uses 200 labor-hours, 66.67 machine 2 hours, and 933.33 kiloliters of chemical D. This activity yields: (i) 800 kiloliters of chemical F and (ii) 133.33 liters of chemical B, which are used by machine 1.

3. Jointly, machine 1 and machine 2 require 303.7 labor-hours, which, given the internal availability of 275 labor-hours, means that 28.7 temporary worker labor-hours must be used.

The solution implies an important feature that may not necessarily be true. A solution of 10.37 batches on machine 1 and 13.33 batches on machine 2 assumes that fractional batches (0.37 on machine 1 and 0.33 on machine 2) can be produced. Although it is possible that fractional batches can be produced, it is much less likely that labor time will be proportional to the size of the batch. Probably, a certain amount of labor is required whether a complete or a fractional batch is produced. If this statement is true, RCW may not have enough labor time to produce 0.37 batches on machine 1 and 0.33 batches on machine 2. RCW may have to round the solution to the next-lowest integer (10 batches on machine 1 and 13 batches on machine 2) and test whether this is a feasible schedule. If decision variables, such as numbers of batches, can only take on integer values (such as 0,1,2, . . . , 12,13,14, . . .), a more complex solution procedure—called a mixed-integer programming algorithm—must be used to obtain the optimal solution subject to specified decision variables taking on only integer values.

The output from the linear program can also be fed into a financial planning model of the type we constructed in the preceding chapter. For example, we can extend the example by assuming that the fixed selling and administrative costs in RCW equal $50,000 and that the fixed manufacturing expenses (including the permanent labor costs) are $30,000 per period.

To review, the major principles to formulate an LP model are as follows:

a. Choose variables to represent activities for which we can directly associate costs. In this case, the activities were the number of batches processed by each machine.

b. Develop three sets of constraints (resource, marketing, and balance).

c. Construct one balance constraint for each product that is produced, irrespective of whether it is sold. The balance constraints link the intermediate and final output variables with the input resource variables.

Beyond demonstrating how to model a manufacturing operation, we showed that it was not necessary, indeed it would have been incorrect, to allocate joint costs to individual products. The management accountant, when approached for cost information about products, resources, or activities, must always understand the purpose for the information before responding. It may not be improper to allocate joint costs (for example, for behavioral or regulatory reasons), but if the information is to be used for economic decision making, then joint-cost allocations should be avoided. An optimal product mix can be determined without assigning all the incremental costs of production to individual products.

A second implication for accounting relates to the sensitivity of the decision to the data provided. The data used in the planning model may not be accurate, thus causing the decision model to select a suboptimal decision. The analyst can use the considerable power of sensitivity analysis and parametric programming from a linear programming model to determine which data have the greatest impact on the solution. Discussion of how to interpret the dual variables and how to perform sensitivity analysis and parametric programming in an LP model is covered in an operations research or a managerial economics course. For our purposes, it suffices to demonstrate that LP formulations are the logical extension to multiproduct C-V-P analysis for determining an optimal product mix when constraints on production and sales exist.

Multiperiod Considerations

We can extend our model to handle multiperiod operations. For example, to develop a two-period plan for Rimouski Chemical Works, we have to define new variables and constraints for the activities, both expense and revenue, undertaken in the second period. We would begin by developing resource, marketing, and balance constraints for the second period that would look virtually identical to those formulated for the first period. The balance constraint for each product in each period would be of the form

Opening inventory + Purchases + Production = Ending inventory
+ Internal uses + Sales

In addition, a new constraint would be needed to link the ending inventory of period 1 to the opening inventory of period 2:

Ending inventory (period 1) = Opening inventory (period 2)

This last constraint ties the balance constraints from the two periods together. If there were out-of-pocket holding costs for inventory, we would associate an inventory holding cost in the objective function to an opening (or closing) inventory level. The solution to the multiperiod production problem would determine the production level of all products in both periods and the optimal inventory level to carry between periods. Sometimes firms provide target ending inventories to represent a minimum level of service for customers; in effect, they constrain the solution to reflect factors (such as safety stocks or customer responsiveness) that have not been incorporated into the LP formulation.

Short-run Bottlenecks and Long-run Planning Considerations

Fixed costs were not considered relevant for short-run planning considerations. The fixed costs provided a level of capacity that we assumed could not be varied in the short run. Management's objective in the short run, therefore, was to use available capacity in its most effective way.

The LP solution indentifies the cost to the firm when a factor of production constrains output. In the above example, the factor constraining production was the permanent force labor-hours that were available, although, in the example, we were able to supplement the permanent labor force with temporary workers. This cost reflects the opportunities that are lost from not having additional capacity. For long-run capacity planning, sufficient capacity should be acquired so that the cost of the last unit of capacity added is reimbursed by the opportunities arising from having the additional unit of capacity. Therefore, fixed costs are relevant in planning for capacity but irrelevant for short-run product-mix decisions once the capacity is acquired. The cost of capacity resources would become relevant if the firm contemplated downsizing or reducing capacity. In this case, we would want to know the net proceeds from disposing of existing capacity.

Recently an important limitation to the deterministic LP formulation has been uncovered. As described above, the LP solution will produce profitable products up to the point where additional production is constrained by one or more bottleneck resources (or perhaps by maximum sales constraints). Therefore, if the LP optimal production plan is followed, bottleneck or constraining resources will be present. In such a situation, even modest amounts of randomness—such as from sales orders arriving in an unexpected pattern, statistical fluctuation in processing times, and unexpected machine breakdowns or product defects—will cause queues to develop in front of the bottleneck resources.[5] Such randomness in order arrival or processing will make it virtually impossible to achieve the optimal production plan because, by definition, no additional capacity exists to work off backlogs in front of bottleneck resources.[6]

More importantly, much higher and unrecognized (in the LP model) costs will be incurred because of the delays, queues, and congestion created by the fluctuations in the order arrival, production-processing times, and uncertain quality of products and machines. The costs include the obvious (but unmeasured) holding costs of work-in-process inventory that has been delayed in the production process. But the costs also include the less obvious costs of congestion and confusion in the factory, plus the cost of delayed orders and shipments to customers. Just how to deal with the impact of statistical fluctuations on bottleneck or constraining resources is now emerging as a contemporary research topic.[7] We mention the problem here to remind readers that unless special steps are taken to buffer bottleneck resources from the effects of statistical fluctuations, a production plan that attempts to fully use available capacity not only is unlikely to be achieved but also may cause the firm to incur considerable inventory-carrying costs, general factory confusion and expediting costs, and loss of customer goodwill. One heuristic of coping with this effect might be to develop a production plan based on, say, 80% to 90% of capacity and allow the unused portion of capacity to serve as protective capacity to handle the short-term surges caused by uncertain arrival and processing of work at prior stages.

Optimal product mix and production planning in real environments turns out to be considerably more complicated than the unconstrained

---

[5] This effect is demonstrated in R. Banker, S. Datar, and S. Kekre, "Relevant Costs, Congestion and Stochasticity in Production Environments," *Journal of Accounting and Economics* (1988).

[6] This effect is vividly and humorously demonstrated in Eli M. Goldratt and Jeff Cox, *The Goal*, rev. ed. (Croton-on-Hudson, NY: North River Press, 1986).

[7] Some solutions are offered in Goldratt and Cox, *The Goal*; and Eli Goldratt and Robert Fox, *The Race* (Croton-on-Hudson, NY: North River Press, 1986).

C-V-P, single-product model introduced at the beginning of the preceding chapter would have led us to believe.

Behavioral Considerations Relating to Corporate Planning Models

Linear programming provides a centralized planning tool. The model developed in this chapter determined the operations for the entire firm simultaneously. Especially for large, complex firms, the requisite information to model the entire organization may be impossible to collect and communicate into one central model. Computational capacity may also limit the size of models that can be solved in practice. One large firm, in order to make its organizational planning model tractable, introduced simplifications that frequently caused the recommended plan of action to be infeasible in practice, since the plan violated some organizational constraints. As a consequence, each time the model was run, a group of senior managers used the LP solution only as a starting point to determine, based on their extensive experience and judgment, the decisions that would actually be implemented. The LP model helped to work out the trade-offs among a complex interaction of products and processes to provide a good starting point for the managers' planning activities.

A centralized LP planning model also eliminates much local discretionary decision making, since the major product-mix and resource utilization decisions are made within the central model. Too much reliance on a centralized resource allocation process could stifle the creativity, ambition, and enthsiasm of the lower-level managers. Thus, the apparent efficiency gains of a centralized solution could be outweighed by the indirect costs of reduced individual motivation and creativity. For example, Weyerhaeuser was unsuccessful in managing its extensive operations with a centralized linear programming model.[8]

Moreover, if a centralized planning model is used in a firm that, nominally, is decentralized and organized by responsibility centers, unintended behavioral effects may occur. People in the operational departments (such as the managers of machine 1 and machine 2 in the Rimouski Chemical Works) may misrepresent their operating characteristics when asked to provide information for the centralized planning model. Misrepresentation may occur because managers wish to build slack into their operating budgets. Thus, in the Rimouski Chemical Works problem, the

---

[8] See H. Thomas Johnson, "Organizational Design versus Strategic Information Procedures for Managing Corporate Overhead Cost: Weyerhaeuser Company, 1972–1986," in *Accounting & Management: Field Study Perspectives*, ed. William J. Bruns, Jr., and Robert S. Kaplan (Boston: Harvard Business School Press, 1987).

manager of machine 1 might hedge against potential material efficiency variances by claiming that each batch of product required 60 kiloliters of chemical B (instead of 50). Such misrepresentation or distortion will probably cause a less than optimal overall solution to be chosen.

Whether such dysfunctional behavior will occur in practice is an empirical question that we cannot answer at this time. But analysts need to be aware of and sensitive to the behavioral implications of their centralized planning models.

Summary

When multiple products share common and constraining production resources, we need to generalize our notions of product profitability. Products with the highest contribution margins may no longer be the most profitable. Selling products with the highest contribution margin per unit of constraining resource will maximize profits. If more than one constraining resource exists, a linear programming model can be used to determine the optimal product mix.

Limitations to the LP formulation include the sensitivity of the solution to the extensive data required for the model, the failure of the model to incorporate the effects of statistical fluctuations on the amount of product that can be processed through the bottleneck resources, and the potential for dysfunctional behavioral effects as decision making is moved away from decentralized managers to a centralized planning model. None of these limitations is fatal to the use of LP in practical situations, but the analyst must be aware of the potential for problems and attempt to control for them when working with an extensive, complex model.

PROBLEMS

3–1   Choosing a Product Mix (C. Horngren)*

Brian Jones has just received a university degree in management. He has taken the position of assistant to the president of a fairly small company in South Africa that manufacturers tungsten carbide drill steels for the gold-mining industry.

Two types of drill steels are manufactured. One has a steel rod of ¾-inch diameter and the other a diameter of 1 inch. The manufacturing takes place in three departments. In the tip-fabricating department, tungsten carbide tips are manufactured from powdered wolfram. In the steel-forging department, the steel rods are slotted and prepared for the insertion

---

* Problem prepared by Charles Horngren for *Cost Accounting*, 5th ed. (Prentice-Hall, 1982); reproduced with permission.

of the tips. The assembly department puts the tips and steel rods together in a brazing process.

Each department has severe capacity limits. The first constraint prohibits further capital expenditure because of a very weak liquid position arising from the past losses; the second is the labor situation in South Africa, which makes the hiring of more labor or the working of overtime virtually impossible. The capacity of each department is as follows:

Tip fabricating (Dept. A)	240,000 hours
Steel forging (Dept. B)	180,000 hours
Assembly (Dept. C)	180,000 hours

The treasurer has just completed the budget for the forthcoming year. Because of the renewed confidence in gold, the company is expected to produce at full capacity.

The treasurer has produced the following profit analysis of the two products, on which a major production decision was based:

	¾″	1″
Selling price	$5.00	$6.00
Direct materials		
Tungsten carbide	$ .75	$1.00
Steel	1.45	2.05
	$2.20	$3.05
Direct labor		
Department A	$ .60	$ .30
Department B	.20	.30
Department C	.20	.15
	$1.00	$ .75
Prime costs (from above)	$3.20	$3.80
Factory overhead	.80	.60
Selling and administration	.50	.60
Total costs	$4.50	$5.00
Profit	$ .50	$1.00

The market survey performed by the sales manager showed that the company could sell as many of either type of rod as it could produce. However, the sales manager urged that the needs of three of the big gold mines must be satisfied in full, even though this meant producing a large number of the ¾-inch rods that had only half the profit of the 1-inch rods. The quantities required by these three gold mines amounted to 270,000 ¾-inch rods and 540,000 1-inch rods.

As the 1-inch rods have twice the profit of the ¾-inch rods, the treasurer suggested that the remaining capacity be used to produce two 1-inch rods for every ¾-inch rod. This would mean producing an additional 135,000 ¾-inch rods and 270,000 1-inch rods. Department B would then be working at full capacity and would be the constraint on any further production.

The treasurer then produced the following budgeted income statement for the forthcoming year. Sales are expected to occur evenly throughout the year.

	¾"	1"
Sales (in units)	405,000	810,000
Sales (in dollars)	$2,025,000	$4,860,000
Direct materials	891,000	2,470,500
Direct labor	405,000	607,500
Factory overhead	324,000	486,000
Selling and administration	202,500	486,000
Total costs	$1,822,500	$4,050,000
Profit	$ 202,500	$ 810,000

Jones, as his first assignment, is asked by the president to comment on the budgeted income statement. Specifically, the president feels that capacity might be better utilized with a different sales mix. He wants to know just how much it is costing the company in lost profits by supplying the full needs of the three big goldmining customers. He feels it might be more profitable to produce only the 1-inch rods.

Jones gathers the following additional information before making his recommendations:

Wolfram is purchased at $10 per kilogram (1,000 grams). The ¾-inch tips use an average of 75 grams and the 1-inch tips 100 grams. The special alloy steel costs $2,000 per 2,000 pounds. The ¾-inch rods use 1.45 pounds and the 1-inch rods 2.05 pounds.

Direct-labor costs per hour follow:

Department A	$2.40
Department B	1.80
Department C	1.50

Tip fabricating (Department A) is a skilled process. The smaller tips require twice as much detailed work. Owing to the nature of the work, most of the labor is considered fixed because it would be difficult to replace. Approximately 200,000 hours per annum in Department A are considered fixed. In the steel-forging process, the bigger rods require more time because of the handling difficulties. In the assembly department, the smaller rods again take more time because of the intricacies of the operations. However, this is not skilled work.

Factory overhead in the budgeted income statement is considered 50% fixed. It has been allocated to the products on the basis of direct labor.

Fixed selling and administrative expenses have been allocated on the basis of the number of units sold. Variable selling expenses are predicted to be 10¢ per unit sold of either size.

Required:

If you were Jones, what would be your recommendations to the president?

3–2 Scheduling a Bottleneck Resource

The OPT Company produces two products, P and Q. The production processes for the products are shown below:

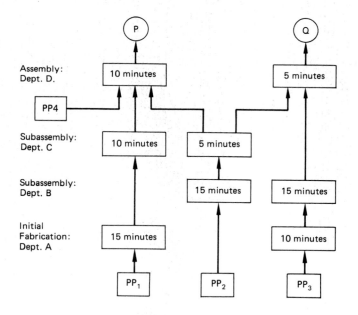

Product P sells for $90 per unit, and product Q sells for $100 per unit. Up to 100 units per week can be sold of P, and up to 50 units per week can be sold of Q. The unit costs of each of the four purchased parts are:

Purchased Part	Unit Cost
PP$_1$	$15
PP$_2$	20
PP$_3$	20
PP$_4$	5

PP$_2$ is processed through Departments B and C and is required for the final assembly stage of both P and Q. The time (in minutes) required to process each component in each department is shown in the diagram above.

Weekly operating expenses, including the cost of direct labor in Departments A, B, C, and D, equal $6,000. Each department—A, B, C, and D—has one worker, who is paid $10/hour. The work in each department is highly specialized, so that workers cannot be transferred from one department to another. The plant operates only one shift (40 hours) per week and no overtime is permitted.

Overhead, equal to operating expense less direct labor cost, is assigned to products as a percentage of direct labor dollars.

Required:

1. Compute the direct labor, material, and overhead costs of products P and Q.
2. Based on this information, which product is more profitable? Which production plan would apparently yield the highest weekly profits based on this information? Compute the profits based on this production plan.
3. Which production plan actually does maximize weekly profits?
4. Compute the amount of time not used in each department under the production plan you recommended in your answer to requirement 3. What should the workers in these departments do with their idle time? What kind of performance measure should be used to evaluate the performance of workers in these departments?

3–3   Scheduling a Production Run

Alberton Fisheries Limited (AFL) is an integrated fish products company. AFL operates a small fleet of trawlers. When the trawlers land their catch, AFL has the choice of selling the whole (round) fish or processing the fish itself.

The processing operation begins by removing the head, tail, skin, bones, and insides of the fish (these byproducts are called offal), leaving two fillets. The fillets represent about 70% of the weight of the whole fish. All of the offal is processed into a fertilizer whose net realizable value is zero. In fact, AFL began the fertilizer-manufacturing operation only to provide a means of disposing of the offal.

The disposition of the fillets depends on the quality. There are three quality grades used. On average, 50% of the fillets are grade 1, 30% are grade 2, and 20% are grade 3. The grade 1 fillets are sold as fresh fish if there is a market available; otherwise they are downgraded to grade 2. The grade 2 fillets are used in the preparation of gourmet entrees that are sold directly by AFL or, under other names, by other distributors. The process involves cooking the fish and then packing the fillet with other products into a container, which is then frozen. If there is an excess supply of grade 2 fillets, the grade 2 fillets are downgraded to grade 3.

The grade 3 fillets are used either to produce the processed, or so-called ketchup-carrier, line of products such as breaded fish sticks, or they are frozen into blocks to be stored for future use or sold.

The processing facility can handle a maximum batch of 100,000 pounds of fish. Any trawler load in excess of this amount has to be sold at whatever price it will fetch, since, given current capacity, the excess fish would spoil before they could be processed.

The cost of processing a batch of fish consists of two components. There is a variable cost of $0.30 per pound of whole fish processed. This cost relates entirely to the unloading and filleting operations and is comprised of wages paid to the factory workers, as well as variable overhead. In addition, there is a fixed cost of $15,000 per batch processed relating to factory depreciation, administrative charges, and salaries.

For fish sold fresh, the only additional costs beyond filleting are the packaging costs, which average $0.10 per pound, and the shipping and handling costs, which average $1.00 per pound. AFL is currently receiving $2.50 per pound of fresh fish.

The maximum amount of fish that can be cooked and frozen per batch is 40,000 pounds. The cost of cooking and freezing is about $0.20 per pound of fish irrespective of whether the fish will be sold as an entree or as a processed product.

For the entree products, the average cost of additional items included with the fish is $1.00 per pound of fish packaged, and the packaging cost is $0.20 per pound of fish. Since the entrees, the processed fish products, and the frozen blocks are sold F.O.B. AFL's factory, there are no shipping costs associated with any of these products. AFL is currently receiving $2.40 per pound of fish sold as an entree.

For the processed products, the average cost of additional material included with the fish is $0.10 per pound of fish packaged, and the packaging cost is about $0.10 per pound of fish. AFL is currently receiving $1.30 per pound of fish sold as a processed food product.

The cost of freezing the fillets into blocks is about $0.10 per pound. The current market price for frozen blocks is about $0.70. The production manager has advised the marketing manager that she can use about 10,000 pounds of frozen blocks next week and will be willing to pay up to $0.80 per pound for the blocks.

Required:

The captain of one of the trawlers has just radioed in that he will land in two days with about 110,000 pounds of fish. The marketing manager, has advised you that he can sell a maximum of 40,000 pounds of whole fish, 20,000 pounds of fresh fish, 28,000 pounds of fish as entrees, 30,000 pounds of fish as processed, and 20,000 pounds of fish sold in frozen blocks. (The last amount excludes the 10,000 that the production manager said she would take.) The marketing manager has also advised you that whole fish can be sold at a price of $0.50 per pound.

What is the optimal disposition of this catch?

3–4 *California Products Corporation: Analyze Product Profitability with Machine Constraints and Fixed and Variable Costs* (F. Kollaritsch)*

History

The California Products Corporation was started in 1955 by several members of the Black family. From 1955 to 1960, Product "I" was the only product produced, and, although profits were not high, they were sufficient to satisfy the family stockholders.

During 1960, the management of the California Products Corporation, mostly members of the Black family, decided to change from absorption costing to direct costing (variable costing) upon the advice of a consulting firm. Product "J" was started into the production line in 1960 and Product "K" was started in 1964.

Since 1960, the company had losses or very small profits. The Profit and Loss Statement for 1965 (see Table 1), shows that the company "broke even" during that year. At the board meeting, held shortly after the financial statements for 1965 were released, optimism was voiced concerning the future profit prospects of the company. The reasons given for this optimism were as follows:

1. Products "J" and "K", it was believed, have overcome starting-up troubles and have finally found acceptance by the public.
2. Products "J" and "K" are both high contribution margin products. (See Table 4.)
3. During 1965 some overtime had been incurred, which it is claimed, cut into profits. It was anticipated that this would not be repeated next year.
4. The sales force had finally become convinced of the necessity of pushing Product "K" because of its high contribution margin.

The Profit and Loss Statement for the year 1966 (see Table 2) was anything but encouraging to the management of the California Products Corporation. The company sustained a loss during this year, and paradoxically had a considerable backlog of unfilled orders. The overtime was not eliminated, although the overall production in unit of output decreased by 50,000 units. (See Table 5.)

---

* Copyright © 1978 by The Ohio State University. Reproduced with permission.

The board meeting which followed the release of the 1966 financial statements was unfriendly and everyone accused everyone else of inability. Without producing any evidence, the vice president in charge of sales accused the production people of gross inefficiency. Evidence was, however, introduced which indicated that sales had to be turned down because production could not supply the goods within the normal delivery time.

The vice president in charge of production accused the sales people of pushing the wrong product. He pointed out that all the troubles started with the introduction of Product "J" and Product "K." He also accused the vice president in charge of finances of "trickery" and stated that the contribution margin (see Table 4) was nothing except "fancy data" which would mislead everyone.

This meeting resulted in ill feelings among the various functional staff managers. The chairman of the board finally obtained their consent to call in a consulting firm to investigate what had happened and to suggest possible means of making the firm profitable.

An investigation into the variable expenses, shown in Table 3, revealed them to be correct, and to include a charge for normally expected overtime. The prices for the products had not been changed for several years and there was no expectation that a price change was feasible in the next few years.

An investigation into the $800,000 fixed expenses, shown in Table 1 and Table 2, showed that $430,000 was a joint fixed cost and that $370,000 was a separable fixed cost attributable to the company's products as follows:

Product "I"	$ 60,000
Product "J"	200,000
Product "K"	110,000
	$370,000

An analysis of the joint fixed costs of $430,000 showed them to be made up of:

Manufacturing Expenses	$ 40,000
Selling & Administrative Expenses	70,000
Depreciation:	
Machine "A"	100,000
Machine "B"	20,000
Machine "C"	200,000
	$430,000

Regardless of the above classification, the full amount of $800,000 was fixed costs and had been properly classified by the company. Information gathered concerning the production process disclosed that each product had to be worked on by each of the three machines and that each of the three products required different machine times on the various machines. (The average production capacity of the machines is given in Table 6.)

It was estimated that each machine was operated about 1750 to 1800 hrs. during a normal year (practical capacity), which takes into consideration maintenance, repairs, resetting, etc. The maximum operational time one could expect from each of these machines during a given year without overtaxing them and incurring unreasonably high additional expenses was 1900 hrs. to 2000 hrs.

TABLE 1
California Products Corporation Profit and Loss Statement Year 1965

	Product "I"	Product "J"	Product "K"	Total
Sales	$1,479,000	$1,320,000	$284,000	$3,083,000
Variable Costs	1,131,000	960,000	192,000	2,283,000
Contribution Margin	$ 348,000	$ 360,000	$ 92,000	$ 800,000
Fixed Expenses				800,000
Net Profit				$ –0–

TABLE 2
California Products Corporation Profit and Loss Statement Year 1966

	Product "I"	Product "J"	Product "K"	Total
Sales	$1,224,000	$1,056,000	$568,000	$2,848,000
Variable Costs	936,000	768,000	384,000	2,088,000
Contribution Margin	$ 288,000	$ 288,000	$184,000	$ 760,000
Fixed Expenses				800,000
Net Loss				$ (40,000)

TABLE 3
California Products Corporation Variable Product Costs

	Product "I"	Product "J"	Product "K"	Total
Materials	$2.00	$3.00	$2.50	$ 7.50
Labor[a]	1.00	1.20	1.00	3.20
Indirect Manufacturing Expenses	.30	.40	.30	1.00
Selling & Administrative Expenses	.60	.20	1.00	1.80
Total	$3.90	$4.80	$4.80	$13.50

[a] Includes reasonable allowance for normal overtime.

TABLE 4
California Products Corporation Contribution Margins

	Product "I"	Product "J"	Product "K"	Total
Sales Price	$5.10	$6.60	$7.10	$18.80
Variable Costs	3.90	4.80	4.80	13.50
	$1.20	$1.80	$2.30	$ 5.30

TABLE 5
California Products Corporation Products Sold (in Units)

	Product "I"	Product "J"	Product "K"	Total
1965	290,000	200,000	40,000	530,000
1966	240,000	160,000	80,000	480,000

TABLE 6
California Products Corporation Average Product Output Capacity per Machine Hour[a]
(in Units)

	Product "I"	Product "J"	Product "K"
Machine "A"	312	260	130
Machine "B"	364	208	156
Machine "C"	520	312	104

[a] Each machine could work at any given time on one product, only.

Required:

Analyze the data of the California Products Corporation given above and summarize your findings in a report to the board of directors of this corporation, addressing your remarks specifically to the questions of overtime, production deficiencies and inefficiencies, the product sales mix, the cost method, the loss during 1966, and the profit potentials of the various products. You might wish to prepare an initial analysis assuming that none of the fixed costs is escapable even were there to be zero production of one or more products. Then you can determine whether your proposed solution remains optimal if the separable fixed costs for products I, J, and K are escapable if there is no production of one or more of these products.

3–5 *Planning the Conversion of Raw Materials into Finished Products*

Williams Lake Forest Products (WLFP) is an integrated paper products firm. Planning for the period's activities begins with the wood lot. The maximum amount of raw wood that can be harvested during this period is 10,000,000 units. Wood is harvested in batches of 1,000,000 units. The cost of harvesting is $300,000 per batch plus $2 per unit of wood harvested.

When the raw wood has been harvested, it is graded. On average, about 30% of the raw wood harvested grades out as sawmill-quality wood, 40% grades out as plywood-quality wood, and 30% grades out as pulp-quality wood.

Sawmill-quality wood can be sold, sent to the sawmill for sawing into lumber, or downgraded into plywood-quality wood. Sawmill-quality wood can be sold on the open market in batches of 1,000 units for $3,000 per batch.

The sawmill processes wood in batches of 100,000 units. The cost per batch processed in the sawmill is $60,000 plus $1.50 per unit of wood processed. The capacity of the sawmill is limited, by the availability of saws, to 2,000,000 units of wood, or 20 batches. Each 1,000 units of wood processed through the sawmill yields product that can be sold for $5,000.

The plywood-quality wood can be sold, downgraded to pulp-quality wood, or sent to the plywood mill to be made into plywood. Plywood-quality wood can be sold in the open market in batches of 1,000 units for $2,500 per batch.

The plywood mill processes wood in batches of 150,000 units. The cost per batch processed in the plywood mill is $75,000 plus $2.50 per unit of wood processed. The capacity of the plywood mill is limited by the capacity of the peeling operation to 3,000,000 units of wood, or 20 batches. Each 1,000 units of wood processed through the plywood mill yields product that can be sold for $6,000.

The pulp-quality wood can be sold or sent to the paper mill to be made into various paper and cardboard products. Pulp-quality wood can be sold in the open market in batches of 1,000 units for $2,000 per batch.

The paper mill processes wood continuously, and thus no batching operation occurs in this mill. The variable cost per unit of wood processed in the plywood mill is $0.80. The capacity of the paper mill is limited to 5,000,000 units of wood. Each 1,000 units of wood processed through the paper mill yields product that can be sold for $3,500.

The accompanying diagram summarizes the operations of WLFP.

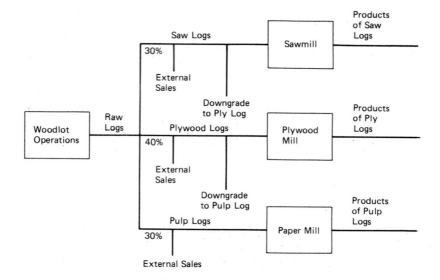

The Marketing Department has advised that the maximum number of **1,000 unit batches** that can be sold during the upcoming period of each of the commodities is:

Saw logs unprocessed	500
Plywood logs unprocessed	750
Pulp logs unprocessed	400
Saw logs processed	1,500*
Plywood logs processed	3,000
Pulp logs processed	4,500

* This number represents the maximum amount of sawmill products that can be sold based on processing 1,500 batches of saw logs.

Required:

1. Formulate an LP to help WLFP determine its best production plan for the upcoming period.
2. Using the LP that you formulated in requirement 1 and LPROG, determine the optimal production plan for the upcoming period.

3–6   *Choosing a Product Mix*

Sheet Harbour Chemicals (SHC) manufactures chemicals used in the paint industry. The process involves three departments.

Chemical A, which is purchased for $3 per liter, is processed through

Department 1 in batches of 100 liters. Each batch of chemicals processed through Department A produces 70 liters of chemical B and 30 liters of chemical C.

Chemical B is sold for $10 per liter. Chemical C is used in Department 2 to produce chemicals D, E, and F. Department 2 processes chemical C in batches of 200 liters. Each batch processed through Department B produces 100 liters of chemical D, 60 liters of chemical E, and 40 liters of chemical F.

Chemical D is sold for $12 per liter. Chemical E is a waste product that is donated to the local municipality to be spread on gravel roads to keep down dust. Chemical F is a hazardous waste product that must be disposed of at a cost of $6 per liter. Alternatively, chemical F can be processed through Department 3 to produce chemical C.

Department 3 processes chemical F in batches of 40 liters. For each batch of chemical F processed, 20 liters of chemical C are produced. In the past, this operation has had a tendency to build up stocks of chemical C. The maximum storage capacity for chemical C is 1,000 liters.

The accompanying diagram summarizes the production activities at SHC.

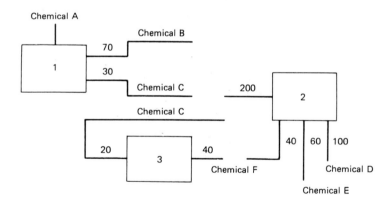

The sales manager indicates that sales of chemical B cannot exceed 35,000 liters in the upcoming period, and sales of chemical D cannot exceed 10,000 liters.

The production manager advises that 7,000 labor-hours are available for the upcoming period. Workers are paid $10 per hour worked. The production manager indicates that the labor-hours required for each batch in Departments 1, 2, and 3 are 10, 15, and 10, respectively. Moreover, because of constraints relating to the mixing vats and storage, the maximum number of batches in Departments 1, 2, and 3 are 600, 80, and 40, respectively. The estimated variable overhead costs per batch in Departments 1, 2, and 3 are estimated as $250, $750, and $100.

Required:

1. Formulate an LP to determine the optimal production plan at SHC for the upcoming period.
2. Using LPROG, solve the LP formulated in requirement 1 to determine the optimal plan.

COST ESTIMATION AND REGRESSION ANALYSIS

Management accountants must understand cost behavior in order to support their planning and control activities. The ability to predict fixed and variable costs as a function of forecasted activity levels is important for several reasons. Managers need to understand the economic consequences of alternative courses of action, such as introducing new products or altering the production level and mix of existing products. Financial models, based in electronic spreadsheets, require estimates of future cost behavior if they are to be a useful management tool. For operational control, actual incurred costs are compared with standard or budgeted amounts. The standards should reflect all the factors that affect costs, such as volume, experience, and inflation.

Engineering Studies

Methods to predict cost behavior have existed for many years. Engineers, especially those active in the scientific management movement during the late nineteenth and early twentieth centuries, spent considerable time studying and analyzing cost functions.[1] Engineering studies require direct physical observation of the production process. Such studies are most useful for understanding repetitive processes that have well-defined relationships between inputs and outputs. The studies are generally expensive and are typically performed to improve the efficiency of the process, not just to set cost standards.

The industrial engineering study produces standards expressed in physical units—hours of labor of given skill, pounds of different input materials, minutes of machine time, number of supervisors. These mea-

---

[1] The role of the scientific management movement, including the development of the standard cost system, is summarized in H. Thomas Johnson and Robert S. Kaplan, "Efficiency, Profit, and Scientific Management: 1880–1910," *Relevance Lost: The Rise and Fall of Management Accounting* (Boston: Harvard Business School Press, 1987) Chap. 3.

surements can then be transformed into costs by multiplying by the appropriate unit prices of the input resources. An engineering study can provide an estimate of the ideal relationship between inputs and outputs, rather than just a measure of the existing, perhaps inefficient, production process. Also, because the study produces physical-unit rather than dollar measures, the cost standards can easily be updated as inflation and relative price changes affect input resource prices.

The engineering method, however, is expensive to implement. The value of highly accurate standard cost information, relative to other estimates of these costs, will rarely be sufficient to justify the expense of such a study purely for accounting purposes.

In addition, many indirect product and production costs are not directly observable from an engineering study. Indirect material, indirect labor, and other support expenses are affected by product and production decisions, but the relationship is subtle and not easily determined even by careful observation of the production process. For these indirect and support costs, historical data analysis and interviews with departmental managers may provide more accurate causal relationships than an expensive engineering study.

The optimal production process may also shift with changes in the relative prices of material, labor, and energy as well as the introduction of new equipment and technology. Therefore, the engineering estimates may become outdated if the production process changes and new estimates are not obtained during the process innovation.

In summary, engineering studies can provide good standards for direct material, labor, and machine time consumption. But these studies are expensive to perform and can quickly become outdated. They also may not provide much insight into factors that lead to a demand for overhead and support resources. Management accountants therefore rely heavily on the analysis of actual historical data in order to explain and predict cost behavior.

Account Classification

The account classification procedure may be the most common method used by companies to estimate their fixed and variable costs. To use this procedure, the management accountant classifies each category of factory costs as being either fixed or variable. The classified costs are then aggregated to develop a picture of overall cost behavior.

Consider the monthly overhead budget for the Machining Department of the Burks Company given in Table 4–1. Supervision is most likely a fixed cost within the planned range of activity. Indirect labor, including material handlers and idle time, probably has variable components. Without knowing the budget or actual costs at a level of activity other than 14,000 machine-hours, we cannot estimate fixed and variable components. Therefore, we initially classify indirect labor as a variable cost and estimate a variable cost per machine-hour of $2,400/14,000 = $0.17. Alternatively, we can make an arbitrary judgment as to the proportion that is fixed and the proportion that is variable. For example, we can assume that half the costs in this category are fixed and half are variable, in which case the fixed-cost component is $1,200 per month and the variable cost is $0.086 per machine-hour ($1,200/14,000). For now, we will assume it is completely variable at $0.17/machine-hour.

TABLE 4–1
Burks Company
Budgeted Overhead Costs at 14,000 Machine-Hours

Account	Budgeted Overhead Cost
Supervision	$ 1,900
Indirect labor	2,400
Supplies	700
Payroll taxes	1,680
Overtime premiums	220
Depreciation	800
Miscellaneous	3,000
Total	$10,700

Supplies costs are probably variable and equal to $0.05 per machine-hour. Payroll taxes, being directly proportional to labor expense, will also be variable (but if indirect labor expense has some fixed components, the payroll taxes associated with these costs will also be a fixed expense). Assuming payroll taxes are all variable, we get an estimate of $0.12 per machine-hour. Overtime premiums will be variable and equal to $0.16 per machine-hour, whereas depreciation will be fixed.

Miscellaneous factory overhead includes charges for building depreciation, insurance, utilities, and janitorial and maintenance expenses. Clearly some of these expenses are fixed, while others (utilities, housekeeping, and maintenance) could have variable components. Further investigation reveals that the factory overhead charge is based on the total cost of these items throughout the factory and allocated proportionally to the square feet of space occupied by each department. Therefore, to a first approximation—neglecting the minor effect on total utility and maintenance cost caused by activity changes in the Machining Department—we can consider the factory overhead to be a fixed cost. Summing up these components yields the classification in Table 4–2. The account classification procedure yields a flexible budget for the department of

Monthly overhead costs = $5,700 + $0.357 * (machine-hours).

TABLE 4–2
Burks Machining Department
Fixed and Variable Costs

Account	Fixed Cost	Variable Cost	Variable Cost/ Machine-Hour
Supervision	$1,900		
Indirect labor		$2,400	$0.171
Supplies		700	0.05
Payroll taxes		1,680	0.12
Overtime premiums		220	0.016
Depreciation	800		
Miscellaneous	3,000		
Total	$5,700	$5,000	$0.357

Obviously this method is easy to implement. Its limitations, however, include

1. A heavy dependence on our classification of an account as fixed or variable. If indirect labor expense is actually entirely a fixed expense, the flexible budget should be $8,100 + $0.186 machine-hours, which represents almost a 50% reduction in the estimated variable-overhead coefficient.

2. A reliance on only a single observation at a single activity level to determine the cost equation. We have no evidence on the cost fluctuation even at the assumed level of 14,000 machine-hours and obviously none on costs at levels other than 14,000 machine-hours.

3. No insight as to whether some costs are partially fixed and partially variable (that is, a mixed cost). If indirect labor expense were actually half fixed and half variable, the flexible budget would become $6,900 + 0.271 machine-hours, producing a 25% reduction in the variable-overhead coefficient.

Some of these problems can be overcome if we have estimates of costs at more than one activity level. Suppose the Burks Company has prepared overhead budgets at four different activity levels, as shown in Table 4–3. We see that supplies is a completely variable cost at $0.05 per machine-hour. Also, depreciation and factory overhead are completely fixed costs. Supervision is a semifixed cost that increases by $300 somewhere between 14,000 and 16,000 machine-hours. Indirect labor expense is a mixed cost with a fixed component of $1,000 and a variable component of $0.10 per machine-hour. Payroll taxes are all variable at the rate of $0.12 per machine-hour. Overtime premium is curvilinear, increasing at a more rapid rate as the activity level increases. Thus, by having budgeted or actual costs at different activity levels, we obtain better indications as to the nature of the cost behavior for each account category.

The account classification method still does not provide evidence on the underlying variability or uncertainty in the cost process from one

TABLE 4–3
Burks Machining Department
Budgeted Overhead Costs

	Volume (machine-hours)			
Account	*10,000*	*12,000*	*14,000*	*16,000*
Supervision	$1,900	$ 1,900	$ 1,900	$ 2,200
Indirect labor	2,000	2,200	2,400	2,600
Supplies	500	600	700	800
Payroll taxes	1,210	1,430	1,680	1,930
Overtime premiums	50	70	220	400
Depreciation	800	800	800	800
Miscellaneous	3,000	3,000	3,000	3,000
Total	$9,460	$10,000	$10,700	$11,730

observation to another. Typically, only the most recent set of observations may be used to estimate fixed and variable costs. Thus, it is a simple and inexpensive method to use, but it requires analysts to make a number of somewhat arbitrary judgments. A deeper understanding of the actual pattern of cost behavior can be obtained by a statistical analysis of historical data.

Regression Analysis for Cost Estimation

The engineering and account classification methods rely on expert opinions and judgments. While relatively easy to explain, these methods can produce quite different results and interpretations depending on the "experts" used. Moreover, unlike regression analysis, neither method provides a means by which the accuracy and reliability of the results can be evaluated.

Regression analysis has now become easy to implement because of the availability of inexpensive computer hardware and software. But like the other methods of cost analysis, regression analysis still requires the use of expert judgment. The widespread availability of computers and software may have increased the possibility for regression analysis to be improperly applied.

Detailed treatments of regression analysis can be found in many statistics and econometrics books. Certainly, it is beyond the scope of a managerial accounting book to provide a complete primer on the subject. The discussion that follows will only review the principal ideas. The concepts will be developed by analyzing a numerical example.

HAMMONDS PLAINS MANUFACTURING

Hammonds Plains Manufacturing (HPM) uses injection molding equipment to manufacture a wide variety of plastic products. Most of the work done by HPM is on a quotation basis. Michelle Sparr, the general manager, wants to develop a better understanding of the firm's overhead costs to help her estimate costs when quoting prices on orders for existing and new products.

Job-cost records are kept for all production runs so that the direct material, direct labor, and machine-hour requirements for any product are readily predictable. Sparr is most concerned about estimating manufacturing overhead costs, about 50% of total manufacturing costs, for products and orders.

Most of the firm's products are produced in stationary molds, which eject products automatically from the molding machines. Operators provide a variety of machine support activities. They maintain an adequate supply of raw plastic in the input hoppers of the molding machines, gather the products as they are ejected from the machines, and attend to any problems that cause the machines to stop. Sparr believes that machine-hours represents the most reasonable measure of the level of activity in the firm.

The data in Table 4–4 summarize the last thirty months of operations. No significant cost inflation or changes in production equipment have taken place over the last thirty months. On average, the plant has operated at about 60% of practical capacity.

Sparr has asked you to undertake an analysis of the behavior of overhead costs to determine whether a relationship exists between the number of machine-hours operated and the level of overhead costs. Up to now, she has been using a popular industry rule of thumb—$23 of variable overhead per machine-hour for injection molding equipment—to estimate costs when she is bidding for new business and pricing contracts.

In estimating the relationship, we will refer to overhead costs—the variable we are attempting to explain—as the **dependent** variable. Machine-hours—the variable used to explain the variation in overhead—will be called the **independent** variable.

Most regression analysis starts by assuming that a linear relationship exists between the dependent variable and the independent variable.[2] In addition to providing an estimate of the linear equation linking the dependent and independent variables, the analysis supplies information about the reliability and the confidence we can have in the estimates.

When only one independent variable exists, it is good practice to start

---

[2] Regression analysis also makes specific assumptions about the nature and the distribution of the error term in the estimated relationship between overhead and machine-hours. Chapter 5 will consider these assumptions in detail as well as procedures for dealing with violations of the classic regression assumptions. In this chapter, we will concentrate solely on developing and interpreting the basic regression equation.

TABLE 4–4
Hammonds Plains Manufacturing Overhead Cost

Month Number	Overhead	Machine-Hours
1	76,667	1,772
2	73,678	1,820
3	80,141	1,634
4	61,985	1,006
5	72,685	1,383
6	87,675	1,957
7	78,450	1,561
8	70,634	1,464
9	63,417	1,545
10	56,057	1,119
11	67,446	1,382
12	72,102	1,320
13	68,533	1,264
14	69,079	1,344
15	85,550	1,803
16	58,197	1,022
17	61,626	1,510
18	80,689	1,793
19	58,256	1,149
20	55,337	1,155
21	85,108	1,847
22	76,485	1,832
23	67,783	1,136
24	56,398	1,136
25	66,622	1,330
26	63,494	1,358
27	89,416	1,882
28	67,518	1,174
29	73,680	1,643
30	66,132	1,381

by plotting the data. Exhibit 4–1 presents a plot of overhead versus machine-hours. Inspection of this plot suggests that the relationship between the two variables is linear. If the plot showed evidence of a nonlinear relationship between the dependent and independent variables, a more complex relationship would have to be estimated.

Let

$$y_t = \text{overhead cost in month } t$$

$$x_t = \text{machine-hours in month } t$$

and assume a linear model of the form

$$y_t = \beta_0 + \beta_1 x_t + \epsilon_t \qquad (4\text{--}1)$$

EXHIBIT 4–1
Hammonds Plains Manufacturing

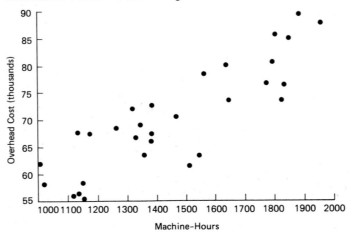

The coefficients β_0 and β_1 are unknown parameters that are to be estimated by the regression analysis. The ϵ_t term represents an error term that incorporates (1) the effects of omitted independent variables (that is, explanatory variables not included in the model) and (2) model errors caused by nonlinear relationships between the dependent and independent variables. It would be rare for all the observations on costs and activity levels to have an exact linear relationship. The error term captures the departures from strict linearity, such as unusual efficiencies or inefficiencies in a month, and factors other than machine-hours that affect overhead costs.

We can interpret the β_0 term in equation (4–1) as the component of total overhead cost that does not vary with fluctuations in the activity level over the range of experience. This estimate does not represent the committed overhead costs, since β_0 can contain discretionary or short-run variable costs, such as the salaries of intermediate-level supervisors, that relate to the level of use of the fixed capacity of the firm rather than directly to the underlying level of activity. Moreover, any estimate of β_0 is only reliable over the range of experience used to estimate the relationship. This range, called the relevant range, is 1,006 to 1,957 machine-hours for the data in Table 4–1. Outside the relevant range, there may be non-linearities in the data or changes in costs relating to the provision of capacity that will cause β_0 to be a poor estimate of nonvariable costs. In other words, we would not literally expect the overhead cost to equal β_0 if the number of machine-hours were reduced to zero.

The β_1 term in equation (4–1) is the estimate of the variable component of overhead in the relevant range of activity. β_1 estimates the increase in overhead costs from each unit increase in machine-hours. If machine-hours increase by one hour, we expect overhead costs to increase by β_1

dollars. The linearity assumption implies that if machine-hours increase by 100 hours, expected overhead costs will increase by 100 β_1 dollars. Knowing the value of β_1 allows Sparr to predict the short-run, out-of-pocket overhead cost once a job's required machine-hours have been predicted.

Typically, the parameters β_0 and β_1 are estimated by an **ordinary least squares** (OLS) regression procedure. The OLS procedure minimizes the sum of the squares of the error terms about the estimated linear relationship.[3] That is, the OLS criterion chooses b_0 and b_1 as estimates of the values β_0 and β_1 to minimize the sum of the squared error terms:

$$(y_t - b_0 - b_1 x_t)^2$$

As long as a constant term is included in the regression, the OLS procedure will cause the sum of the error terms to equal zero. This occurs because the procedure forces the regression line to pass through the point representing the means of the dependent and independent variables.

The calculations for regression analysis can be performed by programmed calculators or computers, so that users need not be concerned with the specific computational procedure for obtaining OLS estimates. The regression equation for the data in the Hammonds Plains Company yields the following estimates:

$$b_0 = 27{,}901 \qquad b_1 = 29.13$$

Thus, the predicted equation for overhead is

$$y_t = 27{,}901 + 29.13\, x_t$$

or, in words, we predict overhead, in the relevant range of activity, to be equal to $27,901 plus $29.13 for each hour the machines are operated. Exhibit 4–2 on the next page shows a plot of the estimated regression line and the actual values of overhead.

Measuring the Goodness of Fit of a Regression Equation

After obtaining the estimated coefficients from the regression routine, we interpret the outcome by careful analysis of the error terms. Table 4–5 tabulates, for each observation, the actual overhead costs, the predicted overhead costs, and the error from the regression.

---

[3] We will discuss the rationale of this criterion in more detail in Chapter 5.

EXHIBIT 4–2
Hammonds Plains Manufacturing

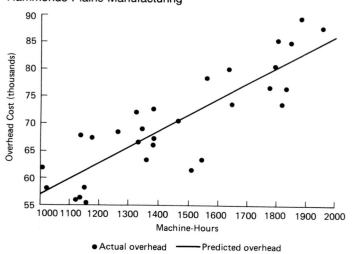

The coefficient of determination, or R^2, provides a measure of how well the linear relationship explains the variation in the dependent variable. With data on only the dependent variable (overhead cost), we would observe only the variation in overhead cost over the thirty-month period. From Table 4–5, we can see that the variance of overhead is 90,276,048. This total variation in the dependent variable is called the **total sum of squares (SST).** Without observing any other variables, we would have to conclude that overhead cost was highly variable from month to month, ranging from a low of $55,337 in month 20 to a high of $89,416 in month 27.

Most of this variation, however, can be explained by the dependence of the overhead cost on machine-hours, which vary greatly from month to month. If there had been less variation in machine-hours, there would have been less variation in overhead cost. We can measure how much of the variation in overhead cost is explained by the variation in machine-hours by computing the explained or regression mean sum of squares.

From Table 4–5, we see that the variance of the predicted value of overhead is 66,914,125. This total variation in the predicted value of overhead is called the **regression sum of squares (SSR).** Since the regression sum of squares represents the amount of variation in the dependent variable that can be explained by the regression equation, the ratio of explained (SSR) to total (SST) sum of squares represents the explanatory power, or R^2, of the regression:

$$R^2 = \frac{\text{SSR}}{\text{SST}} = \frac{66,914,125}{90,276,048} = 0.74$$

TABLE 4–5
Hammonds Plains Manufacturing
Summary of Regression Predictions

Month Number	Actual Overhead	Predicted Overhead	Error
1	76,667	79,527	−2,860
2	73,678	80,925	−7,247
3	80,141	75,506	4,635
4	61,985	57,210	4,775
5	72,685	68,194	4,491
6	87,675	84,917	2,758
7	78,450	73,380	5,070
8	70,634	70,554	80
9	63,417	72,913	−9,496
10	56,057	60,502	−4,445
11	67,446	68,165	−719
12	72,102	66,358	5,744
13	68,533	64,727	3,806
14	69,079	67,058	2,021
15	85,550	80,430	5,120
16	58,197	57,676	521
17	61,626	71,893	−10,267
18	80,689	80,139	550
19	58,256	61,376	−3,120
20	55,337	61,551	−6,214
21	85,108	81,712	3,396
22	76,485	81,275	−4,790
23	67,783	60,998	6,785
24	56,398	60,998	−4,600
25	66,622	66,650	−28
26	63,494	67,465	−3,971
27	89,416	82,732	6,684
28	67,518	62,105	5,413
29	73,680	75,769	−2,089
30	66,132	68,135	−2,003
Mean	70,361	70,361	0
Mean sum of squares	90,276,048	66,914,125	23,361,923
Standard deviation	9,835	8,467	5,003

The statistic, R^2, is also called the coefficient of determination of the regression.

An R^2 of 0.74 implies that 74% of the variation in overhead can be explained by the regression equation we have estimated. We are unable to account for 26% of the variation in the dependent variable with our regression equation. This 26% is attributable to factors, other than machine-hours, that affect overhead. An important assumption of regression is that these omitted factors are random. That is, we assume that no variable has been omitted from the regression analysis that systematically affects overhead.

Many regression packages produce a variant of the R^2 statistic called the R^2 (Adjusted) statistic where

$$R^2 \text{ (Adjusted)} = 1 - \frac{(n - 1)}{(n - k)} * (1 - R^2)$$

where

n = number of observations used to estimate the regression equation

k = number of coefficients estimated by the regression equation

In our example:

$$R^2 \text{ (Adjusted)} = 1 - \frac{(30 - 1)}{(30 - 2)} * (1 - 0.74) = 0.73$$

The adjusted R^2 controls for the number of independent variables (including the constant term) used to estimate the regression equation. The adjusted R^2 can decline when additional independent variables, without much explanatory power, are added to the regression equation.

All other things being equal, the closer the value of the R^2 statistic is to 1, the greater the explanatory power of the predicted equation. Unfortunately, interpreting the R^2 is subjective. A more formal test of the explanatory power of the estimated equation is provided by the F test. The F statistic is computed as

$$F = \frac{\text{SSR}}{(\text{SST} - \text{SSR})} * \frac{(n - k)}{(k - 1)}$$

or, equivalently,

$$F = \frac{R^2}{1 - R^2} * \frac{(n - k)}{(k - 1)}$$

where n and k are defined as before in the equation for the adjusted R^2 statistic.

The F statistic is distributed with $k - 1$ degrees of freedom in the numerator and $n - k$ degrees of freedom in the denominator. Observe that if the regression equation explains none of the variability in the dependent variable, then SSR and the value of the F statistic will be zero. As SSR increases, the regression equation explains more of the variability in the dependent variable. As SSR approaches SST, the point at which the regression equation explains most of the variability in the independent variable, the *F* statistic becomes very large.

In the Hammonds Plains regression, the value of the *F* statistic is

$$F = \frac{66,914,125}{90,276,048 - 66,914,125} * \frac{(30 - 2)}{(2 - 1)} = 80.20$$

and is distributed with 1 degree of freedom in the numerator and 28 degrees of freedom in the denominator. The null hypothesis for the *F* test is that the true values of the slope coefficients are all equal to zero. (The alternative hypothesis is that the true values of the slope coefficients do not all equal zero.) A table of the critical values of the *F* at 95% confidence indicates that the critical value of the *F* statistic in our example is 4.2. Since the *F* statistic of 80.2 greatly exceeds the critical value of 4.2, we reject the null hypothesis and conclude that the true values of the coefficients are not all equal to 0. In other and simpler words, the regression equation helps to explain the variation in the dependent variable, overhead costs.

We can estimate the variance of the error term, ϵ_t, in equation (4–1) by computing the **sum of the squared errors** of the errors, a quantity that also equals the variance of the squared error values. This quantity equals (see Table 4–5) 23,361,923. Note that, as required:

$$\text{SST} = \text{SSR} + \text{SSE}$$

or, in words, the total variation of the dependent variable (SST) equals the explained sum of squares from the regression equation (SSR) plus the sum of squares of the error term (SSE).

The **standard error** of the regression, denoted s_e, measures the variation of the errors about the regression line. It is an unbiased estimator of the standard deviation of the error term in equation (4–1). The standard error is computed as the square root of the sum of the squared error terms from the regression (SSE * n) divided by the value of $n - 2$. In our example,

$$\text{Standard error} = \left(\frac{23,361,923 * 30}{28}\right)^{1/2} = 5,003.$$

We divide by $n - 2$ because two parameters, β_0 and β_1 have been estimated from the data. If we only had two observations, the regression line would fit the data perfectly and there would be no errors. After estimating the two coefficients, b_0 and b_1, the effective number of observations remaining to estimate the standard error equals 28. In general, the number of degrees of freedom is $n - k$, where *n* is the number of observations and *k* is the number of parameters (including the constant) estimated by the regression equation.

Assessing the Confidence of a Regression Equation

Regression analysis is particularly powerful and insightful because it allows us to assess the level of confidence that we can place in the fitted equation. To make these confidence statements, however, we must make explicit assumptions about the probability distribution of the error term. By assuming that the error term is normally distributed, we can avail ourselves of normal distribution theory to make such inferences. In particular, we will develop statements of confidence about two predictions: (1) the estimated coefficients and (2) the predicted value of the dependent variable, given some assumed level of the independent variable.

1. Confidence Statements about Estimated Coefficients

If the error terms are normally distributed, the estimated values b_0 and b_1 will also be normally distributed. Also the estimated values will be unbiased estimates of the true, but unobserved, population values. The standard error of the estimated slope coefficient, denoted s_b, equals

$$\text{Standard error of slope coefficient} = \frac{\text{Regression standard error}}{\text{Sum of squares for } x}$$

where the sum for squares of x, denoted SS_x, equals the square root of the sum of the squared deviations of the independent variable about its mean.[4] In this example, $SS_x = 1{,}538$, so that

$$s_b = \frac{5{,}003}{1{,}538} = 3.25$$

The standard error enables us to test the statistical significance of the estimated coefficient b_1. We can compute the t statistic associated with this estimate by forming the ratio

$$t = \frac{b_1}{s_b} = \frac{29.13}{3.25} = 8.96$$

This statistic is distributed according to a Student's t distribution with $n - 2$ degrees of freedom.[5] By referring to a table of the Student's t distribution, we can determine, for a specified level of confidence, the max-

---

[4] Alternatively, SS_x equals the square root of the variance of the independent variable multiplied by $(n - 1)$.

[5] This statistic is not normally distributed, since we are using an estimate (s_b) of the standard deviation of the true coefficient β_1 rather than the actual standard deviation (which is not observable).

imum probability that we would observe a value of *t* as large as 8.96 if the mean of the distribution that generated the sample value were 0. We test against the value of 0 because if the true value of the coefficient were 0, no relationship would exist between the independent and the dependent variables. The test is formulated as a two-tailed hypothesis test with one-half of the complement of the stated level of confidence in each tail of the distribution. The critical value of *t* with 28 (30 − 2) degrees of freedom and a 95% confidence level is 2.05. For these data, then, we reject the null hypothesis and conclude that a statistically significant relationship exists between the dependent and independent variables.

From a table of the *t* distribution, we can see that at 95% confidence, the critical value of *t*, as the sample size exceeds about 50, is 2. For this reason, a standard rule of thumb is to believe that a regression coefficient is significantly different from zero if the absolute value of its *t* ratio exceeds 2; in effect, to always test with a 0.05 significance (or 95% confidence) level.

Even though we know that a statistically significant relationship exists between the dependent and independent variables, considerable variation still exists in our estimate of the slope coefficient. Knowing the variability of this estimate helps us to quantify the degree of risk from using the estimate for decision-making purposes. A confidence interval for the estimate is constructed by multiplying a *t* value (for the desired level of confidence) by the standard error of the estimate. The confidence interval is

Estimated value $\pm$ *t* $*$ Standard error of the coefficient

In this case, the *t* value associated with 95% confidence is 2.05, and the confidence interval is

$$29.13 \pm 2.05 * 3.25 = [22.5, 35.8]$$

It is often, but incorrectly, stated that the probability is 0.95 that the true value of the variable cost coefficient β_1 lies between 22.5 and 35.8. The correct statement is that we expect that 95% of the confidence intervals constructed in this manner will contain the true value of the coefficient of machine-hours. For any particular confidence interval, such as [22.5, 35.8], the true value is either in the interval or it is not, so that the probability is either 0 or 1 that the true value lies within the computed confidence interval.

The interval [22.5, 35.8] is quite wide, and its breadth may render the estimate impractical for decision-making purposes. A wide range may create the possibility for large opportunity losses. For example, in this case, the industry rule of thumb of $23 is within the range of the estimate. However, if the variable cost is actually $33, then using a number like $23 may lead to accepting jobs or making bids that are not profitable. One solution is to increase the number of observations that are used to estimate the cost equation, perhaps by disaggregating monthly data into weekly or even daily data. The increase in data points should reduce the standard error of the regression and the standard errors of the estimated coefficients.

Regression packages will also compute the standard error and t statistic for the estimate of the constant term β_0 in the regression. For the data above, the standard error of β_0 equals 4,829, so that the associated t statistic is

$$t = \frac{27,901}{4,829} = 5.78$$

We can use this value of t to determine the statistical significance of our estimate of β_0. Note that our test of b_1 concerned whether a statistically significant relationship existed between the dependent variable and the independent variable. For the constant term, b_0, the test concerns whether our estimate of the component of overhead cost that does not vary with machine-hours differs significantly (in a statistical sense) from 0. Since the relevant range is not likely to include very low or shut-down levels of activity, the confidence test involving the value of b_0 is generally regarded as being irrelevant. Many regression programs do not even compute the standard error and t-value associated with the constant term. Nevertheless, if we interpret the value of b_0 as the estimate of fixed costs in the relevant range of activity, a t test allows us to decide whether there is reliable evidence for such a fixed-cost component. If no such evidence is found, we could reestimate the estimated cost function without allowing for a fixed-cost coefficient (although many statistical packages do not provide the option for estimating a regression equation without a constant term).

2. Confidence Statements about Predictions from the Regression Equation

The statistical analysis also permits us to develop confidence intervals for predictions obtained from the regression equation. For example, in Hammonds Plains Manufacturing, we may want, for planning, budgeting, or control purposes, to predict the level of overhead for a planned level of activity (expressed in machine-hours). Suppose the planned number of machine-hours in the upcoming month is 1,850. What level of overhead should we expect given this planned level of activity?

First we must check that the level of activity is within our relevant range of experience. Using an estimated relationship that was developed for one range of activity to predict costs outside of that range can result in large differences between actual and predicted values. To illustrate, consider Exhibit 4–3. Suppose the cost behavior is nonlinear as illustrated. If values of the dependent variable were observed corresponding to values

EXHIBIT 4–3
Nonlinear Cost Curve Outside Relevant Range
of Experience

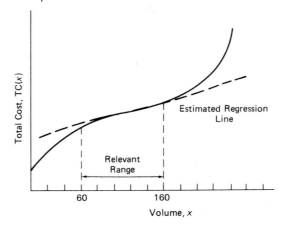

of the independent variable between 60 and 160, the relationship would appear to be linear, which is the approximate behavior of the cost function in the relevant range. However, if this estimated cost function is used to predict the value of the independent variable outside the relevant range, serious prediction errors would occur.

In this case, the projected value of 1,850 is well within the relevant range (from 1,006 to 1,957 machine-hours) of experience. We can now use the estimated equation to predict the overhead cost that will accompany a level of activity of 1,850 machine-hours:

$$\text{Predicted overhead} = y_t = 27{,}901 + 29.13\,x_t$$
$$= 27{,}901 + 29.13 * 1{,}850$$
$$= \$81{,}799$$

At the end of the month, actual overhead turns out to be $95,000. The question arises as to whether the actual overhead differs sufficiently from the predicted value of $81,799 to warrant investigation. The regression equation can provide a signal indicating whether the behavior of overhead has changed from recent experience. We compute an interval for our prediction of overhead cost that represents where we expect overhead costs to lie, given the current level of activity.

When the estimated equation is used to predict a new value of the dependent variable, in this case overhead, discrepancies will arise between the predicted value and the actual value of the dependent variable because of two factors:

1. The standard errors of observations about the estimated regression line—reflecting variables not included in our predictive equation—as measured by s_e

2. Errors from estimating the β_1 coefficient in the regression—how much variation there could be in our estimate of the slope of the regression line

Since the regression line passes through the point representing the mean of the observed values of machine-hours and overhead, errors in estimating the slope are equivalent to rotating the estimated regression line about this point. Therefore, errors in estimating the slope coefficient will have the greatest impact when the independent variable takes on values at the boundaries of our range of relevant experience.

Combining these two errors results in the following formula for the standard error of the forecast, s_f:

$$s_f = s_e * \left[1 + \frac{1}{n} + \frac{(x_f - x_m)^2}{SS_x^2} \right]^{0.5}$$

where x_f is the forecasted value of the independent variable and x_m is the mean of the values of the independent variable. In this case, we have

$$s_f = 5{,}003 * \left[1 + \frac{1}{30} + \frac{(1{,}850 - 1{,}457)^2}{1{,}538^2} \right]^{0.5}$$
$$= 5{,}244$$

In practice, s_f is often approximated as s_e. This approximation is generally satisfactory as long as the sample size, n, is large, the standard error of the regression is not large, and the value of the independent variable, x_f, is not too far from x_m, the mean of the independent variable.

Knowing the standard error of the forecast, we can construct a t statistic to determine whether the actual value lies outside the past range of experience—i.e., whether a different process may have generated the observed value. The t statistic associated with the observation of $95,000 equals

$$t = \frac{95{,}000 - 81{,}799}{5{,}244} = 2.52$$

The probability of a t distribution generating a random variable 2.52 standard errors from its mean is less than .05. We can conclude that it is unlikely that the most recent observation of $95,000 is consistent with the process that generated the thirty preceding observations of overhead cost and machine-hours. This statistically significant deviation implies that an investigation could be warranted, especially if the cost of such an investigation were felt to be below the benefit from finding and correcting the source of the unusually high overhead cost in the most recent month.

Our example started with attempting to estimate the overhead cost for a particular job, but we have analyzed overhead data not for jobs but for monthly periods. Observant readers will notice that the machine-hours for any particular job will be well outside the range of experience we have used to estimate our regression equations. But the monthly total of machine-hours and overhead represents the sum of all jobs worked during the month. Hence, the monthly aggregates are sufficient for estimating the overhead costs likely to be incurred because of individual jobs, since, in total, all jobs worked during the month will sum to the monthly machine-hours in the plant.

Additional Issues in Using Predictions from a Regression Equation

When overhead or other standards are established from statistical analysis of historical cost data, these standards do not necessarily represent efficient or optimal performance. Rather, they represent the level of performance of cost behavior experienced in the past. The standards serve as a basis for determining when current performance has deteriorated (or improved) from previous experience, but they do not imply that past performance represented a reasonable level of efficiency. That would require a more detailed study of the cost center or production process. One danger arises from being satisified if current operations are in fact consistent with recent past experience. Contemporary trends in manufacturing operations emphasize continual improvement activities, so that future operations will be substantially more efficient than current or past operations. Excessive reliance on standards or budgets derived from past experience may not provide the appropriate environment for stimulating continuous improvement activities by managers.

A second danger occurs if high-cost observations are not flagged as "statistically significant" because the standard error of the estimated regression line was high. High standard errors (or, equivalently, low R^2) imply large unexplained fluctuations in overhead costs. Too many large, unexplained fluctuations signal the need for a careful examination of operating procedures so that the erratic cost behavior can be brought under control. The investigation decision can therefore be triggered not just by a shift in the mean (observations more than 2 standard errors from the forecasted amount) but also by a too dispersed distribution of observations in the historical data used to estimate the relationship.

Multiple Regression Analysis

The application of regression analysis would be highly restricted if it could handle only a single independent variable. Regression analysis is easily extended to situations where more than one variable helps to explain the behavior of the dependent variable. The use of more than one independent variable is called **multiple regression analysis.** The statistics that we have already discussed apply equally to multiple regression analysis. The equations and calculations become much more cumbersome, but multiple regression analysis is easily performed by computer programs.

We return to Hammonds Plains Manufacturing to illustrate multiple regression analysis. Suppose that after observing the production process, we believe that the monthly number of production runs will affect the amount of overhead reported during the month. We collect data on the number of production runs performed each month as shown in Table 4–6.

TABLE 4–6
Hammonds Plains Manufacturing
Overhead Cost

Month Number	Overhead	Machine-Hours	Production Runs
1	76,667	1,772	31
2	73,678	1,820	22
3	80,141	1,634	39
4	61,985	1,006	40
5	72,685	1,383	39
6	87,675	1,957	41
7	78,450	1,561	48
8	70,634	1,464	34
9	63,417	1,545	25
10	56,057	1,119	29
11	67,446	1,382	35
12	72,102	1,320	47
13	68,533	1,264	49
14	69,079	1,344	29
15	85,550	1,803	48
16	58,197	1,022	38
17	61,626	1,510	21
18	80,689	1,793	29
19	58,256	1,149	27
20	55,337	1,155	22
21	85,108	1,847	38
22	76,485	1,832	23
23	67,783	1,136	42
24	56,398	1,136	22
25	66,622	1,330	33
26	63,494	1,358	26
27	89,416	1,882	45
28	67,518	1,174	45
29	73,680	1,643	31
30	66,132	1,381	26

A multiple regression analysis using the above data yields the following estimated equation:

Overhead = 11,621 + 28.73 * (machine-hours)
+ 494.3 * (production runs)

The R^2 statistic of this regression is 0.95 (the adjusted R^2 statistic is 0.94), and the standard error of the regression is 2,204. The overall F statistic is 265 and is distributed with 2 degrees of freedom in the numerator and 27 degrees of freedom in the denominator. This value exceeds the critical value (at 95%) of 3.35. The standard errors and t statistics associated with the predictive equation variables are:

	Constant	Machine-Hours	Production Runs
Coefficient	11,621	28.73	494.3
Standard error	2,605	1.43	45.6
t value	4.46	20.0	10.8

The t statistics, distributed with 27 degrees of freedom, are highly statistically significant.

Note that the standard errors associated with this regression equation are much smaller than those associated with our initial equation indicating that we have a much better fit to the data, a situation also revealed by the much higher value of R^2. The newly estimated equation reveals that the cost of a job contains both a fixed-cost component ($494.3) relating to job setup, and a variable-cost component ($28.73) relating to the number of machine-hours required.

The estimate of variable cost per machine-hour is only marginally lower than in the first equation. But the fixed-cost component is much lower. We now understand that part of what we initially thought was a "fixed" cost turned out to be a cost that varied, not with production volume, but with the number of production runs. The failure to understand the production process gave us at first an inaccurate estimate of the incremental cost of additional jobs. The high setup cost ($494 per job) causes small jobs to be much less profitable than the first equation would imply, an important insight for Hammonds Plains Manufacturing, which specializes in custom work that requires many small production runs. Other factors that could be buried in the constant term β_0 by an incomplete analysis include the amount of raw materials handled, product complexity, and number of products produced. Perhaps, in the past, not enough care has been given to controlling and attempting to minimize setup costs for jobs. These costs, as revealed by the second regression equation, are high, so that setups need to be done more efficiently if Hammonds Plains wants to be both competitive and profitable for small jobs.

Summary

In this chapter, we have discussed the use of regression analysis for estimating cost behavior. Ordinary least squares provides a systematic and well-defined approach to isolating the variable- and fixed-cost components of a cost. Moreover, the regression method yields statistics on the confidence, or reliability, of the estimates.

Important assumptions of regression analysis must be satisfied if the estimates and the confidence tests that we have discussed in this chapter are to be valid. The assumptions and nature of violations will be discussed in the next chapter. We will also discuss some techniques to detect when these violations have occurred and approaches to dealing with these violations.

PROBLEMS

4–1 Cost Analysis by Account Classification
(CMA, adapted)

The Tastee-Treat Company prepares, packages, and distributes six frozen vegetables in two different size containers. The different vegetables and different sizes are prepared in large batches. The company employs an actual-cost job-order costing system. Manufacturing overhead is assigned to batches by a predetermined rate on the basis of direct labor hours. The manufacturing overhead costs incurred by the company last year are presented below:

Direct Labor Hours worked	
(000)	<u>2,160</u>
Manufacturing Overhead Costs	
($000)	
Indirect Labor	$ 8,640
Employee Benefits	3,240
Supplies	2,160
Power	1,728
Heat and Light	552
Supervision	2,625
Depreciation	7,930
Property Taxes and Insurance	<u>3,005</u>
	<u>$29,880</u>

The company expects to operate at a 2,300 (000) DLH level of activity this year.

Required:

1. Estimate manufacturing overhead for this year. You can prepare a (1) low, (2) median, and (3) high estimate depending on your assumptions on the amount of fixed and variable expense in each account.
2. For each of your three estimates, compute the average rate used to allocate overhead costs to products and the flexible budget.
3. How can you attempt to obtain better estimates of the fixed and variable cost components for manufacturing overhead? Why would improved estimates be useful to Tastee-Treat?

4–2   Choice of Independent Variable

The Oliver Company wants to develop a flexible budget to predict how overhead costs vary with activity levels. It is unsure whether to choose direct labor-hours (DLH) or units produced, as the best measure of activity for the firm. Monthly data for the preceding twelve months appear below:

Month	DLH	Units	Overhead
1	1250	111	$29,900
2	1497	132	34,600
3	1184	121	28,900
4	1499	147	34,300
5	1356	154	32,400
6	1300	125	31,200
7	1222	122	28,700
8	1259	131	29,400
9	1109	120	27,000
10	1435	144	33,400
11	1121	112	27,700
12	1433	145	34,100

Required:

Determine which measure, DLH or Units, should be used for the flexible budget and obtain the flexible budget for the firm's overhead costs.

4–3   Effects of Price-Level Shifts on Cost Behavior

Indirect labor expense (ILE) for the Parker Company is a simple linear function of direct-labor-hours (DLH). At the start of 1989, this relationship is given by:

$$ILE = \beta_0 + \beta_1 DLH$$

with $\beta_0 = 200$ and $\beta_1 = 8$. Six months of operation occurred with these parameters. At the start of the seventh month, all cost categories in the

Parker Company increased by 10%. Six more months of operation occurred at this price level and at the start of month 13, another 10% across-the-board increase in all costs occurred. The Parker Company operated at this price level for six more months. Data for direct labor-hours and indirect labor expense for these eighteen months are given below.

Month	DLH (000)	ILE (000)	Month	DLH (000)	ILE (000)
1	20	$360	10	29	$475.2
2	25	400	11	27	457.6
3	22	376	12	25	440.0
4	23	384	13	28	513.0
5	20	360	14	32	551.8
6	19	352	15	35	580.8
7	24	431.2	16	34	571.1
8	28	466.4	17	30	532.4
9	26	448.8	18	36	590.5

Required:

1. Plot the data. Verify that the specified linear relationship holds within each six-month period. What values do β_0 and β_1 have during months 7–12 and months 13–18?
2. Fit a straight-line (visually or by using a regression routine) to all 18 data points. What values of β_0 and β_1 do you obtain?
3. Perform a price level adjustment to the data and reestimate β_0 and β_1 using all 18 data points. Assuming no cost increases for month 19, what is your prediction for Indirect labor expense if there were 33(000) direct labor-hours in Month 19?
4. Interpret your results. What causes the difference in the linear relationship estimated in requirement 2 and requirement 3?

4–4   Statistical Inference and Prediction

Stayner Plastics manufactures a variety of plastic products in injection-molding machines. In injection molding, molten plastic is forced into a mold. The mold is then cooled using water or air, which hardens the plastic. Once the plastic is hardened, the mold is opened and the parts are ejected or removed.

One of the products manufactured by Stayner Plastics is a float used to provide buoyancy in fishing nets. These floats must be able to withstand water pressure, an attribute that is jointly determined by the design of the float, the plastic used to manufacture the float, and the cooling time in the mold.

To test the relationship between the cooling time in the mold and the ability of the float to withstand pressure, 30 floats of a particular design were tested. The data on the pressure, in pounds per square inch, at which each float collapsed and the time, in seconds, that each float spent in the mold are shown in the accompanying table.

Stayner Plastics
Results of Pressure Test

Float Number	Pressure Withstood	Cooling Time	Float Number	Pressure Withstood	Cooling Time
1	510	127	16	672	177
2	584	158	17	554	125
3	804	197	18	931	213
4	845	230	19	695	151
5	620	136	20	578	146
6	860	230	21	561	132
7	902	244	22	878	216
8	610	123	23	913	224
9	671	129	24	957	231
10	809	219	25	715	174
11	637	139	26	646	153
12	888	230	27	599	131
13	789	196	28	926	219
14	738	197	29	882	209
15	881	229	30	868	219

The production manager has asked you to study these data to determine the nature of the relationship between the cooling time in the mold and the pressure that the float can withstand. On the basis of the relationship that you uncover, you have been asked to recommend the amount of time that the floats should be allowed to cool in the mold. Stayner Plastics has committed to its major distributors that the probability is less than .05 that a float cannot withstand a pressure of 800 pounds per square inch.

4-5 Estimating a Security's Systematic Risk through Regression Analysis

Waterville Electronics manufactures electronic components used in the computer and space industries. The annual rate of return on the market portfolio and the annual rate of return on Waterville Electronics stock for the last 40 months are shown in the accompanying table.

Waterville Electronics
Stock Return and Market Return Data

Month Number	Market Return	Stock Return	Month Number	Market Return	Stock Return
1	0.123	0.1836	21	0.085	0.0630
2	0.085	0.1320	22	0.130	0.1770
3	0.031	0.0112	23	0.051	0.1012
4	0.123	0.2676	24	0.054	0.2458
5	0.104	0.1738	25	0.162	0.2234
6	0.155	0.3410	26	0.078	0.2086
7	0.057	0.0514	27	0.090	0.2170
8	0.252	0.3574	28	0.132	0.1554
9	0.097	0.2294	29	0.146	0.1972
10	0.078	0.0936	30	0.085	0.1670
11	0.119	0.1868	31	0.132	0.2374
12	0.038	0.0366	32	0.099	0.1938
13	0.010	−0.0450	33	0.092	0.2154
14	0.076	0.0822	34	0.123	0.1456
15	0.049	0.0558	35	0.111	0.1752
16	0.078	0.1746	36	0.149	0.1978
17	0.103	0.1776	37	0.062	0.2184
18	0.120	0.2500	38	0.111	0.1742
19	−0.018	0.0104	39	0.060	0.1070
20	0.018	0.0486	40	0.231	0.3582

The treasurer of Waterville Electronics is considering issuing common stock and has asked you to compute the systematic risk of Waterville Electronic's common stock.

A review of a finance text reveals that the rate of return, in period j, on a security (x_j) is hypothesized to be related to the rate of return on the market portfolio (m_j):

$$x_j = a + bm_j + \epsilon_j$$

where a is the risk-free rate of return, b represents the security's systematic risk, and ϵ_j is an error term.

Using the data available, estimate the systematic risk of the common stock of Waterville Electronics.

4–6   *Using Regression Analysis in Analytic Review*

The auditor of Fort Dodge Manufacturing uses regression analysis during the analytical review stage of the firm's annual audit. The regression analysis attempts to uncover relationships that exist between various account balances. Any such relationship is subsequently used as a preliminary test of the reasonableness of the reported account balances.

The auditor wants to determine whether a relationship exists between the balance of accounts receivable at month-end and that month's sales. The accompanying table contains data relating to these two accounts, which have been accumulated for the last 25 months.

Fort Dodge Manufacturing
Monthly Sales and Accounts Receivable Balances

Month Number	Sales	Accounts Receivable	Month Number	Sales	Accounts Receivable
1	2,239,363	2,545,025	14	1,626,758	2,580,813
2	2,812,525	3,462,323	15	2,145,361	2,485,592
3	2,903,861	3,623,508	16	1,826,522	2,571,181
4	1,978,638	3,247,471	17	2,728,382	2,971,562
5	2,864,199	3,293,639	18	2,718,027	3,359,156
6	2,409,085	3,405,759	19	2,069,679	2,966,645
7	1,575,971	2,434,565	20	1,834,209	2,400,425
8	1,951,929	2,211,205	21	2,238,403	2,663,529
9	1,850,453	2,502,739	22	2,963,719	3,497,009
10	1,606,938	2,218,287	23	2,380,332	3,425,310
11	2,387,561	2,822,624	24	2,634,062	3,061,575
12	1,676,706	2,449,310	25	2,518,412	3,167,496
13	2,572,484	3,199,568			

Required:

1. Is there any statistical evidence to suggest a relationship between the monthly sales level and the closing balance of accounts receivable?
2. During month 26, which is a fiscal year-end month, the sales were $1,800,000. The reported accounts receivable balance was $3,000,000. Does this reported amount seem consistent with past experience?

4–7 *Regression Analysis and a Test of an Income-Smoothing Hypothesis*

The auditor of Hartland Manufacturing is concerned about the number and magnitude of year-end adjustments that are made annually when the financial statements of Hartland Manufacturing are prepared. Specifially, the auditor suspects that the management of Hartland Manufacturing is using discretionary write-offs to manipulate the reported net income.

To test this hypothesis, the auditor has developed a data-set of twenty-five firms that are similar to Hartland Manufacturing in terms of manufacturing facilities and product lines. The cumulative reported third-quarter income, as well as the final net income reported, is shown in the accompanying table for each of these twenty-five firms.

Hartland Manufacturing

Firm Number	Cumulative 3rd-Quarter Income	Reported Annual Income	Firm Number	Cumulative 3rd-Quarter Income	Reported Annual Income
1	3,296,716	5,197,454	14	3,454,048	5,838,526
2	2,182,805	3,902,133	15	3,334,191	4,890,822
3	3,413,178	4,180,006	16	2,432,622	2,906,894
4	1,524,886	2,693,017	17	2,514,495	3,508,272
5	2,875,030	3,209,407	18	1,856,126	3,143,044
6	3,487,535	4,854,346	19	2,413,233	4,193,686
7	2,504,970	3,268,122	20	2,964,661	4,235,616
8	3,356,565	4,838,645	21	3,235,884	5,702,916
9	3,183,830	3,632,840	22	3,364,447	5,629,464
10	3,274,635	5,028,237	23	2,495,817	3,773,179
11	1,628,167	2,853,374	24	2,019,277	3,075,330
12	3,658,482	5,673,593	25	3,789,931	4,849,016
13	2,388,552	3,812,585			

If Hartland Manufacturing reported a cumulative third-quarter income of $2,500,000 and a preliminary net income of $4,000,000, should the auditor conclude that the relationship between cumulative third-quarter income and the annual income for Hartland Manufacturing differs from that of the twenty-five firms in this sample?

4–8   Effect of Omitted Variables

Twin Falls Drills manufactures drill bits. The production of the drill bits occurs in lots of 1,000 units. Due to the intense competition in the industry and the correspondingly low prices, the vice-president of production at Twin Falls Drills has ordered a study of the manufacturing costs of each of the products manufactured by the company. As the senior cost analyst, you have been asked to undertake a cost study of the overhead costs associated with producing the drill bits. On the basis of discussions with senior production personnel, you have determined that the number of lots produced, the direct labor-hours used, and the number of production runs per month might help to explain the behavior of overhead costs. The accompanying table contains the data on these variables that have been collected.

Your assistant has analyzed these data and has prepared a preliminary report on the regression findings. She has suggested that the following regression be used to predict overhead:

Overhead = 59,970 + 3.12 direct labor-hours

+ 914 number of production runs

Twin Falls Drills
Overhead Cost Data

Month Number	Overhead	Lots Produced	Direct Labor-Hours	Number of Production Runs
1	76,506	6,289	3,292	7
2	75,877	6,403	3,316	7
3	75,799	7,467	3,733	6
4	82,398	8,807	4,427	8
5	78,644	8,949	4,605	3
6	78,679	6,784	3,353	8
7	70,470	6,243	3,144	4
8	72,413	5,721	3,014	4
9	80,629	7,476	3,732	9
10	78,737	8,391	4,152	8
11	74,299	6,860	3,422	5
12	73,814	8,566	4,143	3
13	78,367	5,854	3,022	4
14	73,936	5,523	2,842	8
15	80,060	7,663	3,844	6
16	71,895	6,558	3,250	5
17	79,128	7,679	3,826	9
18	72,565	5,644	2,835	4
19	72,516	7,513	3,646	3
20	67,870	7,358	3,497	4
21	76,235	5,221	2,635	8
22	76,713	6,190	3,227	7
23	74,433	7,358	3,706	4
24	80,237	8,379	4,319	5
25	71,639	5,491	2,608	3
26	81,263	8,380	4,109	4
27	76,879	8,788	4,424	4
28	78,761	5,100	2,486	4
29	67,699	5,301	2,707	3
30	75,332	8,030	3,767	4

This regression has an R^2 of 0.49. The standard error of the regression equals 2,828. The t values associated with the estimated coefficients of the independent variables are both significant at the 95% level of confidence.

After studying the report and noting that a statistically signficant relationship has been found, your initial disappointment with the low explanatory power of the regression gives way to a determination to develop a better predictive equation for overhead. After showing your assistant's analysis to one of the production line supervisors, the supervisor comments:

I can believe that labor-hours and the number of production run setups will affect overhead because we use a lot of supplies when we are working on the machines and because the machine setup time for each run is charged to overhead. But your equation is missing something. When the rate of production increases, we use overtime until we can train the additional people that we require for the machines. When the rate of production falls, we incur idle time until the surplus workers are transferred to other parts of the plant. So it would seem to me that there will be an additional overhead cost whenever the level of production changes. I would also say that because of the nature of this rescheduling process, the bigger the change in production, the greater the effect of the change in production on the increase in overhead.

Required:

Develop a variable that will allow you to incorporate the comments of the production supervisor into the regression analysis and then, using this new variable, estimate a new equation to predict overhead. You have been advised that the number of lots produced in the month preceding month 1 was 5,964.

4–9   Understanding the Relationship between Cost and Underlying Activities

Bay City Printers performs all types of printing including custom work, such as advertising displays, and standard work, such as business cards. Market prices exist for standard work, and Bay City Printers must match or better these prices in order to get the business. The key issue is whether the existing market price covers the cost associated with doing the work.

On the other hand, most of the custom work must be priced individually. Since all custom work is done on a job-order basis, Bay City Printers routinely keeps track of all the direct labor and direct materials costs associated with each job. However, the overhead for each job must be estimated. The overhead is applied to each job using a predetermined (normalized) rate based on estimated overhead and labor-hours. Once the cost of the prospective job is determined, the sales manager develops a bid that reflects both the existing market conditions and the estimated price of completing the job.

In the past, the normalized rate for overhead has been computed by using the historical average of overhead per direct labor-hour. Mary Steele, the owner and manager of Bay City Printers, has become increasingly concerned about this practice for two reasons:

1. The approach has not produced accurate forecasts of overhead in the past, leading Mary to believe that it is not reliable.

2. The equipment used by Bay City Printers is becoming more expensive and more automated. As a result, the labor content of jobs is decreasing, and the normalized rate of overhead per direct labor-hour has steadily been increasing.

The accompanying table shows the overhead data that Mary has collected for her shop for the past 50 weeks.

Bay City Printers
Overhead Cost Data

Week Number	Overhead Cost	Labor-Hours	Machine-Hours	Week Number	Overhead Cost	Labor-Hours	Machine-Hours
1	76,890	1,266	339	26	76,695	1,139	333
2	75,671	668	468	27	61,595	772	211
3	84,001	1,474	264	28	70,922	673	414
4	77,643	1,201	239	29	68,090	1,006	272
5	84,703	1,028	400	30	54,247	592	261
6	77,328	1,209	317	31	74,917	1,014	229
7	78,516	618	401	32	97,492	1,396	422
8	64,865	721	248	33	77,308	746	441
9	84,365	850	389	34	84,322	901	456
10	70,247	841	377	35	74,274	755	325
11	62,261	675	216	36	83,259	1,422	276
12	73,207	932	289	37	72,550	1,174	225
13	79,742	1,325	377	38	99,452	1,351	428
14	93,115	1,348	454	39	94,511	1,452	406
15	57,579	618	236	40	93,816	1,444	428
16	90,639	974	454	41	88,372	1,021	473
17	88,547	840	485	42	83,134	1,315	359
18	68,113	1,124	207	43	95,778	1,299	465
19	54,160	565	222	44	84,784	940	460
20	71,695	552	428	45	66,563	669	421
21	69,144	1,096	244	46	91,651	1,204	454
22	62,065	640	454	47	100,873	1,372	440
23	91,539	1,423	374	48	78,837	747	430
24	70,520	1,013	378	49	86,107	1,423	294
25	87,984	863	452	50	67,477	675	356

The average weekly overhead for the last 50 weeks is $78,431, and the average weekly number of labor-hours worked is 1,007. Therefore, the normalized rate for overhead that will be used in the upcoming week is $78 (78,431/1,007) per direct labor-hour.

Mary has asked you to examine the overhead cost data for her firm to determine whether you can develop a more accurate estimate of overhead costs. Mary is now preparing a bid for an important order that may involve a considerable amount of repeat business. The estimated costs for this project are:

Number of labor-hours required	15
Number of machine-hours required	8
Direct labor cost	$150
Direct material cost	$750

Using the existing approach to cost estimation, Mary has estimated the cost for this job as being $2,070 [150 + 750 + (78 * 15)]. Given the existing data, what cost would you estimate for this job?

4–10   *Predicting the Relationship between Price and Product Characteristics*

Clayton Park Electronics manufactures color television sets for sale in a highly competitive marketplace. Recently Bill Pollock, the marketing manager of Clayton Park Electronics, has been complaining that the company is losing market share because of a poor-quality image and has asked that the company's major product, the 25″ console model, be redesigned to incorporate a higher-quality level.

The company general manager, Gord Langdon, is considering the request to improve the product quality but has observed:

> Higher performance costs money and, before we go to the expense, I would like to see some evidence that the consumer is willing to pay for any additional quality we design in.

As the company controller, you have been given the task of determining the cost effectiveness of improving the quality of the television sets manufactured by Clayton Park Electronics. With the help of the marketing staff, you have obtained a summary of the average retail price of the company's television set and the prices of twenty-nine competitive sets. In addition, you have obtained from *The Shoppers' Guide*, a magazine that evaluates and reports on various consumer products, a quality rating of the television sets produced by Clayton Park Electronics and its competitors. The table on the next page summarizes these data.

According to *The Shoppers' Guide*, the quality rating, which varies from 0 to 10 with 10 being the highest level of quality, considers such factors as the quality of the picture, the frequency of repair, and the cost of repairs.

Discussions with the product design group suggest that the cost of manufacturing this type of television set is

$$125 + q^2$$

where q is the quality rating.

Clayton Park Electronics
Market Summary

Product Number	Average Price	Quality Rating	Product Number	Average Price	Quality Rating
1	499	9	16	418	5
2	486	8	17	423	3
3	459	5	18	479	9
4	473	8	19	485	8
5	417	2	20	463	7
6	487	8	21	463	6
7	478	9	22	466	7
8	433	3	23	467	8
9	429	4	24	425	4
10	455	5	25	508	9
11	449	4	26	491	9
12	473	7	27	442	5
13	441	5	28	479	7
14	428	3	29	446	4
15	423	2	30	465	6

Required:

1. Does any statistical evidence from these data indicate that customers will pay for quality? If so, what is the price premium as a function of the quality level of the product?
2. Given the results from requirement 1 is there a preferred level of quality for this product? You should assume that the quality level will only affect the price charged and not the level of sales of the product.

4–11   *Estimating the Sales-Advertising Relationship*

Dauphin Dairy Limited (DDL) produces and sells a wide range of dairy products. Since most of the dairy's costs and prices are set by a government regulatory board, most of the competition between the dairy and its competitors takes place through advertising.

The controller of DDL has developed the accompanying schedule of sales and advertising levels for the last 50 weeks.

The company controller has turned these data over to you with the following comments:

> We are spending a lot of money on advertising. Sometimes I think that we are advertising too much. I know that our contribution-margin ratio is about 10%. That is, 10% of each sales dollar goes toward covering our fixed costs. That means that each advertising dollar has to generate at least $10 of sales or the advertising is not cost effective. I would like

Dauphin Dairy Limited

Week Number	Sales	Current Promotion	Week Number	Sales	Current Promotion
1	227,885	5,823	26	221,519	5,461
2	237,806	7,075	27	219,078	7,707
3	229,854	6,140	28	233,242	6,157
4	222,078	5,544	29	222,690	7,063
5	208,821	5,340	30	228,235	7,138
6	225,181	6,489	31	225,868	5,845
7	227,044	5,742	32	227,933	5,989
8	237,305	7,946	33	222,639	7,577
9	235,280	7,264	34	243,347	6,319
10	234,239	7,089	35	231,268	6,888
11	235,418	6,584	36	237,697	7,853
12	239,299	7,249	37	232,384	5,757
13	242,819	7,618	38	222,187	7,214
14	237,523	5,986	39	233,702	6,646
15	230,684	7,763	40	224,707	5,007
16	245,321	7,852	41	229,841	7,763
17	232,105	6,145	42	228,440	6,535
18	226,502	7,143	43	241,565	5,417
19	231,928	5,832	44	224,190	7,240
20	231,554	6,775	45	226,766	6,174
21	231,003	6,727	46	226,312	5,731
22	220,017	5,098	47	219,681	7,292
23	231,023	7,609	48	224,125	6,971
24	232,824	6,264	49	230,648	6,661
25	222,506	6,557	50	222,718	5,975

you to determine whether our advertising dollars are generating this type of sales response.

4–12 Multiple Regression Analysis

Ward Martin, the owner-manager of White River Home Fuels Company, faces a difficult problem. White River Home Fuels Company sells heating oil to residential customers. Given the amount of competition in the industry, both from other home heating oil suppliers and from electric and natural gas utilities, the price of the oil supplied and the level of service are critical in determining a company's success.

Unlike electric and natural gas customers, oil customers are exposed to the risk of running out of fuel. Home heating oil suppliers therefore have to guarantee that the customer's oil tank will not be allowed to run dry. In fact, Ward's service pledge is, "50 free gallons on us if we let you run dry." Beyond the cost of the oil, however, Ward is concerned about the perceived reliability of his service if a customer is allowed to run out of oil.

To estimate customer oil use, the home heating oil industry has, for many years, used the concept of degree days. A *degree day* is equal to the difference between the average daily temperature and 68 degrees Fahrenheit. Thus, if the average temperature on a given day is 50, the degree days for that day will be 18. (If the degree day calculation results in a negative number, the degree days number is recorded as 0.) By keeping track of the number of degree days since the customer's last oil fill, by knowing the size of the customer's oil tank, and by estimating the customer's oil consumption as a function of the number of degree days, the oil supplier can estimate when the customer is getting low on fuel and can resupply the customer.

Ward has used this scheme in the past but is disappointed with the results and the computational burdens that it places on him. First, the system requires that a consumption-per-degree-day figure be estimated for each customer to reflect that customer's consumption habits, size of home, quality of home insulation, and family size. Since Ward has over 1,500 customers, the computational burden of keeping track of all these customers is proving to be enormous. Second, the system is crude. The consumption per degree day for each customer is computed by dividing the oil consumption during the preceding year by the degree days during the preceding year. This approach has proved to be very unreliable. Customers have tended to use less fuel than estimated during the colder months and more fuel than estimated during the warmer months. This means that Ward is making more deliveries than necessary during the colder months and customers are running out of oil during the warmer months.

Ward has asked you to help him develop a consumption estimation model that is practical and more reliable. As you begin speaking to Ward, you find that he has the following data available:

1. The number of degree days since the last oil fill and the consumption amounts for 40 customers.

2. The number of people residing in the homes of each of the 40 customers. Ward figures that this is important in predicting the oil consumption of customers using oil-fired hot water heaters, since it provides an estimate of the hot-water requirements of each customer. Each of the customers in this sample uses an oil-fired hot-water heater.

3. An assessment, provided by his sales staff, of the home type of each of these 40 customers. The home type classification, which is a number between 1 and 5, is a composite index of the home size, age, exposure to wind, level of insulation, and furnace type. A low index would imply a lower oil consumption per degree day, and a high index would imply a higher consumption of oil per degree day. Ward figures that the use of such an index will allow him to estimate a consumption model based on a sample data set and then to apply the same model to predict the oil demand of each of his customers.

Ward then provides you with the accompanying table containing data on **monthly** oil consumption. He asks whether a statistically reliable oil consumption model can be estimated from the data.

White River Home Fuels

Customer Number	Oil Usage	Degree Days	Home Factor	Number of People
1	381	888	3	3
2	171	176	5	7
3	644	1073	5	4
4	19	126	2	4
5	394	645	5	5
6	153	326	4	6
7	7	1229	1	3
8	319	1218	2	4
9	40	570	2	1
10	121	334	1	7
11	243	738	3	3
12	200	1464	1	5
13	402	880	4	5
14	118	1134	1	5
15	319	1019	3	4
16	185	460	2	3
17	209	257	5	4
18	467	779	5	4
19	50	128	2	4
20	153	371	2	5
21	94	178	3	6
22	574	933	5	3
23	191	295	3	5
24	679	1358	4	5
25	305	626	4	5
26	85	237	2	7
27	87	813	1	6
28	170	385	3	5
29	92	678	1	4
30	35	54	2	3
31	60	314	1	5
32	507	898	4	3
33	148	966	1	6
34	83	84	5	3
35	318	919	3	4
36	85	379	1	4
37	245	512	3	4
38	56	355	2	3
39	303	759	3	3
40	10	777	1	4

chapter 5

TOPICS IN REGRESSION ANALYSIS

In this chapter, we discuss five issues that arise when applying regression analysis to estimate cost functions:

1. What procedures in the recording and accounting process can cause problems for regression analysis?
2. What criteria exist to evaluate the output from a regression analysis?
3. What are the crucial assumptions of regression and why are they important?
4. How can we detect when a regression assumption has been violated?
5. What can we do when we find that a regression assumption has been violated?

The discussion of these five topics can become quite technical, requiring expertise far beyond the reasonable capability of a practicing management accountant. Our discussions will be only of an introductory nature, to identify some of the sources, effects, diagnoses, and cures of the problems that might arise.

Planning for Regression Analysis of Business Data

Before embarking on a statistical analysis of historical data, the analyst needs to verify that the data have been gathered appropriately. Several factors in the business environment can create difficulties that need to be overcome or at least mitigated before the statistical analysis should proceed:

1. Accuracy and honesty in recording data
2. Difficulties in ensuring proper accrual
3. Economies of scale or learning effects
4. Changes in the nature of the production process

5. The tendency of many organizations to operate at a constant level of activity
6. Practices relating to adjustment to expansion or contraction
7. Choosing the underlying activity level

Accuracy and Honesty in Recording Data

Regression analysis must be performed on accurate data. Data that are unreliable will cause the regression analysis to fail to uncover, or possibly to misrepresent, an underlying relationship that may exist.

Inaccuracies can arise in two ways. First, there may be clerical errors in recording the data. This should not be a problem when data are extracted from the financial accounting system, since those data are subject to considerable integrity and validity checks. Frequently, however, the data for a regression analysis will be derived from informal production reports that contain considerable errors because

a. The importance of accuracy is not impressed on the recorder
b. The data are not subject to independent verification or calculation
c. The data may be used in either formal or informal performance evaluation schemes so that the recorder may present the data in the most favorable, rather than the most accurate, way

Difficulties in Ensuring Proper Accrual

Regression analysis, by its very nature, requires the comparison of data that relate to the same period of time. This in turn means that costs must be accurately accrued. Performing a statistical analysis on data generated from a cash, rather than an accrual, system will almost surely yield meaningless output. For example, if a regression analysis is undertaken to determine the effect of changes in the level of production activity on overhead costs, the overhead costs must be accumulated and properly accrued for the same time interval as the production data. Frequently, however, the cost accumulation and the production systems may be out of phase. Production activity may be recorded weekly, daily, or batch by batch, but costs may be accrued monthly or quarterly. Therefore, the analyst must choose a time interval for which both accurate production and financial data will be available.

Improper accruals will lead to errors in two data points. A cost incurred in January but allocated to February because of a late billing will cause January's costs to be understated and February's to be overstated. A similar problem arises if a detected error in one month's report is corrected by adjusting the next month's report rather than restating the initial month's total correctly. Such adjustments may be satisfactory for financial reporting, but they undermine the value of the monthly data for analyzing cost behavior. When selecting an accounting period as the basis for a historical-cost analysis, good closings should occur at the end of each period; accruals of all incurred costs (including the hourly or weekly payroll) should be estimated carefully, all relevant costs incurred during the period should be counted, and errors detected subsequent to the closing should be closed back to the appropriate period rather than handled as an adjustment in some subsequent period.

Problems can also arise from cost aggregation and allocation procedures. For example, suppose the firm allocates corporate overhead in proportion to the level of production. A correlation of overhead cost with production activity will merely reflect this allocation procedure. It cannot be used to imply that corporate overhead is affected by the level of production. The data used in the regression analysis should only include items for which a cause-and-effect relationship is thought to exist. It should exclude arbitrary or formula allocations, such as corporate overhead, that might confuse the regression analysis.

Economies of Scale or Learning Effects

Most regression analyses assume that a linear, or directly proportional, relationship exists between the dependent variable and the independent variables. The regression analysis could be badly flawed if a linear equation were fitted to an inherently nonlinear relationship. Nonlinearity could arise in the presence of learning or experience curve effects. Total or average costs vary nonlinearly with cumulative output, since the learning effect causes more recently produced items to have lower production costs than items produced much earlier.

A second example of a nonlinear relationship between the dependent variable and the underlying activity variable occurs if economies of scale exist. If the firm is able to produce products more efficiently at higher levels of production, a simple linear model will not capture this phenomenon.

Changes in the Nature of the Production Process

Regression analysis assumes a single, stable, and continuing relationship between the dependent variable and the independent variable(s). This assumption is violated if some aspect of the production process is changed, such as when a new piece of important production equipment is installed.

The environment of the firm is constantly changing, and if the assumption of constancy were to be taken literally, regression analysis would never be possible. We can only require that there be no major changes in the production process. Changes in the quality or mix of materials used, the labor classification employed, or the type of equipment used are all examples of changes that would need to be explicitly recognized in the modeling process. If a major change in the production process has occurred, then the regression analysis should analyze the situations before and after the change separately or else model the change explicitly within the regression model.

Operating at a Constant Level of Activity

Operating at a constant level of activity, the production scheduler's ideal, is the worst possible situation for applying regression analysis. It would be impossible to uncover a relationship between cost and the activity level, since there would be observations on only one activity level. Regression analysis will be most effective when the dependent and independent variables are observed over a wide range of values.

Unfortunately, this goal for wide variation in data conflicts with the normal data accrual process. There may be significant day-to-day changes in activity levels, an ideal situation for regression analysis. But if data are accrued and reported on only a monthly basis, then the analysis must be limited to monthly data. Over this period of time, daily variations will average out to much more stable monthly data.

Practices Relating to Adjustment to Expansion or Contraction

Many businesses can expand more responsively than they can contract. Costs, therefore, tend to follow expansion up much more closely than they follow contraction down, since it may be difficult to dispose of excess plant and equipment and many firms are reluctant to lay off skilled or highly valued employees. The asymmetry of costs varying during expansions but remaining fixed during contractions creates problems for regression analysis, since a simple linear relationship will not exist between current costs and current activity levels. The history of how we got to the present level of activity will also help to explain the current level of costs.

Choosing the Underlying Activity Measure

Units of production and direct labor-hours are two activity measures often used in cost analysis. In highly automated production processes, measures such as the machine-hours, amount of raw materials handled, average production flow rate, and number of production-run setups have also been suggested. These latter measures, however, may not be recorded in the official accounting system. As organizations attempt to shift from a direct-labor to a machine-hour basis for distributing overhead, entirely new measurements have to be made and recorded.

All of these attributes of the practical environment of business create potential pitfalls for the application of regression analysis. The analyst must be sensitive to violations of the regression assumptions caused by these phenomena.

Criteria Used to Evaluate Regression Output

Four criteria can be used to evaluate regressions:

1. Plausibility
2. Goodness of fit
3. Confidence
4. Specification tests

1. Plausibility

The regression model should be plausible. Regression analysis measures only the presence or absence of statistical correlation between a dependent variable and one or more independent variables. Regression analysis cannot conclude that a physical or causal relationship exists between variables. Instead regression analysis should be used to confirm or reject beliefs that have been developed from a study of an underlying process.

Many students question the need for, and the relevancy of, determining plausibility. They argue:

> Why does it matter that we do not really understand the nature of the statistical relationship that we have found? If the rise and fall of the stock market is found to be correlated with some other physical phenomenon, such as skirt hemlines, why not use that relationship?

If, after careful study, we cannot understand the nature of the relationship, it could be a statistical fluke due to a spurious correlation in the data. If it is a statistical fluke, the relationship could end at any time and without warning. It would be risky to rely on an implausible correlation when attempting to predict or control future activities.

2. Goodness of Fit

The goodness-of-fit criterion requires measures of how well the model explains the behavior of the dependent variable. The most common goodness-of-fit measure is the regression coefficient of determination, or R^2 statistic, discussed in the Chapter 4. The adjusted R^2 statistic provides a rough indication of whether adding additional independent variables has increased the explanatory power of the model.

3. Confidence

Confidence concerns the statistical confidence, or reliability, that we can place in the regression results. The confidence of the regression results can be measured using the t statistics of the coefficients of the independent variables. Confidence intervals can also be developed for predictions from the regression model, as explained in Chapter 4.

4. Specification Tests

Specification tests are undertaken to ensure that the critical assumptions of regression have been met in a particular application.

Assumption 1: Linearity Linearity requires that the dependent variable be a linear function of the constant and the independent variables. Linearity is a strong assumption that, strictly speaking, will probably not be met in practice. Linearity implies that the effect on the dependent variable of a change in an independent variable is not influenced either by the level of that independent variable or by the level of any other independent variable in the regression equation. If the linearity assumption is violated, then an alternative model, derived by transforming the data or using a nonlinear regression, will be a more efficient (better) estimator of the underlying relationship. (In statistics, the concept of efficiency means that the estimator has the lowest possible standard error for the given sample size and data characteristics.) Violations of linearity can frequently be detected by careful analysis of the estimated error terms (the residuals) from the regression equation. We will provide examples of such analysis later in this chapter.

Assumption 2: The Expected Value of the Error Term Is Zero The expected value of the error term will not be zero if important explanatory variables have been omitted from the regression equation. In this case, actual observations will differ from the predicted values, not because of inherent randomness in the process, but because we have failed to include the omitted variables. Departures from this assumption are difficult to detect because the estimated regression line forces the sum of the residuals to equal zero. The absence of an omitted variable can be detected by systematic patterns in the residuals, such as a definite time pattern, suggesting a nonstationarity in the process that has yet to be reflected in the model.

An omitted variable problem may also be detected by using the estimated regression model on new data from the same process. Frequently, the explanatory power of the model on new data is far below the R^2 of the estimated model. Recall that our goodness-of-fit criterion, R^2, equals the percentage of variation of a dependent variable, *as measured from the mean of the dependent variable*, that is explained by variation in the independent variable. When attempting to predict future values of the dependent variable, we are no longer assured that the mean value of our predictions will equal the mean value of the variable we are trying to predict (the new observations of the dependent variable). If the mean value of these new observations differs significantly from the mean value of our predictions, we have evidence that important variables have been omitted from the model and that we have violated the assumption of a zero mean error term. Because the mean of the predicted values will not equal the mean of the actual observations, the "R^2" of the predicted values could even be negative; that is, the predictions from the regression model explain less of the variation in the dependent variable than if we had just used the ex post mean of these values.

Assumption 3: The Variance of the Error Term Is Constant The ordinary least-squares procedure weights each observation equally. This equally weighted procedure is optimal if the underlying precision or variance is the same for every observation. In other words, the OLS procedure requires that the variance of the error term not be a function of (1) time, (2) the size of any of the independent variables, or (3) the size of the predicted value of the dependent variable. If these three conditions are met, the condition called *homoscedasticity* exists, and the variance of the distribution of the error term is constant for every observation; the variance is independent of time and the magnitude of all the variables in the model. When the data do not have these properties, we describe the data as being *heteroscedastic*. In this case, the OLS estimates will no longer be the *best* (minimum variance) estimates that we can produce from the given set of data. Departures from homoscedasticity can be detected by plotting the data and observing whether error terms seem to vary systematically over time or for large values of the independent variable(s).

In practice, the homoscedasticity assumption is frequently violated; the most common violation occurs when a higher variance exists for large observations of the independent or dependent variables. Attempts to correct this condition, however, rarely make a large change in the estimated parameters, so that a casual benefit-cost analysis suggests that we not devote much more space here discussing this particular problem. The main problem created by heteroscedasticity is that the standard errors from the regression equation may be inaccurate.

Assumption 4: The Error Terms Are Independent When error terms are correlated with each other, we have less precision in our estimates than the statistical procedures would lead us to believe. In effect, we are getting less information than assumed (a smaller effective sample size) because the same information influences more than one observation. In statistical terms, the standard errors produced by the regression will be misestimated, thus invalidating normal confidence statements. For example, positive serial correlation causes the standard errors estimated by the regression to be underestimated. The downwardly biased standard errors will produce confidence intervals, either for coefficient estimates or for predictions from the regression equation, that are too narrow, causing the analyst to assign more precision to estimates than is properly warranted.

A number of tests can be used to detect correlation among the error terms. The most commonly used test is the Durbin-Watson statistic, which provides a measure of association between **successive** values of the error terms. The Durbin-Watson statistic that is computed from the regression data is compared against two tabulated values, d_u and d_l, that depend on the desired confidence level of the test and the degrees of freedom of the data (which is determined by the number of observations and the number of independent variables in the regression).

If the Durbin-Watson statistic is greater than d_u, then we accept the null hypothesis that there is no positive correlation between successive error terms. If the Durbin-Watson statistic is less than d_l, then we accept the alternative hypothesis that there is a positive correlation between successive error terms. If the Durbin-Watson statistic lies between d_u and d_l, the test is inconclusive and we can neither accept nor reject the null hypothesis. To test for negative correlation between successive error terms, we must subtract the computed Durbin-Watson statistic from 4. We then follow the same procedure to test for negative correlation as the procedure used to test for positive correlation.

Roughly speaking, a Durbin-Watson statistic around 2 suggests no evidence of correlation of the successive error terms. A Durbin-Watson statistic less than 1.5 is usually evidence of positive correlation of the successive error terms, and a value greater than 2.5 is usually evidence of negative correlation.

The Durbin-Watson test is confined to testing for correlation between successive error terms (this is called first-order serial correlation): if we let r be the correlation between successive error terms, we can show that the Durbin-Watson statistic approximately equals $2 * [1 - r]$. The regression assumption is stronger than that tested by the Durbin-Watson statistic. The regression assumption requires no correlation of any kind (of any order) between the error terms.

For this reason, some regression packages allow the analyst to compute higher-order correlations of the errors. For example, if a quarterly or seasonal effect exists but is not included in the model, one might find that a fourth-order correlation of the residuals exists in monthly data. (That is, every fourth error term is correlated.)

The most common cause of correlated error terms is a model misspecification error. That is, the model is not a good representation of the actual relationship. The following are common misspecification errors:

1. The omission of an important variable, such as a seasonal effect, that affects the dependent variable. In this case, the omitted variable should be identified and added to the model.

2. The relationship is nonlinear perhaps because of inflationary trends. In this case, the data should be transformed (deflated), or an explicit nonlinear regression should be used.

3. A shift in the production process has occurred, such as a change in the production equipment that is used but has not been incorporated into the model. In this case, the shift should be incorporated into the model, or the regression should be confined to the period since the shift.

Assumption 5: The Independent Variables Are Uncorrelated If the independent variables are perfectly correlated, then, technically speaking, regression analysis is impossible. Of course, in this case the solution is obvious; merely drop one of the perfectly correlated variables from the equation. In practical terms, then, the problem arises with variables that are highly but not perfectly correlated with each other. In this situation, the highly correlated independent variables fluctuate together, and it becomes difficult to obtain reliable estimates about the effect on the dependent variable of each independent variable by itself. Thus, when two or more independent variables are highly correlated, the coefficient estimates of these variables will be unreliable and the standard errors of the coefficients will be high.

One rule of thumb advocates avoiding the simultaneous use of independent variables that have a correlation coefficient whose absolute value exceeds 0.8. Alternatively, Klein's Rule asserts that multicollinearity will not be a problem if the correlation between any two independent variables is less than the multiple correlation coefficient (R) of the regression.

Collinearity only affects coefficient estimates but not the explanatory power (R^2) of the regression. Therefore, collinearity problems may be detected by a regression equation with high R^2 but low t statistics for coefficient estimates or when the signs of one or more coefficients are opposite from those expected. Therefore, if the regression equation is to be used only for prediction of future values of the dependent variable, and not for making inferences about individual coefficient estimates, the presence of multicollinearity may not be a serious problem.

Assumption 6: The Errors Are Normally Distributed This normality assumption is not required in order to obtain OLS estimates to fit a regression line through a set of observations. But our normal statistical procedures—performing F tests and t tests, and constructing confidence intervals—are, strictly speaking, only valid if the error term can be approximated by a normal distribution. In practice, it would be unusual for nonnormality to create serious problems for the analyst. We are unlikely to affect the future of the company because we rejected a hypothesis at a .05 significance level when the true significance level was only .08 or .10. The statistics we compute are designed to be indicative of the goodness of fit and confidence we have in our estimates, not necessarily to be taken literally. Reporting t statistics or confidence levels with four or more significant digits connotes a degree of precision that is not available from the underlying processes and data.

An Example

We will illustrate the diagnostic procedures by examining the following situation.

CHATHAM BOX COMPANY

The Chatham Box Company (CBC) manufactures cardboard boxes in a highly automated factory. Although the company cost accountant suspects that factory overhead is related to the number of machine-hours worked, no study has been undertaken to confirm whether his intuition is supported by evidence.

The company cost accountant has assembled the following data and has provided the following background information:

The accompanying table (on page 139) summarizes monthly operations in the 50 months since the plant opened. No major production line or equipment changes have occurred since we opened. The costs of the supply items included in overhead seem to be increasing by about 1% per month.

We will follow a structured approach to interpreting the regression output.

1. Plausibility

We are contemplating a regression of overhead versus machine-hours. This relationship seems plausible based on the cost accountant's intuition and because using machines should cause an increase in the consumption of overhead items, such as power and machine supplies.

Running the regression, we obtain the following estimated equation:

$$\text{Overhead} = 282{,}133 + 8.42 * (\text{machine-hours})$$

2. Goodness of Fit

The R^2 statistic associated of this regression is .10, which means that the model explains only 10% of the variation in the dependent variable. We do not give this model high marks along the goodness-of-fit criterion.

Chatham Box Company
Production and Overhead Data

Observation Number	Overhead	Machine-Hours	Observation Number	Overhead	Machine-Hours
1	266,983	6,371	26	327,416	5,125
2	311,996	8,927	27	307,833	4,223
3	296,332	9,334	28	368,761	6,548
4	249,135	5,209	29	310,133	3,647
5	304,885	9,157	30	335,758	4,728
6	299,218	7,128	31	317,539	3,869
7	270,628	3,413	32	362,725	7,234
8	268,504	5,090	33	330,913	4,392
9	270,260	4,637	34	411,752	9,129
10	257,595	3,551	35	385,652	5,865
11	298,164	7,032	36	327,969	4,133
12	254,973	3,862	37	406,620	6,701
13	318,526	7,856	38	365,078	4,792
14	277,487	3,640	39	372,341	6,098
15	302,900	5,952	40	354,962	3,319
16	277,617	4,530	41	342,100	4,476
17	346,044	8,551	42	378,318	7,079
18	353,666	8,505	43	417,137	7,382
19	287,789	5,615	44	343,356	3,450
20	289,801	4,565	45	414,324	7,172
21	303,599	6,367	46	389,752	4,766
22	360,447	9,601	47	411,628	5,357
23	325,414	7,000	48	359,014	4,657
24	346,235	8,131	49	401,955	6,459
25	333,117	7,615	50	406,997	6,540

3. Confidence

The *t* statistic associated with the coefficient estimated for machine-hours is 2.34, with 48 degrees of freedom (the number of observations minus the number of coefficients estimated by the regression). At 95% confidence, the critical value of the *t* statistic is about 2. We can therefore reject the null hypothesis that the true machine-hours coefficient is 0.[1] Thus, we believe that a statistically significant relationship exists between the dependent variable and the independent variable.

The *F* (Fisher) statistic can also be used as a measure of the overall confidence, or reliability, of the regression. With only one independent variable, however, the *F* statistic will be statistically significant if and only if the *t* statistic of the slope coefficient (for machine-hours) is significant,

---

[1] Note that this is a two-tailed hypothesis test. Therefore, one-half of the indicated confidence will be distributed in each tail of the distribution.

since the F statistic, with one independent variable, equals the square of the t statistic of that independent variable.

4. Specification Tests

A1. *Linearity* One test for linearity plots the dependent variable against the independent variable(s) to determine whether the relationship is approximately linear. This test should usually be performed before any regression is run. Exhibit 5–1 has a great deal of dispersion (which explains why the R^2 is low), but no violent departures from linearity are evident.

A2. *Expected Value of the Error Term Is Zero* A plot of the error terms from the regression versus a time variable (see Exhibit 5–2) is upward sloping, and the correlation between the error terms and the time variable is 0.94. An important explanatory variable that is correlated with time has probably been omitted from the model. For example, the level of production may have been increasing and the relationship between cost and production levels may not be linear (more specifically, costs increase at a more rapid rate than the increase in the level of production). Alternatively, the cost data could be trending upward because of inflation.

A3. *The Variance of the Error Terms Is Constant* The plots of the error terms from this regression against a time variable, the independent variable, and the predicted value of the dependent variable appear to have a constant width. The width of the plot of the error terms does not seem to vary as

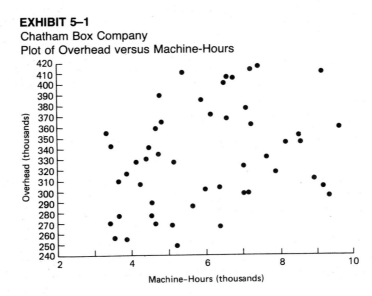

EXHIBIT 5–1
Chatham Box Company
Plot of Overhead versus Machine-Hours

EXHIBIT 5–2
Chatham Box Company
Regression Error versus Time Variable

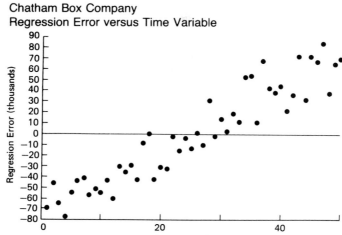

a function of the size of any of these variables. We conclude that no evidence of heteroscedasticity exists.

A4. *Error Terms Are Independent* The Durbin-Watson statistic from the regression is 0.33. From the table of Durbin-Watson cutoff points for 95% confidence, one independent variable, and 50 observations, we find $d_u = 1.59$ and $d_l = 1.50$. Since 0.33 is less than 1.50, we reject the null hypothesis of uncorrelated errors and conclude that successive error terms are positively correlated.

Recall that the Durbin-Watson test relates to only one aspect of correlation between error terms. There may be higher-order correlations among the error terms. When we plot the error terms against time, no evidence appears of a cyclical pattern of residuals, such as a sine wave, that would suggest higher-order correlations. A formal test of higher-order correlation can be undertaken by lagging the residuals and computing higher-order correlations.

A5. *Independent Variables Are Not Correlated* Since only one independent variable has been used in the regression, this assumption is not relevant for the analysis.

A6. *Error Terms Are Normally Distributed* A visual test of normality can be obtained by plotting the residuals from the regression into a histogram and judging whether the plot has a shape that approximates the normal distribution. (Alternatively, many regression packages perform a chi-squared test to test whether the distribution of error terms conforms to a normal distribution.) The shape of the histogram of the error terms from this regression appears to be approximately normal (see Exhibit 5–3).

EXHIBIT 5–3
Chatham Box Company
Histogram of Regression Error

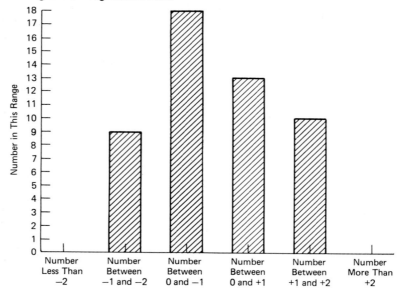

Range of Standard Error of Residual

In summary, the regression line provides a poor fit to the data and violates the error term independence assumption. Both symptoms point to one or more omitted variables or the existence of a nonlinear relationship between the dependent variable and the independent variable.

Correlated error terms can occasionally be fixed by taking first differences between successive observations, subtracting each observation from the preceding observation. This procedure is a mechanical solution that does not provide any insight into the underlying structural cause of the dependency. Recall that the error term in the regression analysis incorporates the cumulative effects of all the variables omitted from the model. Mechanical approaches, such as computing first differences, do not identify the source and nature of these omitted variables. We should attempt to identify the omitted variables or the cause of the time dependency still remaining in the data.

In this case, we can recall the cost accountant's statement about the price increases in the overhead costs. Perhaps if we deflate the data, to eliminate the estimated monthly price increases, we will get a clearer picture of the underlying relationship between machine-hours and overhead.

We divide each of the reported overhead costs by $(1.01)^{n-1}$, where n is the observation number, to reflect the estimate of 1% per month inflation

EXHIBIT 5–4
Chatham Box Company
Deflated Overhead Data

Observation Number	Deflated Overhead	Machine-Hours	Observation Number	Deflated Overhead	Machine-Hours
1	266,983	6,371	26	255,308	5,125
2	308,906	8,927	27	237,661	4,223
3	290,493	9,334	28	281,882	6,548
4	241,807	5,209	29	234,719	3,647
5	292,988	9,157	30	251,597	4,728
6	284,695	7,128	31	235,589	3,869
7	254,943	3,413	32	266,449	7,234
8	250,438	5,090	33	240,674	4,392
9	249,580	4,637	34	296,503	9,129
10	235,529	3,551	35	274,959	5,865
11	269,923	7,032	36	231,517	4,133
12	228,538	3,862	37	284,196	6,701
13	282,675	7,856	38	252,635	4,792
14	243,817	3,640	39	255,110	6,098
15	263,512	5,952	40	240,795	3,319
16	239,125	4,530	41	229,772	4,476
17	295,113	8,551	42	251,582	7,079
18	298,627	8,505	43	274,650	7,382
19	240,596	5,615	44	223,833	3,450
20	239,879	4,565	45	267,423	7,172
21	248,812	6,367	46	249,072	4,766
22	292,477	9,601	47	260,448	5,357
23	261,436	7,000	48	224,908	4,657
24	275,409	8,131	49	249,316	6,459
25	262,351	7,615	50	249,944	6,540

in the data. After this transformation, the overhead data are expressed in terms of month 1 dollars (see Exhibit 5-4).

The estimated regression line for the deflated data is

$$\text{Deflated overhead} = 194{,}667 + 10.73 \text{ machine-hours}$$

The R^2 of the regression is 0.78, a considerable improvement over the 0.10 obtained from the initial regression. We now have a much better fit to the data. The t statistic of the machine-hours coefficient equals 13.0 and is distributed with 48 degrees of freedom. This value is statistically significant at any confidence level one might ever want to use. We have overwhelming evidence of a statistically significant relationship between machine-hours and deflated overhead.

The plot of deflated overhead versus machine-hours (Exhibit 5–5) appears to be approximately linear. Also, a plot (not shown) of the error terms versus time and of the independent and dependent variables does

EXHIBIT 5–5
Chatham Box Company
Deflated Overhead versus Machine-Hours

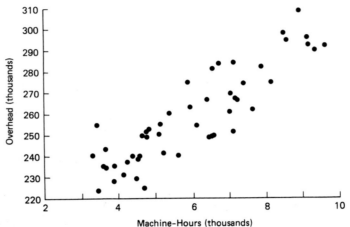

not reveal any systematic patterns that would suggest the expected value of the error term is different from zero.

Plots of the error terms (not shown) against a time variable, machine-hours, and the predicted value of overhead also seem to have a constant width, suggesting that the variance of the error term is not a function of the magnitude of any of these variables.

The Durbin-Watson statistic for the regression equals 1.61. With 50 observations and at 95% confidence, the cutoff points for the Durbin-Watson tests are $d_u = 1.59$ and $d_l = 1.50$. We therefore cannot reject the null hypothesis that successive error terms are independent.

Note that deflating the data by the 1% per month inflation not only dramatically improved the fit of the model but also eliminated the severe autocorrelation problem with the original data. The steady price increase caused early observations to be below the predicted values and the later values to be above predicted values. Thus, if the error term from one observation was negative (positive), it was very likely that error terms from neighboring observations would also be negative (positive). The ability to predict something about nearby error terms violates the independence assumption and is the source of the measured autocorrelation in the original data.

We now have a satisfactory explanation of the dependence of overhead costs on machine-hours worked. Before turning our results over to the cost accountant, we must remember to express the predictions in units that correspond to current measurements. At present, our equation provides an explanation in terms of deflated overhead dollars. To predict the overhead in the current month, we must multiply our overhead estimate by the price index for the current month relative to month 1.

Dummy Variables

The independent variables we have used so far—machine-hours, labor-hours—have been continuous variables, that is, variables that can take on a continuous set of values. Explanatory or independent variables can also be discrete or categorical, taking on only a finite number of different values. For example, in estimating utilities expense, the cost of heating will be higher in winter months than in summer months. To incorporate this effect, a dummy variable can be included in the regression model. The variable will be set equal to 1 during the winter months, and to 0 during all the other months. The coefficient of this variable will then estimate the increased cost during the winter months (when the variable is defined to be 1) relative to all other months.

A dummy variable can also be useful to control for jumps or shifts in fixed costs. Supervision or manning levels may have increased at some point, or increased charges due to new machines or expansion of floor space may have been occurred sometime during the estimation period. The situation is well illustrated by the data shown in Exhibit 5-6.

A simple linear regression of overhead cost (OH) versus direct labor-hours (DLH) yields:

$$OH_t = 16,056 + 5.13 \, DLH_t, \, \overline{R}^2 = 0.16, \, DW = 0.97$$
$$(5.46) \quad (1.77)$$

(*t* statistics are in parentheses below estimated coefficients).

EXHIBIT 5–6
Nonstationary Overhead Costs

Month	Overhead Cost	Direct Labor-Hours
1	20,070	930
2	20,780	1,090
3	20,890	1,010
4	21,350	1,080
5	20,320	1,120
6	20,440	1,010
7	20,780	890
8	23,750	1,190
9	21,100	850
10	22,450	990
11	20,540	900
12	22,350	1,060

The explanatory power of the regression is low, the coefficient of DLH is barely statistically significant (using a one-sided test at the 5% level), and the Durbin-Watson statistic indicates a high degree of positive autocorrelation. A plot of residuals versus time (see Exhibit 5-7) shows that the first six observations have negative residuals while five of the next six have positive residuals. This evidence suggests that around the end of month 6 an increase in fixed costs occurred. To test this hypothesis, we define a dummy variable, JUMP, that equals 0 for observations 1, 2, . . . , 6 and equals 1 for observations 7, 8, . . . , 12. Rerunning the regression with the dummy variable, JUMP, leads to the following output:

$$OH_t = 12,679 + 7.66 \ DLH_t + 1,646 \ JUMP_t, \ R^2 = 0.77; \ DW = 2.4$$
$$(7.55) \quad (4.78) \quad\quad (5.20)$$

The explanatory power of the regression is now quite good. The estimated coefficients of DLH and the JUMP variables are highly statistically significant. Monthly fixed costs increased by $1,646 after month 6. Naturally, this finding should be corroborated with plant personnel to identify the change that would have caused the fixed costs to increase after month 6. Furthermore, by controlling for the jump in fixed costs, we have eliminated the autocorrelation problem signaled in the first regression. If we wanted to predict costs beyond period 12, we would add the coefficients of the intercept and dummy variable together to obtain $OH = 14,325 + 7.66$ DLH.

In another example, perhaps fixed costs increased more gradually because of a steady increase in the price level. In this situation, we could assume a linear increase in costs by defining a variable indexed by the month:

$$OH_t = \beta_0 + \beta_1 \ DLH_t + \beta_2 t,$$

where the coefficient β_2 will measure the assumed linear increase in fixed costs each period. A variable such as t, taking on integer values, would be

EXHIBIT 5–7
Residuals from Overhead Costs versus DLH Regression

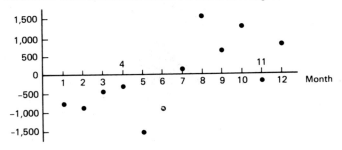

classified as a discrete independent variable rather than a dummy variable whose only possible values are 0 and 1.

Dummy variables also arise when estimating a cross-sectional cost relationship. Suppose we had a company with a large number of retail chains around the country, and we wished to estimate the variable selling expenses as a function of the gross sales of each store. Initially, we might estimate a simple model using the observations in the same period for each store, i:

$$\text{Selling expense}_i = \beta_0 + \beta_1 \text{ sales}_i$$

A more careful study would reveal that wages and expenses are highly variable across the country. Northeastern urban stores may have higher hourly wages than rural southwestern stores. Such variations would cause the estimated relationship to have low explanatory power because of the omitted variables (region, urban/rural).

To control for this systematic variation in wage expense, we could split the stores into mutually exclusive and collectively exhaustive categories in which stores considered to be reasonably homogeneous would be grouped together within a category. For example, we could define the following 0–1 dummy variables:

$$D_1 = \begin{cases} 1, \text{ if northeast} \\ 0, \text{ elsewhere} \end{cases} \quad D_2 = \begin{cases} 1, \text{ if southwest} \\ 0, \text{ elsewhere} \end{cases} \quad \text{etc.}$$

$$S_1 = \begin{cases} 1, \text{ if urban store} \\ 0, \text{ elsewhere} \end{cases} \quad S_2 = \begin{cases} 1, \text{ if suburban store} \\ 0, \text{ elsewhere} \end{cases}$$

$$S_3 = \begin{cases} 1, \text{ if rural store} \\ 0, \text{ elsewhere} \end{cases}$$

The coefficients of these dummy variables will measure the shift in fixed costs associated with having a store in a given region.

When splitting observations into these mutually exclusive categories, we must remember to either omit one category from the regression or estimate the relationship without the constant term. Otherwise we will have a severe problem, since the independent variables will be perfectly collinear. For example, suppose we classify stores into three categories, as above—urban, suburban, and rural—where each store is in one (and only one) of the three categories. The constant term always equals 1, so that for every observation we would have

$$\text{constant} = S_1 + S_2 + S_3$$

With this perfect collinearity, we will be unable to obtain regression estimates. The regression program either will not work or will give nonsense results.

To avoid this problem, simply omit one category, say rural stores, and estimate coefficients for the constant and the remaining categories. We then interpret the coefficient of the categorical dummy variables as the increase (or decrease) in fixed cost relative to the omitted category; that is, the coefficient of S_1 would represent the difference in fixed costs between an urban store and a rural store.

Dummy variables are aptly named. People occasionally use these categorical variables when they have not thought enough about how to measure the relevant effect. It would be preferable to identify the specific factor that causes costs to shift across categories. For example, instead of using a dummy variable—for each season—to explain monthly heating expense, we could use the continuous variable of median monthly temperature or median degree days (a *degree day* measures the number of degrees below a standard temperature, such as 68 degrees Fahrenheit each day). Then if we had an unusually warm or cold month, the regression model would be better able to explain or predict actual heating expense. In the cross-sectional retail store example, we could use median wage levels in each region, a continuous variable available from governmental statistics, rather than a dummy variable for each region. Again, such a variable would do better in tracking costs if there were relative shifts in wages among the various regions in the future.

Dummy variables are best used when we do not believe that the dependent variable will vary linearly with the independent variable. In such cases, we can define separate dummy variables for subsets of the independent variable and not impose a linearity assumption. We can let the data suggest how the dependent variable varies across the range of values in the independent variable.

Nonlinear Transformations

All the cost models we have developed so far have been linear and additive in the independent variables. A departure from linearity occurs if one of the independent variables has a nonlinear effect on the dependent variable. Thus, rather than estimate a simple linear function, we could estimate a quadratic cost function of cost versus output:

$$\text{Cost} = \beta_0 + \beta_1 X + \beta_2 X^2$$

which allows for economies of scale (if β_2 is negative) or diseconomies of scale (if β_2 is positive). Or we could allow for more complex cost behavior with output by adding a cubic term, $\beta_3 X^3$. These models allow for some curvature in the estimated cost function. They are easily estimated by computing and entering the square or the cube of the independent variables. Many statistical packages make such transformations of the data easy to accomplish, but the analyst should ensure that the variables are scaled so that the numbers do not get to be so large that they introduce rounding error into the computerized routines. In practice, strong evidence of nonlinearities is seldom found in the time periods (biweekly or monthly) studied by management accountants. Also, even the quadratic form may be difficult to estimate because, unless there is considerable variation in the independent variables, the variables X and X^2 will be highly collinear.

Other transformations of the data include taking the log or the square root of independent variables. These transformations are occasionally done to reduce the dispersion of the independent variables and obtain better properties of the residuals—for example, to avoid violating the homoscedasticity assumption. Cross-sectional studies, where size of firms or size of different plants is used as an independent variable, may find that the error terms have better properties when the size variable is measured by the log of sales or log of assets. These adjustments are somewhat ad hoc and may be difficult to explain or justify without some underlying reason for the nonlinear transformation.

Multiplicative Model for Nonlinear Cost Functions

If we want to allow the effect of each independent variable to be a function of the level of itself and all other independent variables, then we should attempt to estimate the model in multiplicative form:

$$\text{Cost} = \beta_0 X_1^{\beta_1} X_2^{\beta_2} X_3^{\beta_3}$$

With this model, the effect of a change in any independent variable, say X_2, is a function of the level of X_2 as well as the levels of X_1 and X_3. The estimated coefficient, β_2, represents the percentage change in the dependent variable caused by a given percentage change in the independent variable, X_2. Students of economics will notice that β_2 represents the *elasticity* of cost with respect to the variable X_2. The multiplicative model assumes a constant elasticity β_i for each of the independent variables.

The multiplicative model is most useful when the dependent variable is naturally written as the product of independent variables. For example, total labor expense is the product of total labor-hours and the average wage rate. Interest expense is the product of loans outstanding and the interest rate. In both cases, we would expect the estimated exponential coefficients, β_1 and β_2, of the independent variables to be close to 1. It would be a mistake to estimate either of these relationships as additive in the independent variables, since the cost category is a function of the *product*, not the *sum*, of the independent variables.

The multiplicative model is easily estimated using standard OLS packages by taking the logarithm of the left- and right-hand side of the regression equation to yield:

$$\log Y_t = \log \beta_0 + \beta_1 \log X_{1t} + \beta_2 \log X_{2t} + \beta_3 \log X_{3t}$$

This equation is now linear in the sum of the logarithms of the independent variables. Therefore, we transform the original data by computing the logarithm of the dependent and independent variables and running a standard regression routine on these "logged" values. The estimated coefficients of the logged variables represent the constant elasticities, β_i, in the multiplicative model.

A particularly ambitious application of the multiplicative regression model was used to estimate the cost functions of commercial banks.[2] Data from nearly one thousand commercial banks were collected and used to estimate total bank costs as a function of the banks' many different activities and characteristics. Because of the complexity of a bank's operations and the expectation that the cost for any particular service would depend on the current activity levels of all the services, a multiplicative model containing twelve independent variables was used:

Variable Number	Variable Description
1	Average number of accounts per office
2	Average dollar size of a demand deposit account
3	Average number of debits per account
4	Average number of deposits per account
5	Average number of non-home-bank (transit) checks deposited per account
6	Average number of official checks issued per account
7	Average number of checks cashed per account
8	Average number of transit checks cashed per account
9	Number of offices operated by the bank
10	Ratio of number of regular checking accounts to the sum of regular and special accounts
11	Average annual wage rate per employee
12	Ratio of dollar volume of demand deposits to sum of demand and time deposits

The R^2 of the regression was about 0.93 and yielded the following coefficient estimates:

---

[2] From William A. Longbrake, "Statistical Cost Analysis," *Applied Statistics* (June 1962), pp. 69–78.

Variable Number (i)	Coefficient Estimate (β_i)	t statistic
1	0.950	74.8
2	0.390	15.9
3	0.047	1.7
4	0.140	4.1
5	0.074	5.9
6	0.058	5.3
7	0.018	1.7
8	−0.005	0.4
9	1.020	110.3
10	−0.063	2.5
11	0.430	9.2
12	0.011	0.4

These data indicate that size (variables 1 and 9) is highly significant in explaining bank operating costs. The coefficients near unity for these two variables indicate that a 1% increase in the number of accounts per office or the number of offices per bank causes about a 1% increase in the total operating cost of a bank. The negative coefficient of variable 10 shows that if a regular account is substituted for a special account, costs will decrease. The coefficient of 0.43 for variable 11 indicates that increasing wage rates by 10% leads to a 4.3% increase in total costs.

When a cost function is estimated in multiplicative form, the traditional dichotomy between fixed and variable costs is no longer clear. A relevant consideration is still incremental costs associated with a change in activity levels, but these incremental costs are now a function of the current or proposed activity levels. Analysis and interpretation are therefore more difficult with the multiplicative model.[3]

Comparing the Explanatory Power of Multiplicative and Linear Models

Earlier in this chapter, we described the use of R^2 as a measure of the goodness-of-fit criterion. It would be natural, but incorrect, to estimate both the linear and the multiplicative form of the model and choose the one whose regression had the higher R^2. Even seemingly experienced analysts fall into this trap occasionally. Such a comparison is invalid. The R^2 of the linear model represents the percentage of variation of the dependent variable, Y, explained by the linear model, whereas the R^2 of the multiplicative regression equals the percentage of variation of log Y explained. The two measures are not comparable because they are measur-

---

[3] The interested reader should refer to Longbrake, "Statistical Cost Analysis," for an extensive discussion of how to interpret the output from a multiplicative model.

ing the percentage of variation explained of two different variables, Y and $\log Y$.

Summary

Multiple regression analysis is a valuable tool for cost estimation, but it has many pitfalls for the inexperienced or untrained user. The analyst must be sure that the data are suitable for statistical analysis, must decide how many and which independent variables to include in the regression, and must determine whether to use a linear or a nonlinear model.

The availability of convenient regression packages could be dangerous if used without thinking. Successful applications of regression analysis require more than software. One must verify that the assumptions underlying the application of regression have been met.

This chapter has focused on the assumptions and extensions of regression analysis. You should have a general idea of these assumptions and the tests that can be used to identify when the assumptions have been violated. We have also provided some simple procedures that may remedy problem conditions. But dealing with complex data and models may require more knowledge and sophistication than we can provide in the two chapters devoted to this topic.

An analogy may be useful. You should know enough to stop driving a car when the oil pressure light comes on. You may even know that when this light comes on, the problem may be solved simply by adding oil. But if this simple remedy does not handle the problem, it is time for an expert. If you think you can fix your engine by yourself, fine. But you may have to suffer the consequences of using your car if you try to fix an abnormal situation that you are not qualified to remedy. This chapter has tried to teach you what red lights to look for when estimating regression models and some of the simple remedies. If the simple remedies do not seem to be working, calling in a statistical expert may be indicated.

PROBLEMS

5–1 Relevant Time Period for Statistical Analysis of Cost Data (CMA Adapted)

The Alma Plant manufactures the industrial product line of CJS Industries. Plant management wants to be able to get a good, yet quick, estimate of the manufacturing overhead costs which can be expected to be incurred each month. The easiest and simplest method to accomplish this task appears to be to develop a flexible budget formula for the manufacturing overhead costs.

The plant's accounting staff suggested that simple linear regression be used to determine the cost behavior pattern of the overhead costs. The regression data can provide the basis for the flexible budget formula. Sufficient evidence is available to conclude that manufacturing overhead costs vary with direct labor hours. The actual direct labor hours and the corresponding manufacturing overhead costs for each month of the last three years were used in the linear regression analysis.

The three-year period contained various occurrences not uncommon to many businesses. During the first year, production was severely curtailed during two months due to wildcat strikes. In the second year, production was reduced in one month because of material shortages, and materially increased (overtime scheduled) during two months to meet the units required for a one-time sales order. At the end of the second year, employee benefits were raised significantly as the result of a labor agreement. Production during the third year was not affected by any special circumstances.

Various members of Alma's accounting staff raised some issues regarding the historical data collected for the regression analysis. These issues were as follows.

1. Some members of the accounting staff believed that the use of data from all 36 months would provide a more accurate portrayal of the cost behavior. While they recognized that any of the monthly data could include efficiencies and inefficiencies, they believed these efficiencies/inefficiencies would tend to balance out over a longer period of time.

2. Other members of the accounting staff suggested that only those months which were considered normal should be used so that the regression would not be distorted.

3. Still other members felt that only the most recent 12 months should be used because they were the most current.

4. Some members questioned whether historical data should be used at all to form the basis for a flexible budget formula.

The accounting department ran two regression analyses of the data—one using the data from all 36 months and the other using only the data from the last 12 months. The information derived from the two linear regressions is shown below.

Least Squares Regression Analyses

36 Month Regression[a]

$OH_t = \$123,810 + \$1.60 \quad DLH_t \quad ; \quad R^2 = .32$
(1.64)

12 Month Regression[a]

$OH_t = \$109,020 + \$3.00 \quad DLH_t \quad ; \quad R^2 = .48$
(3.01)

[a] *t*-statistic is in parentheses below estimated variable cost coefficient

Required:

1. Which of the two results (12 months versus 36 months) would you use as a basis for the flexible budget formula?
2. How would the four specific issues raised by the members of Alma's accounting staff influence your willingness to use the results of the statistical analyses as the basis for the flexible budget formula? Explain your answer.

5–2 Conditions for Statistical Estimation of Relationships from Historic Data*

Bob Samuels has just been hired as a consultant to a large local hospital. His mission is to devise improved planning and control procedures that will aid the hospital administrator in managing the organization. Bob believes that improving the cost accounting and reporting system will provide a good project, yielding benefits that can be realized quickly and thereby establishing credibility with the hospital administrator.

At present, the hospital accounting system produces a monthly report on the cost of each department, patient unit, and service center in the hospital. This report (excerpts are shown in Table 1) displays actual costs and the variance from budget for each month and year-to-date.

At present, the administrator reads this report each month, and if costs are too high, he sends a memorandum to the offending department requesting an explanation.

Samuels felt that the basic idea of monthly reporting and follow up seemed sensible but could be improved by controlling for variations in the amount of service delivered each month by a given department. It was possible that a higher than budgeted cost in a department could have occurred because it performed a larger number of procedures or processed a larger number of patients, or, in general, had a higher level of activity than had been expected that month. To the extent that incremental increases in volume lead to increased costs, the department would likely exceed its budget. Conversely, for months in which there was a lower level of service provided than was anticipated when the budget was prepared, departments should be expected to be *under* their budgeted costs. In these cases, Samuels reasoned that the administrator should not be satisfied with actual costs just equaling budgeted costs.

Samuels collected a monthly volume or units-of-service index for as many departments as he could (number of tests performed, hours of anesthesia, etc.) For those departments where no volume index was available,

---

*This example is adapted from Robert S. Kaplan, "Management Accounting in Hospitals: A Case Study," in *Accounting for Social Goals*, ed. J. L. Livingstone and S. C. Gunn (New York: Harper & Row, 1974), pp. 131–48.

TABLE 1
Spending Analysis (000)

Department	Month			Year-to-Date		
		Variance from Plan[a]			Variance from Plan[a]	
	Actual	$	%	Actual	$	%
Professional/Care—Total	$1142	30	3	$6320	200	3
Anesthesiology	60	—	—	300	20	7
Blood Bank	40	(10)	(20)	200	(34)	(20)
Laboratory	175	(15)	(8)	825	(50)	(6)
Nursing Service	250	30	14	1310	90	7
Radiology—Diagnostic	120	10	9	590	74	14
:	:	:		:		
Services—Total	415	(80)	(16)	1600	(30)	(2)
Dietary	120	(15)	(11)	485	12	2
Housekeeping	75	3	4	330	30	10
Maintenance	160	(65)	(68)	530	(80)	(18)
:	:	:		:		
Overhead—Total	220	(8)	(4)	1120	12	1
Business Office	52	(3)	(5)	248	(20)	(7)
Depreciation	60	—	—	300	—	—
:	:			:		

[a] Favorable variance in parentheses.

the number of patient days was used as a surrogate measure of activity. Samuels then estimated a regression model for each major department or cost center:

$$C_{it} = a_i + b_i V_{it} + \epsilon_{it}$$

where

C_{it} = Actual Cost in Department i in Month t

V_{it} = Volume or Units-of-Service Index for Department i in Month t

ϵ_{it} = Error Term

a_i, b_i = Fixed and Variable Cost Coefficients for Department i

These regressions were estimated on the most recent 12 months of data from each major department.

Samuels was greatly chagrined by the results. The variable cost coefficients, b_i, were mostly insignificant and frequently of the wrong sign. The explanatory power of the regressions was low and there was a high degree of serial correlation in the residuals. It appeared as if costs were just increasing over time and that there was no relation between costs and activity levels.

TABLE 2

Department:	Reported Units of Service Index
Radiology—Diagnostic	Running average of the number of procedures performed each month for the prior 12 months.

Month	Actual Number of Radiology-Diagnostic Procedures Performed (Not Reported Outside the Department)
July 1989	4019
August	5805
September	5385
October	4558
November	5885
December	4613
January 1990	5926
February	6146
March	10791
April	8563
May	6874
June	6974
	75539

Before reporting these inconclusive results to the administrator, Samuels decided to investigate further. He concentrated on one department, Radiology-Diagnostic, and examined the monthly reports from this department in as much detail as he could uncover. Excerpts and summaries from this discovery process appear in Tables 2 and 3.

TABLE 3
Radiology—Diagnostic

Month	Salaries (total)	Films and Chemicals	Purchased Services	Equipment and Instruments
July 1989	$ 94,000	$26,800	$4,480	$ 160
August	104,600	21,000	2,900	7,300
September	100,600	20,400	2,800	580
October	103,000	19,400	640	12,540
November	103,000	59,000	4,600	380
December	114,000	16,400	3,800	1,070
January 1990	114,000	16,000	4,400	720
February	96,000	77,000	5,000	580
March	107,400	13,200	6,900	3,850
April	107,000	20,800	25,500	1,000
May	143,200	73,000	6,500	2,700
June	143,400	22,400	44,600	8,900

Required:

Explain why Bob Samuels had trouble fitting his regression model to the monthly data from the hospital. Be specific in identifying as many causes as you can for the poor explanatory power of the regressions. What adjustments would you recommend be made that could improve the use of a regression model for this application?

5–3 Analyzing Time-Series Data

Pas Garment Manufacturing Limited manufactures a line of insulated winter garments. One of the products in this line is the High Arctic winter coat. The following table reflects the labor-cost data associated with manufacturing this coat for the last 50 months. The company accountant has advised you that the cost data have already been deflated to account for the wage increases that have occurred over this period of time.

Your task is to determine the nature of the relationship between the number of coats produced and labor costs. If you find problems with the regression analysis involving the number of coats and labor costs, you

Pas Garment Manufacturing Limited

Month Number	Labor Costs	Coats Produced	Month Number	Labor Costs	Coats Produced
1	110,422	4,989	26	104,651	4,581
2	99,517	3,111	27	108,935	4,952
3	94,497	3,673	28	101,256	3,679
4	93,157	3,574	29	106,896	4,856
5	98,694	3,993	30	106,101	4,625
6	95,956	3,749	31	96,383	3,297
7	92,863	3,313	32	94,291	3,717
8	102,368	4,495	33	97,812	4,016
9	100,463	4,209	34	97,461	3,816
10	106,246	4,664	35	99,618	4,204
11	102,793	4,383	36	97,476	4,049
12	101,119	4,353	37	100,984	4,369
13	99,332	3,934	38	94,885	3,218
14	100,241	4,090	39	88,628	3,113
15	107,215	4,797	40	102,381	4,473
16	100,885	3,530	41	101,777	4,139
17	94,302	3,645	42	95,357	3,284
18	94,738	3,722	43	89,904	3,289
19	99,319	4,103	44	88,214	3,322
20	94,164	3,506	45	98,339	3,950
21	105,175	4,534	46	94,054	3,266
22	96,810	3,111	47	93,927	3,600
23	100,183	4,267	48	99,790	4,123
24	105,005	4,510	49	108,024	4,858
25	101,161	3,534	50	97,983	3,122

should indicate the nature of these problems and undertake any adjustments that you think will be useful. Production records show that 3,792 coats were produced in the month prior to month 1 in the accompanying table.

5–4   Examining Data for Nonlinearities

Hanna Ceramics Limited manufactures a ceramic component used in the electronics industry. Each component manufactured is subjected to exhaustive quality control tests.

Since manufacturing this product ties up over 50% of the company's manufacturing facilities, the company president is evaluating the profitability of this component. As a first step, the president would like to determine the cost of manufacturing this product. The company controller has assembled the accompanying data. The controller has advised you that cost inflation has been minimal over this period.

Hanna Ceramics Limited

Month Number	Production Costs	Units Produced	Month Number	Production Costs	Units Produced
1	730,403	4,573	26	740,402	5,374
2	716,363	4,071	27	745,700	6,142
3	763,990	7,895	28	751,324	7,020
4	746,070	6,225	29	730,540	4,592
5	756,828	7,589	30	740,873	6,006
6	738,234	5,183	31	749,968	7,120
7	750,436	7,090	32	728,453	4,471
8	746,779	6,056	33	717,959	4,086
9	734,426	4,851	34	736,167	4,979
10	722,175	4,133	35	748,830	6,836
11	751,048	7,033	36	728,176	4,410
12	736,450	4,843	37	716,246	4,009
13	742,897	5,634	38	749,705	6,992
14	752,502	7,346	39	729,197	4,450
15	744,895	5,706	40	744,248	5,604
16	736,809	4,894	41	754,882	7,306
17	745,808	6,267	42	740,882	5,463
18	718,763	4,090	43	737,544	4,957
19	734,180	4,547	44	741,071	5,327
20	745,334	6,146	45	741,102	5,408
21	744,070	6,187	46	726,244	4,346
22	746,815	6,299	47	744,580	5,743
23	735,189	5,012	48	760,931	7,668
24	726,539	4,477	49	740,621	5,297
25	736,096	5,011	50	736,606	4,943

Determine the nature of the relationship between the number of units produced and the production costs.

5–5   Attempting to Improve the Fit of a Regression Model

The Powell River Rivetworks manufactures a variety of rivets. Production is measured in lots of 1,000 rivets. Overhead and production data have been accumulated for the last 60 months of operations. Cost inflation has been minimal over this period.

The marketing manager is evaluating an order for a new type of rivet and, in the process, is estimating the cost of filling this order. Your task is to determine the relationship between the number of lots made and the overhead cost. If you find problems with the regression analysis, you should indicate the nature of these problems and make any adjustment that you think would be useful to deal with these problems. Production records indicate that 49,575 lots were produced in the month prior to month 1.

Powell River Rivetworks

Month Number	Overhead	Lots Made	Month Number	Overhead	Lots Made
1	732,975	46,865	31	582,851	32,451
2	690,245	44,758	32	566,296	48,655
3	594,155	30,841	33	631,515	28,373
4	554,520	48,932	34	402,949	24,821
5	725,212	48,762	35	478,004	46,880
6	620,557	27,589	36	685,659	42,123
7	442,809	34,277	37	595,371	35,263
8	549,051	40,330	38	600,940	49,864
9	632,747	46,948	39	612,466	22,122
10	647,056	33,389	40	389,717	32,789
11	451,028	23,298	41	434,337	21,580
12	392,769	31,494	42	436,269	43,455
13	444,717	26,263	43	640,448	41,207
14	428,273	34,512	44	628,572	43,452
15	498,550	30,222	45	603,492	33,340
16	539,355	47,352	46	506,656	34,434
17	610,500	26,305	47	484,274	26,998
18	503,968	49,042	48	453,135	37,396
19	706,416	40,167	49	500,366	25,059
20	623,428	44,420	50	377,214	26,120
21	551,471	21,895	51	466,818	38,910
22	467,764	49,390	52	636,560	48,250
23	614,039	25,272	53	680,827	40,231
24	484,512	48,153	54	523,225	24,909
25	584,354	21,046	55	433,589	37,131
26	347,305	28,387	56	608,141	47,325
27	513,760	46,421	57	672,276	39,292
28	603,461	27,782	58	630,236	46,367
29	381,964	20,437	59	687,243	44,338
30	406,982	42,881	60	589,722	28,464

5–6 *Dealing with Outliers*

Mark Runcie, the owner-operator of Long Grove Printers, wants to develop a standard for the amount of paper required to print a magazine. This knowledge will help him develop prices for special printing jobs.

Mark has gathered the data shown below for the last 40 weeks of operations. Because different magazines are printed in different weeks and because magazines are printed in varying sizes, Mark has counted the number of magazine pages printed each week and divided by 100 (the average number of pages in the magazines that Mark prints) to compute a number that represents the standardized number of magazines printed. (For example, the number of pages printed in week 1 was 9,702,400.)

When Mark ran a regression of the number of units of paper used versus the number of magazines printed, he obtained the following regression result:

$$\text{Units of paper required} = 3.6 + 0.0105 \text{ magazines printed}$$

The r-squared associated with this regression was 0.43, and the t value associated with the estimated coefficient of magazines printed was 5.4. However, Mark goes on to explain:

> Something seemed wrong with this regression. The residuals for observations 3, 23, and 36 were all very large. In all three cases, the amount of paper used far exceeded the amount of paper that the regression predicted.
>
> When I divided each of these three errors by the standard deviation of the error terms, in each case I obtained a value in excess of 3, indicating that each of these three errors was more than 3 standard deviations from the zero mean of all the error terms.
>
> Moreover, when I looked at a histogram of the error terms from this regression, it did not seem to have a shape that even remotely approximated a normal distribution.
>
> With these things in mind, I concluded that these were three unusual events and I dropped observations 3, 23, and 36 from the data set and ran another regression with the remaining 37 observations. I got the following results:

$$\text{Units of paper required} = -115 + 0.0111 \text{ magazines printed}$$

The r-squared associated with this regression was 0.89, the t value associated with the estimated coefficient of magazines printed was 17, and the histogram of the error terms from this regression appears to have the shape of a normal distribution.

Long Grove Printers
Output and Usage Data

Week Number	Units of Paper Used	Magazines Printed	Week Number	Units of Paper Used	Magazines Printed
1	1102	97,024	21	435	44,892
2	583	61,984	22	733	63,633
3	1640	74,655	23	1765	73,949
4	457	48,982	24	595	58,386
5	872	83,984	25	424	53,918
6	307	40,029	26	705	75,793
7	984	103,744	27	979	99,754
8	839	92,050	28	296	54,116
9	602	63,785	29	1060	107,294
10	1208	113,615	30	357	53,966
11	1027	104,025	31	978	90,331
12	749	88,101	32	818	87,093
13	1129	104,948	33	891	94,243
14	960	82,177	34	943	95,483
15	1114	102,183	35	429	58,692
16	668	82,083	36	1759	83,278
17	944	97,633	37	1041	101,880
18	489	40,235	38	1079	103,999
19	991	119,670	39	1275	118,867
20	531	54,643	40	549	65,586

Required:

1. Explain why you agree or disagree with Mark's approach to dealing with this problem.
2. Suppose that, upon investigation, it is discovered that the paper used during weeks 3, 23, and 36 was supplied by a new paper mill at discount prices. Using regression analysis, estimate the change in usage associated with using the paper purchased from this supplier.

5–7 Correlated Independent Variables

Bob Hardy, the cost analyst at Maryville Welded Products, has heard that manufacturing overhead is often a function of both labor-hours and machine-hours. Bob has assembled the data from the last 40 months of operations at Maryville Welded Products and has advised you that the overhead cost data have been deflated to account for the price increases that have occurred over the last 40 months.

Using these data, Bob obtained the following regression results:

Overhead = 23812 + 26.8 machine hours + 6.0 labor hours

Maryville Welded Products

Month Number	Overhead Cost	Labor-Hours	Machine-Hours	Month Number	Overhead Cost	Labor-Hours	Machine-Hours
1	37,149	977	259	21	37,339	1,018	239
2	36,110	1,003	251	22	37,127	1,009	256
3	36,442	902	242	23	32,573	633	167
4	31,165	563	139	24	32,055	633	138
5	33,654	767	190	25	33,449	738	183
6	38,082	1,077	282	26	32,301	753	187
7	34,272	863	212	27	37,038	1,036	269
8	33,965	810	222	28	32,970	654	169
9	33,320	854	210	29	36,168	907	228
10	30,404	624	159	30	32,992	766	180
11	32,683	766	182	31	31,900	652	158
12	32,324	733	178	32	33,982	816	202
13	34,335	703	168	33	33,837	826	182
14	31,749	746	183	34	37,944	1,019	253
15	38,026	994	256	35	36,731	1,088	254
16	31.629	572	157	36	35,448	928	240
17	33,646	836	196	37	32,725	691	167
18	34,205	988	255	38	36,064	951	233
19	32,304	640	174	39	32,145	679	169
20	33,374	643	170	40	34,516	882	205

The *r*-squared associated with this regression is 0.85, and the standard error is 855. The *t* statistics associated with the estimates of the coefficients of machine-hours and labor-hours are 2.1 and 1.8, respectively.

Bob has heard that *t* value of an estimated coefficient "should be around 2" and wonders how to interpret this result.

Required:

1. Replicate this regression analysis to verify the accuracy of Bob's results. Comment on any problems that you see with this result and undertake any corrective action that you feel is necessary.
2. On the basis of scheduled production, Bob figures that during the upcoming month, labor-hours and machine-hours will total 800 and 200 hours, respectively. On the basis of your analysis in requirement 1, what do you feel is the most likely value for overhead in the upcoming month?
3. One of the jobs scheduled for production during the upcoming month will require an estimated 25 labor-hours. No machine-hours will be required, since the work will be done on the customer's machines at the customers's place of business. On the basis of your analysis in requirement 1, what do you feel is the most likely value of the variable overhead associated with this job?

5–8 Choosing Explanatory Variables

Susan Green, the controller of Swift Current Autoparts, a steel fabricator specializing in the manufacture of replacement automotive parts, has undertaken a project to study the behavior of overhead cost. She has assembled data for this month from each of the firm's 30 manufacturing facilities. In addition, all the allocated components of the factory overhead account, such as head office costs, have been eliminated from the factory overhead account balances.

Swift Current Autoparts

Plant Number	Factory Overhead	Labor-Hours	Machine-Hours	Tons of Raw Material Handled	Production Line Setups
1	137,896	2,092	959	414	67
2	174,342	1,617	1,227	623	88
3	168,896	2,215	1,351	437	50
4	178,059	1,584	1,480	479	89
5	166,605	1,930	952	678	52
6	165,320	1,717	986	666	50
7	157,585	2,319	931	585	75
8	165,667	2,312	1,439	479	90
9	155,657	1,880	945	619	94
10	144,605	1,723	869	489	60
11	157,608	1,992	1,171	445	56
12	171,700	2,476	1,228	581	75
13	140,686	2,087	928	446	61
14	171,982	2,256	950	688	99
15	155,252	2,179	1,016	580	78
16	140,793	1,806	902	464	60
17	154,377	1,671	948	610	61
18	150,886	2,019	1,130	532	89
19	159,198	1,585	1,335	415	98
20	145,379	1,747	1,052	517	91
21	152,614	1,618	860	640	64
22	159,450	2,122	1,188	548	61
23	160,983	1,697	1,254	425	56
24	175,393	2,406	1,187	695	58
25	153,031	1,917	948	468	97
26	166,110	1,658	1,015	660	74
27	150,041	2,042	971	478	51
28	170,419	1,757	1,111	652	85
29	169,062	1,952	1,326	619	96
30	157,149	1,536	1,017	513	57

Susan has asked you to develop a model to predict the level of manufacturing overhead.

5–9   *Handling Nonstationarities*

St. Urbain Steelworks (SUS) manufactures a line of steel products. The company controller has developed the accompanying schedule of production and overhead costs for the last 50 months of operations.

St. Urbain Steelworks
Production Data and Overhead Costs

Month Number	Tons Produced	Overhead	Month Number	Tons Produced	Overhead
1	11,978	716,167	26	11,163	592,970
2	8,223	556,691	27	11,904	633,607
3	9,346	611,407	28	9,358	553,480
4	9,147	602,829	29	11,712	614,854
5	9,985	646,189	30	11,249	581,390
6	9,499	609,232	31	8,594	529,275
7	8,626	596,869	32	9,435	512,600
8	10,990	724,377	33	10,032	532,384
9	10,418	676,950	34	9,633	552,799
10	11,327	712,795	35	10,408	582,945
11	10,766	668,988	36	10,097	560,037
12	10,706	699,716	37	10,738	554,994
13	9,868	611,437	38	8,437	529,293
14	10,180	669,470	39	8,226	504,455
15	11,593	702,552	40	10,945	552,257
16	9,061	595,585	41	10,278	549,563
17	9,291	650,887	42	8,568	476,520
18	9,444	626,992	43	8,579	513,172
19	10,206	655,948	44	9,899	526,937
20	9,012	568,270	45	8,645	477,679
21	11,068	727,789	46	8,532	488,097
22	8,223	578,999	47	9,200	544,524
23	10,534	709,064	48	10,245	536,181
24	11,019	689,209	49	11,715	643,976
25	9,068	589,028	50	8,244	499,912

Required:

1. The company accountant has asked you to study these costs to determine if a relationship exists between the tons of steel produced and the monthly overhead. You have studied the accounting system at SUS and have determined that the monthly accruals are both comprehensive and accurate. Moveover, the overhead account contains no allocated costs. Analyze the relationship and comment on the specification.
2. Upon consultation with the plant engineers, you find that more expensive equipment was installed between month 25 and month 26. How can this information be used to improve the fitted relationship?

5–10 Error Terms with Nonconstant Variance

The cost accountant at Northumberland Bakery is attempting to establish a labor standard for the bakery's major product, the round white, a loaf of plain white bread. The accompanying data, relating to labor-hours and production of this bread, have been gathered.

Northumberland Bakery

Week Number	Labor-Hours	Loaves Produced	Week Number	Labor-Hours	Loaves Produced
1	567	32,438	21	992	60,231
2	472	44,205	22	725	84,540
3	860	50,147	23	551	89,066
4	653	96,182	24	830	65,586
5	732	72,065	25	857	93,963
6	677	58,654	26	1031	88,803
7	868	41,441	27	1238	91,286
8	875	99,703	28	511	18,207
9	1598	70,116	29	316	28,118
10	1305	95,538	30	540	70,083
11	754	38,330	31	478	20,314
12	1145	96,310	32	769	37,838
13	584	63,665	33	734	71,194
14	851	46,455	34	440	22,143
15	1277	94,851	35	456	10,382
16	1592	89,932	36	667	44,462
17	485	28,097	37	600	32,688
18	1290	54,610	38	653	28,058
19	637	34,694	39	1240	68,937
20	1000	84,960	40	603	34,260

Required:

1. Run a simple regression of labor-hours versus number of loaves produced. Are there any difficulties with this regression?
2. Create two new variables as follows:
   a. Divide each observation of labor-hours by the corresponding observation of loaves produced. Call this new variable **adjusted labor-hours.**
   b. Compute the reciprocal of loaves produced (that is, compute 1/loaves produced). Call this new variable **adjusted loaves produced.**

Run a regression of adjusted labor-hours versus adjusted loaves produced. How do the results of this regression, including the results of the specification tests, compare with the results of the regression that you ran in requirement 1?

5–11   Modeling Nonlinearities in the Production Process

John Ferguson, the senior cost accountant at North Bay Power Company, has been asked by the chief financial officer to study the cost of producing

166 *Chapter 5*

electricity. North Bay Power Company's regulatory board has requested information concerning the variable cost of generating electricity.

John has assembled the accompanying data for the last 50 months of operations. He has eliminated all allocated costs from the account balance reported for "**Generating Cost.**"

North Bay Power Company

Week Number	Generating Cost (000)	Units of Power Produced	Week Number	Generating Cost (000)	Units of Power Produced
1	1,837	78,945	26	2,787	131,593
2	1,919	83,021	27	1,826	91,816
3	2,759	128,002	28	1,891	84,843
4	1,960	92,375	29	2,029	96,856
5	2,156	108,500	30	1,686	60,978
6	2,901	135,823	31	1,834	77,815
7	1,690	76,450	32	1,727	60,627
8	2,410	117,723	33	3,053	134,412
9	2,252	101,622	34	1,847	74,835
10	1,398	55,209	35	2,001	102,920
11	3,126	133,286	36	1,539	61,534
12	1,946	98,478	37	1,994	94,274
13	1,541	66,823	38	1,686	73,746
14	2,369	118,455	39	1,736	66,945
15	1,876	88,253	40	3,074	138,434
16	1,835	75,714	41	1,798	62,900
17	2,724	119,947	42	2,053	101,150
18	2,426	110,842	43	2,586	121,138
19	2,150	102,063	44	2,026	97,900
20	1,844	82,617	45	1,837	94,624
21	1,585	60,492	46	2,905	126,857
22	1,811	86,686	47	2,768	127,625
23	2,681	123,337	48	2,159	103,858
24	2,235	108,631	49	2,336	106,734
25	1,994	74,196	50	2,138	106,817

Required:
1. Run a regression of generating cost versus number of units of power produced to estimate the cost function for generating power. Do any difficulties exist with this regression?
2. After running the regression in requirement 1, John learned that power requirements over 100,000 units in any particular month are generated by equipment different from that used to generate the first 100,000 units of power. Given this information, estimate an alternative cost function for generating power.

5–12   *Working with Dummy Variables*

Pamela Foster, the manager of Sherlock Homes Real Estate, is developing a model to assess the price of real estate. The model is intended for two purposes: (1) to help clients set a realistic selling price for their homes and (2) to identify undervalued properties for investment purposes.

After undertaking considerable market research, Pamela has decided that the price of real estate in the market served by her office is likely to be a function of three factors:

1. The size of the house (a positive effect on price)
2. The location of the house (the more desirable the area, the greater the price of the house, all other factors constant)
3. The age of the house (a negative effect on price)

Although Pamela figures that interest rates, the general economic climate, and the rate of new home construction can also affect the market prices of houses, she has decided to limit her attention, initially at least, to the above three factors. The model will be updated monthly using the sales data from the preceding month, and therefore these factors will be constants in each estimated model. In addition, Pamela knows that unusual houses, houses in especially good condition, and houses with added features may command premiums in excess of the normal price. Pamela feels, however, that these latter factors are too difficult to quantify for use in a real estate valuation model.

Pamela has gathered information on houses sold during the past three weeks. It is shown in the table on page 168.

Required:

1. Using the data in the table, estimate a real estate pricing model for Pamela. The data in Pamela's model appear in the summary sheet (or cut) for each house offered for sale. The size of the house is given in square feet, the age is in years, and the location parameter is based on a consensus rating about the least desirable (0) to the most desirable (6) areas in the city.
2. A house has just come on the market for $250,000. The house has 3,000 square feet, is two years old, and is located in area number 3. One of Pamela's clients has asked her if this is a good buy, a normal price, or an abnormally high price for this property.

5–13   *Controlling for Seasonal Variation*

Melfort Mining Limited operates an ore extractor. The accompanying table shows overhead cost data associated with operating the ore extractor for the last 50 months. The cost data have already been deflated to account

Sherlock Homes Real Estate

House Number	Selling Price	House Size	House Age	House Location
1	104,307	1,737	11	3
2	196,519	2,744	10	5
3	135,515	1,894	7	2
4	224,496	3,311	8	3
5	154,898	2,334	14	3
6	144,957	1,816	4	5
7	205,938	2,584	5	4
8	173,194	2,013	5	3
9	162,475	2,404	8	0
10	113,892	1,573	4	0
11	107,622	1,919	12	0
12	221,972	2,698	0	4
13	159,906	2,788	10	1
14	120,049	1,612	12	2
15	191,532	2,725	4	5
16	126,075	2,005	12	1
17	156,356	2,182	15	0
18	141,735	1,973	5	0
19	159,674	2,512	14	2
20	150,529	2,536	12	3
21	268,092	3,417	2	4
22	184,895	2,290	5	3
23	161,715	2,001	8	1
24	229,782	3,250	6	5
25	136,160	2,237	9	0
26	231,656	3,450	8	1
27	168,021	2,158	10	2
28	201,238	2,372	1	3
29	209,726	2,588	0	3
30	128,445	1,745	11	4
31	140,519	1,725	9	2
32	204,925	2,804	2	5
33	156,457	2,391	2	0
34	127,887	1,537	2	0
35	225,494	3,250	7	0

for price increases that have occurred in the overhead items over this period of time.

As you begin the task of analyzing the data, the company accountant makes the additional comment:

> I just remembered that we looked at the relationship between overhead cost and tons of ore processed about a year ago. At that time, we could not find a strong relationship, perhaps because we did not include a seasonal factor in the analysis. Production supervisors feel that the variance reporting system does not reflect cost behavior accurately

throughout the year. Costs are always highest in the winter months, lower in the fall and spring months, and lowest in the summer months.

Melfort Mining Limited

Month Number*	Total Overhead	Tons of Ore Processed	Month Number	Total Overhead	Tons of Ore Processed
1	387,338	3,806	26	353,111	3,030
2	389,312	3,764	27	351,931	3,145
3	402,087	4,157	28	300,050	3,222
4	305,625	3,554	29	299,296	3,603
5	313,184	3,513	30	282,504	3,006
6	307,852	3,555	31	280,776	4,034
7	242,530	2,552	32	247,693	2,611
8	272,253	3,562	33	265,782	3,767
9	293,725	4,403	34	361,861	4,010
10	314,191	2,647	35	324,259	3,034
11	381,785	4,489	36	363,713	4,081
12	298,971	2,611	37	427,284	4,452
13	358,286	3,173	38	363,207	3,179
14	356,372	3,074	39	417,376	4,356
15	382,578	3,493	40	319,873	4,125
16	299,763	3,249	41	276,827	2,797
17	288,081	2,813	42	302,456	3,217
18	324,369	3,995	43	276,930	3,516
19	274,262	3,709	44	261,479	3,316
20	275,314	4,164	45	278,204	3,704
21	274,475	3,883	46	353,721	3,549
22	358,207	3,853	47	355,247	3,869
23	342,531	3,434	48	304,034	2,718
24	345,088	3,590	49	327,941	2,613
25	417,842	4,297	50	390,589	3,973

* Month 1 is January.

Required:

1. Without making any adjustment to account for the seasonal factor, determine the relationship between tons of ore processed and overhead costs. Are there any problems evident with this model?
2. After developing a method to account for the possibility of seasonal variations in overhead costs, determine the relationship between tons of ore processed and overhead costs.

5–14 *Dummy Variables for Location and Other Factors*

Monticello Management Consultants (MMC) is a national firm of management consultants specializing in developing accounting systems for their clients. Recently John Shubert, the managing partner of MMC, has been criticized for not providing equal opportunities for women. In particular, the charge has been levied that MMC discriminates against women on the basis of salary. John is distressed by this charge. For one thing, it is bad for the firm's reputation, but, more personally, he felt that had been taking affirmative action to avoid this situation, which he found to be morally offensive.

In response to the recent criticism, and hoping that it is untrue, John has collected the salary records of a sample of 40 management consultants employed across the country and has begun to study the factors that account for the wage discrepancies among the various employees.

MMC has six offices, all located in large metropolitan areas across the country. John knows, from past experience, that certain areas command a wage premium over other areas. Using data from the most recent census, he has assigned each of the offices an office location code ranging from 0 (least expensive city to live in) to 5 (most expensive city to live in). It is John's hypothesis that the salaries in each of the offices will reflect, among other things, the cost of living in that city.

John expects that the years of experience will also be reflected by each employee's salary. This expectation reflects not only increased consulting skills, which MMC's clients readily recognize, but also the rank and billable rates for each employee. John's hypothesis is that the greater the experience, the higher the salary, all other things being equal.

Finally, there is the matter of discrimination on the basis of sex. John has indicated the employee's sex on the summary of the data that he has developed (see page 171) and has asked you to study whether evidence exists to support the change of salary discrimination against women in MMC.

5–15 *Comparing Linear and Nonlinear Models*

Henry Murphy, the marketing analyst for Gotham Motors, wants to understand the critical factors affecting automobile sales in his region. At present, four other automobile dealerships in the city sell the same cars as Gotham Motors. The dealers all provide the same quality of service but differ in their price and advertising strategies. While Henry believes that price and advertising are important for influencing consumers, it is also

Monticello Management Consultants

Employee Number	Salary	Years of Experience	Office Location	Sex
1	34,027	7	1	F
2	92,702	14	4	M
3	36,414	3	2	F
4	42,203	2	1	M
5	47,242	10	0	F
6	42,657	6	2	F
7	65,333	10	1	M
8	56,731	2	5	F
9	69,697	10	4	F
10	67,277	9	4	F
11	36,530	0	3	F
12	67,337	4	4	M
13	86,218	9	5	M
14	81,140	13	1	F
15	55,333	1	5	M
16	97,101	13	5	F
17	113,635	15	2	F
18	39,824	0	4	F
19	31,070	1	1	M
20	90,100	12	3	M
21	53,775	2	3	M
22	67,907	13	0	F
23	71,070	9	5	F
24	84,412	9	2	M
25	85,466	13	3	F
26	45,967	7	0	M
27	32,660	0	5	F
28	88,115	11	2	F
29	64,537	3	4	M
30	81,583	3	4	F
31	33,169	1	1	F
32	67,288	11	1	M
33	117,816	12	5	F
34	79,332	13	2	F
35	59,925	6	3	M
36	45,008	4	5	F
37	35,690	1	1	F
38	63,793	12	4	F
39	48,256	10	3	F
40	76,354	12	0	M

true that many automobile buyers prefer to purchase from a dealer nearby so that the car can be serviced conveniently.

It would usually be impossible to find out the price, advertising, and number of cars sold of competing dealerships, but a recent court case between another dealer in the city and the automobile manufacturer provided an interesting source of data for Henry. During the course of the trial, a witness for the manufacturer presented data on dealer profitability in the city which included data on car sales, average new car margin over dealer cost, and dealer advertising.

Dealer	Average Margin	Advertising	Total Sales
1	$300	$15,000	333
2	260	20,000	337
3	340	9,000	454
4	280	12,000	229
5	290	30,000	370

At first glance, the high sales of Dealer 3 seemed surprising, but Henry recalled that Dealer 3 was located in the most heavily populated section of the city. He decided that a spatial model would give better insights into the pattern of new car sales. Henry subdivided the city into five contiguous regions representing the primary marketing area for each dealer (see below):

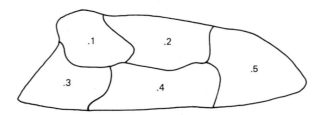

He then estimated the distance between each pair of dealers and the average distance that a purchaser within each dealer's region would have to travel to reach that dealer. This led to a matrix of distance, D_{ij}, representing the average distance a customer in region i would have to travel to reach dealer j:

	D_{ij}	1	2	3	4	5
	1	2	5	4	7	12
	2	5	2.8	8	6	9
i	3	4	8	1.4	5	18
	4	7	6	5	3	6
	5	12	9	18	6	2.2

From census tract data, Henry estimated the population in each of the five regions:

Region	Population
1	20,000
2	16,000
3	30,000
4	25,000
5	10,000

Finally, by a tedious analysis of the zip codes of the purchasers of each automobile, Henry was able to estimate the number of cars sold by Dealer *i* in each region *j*:

Sales of Dealer i *in Region* j

		Region					Total
		1	*2*	*3*	*4*	*5*	
	1	193	27	89	17	7	333
	2	69	180	24	52	12	337
Dealer	3	58	16	325	54	1	454
	4	15	38	39	118	19	229
	5	16	14	8	54	278	370
	Total	351	275	485	295	317	1,723

These data seemed reasonable, since sales of a dealer were highest in its own region and were lowest in regions most distant from the dealership. Nevertheless, because of the joint influence of price, advertising, distance, and population on the amount and distribution of car sales. Henry believed that only a multiple regression analysis could sort out the contributions of these different factors. Henry decided to estimate the following model:

$$S_{ij} = \beta_0 + \beta_1 \cdot \text{Price}_i + \beta_2 \cdot \text{Adv}_i + \beta_3 \cdot \text{Pop}_j + \beta_4 \cdot D_{ij}$$

where S_{ij} = Sales of dealer *i* in region *j*.

Required:

1. Perform this regression; analyze and interpret the results.
2. Henry is disappointed in the results from his linear regression model. Only a minor amount of the variation in the dependent variable, S_{ij}, is explained by the model and at least one of the coefficient estimates has a sign different from what Henry had expected (which one(s)?). Henry reasons that perhaps the relationship is not well specified by a linear model. The effects of the

price and advertising of Dealer 5 on a customer in Region 3, who is 18 miles away, is likely to be different from the effects on a customer in Region 4 or 5 who is much closer. Because of the possibility of such interaction effects, Henry decides to try a model for which the effect of variation in any single variable depends on the level of all the variables in the model. He estimates:

$$S_{ij} = \beta_0(\text{Price}_i)^{\beta_1}(\text{Adv}_i)^{\beta_2}(\text{Pop}_j)^{\beta_3}(D_{ij})^{\beta_4}$$

by taking the logarithm of the dependent and independent variables and estimating the coefficients using his standard OLS package.

Perform this regression for the multiplicative form of the model. Analyze and interpret the results.

3. Which model explains more of the variation in the sales of Dealer *i* to Region *j*? (Optional)
4. What assumptions are implicitly being made about the distribution of dealer sales by both the additive or multiplicative model that limit the usefulness of the model as a means for predicting the number of cars sold by a dealer?

5–16   *Controlling for Known Patterns of Expenditures*

The general manager of Melrose Auto Rentals has decided to implement a spreadsheet-based financial planning and control system. To implement this system, the general manager has requested information on the firm's cost structure.

Besides fuel costs, maintenance is one of the most important cost components in this firm. The general manager wants to know, "Is maintenance cost a fixed or a variable cost?" You have been provided with data on the facing page. Month 1 is January 1986.

Required:
1. Undertake a simple regression of maintenance cost versus mileage to describe the structure of maintenance cost in this firm. Is there any evidence of problems with this simple cost model?
2. Shortly after undertaking the analysis in requirement 1, the maintenance supervisor provides you with the following commentary:

There are two types of maintenance costs in this firm. The first kind, preventive maintenance, includes an examination and repair of each vehicle's electrical systems, braking system, and general body condition. This maintenance is performed on an annual basis and is independent of the mileage that the vehicle has traveled during the preceding year. We do this work in December, January, February,

Melrose Auto Rentals

Month Number	Number of Miles	Maintenance Cost	Month Number	Number of Miles	Maintenance Cost
1	815,878	191,605	19	945,904	201,416
2	984,974	218,729	20	987,671	206,331
3	996,121	234,402	21	909,708	193,930
4	833,775	200,089	22	1,076,580	225,333
5	1,175,694	248,983	23	952,015	206,435
6	865,735	176,498	24	807,454	190,550
7	1,023,222	213,086	25	922,967	219,536
8	1,142,926	240,165	26	868,983	201,076
9	982,324	193,512	27	828,275	194,015
10	943,597	195,598	28	892,705	208,640
11	1,196,376	241,075	29	1,101,835	230,350
12	1,003,004	232,767	30	1,078,521	227,704
13	873,918	198,683	31	1,011,233	209,825
14	803,339	195,094	32	1,099,789	226,484
15	963,587	221,329	33	1,149,039	237,778
16	1,039,869	232,676	34	931,537	202,594
17	1,164,347	233,130	35	1,168,296	240,706
18	878,975	193,897	36	938,835	225,717

March, and April because these are the months in which our vehicle idle time is the greatest.

The second type of maintenance is required maintenance, and this maintenance is scheduled on the basis of the number of miles traveled by the vehicle. This type of maintenance includes oil changes, brake repairs, and tire replacements. This maintenance is performed as required.

Given this information, reestimate the cost model that you estimated in requirement 1. Does your revised model address any of the problems with the regression model that you estimated in requirement 1?

5–17   *Learning Curve Effects*

Elora Electronics Limited (EEL) manufactures a sophisticated radar unit that is used in a fighter aircraft built by Global Aircraft. The first 50 units of the radar unit have been completed, and EEL is preparing to submit a proposal to Global Aircraft to manufacture the next 50 units. EEL wants to submit a competitive bid, but at the same time, it wants to ensure that all the costs of manufacturing the radar unit are fully covered.

As part of this process, EEL is attempting to develop a standard for the number of labor-hours required to manufacture each radar unit. Developing a labor standard has been a continuing problem in the past.

The company accountant has provided you with the accompanying schedule of labor-hours required for each of the first 50 units of production and has asked you to determine whether there is some consistent way to predict the labor required to produce this unit. The company accountant has left you with the following remark:

The number of labor-hours required per unit seems to be falling as a function of time. Perhaps we can predict the labor-hours required per unit simply as a function of time.

Elora Electronics Limited

Unit Number	Direct Labor-Hours	Unit Number	Direct Labor Hours
1	29	26	6
2	18	27	8
3	12	28	4
4	14	29	6
5	12	30	8
6	12	31	8
7	11	32	7
8	10	33	4
9	11	34	7
10	8	35	6
11	12	36	6
12	8	37	5
13	9	38	7
14	7	39	6
15	8	40	6
16	9	41	5
17	7	42	7
18	9	43	6
19	6	44	3
20	7	45	7
21	11	46	5
22	6	47	7
23	7	48	5
24	6	49	6
25	9	50	5

Run a regression of labor-hours versus the time variable. (Thus, this regression model assumes that the labor-hours per unit is a function of time.) Comment on the results of this regression and on any difficulties you see in the results. Can you make adjustments to address any problems that you find with the initial regression?

chapter 6

COST ANALYSIS
FOR PRICING DECISIONS

Firms frequently have considerable latitude in the prices they charge for their products. Such latitude is most likely when a product line consists of a broad range of specialty products, some of which will be unique to individual customers. The pricing decision, in these circumstances, will be strongly influenced by product cost information.

Even when the firm is selling an actively traded, standard commodity product, so that the firm is basically a "price-taker" in the marketplace, it still needs to determine its scale of operation, its production technology, the method and terms for marketing and distribution, and, most importantly, whether to be in the market at all. All these decisions will be influenced by its perception of the product's "cost" and by how much profit it believes it is earning from production and sales of the product.

The Economists' Model

Economists offer a simple yet powerful paradigm for guiding the price-output decisions of firms. They argue and can show—after appropriate assumptions have been made—that firm profits are maximized at the price-output combination where marginal revenue equals marginal cost. To use this paradigm, economists assume that the firm can estimate both the demand curves for its products and the cost curves that portray how total costs vary with changes in output. In the simplifying case where the firm has no control over the market price for its products—the typical example is a farmer selling wheat; the market price for wheat will be unaffected by the quantity sold by any individual farmer—then the demand curve is flat, and the economists' rule instructs firms to produce (and sell) output up to the point where the marginal cost of the last item produced equals the market selling price.

The computations to obtain the profit-maximizing price-output combination are not difficult even with complex revenue and cost functions. Despite the appeal of this model and the lack of computational complexity, firms are rarely observed to use the economic model for price-output decisions. Economists rarely notice that firms do not attempt to set marginal revenue equal to marginal cost because economists rarely attempt to observe the behavior of individual firms. Economists are more concerned with equilibrium behavior in markets, not with the actions of individual economic entities. Thus, the marginal-revenue—marginal-cost rule is intended more as a simplifying assumption to obtain predictions of aggregate market phenomena and should perhaps not be viewed as a normative or prescriptive rule for actual organizations.

Three separate reasons help to explain why the marginal-revenue/marginal-cost prescription provides limited guidance for actual firm decisions. First, demand curves for a firm's products are difficult to estimate. Second, the appropriate marginal-cost curve can rarely be obtained from the firm's accounting records. Attempting to estimate the marginal-cost curve requires considerable analysis, judgment, and, typically, arbitrary allocations of indirect costs. A third reason has just recently been developed: the economists' simple price-output model may be misleading if not outright wrong when applied to realistic, multiproduct organizations. We will discuss each of these three problems in turn.

Demand Curve Limitations

The simple economists' model of demand and price is valuable because it focuses managers' attention on the external environment in which products must be sold. It forces the managers to think not just about what it will cost to manufacture a product but also about what consumers may be willing to pay for it. In practice, however, actual demand curves for products are not readily available. Techniques for estimating demand curves have been developed and have been applied by skilled practitioners for standard products such as agricultural commodities, automobiles, housing, and alcoholic beverages. The techniques, however, have been applied mostly to aggregate demand at the industry level. They have rarely been applied to estimate the demand curves for an individual company.

Demand curve estimation techniques require considerable skill in econometric modeling to ensure that all relevant variables are included in the analysis and that nonstationarities and simultaneous-equation considerations are controlled for in the analysis. Certainly, for major categories of a firm's products, say automobile sales for General Motors or cigarettes for Philip Morris, it could be possible to attempt to estimate demand relationships at a highly aggregated level. But for firms with thousands of different individual products—consider General Motors attempting to estimate the demand curve for each of its brands, models, and variations; or Philip Morris with its myriad of individual cigarette brands, filter, and packaging options—with complex complementarity and substitutability relationships, demand curve estimation is an essentially impossible task.

Apart from the difficulty of estimating even price-quantity trade-offs, the analyst would also need to model the reaction of competitors to price changes by a single firm. The present state of oligopoly theory is not sufficiently developed to offer much specific guidance for such a modeling effort. Going beyond the individual industry level, competitive reactions by producers of substitute products could upset the calculations of demand forecasts if major price changes were to be implemented.

Further complications arise because price is only one factor that contributes to a purchase decision. Much work in the field of marketing has been motivated to bypass head-to-head pricing competition. Considerations such as product characteristics, advertising and promotion, distribution, service, delivery, and credit terms affect firms' gross margins and market share by transforming a homogeneous product into a differentiated product. Studies that look solely at price will see only a portion of all the factors that contribute to a product's sales (and ignore factors such as product design and performance, promotion, and distribution and availability). All these reasons combine to help explain why many firms make pricing decisions without the "benefit" of demand curves for each of their products.

Difficulties in Constructing the Marginal-Cost Curve

The second difficulty in applying the marginal-revenue, marginal-cost paradigm arises when attempting to estimate the appropriate marginal-cost curve. For cost-volume-profit analysis, accountants typically consider costs as variable only if they vary with short-run fluctuations in output volumes. This definition is inadequate for long-term decisions on pricing and product mix, especially for the firm's principal product lines. In order for a product to be profitable over the long run, it must cover not only its short-term variable costs but also

1. The costs of capacity resources required for the product
2. The overhead and indirect costs, including both factory and general administrative, that are required to support the product
3. The cost of capital, including fixed resources and working capital, to support the product

Factor 1, the costs of capacity resources, is usually calculated by accountants as the depreciation on the fixed assets used in the manufacture of the product. But the depreciation schedule derived for financial reporting purposes is unlikely to be a good estimate of the decline in value of the assets through use or the passage of time. Economists are seldom precise in developing an operational definition of capital costs, but, if pressed, they would probably advocate measuring the decline in value as being more relevant than an arbitrary allocation of historical acquisition cost over time. Occasionally, capacity resources produce outputs in fixed proportions (the joint-cost problem), so that measuring the capacity costs of the joint-output products can require arbitrary allocations. And finally, the use of capacity resources for some products will preclude their use for other products, so that an opportunity cost can be associated with the production of the existing product line. Thus, measurement of factor 1 poses challenging problems for estimating economic depreciation, allocating joint costs, and measuring opportunity costs.

Conventional wisdom advocates ignoring fixed factory overhead and general and administrative (G&A) costs (factor 2) when making product-mix and pricing decisions. These costs are considered "fixed" or "sunk" with respect to such decisions. But they are not sunk with respect to decisions about introducing and maintaining products. These costs are incurred because they help the firm produce, design, market, or service its products. Also, recent evidence has shown that these costs have been increasing most rapidly. Thus, these costs are influenced by product decisions and need to be considered part of the long-run cost of production. We will have more to say about how to attribute such so-called fixed costs to products in the next section. For now, we can just cite the difficulty of measuring the long-run variability of overhead costs with products as another barrier for estimating the firm's long-run marginal-cost curve.

The return on capital, factor 3, is called a profit by accountants but is considered a cost by economists—a cost also to be included in the long-run marginal-cost function. The cost of capital must be applied both to the fixed or long-term assets used in the production process and to the investment in net working capital (accounts receivable plus inventory less accounts payable) required for the product. This capital cost is the opportunity cost of the invested capital for the product, and it must also be covered by the firm's pricing decisions.

In summary, the long-run marginal-cost function cannot be obtained by simple calculations from the firm's historical-cost transactions-based cost accounting system. It requires, in addition to short-term variable costs, estimates of the cost of capacity resources, the long-run incremental cost of service and staff departments to support the product, and the cost of invested capital in the product's production, distribution, and sales activities. Thus, while the optimizing calculations to set marginal cost equal to marginal revenue may be quite simple, neither the demand curve used to construct the total revenue function nor the appropriate long-run marginal-cost curve can be obtained without considerable, perhaps enormous, thought, effort, calculation, and subjective judgment.

Limitations of the Economists' Single-Product Model

Recent research has revealed that the single-product model, implicitly assumed in the economists' curves of revenues and cost versus output, seriously misrepresents the economics of multiproduct firms.[1] The model implicitly assumes that increases in output are achieved by increasing the production and sales of a single, homogeneous product. Almost all firms, however, offer many models and variations of their basic products. Most sales increases over time were achieved by expanding the range of models, features, and options. Typically, it is no longer possible to simply count the number of units sold as a measure of output, since substantial variation in unit cost and complexity exist among the various models in a product line. Only by standardizing by some measure of input consumption—such as direct labor-hours or machine-hours—can we obtain a single aggregate measure of output activity in a period.

The total costs of production, however, are very different when a firm produces 1,000,000 units of a single product than when the same equivalent output is achieved by producing between 100 and 100,000 units of two thousand different products in a single-product line. Companies with a more diverse product line have considerably higher costs—for the same nominal output—than pure single-product firms. Thus, it is not only the total volume of output but the composition of the output that determines the cost function of the firm. The so-called fixed overhead and G&A expenses (see factor 2 above) arise mainly to support the diversity and complexity of the firm's product line. Either ignoring these costs or applying them uniformly to products by average markup percentages can lead to substantial distortion of product costs. Such distortions lead to poor pricing decisions and poor decisions about product-line proliferation.

In effect, multiproduct firms can have substantial diseconomies of scope that are suppressed when the cost function is viewed as varying only with total production output. We will develop this point later in the chapter. For now it is sufficient to recognize that cost functions that vary solely with output or with surrogates of output can seriously misrepresent the underlying microeconomics of multiproduct firms.

Full-Cost Pricing

Many companies have resorted to full-cost pricing for determining the prices of their multiple products. In this scheme, an estimate is made of

---

[1] See, for example, Robin Cooper and Robert S. Kaplan, "How Cost Accounting Systematically Distorts Product Costs," in *Accounting & Management: Field Study Perspectives*, ed. William J. Bruns and R. S. Kaplan (Boston: Harvard Business School Press, 1987); and "Measure Costs Right: Make the Right Decisions," *Harvard Business Review* (September–October 1988).

the costs that can be directly traced to the product, such as direct labor and materials. Factory overhead expenses are then applied based on direct labor time, materials dollars, and/or machine processing time. The factory overhead rates are typically determined annually, as part of the budgeting process, by dividing expected departmental expenses by an expected volume measure—such as total number of direct labor-hours or machine-hours.

After all factory costs have been applied to the product, an additional markup over manufacturing costs is applied as an allowance for general, selling, and administrative expenses. Finally, a target profit percentage, expressed as a percentage over total costs, is added to arrive at a price that the company hopes will cover all costs and provide a satisfactory profit percentage. These schemes can become exceedingly complex. We will present a simple example that provides the essential structure of full-cost pricing schemes.

WILSON COMPANY

The Wilson Company produces a variety of machine-tooled products. Some are standard and are sold to a set of regular customers. Throughout the year, however, opportunities arise to bid for new jobs or special orders, some of which may turn out to represent sources of long-term business. The Wilson Company has two principal operating units: the Fabrication Department and the Assembly Department. In addition, it has a sales staff and the normal central staff functions of purchasing, personnel, finance, information systems, and so on. At the end of the year, a budget is prepared for the upcoming year, projecting actual volumes and costs. Such a budget is presented below.

Fabrication		Assembly	
Materials	$150,000	Materials	$ 15,000
Direct labor	225,000	Direct labor	150,000
Variable overhead	75,000	Variable overhead	120,000
Fixed costs	150,000	Fixed costs	180,000
Total costs	$600,000	Total costs	$465,000
Estimated machine-hours	20,000	Estimated labor-hours	10,000

General, selling, and administrative costs $405,000.

The Wilson Company follows a full-cost pricing scheme based on the amount of work performed in its two production departments: Fabrication and Assembly. Materials costs vary widely across different products, and the amount of work performed in the Fabrication and Assembly departments is not strongly correlated with the value of materials being processed. Therefore, materials costs are accumulated separately from labor and factory overhead costs. The Fabrication Department consists of automatic and semiautomatic machines; labor time is spent setting up the machines and monitoring them while they

Cleen-Brite Compounds—Clinton Plant
Forecasted Results of Operations
For the Six-Month Period Ending June 30, 1988
($000 omitted)

	Regular	Heavy Duty	Total
Sales	$2,000	$3,000	$5,000
Cost of sales	1,600	1,900	3,500
Gross profit	$ 400	$1,100	$1,500
Selling and administrative expenses			
Variable	$ 400	$ 700	$1,100
Fixed*	240	360	600
Total selling and administrative	$ 640	$1,060	$1,700
expenses			
Income (loss) before taxes	$ (240)	$ 40	$ (200)

* The fixed selling and administrative expenses are allocated between the two products on the basis of dollar sales volume on the internal reports.

product is manufactured on a separate production line. Annual normal manufacturing capacity is 200,000 cases of each product. However, the plant is capable of producing 250,000 cases of regular compound and 350,000 cases of heavy duty compound annually.

	Cost per Case	
	Regular	Heavy Duty
Raw materials	$ 7.00	$ 8.00
Direct labor	4.00	4.00
Variable manufacturing overhead	1.00	2.00
Fixed manufacturing overhead†	4.00	5.00
Total manufacturing cost	$16.00	$19.00
Variable selling and administrative costs	$ 4.00	$ 7.00

† Depreciation charges are 50% of the fixed manufacturing overhead of each line.

The table on the next page reflects the consensus of top management regarding the price/volume alternatives for the Cleen-Brite products for the last six months of 1988. These are essentially the same alternatives management had during the first six months of 1988.

Regular Compound		Heavy Duty Compound	
Alternative Prices (per case)	Sales Volume (in cases)	Alternative Prices (per case)	Sales Volume (in cases)
$18	120,000	$25	175,000
20	100,000	27	140,000
21	90,000	30	100,000
22	80,000	32	55,000
23	50,000	35	35,000

Top management believes the loss for the first six months reflects a tight profit margin caused by intense competition. Management also believes that many companies will be forced out of this market by next year and profits should improve.

Required:
Each question should be considered independently.

1. What unit selling price should Stac Industries select for each of the Cleen-Brite compounds (regular and heavy duty) for the remaining six months of 1988?

2. Assume the optimum price/volume alternatives for the last six months were a selling price of $23 and volume level of 50,000 cases for the regular compound and a selling price of $35 and volume of 35,000 cases for the heavy duty compound. Should Stac Industries consider closing down its operations until 1989 in order to minimize its losses?

6–2 Pricing a New Product with Nonlinear Opportunity Costs

Ralph Smart, the owner of the Blackburn Garage, is considering the possibility of becoming a *Silencer Muffler* franchise.

Ralph's garage operations consist of eight gasoline pumps and six service bays (areas). Each service bay is dedicated to a specific area of auto repair. These areas are: (a) tune ups, (b) lubrication and oil change, (c) wheel alignment, (d) brake repair, (e) major engine overhaul, and (f) transmission repair.

When a customer brings an automobile in for repair, the job is costed by referencing the "blue book" for repairs. This gives the average cost for the job in the general geographical vicinity of Ralph's garage. Because of the competitive nature of the auto repair business and the quality of work at Blackburn Garage, Ralph's customers have found this "standard cost" approach to pricing very acceptable.

For internal control purposes, Ralph uses a job order costing system to accumulate costs by each job. Parts are charged at cost. Labor and overhead are charged to each job at a rate of $36 per mechanic hour. This must be earned on the operating capital, it becomes possible to determine the standard price of a product—that is, that price which with plants operating at 80 percent of capacity will produce an annual return of 20 percent on the investment.

Standard Volume

Costs of production and distribution per unit of product vary with fluctuation in volume because of the fixed or nonvariable nature of some of the expense items. Productive materials and productive labor may be considered costs which are 100 percent variable, since within reasonable limits the aggregate varies directly with volume, and the cost per unit of product therefore remains uniform.

Among the items classified as manufacturing expense or burden there exist varying degrees of fluctuation with volume, owing to their greater or lesser degree of variability. Among the absolutely fixed items are such expenses as depreciation and taxes, which may be referred to as 100 percent fixed, since within the limits of plant capacity the aggregate will not change, but the amount per unit of product will vary in inverse ratio to the output.

Another group of items may be classified as 100 percent variable, such as inspection and material handling; the amount per unit of product is unaffected by volume. Between the classes of 100 percent fixed and 100 percent variable is a large group of expense items that are partially variable, such as light, heat, power, and salaries.

In General Motors Corporation, standard burden rates are developed for each burden center, so that there will be included in costs a reasonable average allowance for manufacturing expense. In order to establish this rate, it is first necessary to obtain an expression of the estimated normal average rate of plant operation.

Rate of plant operation is affected by such factors as general business conditions, extent of seasonal fluctuation in sales likely within years of large volume, policy with respect to seasonal accumulation of finished and/or semifinished product for the purpose of leveling the production curve, necessity or desirability of maintaining excess plant capacity for emergency use, and many others. Each of these factors should be carefully considered by a manufacturer in the determination of size of a new plant to be constructed, and before making additions to existing plants, in order that there may be a logical relationship between assumed normal average rate of plant operation and practical annual capacity. The percentage accepted by General Motors Corporation as its policy in regard to the relationship between assumed normal rate of plant operation and practical annual capacity is referred to as standard volume.

Having determined the degree of variability of manufacturing expense, the established total expense at the standard volume rate of operations can be estimated. A *standard burden rate* is then developed which represents the proper absorption of burden in costs at standard volume. In periods of low volume, the unabsorbed manufacturing expense is charged directly against profits as unabsorbed burden, while in periods of high volume, the overabsorbed manufacturing expense is credited to profits, as overabsorbed burden.

Return on Investment

Factory costs and commercial expenses for the most part represent outlays by the manufacturer during the accounting period. An exception is depreciation of capital assets which have a greater length of life than the accounting period. To allow for this element of cost, there is included an allowance for depreciation in the burden rates used in compiling costs. Before an enterprise can be considered successful and worthy of continuation or expansion, however, still another element of cost must be reckoned with. This is the cost of capital, including an allowance for profit.

Thus, the calculation of standard prices of products necessitates the establishment of standards of capital requirement as well as expense factors, representative of the normal operating condition. The standard for capital employed in fixed assets is expressed as a percentage of factory cost, and the standards for working capital are expressed in part as a percentage of sales, and in part as a percentage of factory cost.

The calculation of the standard allowance for fixed investment is illustrated by the following example.

Investment in plant and other fixed assets	$15,000,000
Practical annual capacity	50,000 units
Standard volume, percent of practical annual capacity	80 %
Standard volume equivalent (50,000 × 80%)	40,000 units
Factory cost per unit at standard volume	$1,000
Annual factory cost of production at standard volume (40,000 × $1,000)	$40,000,000
Standard factor for fixed investment (ratio of investment to annual factory cost of production; $15,000,000 ÷ $40,000,000)	0.375

The amount tied up in working capital items should be directly proportional to the volume of business. For example, raw materials on hand should be in direct proportion to the manufacturing requirements—so many days' supply of this material, so many days' supply of that material, and so on—depending on the condition and location of sources of supply, transportation conditions, etc. Work in process should be in direct proportion to the requirements of finished production, since it is dependent on the length of time required for the material to pass from the raw to the finished state, and the amount of labor and other charges to be absorbed in the process. Finished product should be in direct proportion to sales

TABLE 1
Illustration of Method of Determination of Standard Price

	In Relation to	Turnover Per Year	Ratio to Sales Annual Basis	Ratio to Factory Cost Annual Basis
Cash	Sales	20 times	0.050	—
Drafts and accounts receivable	Sales	10 times	0.100	—
Raw material and work in process	Factory cost	6 times	—	0.16⅔
Finished product	Factory cost	12 times	—	0.08⅓
Gross working capital			0.150	0.250
Fixed investment			—	0.375
Total investment			0.150	0.625
Economic return attainable, 20%			—	—
Multiplying the investment ratio by this, the necessary net profit margin is arrived at			0.030	0.125
Standard allowance for commercial expenses, 7%			0.070	—
Gross margin over factory cost			0.100	0.125
			a	b

$$\text{Selling price, as a ratio to factory cost} = \frac{1 + b}{1 - a} = \frac{1 + 0.125}{1 - 0.100} = 1.250$$

If standard cost = $1,000
Then standard price = $1,000 × 1.250 = $1,250

requirements. Accounts receivable should be in direct proportion to sales, being dependent on terms of payment and efficiency of collections.

The Standard Price

These elements are combined to construct the standard price as shown in Table 1. Note that the economic return attainable (20 percent in the illustration) and the standard volume (80 percent in the illustration) are long-run figures and are rarely changed;[1] the other elements of the price are based on current estimates.

[1] A Brookings Institution Survey reported that the principal pricing goal of General Motors Corporation in the 1950s was 20% on investment after taxes. See Lanzilotti, "Pricing Objectives in Large Companies."

Differences among Products

Responsibility for investment must be considered in calculating the standard price of each product as well as in calculating the overall price for all products, since products with identical accounting costs may be responsible for investments that vary greatly. In the illustration given below, a uniform standard selling price of $1,250 was determined. Let us now suppose that this organization makes and sells two Products, A and B, with equal manufacturing costs of $1,000 per unit and equal working capital requirements, and that 20,000 units of each product are produced. However, an analysis of fixed investment indicates that $10 million is applicable to Product A, while only $5 million of fixed investment is applicable to Product B. Each product must earn 20 percent on its investment in order to satisfy the standard condition. Table 2 illustrates the determination of the standard price for Product A and Product B.

From this analysis of investment, it becomes apparent that Product A, which has the heavier fixed investment, should sell for $1,278, while Product B should sell for only $1,222, in order to produce a return of 20 percent on the investment. Were both products sold for the composite average standard price of $1,250, then Product A would not be bearing its share of the investment burden, while Product B would be correspondingly overpriced.

Differences in working capital requirements as between different products may also be important due to differences in manufacturing methods, sales terms, merchandising policies, etc. The inventory turnover rate of one line of products sold by a division of General Motors Corporation may be six times a year, while inventory applicable to another line of products is turned over thirty times a year. In the second case, the inventory investment required per dollar cost of sales is only one-fifth of that required in the case of the product with the slower turnover. Just as there are differences in capital requirements as between different classes of product, so may the standard requirements for the same class of product require modification from time to time due to permanent changes in manufacturing processes, in location of sources of supply, more efficient scheduling and handling of materials, etc.

The importance of this improvement to the buyer of General Motors products may be appreciated from the following example. The total inventory investment for the 12 months ended September 30, 1926, would have averaged $182,490,000 if the turnover rate of 1923 (the best performnce prior to 1925) had not been bettered, or an excess of $74,367,000 over the actual average investment. In other words, General Motors would have been compelled to charge $14,873,000 more for its products during this 12-month period than was actually charged if prices had been established to yield, say, 20 percent on the operating capital required.

TABLE 2
Variances in Standard Price Due to Variances in Rate of Capital Turnover

	Product A		Product B		Total Product (A plus B)	
	Ratio to Sales Annual Basis	Ratio to Factory Cost Annual Basis	Ratio to Sales Annual Basis	Ratio to Factory Cost Annual Basis	Ratio to Sales Annual Basis	Ratio to Factory Cost Annual Basis
Gross working capital	0.150	0.250	0.150	0.250	0.150	0.250
Fixed investment	—	0.500	—	0.250	—	0.375
Total investment	0.150	0.750	0.150	0.500	0.150	0.625
Economic return attainable, 20%						
Multiplying the investment ratio by this, the necessary net profit margin is arrived at	0.030	0.150	0.030	0.100	0.030	0.125
Standard allowance for commercial expenses, 7%	0.070	—	0.070	—	0.070	—
Gross margin over factory cost	0.100 a	0.150 b	0.100 a	0.100 b	0.100 a	0.125 b
Selling price, as a ratio to Factory cost $\Big\} = \dfrac{1+b}{1-a}$	$\dfrac{1. + 0.150}{1. - 0.100} = 1.278$		$\dfrac{1. + 0.100}{1. - 0.100} = 1.222$		$\dfrac{1. + 0.125}{1. - 0.100} = 1.250$	
If standard cost equals	$1,000		$1,000		$1,000	
Then standard price equals	$1,278		$1,222		$1,250	

Conclusion

The analysis as to the degree of variability of manufacturing and commercial expenses with increases or decreases in volume of output, and the establishment of "standards" for the various investment items, makes it possible not only to develop "Standard Prices," but also to forecast, with much greater accuracy than otherwise would be possible, the capital requirements, profits, and return on capital at the different rates of operation, which may result from seasonal conditions or from changes in the general business situation. Moreover, whenever it is necessary to calculate in advance the final effect on net profits of proposed increases or decreases in price, with their resulting changes in volume of output, consideration of the real economics of the situation is facilitated by the availability of reliable basic data.

It should be emphasized that the basic pricing policy stated in terms of the economic return attainable is a policy, and it does not absolutely dictate the specific price. At times, the actual price may be above, and at other times below, the standard price. The standard price calculation affords a means not only of interpreting actual or proposed prices in relation to the established policy, but at the same time affords a practical demonstration as to whether the policy itself is sound. If the prevailing price of product is found to be at variance with the standard price other than to the extent due to temporary causes, it follows that prices should be adjusted; or else, in the event of conditions being such that prices cannot be brought into line with the standard price, the conclusion is necessarily drawn that the terms of the expressed policy must be modified.[2]

Required:

1. An article in the *Wall Street Journal*, December 10, 1957, gave estimates of cost figures in "an imaginary car-making division in the Ford-Chevrolet-Plymouth field." Most of the data given below are derived from that article. Using these data, compute the standard price. Working capital ratios are not given; assume that they are the same as those in Table 1.

Investment in plant and other fixed assets		$600,000,000
Required return on investment	30% before income taxes	
Practical annual capacity		1,250,000
Standard volume—assume	80%	
Factory cost per unit:		
Outside purchases of parts		$ 500*
Parts manufactured inside		600*
Assembly labor		75
Burden		125
Total		$1,300

* Each of these items includes $50 of labor costs.

---

[2] This paragraph is taken from an article by Donaldson Brown, then vice-president, finance, General Motors Corporation, in *Management and Administration*, March 1924.

"Commercial cost," corresponding to the 7% in Table 1, is added as a dollar amount and includes the following:

Inbound and outbound freight	$ 85
Tooling and engineering	50
Sales and engineering	50
Administrative and miscellaneous	50
Warranty (repairs within guarantee)	15
Total	$250

Therefore, the 7% commercial allowance in Table 1 should be eliminated, and in its place $250 should be added to the price as computed from the formula.

2. What would happen to profits and return on investment before taxes in a year in which volume was only 60% of capacity? What would happen in a year in which volume was 100% of capacity? Assume that nonvariable costs included in the $1,550 unit cost above are $350 million; i.e., variable costs are $1,550 − $350 = $1,200. In both situations, assume that cars were sold at the standard price established in requirement 1, since the standard price is not changed to reflect annual changes in volume.

3. In the 1975 model year, General Motors gave cash rebates of as high as $300 per car off the list price. In 1972 and 1973, prices had been restricted by price control legislation, which required that selling prices could be increased only if costs had increased. Selling prices therefter were not controlled, although there was always the possibility that price controls could be reimposed. In 1975, demand for automobiles was sharply lower than in 1974, partly because of a general recession and partly because of concerns about high gasoline prices. Does the cash rebate indicate that General Motors adopted a new pricing policy in 1975, or is it consistent with the policy described in the case?

6–4   Price Leadership in an Oligopoly*

Atherton Company

Early in January, 1975, the sales manager and the controller of the Atherton Company met for the purpose of preparing a joint pricing recommendation for Item 345. After the president approved their recommendation, the price would be announced in letters to retail customers. In accordance with

---

* This case was prepared by R. L. Lavoie under the supervision of Robert N. Anthony. Copyright © by the President and Fellows of Harvard College. Harvard Business School case 9–156–002.

company and industry practice, announced prices were adhered to for the year unless radical changes in market conditions occurred.

The Atherton Company was the largest company in its segment of the textile industry; its 1974 sales had exceeded $12 million. Company salespersons were on a straight salary basis, and each salesperson sold the full line. Most of Atherton's competitors were small. Usually they waited for the Atherton Company to announce prices before mailing out their own price lists.

Item 345, an expensive yet competitive fabric, was the sole product of a department whose facilities could not be utilized on other items in the product line. In January 1973, the Atherton Company had raised its price from $3 to $4 a yard. This had been done to bring the profit per yard on Item 345 up to that of other products in the line. Although the company was in a strong position financially, it would require considerable capital in the next few years to finance a recently approved long-term modernization and expansion program. The 1973 pricing decision had been one of several changes advocated by the directors in an attempt to strengthen the company's working capital position so as to insure that adequate funds would be available for this program.

Competitors of the Atherton Company had held their prices on products similar to Item 345 at $3 during 1973 and 1974. The industry and Atherton Company volume for Item 345 for the years 1969–74, as estimated by the sales manager, is shown in Table 1. As shown by this exhibit, the Atherton Company had lost a significant portion of its former market position. In the sales manager's opinion, a reasonable forecast of industry volume for 1975 was 700,000 yards. He was certain that the company could sell 25 percent of the 1975 industry total if it adopted the $3 price. He feared a further volume decline if it did not meet the competitive price. As many consumers were convinced of the superiority of the Atherton

TABLE 1
Item 345, Prices and Production, 1969–74

| Year | Volume of Production (yards) | | Price | |
	Industry Total	Atherton	Charged by Most Competitors	Atherton Company
1969	610,000	213,000	$4.00	$4.00
1970	575,000	200,000	4.00	4.00
1971	430,000	150,000	3.00	3.00
1972	475,000	165,000	3.00	3.00
1973	500,000	150,000	3.00	4.00
1974	625,000	125,000	3.00	4.00

Copyright 1986 by John Leslie Livingstone and Richard Mandel. Reproduced with permission.

product, the sales manager reasoned that sales of Item 345 would probably

a well-known established brand that was sold by its own distribution division to appliance stores, home improvement centers, building and remodeling contractors, and other retail outlets. Under another contract, Baker & Brown manufactured ovens for Mastercraft Stores, which was a mass-market retailer with over a thousand stores throughout the United States. The Samantha and Mastercraft ovens were essentially similar to the Baker & Brown brand ovens.

Within ten minutes, Bob had his three top executives around a conference table and had relayed to them the substance of Carol's call. Jack Hewitt, the plant manager, was saying, "The Samantha and Mastercraft ovens are basically like our own ovens, but they are not as well insulated in their walls or as well sealed at the door opening. The difference in cost is $5 for rockwool insulation and $1 for the door gasket per oven. Labor cost is the same for all three brands.

"Under the contracts with Samantha and Mastercraft, their production is scheduled 90 days in advance—which allows our 'just-in-time' inventory system to be implemented for raw materials. As a result, inventories of raw materials, work in process, and finished goods average about 30 days versus the 100 days of inventory we normally carry for the Baker & Brown brand ovens. Sidney, what are our inventory carrying costs?"

Sidney Cohen, the division controller, tapped his pencil on the table and cleared his throat. "We have carefully studied our inventory carrying costs, and these add up to double the interest rate that we pay on borrowings. Baker & Brown corporate recently issued twenty-year debentures at an interest rate of 10%. We also have a line of credit at two points over prime, with a compensating balance requirement of 20%."

Jack continued: "So, there are definitely manufacturing cost savings on our OEM ovens for Samantha and Mastercraft."

Next to speak was Barbara Craig, the division sales manager. "Our terms of payment are 10 days from invoice for Samantha and Mastercraft, as compared with the normal 60 days of accounts receivable that we carry for our own distributors. Also, Baker & Brown pays the freight on all truckload orders from our distributors. Samantha and Mastercraft pay the freight on all of their OEM ovens to their central distribution points in Dallas and Chicago, respectively.

"Baker & Brown provides a three-year warranty on labor and materials for our own brand ovens, but we do not provide warranties or warranty service on the OEM ovens.

"Incidentally, I hope you aren't thinking of raising our price to Samantha. I've begun discussing with them over next year's OEM contract and they've already told me that they'll consider going elsewhere if we raise the price."

Bob Brown said, "Each of you had identified possible sources of lower costs on our OEM ovens. The question is whether these cost savings add up to enough to justify the lower prices that our OEM ovens sell for. If not, we may be in hot water. I seem to recall there's a law, Robertson-Patrick or some such name, on price discrimination. I hope that's not why the distributors are bringing their lawyer tomorrow.

"Sidney, would you put a report together on this right away. Then let's all get together again this afternoon at four to see how we stand."

Sidney replied, "So they're bringing in their lawyer, are they? Well I don't like to be threatened. We can bring in lawyers too. Isn't there some law against trade conspiracies, Bob? Can't you call our lawyer and see if he can be here for the meeting?"

Bob called the Baker & Brown attorney. He had a previous engagement but agreed with Bob that this appeared, at the very least, to be a Robinson-Patman problem. He promised to send over a summary of that act for use at the four o'clock meeting.

Exhibit 1 is the Income Statement for the oven division for the recently ended fiscal year. Exhibit 2 is the brief summary of the main provisions of the Robinson-Patman Act, dealing with price discrimination, sent to Baker & Brown by their attorney.

EXHIBIT 1
Baker & Brown Corporation
Home Oven Division
Income Statement for the Year Ended December 31 (in $'000)

Sales (net)		30,538
Raw materials	6,894	
Factory wages	8,642	
Factory overhead	7,003	
Cost of goods manufactured		22,539
Add: Beginning inventories		5,079
Less: Ending inventories		5,985
Cost of goods sold		21,633
Gross profit		8,905
Less operating expenses:		
Product warranty service costs	1,256	
Freight out	1,321	
Selling and marketing	958	
Product advertising and promotion	432	
General and administrative	1,623	
Allocated corporate overhead*	329	
Total operating expenses		5,919
Division income before income taxes		2,986

* Note: Corporate overhead includes interest expense.

Ovens Sold	Number	Average Price	Total Sales
Baker & Brown brand	23,673	$626.00	14,819
Samantha OEM brand	17,654	$407.00	7,185
Mastercraft OEM brand	20,966	$407.00	8,533
Totals	62,293		30,537

EXHIBIT 2

The Robinson-Patman Act (the "Act") is actually Section 2 of the Clayton (Antitrust) Act as it has stood since its amendment in 1936. The most relevant portions of the Act are set forth below:

It shall be unlawful for any person engaged in commerce . . . either directly or indirectly, to discriminate in price between different purchasers of commodities of like grade and quality, where either or any of the purchasers involved in such discrimination are in commerce . . . and where the effect of such discrimination may be substantially to lessen competition or tend to create a monopoly in any line of commerce, or to injure, destroy or prevent competition with any person who either grants or knowingly receives the benefit of such discrimination or with customers of either of them, *provided* that nothing herein contained shall prevent differentials which make only due allowance for differences in the cost of manufacture, sale or delivery resulting from the differing methods or quantities in which such commodities are to such purchasers sold or delivered . . . and *provided further* that nothing herein contained shall prevent price changes from time to time where in response to changing conditions affecting the market for or the marketability of the goods concerned, such as but not limited to actual or imminent deterioration of perishable goods, obsolescence of seasonal goods, distress sales under court process, or sales in good faith in discontinuance of business in the goods concerned.

(b) . . . provided however that nothing herein contained shall prevent a seller rebutting a prima facie case [of price discrimination] by showing that his lower price . . . was made in good faith to meet an equally low price of a competitor . . .

(f) It shall be unlawful for any person engaged in commerce, in the course of such commerce, knowingly to induce or receive a discrimination in price which is prohibited by this section.

As is evident from the foregoing, the thrust of the Act is to prohibit the granting of price discrimination or knowing receipt of an individual price discount. A Seller's charging different prices for the same or similar goods to different customers will almost always implicate the Act, putting the burden on the Seller (or the knowingly benefiting Buyer) to justify the practice by reference to the various portions of the Act which excuse the practice under certain circumstances. The most important of these follow:

a) Jurisdictional concerns—As an Act of Congress whose Constitutional underpinning is the power "to regulate Commerce . . . among the several states," the Act prohibits price discrimination only when at least one of the purchases occurs in interstate commerce. It should be noted, however, that in the present judicial climate, it would be extremely difficult in most circumstances to convince a court that any particular business transaction was not in some way involved with interstate commerce.

b) Sales of goods—The Act concentrates its focus on sales of "commodities." Thus, price discrimination in the provision of services or intangible items is not covered by the Act.

c) "Like grade or quality"—The Act prohibits discrimination only in the sale of goods of like grade or quality. The Seller can thus defend his pricing practices by proving that the goods in question are significantly different from each other. It has been held, however, in numerous enforcement proceedings that mere slight differences in the products in question will not take the transactions beyond the reach of the Act.

EXHIBIT 2 (continued)

d) Effect on competition—Only price discrimination which "may . . . substantially . . . lessen competition, . . . tend to create a monopoly . . . or . . . injure, destroy or prevent competition with any person . . ." violates the Act. Thus price discrimination which has no effect on competition is perfectly legal. One must note, however, that a transaction which only "may" accomplish any of the foregoing will encounter the Act's prohibitions. No actual effect need be demonstrated; mere potential will do. In addition, although a general lessening of competition in a product or creation of a monopoly may be somewhat difficult to establish, it is often much easier to demonstrate a negative effect on competition only among the particular Sellers or Buyers involved.

e) Cost—The Act specifically exempts price discrimination which can be justified with reference to the different costs involved in the manufacture, sale or delivery of the product to the different customers involved. Courts have held, however, that the mere existence of differences are not enough; the amount of the cost savings must match the price differentials, since only "due allowance" is allowed.

f) Changing Market Conditions—The Act allows for price differentials which result from legitimate reactions to changing market conditions affecting the marketability of a product. Specifically, the Act exempts price discounts resulting from the perishability of goods, the obsolescence of seasonal goods, sales pursuant to judicial process and good faith "going out of business" sales. Although the Act sets forth these specific examples of relevant market conditions, the Act expressly states that this exception is not limited to these examples.

g) Meeting competition—Regardless of the existence of any other justification, the Act allows any person to practice price discrimination in a good faith response to a competitor's prices, even if the competitor's price cuts might be illegal under the Act. It should be noted, however, that this exception allows one to meet the competition only; undercutting the competition in the absence of independent justification under the Act, remains illegal.

6–6   *Pricing and Strategic Decisions*

MUELLER-LEHMKUHL GmbH (Abridged)

As the largest single manufacturer of apparel fasteners in Europe, we can reap the benefits of economies of scale. At the moment, we are

This case was prepared by Dagmar Bottenrebruch, Research Associate, under the supervision of Professor Robin Cooper. Copyright © 1986 by the President and Fellows of Harvard College. Harvard Business School case 9–189–032.

cost competitive with the Japanese. While the Japanese have lower wages and overhead, we are closer to the market and have lower selling costs.

Currently, the Japanese are pricing 20% below us. It is not enough to offset our quality advantage, but if they can match our quality or drop prices even further, we could have a problem.

Dr. Richard Welkers
President

Introduction

Mueller-Lehmkuhl (ML) is a West German producer of apparel fasteners. In 1986 ML had estimated revenues of $103 million (Exhibit 1).

EXHIBIT 1
MUELLER-LEHMKUHL GmbH
Budgeted Income 1986
($000)

Sales			$103,000
Cost of Goods			
Material (inc. material O/H)		$31,000	
Direct labor (inc. setup labor)		1,610	
Machine overhead		4,500	
General overhead			
Factory support	$ 3,020		
Factory supplies	470		
Technical administration	6,500		
Support departments	6,500		
Machining department	13,350		
Tooling department	3,050		
		32,890	
TOTAL			$ 70,000
Sales, General and Administrative			
Research and development	5,810		
Administration	2,760		
Marketing	7,930		
Shipping	3,170		
Commission	3,830		
			23,500
NET INCOME			$ 9,500

Product Description

Snap fasteners are used by the garment industry to replace buttons and buttonholes. ML produced about 700 different fasteners in 5 major product lines: s-spring socket snap fasteners, ring socket snap fasteners, two open prong snap fasteners (brass and stainless steel), and tack buttons.

Each product line was designed for a specific application. The s-spring fasteners were used for medium thick materials (1.4 to 2.0 mm). They could not be used for stretch materials, since they were attached centrally (through one stud) and would damage the material. The ring spring fasteners were used for thicker materials (up to 6.5 mm) and could be used on materials exposed to heavier strains. The open prong fasteners were especially well suited for use on thin (.25 to .75 mm) and stretchy materials since they did not damage the materials. All fasteners could be washed, dry cleaned, and ironed. Tack buttons were used to replace conventional buttons. They were usually used on blue jeans. Fasteners were customized either by applying various colors of finishes or by embossing the customer's logo on the cap.

As part of their strategy of being an integrated manufacturer, ML also manufactured attaching machines. In 1986, ML manufactured six attaching machines, three manual and three automatic (Exhibit 2). All of the machines could be modified to attach any of the company's fasteners. An operator using a manual machine placed the two parts of the fastener into the machine by hand, positioned the material, and operated the machine. In an automatic machine, one or more of the parts was positioned automatically. The operator still had to position the material manually.

Over the years, the firm had developed a policy of selling the manual machines and renting the automatic ones. Manual machines were sold because, unlike automatic machines, they did not cost much, did not require service, and were easily and inexpensively modified to allow them to attach different fasteners. Automatic machines were rented on an annual basis, though the company was willing to take them back at any time. About 10% of the 7,000 rented machines were returned in the average year. The company inventoried these machines until new orders arrived. They then modifed the old machines to enable them to attach a different fastener. Modification was expensive, as it required replacing all components specific to the fastener. The company estimated that an average modification cost $2,000.

While the rental contract did not specify free service, it was industry practice to provide preventive maintenance and emergency service at no charge. Even though most large customers had downtime insurance, ML viewed reliability and fast service response as an important sales tool. Consequently, it was not unusual for service personnel to be flown to a customer site within hours of an emergency call. In 1986, service was expected to cost about $4.5 million. To partially make up for the cost of providing this service, ML attached two conditions to the rental of a machine: only ML fasteners were to be used on the machine, and at least $10,000 worth of fasteners were expected to be purchased during the year. However, due to uncertain demand and overly optimistic customers, the average rented machine only attached about $7,000 worth of fasteners per year.

EXHIBIT 2

MUELLER-LEHMKUHL GmbH

Characteristics of Attaching Machines

Number	M1	M2	M3	A1	A2	A3
Operation mode	Manual	Manual	Manual	Semi-Automatic	Automatic	Automatic
Motive force	Hand	Foot	Pneumatic	Pneumatic	Pneumatic	Electric
Price[1]	$200	$250	$500	—	—	—
Annual rental fee[2]	—	—	—	$300	$500	$1500
Attachment speed[3]	5/min	6/min	15/min	15/min	25/min	50/min
Application[4]	Low volume	Low volume	Low volume	Low/medium	Medium/high	High
Budgeted production 1986	35	70	105	350	280	420
Budgeted rental base 1986[5]				1,350	2,250	3,500
Life expectancy	20 years	20 years	15 years	10 years	10 years	10 years

[1] Manual machines are sold, not rented.

[2] Automatic machines are rented, not sold. Rental fee equals average paid for all outstanding models.

[3] Average number of fasteners attached per minute.

[4] Low volume is less than 50,000 fasteners per year.
  High volume is greater than 300,000 fasteners per year.

[5] Includes machines manufactured in earlier years and still on rental contracts.

Market Conditions

The European market could be characterized as a stable oligopoly consisting of four firms who together accounted for 65% of the European fastener market (Exhibit 3). An additional 13 firms (including the Japanese) accounted for the rest of the market. Most of these firms sold fasteners and attaching machines. In addition to the fastener manufacturers, there were several companies who only produced attaching machines. Their machines were usually cheaper and of inferior quality to ML's. ML's fastener sales to customers using third-party equipment were thought to be about 10%. The exact percentage was unknown because ML could not be certain on which machines their products were actually used.

The four major players, all providing equivalent services, had over the years settled into peaceful coexistence. They never initiated price wars and rarely tried to steal each other's customers. Customers had helped achieve this stability by sourcing from multiple suppliers. Customers normally identified a primary source but ordered from at least one other firm. If ML attempted to move from a secondary supplier to a primary supplier by price cutting, the adversely affected company could easily retaliate by trying to become the primary source for one of ML's customers.

Several other factors helped to reduce the level of competition between the major players. First, the companies developed longstanding personal relationships with their customers. These relationships coupled to high customer satisfaction made it difficult to lure away any business. Second, the policy of renting machines coupled to designing the fasteners so that they could only be used in the supplier's own machines made switching an expensive undertaking. Third, virtually no standard prices existed. Each customer paid different amounts for their fasteners. This made it difficult to compete on price.

Despite these limitations, the firms did compete on three dimensions.

EXHIBIT 3
MUELLER-LEHMKUHL GmbH
Competitive Analysis—Predicted Sales by Fastener Product Line
($ million)

Name	Country of Origin	S-Spring	Ring	Prong	Tack	Total
M-L	Germany	$ 12	$ 9	$ 60*	$15	$ 96
PILONI	Italy	44	30	16	2	92
BERGHAUSEN	Germany	63	11	11	2	87
YOST & CO.	Germany	12	21	46	4	83
Other		61	46	63	23	193
		$192	$117	$196	$46	$551

* $24 prong brass + $36 prong – Stainless Steel

1. The quality of the fasteners and, in particular, the tolerance to which they were manufactured. The higher the tolerance, the less likely fasteners were to cause machine downtime and the longer their life expectancy once fastened. 2. The performance of the attaching machine, in particular speed, reliability, safety, noise level, and ability to attach fasteners without scratching the surfaces. 3. The quality of service provided.

ML sold its products through agents in some countries, distributors in others, and regional sales offices in yet others. Attaching machines were always purchased or rented directly from Mueller-Lehmkuhl. Agents generally represented a range of associated but noncompetitive products. They promoted ML products and were paid a 6% to 10% commission on fastener sales. Agents did not maintain inventories. Distributors differed from agents by maintaining inventory, thus reducing the uncertainty of local supply. Like agents, they enabled the local customer to deal with a fellow national. Overall, agents and distributors accounted for about 75% of sales. Product purchased through a distributor usually cost about 10% to 15% more than when purchased directly. In countries where local differences were not a major factor or ML maintained a regional sales office, large customers could purchase directly from the firm at reduced prices.

Production Process

ML's production facility was a four story building located next to the head office in Duesseldorf, West Germany. The top floor of the building, which contained the machining and tooling departments, was primarily dedicated to the production of attaching machines. All design and prototype work for the attaching machines was completed in house. This represented about 30% of the engineering staff's activities. In addition to attaching machines, the company manufactured some of its own production machines.

The machining department labor force was split into two groups, one producing attaching and production machines and the other refitting returned attaching machines. Management estimated that 80% of the labor force that was producing machines was dedicated to attaching machine production.

The tooling department, which was also located on the top floor, manufactured and repaired tools that were used in the production of both fasteners and machines. Tools used in the production of fasteners were very costly and were frequently reworked, whereas tools used in the production of attaching machines were relatively inexpensive and usually replaced when they showed signs of wear. No attempt had been made to determine how the tooling department's capacity was split between production and attaching machine tools.

The other three floors of the factory were dedicated to fastener production. Fastener production consisted of three major steps: stamping, assembly, and finishing, and each floor was primarily dedicated to a single step. In stamping, the material components were stamped out of large coils. If the fastener was being produced in very large quantities, then automated machines were used that could produce up to 12 components with a single stamp. These high volume machines required expensive tooling, often costing up to $50,000. At low production volumes, less sophisticated machines were used. The stamping department contained 47 different types of machines. In the stamping department, it was not unusual for a single operator to run several machines simultaneously. In assembly, the stamped components were combined by machine. The type of machine used to assemble the components again depended on the production volume. There were 112 different types of machines in assembly.

Once assembled, the parts were then washed and, if required, heat treated before being sent to finishing. Several different finishes were produced. These included plating (the part was plated to make the surface smooth and shiny), painting or enameling (the part was spray painted in a variety of colors), tumbling (to produce a matte surface) and polishing (to produce a smooth surface). There were 15 different types of machines in the finishing department.

Finished parts were packed ready for shipping. Only minimum work in process and finished goods inventories were maintained, because most fasteners were produced to order.

While, on the surface, fasteners seemed to be simple products requiring fairly low technology, in fact, they had to be machined to within a hundredth of a millimeter. This required precision stamping and high quality control. Similarly, the attaching machines were on the forefront of automated material handling technology. To maintain their technological superiority, the firm maintained a strong research and development department. The introduction of the fashion line required significant R&D resources. Management estimated that at least two-thirds of current R&D projects were related to fastener production with the new high fashion fasteners accounting for about 50%.

Cost Accounting System

The cost accounting system had recently been overhauled. According to Mr. Atwater, the corporate controller, the old system, which consisted of about 70 cost centers, failed to differentiate appropriately between automatic and manually operated machines. The new system contained more cost centers: one per machine class.

Material, after adjustment for scrap, was charged directly to the product. The new cost system also identified a material overhead charge. This included the costs associated with purchasing, material handling, and inventory storage. Products were allocated material overhead on the basis of the material dollars they consumed.

Labor costs, after dividing by the number of machines the operator was running, were charged directly to each product. Setup labor costs were divided by the lot size to produce a per part setup charge. Overhead consisted of two components: machine-specific costs and general overhead. Machine-specific costs, such as floor space, energy, maintenance, depreciation, and an interest charge for invested capital were traced directly to individual machines. The total cost of these items for each machine was divided by the projected direct labor dollars (including setup) expected to be worked on the machine class to give the machine overhead burden rate per direct labor dollar for the coming year. This rate was multiplied by the standard direct labor dollars of a product at that machine to charge machine-specific overhead to products.

General overhead consisted of factory support, factory supplies, technical administration, support department costs, machining department costs, and tooling department costs (Exhibit 4). Where possible, general overhead costs were traced directly to the fastener production departments; otherwise they were allocated to each department on the basis of direct labor dollars (including setup dollars). The general cost pool for each fastener production department was then divided by projected direct labor dollars (including setup) for each department for the coming year to give the departmental burden rate per direct labor dollar. The resulting departmental burden rate was multiplied by the standard direct labor dollar content of each product to give the product cost.

EXHIBIT 4
Mueller-Lehmkuhl Gmbh
Description of General Overhead Accounts

Factory Support included the unallocated supervision, floor space, and janitorial services that were consumed by fastener production. Production management was also contained in this account.
Factory Supplies included oil, grease rags, and miscellaneous tools used in the fastener production departments.
Technical Administration included attaching machine service costs and those engineering costs not included in R&D.
Support Department included costs for production scheduling, fastener inventory control, the apprentice workshop, and the worker council.
Machining Department included material labor and overhead like supervision, depreciation, floor space for the manufacture of production and attaching machines.[a]
Tooling Department included material, labor, and overhead costs for the manufacture of tools.

---

[a] Under German accounting principles, given the nature of the lease agreement, the entire cost of the attaching machines was written off to general overhead in the year in which the machines were manufactured.

In summary, the cost system reported standard product costs in the following manner (the unit of measurement was a "mil" which was equal to 1,000 pieces):

Material	standard cost + material overhead
Labor	standard labor hours × standard pay rate/number of machines operated
Setup	standard set up labor hours × standard pay rate/lot size
Machine O/H	standard labor dollars × machine burden rate
General O/H	standard labor dollars × departmental burden rate

While the different products appeared relatively similar to the inexperienced eye, they could actually have significantly different cost structures (see Exhibit 5 for the cost structures of five representative products).

Japanese Competition

Hiroto Industries (HI), the major Japanese competitor in Europe, was a trading company that sold a broad range of fashion accessory products to the shoe, leather goods, and garment industries.

HI entered the European market in 1973. It faced substantial entry barriers, in particular the longstanding relationships of European companies with customers, its lack of high quality attaching machines, and the absence of a network of distributors and service personnel. To help mitigate these barriers, HI focused on the high volume products, such as workwear, leather goods, and babywear, where the market consisted of a few customers ordering very large volumes of products.

HI also adopted a new marketing strategy. Rather than rent the attaching machines themselves, HI identified distributors that were willing to purchase attaching machines and then rent them to their customers. These machines were purchased from the companies that only manufactured attaching machines because the firms that manufactured both attaching machines and fasteners would only sell or rent their machines to the end user. HI then supplied these dealers with fasteners at about a 20% discount on current European prices. This strategy had several advantages for HI. First, it did not own the machines and consequently did not have to provide service. Second, invested capital was kept to a minimum, and, finally, HI did not bear the risk of returned machines.

The dealers benefited because they could now compete with companies like ML. They had a significant price advantage and could "steal" those customers who were not contractually obligated to use a specific firm's fasteners.

HI's new strategy threatened two segments of ML's market. The first was the small volume customers who used fasteners that were very popular. Several such firms were effectively equivalent to a large volume customer. However, given that these customers owned their own equipment, they were free to purchase fasteners from whomever they chose.

A more worrying trend was when a large volume customer decided to use Japanese fasteners on ML equipment. While most fasteners were customized, some of the really high volume fasteners, such as stainless

EXHIBIT 5

Mueller-Lehmkuhl GmbH

Product Cost Structures of Representative Products

($ per 1,000 units)

	S-Spring			Ring			Prong (Brass)			Prong (SS)			Tack Button		
Average Selling Price	$46.75			$39.83			$15.28			$20.32			$38.40		
	Total	Var	Fixed	Total	Var	Fixed	Total	Var	Fixed	Total	Var	Fixed	Total	Var	Fixed
Material															
Raw Material	9.70	9.70	0.00	8.88	8.88	0.00	6.04	6.04	0.00	5.74	5.74	0.00	11.88	11.88	0.00
Material O/H	0.54	0.13	0.41	0.50	0.12	0.38	0.34	0.07	0.27	0.32	0.07	0.25	0.67	0.15	0.52
	10.24	9.83	0.41	9.38	9.00	0.38	6.38	6.11	0.27	6.06	5.81	0.25	12.55	12.03	0.52
Stamping															
Setup	0.12	0.12	0.00	0.25	0.25	0.00	0.01	0.01	0.00	0.03	0.03	0.00	0.03	0.03	0.00
Labor	0.68	0.68	0.00	0.48	0.48	0.00	0.04	0.04	0.00	0.21	0.21	0.00	0.25	0.25	0.00
Machine O/H	1.31	0.34	0.98	1.28	0.40	0.87	0.17	0.07	0.10	1.13	0.48	0.65	1.11	0.74	0.37
General O/H	22.40	12.49	9.91	14.63	8.06	6.58	0.94	0.49	0.45	5.62	3.18	2.46	8.42	5.91	2.51
	24.51	13.63	10.89	16.64	9.90	7.45	1.16	0.62	0.54	7.01	3.90	3.11	9.81	6.93	2.88
Assembly															
Setup	0.14	0.14	0.00	0.05	0.05	0.00	—	—	—	—	—	—	0.01	0.01	0.00
Labor	0.10	0.10	0.00	0.24	0.24	0.00	—	—	—	—	—	—	0.18	0.18	0.00
Machine O/H	0.25	0.07	0.18	0.45	0.12	0.33	0.00	0.00	0.00	0.00	0.00	0.00	0.26	0.13	0.13
General O/H	1.56	0.74	0.82	3.55	1.85	1.70	0.00	0.00	0.00	0.00	0.00	0.00	2.51	0.52	1.99
	2.05	1.05	1.00	4.29	2.26	2.03	0.00	0.00	0.00	0.00	0.00	0.00	2.96	0.84	2.13
Finishing	5.66	4.14	1.52	8.28	6.02	2.26	1.88	1.38	0.50	0.56	0.40	0.16	3.84	2.80	1.04
TOTAL	42.46	28.65	13.81	38.59	26.47	12.12	9.42	8.11	1.31	13.63	10.11	3.52	29.17	22.60	6.57
Total DL (inc. setup) for All Departments (inc. Finishing)	$1.32			$1.43			$0.14			$0.27			$0.66		

steel spring fasteners, were standardized and could run on anybody's equipment. Certain ML customers, even though contractually obligated to purchase product from ML, were beginning to experiment with the Japanese product. ML had threatened to cancel the equipment leases if they caught any firm violating the contract. Recently, one firm had been caught, but immediately agreed to stop "experimenting" with Japanese fasteners.

Mr. Brune, ML's European sales manager, commented:

> My biggest concern is keeping price levels as high as possible in the face of Japanese competition. We do not want to lose market share to them, but the problem is that their prices are so much lower than ours that matching them would be too expensive. They do not present an immediate threat because our quality is so much higher. However, even though our customers carefully analyze the situation and decide to stay with us, they are left with the feeling that they would be better off if they bought Japanese.
>
> The worst scenario I can think of is the Japanese importing thousands of their attaching machines and pricing their fasteners below cost in an attempt to dominate the European market. If they did that, Europe would become a battlefield.

6–7 *Activity-Based Costing*

JOHN DEERE COMPONENT WORKS (A) (Abridged)

The phone rang in the office of Keith Williams, manager of Cost Accounting Services for Deere & Company. On the line was Bill Maxwell, accounting supervisor for the Gear & Special Products Division in Waterloo, Iowa. The division had recently bid to fabricate component parts for another Deere division. Maxwell summarized the situation:

> They're about to award the contracts, and almost all of the work is going to outside suppliers. We're only getting a handful of the parts we quoted, and most of it is low-volume stuff we really don't want. We think we should get some of the business on parts where our direct costs are lower than the outside bid, even if our full costs are not.

Williams asked, "How did your bids stack up against the competition?" Maxwell replied:

> Not too well. We're way high on lots of parts. Our machinists and our equipment are as efficient as any in the business, yet our costs on

This case was prepared by Research Associate Artemis March, under the supervision of Professor Robert S. Kaplan. Copyright © 1987 by the President and Fellows of Harvard College. Harvard Business School case 9–187–107.

standard, high-volume products appear to be the highest in the industry. Not only are we not competitive with outside suppliers, but our prices are also higher than two other Deere divisions that quoted on the business.

Deere & Company

The company was founded in 1837 by John Deere, a blacksmith who developed the first commercially successful steel plow. One hundred years later, Deere & Company was one of seven full-line farm equipment manufacturers in the world and, in 1963, had displaced International Harvester as the number one producer. During the 1970s, Deere spent over one billion dollars on plant modernization, expansion, and tooling.

During the three-decade, post–World War II boom period, Deere expanded its product line, built new plants, ran plants at capacity, and still was unable to keep up with demand. Deere tractors and combines dotted the landscape throughout America.

During this same period, Deere had diversified into off-the-road industrial equipment for use in the construction, forestry, utility, and mining industries. In 1962, it also began building lawn and garden tractors and equipment. By the mid-'80s, Deere had the broadest lawn and garden product line in the world.

The collapse of farmland values and commodity prices in the 1980s, however, led to the worst and most sustained agricultural crisis since the Great Depression. Several factors exacerbated the crisis. The high dollar reduced U.S. exports and thus hurt both American farmers and American farm equipment producers. Farmers had been encouraged to go into heavy debt to expand and buy land, so when land values and farm prices plummeted, the number of farm foreclosures skyrocketed. Few farmers were in a position to buy new equipment, and resale of repossessed equipment further reduced the market for new equipment.

In response, Deere adjusted its level of operations downward, cut costs where possible, increased emphasis on pushing decision making downward, and restructured manufacturing processes. While outright plant closings were avoided, Deere took floor space out of production, encouraged early retirements, and did not replace most of those who left. Employment was reduced from 61,000 at the end of 1980 to about 37,500 at the end of 1986. It implemented new manufacturing approaches such as just-in-time production and manufacturing cells that grouped a number of operations for more efficient flow-through production and placed quality control directly at the point of manufacture. To add production volume, Deere wanted its captive component divisions to supply other companies and industries.

John Deere Component Works

For many years, all the parts for tractors were made and assembled at the tractor works in Waterloo. To generate more production space in the 1970s, Deere successfully split off parts of tractor production. Engine machining and assembly, final tractor assembly, and product engineering each were moved into new plants in the Waterloo area. By the end of the decade, the old tractor works buildings were used only for component production, ranging from small parts to large, complex components such as axles and transmissions. The old tractor works buildings in Waterloo were renamed the John Deere Component Works (JDCW).

In 1983, JDCW was organized into three divisions. The Hydraulics Division, which was soon consolidated into a nearby, refurbished warehouse, fabricated pumps, valves, and pistons. The Drive Trains Division made axles, transmissions, and drive trains. The Gear and Special Products Division made a variety of gears, shafts, and screw machine parts, and performed heat treating, cast iron machining, and sheet metal work.

As part of a vertically integrated company, JDCW had been structured to be a captive producer of parts for Deere's equipment divisions, particularly tractors. Thus, it had to produce a great variety of parts whose volume, even in peak tractor production years, was relatively low. During the 1970s, operations and equipment had been arranged to support tractor production of approximately 150 units per day; by the mid-'80s, however, JDCW was producing parts for less than half as many tractors. The lower volume of activity had a particularly adverse effect on JDCW's screw machine and sheet metal businesses, since their machines were most efficient for high-volume production.

Internal Sales and Transfer Pricing. Virtually all of JDCW's sales were internal. Deere equipment-producing factories were required to buy internally major components, such as advanced design transmissions and axles, that gave Deere a competitive advantage. For smaller components, corporate purchasing policy placed JDCW in a favored, but not exclusive, position for securing internal business.

Corporate policy stated that transfers between divisions would take place at full cost (direct materials + direct labor + direct overhead + period overhead). Corporate also had a make-buy policy that when excess capacity was available, buying divisions should compare component divisions' direct costs, rather than full costs, to outside bids. (Direct costs equal full costs less period overhead.) Thus, for example, if JDCW full costs were $10, its direct costs $7, and an outside bid $9, the make-buy decision rule held that the buying division should buy from JDCW. But, the transfer pricing policy required the buyer to pay $10 to the component division. Bill Maxwell described the conflict:

The equipment divisions looked only at price, and acted like profit centers rather than cost centers. They are starting to act in the interest of their factory rather than the corporation as a whole. The transfer pricing policy wasn't a problem until times got bad and capacity utilization went down. At Component Works, we said to our sister divisions, "You should look at our direct costs and buy from us." They replied, "We don't want to pay more than it would cost us from outside vendors."

In practice, equipment divisions did not always follow the corporate guidelines for internal sourcing and JDCW lost a portion of the equipment factories' business to outside vendors.

Screw Machine Business

Deere's effort to push decision making down into more manageable units encouraged divisions to view their product lines as stand-alone businesses that sold to external markets. By early 1984, JDCW operations were so far below capacity that managers realized they could not wait for the agricultural market to turn around. In the Gear and Special Products Division, several people thought that screw machine products offered a promising niche.

Screw machines transformed raw materials (primarily steel barstock) into finished components, and were the most autonomous of the division's operations. As one manager put it, "We could shut down the screw machine area and not affect the rest of the plant—except that we would then have to buy machined parts from outside suppliers." Only the master schedule connected the area with the activities of the rest of the plant.

The screw machine operations were organized into three departments. These departments were distinguished by the diameter of the barstock its machines could handle, and by the number of spindles on each machine. A six-spindle machine could handle six different orientations, for example, and thus make more complex parts than a four-spindle machine.

Screw Machine Capabilities and Operations. Screw machines automatically fabricated small metal parts. Raw barstock was brought to a staging area near the machines by an overhead crane, the amount depending on the lot size to be run. Barstock (in round, square, or hexagonal sections) was fed horizontally by the operator into the back of the machine. Multiple stations each performed different operations simultaneously on what would become parts; when the longest cycle time (they ranged from a few seconds to six minutes) was completed, a machine indexed to the next position. Small parts, such as pinions, collars, gears, bushings, and connectors continually emerged from the final station. Finished parts were transported in 50-pound baskets stacked in trailers that carried up to 1500 pounds.

Once set up, automatic screw machines were very fast, had excellent repeatability, and were particularly good at drilling, threading, grooving, and boring out large holes. New, the machines could cost as much as $500,000 each; their replacement value was estimated at about half that amount.

Operators were assigned to a battery of two or three specific machines; they did their own setups and tool changes. Setups, like runs, were timed; operators punched in and out, creating a record of how long setups actually took. Operators were also responsible for quality, machine cleanup, and housekeeping in their areas. Following first-part inspection by an inspector, operators ran the lot. Roving inspectors also checked samples from each lot or basket for conformance to quality standards.

Layout. Component Works had 120 automatic screw machines lined up in four long rows in an 80,000-square-foot building (almost the size of two complete football fields). The chip and coolant recovery system was constructed under the floor, running the entire length of the building. It was connected up to each machine, much like houses are connected to a sewer system, to carry off the tremendous amount of chips generated by the machines as well as to cool and lubricate the machines. The layout of the cooling system made it infeasible to redesign the screw machine layout into cellular configurations that would group attendant secondary and finishing operations together.[1] Screw machines could be shifted around or dedicated to certain parts, but due to the prohibitive expense of duplicating a chip coolant system, they were forced to remain in rows in Building S.

During the 1970s, secondary operations had been moved off the main floor in S Building to make room for more screw machines; this increased material handling distances for most parts. For example, the enormous heat treatment machines were located about one-quarter mile from the main screw machine area.

Process Engineering. To bring a new part into production required extensive process engineering activities. Operations had to be sequenced, and tooling requirements specified for each spindle. If the appropriate specialized tooling did not exist, it either had to be purchased, or designed and built (usually outside). Both setups and runs had to be timed and standards established. Process engineers had to make sure that the process they had designed would in fact make the part correctly. Databases then had to be set up for each machine.

---

[1] Secondary operations included heat treating, cross-drilling, plating, grinding, and milling; most parts required one or more secondary operations.

All of these activities had to be conducted whether or not the part number ever ran. John Gordon, head of the process engineering group for screw machining, commented, "We have to do as much work for a part we run once a year—or one we never ever run—as for one we set up every month or that runs every day."

Recently, process engineering and production people had begin to make changes in how they ran screw machine parts. . . . As Andy Edberg, head of process engineering for the division, noted, "Screw machines are extremely high-volume machines so you want to dedicate them if possible." Process engineers were starting to outsource some low-volume parts or to transfer them to more labor-intensive processes. Edberg pointed to the fundamental nature of the shift:

> We always made all the components for tractors, so we ran lots of part numbers but never really looked at the costs of individual parts. What was important was the efficiency of the whole rather than the efficiency of making the parts.

Competition and Strategy. By 1984, Gear and Special Products had roughed out a general strategic thrust towards marketing screw machine parts to the outside world such as automobile OEMs. Initial efforts to gain outside business, however, soon made it obvious that competing in the external market was going to be harder than anticipated. Competition came in two forms: captive producers of other vertically integrated companies (about whom Deere found it difficult to obtain information), and independent screw machine shops. The latter had sprung up around geographical clusters of end users. On the East Coast, the independent shops fed the defense industry particularly shipyards; on the West Coast they supplied the aircraft industry; and in Michigan and Indiana, they sold to the automotive industry. Dick Sinclair, manufacturing superintendent, observed:

> The key to successful competition in the outside market is price. We found we have a geography problem. We are not in the midst of heavy users, and it is expensive to ship steel both in and out. We also found our range of services to be less useful than we thought they would be.

Bid on 275 Screw Machine Parts

Both excess capacity and its new thrust toward developing stand-alone business motivated Gear and Special Products to bid on 275 of the 635 parts Deere & Company offered for bid in October 1984. All 635 parts had high potential for manufacture on automatic screw machines. Gear and Special Products bid on a subset for which it had the capability, and where the volume was large enough to exploit the efficiencies from its multiple-spindle machines. The buying group consisted of several equipment factories plus a corporate purchasing group; its aim was to consolidate screw machine purchasing by dealing with just a few good vendors, and to gain improved service, quality, and price for these parts. Gear and Special Products had one month to prepare its bid.

Results of the bid are summarized below (dollars are in thousands, and represent the annual cost for the quantity quoted):

Comparison—JDCW vs. Vendor

	Parts with JDCW Low Total Cost	Parts with JDCW Low Direct Cost	Total JDCW Direct Cost High	Total All Parts
Part Numbers	58	103	114	275
JDCW Direct Cost	$191	$403	$1,103	$1,697
JDCW Full Cost	272	610	1,711	2,593
Low Outside Quote	322	491	684	1,507
Percent of $ Value	22%	33%	45%	100%
% JDCW of Low Vendor:				
Direct Cost	58	82	161	113
Full Cost	82	124	250	172

The purchasing group awarded Gear and Special Products only the 58 parts for which it was the low bidder on a full-cost basis. Most of these were low-volume parts that the division did not especially want to make. Gear and Special Products could be the source for the 103 parts on which its direct costs were below the best outside bid only if it agreed to transfer the parts at the same price as the low outside bidder. The division passed on this "opportunity."

The bidding experience generated a good deal of ferment at Gear and Special Products and confirmed the feeling of many that "we didn't even know our costs." Sinclair recalled:

> Some of us were quite alarmed. We had been saying, "Let's go outside," but we couldn't even succeed inside. Deere manufacturing plants in Dubuque and Des Moines also quoted and came in with lower prices— not across the board, but for enough parts to cause concern. If we weren't even competitive relative to other Deere divisions, how could we think we could be successful externally? And when we looked at the results, we knew we were not costing things right. It was backwards to think we could do better in low-volume than high-volume parts, but that's what the cost system said.

JDCW Standard Cost Accounting System

A standard cost accounting system was used throughout Component Works. . . . The standard or full cost of a part was computed by adding up the following:

- direct labor (run time only)
- direct material
- overhead (direct + period) applied on direct labor
- overhead (direct + period) applied on material dollars
- overhead (direct + period) applied on ACTS machine hours

Establishing Overhead Rates. Once a year, the JDCW accounting department re-established overhead rates based on two studies, the normal study, and the process study. The normal study determined the standard number of direct labor and machine hours and total overhead for the following year by establishing a "normal volume." In order to smooth out sharp swings, normal volume was defined as the long term "through the business cycle" volume. One of the measures for setting normal volume was the number of drive trains produced per day.

The process study broke down projected overhead at normal volume among CW's 100-plus processes, such as painting, sheet metal, grinding, screw machines, and heat treating. To determine the overhead rate for each process, accounting computed the rate from actual past charges, and then asked, "Do we expect any changes?" (Accumulated charges were collected by charging the specific process code as production took place.) Applying judgment to past rates, next year's normal volume, and any probable changes, a new overhead rate was established for each process for the coming year.

Evolution of Bases for Overhead Rates. For many years, direct labor run time was the sole basis for establishing overhead rates at Component Works. Thus if $4,000,000 in overhead was generated by $800,000 of direct labor, the overhead rate was 500%. In the 1960s, a separate materials overhead rate had been established. This rate included the costs of purchasing, receiving, inspecting, and storing raw material. These costs were allocated to materials as a percentage markup over materials costs. Over time, separate rates had been established for steel, castings, and purchased parts to reflect the different demands these items placed on the materials handling resources.

Both labor- and materials-based overhead were subdivided into direct and period overhead. Direct (or variable) overhead, such as the costs of setups, scrap, and material handling, varied with the volume of production activity. Period (or fixed) overhead included accounts, such as taxes, depreciation, interest, heat, light, and salaries, that did not vary with production activity.

In 1984, Component Works introduced machine hours as well as direct labor and materials to allocate overhead. With the increased usage of automated machines, direct labor run time no longer reflected the amount of processing being performed on parts, particularly when one operator was responsible for several machines. Every process was studied and assigned a machine hour or ACTS (Actual Cycle Time Standard) rate. Labor hours was retained for processes where labor time equaled machine time; where these were different, ACTS hours were used to allocate overhead. Total overhead (other than materials overhead) was then split between direct labor overhead and ACTS overhead. As before, each overhead pool was subdivided between direct and period overhead.

Launching a Cost Study for Screw Machines

Keith Williams had been aware that the existing standard cost system, although satisfactory at an aggregate level, was ineffective for costing and bidding individual parts. He was experimenting with other ways to apply overhead to products. When Maxwell called him in November 1984, Williams realized that the situation at Gear and Special Products provided an opportunity to demonstrate the weaknesses of the current system and to develop a new approach that would be more useful for decision making.

After his phone conversation with Maxwell, Williams quickly put together a proposal to management at Deere & Company, and to the Division Manager of Gear and Special Products. The study would focus on one cost center—the three screw machine departments—because screw machine ACTS hours were the highest chunk of costs in the bid; more than 60% of total machining for the parts occurred on the screw machines. To conduct the study, Williams chose Nick Vintila, who had begun his career at Deere as a manufacturing supervisor at Component Works. During his second year, Vintila had worked in the screw machine area. Not only had he become very familiar with its operation, but he had worked with people such as Gordon, then in methods, and Edberg, then a manufacturing superintendent, who would now also be working on the cost study. Vintila had subsequently served as a liaison between systems development and manufacturing to implement a labor reporting system that tied into MRP, and then became an accounting supervisor at the Tractor Works.

As a first step, Williams and Vintila studied a sample of 44 of the 275 bid parts. (See *Exhibit 1*.) This examination showed: (a) an enormous range of variation among quotes for many parts; (b) a large dispersion between JDCW and vendor quotes, ranging from 50–60% on some parts and 200–300% on others; (c) that JDCW estimated standard costs exceeded vendor prices by 35%, on average; and (d) that JDCW appeared to be most cost-effective on low-volume and low-value parts. (See *Exhibit 2* for summary measures of the characteristics of the 44 sample parts.) These findings raised numerous questions about the validity of the standard cost system for determining costs of individual parts, and reaffirmed the need for an alternative costing method.

Vintila spent the first half of 1985 working full time on what became known as the ABC—Activity-Based Costing—study. After detailed study of the shop process flow, he and Williams learned that use of overhead resources could be explained by seven different types of support activities: direct labor support, machine operation, setup hours, production order

EXHIBIT 1

John Deere Component Works (A)

Comparison of JDCW vs. Outside Vendor Bids for Sample of 44 Parts

Part Number	Part Description	Quote Volume	JDCW Est		Competing Vendor Quotes							% to JDCW to VDR. 2		Direct Labor $ Each
			Dir. Cost	Mfg. Cost	1	2	3	4	5	6	7	Dir. Cost	Mfg. Cost	
Component Works Low on Full-Cost Basis:														
F382	Fitting	4,009	$ 2,248	$ 3,153	$ 3,940	$ 9,822	$13,550					23%	32%	$0.05
S209	Spacer	950	183	291	399	522	551	$ 1,244	$ 1,244			35	56	0.03
P594	Pin	692	297	430	692	796	817	1,012	1,509			37	54	0.03
T815	Stud	3,150	719	1,162	1,712	1,859	2,158	2,300	3,131	$ 9,356		39	62	0.03
P675	Pin	3,596	1,703	2,649	3,587	3,740	6,024	7,947				46	55	0.07
H622	Hub	4,450	3,207	4,365	5,687	6,324	6,743	7,518	8,463	12,875	$12,875	51	69	0.05
S245	Spacer	4,912	1,249	1,917	2,210	2,335	2,536	3,276	3,585	4,076		53	82	0.03
R647	Sprocket	5,167	6,792	9,196	11,907	12,142	12,400	13,124	16,116	16,674	17,516	56	76	0.10
T501	Stud	4,879	902	1,492	1,537	1,610	1,625	1,820	2,196	2,976	6,294	56	93	0.03
S071	Spacer	5,661	4,896	6,885	8,378	8,433	10,133					58	82	0.09
C784	Cap	71,200	13,101	19,537	17,088	22,072	22,606	23,332	29,832	41,253		59	89	0.04
P583	Pin	3,402	2,775	4,285	4,380	4,467	4,826	5,233	5,391	17,200		62	96	0.09
R410	Sprocket	792	878	1,226	658	1,349	2,162	2,273	2,866	2,946	3,983	66	91	0.08
Total or Average		112,860	$38,949	$56,590		$75,471						52%	75%	$0.05

Component Works Low on Direct-Cost Basis:

R918	Rocker	1,091	$ 663	$ 1,063	$ 905	$ 1,036	$12,655	$14,642	$18,711			64%	103%	$0.05
P220	Pin	3,204	6,685	11,754	9,048	10,413	2,306	2,985				64	113	0.45
P057	Pin	1,281	979	1,675	1,460	1,487	12,628	13,461	18,568			66	113	0.09
T566	Stud	2,452	7,925	12,037	9,563	11,843			13,323	22,983		67	102	0.42
P736	Pin	38,955	6,837	10,475	9,181	10,167	11,492	11,492	3,420			67	103	0.03
P904	Pin	950	1,170	1,801	1,606	1,729	1,767	1,995	4,775			68	104	0.10
H355	Hub	1,155	1,947	3,090	2,552	2,872	2,979	3,026	11,805			68	108	0.13
P423	Pin	3,402	2,661	4,157	2,994	3,912	5,137	5,477		6,846		68	106	0.09
B605	Bolt	10,561	2,239	3,373	2,893	3,273	3,485	3,707	3,970	4,718	$ 4,718	68	103	0.03
H346	Hub	1,088	2,223	3,570	3,007	3,122	3,151	3,242	3,438	4,034	4,128	71	114	0.15
H554	Hub	1,490	1,551	2,214	1,967	1,997	2,077	2,216	2,298	2,459	2,459	78	111	0.06
P244	Pin	7,383	7,438	10,948	7,591	8,786	9,498	10,705	11,270	12,677	23,773	85	125	0.11
L209	Lever	5,351	2,480	3,827	1,578	2,745	3,692	4,334	4,486	4,548	4,826	90	139	0.05
R316	Roller	18,058	2,470	4,610	2,257	2,691	3,250	4,050	4,231	4,939	4,984	92	171	0.03
S451	Spacer	2,785	645	1,226	390	697	852	1,104	1,253	1,276	1,306	93	176	0.04
P333	Pin	4,258	6,818	12,088	6,898	7,324	9,197	11,113	12,008			93	165	0.32
P379	Pin	6,807	6,984	10,249	5,037	7,352	7,760	9,394	9,421	21,919		95	139	0.11
P682	Pin	3,402	4,037	5,880	2,824	4,208	5,035	5,817	11,533			96	140	0.08
Total or Average		113,673	$ 65,753	$104,038		$ 85,654						77%	121%	$0.08
Cumulative		226,533	$104,703	$160,629		$161,125						65%	100%	$0.08

Component Works Not Cost Competitive:

H265	Hub	4,464	$ 15,311	$ 24,341	$13,570	$ 15,236	$17,275	$17,454	$17,901	$20,489		100%	160%	$0.57
A152	Shaft	2,972	7,749	12,841	6,685	7,667	8,470	10,877	7,887	8,868	$ 9,450	101	167	0.38
R717	Sprocket	4,869	6,834	10,003	6,205	6,707	7,421	7,839			2,203	102	149	0.16
S771	Spacer	11,092	971	1,689	909	942	1,053	1,275	1,852	2,107		103	179	0.02
R428	Sprocket	3,180	4,374	6,888	3,637	4,226	4,285	4,293	4,624	4,709	5,599	103	163	0.18
R946	Roller	5,904	6,254	10,727	4,815	6,022	6,199	6,494	7,947	9,269	19,837	104	178	0.14
R157	Roller	3,181	1,651	2,934	1,082	1,565	1,645	1,749	1,890	1,917	2,004	106	188	0.08
B823	Button	18,200	3,296	5,622	2,347	3,094	3,257	3,276	3,314	3,516	6,042	107	182	0.03
T863	Stud	7,120	11,136	17,790	8,231	8,590	9,185	13,243	24,706	16,606		130	207	0.37
T237	Stop	4,258	12,719	18,713	7,877	8,516	9,112	9,623	10,228	8,925	15,640	149	220	0.35
N281	Nut	8,500	6,350	11,322	3,392	3,789	4,114	6,375	7,548			168	299	0.18
T166	Stud	5,645	8,766	16,014	3,912	5,024	5,701	13,209				174	319	0.41
T586	Stud	10,000	15,957	27,273	7,525	8,900	9,540	11,000	11,520	26,700		179	306	0.40
Total or Average		89,385	$101,367	$166,157		$ 80,278						126%	207%	$0.21
Total/Avg. all Parts		315,918	$206,069	$326,786		$241,403						85%	135%	$0.11

EXHIBIT 2
John Deere Component Works (A)
Characteristics of Sample of 44 Parts

Category	Number	Volume	Direct Labor $	ACTS Hours per 100 Parts	Annual ACTS Hours	DL $/ Materials $
Low on Full-Cost Basis	13	4,009[a] [692; 71,200]	.05 [.03; .10]	.04 [0.3; 1.5]	19 [2; 266]	21% [9; 51]
Low on Direct-Cost Basis	18	3,402 [950; 38,955]	.09 [.03; .45]	1.2 [0.3; 2.8]	31 [10; 159]	23% [9; 224]
Not Cost Competitive	13	5,645 [2972; 18,200]	.18 [.02; .57]	1.5 [0.2; 3.4]	70 [18; 150]	57% [22; 480]
Total	44					

[a] Top Number is the Median Value in that category.
The Range [minimum; maximum] appears beneath the Median.

activity, material handling, parts administration, and general overhead. Vintila then went through each overhead account (e.g., engineering salaries, crib attendant costs), asking others and himself, "Among the seven activities, which cause this account to occur? What creates work for this department?" He began to estimate the percentages of each overhead account that were driven by each of the seven activities. He conducted specific studies to estimate the total volume of each of the seven overhead driving activities (such as number of production orders, total machine hours). This work was circulated among people like Maxwell, Edberg, Gordon and Sinclair, who, drawing on their experience and judgment, accepted the seven activities as the key overhead drivers, and adjusted the final percentages for allocating budgeted items to each activity. (See Appendix A for a description of the seven overhead drivers and how Vintila arrived at the seven overhead rates.) When the ABC method was used to allocate overhead, 41% of the overhead shifted to activity bases 3–7 (see *Exhibits 3* and *4*). The data needed to estimate the cost of a particular part are shown in *Exhibit 5*.

EXHIBIT 3
John Deere Component Works (A)
1985 Screw Machine Overhead Allocation
Using Standard Cost System

	Applied Based on Direct Labor		Applied Based on Machine Hours		Total	
					$000s	Total
Direct Overhead:						
Maintenance	$ 32	0.3%	$1,038	10.2%	$ 1,070	10.5%
Labor Allowances	459	4.5	0	0.0	459	4.5
Machine Setups	0	0.0	524	5.2	524	5.2
Other OH Lab	130	1.3	164	1.6	294	2.9
Scrap & Misc.	80	0.8	96	0.9	176	1.7
Employee Benefits	1,296	12.7	556	5.5	1,852	18.2
Total Direct OH	$1,997	19.6%	$2,378	23.4%	$ 4,375	43.0%
Period Overhead:						
Maintenance	$ 127	1.2%	$ 527	5.2%	$ 654	6.4%
Salaries	796	7.8	826	8.1	1,622	15.9
Depreciation	0	0.0	1,790	17.6	1,790	17.6
Gen. & Misc.	227	2.2	717	7.0	994	9.3
Employee Benefits	354	3.5	432	4.2	786	7.7
Total Period OH	$1,504	14.8%	$4,292	42.2%	$ 5,796	57.0%
Total Overhead	$3,501	34.4%	$6,670	65.6%	$10,171	100.0%
Overhead Base	$1,714 DL$		242,000 ACTS hrs.			
Direct Overhead Rate	117%		$ 9.83 per hr.			
Period Overhead Rate	88%		17.73 per hr.			
Total Overhead Rate	205%		$27.56 per hr.			

EXHIBIT 4

John Deere Component Works (A)
1985 Screw Machine Overhead Allocation
Using ABC Method

	Direct Labor Support Overhead		Machine Operation Overhead		Machine Setup Overhead		Production Order Overhead		Material-Handling Overhead		Part Admin. Overhead		General and Administration Overhead		Total	
	$000s	% Total	$000s	% Total	$000s	% Total	$000s	% Total	$000s	% Total	$000s	% Total	$000s	% Total	$000s	% Total
Direct Overhead:																
Maintenance	$ 0	0.0%	$ 899	8.8%	$ 45	0.4%	$ 62	0.6%	$ 63	0.6%	$ 0	0.0%	$ 0	0.0%	$ 1,069	10.5%
Labor Allowances	$ 329	3.2%	$ 47	0.5%	$ 61	0.6%	$ 10	0.1%	$ 12	0.1%	$ 0	0.0%	$ 0	0.0%	$ 459	4.5%
Machine Setups	$ 0	0.0%	$ 146	1.4%	$ 378	3.7%	$ 0	0.0%	$ 0	0.0%	$ 0	0.0%	$ 0	0.0%	$ 524	5.2%
Other OH Lab	$ 0	0.0%	$ 67	0.7%	$ 0	0.0%	$106	1.0%	$122	1.2%	$ 0	0.0%	$ 0	0.0%	$ 295	2.9%
Scrap & Misc.	$ 0	0.0%	$ 141	1.4%	$ 0	0.0%	$ 30	0.3%	$ 6	0.1%	$ 0	0.0%	$ 0	0.0%	$ 177	1.7%
Employee Benefits	$1,100	10.8%	$ 339	3.3%	$ 246	2.4%	$ 77	0.8%	$ 90	0.9%	$ 0	0.0%	$ 0	0.0%	$ 1,852	18.2%
Total Direct OH	$1,429	14.0%	$1,639	16.1%	$ 730	7.2%	$285	2.8%	$293	2.9%	$ 0	0.0%	$ 0	0.0%	$ 4,376	43.0%
Period Overhead:																
Maintenance	$ 10	0.1%	$ 333	3.3%	$ 40	0.4%	$ 9	0.1%	$ 8	0.1%	$238	2.3%	$ 17	0.2%	$ 655	6.4%
Salaries	$ 270	2.7%	$ 179	1.8%	$ 62	0.6%	$243	2.4%	$ 0	0.0%	$421	4.1%	$448	4.4%	$ 1,623	16.0%
Depreciation	$ 27	0.3%	$1,424	14.0%	$ 226	2.2%	$ 25	0.2%	$ 0	0.0%	$ 43	0.4%	$ 45	0.4%	$ 1,790	17.6%
Gen. & Misc.	$ 59	0.6%	$ 323	3.2%	$ 19	0.2%	$152	1.5%	$ 0	0.0%	$ 90	0.9%	$298	2.9%	$ 941	9.3%
Employee Benefits	$ 103	1.0%	$ 147	1.4%	$ 34	0.3%	$103	1.0%	$ 2	.0%	$207	2.0%	$190	1.9%	$ 786	7.7%
Total Period OH	$ 469	4.6%	$2,406	23.7%	$ 381	3.7%	$532	5.2%	$ 10	0.1%	$999	9.8%	$998	9.8%	$ 5,795	57.0%
Total Overhead	$1,898	18.7%	$4,045	39.8%	$1,111	10.9%	$817	8.0%	$303	3.0%	$999	9.8%	$998	9.8%	$10,171	100.0%
Overhead Base	$1,714 DL$		242,000 Annual ACTS Hours		32,900 Annual Setup Hours		7,150 Annual Orders		15,600 Annual Loads		2,050 Part #'s		$10,887 Value Added*			
Direct Overhead Rate	83.4%		$ 6.77 per hour*		$22.18 per hour		$ 39.86 per order		$18.78 per load		—		—			
Period Overhead Rate	27.4%		$ 9.94 per hour		$11.58 per hour		$ 74.41 per order		.64 per load		$487 per part		9.1%			
Total Overhead Rate	111.0%		$16.71 per hour		$33.76 per hour		$114.27 per order		$19.42 per load		$487 per part		9.1%			

$ 1,714 DL$
1,898 DL$ OH
4,045 Mach. Oper. OH
1,111 Setup OH
817 Prod. Order OH
303 Mat. H. OH
999 Part. Adm. OH
$10,887 Value Added

* Rates shown are averages across all screw machines. In practice, separate machine overhead rates were calculated for each major class of machines.

The detailed work to design the ABC system had now been completed. The next step for Williams and Vintila was to test and gain acceptance for their new costing approach.

EXHIBIT 5
John Deere Component Works (A)
Elements for Costing Part A103 in 1985

$6.44 Materials Cost/100 Parts

    Materials Overhead Rates:

2.1%	Direct
7.6%	Period

.185	Direct Labor Hours/100 Parts
.310	ACTS Hours/100 Parts
$12.76	Labor Rate for Screw Machine Operation
4.2 hrs.	Machine Set-up Time
0.176 lbs.	Part Weight

8,000 Quote Volume (annual volume as specified by user)
  2 Runs/Year

6-Spindle Machine Rates:	Direct:	$8.99
(under ABC systems)	Period:	$7.61

Appendix A: John Deere Component Works Activity-Based Costing (A)

ABC Activities for Applying Overhead to Screw Machine Parts

The ABC study used the accounting estimate of normal volume and total overhead costs as its starting point. Overhead costs were then allocated to seven rather than just two activities. A separate overhead rate was derived for each activity. (See *Exhibits 3* and *4* for comparison of the two methods.) Vintila used the following approach to apportion overhead and to develop overhead rates:

1. *Direct Labor Support* overhead was generated by incentive employees working on parts. It included allowances for benefits, break periods, and a percentage of supervision, personnel, payroll, and industrial engineering salaries. All direct labor support overhead costs were summed ($1,898,000 in 1985), and divided by the total amount of direct labor dollars ($1,714,000) to derive an overhead rate for this activity (111%).

2. *Machine Operation* overhead was generated by operating the screw machines, plus an allocation of facility and capacity charges. This activity received most of the costs of machine maintenance, small tools, jigs, and dies, as well as smaller proportions of inspection and defective work, engineering and supervision salaries. Allocations were also made for depreciation, taxes, interest, and utilities. The total dollars required to operate the machines ($4,045,000) were divided by the total number of machine hours (242,000) to develop the $16.70 per hour overhead rate for this activity.

   Whereas the standard cost system used the same ACTS rate for all screw machines, Vintila examined the machines individually, and ultimately developed separate rates for four different size machines. He gathered data on several factors to create machine-specific estimates of the costs of running them. For example, kilowatt hours multiplied by the load factor was used to generate utilities cost; replacement costs to estimate the share of insurance, taxes, and depreciation; square footage to calculate a proportion of facilities costs; and the "spindle factor" to allocate tooling and maintenance costs. The spindle factor took into account the number of spindles on a machine; when multiplied by its annual load (or ACTS hours), it provided a basis for allocating tooling and maintenance costs according to size and use of the machine. For all of these factors, Vintila obtained percentages by dividing the total (e.g., replacement costs of all screw machines) by that for the particular machine. To obtain an overall direct overhead rate for a machine, he divided all its direct overhead by its ACTS hours.

   Once this information had been generated for each of the screw machines, similar size machines were grouped and a single overhead rate determined for each group. In this way, machines that happened to have a lower load would not be penalized by a higher rate.

3. *Setup Hours* overhead was generated by changing the job to be run. It included actual setup costs; a small share of machine and small tool maintenance, supervision, and engineering salaries; and a share of depreciation and other facility costs. These costs ($1,111,000) were divided by the estimated number of setup hours (32,900) to arrive at an hourly overhead rate ($33.80).

   The number of setup hours was estimated through an examination of production control data which showed the average setup time to be 4 hours. This figure was multiplied by the average number (4) of annual runs per part number, and by the 2,050 parts in the system.

4. *Production Order Activity* was generated by shop activity resulting from each production order. The largest cost was material control salaries. Percentages of crib attendant costs, inspection, defective work, and manufacturing costs were also applied. The sum was di-

vided by the total number of annual production orders (7,150) to yield a cost of $114 per production order.

5. *Material Handling* overhead arose from moving barstock to the machines, and then moving the parts to the next operation. The major cost elements were materials handling labor and equipment maintenance. This activity also received a share of inspection and defective materials costs. An overhead rate ($19.42) was derived by dividing the total allocated costs ($303,000) by the number of loads (15,600).

The number of loads was estimated through a six-step process:

a. $$\frac{\text{part weight} \times \text{annual volume}}{\text{runs/year for that part}} = \text{weight/run}$$

b. $$\frac{\text{weight/run}}{\text{pounds/load}} = \text{loads/run}$$
(average of 2000 lbs. per transport container)

c. loads/run + .5, then round result to nearest full integer (a calculation to correct for incomplete loads)

d. multiply result in (c) by # runs of that part/year = # loads/year moved away from machines

e. loads/year × 2 (movement to and from machine) = total # loads/year for that part

f. repeat process for all part numbers, and add # loads/part to obtain total # loads per year

6. *Part Administration* overhead was incurred just by having a part number in the department's repertoire. It included the cost of establishing and maintaining records and systems documentation, and a share of salaries in process engineering, industrial engineering, supervision, and materials control. The sum of $999,000 in overhead, when distributed among the 2,050 parts in the system, generated a head tax of $487 per part number.

7. *General and Administrative* overhead was attributed to the entire factory, not to a particular manufacturing process or activity. It included a large share of taxes, utilities, and depreciation, as well as smaller shares of salaries such as accounting, reliability, and manufacturing engineering. The $998,000 of G&A overhead was prorated to products based on their value added: the sum of direct labor plus the other six overhead activity costs for each part. The value-added sum became the denominator for determining the G&A rate to be applied to the part.

chapter 7

ASSIGNING SERVICE DEPARTMENT COSTS

We can usually distinguish two types of departments in organizations: *production departments*, which directly produce or distribute the firm's outputs, and *service departments*, whose main output is to provide service to other departments. Examples of such service departments include utilities, maintenance, production control, stockroom, material handling, housekeeping, and information systems. Units such as R&D or advertising that produce companywide services may not be included in this analysis unless their output is produced for specific departments or products.

In this chapter, we will discuss the process of attributing or allocating the costs of service departments to operating departments and products. We will attempt, in the initial discussion in this chapter, to distinguish between **attribution** and **allocation** of costs. **Attribution** is the process of assigning a cost that is unambiguously associated with a particular cost object to that particular cost object. Costs that can be attributed are often called **separable** costs. Costs that cannot be attributed can be either joint or common costs that must be **allocated** to cost objects. **Allocation** is the process of assigning a resource cost to a department or a product when a direct measure does not exist for the quantity of the resource consumed by the department or product. Thus, both attribution and allocation assign resource costs to departments or products—attribution based on a direct measure of resource consumption and allocation based on an indirect or surrogate measure.

For example, consider the costs of a Power Department that a company maintains to generate its power internally. If some unit of the company has special power needs, requiring special transformers and distribution equipment that are not used by any other unit of the firm, then the costs of those transformers and distribution equipment can be attributed to that organizational unit. When direct measurement is not performed for a resource, we may still wish to allocate service department costs to consuming units for product costing purposes. We will discuss both possibilities in this chapter.

Why Charge for Using Service Department Resources?

A good cost accounting system should provide incentives for efficient performance by the managers of service departments and for prudent use of service departments' outputs by the managers of revenue-producing departments. If the costs of using an internal service department are not charged to user groups, a number of negative consequences can occur. First, more of the service will be demanded by user groups than is economically reasonable to supply. Without incurring any charge for using a service department's resources, a user will attempt to use the service up to the point where the marginal benefit is zero. Naturally, this will be well beyond the optimal usage, where the marginal benefit from the service equals the marginal cost of supplying it.

Second, without charging for its output, we cannot determine whether the service department is operating efficiently. In the absence of prices charged to profit-conscious departmental managers, the service department must be treated as a discretionary expense center. The budgeted costs, obtained from historical experience, may offer no guarantee that the department is operating efficiently. Also, no signals are available to determine the optimal scale or size of the service department. At times of financial stringency, the output of the service department may be restricted to reduce operating expense. This curtailment of activity may not be desirable if it restricts or downgrades the performance of revenue-producing departments that would be willing to pay for additional amounts of the service.

Third, if a service department's output is not priced, little guidance exists on whether the firm should continue to supply the service internally. For many service activities, firms have the option to purchase the service externally. For example, utilities, data processing, maintenance, housekeeping, consulting, industrial engineering, and security can be either supplied internally or purchased externally. Without a price system to compare relative costs, it may not be obvious when an internal service center is more expensive than external alternatives, because of either internal inefficiencies or an uneconomically small scale of operation.

Finally, without a pricing system for service department outputs, managers will have little guidance about the level of service to be provided or demanded. A service department may wish to avoid complaints from users and obtain satisfaction by providing service of excellent quality, based on acquisition of sufficient resources to provide the best and most responsive service possible. If user departments were made to see the cost of receiving this level of service, they might opt for a more economical service level—functional, without frills, and less expensive. But without the incentives and signals emanating from a pricing system for the output of a service department, a user department has little opportunity to communicate its preferences on the price-versus-service-level dimension.

By charging for the output of a service department, we can overcome these four difficulties. Managers of consuming departments who are charged for the output of a service department will (1) exercise more control over the consumption of that output in their departments, (2) compare the costs of using the internal service department with the costs of comparable services purchased outside the firm, and (3) attempt to communicate to the service department the quality level of services desired, including showing their willingness to pay more to receive higher-quality service or to accept lower quality in order to pay less. Managers of service departments whose output is charged directly to user departments become aware that such prices will be reviewed critically by profit-conscious departmental and divisional managers; hence they will be motivated to keep departmental costs down. They may become more entrepreneurial and innovative as they attempt to provide a level and quality of service that will be demanded by user departments. Service department managers should therefore become more responsive to the demands of user groups rather than offering service on a take-it-or-leave-it basis.

Charging for the output of service departments also helps the firm in internal resource-allocation decisions. Short-run capacity limits may constrain the output from some departments, such as utilities, data processing, or departments with skilled personnel. If demand is high for the output from these service departments, the firm may find it difficult to allocate the available supply among all the user groups. Prices, however, can be set above the actual costs of service departments so as to ration the excess demand to those user departments that most value the service. If enough user groups are willing to pay a high price for a service, the firm can use this market clearing price as a signal to invest in additional (and costly) capacity for the service department. If, conversely, a service department is unable to recover its long-run marginal costs when it prices its output to users, the firm has a good signal that the department has more capacity than is economically warranted over the long run. Service departments unable to cover even their short-run variable costs through charges to user departments should be identified for special attention. Such departments should be examined closely by top management to determine why their cost structure is so high or their output so lightly demanded.

We have been focusing on the use of prices to control the demand and supply of the output from a service department. In principle, the prices could be determined by reference to potential outside suppliers of these services. This possibility will be extensively discussed in Chapter 14 on transfer pricing. Using externally referenced prices would treat service departments as profit centers and, if carried to its logical conclusion would allow revenue-producing centers the choice of acquiring the service either from the internal service department or from an outside supplier. Typically, however, the charges for use of service departments are based on the budgeted or actual costs of these departments. We will follow a cost-based pricing scheme for service departments throughout this chapter and will defer the consideration of a market-referenced pricing system until the transfer price discussion in Chapter 14. Most of the benefits of a service department pricing system can be achieved even when prices are based on the costs of the service department.[1]

When service department costs can be directly attributed to production departments, these costs can then be readily included in product costs as well. But even when direct consumption measures of service departments do not exist, product costs still require an estimate of the consumption of service department outputs by the individual products, as we discussed in the preceding chapter on pricing strategies.

Financial reporting requirements provide a final reason for allocating service department costs to producing departments and subsequently to final goods and services. Generally accepted accounting principles require that the full costs of production be allocated to products sold and placed in inventory during a period. The cost allocations for financial accounting purposes, however, can and probably should be done separately from the system used to encourage operational efficiencies.[2] In this chapter, we will focus on attributing service department costs to production departments for the reasons given before, not on allocating such indirect costs to products.

Measuring Costs of Using Service Departments

Service department costs are attributed to other departments based on a measure of usage of the service department's output. Thus, for each service department, we need to choose a measure of activity to cost and charge for its output. Ideally, we will be able to choose a direct measure of output from that service department—for example, kilowatt-hours or pounds of steam from a utility department, or number of purchase orders filled for a purchasing department. If a service department provides a variety of different kinds of services, then multiple measures of activity can be used to reflect the consumption of the different types of activities. For example, with a data processing department, separate charges could be incurred for CPU hours, disc-memory storage, pages of output printed, and connect time. For some departments, we will have to settle for input measures,

---

[1] See, for example, the methods described for attributing corporate overhead costs to operating divisions in H. Thomas Johnson and Dennis A. Loewe, "How Weyerhaeuser Manages Overhead Costs," *Management Accounting* (August 1987); and for charging for information systems resources in Brandt Allen, "Make Information Services Pay," *Harvard Business Review* (January-February 1987).

[2] See Robert S. Kaplan, "One Cost System Isn't Enough," *Harvard Business Review* (January-February 1988), pp. 61–66.

such as hours of maintenance supplied, rather than an output measure, such as improvement in equipment performance.

More problematic is whether the costs of service department outputs should be charged to production departments where direct measures of consumption do not exist. When only surrogate but not direct measures exist for the consumption of service department outputs (such as machine horsepower for charging utility expenses to unmetered departments, square footage of space occupied for housekeeping expenses, total direct costs for a controller's department, or direct labor-hours for many categories of factory overhead costs), there may be little benefit and, in fact, some harm incurred by attempting to allocate service department costs to production departments. Direct measures may not exist because the cost of obtaining such measures, for example by metering individual production departments or by monitoring the amount of time the housekeeping staff spends in each department, greatly exceeds any potential benefit from using these direct measures.

The exercise of charging production departments for the costs of service departments will be most useful when direct measures exist for the quantity of service department output that has been consumed by individual production departments. Little benefit and some harm may result from allocating service department costs when direct measures do not exist and surrogate measures, which bear no causal relation to consumption of service department outputs, are used to allocate service department costs to production departments. Because the assigned cost will be based on a measure unrelated to the demands the production department made on the service department, the cost will not be the direct consequence of actions taken by the manager or workers in the production department. Therefore, the cost signal cannot provide useful feedback on operating performance in the production department during the period.

How might a manager respond to a cost signal based on an arbitrary allocation of costs? First, she might ignore the signal entirely, perhaps the optimal action, recognizing that the signal does not provide any useful information about actions taken in the recent past or likely to be taken in the near future. Two circumstances may prevent the manager from ignoring the signal entirely. First, managers are frequently requested to respond to variances in their periodic operating report and to reconcile the signal with other records, such as from the production control system. Thus, some amount of the manager's time must be committed to responding to reported cost variances, regardless of their source or accuracy.

Second, if the report will be considered when evaluating the manager's performance, the manager will naturally attempt to influence the signal that does get reported. Since the signal, by assumption, cannot be directly affected by the manager's actions in the production department, the manager can influence the signal only by arguing about and negotiating the allocation procedure with other managers, of both production and service departments, or the manager's superiors. These discussions clearly detract from the amount of time the manager has to improve efficiency, productivity, and quality within her own department. By allocating a cost that does not reflect resource consumption by a production department, but continuing to hold managers responsible for such a cost, the company has signaled that managers of such departments should spend some amount of their time discussing and negotiating about allocation percentages with other managers.

Despite these limitations, the practice of cost allocation is widespread. A study of cost allocation for the National Association of Accountants reported that 85% of the respondent firms engaged in some form of service department cost allocation.[3] The primary objectives of cost allocation were to support: the performance evaluation process, cost-based pricing, decision analysis, and financial reporting.

The Cost Accounting Standards Board, which specified cost accounting practice for firms engaged in contracting with the U.S. government, argued that cost allocation practice should reflect the actual costs of the services used to complete a job. With this point of view, the CASB developed a hierarchy of cost allocation bases:

1. The preferred basis of cost allocation is direct attribution. That is, all costs that can be uniquely associated with a cost object should be attributed to that cost object. A cost object can be any unit for which the firm wants to accumulate costs. Examples include a job (such as a building), a production run, a product line, or even a unit of production. The work or inputs that went into the cost object are determined, and costs are attributed to the cost object based on the specific work or input for that cost object.

2. For costs that are common or joint to several products, the CASB preferred an approach that allocates these costs in proportion to the service provided by the service center to each cost object. For example, if the cost object used 10% of the output of a machine shop, that cost object should be assigned 10% of the machine shop's costs.

Several cost pools, reflecting different causes of overhead cost (called cost drivers), may exist within a single service department. Each pool would be allocated to cost objects using different allocation bases. For example, the costs of running a machine shop may be caused primarily by the use of alternative machines, the use of indirect labor, the handling of raw materials, and the number of production line setups. The costs accumulated in each of these cost pools should be allocated to the different cost objects using an allocation basis that best explains the increase of costs in that pool. For example, the number of machine-hours for the machine cost pool, the number of hours of indirect labor for the indirect labor cost pool, the number of tons (or type) of raw materials handled for the raw materials handling

---

[3] J. M. Fremgen, and S. S. Liao, *The Allocation of Corporate Indirect Costs* (National Association of Accountants: New York, 1981).

cost pool, and the amount, or nature, or production line setups for the production line setup cost pool.

3. In cases where it is not possible to measure the work done for individual cost objects, the CASB proposed other measures of cost allocation based on the activities of the cost objects. These measures are intended to be an approximation of the work that was done, but not measured. For example, the cost of a corporate administrative department could be allocated to organizational units on the basis of the number of employees in each unit.

Using the terms we developed earlier in this chapter, CASB rule 1 is consistent with the attribution approach (when we assumed a direct quantity measure of consumption exists), whereas, at the other extreme, rule 3 represents an arbitrary allocation.

At least part of the rationale for arbitrary cost allocations can be derived from external reporting requirements—for financial accounting, for the CASB, or for other regulatory agencies. We should not confuse the existence of allocations for these external constituencies as justifying arbitrary allocations for internal managerial purposes. But Zimmerman has proposed that cost allocation serves multiple managerial roles as well; to decompose complex problems, to motivate decision makers, and to coordinate the decisions of decentralized decision makers.[4] A common theme underlying the NAA study findings and Zimmerman's suggestion is that the cost allocation should reflect the opportunity costs of the services provided by the service center, in effect a market price to support decentralization by providing relevant economic signals to accompany and direct resource usage and to evaluate the results of operations.

We agree that cost allocation plays an important role, where direct measurement does not exist, for estimating the costs of resources consumed by products. In fact, we argued for just such a role in our discussion of product costing for pricing purposes in the preceding chapter. We do not believe, however, that cost allocations are useful for short-term performance evaluation of operating managers when accurate measures of the quantity of service department output consumed do not exist.

A Fundamental Cost Accounting Equation

Any cost can be decomposed into a quantity and a price component. We can write a cost, C, as the product of a quantity, Q, of a resource multiplied by the unit price, P, of that resource:

[4] J. Zimmerman, "The Costs and Benefits of Cost Allocations," *Accounting Review* (July 1979), pp. 504–21.

$$C = P \times Q$$

For example, utility expense can be represented as the product of kilowatt-hours (kwhr) consumed (the Q measure) multiplied by the cost per kilowatt-hour (the P measure). When we have referred to the existence of a direct measure on service department consumption, we meant that we have an accurate measure of the **quantity**, Q, of the service department's output (e.g., the number of kwhr) consumed by a production department. Even with such a direct accurate quantity measure, the amount charged to a production department could still include allocations when the price measure, P, includes allocated costs. The price measure could include cost allocations from depreciation or floor space charges, or charges from other service departments.

We believe that the crucial issue, however, is not whether allocations are included in the price measure. More important is whether the quantity Q is measured directly or whether it is a rough estimate based on a surrogate measure. With a good measure of quantity consumed, the price measure would have to be substantially in error before it would adversely affect managerial decisions. As long as operating managers are charged based on an accurate quantity measure, they will probably not spend much time arguing about minor fluctuations in its unit price. Instead they will act to use the quantity of the resource they consume efficiently and effectively.

If, however, the quantity Q is measured inaccurately, such as when costs of service departments are arbitrarily allocated to operating departments based on head count, floor space, or direct labor-hours, then operating managers are not rewarded or punished for the quantity of the demands they place on service departments. In this case, the use of a surrogate, unrepresentative measure of Q has caused the cost signal to be ineffective in motivating operating efficiences. Thus, cost attribution to operating departments can be performed when an accurate Q measure exists. But we create an undesirable, perhaps dysfunctional, cost allocation when we use an arbitrary measure for Q that does not represent the actual demands that an operating department makes on a service department.

One exception to this rule can be noted. Seemingly arbitrary cost allocations may be useful to force periodic managerial discussions and negotiations. For example, some corporations deliberately allocate all corporate overhead expenses to operating departments with allocation bases (such as sales dollars, head count, or total costs) that have little to do with the consumption or causes of the overhead costs. Senior managers apparently want operating managers to be aware of centrally determined and controlled costs. Perhaps the fully allocated costs are meant to encourage more aggressive pricing decisions by the decentralized managers (which may or may not be a good idea). But they may also serve to enlist operating managers' support in curtailing the growth of corporate expenses. Only by having all responsible managers see the costs of company planes, corporate headquarters' buildings and furnishings, and other such discretionary expenses, may countervailing forces be set in motion to limit the growth and escalation of the costs.

The use of cost allocations to stimulate negotiations was documented in a recent study.[5] A high-tech company assigned marketing expenses and revenues to the managers of product-development departments, and it assigned product-development expenses to marketing managers. The product-development managers had no marketing authority and the marketing managers had no product-development authority; yet each was held responsible for the actions of the other, seemingly an arbitrary exercise in allocating noncontrollable costs and revenues. The plausible and defensible rationale for this practice was to force active and continual dialogue among product-development and marketing managers on the needs of the marketplace and the marketability of proposed products. In this case, the discussions and negotiations that accompanied the arbitrary allocation of costs and revenues were exactly the actions that the senior management of the company wanted to encourage.

To summarize, if we want operating managers to promote efficiencies, improve productivity, and learn more about the characteristics of production processes under their control, then we should send them accurate measures of quantities and good estimates of prices of input resources consumed. If such accurate measures do not exist, then arbitrary quantity measures should not be substituted—in effect, transforming a desirable cost attribution into an undesirable cost allocation.

If, however, we want managers to spend much of their time away from their areas of direct responsibility and authority, in discussions and negotiations with other managers about each other's actions, then arbitrary allocations will motivate this behavior. A useful compromise between these conflicting objectives can perhaps be made. Any arbitrary allocation of costs should be done infrequently, say annually, to signal the need for occasional outside discussions and negotiations. Or, alternatively, the company can report to each operating department the total periodic cost of any common or joint corporate resource, without assigning, as the responsibility of individual operating department managers, arbitrarily carved-up pieces of these common or joint costs. The regular periodic operating reports, however, should be left relatively uncontaminated from data that do not accurately reflect actual resource consumption by operating units.

---

[5] Jeremy Dent, "Tension in the Design of Formal Control Systems: A Field Study in a Computer Company," in *Accounting & Management: Field Study Perspectives*, Robert S. Kaplan and William J. Bruns, Jr. (Boston: Harvard Business School Press, 1987), Chap. 5, pp. 119–45.

Controlling for Differences between Actual and Budgeted Costs

We assume now that we have direct, accurate measures of the consumption of service department output by production departments. Even with a good set of activity measures for each service department, pitfalls await the unwary analyst when attributing service department costs. To illustrate these pitfalls, let us look at an example.

MAXWELL COMPANY

The Maxwell Company has a utility department that provides its three operating departments with power. The three operating departments have the following standard and actual demand for power:

	Operating Department			
	1	2	3	Total
Practical capacity (kwhr)	70,000	100,000	30,000	200,000
Normal activity (kwhr)	60,000	85,000	25,000	170,000
Actual activity in January (kwhr actually used)	60,000	50,000	27,000	137,000
Standard kwhr allowed for output actually produced in January	55,000	50,000	28,000	133,000

At the normal activity level of 170,000 kilowatt-hours, the utility department's standard cost is $8,500. Power costs are budgeted to the operating departments at a rate of $0.05/kwhr to fully recover the utility department's standard cost at normal activity levels. The actual charges to the operating department, however, are done at the end of each month based on the actual cost of the utility department and the actual number of hours used by each operating department. During January, the utility department incurred costs of $8,220. For fluctuations up to 25% on either side of the normal activity level, the variable cost of the utility department is $0.02/kwhr.

As a first pass at analyzing the cost of power to the three operating departments, we compute the variance between actual and budgeted costs for the month of January. During this month, power is billed at a rate of $0.06/kwhr, a figure obtained by dividing the $8,220 actual cost by the actual number of kilowatt-hours, 137,000. For the three departments, we have the following variance report:

	1	2	3	Total
Actual costs (actual kwhr × 0.06)	$3,600	$3,000	$1,620	$8,220
Budgeted costs (allowed standard kwhr × 0.05)	2,750	2,500	1,400	6,650
Variance	$ 850U	$ 500U	$ 220U	$1,570U

where *U* represents an unfavorable variance. Clearly, something is wrong with this scheme. Department 3 has used more than the normal number of kilowatt-hours (which should produce a favorable variance because variable costs are well below full costs) and has actually used less than the standard number of kilowatt-hours for the output it produced—yet it shows an unfavorable variance on power costs.

A clearer picture emerges when the total variance is decomposed into a price variance and a usage (or quantity) variance:

	1	2	3	Total
Price variance:				
Actual kwhr (actual rate − budgeted rate)	$600U	$500U	$270U	$1,370U
Usage variance:				
(Actual kwhr − allowed standard kwhr) × 0.05/kwhr	250U	0	50F	200U
Total variance	$850U	$500U	$220U	$1,570U

We now see that most of the unfavorable variance is caused by the $0.01 increase in the rate per kilowatt-hour charged for power. The manager of Department 3 has been penalized for two factors not ordinarily under his control: (1) the total amount of power consumed by the other two departments and (2) the unit price and efficiency of the utility department. These two uncontrollable factors produce the $270 unfavorable price variance shown for Department 3. Note that if Department 2 had used its normal amount of 85,000 kwhr instead of the 50,000 kwhr it actually used, the cost per kilowatt-hour would have declined significantly for all departments. The fixed costs of the utility department would have been spread over many more actual hours of service. In effect, by working many fewer hours than normal, Department 2 has generated an unfavorable price variance for itself and for the other two departments.

Also contributing to the unfavorable price variance are inefficiencies in the utility department. With variable costs equal to $0.02/kwhr, the reduction in actual number of kilowatt-hours demanded should have reduced costs by

$$(\text{Normal kwhr} - \text{Actual kwhr}) \times \text{Variable cost/kwhr}$$
$$= (170,000 - 137,000) \times 0.02$$
$$= \$660$$

The actual reduction in costs was $8,500 − $8,220 = $280. Thus, a spending or efficiency variance of $660 − $280 = $380 has been incurred in the utility department, which is being passed on to the operating departments through a higher average hourly rate. The present scheme charges a manager for the costs of activities and inefficiencies in departments over which the manager has little or no control. The operating departments are also being charged on an average—rather than marginal—cost basis. Thus, their managers might be turning down profitable opportunities they might have accepted had they known that incremental power cost them $0.02 to $0.03/kwhr rather than the current budgeted figure of $0.05/kwhr.

An improved system for attributing service department costs would have the following characteristics:

1. The level of activity and inefficiency in any single operating department should not affect the evaluation of other operating departments.
2. Efficiencies or inefficiencies in the service department should be reflected in the evaluation of the service department, but not in the evaluation of any operating department.
3. The evaluation of the service department should not be affected by factors beyond its control, such as unanticipated fluctuations in the quantity of service demanded of it.
4. The operating departments should be encouraged to expand the use of the service department as long as the incremental benefits to them exceed the company's marginal cost of supplying the service.
5. The long-term costs of the service department should be paid by the users of its service. If a service department is being used to capacity under the pricing system, this can be viewed as a reliable signal to expand its capacity. If operating departments balk at paying long-run costs, the service activity can be contracted over time or perhaps made more efficient.

One relatively simple scheme achieves most, if not all, of these benefits. We consider a scheme in which

1. Each department is charged for the actual quantities of service department output consumed but at a budgeted service department rate, not a rate computed based on actual costs incurred in the service department.
2. Charges are separated into fixed and variable costs. Under this scheme, each operating department would be charged $0.02/kwhr actually used. The $0.02 figure is the budgeted variable cost of the service department. Charging at this rate reflects the underlying cost driver (kwhr) for the variable cost of the service department.

The fixed costs of the service department can be estimated as

$$\$8,500 - \$0.02(170,000) = \$5,100$$

The allocation of this $5,100 to the operating departments is rather arbitrary but probably useful. It alerts the managers of these departments to the cost of supplying capacity in the power department. It is a reservation price to have access to the relatively low cost ($0.02/kwhr) power on a variable-cost basis. It can also be considered the long-run component of marginal cost.

Long-run planning for the service department requires that its long-run costs be considered. For example, if we are estimating the future maintenance costs of a building about to be constructed, then we must consider the long-run maintenance costs. When considering a short-run decision, however, such as whether to undertake a particular maintenance job, we must consider the short-run costs and benefits of the maintenance. The key idea is that different costs are relevant depending on whether we are making a long-run or a short-run demand on maintenance services. These considerations motivated our recommendation that the fixed costs be assigned to production departments based on planned use and that the variable costs in the pool be attributed to departments based on the quantity of output actually used.[6]

Two reasonable possibilities for assigning the fixed-cost component are (1) proportional to practical capacity and (2) proportional to normal activity levels:

	Department			
	1	*2*	*3*	*Total*
Practical capacity	70K	100K	30K	200K
Percent of total	35%	50%	15%	100%
Assigned fixed costs	$1,785	$2,550	$765	$5,100
Normal activity level	60K	85K	25K	170K
Percent of total	35.3%	50%	14.7%	100%
Assigned fixed cost	$1,800	$2,550	$750	$5,100

In this example, little difference exists between the two assignment bases. In practice, however, we should attempt to use the base that most closely represents the demand for long-run capacity; in effect, try to determine and then select the cost driver for capacity costs.

Under the proposed scheme, and assigning fixed costs based on

---

[6] We deliberately used the word *assigned* rather than *attributed* or *allocated* in describing the fixed-cost charge. One can argue that the cost is attributed because it is a function of a quantity measure—planned usage—known and under the control of the operating manager. Alternatively, one can make the argument that the fixed-cost charge is allocated, since it is not a function of the actual quantity of energy demanded by the operating unit. We prefer to let readers make their own choice between which term is more useful in this circumstance rather than bog our discussion down further in semantic hair-splitting.

normal activity levels, the power department costs charged to the three operating departments in January would be:

1	$1,800 +	60,000($0.02)	=	$3,000	
2	2,550 +	50,000($0.02)	=	3,550	
3	750 +	27,000($0.02)	=	1,290	
Total	$5,100 +	137,000($0.02)	=	$7,840	

The only variance recognized in the operating departments arises from using a nonstandard amount of power for the amount of output produced. In Department 1, 60,000 kwhr were used instead of the standard allowance of 55,000 kwhr. This generates an unfavorable usage variance of (5,000)(0.02) = $100. Department 2 shows a favorable usage variance of $20, since it used 1,000 fewer hours than the standard allowance (1,000 hours at $0.02 = $20). The utility department shows an unfavorable spending (or efficiency) variance of

$$\text{Actual costs} - \text{Budgeted costs at actual volume}$$
$$= \$8,220 - \$7,840 = \$380$$

Note that this method eliminates the influence of rate fluctuations and usage by other departments from the evaluation of services consumed by an individual department. Each production department manager should understand that utility costs being charged to the department are the direct consequences of activities undertaken by and under the control of people in that department. The managers in each operating department will be motivated to use the output from the service department for applications in which the benefit exceeds the $0.02/kwhr short-run variable cost. But the operating managers will still see some of the capacity or longer-run costs of operating the service department through the assigned fixed-cost charge. The manager of the service department will be evaluated on a flexible budget so that his performance will not be affected by fluctuations in demand for his service. Any inefficiencies in the service department will be reflected in a spending variance for the service department and not passed on as higher charges to the operating departments.

By using standard costs that reflect expected performance, consuming departments have a guideline for short-run planning decisions, and service departments will absorb their own short-run production efficiencies or inefficiencies. If, however, the service department faces predictable short-run efficiencies or inefficiencies, perhaps the users of the outputs of the service department should see these cost shifts so that they can respond to the new cost structure. This implies that the short-run standard cost should be modified when actual service department costs are known to have shifted, especially when the resource—such as energy—is critical to the strategic success of the firm.

The Nature and Problems
of Reciprocal Services

If service departments only provided services to production departments, our task in this chapter would be concluded. It would be unusual, however, for multiple service departments to have no interaction among themselves. In general, service departments provide service to other service departments. For example, a personnel department hires and oversees people for all departments in the organization; a utility department provides heat and light to all departments (including itself), a data processing department provides computer services and output to many service departments, a housekeeping department cleans all facilities, and a maintenance department repairs machinery throughout a facility. With such interactions, an analysis that charges all the costs of each service department directly to production departments will not give an accurate picture of cost dependency.

At first glance, it would seem simple to attribute the costs of each service department to all departments that use its output, both production and other service departments. But one soon realizes that once the process begins, exactly what "the costs" of a service department include is no longer clear. Besides the traceable costs incurred, each service department will start to accumulate charges from other service departments from which it receives services, and these must be reassigned back to its user departments.

Three major alternatives have been proposed to deal with this interacting, or reciprocal, service department situation:

1. The direct method (which ignores the reciprocal services)
2. The step method (which has the potential of only partially considering the reciprocal services)
3. The reciprocal method (which models any reciprocal services exactly)

Until the mid-1970s, the direct method was virtually the only method known and used in practice. This situation changed when the CASB proposed that the reciprocal method be used instead of the direct method. The proposal instantly legitimized the reciprocal method as the accurate method. Subsequently, the CASB relented when companies complained that they had neither the expertise nor the computing capability to implement the reciprocal method. The CASB then adopted the step method as an acceptable alternative to the preferred reciprocal method and indicated that the direct method was only permissible if it produced costs that approximated the step method.

During the period when they were reimbursed on the basis of costs incurred, hospitals had elaborate procedures for allocating their support department costs to units that delivered services directly to patients, such as in-patient care, operating rooms, recovery rooms, pharmacy, radiology, and pathology. The traditional step method for allocating support department costs began to be supplanted by the reciprocal method when computing resources became more available to health-care providers. Since the direct and step down methods are straightforward and illustrated in most introductory textbooks, we will deal only with the reciprocal method.

A Numerical Example

FALL RIVER COMPANY

The Fall River Company is organized into four units: Power, Water, Division 1, and Division 2. The Power Department supplies power, generated by steam, to the four units using its equipment and consumes water supplied by the Water Department. The Water Department supplies water to the four units from a private reservoir and its water purification equipment. Division 1 and Division 2 are engaged in the primary manufacturing operations of the firm. The firm's management has dictated that all service department costs must be distributed to the two production divisions.

During the past year, the activities of the two service departments (Power and Water) were as follows:

| | | Units of Service Provided to | | | | |
		Power	Water	Div. 1	Div. 2	Total
Units of service provided from	Power	20,000	30,000	80,000	70,000	200,000
	Water	70,000	10,000	30,000	50,000	160,000

All the costs of the two service departments are assumed to be variable. That is, all the costs vary directly with the number of units of service supplied. Later this example will be extended to consider fixed costs. The variable costs are $3,000,000 in the Power Department and $1,600,000 in the Water Department.

The reciprocal method of cost assignment operates in two steps. The first step considers all service department interactions and computes a charge rate for each service department. In the second step, the charge rate computed in the first step assigns the costs of the service department to each user in proportion to the service levels provided to that user.

The initial objective in the reciprocal method of cost attribution, then, is to find a charge rate for the service departments such that the total charges out of each service department equal the total charges incurred by, and assigned to, each department. In this problem, the required rates are $22.57 for the Power Department and $15.18 for the Water Department.

EXHIBIT 1

Fall River Company—Service Department Cost Assignment: Reciprocal Cost Method

	Power	Water	Div. 1	Div. 2
Initial cost	$3,000,000	$1,600,000	N/A	N/A
Assigned by power*	451,400	677,100	$1,805,600	$1,580,000
Assigned by water*	1,062,700	151,800	455,400	759,000
Assigned out†	−4,514,100	−2,428,900	0	0
Net cost assigned	0	0	$2,261,000	$2,339,000

* Total service units consumed (the quantity measure) multiplied by the charge rate per unit.

† Total service units provided (the quantity measure) multiplied by the charge rate per unit.

(The details of the calculations are provided in Appendix 1.) Exhibit 1 demonstrates that these rates have the property of clearing the internal accounts.

The method of finding the charge rates for the two service departments involves constructing a system of simultaneous equations to represent the interactions between the departments and solving the equations to find the appropriate charge rates. The total cost to be assigned from the Power Department (called the Power Department's reciprocal cost, PDRC) is computed as

$$PDRC = \text{Initial cost incurred} + (20{,}000/200{,}000) * PDRC$$
$$+ (70{,}000/160{,}000) * WDRC$$

where WDRC is the Water Department's reciprocal cost. Note that the reciprocal cost is computed by adding, to the initial cost incurred in the service department, amounts that reflect the Power Department's share of the reciprocal cost of all the service departments including its own.

The above equation cannot be solved, since it contains two unknown variables, PDRC and WDRC. A second, and comparable, equation in the two unknown variables can be written for WDRC:

$$WDRC = \text{Initial cost incurred} + (30{,}000/200{,}000) * PDRC$$
$$+ (10{,}000/160{,}000) * WDRC$$

In general, we would construct one reciprocal cost equation for each service department.

The formulas can be simplified to

$$(0.9) * PDRC - (7/16) * WDRC = 3{,}000{,}000$$
$$-(3/20) * PDRC + (15/16) * WDRC = 1{,}600{,}000$$

When these equations are solved, the reciprocal costs and the indicated charge rates can be computed. Fortunately, it is easy to write a computer program to solve quite large systems of simultaneous linear equations so that we do not have to study how to do the calculations by hand.

The Economic Insights of the Reciprocal Method

To this point, we have developed what seems to be just another approach for assigning service department costs to production departments. What remain to be shown are the unique properties of the reciprocal cost method.

It turns out that the charge rate (for variable costs) per unit of service, computed by the reciprocal method, actually represents the out-of-pocket, or marginal cost, of supplying the service to production departments and other service units. In our numerical example, if the total demand by the production divisions on the Power Department were reduced by one unit, the total variable costs in the system would fall by $22.57. This charge rate, therefore, provides an accurate calculation of the marginal cost of providing the service. If an outside bid to provide this service were received, the computed charge rate would be appropriate to compare with the outside quoted price.

Specifically, if an outside utility offered to provide power at the rate of $21 per service unit, the bid could be accepted (since it is less than the inside incremental cost of $22.57 per service unit). Of course, this analysis assumes that none of the fixed costs of the service facility would be avoidable if the service facility were to be closed. If some of the fixed costs are avoidable, then these costs must be added to the variable cost in order to develop a total cost to compare with the outside quote to provide the service.

In general, neither the step-down method nor the direct method will compute sufficiently accurate service department costs when extensive interactions exist among service departments. The accuracy and relevance of the reciprocal method derives from its recognition of the reciprocal relationship of costs among service departments. Since the Power Department uses such a large part of the output of the Water Department, the cost of supplying an additional unit of power must reflect not only the direct costs incurred in the Power Department but also the indirect costs incurred in the Water Department.

The Treatment of Fixed Costs

To this point, all costs have been assumed to be variable. With the basic model in place, we can now abandon that assumption. But first we must develop two more insights from the information provided by the reciprocal method.

As we argued above, the primary reason for assigning variable and fixed costs separately arises from their different causal factors, or cost drivers. The cost driver for variable cost is short-run usage, while the cost driver for fixed costs is planned long-run usage. Therefore, we require a dual-rate system (one rate for variable costs and one rate for fixed costs) to assign service department costs. Since variable costs are directly attributable to the user demanding the service, it is economically sound and equitable (if that is a consideration) to attribute variable costs on the basis of the actual quantity consumed.

We will assign the fixed costs in proportion to the planned use of capacity. If one division plans to use 20% of the output of a facility, then that division should be assigned 20% of the fixed cost of the facility. While this seems like an arbitrary allocation based on equity principles, an economic basis for this suggestion does exist.[7] This approach, called peak-load pricing, asks users to bear the system costs in proportion to their use of the facility when it is operating at capacity. It has been widely used in utility regulation in North America and Europe.

Thus, when we assign service department costs, we begin by separating the department's costs into fixed and variable components. The variable component will be attributed on the basis of actual usage, and the fixed portion will be allocated (or attributed, depending on your point of view) on the basis of planned usage.

Make-or-Buy Decisions and Cost Assignments

If a service department in a reciprocal services situation is shut down, the number of service units purchased externally will be lower than the current production of the internal service department. When the units of service are purchased outside, the current reciprocal pattern of consumption is altered, since the remaining departments do not have to provide service to the external supplier. In the illustration, the Power Department currently supplies power to the Water Department and consumes water provided by the Water Department. Indirectly, then, the Power Department is consuming some of its own output.

The reciprocal method provides information about the number of outside units of a service that would have to be purchased if internal production were discontinued. In this example, if the firm discontinued internal production of power, 166,000 units of power would have to be purchased externally. If water production were discontinued, the firm would have to purchase 138,333 units externally. (Details of these calculations can be found in Appendix 1.) We can see, then, that the Power

---

[7] See, for example, W. J. Baumol, "Optimal Depreciation Policy: Pricing the Products of Durable Assets," *Bell Journal of Economics and Management Science* (Autumn 1971), pp. 638–56.

Department consumes 34,000 (200,000 − 166,000) units of its own output. If the power were purchased outside, this indirect consumption would be eliminated.

Another piece of information provided by the reciprocal method is a reciprocal factor for each service department. In this example, the reciprocal factor for the Power Department is 1.2048, and the reciprocal factor for the Water Department is 1.1566. The reciprocal factor for a service department tells us how much the total production of the service department will fall if the external demand on the service department is reduced by one unit.

With the knowledge of the outside units required and the reciprocal factor, we can now evaluate the make-or-buy decision. Kaplan[8] showed that the total variable cost avoided when a service department is shut down can be computed as

$$\text{Variable cost avoided} = \frac{\text{Reciprocal cost for Department } i}{\text{Reciprocal factor for Department } i}$$

Applying this rule to the example, the variable cost avoided if the Power Department is shut down equals \$3,746,680.[9]

Next we must consider the fixed cost saved if the department is shut down. Suppose the power-generating facilities can be sold and fixed costs of \$2,000,000 avoided. The total of all costs avoided would be \$5,746,680 (3,746,680 + 2,000,000).

Finally, we can compute the maximum price that we would pay to an external supplier. Since the external number of units required is 166,000, the maximum price the firm would be willing to pay, per unit provided, to an external supplier is \$34.62.[10]

Implementation of the Reciprocal Cost Method

We pointed out earlier that the implementation of the reciprocal method had been delayed because of the computational demands it placed on users. It is easy, however, to program a computer for the calculations. A worksheet (COSTALLO) to perform direct, step-down, and reciprocal cost allocations has been prepared to accompany this chapter so that the reciprocal method can be used even with a modest personal computer. The program only requires that fixed and variable costs be segregated.

---

[8] R. S. Kaplan, "Variable and Self-Service Costs in Reciprocal Allocation Models," *Accounting Review* (October 1973), pp. 738–48.

[9] (4,514,000/1.2048).

[10] (5,746,680/166,000).

Summary

Assigning the costs of service departments to production departments sets up an internal market for the supply and demand of internally produced services. By charging for service departments' output, we can

- Ration demand from user departments
- Provide signals on service department efficiency
- Facilitate comparison with externally supplied service
- Provide opportunities for price-quality trade-offs

When charging for service department costs, a user department's charges should not be affected by activity levels in other user departments or by inefficiencies in the service department. Also, fluctuations in demand by user departments should be charged on a marginal-cost basis. We have proposed the following scheme:

1. Assign any of the costs of a service department that are directly attributable to a specific organization unit to that unit.
2. Assign the remaining costs in the service department to cost pools based on the factor (the cost driver or quantity measure, as we have referred to it here) that causes each cost to vary in that pool. This will mean that costs will be segregated both by function and whether they are fixed or variable.
3. Assign the costs in each cost pool to other organization units based on accurate quantity measures of each organization unit's use, or consumption, of the cost driver.

When budgeted rather than actual costs are used to assign service department costs, cost shifts or inefficiencies will be isolated within the service department and not passed on to production departments.

A special problem arises when service departments provide service to each other as well as to production departments. In this case, the costs of the interacting service departments can be assigned using a simultaneous-equation technique (the reciprocal method). The reciprocal method is essential if we want an accurate estimate of the marginal cost of internally supplied service or when attempting to decide whether to replace an internal service department by purchasing the service externally.

Appendix 1: The Reciprocal Cost Procedure

This appendix provides the algebraic basis for the reciprocal service department assignment procedure described in the chapter. Begin by observing that the reciprocal process can be represented by a system of simultaneous equations defining the reciprocal costs. The equations for the problem discussed in the chapter are repeated here:

$$(0.9) * PDRC - (7/16) * WDRC = 3,000,000$$

$$-(3/20) * PDRC + (15/16) * WDRC = 1,600,000$$

These equations can be expressed in algebraic terms as

$$[I - A] [B] = [C]$$

where the items in brackets represent matrices or vectors. Thus, in this case:

$$[A] = \begin{bmatrix} 2/20 & 7/16 \\ 3/20 & 1/16 \end{bmatrix} \quad [I] = \begin{bmatrix} 1 & 0 \\ 0 & 1 \end{bmatrix} \quad [B] = \begin{bmatrix} PDRC \\ WDRC \end{bmatrix}$$

$$[C] = \begin{bmatrix} 3,000,000 \\ 1,600,000 \end{bmatrix}$$

The $[A]$ matrix indicates the usage proportions. The element in the ith row and jth column of this matrix represents the fraction of the total output of service department j consumed by service department i. The $[I]$ matrix is an identity matrix. The $[B]$ vector is the vector of reciprocal costs. The $[C]$ vector is the vector of variable costs initially recorded in each of the service divisions. We can solve for matrix $[B]$ by observing that

$$[B] = [I - A]^{-1}[C]$$

where $[I - A]^{-1}$ is the inverse of matrix $[I - A]$, if one exists. This point, incidentally, is where the computer is useful. Functions that compute inverses are provided in most programming languages.[11] In the case of the example in the chapter:

$$[I - A]^{-1} = \begin{bmatrix} 1.2048 & 0.5623 \\ 0.1928 & 1.1566 \end{bmatrix}$$

and

$$[B] = \begin{bmatrix} 4,514,056 \\ 2,428,915 \end{bmatrix}$$

---

[11] In fact, some popular worksheet packages, such as Lotus 1-2-3, provide the facility to invert matrices.

The numbers on the main diagonal (the line running from the upper left to the lower right) of the $[I - A]^{-1}$ matrix provide the reciprocal factors that is useful for decision making. There is, by construction, one reciprocal factor on the main diagonal for each of the service departments. In the case of our example, the first factor, 1.2048, relates to the Power Department and the second factor, 1.1566, relates to the Water Department. These are the reciprocal factors.

If the reciprocal (variable) cost of a service department is divided by its associated reciprocal factor, we obtain the cost avoided if that department is shut down. Moreover, if the number of units of service currently provided by a service department is divided by the department's reciprocal factor, we obtain the number of units required if the service is acquired externally. The charge rate per unit of service provided by the service department is given by the ratio of the department's reciprocal cost divided by the number of units of service provided. Thus, the charge rate for the Power Department equals 4,515,056/200,000 = \$22.57.

As we have seen in the example, the cost to be assigned to the production division equals the product of the service department's charge rate and the number of units of service provided to the division. The indicated assignment can also be obtained by extending the algebraic model developed above. Define a matrix $[D]$ such that the element in the ith row and the jth column represents the fraction of the total output of service department i consumed by production division j. Then $[E]$, the vector of service department costs to be assigned to the production divisions, is given by

$$[E] = [B]^T[D]$$

where $[B]^T$ is the transpose of the vector of the reciprocal costs.

In the case of the example:

$$[B]^T = [4{,}514{,}056 \quad 2{,}428{,}915]$$

$$[D] = \begin{bmatrix} 80{,}000/200{,}000 & 70{,}000/200{,}000 \\ 30{,}000/160{,}000 & 50{,}000/160{,}000 \end{bmatrix}$$

$$[E] = [2{,}261{,}044 \quad 2{,}338{,}956]$$

This means that a total of \$2,261,044 of the service department costs is assigned to Division 1, and \$2,338,956 is assigned to Division 2.

The analysis can easily be extended to any number of service and production departments.

PROBLEMS

7–1   Allocating Central Service Department Costs

"I can't believe it. We just went through a study showing how my department could save money by using the central data processing facility. But the first month using this facility shows that my costs are up more than 20 percent." Don Thompson, the general manager of the Delta Division of ABC Products, had just received his monthly bill from the Data Processing Service Division and he was obviously upset.

Prior to converting to the central facility, the Delta Division had used outside vendors for its data processing services, at a cost of $15,000 per month. An internal task force, investigating the use of outside services that were also available internally, had found that all the data processing needs of the Delta Division could be handled internally. At present, there was time available at the central computing facility and the services required by Delta could be supplied at an incremental cost of $10,000. After some assurance that his division's data processing services could be supplied at this lower incremental cost, Don Thompson agreed to convert from external to internal supply of services.

After receiving a monthly bill for more than $18,000 from the Data Processing Division, Thompson demanded an explanation. Phil Johnson, the manager of Data Processing, provided the following data. Table 1 shows

TABLE 1

Division	CPU Minutes	Percentage	Allocated Costs
Able	6,000	50%	$ 60,000
Baker	4,000	33%	40,000
Carter	2,000	17%	20,000
	12,000	100%	$120,000

the allocation of the monthly data processing costs of $120,000 to the three other divisions of ABC Products, prior to handling Delta's requirements: As Johnson explained, "We have to charge out the costs of our division in some equitable manner. We've decided that an allocation based on CPU minutes used is as good as any." Johnson then showed (see Table 2) how the allocation to Delta was derived based on incremental costs of $10,000 and the 2,000 CPU minutes required to provide the data processing services to Delta.

TABLE 2

Division	CPU Minutes	Percentage	Allocated Costs
Able	6,000	42.9%	$ 55,700
Baker	4,000	28.6%	37,100
Carter	2,000	14.3%	18,600
Delta	2,000	14.3%	18,600
	14,000	100%	$130,000

Required:

1. Comment on the method used by Johnson to charge for the use of data processing services in ABC Products. Why does this method cause Delta's charges to increase from $15,000 to $18,600 per month?
2. Suggest alternative methods for charging for the use of this internal service department that would provide better incentives for use of this department.

7–2 Allocating Service Department Costs— Fixed and Variable; Actual and Budgeted

"I get overcharged by the Printing Department each month," declared Bud Perles, the manager of the Greene Company's Advertising Department. "Even though my usage is down during the month, the total amount I have to pay keeps going up. The work done by our Printing Department is certainly high quality, but if these charges keep escalating, I'm going to start taking my business to outside printers."

The Printing Department of the Greene Company provides services to many departments throughout the company. The cost budget for the Printing Department at a normal volume of 800 service hours, as well as the actual expenses for September (when 700 hours were actually used) appears below:

	Budget at 800 hours		Actual in September
	Amount	Fixed (F) or Variable (V)	
Labor	$10,000	V	$ 9,000
Supervision	2,000	F	2,000
Indirect labor	3,000	V	2,800
Supplies	11,000	V	10,500
Depreciation	6,000	F	6,200
Rent	4,000	F	4,500
Total	$36,000		$35,000

Depreciation charged each month is a fixed percentage of the original cost of equipment installed in the Printing Department. The rental charge is an allocated share of total monthly building costs. The allocation is proportional to the space occupied by each department.

The cost of the Printing Department is charged to other users on the basis of average *actual* departmental costs during the month multiplied by the number of printing hours used during the month.

The Advertising Department of the Green Company is a heavy user of the Printing Department's services. Normally the department uses 100 hours each month from the Printing Department, but during September it used 95 hours. The quote at the beginning of the problem was made when Bud Perles received his bill for September usage from the Printing Department.

Required:

1. Compute the budgeted charge to the Advertising Department at normal volume. Also compute what the budgeted charge would be if the Advertising Department uses 95 hours in a month (assume that total demand for the Printing Department remains constant at the budgeted 800 hours).
2. Compute the actual charge from the Printing Department to the Advertising Department during September.
3. Analyze the difference between what Advertising might have expected to pay at its normal volume of 100 hours, from what it actually had to pay for the 95 hours it used during September. Indicate who is responsible for various differences between budgeted and actual costs.
4. Comment on any changes you would recommend in charging for the Printing Department.
5. Alice Deming, the manager of the Printing Department, responds to Perles's criticism: "We do the best we can in controlling our costs, but it has been difficult because the number of hours we've been working has decreased over the past several years. At the same time, however, we've had to acquire more expensive and sophisticated printing equipment to handle the requests being made by the Advertising Department. That department has been a heavy user of these machines which the other departments in the company hardly use. If anything, we should charge the Advertising Department more for our services." How did this situation develop and should a change in the pricing method for the Printing Department's services be made in light of this new information?

7–3 Allocating Fixed Costs of Central Facility

Squirrel Hill Distributors is a decentralized firm specializing in the distribution of consumer products. The firm is divided into three operating divisions along the major product lines: Tru-Fit Hardware Supplies, Mudd Beauty Products, and Atomo Lighting Fixtures.

$$2.46 \times .04 = \qquad\qquad .0984$$
$$0.96 \times 1.00 = \qquad\qquad .9600$$
$$(100 \times 2.46) \times .0016 = \qquad .3936$$
$$1665 \times .0002 \qquad\qquad \underline{.3330}$$

Equivalent Accounting Minutes   1.7850

Cost/Job = 1.785 × $2.10 = $3.75

EXHIBIT 3

Laughton Service Corporation
Calculation of Cost Per Accounting Minute in August 1971

Cost Component	Monthly Anticipated Use	Weighting	Total Accounting Minutes
Elapsed Time on Computer (Minutes)[1]	243,000	.04	9,720
CPU TIME (Minutes)[2]	40,500	1.00	40,500
Charge/1K Core Used Per Minute[3]	14,515,000	.0016	23,220
Accesses (Disk, Tape, Print, Read)	105,000,000	.0002	21,000
Total Weighting Points			94,440

[1] 3 processors running 450 hours/month (27,000 min) each with an average of 3 Programs in Internal Memory.

[2] 3 processors running 450 hours/month with 50% CPU use by Application Programs.

[3] 3 processors each with 256 K core assuming a 70% average Internal Memory use by Application Programs

Total Computer Operations Cost	$198,320
Total Accounting Minutes	94,440
Cost/Accounting Minute	$2.10

Mr. Allen's proposal was explained to the head of the other divisions where it met with immediate and strong opposition. First to express disapproval were the heads of other divisions that had work totaling the following amounts done by the Computer Operations Department each month.

	Elapsed Time	CPU Time	Core Utilization Ave/Elapsed Min	No. of Accesses
Accounts Service Division	2,000 minutes	400 min.	30K	1,000,000
Economic Services Division	800	30	90K	101,000
Business Services Division	4,000	400	20K	280,000

These managers thought it was unfair to change a sizeable part of their department's costs, especially since they had no control over the cost incurred in the Computer Operations Department.

Mr. Ahearn, manager of the Accounts Services Division, was very much against the proposal: "The computer department does the basic processing for all the data handled by my department. If you raise my costs on this work, I'll never be able to stay within my budget, because the computer department is already charging me more than I could do the work for in my own department."

The sales manager of the Economic Services Division was also against the proposal: "If you start monkeying around with our cost system, we'll have to start changing our prices, and we're having enough trouble with price competition from the major companies as it is. After all, our complete service bureau line is showing a profit. You have to carry some items for sales reasons regardless of their profitability, so why worry about the very small variation in cost between different items."

The head of the payroll department of the Business Services Division also opposed the change: "I'm too busy to fool with more paper work. It takes all my time to get the product out without trying to keep up with this stuff, section by section. And my supervisors in the sections don't have time for it either. The department is carrying all its costs now, so why put in an extra gimmick?"

Mr. Dennison remained neutral on the question. He was most interested in whether or not the added cost and trouble of the proposed system would be justified by the benefits the system would give.

Required:

1. What is the difference in the cost of the Bank Deposit run under the proposed method as compared with that under the present method? In value of scientific work? In the cost work done for other divisions? Are these cost differences significant?
2. What causes the difference in cost given by the proposed method as compared with the present method?
3. Suppose that the company upgraded because of peak period difficulty to a faster central processor increasing monthly costs by $10,000. As a result, the total CPU time would be reduced by 30% (elapsed time by about 10%). Operations expense is directly variable with elapsed time and about 20% of the burden is variable with respect to CPU time.
   a. Calculate what the total cost per CPU/minute would be after the new CPU's are in operation if there were only one cost allocation in the Computer Operations Department. Assume that the job stream and other factors are the same in August in all other respects.
   b. Calculate what the total cost per hour would be if Mr. Allen's more disaggregated approach were adopted.

c. What would happen to the computed cost per month of producing Bank Deposits with a single cost center, after upgrading the CPU's as compared with the cost before the upgrade? For the scientific programs?

d. What would happen to the computed costs per month of Bank Deposits with Mr. Allen's new approach after upgrading the CPU as compared with the cost before the upgrading? For the scientific programs?

e. What do you conclude about the relative usefulness of the two methods (single charge rate versus a compound charge rate)?

4. What management benefits, if any, would you expect from the proposed system? Consider this question from the standpoint of (a) product pricing, (b) cost control, (c) charges to other departments. Do you think these benefits would outweigh the cost of collection of the necessary data?

7–10   *Allocating Costs in a Joint Venture**
(Edward Deakin)

Eastern Refineries, Ltd.

In 1966 American Oil Corporation and United Petroleum (two large integrated petroleum companies) entered into an agreement to construct and operate a petroleum fuels refinery in the Far East. A corporation named Eastern Refineries Limited was formed to operate the refinery. At the time the agreement was drawn up, American provided 70 percent of the capital while United provided 30 percent.

The sponsoring companies received capital stock in Eastern in proportion to the capital provided by them.

The Refinery

A refinery processes crude oil through various heat, pressure, and chemical operations to extract as much gasoline from the crude as possible. Other products such as sulphur, kerosene, distillate fuels, and asphalt are produced as byproducts. A certain quantity of fuel extracted from the crude is used to provide the heat necessary to operate the refinery as well as to provide heat and power for the refinery administrative and service support functions.

The original Eastern fuels refinery consisted of five principal processing units as diagrammed in Exhibit 1. Crude oil was shipped to the refinery and piped to the crude splitter. This unit separates the crude oil into two products: "Overheads" which consist of the lighter fractions from

---

* Copyright 1982 by CIPT Co. Reproduced with permission.

EXHIBIT 1
Flow of Product Through the Eastern Fuels Refinery

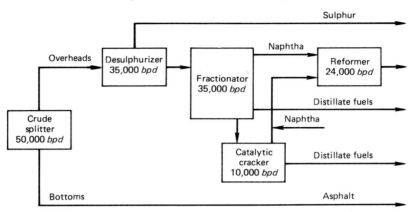

the crude, and "Bottoms" which contain the heavier fractions. Bottoms have relatively little energy content and are, therefore, usually sold as asphalt with very little further processing.

The overheads contain naphtha, a very light fraction; fuel oil, an intermediate product, and sulphur. Some overheads are immediately usable as refinery outputs. Others must flow through the remaining system. Sulphur is removed before the overheads are processed into finished products. A desulphurization unit extracts the sulphur from the overheads. The remaining overhead flow is then distilled in the fractionator. The products with the lower boiling point (i.e., the lighter fractions) vaporize as the temperature in the fractionator equals the boiling point of the respective fraction. The vaporized fractions are then cooled and return to their liquid state.

Naphtha, one of the lighter fractions, is used to make gasoline. With the use of heat and pressure in the reformer unit, naphtha is converted into gasoline. The remaining fractions are then directed to the catalytic cracker. This unit employs chemical and heat processes to convert some of the heavier materials from the fractionator into the more valuable naphthas. The naphthas from the catalytic cracker are then processed through the reformer in the same manner as the naphthas from the fractionator. The remaining output from the catalytic cracker is sold as distillate fuel products such as kerosene, jet fuel, and heating oil.

Refinery Investment Costs

The costs to construct the initial refinery totalled $60 million. These initial costs were related to different units and support functions as follows:

Unit	Investment Cost ($000)
Crude Splitter	$10,000
Desulphurizer	6,000
Fractionator	13,000
Catalytic Cracker	15,000
Reformer	9,000
Administrative, support and other	7,000
TOTAL	$60,000

The sponsoring companies entered into a contract for the processing of crude oil through the refinery. Each sponsor was permitted to utilize the refinery capacity to process crude oil in the same ratio as its equity investment. Thus, American was permitted to process 35,000 barrels per day (70 percent of 50,000 bpd capacity). The refinery does not take title to the crude it processes, but rather acts as a processing service which receives the crude, processes it and delivers the end products to each processor. To recover its costs, the refinery charges a processing fee to each of the sponsors. The processing fee consists of a variable charge based on the crude oil actually processed during a period plus a fixed charge based on the sponsor's share of refinery capacity.

Certain operating and cost data related to refinery processing during the years 1980 and 1981 are shown in Table 1.

Expansion Proposal

American had been utilizing close to its share of capacity for several years. Indeed, to supply all of its customers in the market area served by this refinery, it was necessary to import finished distillate fuels from other, distant refining facilities. On occasion, to supply its customers, the company was required to purchase distillate fuels on the spot market.

As a result of market conditions, company management proposed that parts of the Eastern refinery be expanded. The expansion would provide additional distillate fuels for American's local needs and, in addition, would provide naphthas which could be transported to another American refinery for further processing. There would be a net reduction in the company's transportation costs as a result of the savings in distillate fuels transportation. As a result of this, and by eliminating the need to make spot market purchases, American management estimated it could obtain net after tax cash savings of $2,500,000 in each of the estimated twenty years' life of the refinery expansion. The return on investment for the project was quite high because the project could utilize the tankage, wharf and piping systems that were already in place at the refinery site.

According to the agreement between the sponsors of Eastern, any sponsor could request that the refinery company construct an expansion

TABLE 1
Summary Operating and Cost Data (000 omitted)

	1981	1980
Crude processed (barrels):		
American	12,700	12,775
United	4,100	4,050
Total	16,800	16,825
Variable Costs:		
American	$3,061	$2,965
United	1,008	954
Total	$4,069	$3,919
Fixed Costs:		
American	$6,510	$6,447
United	2,790	2,763
Total	$9,300	$9,210
Products Delivered:		
American		
Gasoline (bbls)	6,126	6,103
Distillate Fuels (bbls)	2,780	2,759
Sulphur (tons)	16	16
Asphalt (bbls)	417	408
United		
Gasoline (bbls)	2,362	2,376
Distillate Fuels (bbls)	591	597
Sulphur (tons)	7	8
Asphalt (bbls)	134	136

or modification to increase the maximum capacity of the refinery. If one of the sponsors proposed an expansion, it had to advise the other sponsor of the nature of the project, the estimated investment costs of the project together with an estimate of the fixed costs that would arise from the expansion. The other sponsor could elect to join in the project or could decline. If this sponsor declined participation the expansion could still be conducted, but all of the investment costs would then be charged to the sponsor that proposed the expansion.

The agreement between the sponsors further provided that any such expansion would become a part of the refinery but that the sponsor who financed the expansion would receive the exclusive right to use the expansion. In addition, appropriate adjustments were to be made to the accounting procedures to reflect the existence of the expansion and to make certain that neither party was adversely affected by the expansion. The definition of "appropriate adjustments" was not specified in the agreement.

In 1980, American submitted a proposal to expand the crude splitter, desulphurizer and fractionator. Summary data concerning the estimated incremental costs, investment required and capacity expansions for the units are shown in Table 2. Information concerning American's estimated cash savings from the project were not disclosed because those data are proprietary.

TABLE 2
Proposal for Expansion Units to Be Expanded: Crude Splitter, Desulphurizer, and Fractionator

	Expansion Details (dollars in thousands) Crude Splitter	Desulphurizer	Fractionator
Incremental Capacity	30,000 bpd	10,000 bpd	10,000 bpd
Projected Costs of Investment	$4,000	$800	$2,200
Projected Incremental Fixed Costs (Per Year)	$ 300	$100	$ 150

After reviewing the proposal, United notified Eastern that it did not wish to participate. United objected to Eastern's construction of the proposed expansion on the grounds that it would suffer a reduced ability to compete with American should American obtain the proposed additional ability to produce distillate fuels.

American agreed to finance all of the costs of the expansion and to pay the fixed costs of the expansion. The expansion was constructed for the investment costs shown in Table 2. The new units were placed in service at the start of 1982.

At the end of 1982, a report of operating and cost data was prepared. This report is reproduced in Table 3. The fixed costs included $9,500,000 attributed to the original refinery plus $560,000 considered related to the expansion.

Upon receipt of this statement, United immediately objected to the allocation of fixed costs. In a memorandum to the Board of Directors of the refinery, United management stated:

As you know, we objected to the expansion of this refinery because we believed such an expansion was not in the best interest of the refinery and would be harmful to our competitive position in the local market.

Our agreement calls for the allocation of fixed costs on the basis of the maximum capacity of the Eastern refinery. Whereas we previously had 30 percent of that maximum capacity and paid 30 percent of the fixed costs, we now only have 18.75 percent of that capacity. However, you have charged us 28.3 percent of the total fixed costs. Our share of the fixed costs should not exceed 18.75 percent and we request an immediate adjustment to our account.

We note that under your allocation scheme our fixed costs per barrel amounted to $.74 this year but the fixed costs allocated to Amer-

Table 3
Summary Operating and Cost Data
(000 omitted)

	1982
Crude processed (barrels):	
American	23,750
United	3,840
Total	27,590
Variable Costs:	
American	$ 5,556
United	1,150
Total	$ 6,705
Fixed Costs:	
American	$ 7,210
United	2,850
Total	$10,060
Products delivered:	
American:	
Gasoline (barrels)	6,128
Distillate (barrels)	6,320
Sulphur (tons)	25
Asphalt (barrels)	830
Naphthas (barrels)	3,975
United:	
Gasoline (barrels)	2,337
Distillate (barrels)	610
Sulphur (tons)	7
Asphalt (barrels)	133

ican only amounted to $.30. This disparity clearly demonstrates that
your method of allocation is incorrect.

Finally, it is apparent that the wharf and related facilities which
we helped construct is being utilized to a much greater extent now
that American is processing a greater share of the refinery throughput.
We believe that American should be required to reimburse us for the
difference between our 30 percent investment in the wharf and our
usage which this year only amounted to 13.9 percent.

We trust this matter can be resolved promptly at the next meeting
of the Board.

The Chairman of the Board of Eastern has directed this memorandum
to the Controller's Office with the following comment:

The points raised in this letter will be discussed at next week's meeting
of the Board. It is imperative that we straighten this out at once. The
points appear logical, and I hope that any error in your office can be
corrected.

What is the amount by which they appear to have been over-charged? How would their method affect the economic viability of the expansion? What accounting principles did you use in arriving at your method of allocation?

Required:

The controller has asked you to prepare a draft of a response to the Chairman of the Board together with any supporting schedules or documents that would be required. Your response should address each of the points raised in the letter from United.

chapter 8

JOINT COSTS

Joint products arise whenever a single resource or process produces more than one output. Examples of joint products are the various cuts of beef produced when a steer is processed (steaks, roasts, hamburger), the products yielded by refining a barrel of crude oil (naphtha, benzene, gasoline, fuel oil), and the capital costs of an asset (which are joint to all the years over which the asset is used). We are in a joint-cost situation when an intermediate or final product cannot be produced without also producing, simultaneously, all the other joint products. The production of the joint products may be in fixed proportions (the proportion of each joint product produced cannot be changed) or in variable proportions (the amount of each joint product produced can vary under the control of the decision-maker). The joint cost of such a process equals the cost of acquiring and processing the initial resource until the joint products are split off to be sold separately or processed separately.

The discussion in Chapter 7 argued that attributing service department costs to user departments helped the persons demanding the services to understand the costs of providing these services. Also, the cost of the services could be reflected in the total costs of products.

Joint-cost allocation is not a process of cost attribution. Cost allocation is an **arbitrary** assignment of costs that **cannot** be attributed to individual products. To reinforce the difference in meaning between **attribution** and **allocation,** we say that we can **attribute** the joint cost of producing the joint products to the entire collection of joint products, but we can only **allocate** the joint cost to any individual product.

Some of the greatest controversies in accounting concern the treatment of joint costs. Joint costs need not be allocated to the individual joint products in order to determine the optimal amount of the initial resource to process into joint products. Therefore, economists have questioned the need to perform any joint-cost allocation, particularly in a decision-oriented, management accounting context. But, in practice, joint-cost allocations are pervasive. Two credible reasons may help to explain the persistence of joint-cost allocations:

1. To provide the product valuations required for financial accounting and other regulatory purposes
2. To coordinate the activities of decision makers in a decentralized firm

In this chapter, we will discuss these two justifications for joint-cost allocations and their implications for the types of cost allocations that might prove useful.

Inventory Valuation

Financial accounting requirements place only loose restrictions on cost allocation processes. Even these broad guidelines, however, have some interesting implications and economic interpretations.

For example, the doctrine of conservatism in financial accounting provides that the cost assigned to an asset for financial statement purposes should not exceed the value of the asset. This rule helps to prevent situations where assets of firms are overstated. When we apply the lower-of-cost-or-market rule to joint products, the rule implies that the costs allocated to the joint products should not exceed the value of the joint products. Of course, this condition will hold whenever the initial resource giving rise to the joint products has been acquired in an economically rational manner.

This reasonably simple financial accounting rule suggests that the joint-cost allocation could be based on the relative value of each product. Such a procedure should ensure that the joint cost allocated to a particular product will never exceed the product's market value. While this simple observation does not define a unique approach to joint-cost allocation, it does cut down rather significantly on the number of alternatives to be considered.

Cost allocation based on physical units appears to be the method most commonly used in practice. That is, joint costs are allocated to the joint products in proportion to the number of units of the joint products that are produced. For example, both the weighted-average method of inventory valuation and process costing rely on the physical units approach to cost allocation. While the simplicity of this method is its main virtue, its major defect is that the costs allocated to individual products may exceed the market value of the products. Not only does this allocation violate a financial reporting convention (that the inventory cost should be less than market) but many unfortunate decision-making contexts can also arise.

For example, when the cost allocated to a joint product exceeds its market value, managers frequently allow the product to pile up in inventory. Were the joint product to be sold, a loss would be reported on the sales of that product, which, in turn, would adversely affect the managers' rewards. Therefore, the managers leave the allocated cost suspended in inventory, incurring implicit holding costs, rather than release the cost to the income statement by selling the joint product for the market price.

The net-realizable-value (NRV) method, while not the most popular method used in practice, is at least consistent with the financial accounting guideline. The NRV rule can be explained using the following example.

ERB MANUFACTURING CORPORATION

The Erb Manufacturing Corporation manufactures two chemicals using the following simple process:

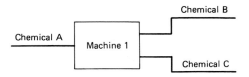

The cost of chemical A per batch in machine 1 is $500. In addition, the cost per batch to process A through machine 1 is $700. Each batch from machine 1 yields 20 units of chemical B, which have a net realizable value of $1,500, and 10 units of chemical C, which have a net realizable value of $1,000.

The production process is economically desirable, since the net realizable value of chemicals B and C ($2,500) exceeds the total joint cost of $1,200 to operate machine 1. No joint-cost allocation of the $1,200 to chemicals B and C is required to reach this conclusion.

The net-realizable-value method of cost allocation would allocate the joint costs as follows:

$$\text{To chemical B:} \quad \frac{1,500}{2,500} * 1,200 = \$720$$

$$\text{To chemical C:} \quad \frac{1,000}{2,500} * 1,200 = \$480$$

The net realizable value becomes more complicated when one or more of the joint products can be processed before being sold. For example, suppose chemical C can be sold as it leaves machine 1, or, alternatively, it can be passed through machine 2 at an incremental cost of $2,000. Each batch of 10 units of chemical C processed through machine 2 produces 10 units of chemical D with a net realizable value of $1,000 and 20 units of chemical E with a net realizable value of $2,500.

The manufacturing process now appears as follows:

are not mandated or regulated. Perhaps the cost allocations serve to approximate the long-run cost of resources so that in a large, decentralized firm, where many alternative uses for a joint product exist, the decision-making process can be decomposed and simplified. In this context, managers use the cost allocation as a signal to coordinate and evaluate the resource allocation process.

PROBLEMS

8–1 Joint-Cost Allocations and Processing a Product Further

The Spencer Company processes a basic chemical through a manufacturing process that yields three intermediate substances. Each of these three substances is processed further into final products designated product A, product B, and product C. At present, 1,000,000 pounds of the basic chemical are processed each year into 500,000 pounds of A, 300,000 pounds of B, and 200,000 pounds of C. The manufacturing process always produces these three outputs in fixed proportions (10 pounds of chemical will produce 5 pounds of A, 3 pounds of B, and 2 pounds of C. The budgeted product-line income statement for next year is shown in Table 1.

TABLE 1
Product Line Income Statement

	A	B .	C	Total
Pounds produced	500K	300K	200K	1,000K
Selling price/pound	$1.20	$ .70	$1.50	
Revenues	$600K	$210K	$300K	$1,110
Manufacturing process cost	$250K	$150K	$100K	$500K
Incremental costs of further processing (all variable)	$120K	90K	100K	310K
Net income	$230	$(30K)	$100K	$300K
(Cost per pound	$0.74	$0.80	$1.00)	

Required:

1. What technique is being used to allocate the cost of the initial manufacturing process?
2. The treasurer of Spencer Company points out that product B should not be processed and sold, since it shows a loss of $.10 per pound. Do you agree? Be sure to give your reasons.

3. A recently hired analyst from the controller's department recalls that the net realizable value method can be used to allocate joint costs and that this method provides costs indicative of the relative revenue generating capability of products. Prepare a budgeted product-line income statement for the three products using the net realizable value method for allocating the $500K manufacturing cost.

4. Product C can be processed further to yield a new product, called product D, that sells for $2.40 per pound. From 200,000 pounds of product C, we can obtain 150,000 pounds of product D at an additional processing cost of $75,000. The marketing manager advocates promoting product D because of its higher margin. Should the Spencer Company shift its activities from selling product C to selling product D? How does the cost of $1.00 per pound of C in Table 1, or the cost you derived in requirement 3, help you in this analysis?

5. The Spencer Company has an opportunity for a special order next year for product A. The order will be for 200,000 pounds of A at a price of $1.10 per pound. Since this is above the cost of producing product A (see Table 1), management will likely accept the order. Do you agree? Briefly give your reasons and analysis.

6. (Ignore previous requirements of this problem.)

   Suppose that each product line in its uncompleted state (after the joint manufacturing process) can be either sold immediately after split-off or processed further. Each product requires a different amount of processing time on a common resource to obtain the finished form. Details are shown below:

	Product Lines		
	A	B	C
Pounds produced	500K	300K	200K
Selling price per unit of unfinished product	$0.40	$0.30	$0.60
Unit cost of further processing (all variable)	$0.24	$0.30	$0.50
Rate of processing	10 lbs/hour	100 lbs/hour	5 lbs/hour
Selling price per unit of finished product	$1.20	$0.70	$1.50

To produce all three finished products will require 93,000 hours of resource time:

Product	Pounds	Processing Rate per Hour	Total Hours Required
A	500K	10 lbs.	50K
B	300K	100 lbs.	3K
C	200K	5 lbs.	40K
			93K

If less than 93,000 hours of resource time are available, how should the Spencer Company decide on which products to finish and which to sell in the unfinished state? Be as specific as you can using the data provided.

8–2   Joint Cost Allocations and Product Decisions

The Thompson Company processes 10 pounds of Material X in Department 1 to yield 4 pounds of product A and 2 pounds of product B. Product A can either be sold at the split-off point as A* or be processed further in Department 2 and sold as A'. Similarly, product B can either be sold at the split-off as B* or be processed further in Department 3 and sold as B'.

Product X costs $2 per pound. The costs of operating Departments 1, 2, and 3 are:

	Department		
	1	*2*	*3*
Fixed costs	$80,000/month	—	—
Variable costs	$1/lb. of X	$6/lb. of A	$4/lb. of B

Also: Selling Price

A*	$8/lb.
A'	15/lb.
B*	7/lb.
B'	10/lb.

At present, only 80,000 pounds of material X are available each month: all of this is processed in Department 1. All of intermediate products A and B are processed further and sold as A' and B'. A product-line profit analysis appears below.

	Profit Statement	
	A'	*B'*
Selling price	$15	$10
Processing costs	6	4
	$ 9	$ 6
Joint costs	7.5	5
Profit/lb	$ 1.5	$ 1.0

Required:

1. What method is being used to allocate the cost of acquiring and processing material X?
2. What is the monthly profit being earned by Thompson? Is Thompson earning the maximum possible profit from its operations?

3. Product A' can be processed further to yield a new product, called product C, that sells for $25 per pound. From 32,000 pounds of A' we can obtain 20,000 pounds of C with incremental processing costs of $40,000. The marketing manager advocates promoting product C because of its higher price. Should Thompson shift its activities from selling product A' to selling product C?

4. (Ignore the option in requirement 3.) Suppose Departments 1, 2, and 3 require processing time on a common resource. The resource is such that the following production rates are achievable: 20 lbs. of X per hour, 8 lbs. of A per hour, 10 lbs. of B per hour. Only one product at a time can be processed on this resource, and a maximum of 6,000 hours of resource time are available each month. Show how the Thompson Company can determine a product mix that will maximize its profits.

8–3   *Joint-Cost Processes and Linear Programming*

Dartmouth Chemical manufactures chemicals used in the resource extraction industry. The production operation consists of two main processes as follows:

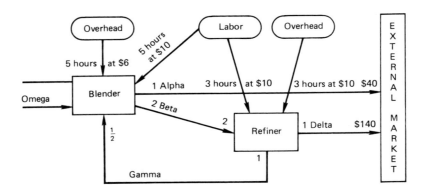

In the blender, ½ gallon of Gamma, 2 gallons of Omega at $12 per gallon are combined with 5 labor-hours at $10 per hour, and 5 overhead hours at $6 per hour to produce 1 gallon of Alpha and 2 gallons of Beta.

Alpha is sold in the external market for $40 per gallon.

Beta is used internally in the refiner to produce Delta and Gamma. In the refiner 2 gallons of Beta, 3 labor-hours at $10 per hour, and 3 hours of overhead at $10 per hour are combined to produce 1 gallon of Delta and 1 gallon of Gamma.

Delta is sold in the external market for $140 per gallon.
There is no external market for Gamma or Beta.

Since the chemicals are unstable and cannot be stored for any prolonged period, in the past excess stocks of Gamma and Beta have been
dumped, surreptitiously, in a local swamp.

Elmo Slack, the factory analyst, recently developed the following analysis to model the firm's operations.

Notation

$$x_1 \text{ units of activity of blender}$$
$$x_2 \text{ units of activity of refiner}$$
$$x_3 \text{ units of Alpha produced and sold}$$
$$x_4 \text{ units of Delta produced and sold}$$

Costs

The out-of-pocket cost per unit of activity of x_1:

Cost of Omega:	2 gallons at $12 =	$ 24
Labor:	5 hours at $10 =	50
Overhead:	5 hours at $ 6 =	30
		$104

The out-of-pocket cost per unit of activity of x_2:

Labor:	3 hours at $10 =	$30
Overhead:	3 hours at $10 =	30
		$60

Objective Function

$$\text{Max} - 104x_1 - 60x_2 + 40x_3 + 140x_4$$

Constraints

				Associated Dual Variable
a.	Alpha:		$x_1 \geq x_3$	
		OR	$-x_1 + x_3 \leq 0$	(y_1)
b.	Beta:		$2x_1 \geq 2x_2$	
		OR	$-2x_1 + 2x_2 \leq 0$	(y_2)
c.	Delta:		$x_2 \geq x_4$	
		OR	$-x_2 + x_4 \leq 0$	(y_3)
d.	Gamma		$x_2 \geq \frac{1}{2}x_1$	
		OR	$.5x_1 - x_2 \leq 0$	(y_4)

In addition, it was discovered that a maximum of 368 labor hours are available per period.

e. Labor $5x_1 + 3x_2 \leq 368 \ (y_5)$

Elmo solved the linear program and obtained the following optimal solution.

$$x_1 = 46 \qquad y_1 = 40$$
$$x_2 = 46 \qquad y_2 = 37$$
$$x_3 = 46 \qquad y_3 = 140$$
$$x_4 = 46 \qquad y_4 = 0$$
$$y_5 = 2$$

Excess Gamma $= 23$.

Required:

1. Explain the meaning of this solution. If there are any interrelationships among the marginal values, explain them. Are there any accounting applications suggested by these relationships?
2. Charlie Nelson, the company president, reports that local citizen groups are getting suspicious about the firm's disposal operations and are prepared "to make trouble for Dartmouth Chemical."
    The company has only two alternatives for disposal:
    a. A contractor has been found who can reclaim Gamma for use as a weed killer. This contractor will take, if paid $6 per gallon, all the Gamma that Dartmouth Chemical wishes to dispose of.
    b. Use 1 gallon of Gamma, 1 gallon of Alpha, 1 gallon of Beta, 1 hour in the refiner process, and 1 labor-hour to produce 3 gallons of a new product which will sell for $30 per gallon.
    What is the cost to the firm of producing three gallons of the new product? Should three gallons of the new product be produced? In responding to this question, use the data to illustrate the concept of opportunity cost.

8–4 *Use of Linear Programming to Determine when to Process an Intermediate Product Further* (R. Manes)

The Hartley Company processes a Raw Material Y into two unrefined (intermediate) Products A' and B'. These two intermediate products can be sold in the market, for $20 and $8 respectively, after incurring incre-

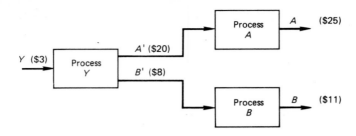

mental costs after split-off of $8 and $4 respectively, for collecting, packaging and delivering the unrefined Products, A' and B'. The Hartley Company also has the option of processing A' and B' further into refined Products A and B. In this case its saves $1 of delivery charges associated with intermediate Products A' and B', but it incurs an additional $4 and $2 per unit respectively for processing Products A' and B' into A and B respectively.

Other Production and Marketing Conditions

1. The Raw Material Y costs $3 per unit. One unit of Y produces 3 units of A' and 2 units of B'.

2. All the processing of Product Y and to refine Products A' and B' into Products A and B requires the same equipment. The processing time per unit of each product is:

Process	Hours per Unit
Y	2.0
A	2.5
B	0.5

Available equipment time is limited to 100,000 hours per period.

3. Raw Material Y can be purchased up to a maximum amount of 16,000 units per period.

4. Maximum sales per period are:

Product	Max. Sales
A'	50,000
B'	8,000
B	10,000

Required:

1. Solve the problem to find the optimal production and sales schedule. Interpret the solution.

2. In the solution to requirement 1, how would profit be affected if Hartley had 1,000 hours of extra equipment time per period? How would profit be affected if Hartley could sell another 100 units of product B?

8–5 *The Williamson Chocolate Company, Ltd.**
(David Solomons)

The Williamson Chocolate Co., Ltd., which has its headquarters and principal factory in Leicester, England, has been engaged in the production of chocolate and cocoa products since the beginning of this century. Subsidiary companies have been established in Canada, Australia, and South Africa, and each of the subsidiaries manufactures the more important of the company's products and markets them in its home market.

The Australian company is located in Melbourne, where all of its manufacturing activities take place, and warehouses for local distribution are also maintained in Sydney, Adelaide, and Perth. The main output at the factory is chocolate in bars. Cocoa beans, the principal raw material for the manufacture of chocolate, are imported from abroad. As a rule, the beans are cleaned, roasted, ground, and then passed through a press. In the press, cocoa butter is separated from cocoa powder. The cocoa butter leaves the press in liquid form because of the heat that is generated during the press operation. The cocoa butter is then stored in large tanks, ready for use in the current production of chocolate.

The Melbourne factory was a net user of cocoa butter, that is, its chocolate production called for more cocoa butter than could be obtained from the pressing of cocoa beans for powder manufacture. This extra cocoa butter could have been imported but it was subject to a heavy import duty, and the local management believed that it was cheaper to import beans and extract the cocoa butter from them. As a result of implementing this policy the factory found itself with a steadily mounting stock of cocoa powder.

The following figures show how the stock of cocoa powder (in pounds) increased during the period 1968–70:

1968:
Stock at January 1, 1968	30,500
Output of press	416,975
	447,475
Less: Usage in 1968	324,500
Stock at December 31, 1968	122,975

---

* Reproduced with permission.

1969:

Output of press		638,750
		761,725
Less: Usage in 1969	506,420	
Sales in 1969	35,500	541,920
Stock at December 11, 1969		219,805

1970:

Output of press		792,125
		1,011,930
Less: Usage in 1970	641,600	
Sales in 1970	43,385	684,985
Stock of cocoa powder, December 31, 1970		326,945

These large stocks of cocoa powder held at the factory caused a serious storage problem, and the local management made continuous efforts to find profitable outlets for the excess cocoa powder. However, the sale of this powder on the Australian market raised a question as to its proper valuation. In accordance with accounting instructions issued by the head office in London some time before the last war, the cost of the cocoa beans purchased together with the labor and overhead costs of the pressing process had to be allocated between the cocoa butter and the cocoa cake on the basis of the fat content remaining in these two products after the pressing operations. This gave a cost for cocoa powder of about $0.23 a pound or about 50 percent above its current market price at the end of 1970. The company was therefore unable to dispose of its excess stock of cocoa cake without incurring a considerable loss. For balance sheet purposes, however, the company made a provision in its accounts in order to bring the book value of its stock of cocoa down to the market value.

During 1971, cocoa prices fell further and the subsidiary was unable to sell any large quantities of its excess stocks, because its costs were too high. There was practically no internal market for cocoa powder. It did succeed however, in exchanging 13,000 pounds of powder against 2,000 pounds of cocoa butter with another manufacturer.

In the middle of 1971, Mr. Cannon, the marketing manager, brought forward a scheme to market a new cocoa preparation for making a hot chocolate drink. The marketing prospects seemed good as long as the selling price could be kept low enough. This new product offered a promising means of disposing of the excess stocks of cocoa powder but only if they were costed out at substantially less than the cost allocated to them in the books.

The production manager, Mr. Parker, supported this proposal with enthusiasm. He had repeatedly drawn the attention of the subsidiary's managing director, Mr. Woodstock, to the storage problem created by the cocoa stocks, and he welcomed the possibility which now opened up of deaing with this problem once for all. Besides, he said, he had never been able to see the logic of basing the cost of cocoa powder on its fat content. It was its flavor which was important, and fat content had little to do with flavor.

Both Cannon and Parker were surprised to find that Mr. Woodstock was not unreservedly enthusiastic about Cannon's proposal. He pointed out that if cocoa powder were charged to the new product at present cost levels, the product would never show a profit; and without a drop in the price of cocoa beans greater than anyone could at present foresee, the only way to reduce the cost of cocoa powder would be to change the basis of cost allocation between cocoa powder and cocoa butter. This could not be done without permission from London and he was by no means certain that such permission would be given unless some basis of cost allocation which was clearly better than the present one could be proposed. It was all very well to attack the present basis of allocation, as Mr. Parker had done. But unless he or somebody else could suggest a better one, why should London agree to a change?

Mr. Woodstock went on to point out that there was another aspect of the matter which made him reluctant to approach London. If the allocation of costs to cocoa powder were reduced, with a consequent increase in the cost of cocoa butter, the calculation which had been supplied to London in 1967 to support the expenditure of $40,000 on a new cocoa press would be completely undermined. Only on the basis of the present cost of producing cocoa butter as compared with the cost of importing it could investment in the press be justified. If more cost were to be allocated to cocoa butter, it might be shown that it ought to be imported after all, and the investment in the press could be shown to have been misguided.

What should Mr. Woodstock tell London? Should he recommend a change in the allocation method?

8–6   Craik Veneer Company

The sales manager of the Craik Veneer Company received from the Groton Company an offer of $8 per thousand surface feet for 1,000,000 feet per month of sound "backs" of 1/24" birch veneer for the next twelve months. The sales manager wanted to accept the offer, but the production manager argued that it should not be accepted because the cost of production was at least $10 per thousand feet and probably more. The president was inclined to agree with the sales manager because the Groton Company's credit was good and because he wanted to be sure the company could sell all the backs produced, but he asked the controller to examine the

This case is copyright © 1954 by the President and Fellows of Harvard College. Harvard Business School case 9–154–002.

cost situation and to determine whether sale of the backs at $8 would, or would not, result in a profit.

The Craik company manufactured rotary cut birch veneer from high-grade yellow birch logs bought in Vermont. Selected sections called "blocks" were cut out of those logs, the length of the block varying from 84" to 98" depending on the length along the grain of the veneer being produced.

These blocks, as cut for the lathe, cost an average of $200 per thousand board feet. A thousand board feet, log measure, was an amount of logs which being sawed would produce a thousand board feet of lumber. (A board foot is one square foot one inch thick.) Although veneer logs were never reduced to lumber, they were bought on board feet, log measure, by one of the standard rules used to measure logs.

After cutting, the blocks were put in vats filled with hot water and left there for from 24 to 48 hours until the entire log was heated through. This made the wood easier to cut and improved the quality of veneer.

In the rotary veneer process the block was put in a lathe in which a knife longer than the block, with a heavy frame, guide bars and pressure bars, was brought against the side of the block so that it cut off a thin slice of wood the entire length of the block. The process was similar to unrolling a large roll of paper held on a horizontal shaft.

The process could be controlled with skillful operation so it would produce veneer of uniform thickness. The Craik company produced principally 1/24" veneer, and for the purposes of this case it may be assumed that all of its product was 1/24". This veneer was .04166" thick, and it was expected that this thickness could be held, after drying, within ± .002".

The sheet of veneer from the lathe, for instance from a 98" block, was brought onto a clipping table approximately 60 ft. long. This table had rubber belts on its upper surface which moved the veneer along to the clipper. At this point the veneer was like a long sheet of paper moving along the table, the veneer being 98" along the grain.

At the other end of the table was a clipper, which consisted of a long knife extending entirely across the table. The clipper operator was one of the most highly skilled men in the plant. One electrical control connected to the drive of the rubber belts on the table enabled him to move the sheet of veneer under the clipper. Another electrical control brought the clipper down to cut the veneer along its 98" grain and exactly perpendicular to the ends.

The clipper operator constantly inspected the sheet of veneer. He first took one cut to get a straight edge, then advanced the sheet. If the next section of the sheet was of high quality, he advanced the sheet not over 3'8", depending on customers' requirements. If the sheet showed a defect within three feet eight inches he made his cut just short of the defect. A man called the "off bearer" piled these sheets on a hand truck reserved for high-grade or "face" veneer.

If the defect was a knot, the clipper operator then advanced the sheet enough to clear the knot and took another cut, making a piece of waste possibly 3″ wide. If he decided that a section of the sheet was not of face quality, he cut it for "backs," either 3′8″ or in lesser widths. Backs were put on another hand truck.

The clipper operator thus separated the whole sheet of veneer into faces, backs and waste. The faces consisted of pieces of veneer 98″ long along the grain and 6″ to 3′8″ wide. The sound backs were of the same size. The waste went to a chipper; in this company the chipped waste was burned to get rid of it.

The term "faces" came from the fact that these veneer sheets were substantially perfect and could be used on the exposed parts of furniture or on the best face of plywood.[1] The backs had minor defects and were so called because they were used on the back of plywood panels.

The quality required for faces was established by specifications and by the custom of the industry. The dividing line between sound backs and waste was similarly established. The Craik company had a reputation for using high-grade logs and for producing a high grade of veneer both on faces and backs.

The Groton Company was a manufacturer of high-grade furniture, principally of yellow birch, which, over a term of years, had become the leading American cabinet wood. The white sap wood was used for the "blond" or lighter finishes which were in high demand; the heart was used for darker finishes which were utilized in many colonial lines. Solid yellow birch lumber was expensive; for instance, the lumber cost for clear 4/4 (1 inch) birch used in the top of a dresser was 40 cents to 50 cents per square foot.

The Groton Company's research and development department had developed two new lines of furniture, one in blond modern and one in colonial, in which the table tops, dresser tops, and panels, drawer fronts and other exposed parts were of birch veneer over lower grade birch or poplar cores, with table legs, dresser frames, etc., of solid birch.

The Groton research people knew that while all sheets of backs contained defects, 50% to 60% of the area of backs as produced by Craik were of face quality. They had discovered that by buying backs 84″ to 98″ long they could cut clear face quality veneer in lengths which would match their use requirements: enough 54″ for their longest dresser tops and enough of other lengths down to 14″ drawer fronts. The remainder of the veneer which was not of face quality could be used for such purposes as making plywood for drawer bottoms.

The methods developed in the research department had been tested by cutting up several carloads of backs bought from Craik and by the

---

[1] Veneer is a single thin sheet of wood. Plywood consists of several sheets (three, five or nine) glued together with the grain of alternate courses at right angles to add to the strength.

manufacture and sale of the furniture. The quality of the furniture was high, the cost of the finished furniture was favorable in comparison with competition, and the furniture sold well.

On the basis of this experience the Groton Company offered Craik $8 per thousand feet for 1,000,000 feet per month of sound backs in 1/24″ birch veneer for the next twelve months.

The Craik company cut an average of 12,000 board feet of logs per day in one eight-hour shift. With the high quality of logs it bought, it got a yield of 18,000 surface feet of 1/24″ veneer per 1,000 board feet cut; this graded on the average 50% faces and 50% backs.

Labor and factory overhead costs together averaged $8 per thousand surface feet of veneer; selling costs averaged $1.50. Both the cost of the blocks and operating costs for the heating, lathe turning and clipping operations were joint costs; backs had to be produced in order to get the faces. The remaining operations in drying, a slight amount of reclipping, storing and shipping were in a sense separate costs as the operations were done on backs separately, although with the same equipment. The labor and factory overhead costs through clipping averaged $6.75 per 1,000 surface feet of veneer, those for drying and later operations, $1.25.

The selling price of 1/24″ birch faces 84″ to 98″ long was $40 per 1,000 square feet. Face veneer 84″ to 98″ had a high price because it could be used on large surfaces such as flush birch doors which require lengths up to 8 feet. The shorter veneer in length along the grain, made from recutting backs, had a somewhat lower price because it could not be used for these purposes. Unlike faces, the price of backs fluctuated widely. Sometimes Craik could get $10 per thousand feet, but the insistence of the production manager on $10 had led to the accumulation of a heavy inventory of backs. Faces were easy to sell and were shipped substantially as fast as they were produced.

More effort was required to sell backs than to sell faces, although both were sold to the same customers by the same salesmen. Sometimes buyers of faces were required to take a percentage of backs in order to get a car of faces. For these reasons the offer of the customer was attractive to the sales manager.

When the production manager was first informed by the sales manager of the offer of $8 per thousand surface feet, the production manager contended that "your salesmen are so lazy, they would give veneer away if nobody watched them." The production manager went on to say, "If a birch block cost $200 per thousand and we get 18,000 feet of 1/24-inch thick veneer from every thousand board feet of the block, the cost of the block to be allocated to a thousand feet of veneer, whether backs or faces, is $200 divided by 18,000 feet or about $11.11 per thousand feet. A little simple arithmetic proves that selling backs at $8 per thousand doesn't even pay for the material, let alone labor and overhead."

The sales manager countered that this argument was fallacious. "Allocating the cost of the block to the veneer in this manner," he said, "implies that backs are as valuable as faces, which is not the case. The $11.11 material figure for a thousand feet of veneer that you get is merely an average of the value of faces and backs. The material for faces is worth considerably more per thousand feet than this figure; the material for backs is worth considerably less."

The sales manager suggested that the proper procedure was to allocate the cost of the block to faces and backs in proportion to the amounts for which the products were sold. Using this method, the ratio that the revenue of one of the two grades of veneer bore to the revenue received from both grades of veneer would be applied to the total cost of the block, the result representing the cost to be allocated to that particular grade. To illustrate this method, assume a block of 1,000 board feet cost $200, and the selling prices and quantities of faces and backs are as shown in the following table:

Grade	1/24 Inch Veneer in Ft.	Sales Revenue per 1,000 Ft. 1/24" Veneer	Net Value	Per Cent of Total	Cost Applicable to Each Product
Faces	9,000	$40	$360	83.3%	$166.67
Backs	9,000	8	72	16.6	33.33
	18,000		$432	100.0%	$200.00

The material cost applicable to each product, then, per thousand feet of 1/24-inch veneer would be ($166.67/9,000 feet × 1,000 feet) or $18.52 for faces and ($33.33/9,000 feet × 1,000 feet) or $3.70 for backs.

The production manager contended that this method of allocating cost was artificial in that it was based on sales value and did not represent the true material cost which was the same for both products. "Furthermore," the production manager said, "under your method the material cost allocated to either faces or backs would be a function of their relative selling prices. If the selling price of faces fell from $40 per thousand to $20 per thousand and the price of backs remained the same, you would then charge much more material costs to backs, and much less to faces. Your method of allocating cost is certainly not justified."

The sales manager, at this point said, "O.K., if you don't think that method is justified, then let's reexamine our products and see if we're not going about this problem of allocating costs in the wrong way. I think you'll agree that we would prefer to be making faces all the time, yet we can't because backs are a necessary byproduct. As long as we manufacture faces, we're going to produce backs as an undesirable consequence. Now, if we consider faces as the main product and backs as the byproduct, we can charge all block costs to faces. The net proceeds from the sale of backs, after allowing for all conversion, selling and administrative expenses, can be credited to the raw material cost of faces." The sales manager went on to point out that this credit would represent, in theory, the cost of raw material furnished to the byproduct. The net effect would be to charge the byproduct only with the net proceeds of its sale, and all profits and losses of the business would be borne by the main product. The production manager, however, pointed out again that the cost of material allocated to faces would still be a function of the selling price of backs and, furthermore, there would be some difficulty in trying to value inventories at the end of an accounting period. The production manager went on to mention that any profits arising from the sale of backs would be hidden since it would be included in the credit to faces. "It is important to determine the profit or loss being realized on the sale of backs so we can establish a firm sales policy," he said.

Because of their inability to resolve this question, the production manager and the sales manager consulted the president of the Craik Veneer Company who, in turn, asked the controller to examine the cost situation to determine whether the $8 per thousand surface feet of 1/24" backs would, or would not, result in a profit.

Required:

1. As controller, what method of allocating raw material costs would you recommend? What similarities and differences would be encountered in allocating labor and overhead costs as compared with material costs?

2. Should the sales manager accept the $8 per thousand feet offer that he received for the 1/24" backs?

3. If a group of blocks containing 1,000 board feet costs $205, what would be the cost applicable to faces and backs under each of the methods of allocating costs described in the case, and other methods that you may devise, if the following conditions existed:

   a. The current market price of 1/24" faces is $40 per thousand feet, 1/24" backs are currently selling at $9 per thousand.

   b. 10,000 feet of 1/24" faces and 8,000 feet of 1/24" backs were produced from a group of blocks.

   c. Factory labor and overhead cost averaged $8 per thousand feet of veneer ($6.75 for operations through clipping and $1.25 for drying and later operations). Selling costs averaged $1.50 per thousand feet of veneer. If backs were not manufactured (i.e., if they were treated the same as waste), labor, overhead, and selling costs amounting to roughly $2 per thousand feet of backs might be saved.

8–7

Elora Semiconductor Limited

(This problem is loosely based on the description of the semiconductor manufacturing process found in the following article: William L. Cats-Baril, James F. Gatti, and D. Jacque Grinnell, "Joint Product Costing in the Semiconductor Industry," **Management Accounting,** February 1986, pp. 28–35.)

Elora Semiconductor Limited (ESL) manufactures memory chips and computer memory boards. The manufacturing process begins in the Fabrication Division where silicon wafers are photolithographed and baked at high temperatures. Each wafer has the potential of yielding 20,000 memory chips of identical design. The joint cost associated with each wafer to this point is $90,000.

After the baking operation, the chips are individually tested and classified. This testing and classification costs about $3 per chip. The testing determines the number of usable memory bytes in each chip and the speed at which information can be accessed in each chip. The chips are classified into five categories:

1. Unusable
2. Low speed, low memory (type 1)
3. High speed, low memory (type 2)
4. Low speed, high memory (type 3)
5. High speed, high memory (type 4)

Because of the nature of the photolithographing and baking process, it is not possible to fix the distribution of chips that results from each wafer. The distribution is affected by factors including the cleanliness of the air in the furnace, the quality of the silicon wafers, and the quality of the production line equipment and the workers. On average, the distribution of chips is as follows:

Unusable chips	25%
Type 1 chips	10%
Type 2 chips	20%
Type 3 chips	30%
Type 4 chips	15%

The chips classified as unusable are sold to a wholesaler for $5 per chip.

The remaining chips are used to manufacture one of three modules in the Assembly Division. In the Assembly Division, the chips are encapsulated in ceramic and wired for assembly into a memory module or board.

The cost to assemble each module is $3.80. The chip requirements for each of the modules are as follows:

Type A module	1 type 1 chip and 1 type 2 chip
Type B module	1 type 2 chip and 1 type 3 chip
Type C module	1 type 3 chip and 1 type 4 chip

In assembling the modules, chip downgrades are permitted. Chips classified as type 2, type 3, or type 4 can be substituted for type 1 chips. Chips classsified as type 4 can be substituted for type 2 or type 3 chips. Any chips not used in the assembly of modules are sold for $10 per chip.

Once all the modules are produced, the firm makes a decision regarding how many of each type of module are to be subjected to a stress test. In the stress test, which costs $2.85 per module tested, the module is exposed to extreme conditions. The modules that survive the stress test are classified as extended life modules and command a higher market price. On average, 80% of the modules that are subjected to the stress test survive. The modules that do not survive the test are scrapped for a salvage value that just equals their disposal cost.

Next, 5% of each type of module (the normal and extended life versions of each module type are regarded as different types of modules) is selected for a reliability test which is destructive. This reliability test, which costs $38 per module tested, is a quality control test and is undertaken, without fail, for all products. If the results of the reliability test for any type of module are unacceptable, the entire batch is sold to a discounter for 50% of the normal market price of that module. On average, such dispositions occur about 7 times for every 100 batches of modules tested.

Finally, the completed modules are packed, at a cost of $1 per module, and moved to the warehouse for shipping to customers.

The prices for each of the normal modules are as follows:

Type A module—normal	$60
Type B module—normal	$70
Type C module—normal	$80

The extended life modules command a 30% premium over the prices of the comparable normal life modules.

Because of the quality of these products, ESL can sell all of any modules or chips that it can produce. The sole limitation on the process is that a maximum of 100 wafers can be produced each year.

Required:

Suppose the fiscal year of ELS has just ended. The only inventory is one wafer that has just been tested. The chips on this wafer follow the average distribution of chips exactly. That is, there are 5,000 rejects, 2,000 type 1 chips, 4,000 type 2 chips, 6,000 type 3 chips, and 3,000 type 4 chips on this wafer. Develop an inventory cost, for financial reporting purposes, for each of these chips.

8–8 *Effect of Joint Cost on Product Profitability and Capital Budgeting Analysis** (John Shank)

Ajax Petroleum

Bill MacGregor was still puzzled as he thought about the financial report lying on his desk (see Table 1). The report summarized the key financial statistics for a capital expenditure project which one of MacGregor's subordinates was recommending. MacGregor was the general manager for Ajax Petroleum's Middletown, Ohio, refinery. Although he was a chemical engineer by training, his policy was to rely on the people reporting to him for recommendations about the technical side of the business. He strongly objected to second-guessing his managers on things for which they were responsible.

John Patterson, general superintendent for the catalytic cracking unit ("cat cracker") was pushing strongly for MacGregor's approval of a proposal to install a solvent-decarbonizing unit (SDU) in the refinery at a cost of roughly $30,000,000. The function of an SDU is to clean and purify residual fuel so that it can serve as raw material ("feedstock") for the cat cracker. The cat cracker would then convert this feedstock into gasoline. Residual or No. 6 oil is one of the outputs when crude oil is refined. However, it represents, literally, what is left after the desirable end products are extracted from the barrel of crude. As the dregs, "resid" is dirty, smelly, and so viscous that it will not even flow at room temperature. It was considered in Ajax to be more a nuisance than anything else. However, there is an established nationwide market for resid, at a low enough price, with uses ranging from heating apartment buildings to generating electricity to powering other equipment designed to run on low-grade fuels. John Patterson was convinced that converting resid into more gasoline was a great idea, particularly since gasoline prices at the refinery were stable at $39/bbl. while resid prices were very volatile, having been as low as $18/bbl. in recent weeks. There was sufficient excess capacity at the cat cracker to process the extra feedstock, and no alternative external source of additional feedstock was available.

---

* This case was prepared by Professor John K. Shank with the cooperation of a major oil company. All data in the case are generally realistic as of April 1980, but proprietary information has been disguised. This case appears in John Shank, *Contemporary Managerial Accounting* (Prentice-Hall, 1981). Reproduced with permission.

TABLE 1
Memorandum

March 17, 1980

TO: W. MacGregor
FROM: B. Anderson, Economic Analyst
RE: The Solvent Decarbonizing Unit Proposal

Here is the information you requested concerning the economics of the SDU project. I have the backup file if you want to dig deeper.

1) Investment cost $30,000,000 (delivered and installed)
     Less Investment Tax Credit   3,000,000 (10% of cost)
               Net Investment $27,000,000

2) Annual Operating Costs (three-shift basis) $ 3,300,000 (Labor, maintenance, insurance, property taxes, supplies)

Per Barrel of Cracking Stock Produced

3) Fuel $ 2.90/bbl. (See Note 1 below)
4) Feedstock Cost $ 32.30/bbl. (See Note 2 below)
5) Value of Cracking Stock Produced $ 37.50/bbl. (See Note 3 below)(
6) Thruput is 9,000 bbls. per day (assuming an average of 90% utilization of theoretical capacity on a 365-day/year basis). One bbl. of resid will produce one bbl. of cracking stock.
7) Economic life is 20 years. (This is also the depreciable life for tax purposes. The current tax rate is 46%.) Use straight-line depreciation for simplicity and to be conservative.
8) Inflation in costs and prices is ignored. This would tend to offset for a project like this one.

Project Profitability

     Payback = 9.10 years
     Net Present Value (at 20% after taxes) = negative $12.6 million
     Economic Rate of Return = 9%
     Profitability Index = .72
     Return on Capital Employed = 19.8%

Note 1   The SDU runs on fuel gas[a] to which Ajax currently assigns a cost of $29.00 per equivalent bbl. It takes .10 bbl. of fuel gas to produce a barrel of thruput at the SDU. Thus, fuel gas costs $2.90 per barrel of thruput.

Note 2   Feedstock for the SDU is No. 6 oil. The cost of No. 6 is computed by assigning crude oil cost and crude-still operating costs to the set of outputs at the crude still, based on relative production volumes for each product. With crude running $29.00 average for the refinery, this equates currently to about $32.30/bbl. for resid.

Note 3   Gasoline is currently selling for about $39/bbl. at the refinery. The cost is about $1.50/bbl. at the cat cracker to convert feedstock into gasoline. Thus, the net realizable value of thruput at the SDU which feeds the cat cracker is $37.50/bbl. ($39 minus $1.50).

---

[a] "Fuel gas" is generated at the crude still in a gaseous state as one of the products when a barrel of crude is "cracked." It is not feasible to convert the fuel gas into a salable end product, but it can be used as fuel to power the various production units in the refinery. The DOE–approved guidelines for measuring the allowable cost of gasoline for price control purposes charge fuel gas for a proportionate share of the average cost of crude oil but not for any portion of the operating costs of the crude still. Currently, about 5% of the equivalent volumetric production at the crude still is fuel gas. With crude cost at $30.45 for the incremental barrel and $29.00 on average, Ajax followed the DOE–approved approach and costed fuel gas at $29.00 per equivalent barrel.

316

MacGregor had been intrigued by Patterson's idea because he was no great fan of No. 6 oil either. Because of wide seasonal swings in demand and supply and a relatively thin market, residual prices were notoriously volatile and unpredictable. MacGregor knew that the current price was about $25/bbl., but it had been as low as $18/bbl. and as high as $35/bbl. in recent months. Patterson had also told MacGregor that many of Ajax' competitors already had SDUs in their refineries and that there was always a waiting list for installation of an SDU, so they must be a good investment. MacGregor wasn't particularly impressed by these arguments, however, because he knew that the major oil companies often differed on strategic issues. Just because Ashland and Marathon were deemphasizing heavy oil (No. 6) to yield more light oil (gasoline) from the barrel of crude did not mean Ajax should automatically follow along. In fact, this might make the heavy-oil business a lot better for the remaining suppliers. MacGregor had heard that Exxon, for one, still considered heavy oil to be a viable item in the product line. Also, MacGregor knew that the Ajax marketing department might not agree with deemphasizing resid since there were residual oil sales managers in each sales district and many long-standing customer relationships involved, including many electric utilities in the politically sensitive northeast. MacGregor did know, however, that the additional gasoline could easily be sold in the wholesale market. Long-run prospects for gasoline demand were less certain.

MacGregor had told Patterson that the key in selling the SDU idea would be return on investment. He told Patterson to work with the economic analysis department to pull together the numbers for the SDU proposal. If it was such a good idea the numbers would show it and MacGregor could then recommend the project to the corporate capital expenditures committee. The corporate "hurdle rate" for new investment proposals was currently 20%, after taxes. Patterson had eagerly accepted this idea, noting that an acquaintance of his at Ashland Oil had called the SDU in his refinery one of the more profitable investments he had seen in 20 years in the business. When MacGregor received the financial summary report, he was puzzled because the numbers for the SDU project just didn't look that good.

When MacGregor showed the report to Patterson, the latter accused the "bean counters" of trying to scuttle the project with "funny numbers." He took exception to two items in the report, the cost of $29.00/bbl. for fuel gas and the cost of $32.30/bbl. for residual oil. He said that fuel gas was really free because there wasn't anything else to do with it except use it as fuel. He argued that since the refinery gets it automatically when a barrel of crude is processed and it has no sales value, it should be considered as free. In fact, he said, fuel gas should show a negative cost since it costs money for equpment to flare it off if it isn't used. He should be encouraged to use it up, he said, to save this cost and to save the hassle with EPA about the air pollution when fuel gas is flared. He was even more unhappy with the reported cost of $32.30/bbl. for resid. He said it was absolutely crazy to show resid at a higher cost than crude itself when, in fact, resid is what's left after you take all the desired products out of the crude. Why should resid show a higher value than raw crude when it was dramatically less desirable to customers? Raw crude itself, although dangerous to handle because of static electricity buildup, is a substitute product for resid in nearly all applications. Patterson had said that he had never been much interested in cost calculations because he figured that the accountants were accurate, but if this report was an example of how they think, Ajax was in trouble. MacGregor had agreed that Patterson's points seemed to make sense.

MacGregor had subsequently called in Ben Anderson to discuss Patterson's objections to the cost calculations in Anderson's report. Anderson had assured MacGregor that he had no desire to scuttle Patterson's idea. In fact, he said, the analysis in the report was slanted in favor of the proposal and he had even felt guilty about leaning over backward to make the project look good. The problem with the report, he said, was that fuel gas should be costed at $32.30/bbl. rather than $29.00. It is true, he continued, that fuel gas shows an actual cost of $29.00 per equivalent barrel under Ajax' cost accounting system and that this is the cost approved by DOE for determining gasoline "ceiling" prices. However, he said, actual historical cost was not relevant for the proposed new capital investment. Anderson noted that about one-half of the refinery's current fuel needs were being met by fuel gas and the other half by residual oil. The SDU project would not increase the amount of fuel gas generated at the crude still, but it would consume as fuel some of the fuel gas already being generated. The net result for the refinery as a whole would be to increase the consumption of resid used as fuel by an amount equal to the fuel needs of the SDU. Since resid costs $32.30/bbl., fuel cost for the SDU project should be $32.30. Anderson called this the "opportunity-cost" concept, as opposed to actual historical cost.

Regarding the question of what No. 6 costs, Anderson said he sympathized with Patterson but that the $32.30 was a factual number. In fact, he said, the refinery *does* produce a set of products at the crude still, *including* residual oil, and these products *must each* carry a share of the costs incurred in producing them. A barrel of residual oil thus costs whatever a barrel of crude oil costs, plus some share of the operating costs at the crude still. These crude-still operating costs, he said, could be allocated based on value of products produced, volume of products produced, total energy value (BTUs) of products produced, or some other basis. But under any allocation scheme, outputs from the crude still will cost more than crude oil. Anderson concluded by saying that with fuel gas and resid at $32.30, the SDU actually would be even less profitable than as shown in Table 1 and that the project just couldn't be justified on economic grounds.

But, since more companies use historical costs rather than opportunity costs in their accounting systems, he (Anderson) could "bend" as far as the analysis in the report, as an accommodation to Patterson. The meeting had ended with MacGregor agreeing that Anderson's points seemed to make sense.

MacGregor's background included very little training in cost accounting. He had always considered this area as a technical specialty for which general managers could hire the expertise they needed. He was, however, feeling very frustrated about which cost numbers to believe for the solvent decarbonizing project. He also felt a little foolish for agreeing with both Patterson and Anderson when they talked to him.

He asked his plant controller, Fred Morton, to have lunch with him one day to look at Ben Anderson's report and comment on John Patterson's objections to it. Morton said the basic issue was what cost to show for No. 6 oil in the calculations. He said that Anderson was currently using the cost numbers generated by Ajax' cost accounting system. Resid was considered to be one of the joint set of products produced in the refinery and, accordingly, was assigned a cost of $32.30/bbl. (as compared to middle distillate at $32.90 and gasoline at $34.80). He agreed that the *particular* allocation scheme (weight, volume, heat value, etc.) was essentially arbitrary, but he emphasized that charging a share of refining cost to resid makes it more costly.

He said that one way to show significantly lower cost on resid would be to consider it a "by-product" rather than a "joint product." A by-product has the following characteristics:

1. It is not a desired output from the production process; it just happens to be created in the process of making the desired products.
2. It is low in sales value relative to the main products.
3. It is produced in relatively small quantities.

A clear example of the distinction between a by-product and a joint product is pigs feet versus bacon to a hog butcher. Morton went on to say that normal cost accounting procedure shows a zero cost for by-products. They are just sold for whatever the market will bring, and the sales revenue is netted back against the costs which must be assigned to the desired products. For the refinery, this would mean allocating the sum of crude cost plus crude-still operating costs minus resid sales revenue to gasoline and middle distillate (jet fuel, diesel fuel, and home heating oil), with resid showing a zero cost for accounting purposes. He noted that several of the major oil companies follow this approach, although several others use the same approach as Ajax.

Under the by-product approach, resid would be valued in the capital expenditure analysis at whatever you could sell it for if you didn't convert it to cracking stock or use it as refinery fuel. With gasoline selling for

$39/bbl., he thought resid would average around $20 over its price cycles. However, he added that the long-run average price of resid would certainly be heavily influenced by regulatory pressures to stop utilities from burning resid and by trends in gasoline consumption. The average price by 1985 could be as low as $17/bbl. or as high as $25/bbl., even if crude prices didn't change. Morton said this is what Anderson termed the opportunity-cost approach, as opposed to the historical-cost approach. He concluded by saying that this same idea applies to the fuel gas item. The reported cost incurred is $29/bbl. and the opportunity cost will average around $20/bbl. (the revenue forgone by not selling a barrel of resid).

MacGregor went back to Anderson the next day and asked him to refigure the SDU project showing both the joint product costing and by-product costing approaches for resid and both recorded cost and opportunity cost approaches for fuel gas. Anderson said that would be no problem and agreed to get the information to MacGregor by the next day. MacGregor wondered how much impact these accounting questions would have on the profitability of the SDU project. He couldn't imagine that bookkeeping issues would be that important to the overall analysis. He was anxious to see Anderson's revised report.

Required:

1. Using the same format as in Table 1, recalculate the economic return for the project, using both joint product costing ($32.30) and by-product costing ($20.00) for resid and using DOE costing ($29.00) and opportunity costing for fuel gas ($20.00 or $32.30, depending on the assumed cost of resid). All the basic data will be the same as in Table 1 except for the cost of fuel gas and resid.

2. What do you believe is the best accounting method for fuel gas and residual oil? Why? Which set of accounting numbers produces the most meaningful economic return calculations?

3. Is the proposed solvent decarbonizing unit profitable enough to justify the investment?

4. As MacGregor, would you recommend the SDU project to headquarters? What economic analysis would you present to support your recommendation? What qualitative (versus quantitative) factors influence your decision?

chapter 9

SALES, PROFITABILITY, AND PRODUCTIVITY VARIANCES

Sales and Profit Analysis

Variance analysis is typically performed for the production costs of manufactured goods. But conventional procedures for decomposing a cost variance into its quantity and price components can also be extended to explain deviations of actual from planned profitability. Such an extension permits a profit variance to be decomposed into components due to changes in sales activity, price recovery, and productivity.

Before developing this comprehensive variance analysis, we must first define a **mix variance** to explain shifts in the mix of products sold. Consider the Malone Company, which produces two models, Regular and DeLuxe, of a single product. The budgeted monthly sales volume and contribution margin (price less short-run variable costs) for the two products are shown in Exhibit 9–1.

EXHIBIT 9–1
Budgeted Sales and Contribution Margins

	Regular	DeLuxe
Sales (units)	4,000	1,000
Contribution margin	$16	$30

The budgeted monthly contribution margin for the Malone Company is

$$4,000 \, (\$16) + 1,000 \, (\$30) = \$94,000$$

Suppose that during January, actual sales were 4,400 units for the Regular model and 700 units for the DeLuxe model. Contribution margins for the two products were exactly as budgeted. In this case, the actual contribution margin during January was

$$4{,}400 \ (\$16) \ + \ 700 \ (\$30) \ = \ \$91{,}400$$

and an unfavorable variance of \$2,600 would be reported. Even though more units were sold than anticipated (5,100 rather than the budgeted 5,000), and the contribution margins of both units were exactly as budgeted, the total contribution margin for this product line was below the budgeted amount. The reason, of course, arises from having sold more of the low-margin Regular items and fewer of the high-margin DeLuxe items.

The sum of the total contribution-margin variances for the two products reveals the unfavorable variance:

$$(4{,}400 \ - \ 4{,}000) \ (16) \ + \ (700 \ - \ 1{,}000) \ (30) \ = \ -\$2{,}600,$$

but this analysis does not reveal whether the variance was caused by a decrease in the total number of units sold (a sales-volume variance) or by an unfavorable mix of products sold (the actual situation in this case).

We can remedy this ambiguity by decomposing the total variance of $-2{,}600$ into a component due to sales-volume changes (holding the product mix constant) and a component due to changes in the sales mix. A total sales-activity (or total contribution-margin) variance could be split many ways into volume and mix components. We will present one method that yields intuitive properties for these two variance components.

First, we compute a budgeted average contribution margin per unit, m^*, as

$$m^* = \frac{\text{Total budgeted contribution margin}}{\text{Total budgeted sales units}} = \frac{(4{,}000)(16) \ + \ (1{,}000)(30)}{(4{,}000 \ + \ 1{,}000)}$$

$$= \frac{94{,}000}{5{,}000} = \$18.80$$

The quantity m^* represents the average unit contribution whenever all products are sold in proportion to the planned product mix. With this definition, we can compute the sales-volume variance as

$$
\begin{aligned}
\text{Sales-volume variance} &= (\text{Total change in units sold}) \ (m^*) \\
&= [(4{,}400 \ - \ 4{,}000) \ + \ (700 \ - \ 1{,}000)] \ (18.80) \\
&= (+100) \ (18.80) \\
&= +\$1{,}880
\end{aligned}
$$

The variance is positive (favorable), since actual units sold exceeded budgeted sales units.

To compute the second component, the sales-mix variance, we first multiply the change in sales units for each product by the difference between the budgeted contribution margin and the average budgeted contribution margin, m^*. Then we sum across all products:

$$\begin{aligned}
\text{Sales-mix variance} &= (4,400 - 4,000)(16 - 18.80) \\
&\quad + (700 - 1,000)(30 - 18.80) \\
&= (400)(-2.80) + (-300)(11.20) \\
&= -\$4,480
\end{aligned}$$

The sales-mix variance is made positive (favorable) by either (1) selling more of higher-than-average contribution-margin products (such as the DeLuxe model) or (2) selling less of lower-than-average contribution products (such as the Regular model). Conversely, the mix variance is driven negative by selling more of the low-contribution (Regular) products and less of the high-contribution (DeLuxe) products. In this example, the mix variance for both the Regular and DeLuxe models is negative, since we sold more of the low-margin product and less of the high-margin product.

It is easy to verify that the sum of the sales-volume variance ($+\$1,880$) and the sales-mix variance ($-\$4,480$) equals the total sales-activity variance of $-\$2,600$.

By separating the sales-activity variance into two components, we can decompose the profit variance into a component caused by a shift in the total physical volume of sales and a component due to a shift in the relative mix of products. The decomposition demonstrates that increasing total physical units of sales, or maximizing sales volume, may not be as desirable as promoting the sales of the most profitable mix of products, even when this action must be accompanied by some decrease in unit sales volume.

Production-Mix and Yield Variances

We can extend the analysis to study the mix of input materials used in a production process. In some production processes, operating managers can vary the mix of input materials and affect the yield. Such substitution could occur as a conscious response to changes in material prices. Or perhaps the substitution was unintended and could be attributed to lax supervision. By computing a mix and yield variance, we can provide a preliminary assessment on the consequences of variations from the standards established for the input mix. The yield variance would be analogous to the sales-volume variance in the profitability variance analysis we have just illustrated.

As a simple example, consider the manufacture of a chemical, Kopane, produced by mixing two chemicals, ethyne and butene. Each pound of Kopane requires 1 lb of ethyne and 0.5 lb of butene (some material loss occurs in the mixing process). Ethyne costs $5/lb and butene costs $3.50/lb. Thus, the standard cost for each pound of Kopane is $6.75 (computed as $1.0[5.00] + 0.5[3.50]$).

In January, the actual production of Kopane was 5,000 pounds. In

Exhibit 9–2, the standard cost system reveals the standard quantities and prices for the raw materials to produce this output.

EXHIBIT 9–2
Budgeted Quantities and Unit Prices

	Ethyne	Butene
Standard quantity (lb)	5,000	2,500
Standard unit price	$5.00	$3.50
Total costs	$25,000	$8,750

The actual purchases and uses of raw materials in January were:

	Ethyne	Butene
Actual quantity (lb)	4,500	3,500
Actual unit price	$4.10	$3.90
Total costs	$18,450	$13,650

The actual total cost of $32,100 (= 18,450 + 13,650) is slightly below the standard cost of $33,750 (= 25,000 + 8,750), producing a favorable input-materials variance of $1,650. The input-materials variance can initially be decomposed into price and quantity variances:

$$\text{Price variance} = \text{Change in input prices evaluated at}$$
$$\text{actual input quantities}$$
$$= (4.10 - 5.00)(4,500) + (3.90 - 3.50)(3,500)$$
$$= -\$2,650 \text{ (favorable)}$$

and

$$\text{Quantity variance} = \text{Change in input quantities evaluated at}$$
$$\text{standard input prices}$$
$$= (4,500 - 5,000)(5.00) + (3,500 - 2,500)(3.50)$$
$$= +\$1,000 \text{ (unfavorable)}$$

Note that the signs of the production variances are reversed from those used in the sales-volume and mix variances. When analyzing production inputs, using more materials at higher prices is unfavorable, whereas with sales, having higher selling prices and greater unit sales is favorable. Sign conventions are arbitrary, although the analyst should be able to tell when the sign for a particular variance is favorable or unfavorable.

The quantity variance can now be decomposed further into yield and mix components. As before, we first compute an average price, p^*, per pound of raw material input:

$$p^* = \frac{\text{Total budgeted cost of inputs}}{\text{Total quantity of inputs}}$$

$$= \frac{(5,000)(5.00) + (2,500)(3.50)}{(5,000 + 2,500)} = \frac{33,750}{7,500}$$

$$= \$4.50$$

Then we can compute mix and yield variances:

Yield variance = Change in input quantities evaluated at p^*
$$= (4,500 - 5,000)(4.50) + (3,500 - 2,500)(4.50)$$
$$= \$2,250 \text{ (unfavorable)}$$

Mix variance = Change in input quantities multiplied by (budgeted price minus p^*)
$$= (-500)(5.00 - 4.50) + (1,000)(3.50 - 4.50)$$
$$= -\$1,250 \text{ (favorable)}$$

The yield variance is unfavorable because the actual total consumption of input materials (8,000 lb) exceeded the standard quantity budgeted (7,500 lb) for the amount of Kopane actually produced. The mix variance is favorable for both input materials because less was used of the higher-priced ethyne and more was used of the lower-priced butene. As in the sales-profit variance analysis, the sum of the yield and the mix variances (2,250 − 1,250) equals the quantity variance of +1,000.

Thus, the preliminary evaluation of the favorable input-materials variance of $1,000 finds a favorable price variance of $2,650 arising from an 18% price decline in the more expensive and heavily used ethyne material, only partially offset by an 11% increase in price for the less-expensive and less heavily used butene material. The favorable price variance is negated somewhat by an unfavorable $1,000 quantity variance arising from a large ($2,250) decrease in yield, since total input materials exceeded the standard to produce the actual output. But a favorable mix variance ($1,250), from using more of the low-cost butene and less of the high-cost ethyne, helped to reduce the unfavorable yield variance.

The manager of the Kopane process could argue that she tried to shift the production process so that more of the low-cost ethyne was used to replace high-cost butene. Whether the extra usage of 1,000 pounds of butene can be explained by the 500 fewer pounds of ethyne requires more knowledge than the problem statement gives us of the production process and the degree of substitutability between the two materials. If the manager did attempt such a substitution between the two input materials, she chose an unfortunate month, since the price of ethyne dropped just when the price of butene increased. A more detailed and formal analysis of these variances would require an explicit model of the production function for the Kopane process that would shed further light on the efficacy of input product substitutions. For our purposes here, the decomposition of the total $1,000 materials variance for Kopane into price, yield, and mix variances helps to highlight different aspects of the production process that have different degrees of controllability and responsibility.

A Complete Variance Decomposition Analysis

We are now ready to develop a complete variance analysis of period-to-period operations.[1] The ideas will be illustrated with a relatively simple numerical example. We will show the numeric calculations in the chapter's text as we proceed through the example. Students who have access to a spreadsheet language can find the data and tables stored on the course diskette under the name Matony.wkl. Performing the indicated calculations with the worksheet in parallel with reading the text will greatly enhance the student's understanding of this material.

The Matony Corporation produces three models of a product. The production process is simple, requiring only a single input material, a single type of direct labor, and a single energy input, electricity. The plant, equipment, and indirect labor are shared by all three product models. The standard costs, budgeted sales, and forecasted selling prices for the three models are shown in Exhibit 9–3.

EXHIBIT 9–3
Budgeted Inputs and Sales: Matony Corporation

	Model 1	*Model 2*	*Model 3*
Labor hours per unit	0.20	0.25	0.40
Material lb per unit	1.0	1.1	1.3
Kilowatt hours (kwhr) per unit	0.5	0.6	0.8
Budgeted sales (units)	10,000	6,000	2,000
Forecasted price ($)	15	20	40

The unit costs for the input resources are:

Labor	$20/hour
Material	$ 4/unit
Energy	$ 6/kwhr

and the committed factory overhead is expected to cost $80,000 per period. For simplicity and expositional purposes, we are not including any dis-

---

[1] The analysis presented here was formulated in R. Banker, S. Datar, and R. Kaplan, "Productivity Analysis and Management Accounting," *Journal of Accounting, Auditing and Finance* (1989).

cretionary overhead costs that could vary with the diversity or complexity of the product mix.[2] With these data, we can compute the standard costs and variable contribution margin of each product (see Exhibit 9–4).

EXHIBIT 9–4
Standard Product Costs and Contribution Margins

		Model 1	Model 2	Model 3
Selling price		$15.00	$20.00	$40.00
	Labor	$ 4.00	$ 5.00	$ 8.00
	Materials	4.00	4.40	5.20
	Energy	3.00	3.60	4.80
Variable costs		$11.00	$13.00	$18.00
Contribution margin		4.00	7.00	22.00

The budgeted income statement for the period (see Exhibit 9–5) can be obtained by multiplying the individual cost components by the quantities produced and sold of each of the three products, and then summing across the three product models.

EXHIBIT 9–5
Matony Corporation: Budgeted Income Statement

Sales			$350,000
	Labor	$86,000	
	Materials	76,800	
	Energy	61,200	
Variable costs			224,000
Committed overhead			80,000
Profits			$ 46,000

The actual financial results for the Matony Corporation are shown in Exhibit 9–6.

EXHIBIT 9–6
Matony Corporation: Budgeted Income Statement

Sales			$385,000
	Labor	$109,452	
	Materials	96,448	
	Energy	61,671	
Variable costs			267,571
Committed overhead			84,000
Profits			$ 33,429

---

[2] See Banker *et al.* for a description of how transactions-driven overhead could be incorporated into the analysis.

The crudest form of profit variance analysis just compares actual with budgeted profits:

Actual profits	$33,429
Budgeted profits	46,000
Profit variance	($12,571) unfavorable

This initial level of analysis reveals that profits were $12,571 below expectations, a decline of more than 27%.

At the next level of analysis, we could expand the variance report to compare actual and budgeted levels of performance for each major line item in the income statement.

EXHIBIT 9–7
Line Item Income Statement Variance Analysis

	Actual	Budgeted	Variance	%
Sales	$385,000	$350,000	$35,000 (F)	10.0
Labor	109,452	86,000	23,452 (U)	27.3
Materials	96,448	76,800	19,648 (U)	25.6
Energy	61,671	61,200	471 (U)	0.8
Variable costs	267,571	224,000	43,571 (U)	19.5
Committed				
overhead	84,000	80,000	4,000 (U)	5.0
Profits	$33,429	$ 46,000	$12,571 (U)	27.3

Exhibit 9–7 shows a favorable sales variance, since gross revenues increased by 10%. But all expense categories also increased, especially labor and materials costs, which had increases of more than 25%. In general, we are not surprised that revenue and variable expense variances have opposite signs. Higher sales, caused by an increase in the number of units produced and sold, imply higher variable costs. Conversely, when sales decline, variable costs will also tend to decline. At this stage of analysis, however, we can not tell whether the sales or cost increases are caused by a larger quantity of items produced and sold, or whether they are caused by other factors such as increases in prices, changes in mix, or inefficient use of input resources.

The analysis performed so far follows a traditional path, attributing profit changes to revenue changes less cost changes (see Figure 9–1). This approach arises naturally when a line-item financial income statement, with its separation of revenues and expenses, is used as the departure point for analysis. Extending the analysis one step further, to distinguish price and quantity effects (just as we separate price from usage variances in a standard-cost variance analysis), we can decompose the revenue change into a component due to changes in quantities sold and a com-

FIGURE 9–1

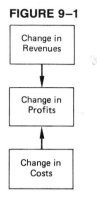

ponent due to changes in unit selling prices. Similarly, the change in costs can be decomposed into quantity and unit input cost components (see Figure 9–2). Such a decomposition almost exhausts the capabilities of conventional variance analysis.

FIGURE 9–2

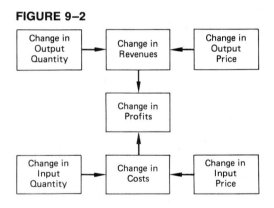

We can see, however, from Figure 9–3 that an alternative decomposition of profit variance is possible by combining the changes in quantities and prices vertically rather than horizontally. Connecting the left-hand boxes in Figure 9–3 requires calculating both a productivity and a sales-activity variance. The sales-activity variance assumes standard consumption of inputs and explains changes in inputs consumed caused by fluctuations in the volume and mix of sales. The productivity variance, computed at the actual level of output achieved, explains changes in inputs consumed caused by efficient or inefficient use of input resources:

FIGURE 9–3

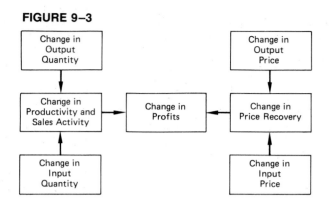

$$\text{Sales activity} + \text{Productivity change} = \frac{\text{Change in product (output) quantity}}{\text{Change in resource (input) quantity}}$$

Similarly, by connecting the two right-hand boxes, we can compute a price-recovery variance that arises from changes in the prices of outputs relative to changes in the prices (or costs) of input resources:

$$\text{Price-recovery variance} = \frac{\text{Change in product (output) prices}}{\text{Change in resource (input) costs}}$$

Combining these new variances or explanations of profit change, we obtain:

$$\text{Profit change} = \text{Productivity variance} + \text{Sales-activity variance} + \text{Price-recovery variance}$$

Such a presentation is appealing because it makes the causes of changes in profitability more visible. For example, many U.S. firms achieved good profit growth during the 1970s by raising prices faster than their input costs were increasing, a strategy that was possible because the inflationary times permitted price increases to be sustained. Also, the weak U.S. dollar protected domestic producers from overseas competition and helped to sustain their market share overseas. When inflation subsided in the 1980s and the dollar was revalued, U.S. companies found that they now suffered from a severe competitive disadvantage because their productivity growth had been far below that of their foreign competitors. The relative deterioration in productivity had been masked by accounting measurements that focused on aggregate profits rather than on how these profits were achieved.

We will now show the calculations that permit profit changes to be decomposed into sales-activity, price-recovery, and productivity variances.

The more detailed level of analysis requires additional information about both unit prices (or costs) and quantities of outputs and inputs. Fortunately, the Matony Corporation kept detailed records on its inputs and outputs, and we discover additional information about operations during the period.

EXHIBIT 9–8
Quantities and Prices of Outputs and Inputs

	Outputs			*Inputs*	
	Quantity	*Price*		*Quantity*	*Price*
Model 1	12,000	$16	Labor	5,212 hr	$21.00
Model 2	5,500	22	Materials	21,920 lb	4.40
Model 3	1,800	40	Energy	10,633 kwhr	5.80

The data in Exhibit 9–8 provide all the additional information we require in order to decompose the unfavorable $12,571 profit variance into components due to differences in sales activity, productivity, and price recovery. The analysis will provide a comprehensive explanation of the factors that contributed to the 27% decline from the profits budgeted at the beginning of the period.

We start by isolating the effects of the changes in the level of business activity from the effects due to changes in costs, prices, and operating efficiencies. Obtaining a flexible budget based on the actual sales activity during the period provides the key computation for such a separation. The flexible budget in Exhibit 9–9 indicates what the expected profits would have been given perfect foresight about the actual sales volume and mix.

EXHIBIT 9–9
Flexible Budget at Actual Sales Volumes

	Actual Sales (Units)	*Contribution Margin per Roll*	*Total Contribution Margin*
Model 1	12,000	$ 4.00	$ 48,000
Model 2	5,500	7.00	38,500
Model 3	1,800	22.00	39,600
Budgeted contribution margin at actual sales volume			$126,100
Period expenses (budgeted)			80,000
Net income			$ 46,100

The $46,100 figure in Exhibit 9–9 represents the budgeted net income at the actual level and mix of sales. It assumes that all output prices, input costs, and production efficiencies equaled the budgeted amounts. From this figure, we can compute three aggregate variances: sales activity, price recovery, and productivity.

Sales-Activity Variance

The sales-activity variance represents the change in profits due to deviations from budget in the actual number and mix of units sold. It assumes that all prices, costs, and resource usages were exactly as budgeted. The computation is shown below:

$$
\begin{aligned}
\text{Sales-activity variance} &= [\text{Actual output} - \text{Budgeted output}] \\
&\quad * \text{Standard margin} \\
&= [(12{,}000 - 10{,}000) * 4 + (5{,}500 - 6{,}000) \\
&\quad * 7 + (1{,}800 - 2{,}000) * 22] \\
&= \$100 \text{ (favorable)}
\end{aligned}
$$

The favorable variance indicates that changes in the volume and mix of sales should have increased actual profits by $100. The sales-activity variance explains why the flexible budget at the actual sales volume equals $46,100, which is $100 higher than the income budgeted at the start of the period (see Exhibit 9–5).

The sales-activity variance can be decomposed further into two components, a sales-volume and a sales-mix variance. Recall from earlier in the chapter that we first compute the weighted-average contribution margin, m^*:

$$
m^* = \frac{\text{Total budgeted contribution margin}}{\text{Total units sold}}
$$

$$
= \frac{\$126{,}000}{18{,}000} = \$7.00
$$

We can now compute the sales-volume variance as the change in expected contribution margin caused solely by changes in the number of units sold (holding mix constant):

$$
\begin{aligned}
\text{Sales-volume variance} &= \text{Change in unit sales} \\
&\quad * \text{Average contribution margin} \\
&= [(12{,}000 - 10{,}000) + (5{,}500 - 6{,}000) \\
&\quad + (1{,}800 - 2{,}000)] * 7.00 \\
&= [2{,}000 - 500 - 200] * 7.00 \\
&= \$9{,}100 \text{ (favorable)}
\end{aligned}
$$

Thus, holding mix constant, the extra 1,300 units sold should have produced a favorable $9,100 increase in profits. But an unfavorable shift occurred in the mix of products sold, as revealed by the sales-mix variance:

$$\text{Sales-mix variance} = \text{Change in unit sales}$$
$$* \text{(Budgeted} - \text{Average) contribution margin}$$
$$= [2,000 * (4 - 7) + (-500) * (7 - 7)$$
$$+ (-200) * (22 - 7)]$$
$$= [-6,000 + 0 - 3,000]$$
$$= -\$9,000 \text{ (unfavorable)}$$

The sales mix is highly unfavorable because the Matony Company increased the percentage of sales of the low-margin Model 1 and decreased the percentage of sales of the high-margin Model 3. We can now see that the favorable $100 sales-activity variance was produced by two offsetting variances, a favorable $9,100 increase based on increased total unit sales less $9,000 due to an unfavorable shift in the mix of products sold.

Price-Recovery Variance

The price-recovery variance measures the change in profits caused by differences in the average prices received for outputs produced and paid for input resources consumed. The variance is computed using the actual (not the budgeted) quantities of outputs and inputs. The price-recovery variance shows whether, at actual outputs and inputs, selling prices have risen enough to compensate for cost increases of inputs; in effect, how much of the increase or decrease in profits can be attributed to relative price increases rather than to changes in sales activity or productivity.

The price-recovery variance is computed in two stages. First, the sales-price variance is obtained as the difference in actual from budgeted prices, measured at actual units sold:

$$\text{Sales-price variance} = [\text{Actual price} - \text{Budgeted price}]$$
$$* \text{Actual sales volume}$$
$$= [(16 - 15) * 12,000 + (22 - 20)$$
$$* 5,500 + (40 - 40) * 1,800]$$
$$= [12,000 + 11,000 + 0]$$
$$= \$23,000 \text{ (favorable)}$$

Second, we compute the input-cost variance as the difference between actual unit costs and standard unit costs for input resources, multiplied by the actual inputs consumed. The computations are shown in Exhibit 9–10.

The price-recovery variance can now be computed as the difference between the sales-price and the input-cost variances:

$$\text{Price-recovery variance} = \text{Sales-price variance} - \text{Input-cost variance}$$
$$= \$23,000 - \$15,853$$
$$= \$7,147$$

EXHIBIT 9–10
Input-Cost Variances

	Actual Unit Costs	Budgeted Unit Costs	Differ-ence	Actual Inputs	Input-Cost Variance
Labor	$ 21.00	$ 20.00	$ 1.00	5,212	$ 5,212
Materials	4.40	4.00	0.40	21,920	8,768
Energy (kwhr)	5.80	6.00	−0.20	10,633	(2,127)
Committed over-head	84,000	80,000	4,000	1	4,000
Input-cost variance					$15,853

The favorable variance shows that profits improved by $7,147 because the Matony Corporation was able to raise its selling prices by more than its costs were increasing.

We have now controlled for changes in sales activity and changes in unit prices and costs. Still remaining is to identify the profit change caused by productivity increases or decreases.

Productivity Variance

The productivity variance can be computed as the sum of individual usage variances. The impact of usage variances in material, labor, and variable overhead (energy) is calculated at actual output levels and budgeted (or standard) prices. The calculations are shown in Exhibit 9–11.

EXHIBIT 9–11
Productivity Variance

	Standard Consumption @ Actual Output				Act. Cons.	Differ-ence	Stand. Price	Usage Var.
	Model 1	Model 2	Model 3	Total				
Labor	2,400	1,375	720	4,495	5,212	717	$20	$14,340
Materials	12,000	6,050	2,340	20,390	21,920	1,530	4	6,120
Energy	6,000	3,300	1,440	10,740	10,633	−107	6	(642)
Productivity variance								$19,818

The entries for the Standard Consumption columns are obtained by combining the data in Exhibits 9–3 and 9–8. For example, the entry for Standard Materials Consumption for Model 2 is computed as

$$\text{Standard materials, Model 2} = \text{Actual output, Model 2}$$
$$* \text{ Materials per unit}$$
$$= 5,500 * 1.1$$
$$= 6,050 \text{ lb}$$

The unfavorable productivity variance of $19,818 arises from using more labor and materials than the standard allowance to produce the actual output. The productivity variance represents the increase in profits from better usage of individual input resources, including variable overhead components, to produce a given quantity of outputs. Shifts in the actual volume and mix of outputs, prices of output products, and prices (or costs) of input resources have already been controlled for in the sales-activity and price-recovery variances. Therefore, the productivity variance is not influenced by production and sales activity or by relative price effects.

Some productivity measurement systems include the sales-activity variance in the productivity measure, thereby enabling companies to show favorable productivity gains during periods of increasing production and sales.[3] We believe it is preferable to separate profit improvements due to increases in sales from profit changes caused by better processes for using materials, labor, energy, capital, and support departments. In effect, we distinguish between increases in output produced by working more hours at the same level of efficiency and increases due to producing more output per unit of hour worked.

In summary, the unfavorable profit variance of $12,571 (see Exhibit 9–7) can now be explained by the three variances:

Actual profit	$ 33,429
Budgeted profit	46,000
Profit variance	$(12,571)
Sales-activity variance	$ 100
Price-recovery variance	7,147
Productivity variance	(19,818)
Total variance	$(12,571)

Each of the aggregate variances already computed can be split into more detailed components. We have already shown how the sales-activity variance could be decomposed into volume and mix effects. The sales-volume variance could be split further into a component attributed to increases in the overall size of the market (representing total industry sales) and a component due to changes in the market share of the Matony Corporation in this market. The sales-mix variance could be decomposed into variances for each individual model. Selling-price and input-cost components could be attributed to the individual products and resources.[4]

---

[3] See, for example, the capacity usage variance in the productivity measurement scheme of B. J. van Loggerenberg and S. J. Cucchiaro, "Productivity Measurement and the Bottom Line," *National Productivity Review* (Winter 1981–82).

[4] These extensions are discussed in J. Shank and N. Churchill, "Variance Analysis: A Management-Oriented Approach," *Accounting Review* (October 1977), pp. 950–57.

And productivity variances could be assigned to individual resources and the consumption of each resource by each product.

The process could be continued even further. Market-share changes could be computed by product line and region. Sales-mix variance could be decomposed by region and customer or by subproduct grades such as color, style, or size. Sales-price changes could be split between list-price changes and discounts or returns from list. The analysis should stop at any level for which the next level of information either is unavailable or is not deemed sufficiently useful to warrant the complexity of additional computations or data collection.

Productivity Ratios

The accounting variances computed in the preceding section help to separate a total profit variance into components caused by increases in the volume of sales, changes in relative prices between outputs and inputs, and productivity effects. But the variance components are themselves absolute numbers and do not translate readily into percentage improvements. Managers generally find it easier to evaluate productivity improvements by percentages, such as by specifying a target for overall productivity improvement of, say, 7% per year. A percentage summary also facilitates comparison both to the scale of operations and to previous years. A favorable productivity variance of $200,000 is more impressive when total operating costs are $2 million than when they are $200 million. And a company that is attempting to increase productivity by 7% each year will not find it immediately informative to learn that its productivity variance for the year was a favorable $200,000.

It is straightforward to obtain percentage measures for the three aggregate variances we computed in the preceding section by choosing an appropriate denominator to scale or normalize each variance. No unique way exists to select denominators for the three variances so that the resulting percentages will depend directly on which denominators are chosen. Nevertheless, the following three choices represent plausible bases to consider:

Accounting Variance	Denominator	Magnitude
Sales activity	Standard contribution margin at budgeted output	$126,000
Price recovery	Standard income at actual quantities of outputs and inputs	26,282
Productivity	Total standard costs at actual output	235,900

The calculation for the sales-activity denominator comes directly from Exhibit 9–5. The denominator for the price-recovery variance comes from the calculations in Exhibit 9–12.

EXHIBIT 9–12
Standard Income Computed at Actual Quantities of Outputs and Inputs

	Budgeted Price	Actual Units Sold	Total
Model 1	$15	12,000	$180,000
Model 2	20	5,500	110,000
Model 3	40	1,800	72,000
Total			$362,000
	Budgeted Cost	Actual Inputs Consumed	Total
Labor	$20	5,212	$104,240
Materials	4	21,920	87,680
Energy	6	10,633	63,798
Committed overhead	80,000	1	80,000
Total			$335,718
Standard income			$ 26,282

The denominator for the productivity variance, standard costs at actual output, is computed in Exhibit 9–13.

EXHIBIT 9–13
Total Standard Costs at Actual Output

	Standard Cost	Actual Units Sold	Total
Model 1	$11	12,000	$132,000
Model 2	13	5,500	71,500
Model 3	18	1,800	32,400
Total standard costs			$235,900

We can now compute the productivity ratios to explain the 27.3% decrease in profits during the year. The $100 favorable sales-activity variance represents an 0.08% increase in contribution margin from the budgeted contribution margin of $126,000. The $7,147 favorable price-recovery variance is a 27.2% improvement relative to the standard income of $26,282 computed with standard prices and costs at the *actual* quantities of outputs sold and inputs consumed. Finally, the unfavorable $19,818 productivity variance represents an 8.4% reduction in actual costs measured with respect to the standard costs computed at the *actual* volume and mix of outputs (see Exhibit 9–14).

EXHIBIT 9–14
Sales-Activity, Price-Recovery, and Productivity Ratios

Actual profits	=	$ 33,429
Budgeted profits	=	$ 46,000
Total profit variance	=	$(12,571)

$$\text{Percentage change in profits} = \frac{(12,571)}{46,000} = -27.3 \ \%$$

Sales-activity ratio	= 100/126,000	=	0.08%
Price-recovery ratio	= 7,147/26,282	=	27.2 %
Productivity ratio	= (19,818)/235,900	=	−8.4 %

	(1) Ratio	(2) Elasticity Weights	(3) = (1) * (2) Impact on Profits
Sales activity	0.08%	$\frac{126,000}{46,000} = 2.74$	0.2%
Price recovery	27.2	$\frac{26,282}{46,000} = 0.57$	15.5
Productivity	−8.4	$\frac{235,900}{46,000} = 5.13$	−43.1
Total profit variance			−27.3%

To combine the three ratios, each normalized by a different activity base, into an overall measure of profit improvement, we compute elasticity weights (see column 2 of Exhibit 9–14) equal to the ratio of the denominator weights (used to compute the ratios in column 1) to the budgeted profits of $46,000. Multiplying each weight in column 2 by the respective ratio in column 1 yields the weighted percentage changes shown in column 3 of Exhibit 9–14. Adding the three percentage changes in column 3 produces the overall percentage decrease in profits of 27.3%. We can now explain the 27.3% decrease in profits by a 0.2% increase in sales activity, a favorable 15.5% improvement in price recovery, less a 43.1% drop in productivity (measured relative to the budgeted profits of $46,000).

In addition to decomposing the percentage change in profits into sales-activity, price-recovery, and productivity components, we can interpret the elasticity weights (column 2 in Exhibit 9–14) as the percentage change in profits produced by a given percentage change in each of the three components. For example, the productivity weight of 5.13 implies that every 1% improvement in productivity produces a 5.13% increase in total profits (holding output quantities and all input and output prices constant). The price-recovery weight of 0.57 implies that a 1% improvement in gross margin, due to changing output and input prices, will produce a 0.57% increase in profits; and the sales-activity weight of 2.74 indicates that each 1% increase in aggregate output will produce a 2.74% increase in profits (holding productivity and prices and costs constant). Thus, the weights computed in Exhibit 9–14 can be interpreted as elasticity factors that estimate the sensitivity of profits to percentage changes in operating and activity factors.

Of course, the three variance ratios and the associated elasticity weights (shown in columns 1 and 2 of Exhibit 9–14) are a direct function of the particular denominators used to normalize the accounting variances. If different denominators are chosen, the ratios and the weights will differ. But the percentages shown in column 3 of Exhibit 9–14 will be the same regardless of how the normalizing denominators are chosen, since they represent the ratio of each accounting variance to the budgeted profits (of $46,000).

Measuring Productivity Year to Year

All the analysis accomplished so far in this chapter has simply explained the difference between actual and budgeted profits in a period. Traditional standard cost-variance analysis provides a one-period retrospective analysis of performance. We have expanded this analysis by splitting a total variance into sales-activity, price, and productivity components. But the most important goal for a productivity measurement system is to compute period-to-period improvements in productivity. A productivity measurement system should enable companies to determine their ability to produce the same (or higher) outputs with fewer quantities of input resources. A productivity measurement system attempts to explain period-to-period changes in *actual* profits. In fact, because productivity measurement has traditionally been applied only to changes in actual performance, there has been no role for standards or budgets.[5] In effect, the base period (period 1) serves as the performance standard for all future periods.

The proposed system for reconciling actual performance in successive periods can be represented by the diagram in Figure 9–4. The sales-activity and price-recovery variances in Figure 9–4 are analogous to those computed earlier in this chapter except that the actual unit quantities and prices in Year 1 serve as the "budgeted" figures for Year 2. Three productivity variances are required. The Year 1 productivity variance links actual op-

---

[5] The problems that arise in traditional productivity measurement systems when information on standard usage is not exploited are documented in Banker, Datar, and Kaplan, "Productivity Analysis."

FIGURE 9-4

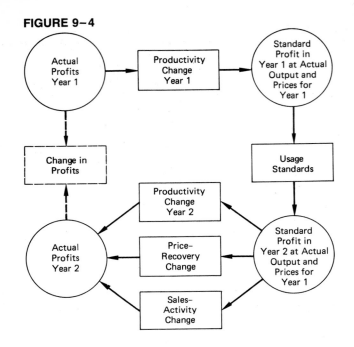

erating performance in Year 1 to the standards for that year; the Year 2 productivity variance explains operating differences between actual and standard Year 2 performance. And a new variance, the usage-standards variance, must be introduced to control for changes in the standards between successive periods. It measures the impact of changes between the two years of the usage standards for the input quantities.

As before, we will illustrate the analysis with a simple numerical example (see Exhibit 9-15).

The top portion of Exhibit 9-15 contains the standards, during two consecutive years of operations, for the quantity of inputs required for each unit of output. The actual sales and consumption of inputs during these two years is displayed in the bottom portion of Exhibit 9-15. The Year 2 data are identical to data analyzed previously in this chapter (see Exhibits 9-3 and 9-8). Our objective now is not to compare Year 2 actual with the standards for Year 2, but to explain the difference in actual profits between Year 2 and Year 1 so that we can determine the causes for the decrease in profits between the two years:

Year 2 actual profits	$33,429
Year 1 actual profits	40,597
Profit decrease	$ 7,168

EXHIBIT 9–15
Production and Sales Data for Two-Period Productivity Example

	Year 1			Year 2		
Technology Specification	*Model 1*	*Model 2*	*Model 3*	*Model 1*	*Model 2*	*Model 3*
Labor-hours per unit	0.22	0.25	0.42	0.20	0.25	0.40
Material lb per unit	1.05	1.16	1.40	1.00	1.10	1.30
Kwhr per unit	0.52	0.64	0.82	0.50	0.60	0.80

	Actual Performance					
	Year 1			Year 2		
	Value	*Quantity*	*Price*	*Value*	*Quantity*	*Price*
Sales						
Model 1	$150,000	10,000	$15.00	$192,000	12,000	$16.00
Model 2	102,720	4,800	21.40	121,000	5,500	22.00
Model 3	93,600	2,400	39.00	72,000	1,800	40.00
Total	$346,320	17,200	$20.13	$385,000	19,300	$19.95
Costs						
Labor	$ 97,922	4,996	$19.60	$109,452	5,212	$21.00
Materials	73,613	20,448	3.60	96,448	21,920	4.40
Kwhr	59,189	10,032	5.90	61,671	10,633	5.80
Overhead	75,000	1	75,000	84,000	1	84,000
Total	$305,723			$351,571		
Profits	$ 40,597			$ 33,429		

Sales-Activity Variance

We start by explaining changes in the actual volume and mix of sales between the two years. Unlike the intraperiod analysis illustrated before, we now use the actual Year 1 prices when computing the sales-activity, volume, and mix variances. The sales-activity variance analyzes just the change in the volume and mix of sales between the two years. We must hold all other factors constant so as not to confound the analysis. Therefore, we analyze the sales difference using the actual prices and costs realized in the base period (Year 1). Other than this change, the calculations follow those done in the single-period analysis and hence are reproduced in Exhibit 9–16 without further explanation.

The sales-volume variance is favorable because 2,100 more units were sold in Year 2 than in Year 1. The mix variance is unfavorable because the large increase in sales occurred in the lowest-margin product, Model 1, and a decrease in sales occurred in the highest-margin product, Model 3.

EXHIBIT 9–16
Sales-Activity Variance: Two-Period Example

	Model 1	Model 2	Model 3
Selling price	$15.00	$21.40	$39.00
Labor (@ $19.60/hr)	$ 4.312	$ 4.900	$ 8.232
Materials (@ $3.60/lb)	3.780	4.176	5.040
Kilowatt-hours (@ $5.90/kwhr)	3.068	3.776	4.838
Variable costs	$11.160	$12.852	$18.110
Contribution margin	$ 3.840	$ 8.548	$20.890

	(1) *Year 1* *Margins*	*(2)* *Output—* *Year 2*	*(3)* *Output—* *Year 1*	*(4) = (2) − (3)* *Difference*	*(5) = (1) ∗ (4)* *Sales-Activity* *Variance*
Model 1	$ 3.840	12,000	10,000	2,000	$ 7,680
Model 2	8.548	5,500	4,800	700	5,983
Model 3	20.890	1,800	2,400	(600)	(12,534)
Total		19,300	17,200	2,100	$ 1,130

Average contribution margin, Year 1 = Total margin/Units sold
$$= 129,566/17,200 = 7.533$$

Sales-volume variance = 2,100 ∗ $7.533 = $15,819

Sales-mix variance = [2,000 ∗ (3.840 − 7.533)] + [700 ∗ (8.548 − 7.533)] + [(−600)
$$∗ (20.890 − 7.533)]$$
$$= −7,386 + 711 − 8,014$$
$$= −$14,689$$

To summarize Exhibit 9–16:

Sales-activity variance:	$ 1,130	favorable
Sales-volume variance:	$ 15,819	favorable
Sales-mix variance:	(14,689)	unfavorable

Price-Recovery Variance

We next compute the price-recovery variance to represent the change between prices and costs in the two years. As with the sales-activity variance, the computations are identical to those done in the single-period model except for the substitution of Year 1 actual prices and costs to serve as the "budgeted" figures for the Year 2 data. Recall that we are attempting to explain the difference between the *actual* profits in Years 1 and 2. The calculations are shown in Exhibit 9–17.

EXHIBIT 9–17
Price-Recovery Variance
Output-Price Variances

	Year 2 Prices	Year 1 Prices	Differ- ence	Units Sold—Year 2	Price Variance
Model 1	$16.00	$15.00	$1.00	12,000	$12,000
Model 2	22.00	21.40	0.60	5,500	3,300
Model 3	40.00	39.00	1.00	1,800	1,800
Sales-price variance					$17,100

Input-Cost Variances

	Unit Costs— Year 2	Unit Costs— Year 1	Differ- ence	Actual Inputs	Input Cost Var.
Labor	$ 21.00	$ 19.60	$ 1.40	5,212	$ 7,297
Materials	4.40	3.60	0.80	21,920	17,539
Energy (kwhr)	5.80	5.90	−0.10	10,633	(1,063)
Committed overhead	84,000	75,000	9,000	1	9,000
Input-cost variance					$ 32,770
Price-recovery variance					$(15,669)

The calculations in Exhibit 9–17 show that the increase in prices failed to recover all the cost increases that occurred in Year 2. In particular, materials costs increased by more than 20% and committed overhead increased by 12%, whereas the largest sales price increase was less than 7%.

Productivity Variances

Having controlled for changes in the level and mix of sales, and for changes in selling prices and input costs, we need only explain the change in productivity in order to get a comprehensive explanation of the profit differential between the two years. Three separate calculations are required. First, productivity in Year 2 is computed relative to the standards in that year. Then, the component in year-to-year productivity already reflected in the different standards between the two years must be calculated. Finally, since we are explaining differences in actual performance between the two years, we need to compute the productivity variance of actual versus standard usage in Year 1. These three components can then be combined into an overall productivity variance between the two years (see Figure 9–5).

The calculations of productivity in Year 1 and Year 2 are identical to those performed in the single-period situation. They are shown in Exhibit 9–18.

344 *Chapter 9*

EXHIBIT 9–18
Productivity Variance—Year 1

	Model 1	Model 2	Model 3	Total	Act. Cons.	Dif- ference	Stand. Price	Usage Var.
Labor	2,200	1,200	1,008	4,408	4,996	588	$19.60	$11,525
Materials	10,500	5,568	3,360	19,428	20,448	1,020	3.60	3,672
Energy	5,200	3,072	1,968	10,240	10,032	– 208	5.90	– 1,227
Productivity variance—Year 1								$13,970

Standard Consumption @ Actual Output spans Model 1–Total.

Sample calculation:
  Materials, Model 1 = 10,000 units sold * 1.05 standard lb per unit

Productivity Variance—Year 2

	Model 1	Model 2	Model 3	Total	Act. Cons.	Dif- ference	Stand. Price	Usage Var.
Labor	2,400	1,375	720	4,495	5,212	717	$19.60	$14,053
Materials	12,000	6,050	2,340	20,390	21,920	1,530	3.60	5,508
Energy	6,000	3,300	1,440	10,740	10,633	– 107	5.90	– 631
Productivity variance—Year 2								$18,930

Sample calculation:
  Materials, Model 1 = 12,000 units sold * 1.0 standard lb per unit

The productivity variances for the two years are both unfavorable (13,970 in Year 1, and 18,930 in Year 2).

The final calculation reconciles the difference in the standards between the two years. The standards for variable input usage per unit of each type of output appear in the top portion of Exhibit 9–15. The effect of the changing standards, called the *usage-standards variance,* is evaluated using the actual output quantities of Year 2 and the actual unit costs of Year 1. The calculations are shown in Exhibit 9–19.

The usage-standards variance equals $12,332 favorable. It is favorable because the standards for Year 2 were tightened relative to those in existence for Year 1.

The calculation of the usage-standards variance makes it clear that we cannot get an accurate measure of productivity performance in Year 2 just by comparing standard with actual performance in that year. Missing from such a calculation is a measure of how much the standards were tightened or loosened between Year 1 and Year 2. The usage-standards variance provides just that link. Thus, the productivity performance between Years 1 and 2 requires three component calculations: actual performance relative to standard in Year 1 (see upper portion of Exhibit 9–18), changes in standards between Years 1 and 2 (Exhibit 9–19), and actual performance in Year 2 relative to standard (lower portion of Exhibit 9–18. These three calculations can now be summarized:

– Productivity, Year 1	$ 13,970	
Usage-standards variance	12,332	
Productivity, Year 2	(18,930)	
Total	$ 7,372	favorable

Overall Comparison: Year 2 with Year 1

We can now combine the sales-activity, price-recovery, and three productivity variances to explain the $7,168 decrease in profits between Year 1 and Year 2 (see Exhibit 9–20).

Exhibit 9–20 shows that the cost increases for materials and labor that were not offset by higher output prices accounted for the decline in

EXHIBIT 9–19
Usage-Standards Variance

	Output Year 2	Standard Consumption @ Year 1 Standards		
		Labor	Materials	Kwhr
Model 1	12,000	2,640	12,600	6,240
Model 2	5,500	1,375	6,380	3,520
Model 3	1,800	756	2,520	1,476
Total		4,771	21,500	11,236

	Output Year 2	Standard Consumption @ Year 2 Standards		
		Labor	Materials	Kwhr
Model 1	12,000	2,400	12,000	6,000
Model 2	5,500	1,375	6,050	3,300
Model 3	1,800	720	2,340	1,440
Total		4,495	20,390	10,740

	Std. Consump. Year 2 Stds.	Std. Consump. Year 1 Stds.	Difference	Unit Costs Year 1	Usage-Stds. Var.
Labor	4,495	4,771	– 276	$19.60	$ (5,410)
Material	20,390	21,500	– 1,110	3.60	(3,996)
Energy	10,740	11,236	– 496	5.90	(2,926)
Total usage standards variance					$(12,332)

EXHIBIT 9–20
Sales-Activity, Price-Recovery, and Productivity Variances

Sales-activity variance	(Exhibit 9–16)	$ 1,130
Price-recovery variance	(Exhibit 9–17)	(15,669)
– Productivity, Year 1	(Exhibit 9–18)	13,970
Usage-Standards Variance	(Exhibit 9–19)	12,332
Productivity, Year 2	(Exhibit 9–18)	(18,930)
Total Profit Variance		$(7,168)

profits between Year 1 and Year 2. There was a net productivity gain of $7,372 between the two years and a small increase in profits due to a higher volume of sales, although this sales increase would have generated even higher profits if it had not been concentrated in the low-margin product (Model 1) and accompanied by a sales decline in the high-margin product (Model 3).

Computing Multiperiod Variance as Percentages

The variances summarized in Exhibit 9–20 can be normalized as we did for the single-period variance analysis to obtain ratio measures:

Accounting Variance	Denominator
Sales activity	Standard contribution margin at actual Year 1 quantities and prices
Price recovery	Net income, computed with Year 1 prices and Year 2 quantities of outputs and inputs
Productivity	Total standard costs at actual outputs with standard input consumption
Usage standards	Total standard costs at actual outputs in Year 2 with Year 1 standard input consumption

The details of this calculation in tabular form follow.[6]

_____

[6] The calculations are similar to those performed in the single-period situation. Readers not interested in these details can skip to the Summary at the end of the chapter without loss of continuity.

A. Computing Denominators to Normalize Each Variance

1. Sales Activity The denominator for the sales-activity variance equals 129,566, the budgeted contribution in Year 1 based on the actual output and mix in Year 1. We obtain this number by extending the data used to construct Exhibit 9–16:

	(1) Year 1 Margins	(2) Actual Output— Year 1	(3) = (1) * (2) Budgeted Contribution Margins
Model 1	$ 3.840	10,000	$ 38,400
Model 2	8.548	4,800	41,030
Model 3	20.890	2,400	50,136
Total		17,200	$129,566

2. Price Recovery The denominator for the price-recovery variance equals 49,098, the gross margin computed with Year 1 prices and Year 2 quantities of outputs and inputs. The data are extracted from Exhibit 9–17 and the calculations are shown below.

	Year 1 Prices	Units Sold—Year 2	Revenues
Model 1	$15.00	12,000	$180,000
Model 2	21.40	5,500	117,700
Model 3	39.00	1,800	70,200
Total			$367,900

	Unit Costs— Year 1	Actual Inputs	Input Costs
Labor	$19.60	5,212	$102,155
Materials	3.60	21,920	78,912
Energy (kwhr)	5.90	10,633	62,735
Committed overhead	75,000	1	75,000
Total			$318,802
Gross margin			$ 49,098

3. Productivity, Year 1 and Year 2 The denominators for the two yearly productivity variances equal the total standard costs for each year, computed at actual output levels and standard quantities of consumption for these output levels. The calculations appear on the next page (data extracted from Exhibit 9–18).

Year 1
Standard Consumption
@ Actual Output

	Model 1	Model 2	Model 3	Total	Standard Price	Input Costs
Labor	2,200	1,200	1,008	4,408	$19.60	$ 86,397
Materials	10,500	5,568	3,360	19,428	3.60	69,941
Energy	5,200	3,072	1,968	10,240	5.90	60,416
Total (Year 1 productivity denominator)						$216,754

Year 2
Standard Consumption
@ Actual Output

	Model 1	Model 2	Model 3	Total	Standard Price	Input Costs
Labor	2,400	1,375	720	4,495	$19.60	$ 88,102
Materials	12,000	6,050	2,340	20,390	3.60	73,404
Energy	6,000	3,300	1,440	10,740	5.90	63,366
Total (Year 2 productivity denominator)						$224,872

4. Usage Standards Finally, the denominator for the usage standards variance, $237,204, equals the total standard costs at actual Year 2 outputs, computed with Year 1 standard consumption of inptus (data extracted from Exhibit 9–19).

	Output— Year 2	Standard Consumption with Year 1 Standards		
		Labor	Materials	Kwhr
Model 1	12,000	2,640	12,600	6,240
Model 2	5,500	1,375	6,380	3,520
Model 3	1,800	756	2,520	1,476
Total input quantities		4,771	21,500	11,236
Year 1 prices		$ 19.60	$ 3.60	$ 5.90
Total costs		$93,512	$77,400	$66,292	$237,204

B. Computing Percentage Changes of Each Variance

Variance	Quantity	Denominator	Percentage
Sales activity	$ 1,130	$129,566	0.9 %
Price recovery	(15,669)	49,098	(31.9)
Productivity—1	13,970	216,754	6.4
Productivity—2	(18,930)	224,872	(8.4)
Usage standards	12,332	237,204	5.2
Total	$ (7,168)		

C. Decomposing Percentage Change in Profits into Components

Actual profits: Year 2	$33,429	
Actual profits: Year 1	40,597	
Change in profits	$ (7,168)	
Percentage change in profits	(7,168)/40,597 = (17.7)%	

Component	Percentage Change	Elasticity Weights	Total Impact on Profits
Sales activity	0.9 %	129,566/40,597 = 3.19	2.9 %
Price recovery	(31.9)	49,098/40,597 = 1.21	(38.6)
Productivity—1	6.4	216,754/40,597 = 5.34	34.2
Productivity—2	(8.4)	224,872/40,597 = 5.54	(46.5)
Usage standards	5.2	237,204/40,597 = 5.84	30.4
Total			(17.7)%

This final calculation shows that the 17.7% decline in profitability between Year 1 and Year 2 could be attributed to a small (2.9%) improvement in sales activity, a large (38.6%) component caused by costs increasing much faster than prices, only partially offset by a significant net gain in productivity (18% = 34.2 − 46.5 + 30.4) between the two years.

Summary

We have shown how to analyze the operating performance for a period into managerially relevant components of sales activity, price recovery, and productivity. These three "buckets" provide a convenient way to aggregate the myriad of variances reported by traditional standard-cost systems into a report that explains differences between actual and planned profits. The single-period analysis can be extended to analyze operating performance over time. In particular, year-to-year changes in profitability can also be explained by changes in sales-activity, price-recovery, and productivity components.

Firms attempting to become low-cost producers should expect profit improvement through favorable net productivity variances each period. For such firms, profit improvements earned by short-term increases in prices over costs will probably not be sustainable and should therefore not be interpreted as favorable performance, relative to their long-term goal of reducing costs and increasing productivity. By explicitly recognizing the profit change component caused by changes in the mix and volume of outputs (the sales-activity variance), we do not permit the confounding effects of increases or decreases in sales to distort the measurement of productivity or price-recovery changes.

The aggregation of usage variances into an overall productivity variance provides a convenient and interpretable aggregation of what would otherwise be a myriad of individual, detailed local variances. Also, the productivity variance extends the traditional standard-cost focus on direct labor and materials to also include productivity performance with respect to variable overhead resources. Traditional standard-cost systems can report overhead efficiency variances, but these are not decomposed into price and quantity components. Measuring productivity performance with respect to overhead resources should be especially valuable as overhead resources become a larger proportion of total manufacturing costs.

Extending the variance analysis to compute percentage changes in productivity, sales activity, and price recovery provides two additional benefits. First, we can link single-period percentage changes into multiple-period measures, since changes in activity levels from period to period are controlled for. Second, we obtain elasticity measures that relate percentage improvements in the individual components to overall changes in profitability.

Finally, the multiple-period perspective enables us to develop period-to-period productivity improvement measures even when standards are changing each period. Thus, we can obtain a dynamic productivity measure that will not be distorted by changes in sales volume and mix, or by changes in the standards.

PROBLEMS

9–1   Profit Variance Analysis

POST ELECTRIC CORPORATION

John Swann, managing director of Post Electric Corporation, glanced at the summary profit and loss statement for 1989, which he was holding (Table 1), and tossed it to Randy Cunningham. Swann looked out the window of his office and declared, somewhat smugly:

> As you can see, Randy, we exceeded our sales goal for the year, improved our margin, and earned more profit than we had planned. Although some of our expenses seemed to grow a little faster than sales, 1989 was a pretty good year for us, don't you think?

TABLE 1
Post Electric Corporation 1989 Operating Results (000)

	Budget	Actual
Sales	$5400	$5710
Manufacturing costs	2000	2090
	$3400	$3620
G & A expenses	1500	1650
Net income before taxes	$1900	$1970

Randy Cunningham, a recent graduate of a highly touted business school, was serving a training period as executive assistant to Swann. He looked over the figures and nodded his agreement. Swann continued:

> Randy, I'd like you to prepare a short report for the board meeting next week summarizing the key factors that account for the favorable overall profit variance of $70,000. I think you're about ready to make a presentation to the board if you can pull together a good report. Check with the controller's office for any additional data you may need or want. Remember, the board doesn't want a long complex presentation. See what you can come up with.

Randy Cunningham agreed to the assignment and gathered the data shown in Table 2. How can he present an analysis of 1989 operating results to the board?

TABLE 2
Additional Information*

	Meters		Generators	
	Budget	Actual	Budget	Actual
Price	$30	$29	$150	$153
Manufacturing cost	15	16	40	42
Margin	$15	$13	$110	$111
Units sold	80,000	65,000	20,000	25,000
Industry sales (units)	800,000	700,000	200,000	250,000

* Post's products are grouped into two main lines of business for internal reporting purposes. Each line includes many separate products which are averaged together for purposes of this problem.

9–2   *Profit Variance Analysis*

Chapel Hill Foods distributes a line of frozen meats. The company's three "products" are in fact, three different packages, each of 500 pounds, of assorted cuts of beef wrapped in a manner suitable for freezing.

For purposes of planning and control, the company prepares an annual budget on both a product and an aggregate basis.

The company's budget and actual results, for the year just ended, appear in Table 1. Industry volume in Chapel Hill's market was forecasted as one million tons. Actual industry volume was 1.2 million tons.

TABLE 1

	Budget			
	Economy Package	Custom Package	Deluxe Package	Total
Sales—pounds	2,000,000	3,000,000	1,000,000	6,000,000
Revenue	$4,000,000	$8,400,000	$3,500,000	$15,900,000
Variable costs	3,000,000	6,000,000	2,500,000	11,500,000
Contribution margin	$1,000,000	$2,400,000	$1,000,000	$ 4,400,000
Traceable fixed costs	500,000	800,000	200,000	1,500,000
Traceable margin	$ 500,000	$1,600,000	$ 800,000	$ 2,900,000
Allocated fixed costs*	200,000	300,000	100,000	600,000
Division income	$ 300,000	$1,300,000	$ 700,000	$ 2,300,000

	Actual			
	Economy Package	Custom Package	Deluxe Package	Total
Sales—pounds	2,500,000	2,500,000	500,000	5,500,000
Revenue	$5,250,000	$5,750,000	$1,400,000	$12,400,000
Variable costs	4,000,000	5,000,000	1,200,000	10,200,000
Contribution margin	$1,250,000	$ 750,000	$ 200,000	$ 2,200,000
Traceable fixed costs	550,000	700,000	200,000	1,450,000
Traceable margin	$ 700,000	$ 50,000	$ 0	$ 750,000
Allocated fixed costs*	295,455	295,455	59,090	650,000
Division income	$ 404,545	$(245,455)	$ (59,090)	$ 100,000

* Allocated on the basis of sales in pounds.

Required:

Charles Krep, president of Chapel Hill Foods, is very dismayed with results. Charlie grouses, "We came within 8.3 percent of our beef poundage sales target but profits are only 4.3 percent of budgeted." Prepare an analysis of sales and profits.

9–3 Materials Price-Mix-Yield Variances(CMA)

The LAR Chemical Co. manufacturers a wide variety of chemical compounds and liquids for industrial uses. The standard mix for producing a single batch of 500 gallons of one liquid is as follows:

Liquid Chemical	Quantity (in gallons)	Cost (per gallon)	Total Cost
Maxan	100	2.00	$200
Salex	300	.75	225
Cralyn	225	1.00	225
	625		$650

There is a 20 percent loss in liquid volume during processing due to evaporation. The finished liquid is put into 10 gallon bottles for sale. Thus, the standard material cost for a 10 gallon bottle is $13.

The actual quantities of raw materials and the respective cost of the materials placed in production during November were as follows:

Liquid Chemical	Quantity (in gallons)	Total Cost
Maxan	8,480	$17,384
Salex	25,200	17,640
Cralyn	18,540	16,686
	52,220	$51,710

A total of 4,000 bottles (40,000 gallons) were produced during November.

Required:

1. Calculate the total raw material variance for the liquid product for the month of November and then further analyze the total variance into a
   a. Material-price variance
   b. Material-mix variance
   c. Material-yield variance
2. Explain how LAR Chemical Co. could use each of the three material variances — price, mix, yield—to help control the cost to manufacture this liquid compound.

9–4 Sales-Profit-Cost Variance Analysis (CMA)

The Markley Division of Rosette Industries manufactures and sells patio chairs. The chairs are manufactured in two versions: a metal model, and a plastic model of a lesser quality. The company uses its own sales force

	Plastic Model	Metal Model
Raw material	$5.00	$ 6.00
Direct labor		
⅙ hour @ $6.00 per DLH	1.00	
¼ hour @ $8.00 per DLH		2.00
Variable overhead		
⅙ hour @ $12.00 per DLH	2.00	
¼ hour @ $8.00 per DLH		2.00
Standard variable manufacturing cost per unit	$8.00	$10.00
Budgeted fixed costs per month		
Supervision	$4,500	$3,500
Depreciation	4,000	3,000
Property taxes and other items	600	400
Total budgeted fixed costs for month	$9,100	$6,900

Required:

1. Analyze the causes of the $32,600 unfavorable income variance.
2. Based upon your analysis:
   a. Identify the major cause of Markley Division's unfavorable profit perform-ance.
   b. Did Markley's management attempt to correct this problem?
   c. What other steps, if any, could Markley's management have taken to im-prove the division's operating income?

9–5   *Mix and Yield Variances in a Decision Setting**

SAGEBRUSH FEED COMPANY

The Sagebrush Feed Company produces a cattle feed that can be made from various combinations of four raw materials. The assumptions and constraints on this product include:

1. Each batch of feed must contain at least 18 percent protein.
2. Each batch must contain no more than 20 percent of Raw Materials 2 and 3.
3. Other processing and input factor costs are independent of the raw ma-terials mix.

---

* This problem is adapted from Harry Wolk and A. Douglas Hillman, "Materials Mix and Yield Variances: A Suggested Improvement," *Accounting Review* (July 1972), pp. 549–55.

The characteristics of the four input raw materials are:

Raw Material	Percent Protein	Standard Cost per Ton
1	50	$45
2	10	30
3	15	25
4	35	40

At present, Sagebrush produces each ton (2000 lbs.) of feed by using 400 pounds of Raw Material 3 and 1600 pounds of Raw Material 4.

Required:

1. Verify that this mixture meets the protein constraint. Compute the standard cost per ton of feed with this mixture.
2. Raw Material prices fluctuate during the period so that the actual average prices for the four raw materials are:

Raw Material	Current Cost per Ton
1	$45
2	25
3	28
4	32

The company, however, followed its standard practice of mixing each ton of feed with 20 percent of Raw Material 3 and 80 percent of Raw Material 4. Compute the price variance from following this plan.

3. A newly hired employee in the controller's department observed that with the current set of prices, the firm is no longer producing at minimum cost. Set up and solve (perhaps by inspection) the linear program that enables him to obtain the minimum cost mix of raw materials for each ton of feed produced.
4. Suppose the revised optimal production plan (computed in requirement 3) has been implemented during the period. Compute the price, mix, and yield variances from following this plan. Interpret the implications of these variances.
5. Can you think of improved methods for computing mix and yield variances when substitution is possible among input factors as specified by a well-defined decision model of the production process?

into a new product line area, urea formaldehyde foam—see Exhibit 1.

EXHIBIT 1
Lancaster Corporation (A & B)
Sales by Product Line
(thousands of dollars)

	1973		*1974*		*1975*	
Alliston-Cambridge (air compressors)	946.7	32.2%	1,118.2	34.7%	986.9	30.0%
Wakefield Equipment (spray painters)	369.3	12.6	379.7	11.8	312.8	9.5
Minnesota Pumps (air driven pumps)	212.6	7.2	203.5	6.3	280.1	8.5
Nailhead (nails & nailers)	842.2	28.6	798.5	24.8	604.9	18.4
Melrose Paint Equipment (electrostatic painting)	292.9	10.0	199.5	6.2	128.8	3.9
Revere Foam (foam)	?				585.4	17.8
Other	276.3	9.4	522.5	16.2	393.9	12.0
TOTAL	2,940.0	100.0%	3,221.9	100.0%	3,292.8	100.0%

The Proposal

When Bill Edwards arrived in 1975, he faced a weak sales forecast and a deteriorating relationship with Alliston-Cambridge—it had increased Lancaster's 1975 sales quota to 240% of its 1974 performance. Keith and Bill believed that the profits on Alliston-Cambridge equipment were less than on other lines and that the sales force was "selling sales dollars rather than gross profit." As Bill told Keith, "We are making money this year, but we really don't know how much comes from where. Our gross margin is averaging 25% yet on the spot checks I have made, the margins vary from 10 to 40%." Thus, in 1976, Cambridge began developing and implementing an information system designed to help management improve profitability.

The first phase of this effort involved providing management and the sales force with cost and gross margin information for 1977 by product line, by customer, by territory and by salesperson. Then for 1977, they planned to give the sales force the sales and cost information they developed, give them authority to set prices at any level above 125% of cost without prior approval, and provide the motivation for profit maximization by paying the sales force a commission of 17% of gross profit on sales.

The "pricing authority" decision was greeted with some concern. The sales manager was afraid that the sales force would cut prices to get volume and "Lancaster would lose all its margin." Bill Edwards countered by saying that the 17% commission on gross margin was incentive enough to keep this from happening. Further, rewarding the sales force on margin rather than sales dollars would motivate the sales force to sell the high margin products which was what the company wanted.

The Results

Lancaster installed the new sales reporting system in November of 1976 and instituted the proposed pricing and compensation systems for 1977.

In early 1978, Bill Edwards was reviewing the results of the policy changes.

It's been quite a year. We beat our sales and gross margin budgets and made record profits—see Exhibit 2 [on page 362]. The new information system is working the way we planned it; all but one of the salespeople took to the new commission system like ducks to water—and they seem to have made more money in the bargain. We had good luck with our pricing policy, too. Instead of the salesmen coming back and saying, "Oh boy, I've got a $500 order," he now comes in saying, "I got an order for $375 and more profit in it than last year's order at $500." He's thinking in terms of profit and that is the key.

I still have work to do to get the salesmen to fully understand the information they are getting—but they are learning. Take a look at the product line results—Exhibit 3 [on page 363]. Alliston-Cambridge is down on budget. But if you would break that down further, you'd see that we made 115% of our small compressor quota but only 60% of quota on the big ones. Now, Alliston-Cambridge is blaming this on "that guy Edwards paying more on small compressors," but it is not true. The salesmen are finding out that on a small $3000-compressor, they can get 25% to 30% gross but on a $20,000-compressor, particularly in last year's market, you're lucky to get 7%. The emphasis of our sales force has changed and Alliston-Cambridge doesn't like it. Overall, we made 19% gross on compressors and that is pretty close to break even on a net basis—which we figure is around 15%.

We are pleased with the system. While we knew in general what was going on, we learned a few things. Alliston-Cambridge presents their product line as being, in the big compressors, a 20% profit item. We know that in the competitive press of the market, it is less than 15%. Nails proved to be even more profitable than I thought and foam, of course, was a panacea. We also get monthly sales and gross product figures and that is a big help when things are changing.

We have some ideas for expansion. We are forming a subsidiary for installing the foam we sell and exploring another "air-related product line" but with a broader market. Our systems will help us here but its real impact is in moving our salespeople to rethink what they are doing. I think we're on the right track.

EXHIBIT 2
Lancaster Corporation (A & B)
Statement of Income
for the year ended December 31, 1977
(Thousands of dollars)

Sales	5,560	100%
Cost of Sales	3,901	70.2
Gross Margin	1,659	29.8%
Operating Expenses	1,404	25.3
Operating Income	255	4.6
Non-operating income less Interest Expenses	69	.2
Net Income Before Taxes	246	4.4%

Required:

1. Were the fears of the sales manager realized?
2. Did the expectation of Bill Edwards come about?

9–8 General Foods—Productivity Measurement Program (Abridged)

After several hours of discussion of the history, current status, and direction of their productivity measurement program, William Brady (Manager of Industrial Engineering) and Edward McNesby (Manager of Cost Systems) for the General Foods Corporation summarized for the casewriter some of the issues currently facing them as follows:

> We're fairly satisfied with our technique for measuring productivity and its acceptance up to now in the organization. So far, however, it has only been used for measuring the performance of plants—and therefore, in effect, plant managers. It has also been incorporated into their bonus program. As a result, their cost consciousness has risen significantly. But we still have a long way to go, and there are a variety of directions in which we can proceed.
>
> For example, we would like to find a way to get this concept down into the plant infrastructure, so that it can influence the everyday actions of people at every level. To do that, we have to be able to translate

© Copyright 1982 by the President and Fellows of Harvard College. Harvard Business School case 9–682–072.

EXHIBIT 3

Lancaster Corporation (A & B)
1977 Budget and Results

	1976 Sales	1977 Sales			1977 Margin $			1977 Margin %	
		Target	Actual	% Target	Target	Actual	% Target	Target	Actual
Alliston-Cambridge	$1,426,203	$1,598,000	$1,320,896	82.7%	$ 327,590	$ 250,970	76.6%	20.5%	19.0%
Wakefield Equipment	287,504	310,000	282,502	91.0%	82,460	77,123	93.5%	26.6%	27.3%
Minnesota Pumps	392,343	485,000	417,973	86.2%	142,590	122,884	86.2%	29.4%	29.4%
Nailhead	745,758	984,000	827,350	84.0%	314,880	238,277	75.7%	32.0%	28.8%
Melrose Paint*	131,987	164,000	167,977	102.6%	49,200	63,999	130.1%	30.0%	38.1%
Revere Foam	835,374	1,288,000	1,958,986	152.1%	483,000	668,014	138.3%	37.5%	34.1%
Other	384,057	450,000	571,298	126.3%	104,400	161,106	154.3%	23.2%	28.2%
Total	$4,203,226	$5,279,000	$5,546,982	105.0%	$1,504,120	$1,582,373	105.2%	28.49%	28.53%

* Terminated line 10/31/77

overall productivity, as we have defined it, into a set of subordinate measures that relate to specific kinds of tasks. We don't want plant personnel simply to be measured by our data, but to use constructively the information we provide them with.

There is also interest in applying a similar kind of measurement at levels above that of the plant manager—at the divisional and corporate level, say. Right now, plant managers do not have control over some of the important variables that affect productivity. Division management, not plant management, is responsible for making such critical decisions as the overall production level, the product mix, new product introductions, purchasing and distribution. Union contracts, on the other hand, are negotiated at the plant level with some constraints, mostly monetary, from the corporate level. There ought to be a way of measuring the effectiveness of these decisions on productivity as well.

We would also like to proceed horizontally, by expanding our system to other plants within the company. And, finally, as we move to a wider variety of plants, we may need to refine or alter the procedure we are currently using.

General Foods' Productivity Measurement Program

The impetus for General Foods' Productivity Measurement Program came during the mid-1970s. Mr. Harold Golle, who was corporate Operations Vice President, was becoming increasingly uneasy about his company's cost reduction activities. "Our learning curve was almost flat," he recalled, "and it was hard to find out where the problem was or how to correct it. I had access to a lot of reports regarding plant operating results and cost reduction efforts, but I needed some way to pull everything together into a summary number for each plant. Moreover, Mr. Ferguson had established the goal that we should be the low-cost producer in our industry, and I had to find ways both to achieve that goal and to document that achievement." Golle participated in a Business Roundtable study group where productivity, along with various measures of it, were discussed. He found that very few other companies were making any attempts to institute effective programs for monitoring productivity.

In 1975, Golle asked Bill Brady and Ed McNesby to take on the task of designing such a productivity program for General Foods that focused on the most leverageable competitive cost elements. Frequently these were raw and packaging material costs rather than labor, which suggested that a measure of "total factor productivity" would be more appropriate for GF's business than the usual simple measure of labor productivity. Ed McNesby, with his knowledge of GF's cost system, developed an approach which was reviewed with Western Electric. (See the Appendix.)

They then began the process of testing the approach and presenting it to Operations Managers and Plant Managers. Two plants agreed to be the test plants, and researched the data necessary to develop a three-year history of their plant's productivity. The results confirmed the original positive feelings about the approach. In May, 1976, the system approach and principles and the results at the two test plants were presented by McNesby and Brady at a Corporate Operations meeting.

Mr. Charles Adamo, who was the Operations Manager for the Maxwell House coffee business unit (whose Houston plant was one of the pilot units), volunteered to try out the system more broadly. Adamo's interest was triggered by a rather unusual competitive and internal environment. The sales revenues and earnings from GF's coffee products (which accounted for about 40% of total corporate sales) had historically been quite volatile because of the boom-and-bust cycle of coffee bean prices.

> The coffee business is intensely competitive. The total U.S. demand for coffee has been stagnant for several years, and material costs account for 75–80% of the total cost of production. We pay the same for our coffee beans as our competitors, so productivity improvement is an important way we can increase our profit margins and gain an advantage versus competition.

His motivation to introduce the new system increased abruptly in 1975, when heavy frosts in Brazil caused coffee bean production there to fall drastically. As a result, world coffee bean prices more than tripled for a while, and demand for coffee dropped. Adamo was faced with idle capacity in his plants and deteriorating profitability.

The Maxwell House division operated four plants, three of them east of the Rocky Mountains. These plants competed against each other, in the sense that Adamo's staff established each plant's production rate on the basis of comparative cost data. Over time this had resulted in increasing production volumes being allocated to newer plants in the south and west U.S., at the expense of an older plant in the Northeast. The manager of this plant complained that his plant's future was being jeopardized by this system. His comparatively high labor costs (because of older workers and the higher wage rate prevailing in his region of the country) and older equipment were causing production volume to be taken away from him, which led to underutilized capacity and still higher average production costs. He was enthusiastic about the idea of introducing a new measure of performance which would provide a more accurate indication of the efficiency of his plant's operations.

Current Status of the Productivity Measurement Program

By mid-1981, 13 of GF's U.S. plants were using the new system, and it was being introduced in plants in Canada and England. All of its domestic "processing plants" (GF characterized its plants as either being "processing" or "mix and pack"; the former were more complicated, capital-intensive, and offered a richer array of opportunities for operating improvement) except those processing frozen foods had adopted the system. Plant managers' reactions to the system were mixed, but generally positive.

Some complained that the new measurement "wasn't fair" because it didn't compensate adequately for factors which were outside their control, such as the total production volume and new product introductions. Others felt that it left out certain critical variables that were peculiar to their particular process and location, and therefore invited unfair comparisons between plants producing different products in different regions of the country. If they wanted their productivity measure to look good, they argued, they had to take actions which would make their ROI look bad over the short term.

Even those who felt that the system generally did a good job of measuring variables that differentiated between good and weak plant management (such as overall manning levels, raw material yields, machine and labor utilization ratios, process improvements, and energy costs), however, felt that the system was overly sophisticated, rigid, and complex. It had not been computerized as yet, and therefore plant controllers were being forced to collect data and perform calculations that they had not been responsible for before. Because of the amount of work required to calculate the measure, most plants only attempted to measure their productivity once per year, and productivity results didn't become available until six months or so after the close of the year.

These concerns were offset by the general awareness of the program's benefits. It brought together a number of disparate pieces of information into a single comprehensive measure, and therefore discouraged the kind of "back door" cost reduction proposals (which simply transferred costs from one department to another within the same plant) which had sometimes slipped through previously. It also had encouraged greater investment in process improvements and the write-off of outdated equipment. Finally, it had permitted better analysis and understanding of the reasons behind unusually large improvements or fall-offs in plant performance, and provided a means for learning from the success of high performing plants. Because of these effects, it was having an increasing impact on the plants' budgetary and planning processes, which are under the supervision of the plant managers.

There had been another, more subtle, impact which was particularly satisfying for Bill Brady. "Up until a couple of years ago, the I.E. group in one division had been allowed to decline," he remarked. "The scope of their activities was reduced. Now, the Industrial Engineering function is gradually being strengthened as division management recognizes that productivity improvement must come from many sources." But, he was also concerned that the I.E.'s in the plants were not taking full advantage of the opportunities available to them through this form of productivity measurement.

> My biggest current frustration is getting the I.E.'s in the plants to use this new data to channel their efforts to the cost areas of greatest leverage and opportunity. Since the Productivity Index is calculated by the plant's Controller, the I.E. Manager may not be aware of how it is developed and used and how it may be of value to him. Whenever I visit a plant, I make sure that the I.E. Manager is involved and is using the results and the data behind the Productivity Index.

Appendix: The Mechanics of GF's Productivity Measurement System

The productivity measurement procedure that Ed McNesby and his colleagues devised had several objectives. Most basically, it sought to provide an accurate measure of how effectively a plant used the resources available to it in producing products, separating out the impact of inflation. It could then use this measure in assessing the comparative performance of individual plants over time, and comparing the company as a whole against the rest of its industry. Through such measurement it sought to encourage plant managers to take actions that would improve their plant's productivity: capital investment, energy conservation, layout and work flow rationalization, inventory control and overhead reduction. Finally, it sought to help identify the key cost leverage points where management attention would have the biggest payoff. Without such guidance, according to McNesby, plant managers found it difficult to see through the shower of fragmented cost-oriented reports (labor efficiency, line utilization, standard cost variances, raw material yields, packaging material spoilage, inventory turnover, capital investment paybacks, etc.) that inundated their desks, and focus their attention on the most critical action items.

The basic philosophy of GF's approach was different from that adopted by most other companies that were in the process of trying to develop productivity measurement systems. Rather than simply trying to calculate a series of "partial productivity" measures (such as the familiar labor productivity ratio—output divided by labor hours—that was almost synonymous with the word "productivity" in many people's minds), GF's system combined these measures into one overall "total factor productivity" measurement. Because plant managers did not have control over the purchasing of the raw materials used in their plants, the cost of raw materials was not included in the calculation of either the plant's "output" or its productivity. The wastage of raw material did enter into the calculation, however, because this was almost totally under the plant's control.

The procedure required that a "Base Year" be chosen, and the ratios of the plant's unit output to each of the major inputs (labor, overhead, raw and packaging materials) be calculated for each product. The total product cost, based on these ratios and the costs of their associated inputs, was then calculated for this Base Year. These Base Year costs were then used in subsequent years to calculate the output value and input costs for the plant; this eliminated the effect of price and cost inflation on the productivity measure. In the case of inputs which were too minor to warrant developing efficiency ratios, government-published indices were used to deflate current costs to constant Base Year dollars. Examples of the calculations of the productivity measure are contained in Exhibits A–1 through A–5.

EXHIBIT A–1
The Mechanics of GF's Productivity Measurement System
How It Works

Input
Procedure example:

Input Item	U/M	Base Year Cost per U/M	Actual U/M's	Input
Material X	Lbs. lost	$ 2.00	55,000	$110,000
Hourly labor	Hrs. worked	7.00	30,000	210,000
Salaried labor	No. of people	15,000	6	90,000
Electricity	KWH	.04	750,000	30,000
Subtotal				$440,000

	Current Year Cost	Deflator Index	
Minor ingredients/supplies	$ 22,000	110%	$ 20,000

	Investment Increase (Decrease) vs. Base Year	% Cost of Capital	
Inventories	$100,000	15%	15,000
Land, buildings, equipment	(50,000)	15%	(7,500)
Subtotal			$ 7,500
Total input			$467,500

EXHIBIT A–2
The Mechanics of GF's Productivity Measurement System
Plant "A" ($ Millions)

Output	1973	1974	1975	1976	1977	1978 Plan
Raw materials lost in production[1]	$ 42.6	$ 41.9	$33.2	$39.8	$35.5	$35.3
Packing materials lost in production	.3	.3	.3	.3	.3	.3
Labor & overhead	25.4	25.5	19.2	22.7	19.9	19.4
Total output	$ 68.3	$ 67.7	$52.7	$62.8	$55.7	$55.0
Input						
Raw materials lost in production[2]	$ 42.6	$ 41.0	$32.4	$37.9	$34.2	$32.7
Packing materials lost in production	.3	.3	.3	.4	.3	.3
Labor & overhead	25.4	25.3	26.2	28.1	25.3	25.9
Increase in cost of capital	—	—	.4	(.9)	(1.0)	(1.4)
Total input	$ 68.3	$ 66.6	$59.3	$65.5	$58.8	$57.5
Productivity index (output ÷ input)	1.000	1.017	.888	.958	.947	.956
Volume (millions of units)[3]	18.1	17.6	14.5	16.2	13.5	12.5

Note: Input data does not reflect cost reduction program

[1] Total costs at base year prices and base year efficiency ratios.

[2] Total costs at base year prices and actual efficiency ratios.

[3] "Units" represent a mix of roasted coffee units and soluble coffee units. Producing a unit of soluble coffee requires a different input of labor, and results in a different ratio of lost material, than does a unit of roasted coffee. Therefore, changes in the mix of the two products can cause the various "output" values to change at different rates than unit volume.

EXHIBIT A–3
The Mechanics of GF's Productivity Measurement System
Plant "B" ($ Millions)

Output	1973	1974	1975	1976	1977 L/E	1978 Plan
Raw materials lost in production	$ 22.7	$ 22.6	$ 20.5	$ 23.8	$ 24.6	$ 23.2
Packing materials lost in production	.2	.2	.2	.2	.2	.2
Labor & overhead	11.4	12.0	10.9	12.8	12.7	12.1
Total output	$ 34.3	$ 34.8	$ 31.6	$ 36.6	$ 37.5	$ 35.5

EXHIBIT A–3 (continued)
The Mechanics of GF's Productivity Measurement System
Plant "B" ($ Millions)

Input	1973	1974	1975	1976	1977 L/E	1978 Plan
Raw materials lost in production	$ 22.7	$ 22.2	$ 19.9	$ 22.3	$ 22.2	$ 21.3
Packing materials lost in production	.2	.2	.2	.2	.2	.2
Labor & overhead	11.4	11.3	10.9	11.9	12.1	11.9
Increase in cost of capital	–0–	(.4)	(.3)	(.8)	(.9)	(1.1)
Total input	$ 34.3	$ 33.3	$ 30.7	$ 33.0	$ 33.6	$ 32.3
Productivity index (output ÷ input)	1.000	1.045	1.029	1.090	1.112	1.099
Volume (millions of units)	18.5	18.7	17.1	19.9	19.9	19.9

Note: Input data does not reflect cost reduction program.

EXHIBIT A–4
The Mechanics of GF's Productivity Measurement System
Plant "B" Plant Productivity Index Impact of 1978 Cost Reduction Program ($ 000's)

Project Title and Description	Annual Net Savings (1978 $)	Annual Net Savings (1973 $)	Cost of Capital (1973 $)	$ Change in Plant Input
Packing material specification changes	$ 80	$ 49	$ (8)	$ 41
New blending system	45	24	(11)	13
Vacuum pump	20	7	(1)	6
Recirculate cooling water to vacuum pumps	13	4	(2)	2
Agglomerator	20	7	(2)	5
2 lb. lid applicator	30	19	(2)	17
New scale—can line no. 1	120	37	(9)	28
Yield improvement of 1.0% on Product X	670	214	—	214
Yield improvement of .8% on Product Y	232	74	—	74
Yield improvement of .2% on Product Z	134	43	—	43
Sewer connection charge not needed	200	138	—	138
Reduce efficiency loss on processing equipment to 4%	150	103	—	103
Other opportunities	86	36	—	36
Total plant	$1,800	$755	$(35)	$720

1978 Productivity index: 1.098
1978 Index if all cost reduction is achieved: 1.123

EXHIBIT A–5

The Mechanics of GF's Productivity Measurement System
Productivity Index Analysis of Change, Total Division ( ) = Unfavorable

	F1976 Base	F1977 Actual	F1978 Actual	F1979 L/E	F1980 AFP
● Raw materials lost in production	—	0.03	0.11	0.14	0.17
● Pkg. materials lost in production	—	—	—	—	—
● Labor and overhead:					
—Plants	—	(0.03)	(0.12)	(0.09)	(0.03)
—Headquarters	—	—	—	—	(0.01)
● Change in cost of capital					
—Plants:					
—M&E (Plant X)	—	—	0.01	0.01	0.01
—M&E, Bldg. (Plant Y)	—	—	—	0.02	0.02
—Others	—	0.01	0.01	0.03	0.03
—Headquarters—F.G. Inventory	—	—	—	0.01	0.02
Total change in cost of capital	—	0.01	0.02	0.07	0.08
Total change in Division P.I.	—	0.01	0.01	0.12	.21
Productivity index	1.00	1.01	1.01	1.12	1.21
Volume index	1.00	.93	.75	.80	.85

chapter 10

MEASURING QUALITY

Companies throughout the world are now recognizing the need for dramatic improvements in their manufacturing operations. Success in the global competitive environment requires that companies commit to order-of-magnitude improvements in quality, enormous reductions in inventory, and successful adoption of advanced manufacturing technology. In the next two chapters, we will briefly describe these innovations and identify the management accounting changes required for the new manufacturing environment.

Total Quality Control

The recent North American approach to quality emphasized that bad quality was the fault of workers. Because quality was a "worker problem," the only way to achieve acceptable outgoing quality was to "inspect it in" by adding more inspectors and more inspection stations. Thus, statistical sampling of items was performed to ensure (with, say, a 95% confidence level) that the number of outgoing defective items did not exceed a specified percentage. Occasionally, if demands to meet production targets and sales orders were high, marginally defective items were passed through final product inspection. After all, that's why the company had a field service force and a warranty reserve; failures, if they occurred, could be fixed in the field. In the meantime, production targets could be met and fixed costs absorbed into production (of both good and defective items).

This casual approach to quality had predictable consequences. Factories had high levels of inventory at each production stage to protect against shortages caused by uncertain quality from previous stages; incurred large costs for inspection, rejects, rework, scrap, and warranty repairs; and produced general confusion on the factory floor as production schedules were interrupted by parts and material shortages due to defective items, and by numerous production schedule changes required in order to reprocess defective items. Large areas of the factory were used to house defective items that were waiting to be reprocessed (and were even given a name, the "rework area").

Such activities were not a problem for traditional standard-cost systems. A "normal" allowance for scrap, waste, and rework was estimated and built into the standard costs for the process. Thus, as long as the production process did not deteriorate drastically from year to year, the costs of defective production could be assigned to the good items actually produced and unexpected variances would therefore be avoided. Also, some of the costs incurred to produce defective items could be recovered by higher prices in the marketplace.

The philosophy of emphasizing production volume over quality worked fine for U.S. manufacturers from the mid-1940s through the 1970s. Few of their domestic competitors were emphasizing manufacturing quality, and companies in the rest of the industrial world were rebuilding their factories from the destruction wreaked during World War II, so that they could not compete effectively in the market for manufactured goods.

During this time, however, several innovative Japanese companies and some West European manufacturers, especially in Germany, Switzerland, and Sweden, adopted a total quality control philosophy in which the only acceptable quality level was zero defects. The zero defect goal was not expected to be achievable, but it provided a target so that a company would never be satisfied unless it was reducing the incidence of defects by substantial amounts year after year.

For these companies, defects were measured not as a percentage of outgoing items, but as a *parts-per-million* (PPM) ratio of defects to items produced. Many activities had to be done correctly in order to achieve continual reductions in PPM defect rates. Most important was to recognize that quality had to be designed in, not inspected in. For example, products designed with fewer parts generally place less-severe demands on the quality of each component in order for the entire product to achieve a given reliability level. Also, when product designers thoroughly understand the manufacturing process, they will be less likely to design products that make stringent requirements on fabrication and assembly processes. The IBM Pro-Printer was designed so that it could be assembled by robots, without manual intervention. The parts were designed so that they fit together with only one orientation. As a consequence of the care taken during the design stage, the product can also be reliably assembled even by an unskilled worker without any mechanical tools, thereby greatly reducing the errors that might otherwise be introduced in the assembly process. Many manufacturing problems arise because of the difficulty of reliably producing a product that has been designed for performance, but not for manufacturability.

The traditional separation of functions in U.S. companies kept product designers far apart from manufacturing and process engineers. With the emphasis on developing better-performing products, containing more and more special features, the design engineers represented the elite group in advanced technology companies. Manufacturing and process engineers were relegated to secondary (and tertiary) roles; their job was to somehow figure out how to produce the products with sophisticated design features that were thrust upon them late in the planning cycle. It was not surprising that the initial production runs of products contained a high fraction of defective items and that production problems could never be completely eliminated.

The problems of poor production processes for new products frequently became rationalized by referring to them as "learning problems." Companies built learning or experience curve effects into their cost-planning estimates. They failed, however, to investigate how much "learning" occurred merely because they started from such an ignorant or inefficient base during initial production.

Today, companies striving for zero defect production recognize that manufacturing considerations must be made part of any new-product design. All new-product design teams include people with extensive production and procurement experience. Quality experts assert that only 20% of quality defects can be traced to the production line. The other 80% become locked in during the design stage or by purchasing based on low price rather than on the quality of parts and materials.[1]

Additional steps include extensive training of all personnel—workers and management—in how to achieve zero defect goals. The responsibility for detecting nonconforming items has been shifted from quality control inspectors to the persons actually performing the work. Operators now maintain their equipment, operate the machines well within acceptable and rated limits, and are expected to produce zero defect output. In some advanced manufacturing installations, the machines themselves perform quality checks, using computerized gauging devices, as the items are produced. Extensive use of statistical process control (SPC) is employed throughout the factory floor to ensure that all production processes continually operate in control. Other techniques are often employed to reduce the incidence of defective production. The Taguchi method attempts to design equipment methods and products that are "robust against noise," such as product deterioration, manufacturing imperfections, and environmental factors. The adverse effects from such noise are reduced instead of attempting to eliminate the noise. This permits products to perform more consistently in service under a variety of conditions.[2]

---

[1] See "The Push for Quality," *Business Week* (June 8, 1987), p. 135.

[2] See R. N. Kackar, "Taguchi's Quality Philosophy: Analysis and Commentary," *Quality Progress* (December 1986); and L. P. Sullivan, "The Seven Stages in Company-wide Quality Control," *Quality Progress* (May 1986).

Quality requirements were also imposed on suppliers. Companies have gone through several phases in their relationships with suppliers; shifting from the old policy of acceptance sampling of incoming items, to 100% inspection (with the entire batch returned if any defects were detected), to the current policy of performing no inspection at all of incoming items. To achieve this last goal, companies have worked with their suppliers, instructing them in statistical process control and, in some cases, showing how new equipment and procedures can be used to produce zero defect output. Suppliers become certified when they demonstrate that they can produce zero defect output. Their deliveries can then enter the production process with no incoming inspection performed. Any subsequent detection of defective items, of course, could lead to unhappy discussions between buyer and supplier.

One materials manager, with tongue planted firmly in cheek, explained that his company understood

> how difficult it is to produce perfect parts and that we will accept a few rejects from our suppliers. We insist only that our suppliers first separate their bad parts from their good ones and ship them separately. Furthermore, if a delivery is going to be late, our materials manager requests only that the supplier's vice president of marketing give our production workers a presentation on satisfying customers while they wait for the material to arrive.[3]

Many people are skeptical about this total commitment to reduce defects. Implicitly, their view would be represented by Figure 10–1, which shows that too much of a good thing becomes excessively expensive; they argue that a trade-off exists between cost and conformance quality. With this view, quality efforts should be curtailed at the point where the marginal benefit from further defect reduction is below the marginal cost.

Companies striving for Total Quality Control (TQC) consider themselves fortunate when their competitors believe the above conventional wisdom. These companies have learned that, based on all their experience, quality is indeed free,[4] as represented by the diagram in Figure 10–2.

Total manufacturing cost (including warranty and service costs) declines as the incidence of defects decreases. It turns out, not surprisingly when one thinks about it, that it is cheaper to build all the items correctly the first time rather than waste resources building substandard items that have to be detected, reworked, scrapped, fixed in the field, or reclaimed from customers. The conventional wisdom that attempts to "optimize" the number of defects has probably grossly underestimated the costs im-

---

[3] See Richard C. Walleigh, "What's Your Excuse for Not Using JIT?" *Harvard Business Review* (March–April 1986), p. 39.

[4] This point has been publicized in Philip B. Crosby, *Quality Is Free* (New York: McGraw-Hill, 1979).

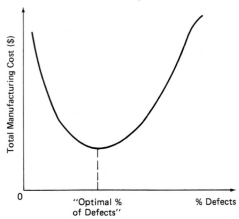

FIGURE 10–1
Traditional View of Quality-Cost Trade-Off

posed on the factory by having to inspect, move, store, reschedule, and rework defective items, as well as the loss in reputation caused by shipment delays and delivering defective items to customers. A leading Japanese industrialist estimates that the "true" losses due to defectives are six times the measured losses. Companies that have committed to achieving zero defect manufacturing are enjoying significant advantages over their competitors who are "optimizing" the number of defects (at a level different from zero).

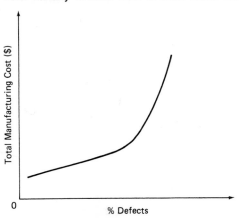

FIGURE 10–2
Total Quality Control View of Cost Trade-Off

Quality Measures

As companies adopt new manufacturing practices to achieve TQC, they will need to devise measures to motivate and evaluate their TQC objectives. Traditional cost accounting measures, such as variances on labor, material, and overhead, will not motivate and evaluate a company's performance in achieving quality goals. For example, many operating managers have been motivated by their cost accounting system to increase output to absorb overhead and thereby avoid unfavorable volume variances. This tendency is reinforced by local efficiency measures, such as the ratio of earned hours to total hours, for workers and machines. This measure encourages keeping workers and machines busy, but frequently little attention is paid at the time of production as to whether the units produced meet specifications. As long as aggregate activity (the total standard direct labor-hours of units produced) is high enough to absorb, or overrecover, period overhead, and worker and machine efficiency measures are high, the manufacturing manager receives good feedback from the traditional cost accounting system. Several companies have found they must shut off the "efficiency" or volume variances computed by their traditional financial accounting systems if they are to motivate quality production.

The purchase-price variance is another traditional cost accounting measure that provides disincentives to zero defect performance. Some purchasing managers have shifted to lower-quality suppliers in order to achieve favorable performance on their purchase-price variance measure. Companies committed to a TQC program recognize that suppliers should not be chosen based on quoting the lowest price. Rather, long-term relationships with suppliers have to be forged to reduce the "total cost of ownership" of purchased parts and materials. The total cost of ownership includes not only the actual purchase price but also the cost of scheduling, receiving, inspecting, and using purchased parts and materials.

One company categorized its vendors into two categories:

Good Vendors: Deliver on time, right quantity
Part requires no incoming inspection
Fair price, terms
Willing to work together to solve problems

Bad Vendors: Deliver late or early, wrong quantity
Part requires incoming inspection
Price, terms not acceptable
Not willing to work together to solve problems

It then announced:

All *bad* vendors have until October to become *good* vendors. At that time, we will terminate all bad vendors if at all possible.

As another example of a dysfunctional cost accounting procedure, standard-cost systems, designed to accumulate costs for financial reporting purposes, estimate normal scrap allowances so that production costs can be spread to the good units produced. Process-costing chapters in traditional cost accounting textbooks provide extensive instruction on how to allocate the "units lost units cost" to the remaining good items. The new manufacturing environment does not want to budget for or allocate the costs of defective items. It demands that we make the costs of defects and yields below 100% more visible so that engineers, operations managers, and workers can attempt to continually reduce the incidence of defective production and low yields. Thus, standards for internal control purposes should be computed based on zero defects and 100% yields, with any deviations flagged as an opportunity for improvement in future periods.

Beyond disconnecting several of the dysfunctional measures currently computed and reported by traditional standard-cost systems, new measures, primarily nonfinancial, will need to become part of the periodic reports for motivation, control, and performance measurement.

Nonfinancial Measures of Performance

One immediate step for improving performance would have management accountants producing information on a much more timely basis for operating managers. Many companies prepare departmental accounting reports only monthly, to correspond to the cycle used to prepare financial statements within the firm. But the cycle for preparing financial statements has little relevance for measuring and monitoring quality improvement work on a continual basis. Management accountants can help companies attempting to continually reduce defect rates by supplying timely—daily, hourly, or even batch by batch—measures of performance.

We can think about developing quality measures in three areas of operation: vendor performance, plant manufacturing performance, and customer acceptance.[5]

Vendor Performance

Many companies have recently developed supplier rating systems. They identify which vendors have been certified—for direct, on-floor delivery without inspection—and which vendors require inspection for incoming items. Quality measures, both the frequency of defects and the percentage of dollars defective, are computed and tracked for each vendor. In addition to such incoming quality measures, the company would track on-time performance and price trends.

---

[5] Robert A. Howell and Stephen R. Soucy, "Operating Controls in the New Manufacturing Environment," *Management Accounting* (October 1987), pp. 25–30.

Plant Manufacturing Performance

In-house manufacturing performance would be measured by part-per-million (PPM) defect rates, percentage yields, scrap, rework, and unscheduled machine downtimes. First-pass yields, the percentage of items completed without requiring any rework, are a particularly important quality measure. Some U.S. managers were shocked to learn that Japanese competitors were achieving scores above 90% on this measure when less than 15% of their own items became finished goods without any rework performed on them.

Many quality improvements result from suggestions contributed by employees, especially shop-level workers. Visitors to Japanese factories frequently see wall charts that graph the number of employee suggestions made each month. In some factories, the number of employee suggestions is the primary measure for evaluating the plant manager's performance.

Quality refers to more than just the physical production process. It extends to operations in general so that measures on safety (number of days between accidents), housekeeping, and adherence to delivery schedules (percentage of delivery commitments met each period) also provide indicators on the quality of operating processes. Measures on design quality could include the number of parts in a product, the percentage of common versus unique parts in a new product, and the number of subassembly or bill-of-materials levels required. Reductions in the incidence of Engineering Change Orders (ECOs) to items currently in production provide a trend indicator of the quality of product and process designs. Several Japanese companies have fewer ECOs each year than comparable U.S. companies have each month.

Customer Performance

Customer acceptance may be measured by the number of customer complaints. Some companies are more pro-active than others, and they conduct systematic surveys of their customers and compute a customer-satisfaction index to measure how their performance is viewed. Objective measure of quality delivered to customers include the incidence of failures at customers' locations, returns and allowances, warranty expense, and field service expense.

Cost of Quality

Before 1980, quality advocates found it difficult to get senior management attention and commitment to a total quality control program.[6] While agree-

---

[6] See Crosby, *Quality Is Free*; A. V. Feigenbaum, *Total Quality Control*, 3rd ed. (New York: McGraw-Hill, 1983); and J. M. Juran and F. M. Gryna, *Quality Planning and Analysis*, 2nd ed. (New York: McGraw-Hill, 1980).

ing in principle that better quality was preferable to lesser quality, the executives still devoted their efforts to actions that promised immediate impact on short-term financial performance as measured by earnings-per-share and return-on-investment. Relative to these financial measures, improvements in quality represented an abstract, somewhat intangible, target.

To overcome this indifference to quality improvement, quality advocates devised a financial approach to quality that they hoped would capture the attention of senior, financially oriented managers. The Cost of Quality (COQ) approach collects all costs currently being spent on preventing defects and fixing them after they have occurred. The Cost of Quality, also called the cost of nonconformance, attempts to compute a single aggregate measure of all the explicit costs attributable to producing a product that is not within specifications. It is a comprehensive, plant or companywide financial measure of quality performance.

The costs of nonconformance can be classified into four categories:[7]

1. Prevention:
The costs of designing, implementing, and maintaining an active quality assurance and control system; includes the costs of design and process engineering, quality control systems, quality planning, and quality training

Quality prevention costs include
- The costs of engineering studies for improved production processes that will produce higher-quality products
- The cost of equipment to produce higher-quality products
- The cost of improved raw materials and supplier training
- The cost of preventive maintenance programs

2. Appraisal:
The costs of ensuring that materials and products meet quality conformance standards; includes the costs of inspecting raw materials and purchased parts, inspecting in-process and finished products, lab tests, quality audits, and field tests

3. Internal Failure:
The costs of manufacturing losses from materials and products that do not meet quality standards; includes the costs of scrap, repair, rework, upgrade, downtime, and discounts on sales of substandard parts and materials

4. External Failure:
The costs of shipping inferior quality products to customers; includes the costs of handling customer complaints and claims, warranty and replacement costs, and freight and repairs of returned merchandise

---

[7] See Wayne Morse and H. P. Roth, "Let's Help Measure and Report Quality Costs," *Management Accounting* (August 1983), pp. 50–53; and John Clark, "Costing for Quality at Celanese," *Management Accounting* (March 1985), pp. 42–46. Also W. Morse and H. P. Roth, *Quality Costs* (Montvale, NJ: National Association of Accountants, 1987).

All these costs are currently being recorded somewhere in the company's cost system; the costs do not include unrecorded or opportunity costs (such as lost future sales) or the difficult-to-measure costs of disruption caused by out-of-specification purchased materials and produced goods. The goal of a Cost of Quality measurement exercise is simply to identify how much the organization is currently spending on quality. Most companies are surprised to learn that they are currently spending between 15% and 20% of sales revenue on quality-related costs. This figure can then be used as the lever to get top management's attention that perhaps this large amount can be reduced significantly by a wiser allocation among the four quality categories.

In particular, companies that have been paying little attention to quality, choosing implicitly to inspect quality in rather than to design it in, incur large costs in the internal and external failure categories (fixing bad items after they have been built). They also spend heavily in the appraisal category. One semiconductor company adopted a total quality control program after it estimated that it would need more inspectors than workers to achieve, under current operating procedures, the quality levels demanded by its customers. An electronics instrument company learned that it was far cheaper to detect and replace a faulty two-cent resistor at the start of the production process than to repair and perhaps replace the $5,000 piece of equipment containing this part, after the instrument had been installed at the customer's site.

Such companies discovered that by spending more in the Prevention category, they could greatly reduce the amount spent in the Internal and External Failure categories. As product design, vendor relations, and process control improved (again by increasing investments in Prevention), the company could also substantially reduce the costs it incurred in the Appraisal category. Far less inspection was required once quality was designed into products and processes. Thus, by monitoring total Costs of Quality and their distribution among the four categories, a company could assess the decline in total quality costs as it shifted efforts from inspection and repair back into prevention.

While Cost of Quality measurement is attractive when used in the above fashion, it cannot be the sole basis for monitoring a TQC effort. First, there is no long-run target for the "optimal" level of quality costs. While spending 15% to 20% of sales dollars on quality-related costs is clearly excessive, the optimal level for Cost of Quality spending is unknown and undoubtedly varies from company to company. Companies have found that they can drive quality costs down to about 5% of sales, but further reductions may be counterproductive. Also, while there are high payoffs from initially shifting quality costs from the Appraisal, Internal Failure, and External Failure categories to the Prevention category, the most desirable distribution among these four categories is unknown. Furthermore, the allocation of quality costs in and among the four categories is a subjective exercise that requires reasonable but still arguable judgments. Thus, the data provide a useful managerial summary of quality efforts and progress, but they probably do not provide a good basis for performance evaluations.

However the existing costs are aggregated among the four Cost of Quality categories, the total cost of producing bad-quality items will still be underestimated. Omitted from the calculation are the costs of disruption in operations caused by out-of-conformance purchases and production, and the loss of sales caused by actual external failures and associated reputational effects. While some of the cost of production scheduling, setups, and engineering change orders can be assigned to one or more of the categories, the implicit cost of factory confusion and excessive inventory levels may be difficult to track down.

In summary, the Cost of Quality measurement appears to be valuable as an attention-getting, public relations effort for senior management; to make them aware of, first, how much the company is currently spending to produce out-of-conformance items and, second, how by reallocating effort from detection and repair categories to prevention, it can realize substantial benefits. But nonfinancial quality measures (e.g., yield, PPM defect rates—both internal and external, and measures of scrap, rework, and unscheduled machine downtime) are also needed to provide more timely, objective feedback and as better targets for quality improvement efforts.

Summary

The past ten years have seen quality reemerge as a key success factor for all organizations. Quality has become elevated to a major concern of managers. Management accountants can play a valuable role in helping organizations achieve their quality goals by providing a variety of measures and reports to motivate and evaluate the quality-improvement efforts of managers. The measures could include financial measures, such as the Cost of Quality, and better estimates than we now have of the total cost of defective production and out-of-specification purchased parts and materials. And the measures should also include a variety of nonfinancial measures, provided on a timely basis to operating managers, on part-per-million defect rates, yields, scrap, rework, and first-pass yields.

PROBLEMS

10–1   Computing Percentage Defective Items

The Juran Company has a simple production process for its basic product. Two metal sections are fabricated in separate production processes and are joined together in an assembly operation. Each of the two production processes produces, on average, 5% defective items, and the assembly process also operates with a 5% defect rate. To prevent bad items from being shipped to customers, inspection is done only after the assembly process.

Required:

1. What defect rate will be noted in the inspection process?
2. How much will the percentage of defects found during inspection drop if the production and assembly processes improve from 95% good parts to 99% good parts?
3. Another product of the Juran Company goes through ten consecutive processing stages. What must be the yield of good items from each stage if the company wants to have a failure rate below 1% of items going through final inspection? What parts-per-million (PPM) defect rate does this correspond to for each stage?

10–2   The Way Things Were

"Hi, John. How are things going out on the line?"

"Hi, Fred. Not bad, not bad at all, though I had to be careful the last couple of days. Someone from IE standards was following me around and I had to go back and work the way we used to do it. I didn't want to get him all upset by seeing the new way we go about our jobs."

"What do you mean? Have you found a new way to sandbag without them noticing?"

"Not at all. We're working smarter, thanks to our department manager, Monty. It all started several months ago when our output went way down even though all the efficiency measures said we were on target."

"How can that occur?"

"Basically, Monty discovered that most of our time was not spent working on producing good items. Let me give you an example. For one of our products we have to perform four welds to attach some metal parts together. We have detailed standards telling us how long it should take to do each step.

"One day, Monty watched Mike do these welds. Everything was done by the numbers. Mike walked over to the WIP storage area, picked out enough parts to prepare 10 products, put them on a dolly, and wheeled them over to his work station. Then he read the job card telling what he had to do and which tools were needed. He grabbed the right tools from his tool crib, set his jig to fixture the parts into place, and proceeded to weld the parts together into the 10 units. After finishing the 10 units, Mike inspected them all, rejecting one because the hole in one of the parts had been drilled incorrectly in a previous operation, put the 9 good parts on the dolly, wheeled them to the next storage area, and then put the one rejected part into the rework area.

"The whole process took about 100 minutes from start to finish—100 minutes to produce 9 good subassemblies. But then Monty watched what happened to the 9 items Mike had just finished. An inspector in a white coat was testing the welds in some kind of new X-ray device we had bought, and ended up rejecting two more subassemblies. Then another guy came around to put tags on the two rejected items with a brief description of the problem, and then took them to the rework area. And that wasn't all. Monty noticed someone counting inventory to make sure it corresponded to the job card attached to the batch and other people doing tests on tools and fixtures. There were more people checking work and moving parts than there were actually doing the work.

"Monty went bananas. He called over one of the IEs who (unfortunately for him) happened to be walking by at the time. Monty yelled at him, 'I just watched one of my workers spend 100 minutes to weld parts for 10 subassemblies, and three of them were rejected after finishing. 100 mintues to get 7 good parts, 28 good welds. Near as I can tell, each weld takes about one minute to do. Is this normal; to spend 100 minutes to get 28 good welds?'

"The IE attempted to explain to Monty about scientific management and how standards for work and productivity were computed. First the IE confirmed Monty's observation. The standard time to do one weld is one minute and 7 seconds. But there were standards for getting the parts and fixturing them into place, standards for assembling and preparing tools, standards for inspection and small repairs, and standards for moving the parts to the next storage area. They even had an allowance for break time and idle time due to line imbalances. Everything had been measured and accounted for. In fact, the total standard time for the 10 units that Mike had done came to 108 minutes, so Mike's 100 minutes was considered good performance; about an 8% productivity improvement.

"This really got Monty riled up. Monty figured that he got 28 good welds from Mike which, according to the IEs stanards, should have taken a little over 30 minutes. So right away, Monty figures that productivity was only around 30% of what's possible, not the 108% the IE was attempting to explain to him. Then he started thinking about all the other people who were standing around inspecting and moving things but who never did any work on the parts themselves. By the time he finished estimating the number of people he had in quality control, maintenance, and storing and handling things, he figured that there was at least one indirect worker for each guy like Mike who actually worked on products. Therefore actual productivity was only about half the 30% he computed initially."

"I can imagine he was upset. But what did he do about it?"

"Monty had the QC people analyze what caused the problems with the two parts that had been rejected after Mike had welded them. It turned out the materials were not exactly within specification and therefore didn't take the welds the way they were supposed to. So Monty took off down to the Purchasing Department to see why substandard materials had gotten through the system. He found out that this particular batch of materials had been bought from a new supplier. The purchasing guy was spending all his time trying to lower costs, and he had just uncovered this new vendor who agreed to supply parts 4% cheaper than the standard purchase price. I wish I had been there when the head of Purchasing attempted to explain to Monty why it was cheaper to buy from this new supplier, when 20% of the subassemblies eventually had to be reworked or scrapped."

"All that running around and screaming couldn't have made Monty very popular."

"Wait—he wasn't finished. A few days later, a rush job that was already several weeks late got delayed further when a machine broke down in the middle of the run. It took maintenance people several days to get replacement parts and another couple of days to install them and get the machine running properly again. During this time when everyone was waiting for the repairs so that we could finish the job, Monty dispatched a couple of workers to find out when the machine had last been maintained. Apparently there is a schedule for preventive maintenance, but the shop had been so busy that no one wanted to interrupt work to do maintenance; so it had gotten delayed and eventually the Maintenance Department had apparently forgotten to reschedule it. This didn't bother the maintenance foreman too much because his people were so busy responding to emergencies, like the one we had, that they didn't have much time to do regularly scheduled maintenance.

"Many of the foremen don't like to have maintenance done on their shift either. They get evaluated by labor and machine efficiency; some kind of ratio of earned hours to hours actually paid. A sure way to get the plant accountants sending nasty letters to you is to stop producing items in order to grease the machines and replace some parts that haven't worn out yet. The accountants claim this kind of work lowers efficiency, since nothing is getting produced and the workers are idle."

"I bet Monty had his hands full doing battle with the Purchasing and Maintenance Departments."

"Not quite. He's a scrappy fellow who doesn't let a few disagreements stop him from doing what he thinks is right. Last month he took off after his monthly performance report. I don't understand all the details of what's in these reports or how they're calculated, but he started muttering about space charges. I think that lots of overhead costs get charged to departments based on the space they take up in the factory. Monty wanted to know why the department occupied so much space. He dragged in one of the IEs and had him do a quick study on how much room was needed for the machines and the people who actually worked on the product. Less than 25% of the space was taken up for machines and workers. What really set him off again was learning that the testing and rework area took up about as much space as the productive workers and machines. Monty thought it dumb that as much space was used to test for and store bad items as to produce good items."

"Sounds like you've had an interesting few months here."

"You better believe it. I've seen more changes in the last few months than we've had in the past 20 years."

Required:

What operating changes do you think Monty instituted? What changes in the accounting and measurement system would be necessary to support the operating changes?

10-3   Signetics Corporation: Implementing a Quality Improvement Program (A)

In 1979, as part of a four-year planning process at Signetics, Mr. D. C. McKenzie, Director of Corporate Quality Control, was asked to forecast his department's growth through 1984. McKenzie believed that "quality" would become the battleground of the future. However, his management and budget forecasts—showing exponential increases in inspectors and QC activities—convinced him that if Signetics were to compete successfully against other U.S. and Japanese manufacturers, it would require the complete reorganization of the quality control function. A new philosophy would have to be implemented—one that would hold every employee accountable for quality and that would have zero defects as its goal.

During the fall of 1979, McKenzie held several meetings with his staff to define a major program for implementing this new philosophy. That program also incorporated quality as a measure in all Signetics' managers' semiannual performance reviews.

Reprinted with permission of Stanford University Graduate School of Business, © 1982 by the Board of Trustees of the Leland Stanford Junior University.

Company Background

Signetics Corporation was founded in Sunnyvale, California, in 1961. It was the first company in the world established for the sole purpose of designing, manufacturing, and selling integrated circuits (ICs). By 1980 Signetics had become the sixth largest U.S. semiconductor company and it offered one of the broadest lines of integrated circuits in the industry. Since 1972, the company had experienced a compound annual growth rate of 26 percent. In 1980 gross sales were expected to exceed $360 million.

From 1962 to 1975 Signetics was owned by Corning Glass Works. In 1975 Signetics was purchased by the U.S. Philips Corporation, a subsidiary of N. V. Philips of the Netherlands.

Company Products and Markets

Signetics had developed several thousand different circuits for such diverse markets as data processing, industrial controls, instrumentaion, consumer products, telecommunications, automotive, and defense. Product lines included PROMs (Programmable Read Only Memory), Fuse Programmable Logic Arrays, LSI (Large Scale Integration), logic and analog circuits. Signetics' major U.S. competitors were: Texas Instruments, National Semiconductor, Motorola, Intel, and Fairchild Camera.

Semiconductors had been dubbed "the crude oil of the 1980s," partly because of the size and growth anticipated in the semiconductor industry and partly because of the pervasiveness of the applications of ICs. Many other manufacturers were expanding their commitment and capabilities in the field, most notably the Japanese, who, owing in part to their product quality record, were making significant inroads in world markets.

In addition to an extensive program to develop its own new products, Signetics had joined with Motorola, Inc., to manufacture that company's family of 16-bit microprocessors. Through this agreement, Signetics was able to offer one of the most sophisticated 16-bit microprocessors available. In keeping with the company's family-of-products philosophy, Signetics had begun to offer a line of higher-performance peripheral input/output and communication chips as well.

Making semiconductor devices involved more than 150 steps and required extremely intricate manufacturing processes. A silicon ingot was sliced into thin wafers. Through miniaturization involving photographic reduction and photo lithography, some 200 to 3,000 elaborate chips were created on each wafer. Following the proper buildup of layers of metals and chemicals, each wafer was cut into individual dice (or chips), gold leads were attached, and each die was packaged on a frame with electrical connectors to become a final unit.

Development of the Quality Improvement Program

Before the fall of 1979, the Quality and Reliability (Q&R) philosophy at Signetics had functioned as though Q&R staff had full responsibility for quality, while production was responsible only for output. D. C. McKenzie expressed a firm conviction as to why the quality control concept within the company had to be revamped:

> My feelings about the inappropriateness of our philosophy came to a head in the fall of '79 when I began to prepare my part of a long-range corporate growth plan. I concluded that the number of Q&R personnel operating as "police people" would have to expand exponentially to keep pace with Signetics' forecasted growth in volume. Q&R had been concentrating on establishing test procedures and setting specifications (commonly thought of as appraisal and gating/screening activities) and then trying to make sure that everyone adhered to our specs. It was just hopeless to continue down that path. The requirements of the future clearly called for quality performance levels possible only through more sophisticated prevention programs.

McKenzie's Q&R staff had met to examine two options—continue past practices or initiate change. During the spring of 1979 alternatives to past practices were discussed. Determined to explore those further, McKenzie organized an off-site three-day planning meeting in September 1979 for all the corporate Q&R managers. He enlisted the help of one of Signetics' Organization Development staff, who opened the meeting with an introduction to a problem-solving technique called A-B-C. As McKenzie explained it:

> ABC stands for Assumptions, Behavior, and Consequences. The idea is that by looking at the current state for each of those three areas, and then looking at what is desired, it's possible to concentrate on problem solving without having to point blame.

McKenzie then presented the problem he wanted his staff to focus upon—that the philosophy that Q&R should act as a police force in Signetics operations needed to be changed radically.

> I was nervous when I got through writing it on the board and turned back to get my staff's response; but right off the bat four of the six agreed with me 100 percent and the other two agreed as soon as they understood more about it. The two who weren't right with me at first don't work directly in the police force role.
>
> We spent the rest of the meeting outlining the before-and-after contrast of a quality philosophy and the details of the transition plan. (See Exhibits 1 and 2)

EXHIBIT 1
Signetics Corporation (A)
Before and After Contrast of Quality—Fall 1979

Before	*After*
Screen for quality	Plan for quality
Quality is Q&R's responsibility	Quality is everybody's responsibility
Some mistakes are inevitable	Zero defects is possible
Quality means inspection	Quality means conformance to
Scrap and rework are the major	requirements
costs of poor quality	Scrap and rework are only a small part
Quality is a tactical issue	of the costs of nonconformance
Production units are where quality	Quality is a strategic imperative
should be measured	Individual accountability is where quality
	should be measured

EXHIBIT 2
Signetics Corporation (A)
Rough Outline of a Four-Year Quality Improvement Program

1980–1981
  Raise the quality consciousness level of all personnel
  Division and Plant Managers begin active leadership roles
  Quality tied to everyone's performance review

1981–1982
  Utilization of the cost of nonconformance as an improvement planning tool
  Zero defects a part of the culture—ppm is standard notation
  Greater emphasis on technical planning
  Major quality improvements made through the quality improvement teams

1983–1984
  Logistics and technical data systems working
  Cooperating routinely with key customers on special programs

Initial Q&R Program Actions

As a skeletal framework for the new Q&R philosophy, McKenzie introduced a fourteen-point program based on the book, *Quality Is Free*, by Philip B. Crosby.

While the group viewed Crosby's program, originally developed for ITT, as not totally complete, it felt the need to have an anchor and a method of instruction—one that had been articulated and would be recognized by other companies and in some published works. In addition, the initial success was based on the humanistic aspects of the program, and not its technical content.

Throughout the fall of 1979, the Q&R managers held a series of meetings to develop the methods required to implement the program. A division was chosen for a pilot program, the training that would be required was defined, the people who could do the training were identified, and the changes in responsibilities that would result from the new philosophy were examined.

In early 1980 the Q&R staff met with Signetics president Chuck Harwood to ask his approval and support for the detailed pilot program. It proposed that all the basic elements be in place by late 1980: throughout the company the Q&R police role would be replaced by individual accountability with a goal of zero defects. In describing their program to Harwood, the Q&R staff even made rough comparisons of how each manager's Responsibility, Measures, and Objectives (RMO) goals (a management by objectives type system in place throughout Signetics) would change after the pilot program. Harwood was asked to communicate his personal support by presenting the program to employees and key customers and by chairing a corporate quality committee that would meet monthly to review the program's progress.

Harwood agreed to the program, but one of the group vice-presidents had serious concerns, typical of the conventional wisdom, about the quality department abdicating its role of keeping the people honest with regard to quality. Since the manager of the division chosen to serve as the pilot site was anxious to get going on the program, approval to begin was given with the understanding that such questions would be answered to corporate satisfaction before the program was adopted company-wide.

Reorganization of the Quality Department

The first of two organizational steps was taken in early 1980. This step included a series of organization changes that decentralized the quality functions into the operating groups. Starting in the Analog Division, the plan was to proceed throughout the other product divisions and manufacturing operations so that by the end of 1980 the transition would be completed. As McKenzie explained:

> The essence of the reorganization consisted of consolidating the various quality activities—Wafer Fabrication Quality Control (QC), Product Assurance, Electrical Sort Quality Control, Quality Engineering, and Reliability Engineering—under the Divisional Quality/Reliability Assurance (QRA) managers. The QRA managers became direct members of the Division Vice Presidents' staffs; the previous structure had them reporting to Corporate Q&R. In the manufacturing/operations groups, a similar transition was accomplished with Assembly and Incoming QC. The Assembly QC functions became part of the Sunnyvale Manufacturing operation and Incoming QC was transferred to Material Control (Purchasing).
>
> The fundamental reason behind this organizational change was to put the control tools into the hands of the responsible parties. We hoped this would generate a team atmosphere and a sense of own-

ership. By eliminating the check-and-balance system which had existed, it was hoped that there would be an intensification in the involvement with quality at the earliest possible time and lowest possible level. The greatest benefit was expected to come from stressing prevention, instead of inspection and corrective action after the fact.

By the end of 1980, Corporate Q&R would consist of the five functional activities it had prior to the transition, but with different objectives. Elimination of the inspection function would make it possible for Corporate Q&R to improve planning and overview activities. In addition to previous activities—such as qualification programs, corrective action, and monitors/audits—anticipated new corporate responsibilities included data compilation/trend analysis, corporate quality systems standards/procedures, training, quality improvement, and prevention programs.

Status of the Quality Improvement Program (April 1980)

While the pilot program had been set up to run from early 1980 through November of 1980, by April, McKenzie and his Q&R management people felt a need to reassess their progress to date and decide just which avenues should be pursued, and how fast, over the next several months. While external (competitor and customer) pressures were adding support to the types of ideas incorporated in the quality improvement program, McKenzie and his people were concerned that they not confuse their own enthusiasm for and agreement on the program with that in the rest of the organization. Thus, in late March, McKenzie asked his group to provide him with information on the progress they thought Signetics had made over the preceding several months and to identify some of the major options that might be pursued as further steps in Signetics' quality improvement efforts.

As McKenzie reviewed these reports, he concluded that significant progress had been made among his own quality and reliability management people with regard to terminology and definitions. Some things that seemed to be clearly in place included:

1. The Q&R managers generally understood the philosophy change represented by the decentralization of the Q&R function. While that decentralization was still in progress, at least those managers whose reporting relationships would be directly affected seemed to have a good understanding of what those organizational changes hoped to accomplish.

2. "Quality" had been redefined as "conformance to specification." Q&R people seemed to be in general agreement that everyone should "perform exactly like the stated requirements or cause those requirements to be officially

changed to what the process could produce and what the customers really needed."

3. The Q&R group agreed that the major thrust of the improvement program was to stress prevention rather than correction. The notions that "it is better to plan for quality than to screen for it" and that "mistakes are not a way of life" seemed to be tying in nicely with the belief that a zero defects philosophy could be developed.

While McKenzie felt confident that a strong consensus had formed within his own Q&R group, it was clear that others within the company still had a long way to go. One aspect of this was that of measurement and reporting. As part of the quality improvement program, McKenzie and his group had decided that the cost of nonconformance should be used as the performance measure for quality. Working with the financial controller, they proposed measurement procedures aimed at identifying the cost of "not doing things right the first time." As shown in Exhibit 3, this approach required data gathering and reporting on a variety of dimensions. While those procedures were not yet functioning, it was clear that there was already some growing opposition to this whole notion of the cost of poor quality. For some in accounting, this looked like a lot of work and they were already under pressure as an "overhead group" to keep the costs of accounting under control. A number of line managers had voiced

EXHIBIT 3
Signetics Corporation (A)
Cost of Nonconformance

Internal
- Rework
- Scrap
- Yield loss—standard is 100%
- Screens
- Corrective actions

External
- Customer returns
- Failure analysis (field failures)

Appraisal
- Quality costs (QA/QC—inspections)
- Production-test/inspection
- Reliability engineering monitors (sure)

Prevention
- Training
- Reliability (testing/qualifications)
- Quality activities—Quality Circles/Qualification Engineering
- Preventative maintenance/calibrations
- Design reviews and process release reviews

considerable doubt, as to the likelihood of ever getting and maintaining accurate data on the factors in Exhibit 3 and the negative motivational impact of telling manufacturing that their poor quality was the source of 15–20% (the preliminary number cited by Q&R) of total costs.

A second aspect of measurement and reporting that was still in the early stages of implementation was the inclusion of quality both in each manager's job specifications and in his or her Responsibility, Measures, and Objectives statement. While those involved in the pilot program seemed to be making good progress on this, it had been hoped that the entire organization would adopt it in 1980. However, the results seemed to be mixed, depending on the division and the level of support coming from division senior management. For many managers it looked like another "procedure" that kept them from their real task of producing product to meet customer needs at a profit (that is, emphasis on volume, delivery and profit.)

McKenzie and his people also had been able to gather some information about the attitudes of managers throughout the company. As McKenzie had anticipated, the behavior and response varied from extremely negative to extremely positive. At the former end of the spectrum was the whole notion of the quality improvement program of keeping people honest and quality having to compete with productivity, which was already lower than it should have been. Clearly, they hadn't made much progress in areas where such a view prevailed.

At the other end were the results achieved to date in the Orem, Utah, plant, which was part of the pilot program. The plant manager, Dennis Peasenell, was extremely enthusiastic about the program and performance statistics already indicated that:

- Wafer lines were running at rates consistently higher than both the U.S. industry average and the plant's own 1979 performance.
- The number of defective circuits uncovered in destructive physical analysis performed in Sunnyvale on Orem-made products had plummeted from 12% to something down in the 1 to 2% range.
- One fab line seemed well on its way to doubling the number of good dies per wafer and expected to reach that goal in another three months.
- Reworks had declined from 20% in 1979 to what the plant manager projected would be 2% by the end of 1980 if the current trend continued.

McKenzie and his people were extremely pleased with the results at the Orem plant. The plant manager was highly committed, as was his boss; several other people were also playing key roles, including the workforce, which seemed to be particularly receptive to the whole idea. The results had come not from simply following a 14-step program, but from broad-based support and commitment to the entire philosophy.

Major Options for Future
Quality Improvement Actions

McKenzie had also asked his managers to think about what additional projects might support Signetics' quality improvement activities.

One type of activity would amount to a shock treatment for Signetics' suppliers. The Signetics purchasing manager, who had been with the firm eighteen years, prided himself on never shutting down a production line because of a lack of components. Although that was an admirable record, Q&R had found that many incoming materials did not meet Signetics' stated specifications (specs). Incoming materials were being put into one of three categories when they arrived at the plant: Acceptable, because they met specs; Returned to the Vendor, because they were totally unacceptable; or Set Aside, because even though they did not fully meet specs they probably could be used with some modification to keep production lines running. As Q&R had examined Signetics' behavior with regard to these three categories, they found that those items traditionally set aside (about 15% of all incoming materials) eventually got "waived" into production because they were needed immediately. It was then Production's job to make them usable.

A radical approach to dealing with vendor quality would require convincing the purchasing and production managers to eliminate the "waived" category so that there would be only two categories in which materials could be placed upon receipt—either they would meet specs and move into production or they would not meet specs and would be returned immediately. McKenzie knew that Purchasing would view an immediate shift to such a policy as disastrous to the company's reputation among its vendors. Production, too, would view such a policy as disastrous to its productivity and shipment schedules. Thus, if such a program were to be undertaken, Q&R would have to convince Signetics' own purchasing department that it made sense, and also to convince vendors of the need to change their behavior. Moreover, they would need the cooperation of the plant, so that materials would be rejected when they didn't meet specifications, no matter how badly they were needed.

Although there were several drawbacks to such an approach (and considerable risks if it was adopted and failed), McKenzie also thought it had many attractions. One of these was that if it could be done and adhered to, he felt certain that most vendors would get very involved in figuring out either how to meet Signetics' specs or convincing the company as to why a different and more appropriate set of specs should be adopted. This source of ideas for quality improvements might be very helpful throughout the Signetics organization and lead to higher-quality products going to customers. He also felt that such a radical change in policy would provide a clear signal, not only to vendors but to everybody within Signetics, that the company was serious about quality and was making a major reorientation in its position.

An alternative project linking Signetics' efforts directly with customer efforts had recently surfaced in the Automotive Division and was referred to as the Parts-Per-Million program. This program represented a radical departure from what had been Signetics' traditional relationship with its customers. In fact, it was a type of approach that Signetics had rejected, at least implicitly, a few years earlier.

During the last half of the seventies, Signetics, like many other American semiconductor manufacturers, had been approached by Japanese firms looking for additional suppliers. However, Japanese quality requirements appeared formidable and unfamiliar to most potential American suppliers, including Signetics. Since World War II, American manufacturers had largely utilized the AQL (acceptable quality level) criterion. AQLs that allowed more than one percent defects were common in U.S. industry.

In the late 1970s, potential Japanese semiconductor customers required much lower levels, stating quality requirements in terms of PPM (parts-per-million). These firms were perceived as asking for legal guarantees on the level of commitment that a firm like Signetics would make to improve quality and specifying targets of performance that would change over time. Under such a PPM program, defect levels less than 0.1 percent were not uncommon goals. Because of the liability issue and the difficulty of working with an entirely new type of customer under such stringent specifications, Signetics had chosen not to negotiate contracts with Japanese firms.

In late 1979, Signetics was approached by a U.S. automotive parts manufacturer which required extremely high IC quality levels to assure reliability through a five-year, 50,000-mile auto warranty period. In a presentation to Signetics management, the manufacturer spelled out its quality requirements for the coming years, which included a failure rate of no more than 200 parts-per-million, a level significantly lower than that achieved by most U.S. IC manufacturers.

Military contracts had required similar low defect rates for years, but the semiconductor industry had traditionally filled those contracts through 100% testing. While this tended to weed out any defective parts before delivery to the customer, such testing was applied to normal production runs, significantly increasing the cost per unit shipped. Generally, military contracts for high reliability (hi-rel) products had been priced at levels that covered the additional testing and screening costs incurred by the semiconductor manufacturers, and still made the business very attractive.

With a major prospective automotive customer wanting a parts-per-million program, there was a sudden interest on the part of Signetics in considering such an agreement. In addition, with increasing pressure for improved quality coming from international competitors, it was clear that this particular proposal might be a good learning experience for the company. This prospect made Signetics somewhat nervous, however, since it required not just higher testing levels but a commitment to eliminate the causes of poor quality, that is, potential problems in engineering/design, manufacturing processes, workforce procedures, material defects, etc.

McKenzie felt that this option had perhaps the greatest leverage of any being considered, but also held some of the greatest risks. On the positive side, the parts-per-million concept complemented the zero defects philosophy that Signetics was already introducing internally. Both approaches defined quality as "performance to specification." PPM, however, was both a concept and a precise measurement of defects arrived at through statistical analysis, testing, materials, and assemblies. If pursued, it was intended to reduce the level of unacceptable product being produced by at least an order of magnitude. Zero defects, on the other hand, offered an overall philosophy but did not necessarily include such precise and significant targets.

Such a PPM program would clearly demonstrate commitment to those within Signetics' own organization, as well as to customers. There was the possibility, however, that in order to solve some problems within the PPM framework, Signetics would have to commit significantly more resources than was currently envisioned. That is, until the contract was undertaken and the feedback loops started to operate, Signetics would not know just what kinds of resources and what level of resource commitments would be required. Thus, it could find itself having to choose between not living up to its part of the contract and committing resources that would cause the contract to be unprofitable.

Worse, this might prevent Signetics from committing resources to other potentially more profitable projects and products. Thus, if this approach were to have any hope of being successful, Signetics would have to commit itself philosophically and then follow through, even if, operationally, it became uncomfortable to do so. McKenzie wasn't sure the company was far enough along in its own internal quality improvement efforts to make such an ironclad commitment.

Required:

1. What changes in the accounting and measurement system would be needed to support Signetics' Quality Improvement Program?
2. What accounting and measurement changes would be needed for the two options being considered?
   a. The new approach to Vendor Quality
   b. The PPM program for the automotive supplier

10–4   *Texas Instruments: Materials & Controls Group*

Although you can find a technical fault with every number, the Cost of Quality system has been successful in meeting its intended objectives. But the Cost of Quality figure probably includes only half of all the costs associated with quality and may no longer provide sufficient incentives to drive further improvements. Cost of Quality numbers should be as high as possible to aid in identifying areas for improvement. During the past five years, we have reduced the biggest boulders. Now we have a conflict between comparability and the need to redefine our measurements so that the smaller rocks become visible. Today's opportunities are mostly in indirect areas but it would take a dramatic shift in attitude to focus on measuring indirect quality costs.

Werner Schedule
Vice President
People & Asset Effectiveness

Introduction

The Materials & Controls Group was the third largest of seven major businesses within Texas Instruments. The M&C Group's activities centered on two primary technologies:

- METALLURGICAL MATERIALS—M&C was currently the world's leading designer and manufacturer of industrial and thermostatic clad metals. Clad metals consisted of two or more wrought metal layers that were metallurgically bonded together to offer properties not available in conventional metals. Examples of this technology included copper-clad aluminum wire, which combined the electrical conductivity of copper with lighter and lower cost aluminum; stainless steel-clad aluminum, offering the luster of stainless and the corrosion-protection of aluminum; and thermostatic metals, which enabled the controlled movement of thermostat components through the bonding of two metals with different coefficients of expansion. M&C had pioneered the application of these layered materials in uses as diverse as cookware, coinage, cable and wire shielding, integrated circuits, and corrosion-inhibiting trim for automobiles.

- CONTROL PRODUCTS—The Control Products business manufactured a wide range of products combining electronic and electromechanical technologies with TI's semiconductor and clad metals expertise. The business operated plants worldwide in support of a strategy based on strong, long-term customer relationships, primarily at the OEM level. Principal markets

This case was prepared by Christopher Ittner, under the supervision of Professor Robert S. Kaplan. Copyright © 1988 by the President and Fellows of Harvard College. Harvard Business School case 9–189–029.

included the automotive, appliance, heating/ventilating/air-conditioning, general industrial and aerospace/defense industries. The business's products offered control, regulation, signaling, and protection functions in applications such as motor protectors, relays, automotive engine controls, pressure switches, circuit breakers, thermostats, and electronic sensors.

The last decade had brought increased competition as companies from Japan, Italy, and Brazil had improved their products while lowering costs. M&C had responded by improving quality and service so that it could compete on factors other than price alone.

Organization

The Product Customer Center (PCC) served as the organizational building block within TI. PCCs had profit and loss responsibility for products and customers. M&C had eleven PCCs and two Fabrication Customer Centers (FCCs) located within four operating divisions (two domestic and two international). Three additional PCCs were located in a Latin American division. Each PCC had its own marketing, engineering, finance, and manufacturing functions. FCCs manufactured components and subassemblies that were common to PCCs in order to capitalize on economies of scale and specialized expertise.

Four staff support activities existed at the group level: Research and Development, Finance, People and Asset Effectiveness (responsible for quality assurance, training, purchasing, and materials management), and Personnel/Group Services (responsible for facilities, tool making, automation, and human resources).

Quality at TI

Productivity, teamwork, and problem-solving had always been important at TI. During the 1950s, work-simplification programs, the forerunner of what are now called "quality circles," had been estabished. In the 1960s and 1970s, TI's productivity programs were expanded to include asset management as well as people effectiveness. As international competition intensified in the late 1970s, TI's People and Asset Effectiveness activities began to focus more specifically on quality improvement. Despite these trends, however, TI continued to emphasize financial controls and a quality philosophy which, while never formally stated, expected a certain amount of defective product to be returned by the customer.

In 1980, the short-run economic trade-off approach to quality was abandoned when the company decided to commit to a "Total Quality Thrust." The new thrust was triggered when Hewlett-Packard, an important

TI customer, publicized a study that had found the products of its best American suppliers to be inferior to those of its worst Japanese suppliers. TI management understood well the message from this study: that its long-run competitive success required a greatly expanded commitment to quality control.

The TI "Total Quality Thrust" was based on the following principles:

1. Quality and Reliability (Q&R) is management's responsibility.
2. Q&R is a responsibility of all organizations.
3. Managers' performance on Q&R will be a key criterion in performance evaluation.
4. Managers' commitments to Q&R will not be measured—only the outcomes.
5. The only acceptable goal for Q&R is a level that surpasses TI's best worldwide competitors at any time.

In order to emphasize that quality was not just a program but had to become TI's normal way of doing business, a Vice President of People and Asset Effectiveness was appointed at the corporate level. A written policy statement, signed by the CEO, was developed and communicated. It stated:

> For every product or service we offer, we will understand the requirements that meet the customers' needs, and we will conform to those requirements without exception. For every job each TIer performs, the performance standard is: Do it right the first time.

A massive training program for all operating personnel on the fundamentals of quality improvement was undertaken. During the first phase, 450 top managers, including 22 from M&C, were sent to quality training courses conducted by Philip Crosby, a leading quality expert. Subsequently, a series of 16 tapes on the quality improvement philosophy and techniques of Joseph Juran, another leading quality expert, was shown to all exempt employees within M&C, with classes taught by senior and operating management. Managers and operating personnel were also trained in quality tools such as control charts and statistical process control. The classes helped to instill awareness and communicate the corporate commitment to quality improvement.

A quality reporting system was implemented to supplement TI's extensive system of financial indicators. For years TI had evaluated the profit-and-loss performance of each business with a series of financial indices published each month in the "Blue Book." In 1981, TI began a "Quality Blue Book" with indices such as product reliability, customer feedback regarding TI quality, and data on the cost of quality. The "Blue Book" format was deliberately chosen to communicate to TI managers that quality performance was now to be judged on the same level as financial performance.

Quality Blue Book

Like its financial counterpart, the Quality Blue Book contained three pages of indices presenting actuals vs. goals, previous period comparisons, and three-month forecasts. Unlike the highly structured Financial Blue Book, however, the Quality Blue Book performance indices were generally determined by the responsible PCC manager. This allowed managers to tailor the report to reflect the key quality indicators in each business. Performance indicators for the unit are defined in Exhibit 1.

Cost of Quality

Cost of Quality (COQ) was one of the performance measures that had to be included in every business unit's Quality Blue Book. COQ represented expenditures that arose because poor quality had occurred or to prevent poor quality from occurring in the future. The COQ measure was designed to highlight the cost of poor quality, the cost of doing things wrong. Explained J. Fred Bucy, TI's President and Chief Operating Officer, in a statement to the company's employees:

> Some people think that quality costs money, because they see the costs of quality in terms of new testing equipment, added inspectors, and so on. But these are the costs of doing it wrong the first time. If we design a product right the first time, and build it right the first time, we save all the costs of redesign, re-work, scrap, re-testing, maintenance, repair, warranty work, etc.
>
> Consider how much of your time is spent in doing something over again. How much of your assets are tied up in re-work, re-testing, repair, and making scrap? How much material is wasted at TI? If we could eliminate these costs by doing things right the first time, we would have true People and Asset Effectiveness, and improved profitability, without having to add a dollar to billings.

The Cost of Quality system was a key component of the "Total Quality Thrust." By measuring quality in financial terms, the COQ system allowed M&C management to create a major cultural change by using terms familiar to everyone—the bottom line. Tom Haggar, Controller of the Metallurgical Metals Division, observed:

> COQ ties quality progress into what we're here for—to be a profitable world class manufacturer constantly improving quality. COQ numbers shocked PCC managers. We initially showed them COQ figures of 10%: 10% of sales value, and an even greater percentage of profits, down the hole. It is now down to a less shocking 4–5%. Managers are saying that they haven't found all of the costs but that the trend is right. Even

EXHIBIT 1
Quality Blue Book Performance Indicators

Concurrent Indicators

Lot Acceptance %	Percentage of lots accepted by Outgoing Quality Control. Tracked by product line.
Avg. Outgoing Quality Level	Defective parts per million. Tracked by product line.

Lagging Indicators

RMR % Quality	Returned Merchandise Report percentage. Percentage of shipments returned from customers due to poor quality.
RMR % Total	RMR % Quality + percentage of shipments returned for reasons other than poor quality. These included incorrect quantity shipped, wrong parts, incorrect packaging, etc.
Customer Report Card	Customer lot acceptance level. A sample of customers was interviewed to get feedback on M&C quality. Lack of record keeping by customers limited the availability of quantified data on this indicator.
Competitive Rank	Subjective self-ranking of competitiveness. Ranking was done by marketing and field sales personnel. The fraction presented in the report represented M&C's competitive ranking relative to the number of competitors in that product line.
On Time Delivery	Shipment of at least 90% of the order on or before the acknowledgement date (indicator added in 1984).[1]

Leading Indicators

First Pass Calibration Yields	Most products produced by this PCC were calibrated to open at a specified temperature. After processing, 100% of the units were tested either manually or automatically to determine that the units were calibrated correctly. This indicator reflected the percentage of units that passed this inspection.
Cost of Quality	Calculated as the percentage of quality costs to net sales billed. Quality costs were defined as costs that were incurred due to poor quality or to prevent poor quality from occurring.

---

[1] Some debate existed as to whether "on time delivery" represented a quality indicator to be put in the Blue Book. Only in the last quarter of 1987 did most divisions in the group incorporate this measure. The "on time delivery" percentage was calculated on events rather than dollars to ensure that shipments to smaller customers received equal weighting. The previous measure of delivery performance was whether or not a customer was ever forced to shut down, ignoring instances in which customers were forced to reschedule production due to late delivery. In 1981, on time delivery was less than 50%. By 1987, 97% of the 2,000 shipments per week were delivered on time.

today's lower percentage is not making them comfortable. A cultural change was needed from the old to the new. For example, we used to budget for 5% scrap but no longer. We now recognize that budgeting for bad quality production is ridiculous.

Implementation of the COQ system began in the fourth quarter of 1981 when the Quality Department undertook a quick top-down exercise to determine quality costs. By the following quarter, an on-going system based on accounting data was in place. At present, Control and Finance provided the PCC's Quality Department with data from the accounting system on the sixth working day following the close of the month. The Quality Department then processed this information into the Quality Blue Book.

The initial list of COQ variables included 77 items, a number that had since been reduced to 19 through the elimination of semantic overlaps between divisions and the merger of insignificant categories into other cost elements. The variables were grouped into four broad categories:

1. *Prevention Costs*—Costs incurred to prevent non-conforming units from being produced.

2. *Appraisal Costs*—Costs incurred to ensure that materials and products that failed to meet quality standards were identified prior to shipment.

3. *Internal Failure Costs*—Scrap costs and costs incurred in correcting errors caught at appraisal, before delivery of the product to the customer.

4. *External Failure Costs*—Costs incurred in correcting errors after delivery of the product to the customer.

The variables included in each category differed somewhat among PCCs, depending upon the nature of the business. The cost elements utilized by the Motor Controls PCC are shown in Exhibit 2.

Several categories of quality costs, such as indirect costs and losses considered inherent to the manufacturing process, were not captured in the COQ system. Indirect quality costs arose from support department personnel repeating tasks because of problems with shipments (defective or incorrect parts, over- or undershipments, late deliveries, etc.) or because the tasks were not done correctly the first time. Examples included the cost of retyping orders, rebuilding tools, and rebilling customers as well as correcting paperwork errors and incorrect journal entries. Efforts were underway to determine the level of indirect quality costs through "Hidden Factory" reviews.

When originally implemented, the COQ system excluded costs that were considered to be a standard part of the manufacturing process. For example, a calibration process in production may have been imperfect, requiring parts to be manually checked on the line. The costs of the manual checking were not included in COQ, leading to an understatement of quality costs. Scrap costs were also under-reported by a number of PCCs. The PCC managers argued that "engineered scrap," such as the material

EXHIBIT 2
Cost of Quality Variables
Motor Controls PCC

Prevention Costs

Quality Engineering	Total Quality Engineering expense from the monthly actuals report.
Receiving Inspection	Total Receiving Inspection expense from the monthly actuals report.
Equipment Repair/ Maintenance	Estimated percentage of actual repair and maintenance expenses spent on preventive maintenance. An estimate of 15% of total R&M expenses was developed by PCC management in 1981. This percentage had not been revised since the original estimate was made.
Manufacturing Engineering	Estimated percentage of actual Manufacturing Engineering expenses spent on prevention. The estimated percentage was revised every six months by the manager of Manufacturing Engineering.
Design Engineering	Estimated percentage of actual Design Engineering expenses spent on prevention. The estimated percentage was revised every six months by the manager of Design Engineering.
Quality Training	Actual cost of quality training from the labor reporting system. Quality training time was charged to a special labor link (charge) number.

Appraisal Costs

TSL Laboratory	Total Technical Services Laboratory expense from the monthly actual report. The Technical Services Laboratory was responsible for sophisticated quality-related testing.
Design Analysis	Estimated percentage of actual Design Analysis expenses spent on appraisal. The percentage was revised every six months by the manager of Design Analysis.
Product Acceptance	Total inspection (quality control) expenses from the monthly actual report.
Manufacturing Inspection	Actual cost of manufacturing inspection from the labor reporting system. Manufacturing inspection was charged to a special link (charge) number.

Internal Failure Costs[1]

Quality Scrap	Calculated as (Material issued at standard)—(Material scheduled for production at standard) multiplied by a labor and overhead factor. The labor and overhead factor represented the amount of labor and overhead costs incurred in the assembly prior to its scrapping.[2] Obsolete parts scrapped out of inventory were not included in this measure.

---

[1] Internal Failure and Net RMR costs were available at the product line level. All other elements were captured at the product (PCC) department level.

[2] In 1981, a study was conducted to determine at which point in the assembly process products were being scrapped. As a result of this study, a factor of 88% above scrapped material costs was calculated to account for labor and overhead. This factor had not been changed since the original study.

EXHIBIT 2   (continued)
Cost of Quality Variables
Motor Controls PCC

Rework	Actual cost of rework from the labor reporting system. Rework was charged to a special link (charge) number.
Manufacturing/Process Engineering	Estimated percentage of actual Manufacturing/Process Engineering expenses spent on internal failure. The estimated percentage was revised every six months by the manager of Manufacturing Engineering.
External Failure Costs	
Net RMR Cost	Cost of returns less good material to inventory.[3]
Marketing	Estimated percentage of actual Marketing expenses spent on external failure. The estimated percentage was revised every six months by the Marketing manager.
Manufacturing/Process Engineering	Estimated percentage of actual Manufacturing/Process Engineering expenses spent on external failure. The estimated percentage was revised every six months by the manager of Manufacturing Engineering.
Repair	Actual cost of repair from the labor reporting system. Repair time was charged to a special link (charge) number.
Travel	Actual travel costs related to quality problems. Computed from the monthly actual report.
Liability Claims	Infrequent claims. Liability claims were included when incurred or when a reserve was taken. Legal fees, which did not hit the Group profit-and-loss statement, were not included.

[3] If a $5 product was returned due to defects, it could either be scrapped or reworked and returned to inventory. If the item were scrapped, the Net RMR Cost would be $5. If, on the other hand, the item was reworked at a cost of $1, Rework Costs of $1 would be reported and no costs would be included in Net RMR.

left when a round part was punched out of a square piece of metal, was inherent to the process.

The COQ system had been easy to implement since it used data that already existed in the accounting system. Now, however, the desire to maintain consistency over time, so that trends would be visible, had made it difficult to add new measures such as indirect quality or engineered scrap costs. In effect, attempts to update the COQ system to make it more accurate and relevant were in conflict with the need to maintain comparability across periods.

Uses of COQ Data

Initially, the COQ system was resented as just another number to be judged against. Carl Sheffer, General Manager of the Motor Controls PCC, recalled his concern:

I resented the system, feeling that quality was a virtue in its own right. Attempting to assign costs to quality diminished its value. Value is not in the numbers but in the areas they represent.

By 1987, however, the quality indicators and the COQ data in the Blue Book had become widely utilized management tools at M&C. Two factors had contributed to the system's widespread acceptance. First, quarterly financial forecast reviews were supplemented by quality reviews. PCC managers were now allowed to present the results of operations in a less structured format with emphasis on the areas of importance to each business.

Second, the Quality Blue Book was not used to "hammer" the PCC managers. Performance was not measured exclusively on the achievement of quality goals nor were quality measures compared across businesses. Rather, the quality measures were used to focus on long term trends of quality improvement and to highlight potential sources of quality problems.

The Quality Blue Book was distributed to the Group President, Controller, Vice President of People and Asset Effectiveness, and to the responsible Division and PCC managers on a monthly basis. Although not formally distributed to operating personnel, the information was widely available to them. Jim Meehan, PCC Quality Manager, noted:

> I don't distribute Quality Blue books to anyone below the level of the PCC manager. The PCC manager must take responsibility for getting copies to all the operating functions. Everybody probably sees them and anyone who asks me can have a copy. Different people use different measures—the PCCs use Cost of Quality, manufacturing uses internal failures, operations is interested in on-time delivery and marketing wants to know about external failures.

Carl Sheffer discussed his use of the data:

> The reports go to all of my managers and team members. I take personal interest in Cost of Quality and ask for the numbers. At monthly meetings, the COQ numbers are discussed with the non-exempt employees. I highlight product lines that have improved and lines that have deteriorated. We primarily focus on Internal Failure and RMR [Returned Material Reports] because they are "hard" numbers. The others are more helpful for trends.
>
> This year, the Cost of Quality numbers provided the single best indicator that problems had arisen in production, problems that had caused a bad P&L performance. The Cost of Quality showed deterioration in Internal Failure when the department claimed that scrap rates were down. The discrepancy arose from the department not realizing that it had not reduced the amount of overage (material in excess of the minimum required) issued from the stockroom. Eventually, a physical inventory check found unused material all around

the shop. So, the Cost of Quality report signaled a problem that may have gone undiscovered for a while.

In addition to Quality Blue Book reports, Sheffer had developed special COQ reports for his area (see Exhibits 3–5). Problems reflected in the COQ reports were not always indicative of actual quality shortcomings however. Continued Sheffer:

> A couple of years ago, we saw continually worsening trends in the Cost of Quality. After investigating, we found that the selling price had been reduced 10%. The same scrap rate led to the Cost of Quality, measured as a percent of Net Sales Billed, to go way up. This is a profitability problem but not one caused by a quality problem.

EXHIBIT 3
Texas Instruments: Materials & Controls Group
Motor Controls PCC
Product Line Failure Costs

Product A	Sep.	Oct.	Nov.	YTD '87
Activity $	$522,833	$467,380	$424,051	$5,398,635
Intl Fail COQ $	14,637	28,597	2,170	232,221
Extl Fail COQ $	425	0	85	4,420
Total Fail COQ $	15,062	28,597	2,255	236,641
Non-Conf COQ %	2.88%	6.12%	0.53%	4.38%
Var Pr Yr %	0.38%	−2.86%	2.73%	−1.12%
Var Pr Yr $	$1,982	($13,361)	$11,569	($60,645)
Cumulative $	($58,853)	($72,214)	($60,645)	

COQ Projects

Quality improvements were aided by management's willingness to expend funds on projects that produced intangible benefits, such as quality and service, without rigorous financial justification. Concurrent with the financial planning cycle, Quality Improvement Teams, consisting of department managers, their staff, and representatives of support organizations such as Marketing, Engineering, Manufacturing, Production Control, Quality, Finance, and Purchasing, met to establish Cost of Quality improvement projects, using COQ system numbers as priority setting mechanisms. Anticipated savings from the COQ improvement projects were estimated and incorporated into the product line's profit forecast. COQ savings by project were subsequently tracked by the Manufacturing Engineering department (see Exhibit 6). Bob Porter, Vice President of Quality Assurance and Reliability, felt that the identification and implementation of COQ projects were the keys to instilling quality awareness and improving quality performance within the group:

EXHIBIT 4

Texas Instruments: Materials & Controls Group
Motor Controls PCC
Failure Rates by Product

		Jan	Feb	Mar	Apr	May	June	July	Aug	Sep	Oct	Nov	Dec	Year
Product A	Overage %	7.1%	8.7%	10.6%	11.5%	8.9%	1.7%	7.1%	-2.1%	15.8%	3.7%	4.4%	—	7.1%
	Internal Failure	7031	8973	13548	11278	8310	2474	7031	-1595	15341	3995	5914	—	82300
	External Failure	2805	3740	1020	0	340	0	85	8670	0	0	0	—	16660
	COQ %	5.6%	5.3%	5.6%	4.4%	3.5%	0.9%	5.1%	3.6%	7.3%	1.8%	2.8%	—	4.1%
Product B	Overage %	3.6%	4.0%	5.7%	4.2%	2.9%	3.7%	7.6%	1.2%	2.6%	3.7%	-8.5%	—	2.3%
	Internal Failure	932	874	1506	1393	1107	1045	1523	600	1255	1543	-2894	—	8884
	External Failure	0	0	0	0	0	0	0	0	0	0	0	—	0
	COQ %	2.8%	4.1%	4.6%	3.7%	2.3%	3.0%	14.2%	1.0%	2.0%	4.0%	-6.6%	—	2.1%

EXHIBIT 5
Texas Instruments: Materials & Controls Group
Motor Controls PCC
Departmental Non-Conformance Costs

			YTD Through November		
*NC Savings vs. 1986**			*YTD NC COQ % NSB*		
Product A	$89K		Product A		1.6%
Product B	61K		Product B		2.1%
Product C	52K		Product C		3.1%
Product D	20K		Product D		3.3%
Product E	16K		Product E		3.4%
Product F	8K		Product F		3.5%
			DEPT AVG.		3.1%

* Represents the difference between actual 1987 quality costs and the quality costs that would have been incurred at the 1986 COQ percentage. Includes internal and external failure costs only.

EXHIBIT 6
Texas Instruments: Materials & Controls Group
Motor Controls PCC
Cost of Quality Project Savings

	1987 Cost Reductions ($K)					Variance from Annual Plan
COQ Projects	*1Q*	*2Q*	*3Q*	*4Q*	*YR87*	
Yield Improvement	26	61	55	54	196	150
Upgrade Assy Machine	20	24	32	44	120	53
Redesign Molded Part	16	20	24	53	113	(55)
Non-Destruct Testing	10	11	14	17	52	13
Laser Coding	9	10	9	10	38	30
Flash Reduction	8	9	11	10	38	22
Stat. Process Contl.	93	119	128	127	467	(90)
Total	182	254	273	315	1024	123

The critical issue is the "process." By that I mean getting management involved in identifying opportunities for quality improvement, establishing priorities, helping ensure that resources are available, and monitoring progress. We need to speak the right language on each of these issues, and COQ is the language of management.

Two of the organizational mechanisms that support the process are the Quality Improvement Teams (QIT) and the People & Asset Effectiveness (P&AE) reviews. The QITs, which are in place at the group, division, and department levels of the business, consist of natural work groups of managers and professionals who meet regularly to steer the quality excellence process. The quality (P&AE) reviews, which are held quarterly, are high-level management reviews in which business managers review progress against their short- and long-term quality goals.

Early in the year, the lowest level QITs identify quality improvement opportunities. Frequently senior management attends these department QITs where the champions of these projects discuss the opportunities. These projects are dollarized, time phased, assigned champions, and summarized at the division level. The forecasted COQ savings are recognized in the annual plan. Key COQ projects are summarized at the group level. The COQ trend is tracked and reviewed at every group and division QIT meeting.

At the P&AE reviews, the operating departments discuss their short- and long-term goals. Much of this is focused on the progress of key COQ projects—how the QITs are using quality tools such as statistical process control to drive continuous improvement in COQ. This process is not treated as an exact science. It is not preoccupied with testing the validity of the numbers or comparison of one entity vs. another. It is focused on who, what, and when, and closing the loop on results.

In summary, the operating businesses have ownership. They establish priorities and wrestle with the resource trade-offs. The quality organization provides lots of support, but quality improvement is clearly not a program of the quality organization. Operations managers work to achieve goals they helped to establish. Progress is monitored against milestones throughout the year at the QITs and P&AE reviews.

If this process works well, the COQ numbers will take care of themselves. Without the COQ numbers, however, this process wouldn't work.

System Results

Between the formal inception of the COQ system in 1982 and the end of 1987, Cost of Quality as a percent of net sales billed had fallen from 10.7% to 7.8%. Reductions had occurred in each category of quality costs (see Exhibit 7). The system had also focused increased attention on the impact of improved quality on costs and profitability. Carl Sheffer, though, still had mixed feelings about the current COQ system:

EXHIBIT 7

Texas Instruments: Materials & Controls Group
Materials & Controls Group
Cost of Quality, % of Net Sales Billed

	1982	1983	1984	1985	1986	1987
Prevention	2.3	2.0	2.0	2.1	2.3	2.3
Appraisal	2.2	1.9	1.7	1.9	1.9	1.8
Internal Failure	5.3	4.8	4.5	4.2	3.6	3.3
External Failure	0.9	0.7	0.6	0.4	0.4	0.4
Total COQ	10.7	9.4	8.8	8.6	8.2	7.8

Motivating senior management wasn't a problem. They already knew that quality was critical. COQ was most helpful for middle managers to see the consequences of poor quality on overall income. COQ gives one number that focuses several things together. If we focused just on scrap, we would get lower scrap costs but would go out of business as we passed scrap on to the customer. On the other hand, if we tried to focus on reducing external failures through inspection alone, without actually reducing manufactured defects, we would become uncompetitive cost wise. COQ forces us to think about an optimum relationship among the various factors. You have to improve the whole, not pieces at a time.

The COQ system has proven to be a good attention getter, has forced priority setting and has stimulated quality improvement activities. It also ends up being a good scorecard. It does much less well as a diagnostic tool, partially because it uses accounting techniques.

chapter **11**

NEW TECHNOLOGY FOR MANUFACTURING OPERATIONS: JIT AND CIM

Just-In-Time Production

Just-in-Time production attempts to have all work processed continually, without interruptions. The goal is to replicate continuous production processes, such as for manufacturing chemicals, for all manufacturing processes. If this goal is achieved, then throughput times will be minimized, inventory holding costs almost eliminated, and large gains realized in productivity and quality.

The throughput time for any manufactured part equals the time interval between when a part is started into production and when the manufacturing process has been completed and the part is ready to be shipped to a customer. We can represent the total throughput time as

Throughput time = Processing time + Inspection time
+ Conveyance time + Waiting time

In many factories, processing time is less than 10% of throughput time; that is, for a total throughput time of one month (22 working days), only eight hours of actual processing time may actually be required. During the remaining time, the part would be waiting, either in storage or on the factory floor, or just before or just after a processing operation, until the next operation could be scheduled and the part fixtured into place. In an ideal JIT system, the throughput time for a part exactly equals its processing time. While this goal, just like zero defects, may be unattainable, it sets a target by which progress can be measured.

The Japanese manufacturers who have led the way in devising and implementing JIT systems emphasize the importance of reducing throughput time by rewriting the above equation as

Throughput time = Value-Added time + Non-Value-Added time

where *value-added time* equals processing time, the times during which work is actually being performed on the product, and *non-value-added time* represents the time the part is waiting, being moved, or being inspected. Many Japanese manufacturers also refer to the non-value-added time as *waste time* to highlight that no value is being created for the customer when the product is not being processed. The time has been wasted by inefficiencies in the manufacturing process.

Poor and uncertain quality is a prime source of delays. Time required to inspect parts, rework parts, replace a scrapped part by starting a new item into production, or wait for a machine breakdown to be repaired all contribute to lengthening throughput times. Thus, as a firm reduces its incidence of in-process failures (as described in the preceding chapter), it can also reduce its production throughput time.

Perhaps the major source of delays in conventional manufacturing processes arises from producing quantities of products in excess of current demand. The traditional rationale for such excess production is the need to economize on setup and ordering costs. In effect, the existence of large setup and ordering costs makes small lot sizes uneconomical. Conventional wisdom in U.S. businesses and universities led managers to attempt to optimize lot sizes through the use of mathematical models. Engineers and operations analysts computed Economic Order Quantities (EOQ) that seemingly provided an optimal balance among setup or ordering costs, storage and holding costs, and stockout costs. Needless to say, this treatment understated considerably the cost of creating inventory. Also, the large EOQ lot sizes led to substantial throughput delays—first to complete the batch production run, and then to move it into storage until the subsequent processing operation could be freed-up to handle the large batch of work.

The approach of attempting to optimize lot sizes was similar in philosophy to the erroneous search for the optimal number of defects in order to minimize manufacturing costs. As described in Chapter 10, leading manufacturers no longer believe that a trade-off exists between total manufacturing costs and defect rates, so that they are now striving to continually reduce PPM (parts-per-million) defect rates. Analogously, many of these same companies are attempting to drive their setup times to zero.

Reliance on the EOQ formula had a further and more subtle insidious effect on production processes. Because people believed that the economics of lot sizes and setups had been well handled by the EOQ formula, little attention was paid to the time spent on setups or whether production orders were being completed on time. Toward the end of the month, when productions and sales quotas had to be met, or when an important customer complained bitterly about a delayed shipment, production specialists—called expediters—were empowered to "hot wire" a production order through completion, overriding the "scientifically" computed production plan.

The Just-in-Time philosophy takes a more dynamic view of how to optimize production. The EOQ formula accepted existing setup or ordering costs as given, and it attempted to choose lot sizes that were optimal with respect to these parameters. With the JIT approach, lot size is not optimized; it is minimized by attempting to drive setup times to zero. In JIT, inventory is viewed as a form of waste, a cause of delays, and a signal of production inefficiencies that must not be submerged or circumvented by creating mounds of inventory to buffer production stages from one another.

Quality Factor

One factor leading to higher inventory is the need to protect production stages from poor quality or uncertain production at earlier stages. If the machine directly preceding a work station breaks down unexpectedly, then the worker at the work station needs to have a buffer stock of items to work on until the problem at the preceding stage is solved. Or if the next item pulled from the bin to be processed is defective, then the worker had better have another item in the bin or else he or she will become idle. Similarly, if a company is not sure about the quality of items obtained from suppliers, it will need to order more items than are actually needed. Rather than just-in-time, such a production process is characterized by large quantities of inventory for just-in-case; regardless of what goes wrong, a backup exists to keep production flowing.

Once a company adopts a Total Quality Program for itself and its suppliers, the quality problem disappears and unexpected machine breakdowns and defective parts become rare occurrences. The company no longer needs to hold inventory just-in-case, to protect against shortages caused by poor-quality production. Thus, one important source of demand for in-process inventory would be eliminated.

When operating in a JIT environment, any problem at a work station will soon lead to a plantwide shutdown, since no inventory exists to buffer production stages from one another. In this environment, workers are usually provided with a button to press that stops the production line (and sets off lights and bells) to signal that a problem has arisen that needs the attention of everyone in the shop.

While improving quality reduces the need for holding inventory, reduced inventory also leads to higher quality—a causal link in the other direction. When items are produced in large batches (without in-line process control), defective materials or a defective process may only be detected during a subsequent processing stage. In this situation, the entire large batch may have to be reworked or even scrapped. Much engineering time must then be committed to salvaging large batches of defective items, either devising a modified product that could use the substandard items or developing a rework program to get the items back into conformance.

When items are produced in small batches and flow smoothly from one stage to the next, defective items are detected much sooner at subsequent stages. Any problem can be fixed before even the small production lot has been completed. Thus, the amount of defective items produced declines dramatically, and the amount of material to be reworked or scrapped becomes negligible. Engineers no longer have to devise schemes to salvage tens of thousands of defective items and can devote their time to process improvements and to new product designs that can be manufactured during the time formerly used to produce defective items.

Setup Times

Long setup and changeover times of equipment provide the second source of demand for high inventory levels in traditional manufacturing environments. The difference in optimal EOQ batch sizes between a U.S. automobile manufacturer that took six hours to change stamping dies and a comparable Japanese firm that took four to six minutes was enormous. U.S. industrial engineers have concentrated their attention on speeding up production processes; their Japanese counterparts worked continually to reduce changeover times. Changeover times can be reduced through a combination of training, organization, and equipment.

The difference can clearly be understood by anyone who watches how fast a tire is changed during pit stops in the Indianapolis 500 auto race (15 seconds) versus how the average driver fixes a flat tire on the highway during a weekend drive (perhaps requiring an hour or more). The faster changeover times during a high-stakes auto race are achieved through extensive specialization and training of the changeover team, careful preparation in anticipation of the change (new tires and tools are ready well before the changeover starts), and special technology installed for accomplishing a speedy changeover (wheels fastened to the car with only one lug nut, a special hydraulic valve built into the car for instant elevation). In summary, training, preparation, and technology can be combined to produce order-of-magnitude reductions in changeover times. One U.S. company was able, within six months of installing a JIT program, to achieve reductions in changeover times from 20 minutes to 2 seconds at one piece of equipment, from 2.5 hours to 2.5 minutes at another, and from 6 hours to 1.7 minutes at a third.[1]

The JIT approach works to reduce and eventually eliminate setup times so that the optimal lot size can be one. With a lot size of one, the work can flow smoothly to the next stage, without the need to move it into inventory and to schedule the next machine to accept this item.

---

[1] The experience was reported on pages 179–81 in Robert S. Kaplan, "Accounting Lag: The Obsolescence of Cost Accounting Systems," *California Management Review* (Winter 1986), pp. 174–99.

Uncertain Supplier Delivery and Quality

Uncertainty in delivery from suppliers provides a third motive for holding inventory. With the JIT approach, companies work with many fewer suppliers but have much longer-term relationships and commitments to these suppliers. Selection of suppliers is influenced less by short-term price concessions and more by the supplier's ability to provide defect-free materials and components on a timely basis. Frequently, purchasing companies link their computer systems so that production orders, invoices, and payments can all be done automatically, without requiring any paperwork, and, in some circumstances, without human intervention.

When a supplier is certified by the buying company as being able to produce with zero defects, the incoming materials and parts can be placed directly into production without any need for receiving, inspection, and storage. It is not unusual for a supplier's truck to drive directly onto the factory floor to deliver a small batch of materials directly to the machine when and where it is needed. A visitor to a Toyota assembly plant reported seeing the driver of a supplier's truck insert a card into the automatic sensing device on the factory gate, with the gate not rising to let the truck onto the premises until the production process was ready for the delivery. The objective was not to have lots of trucks circling around the parking lot waiting to be admitted (that would only shift inventory costs from Toyota to its suppliers). Rather, the programmed gate was used as a dramatic signal to suppliers to organize their production and distribution processes so that they could be synchronized with Toyota's production schedule, and thereby reduce inventory throughout the logistics system.

Factory Layout

With the small production lot sizes in a JIT environment, successive production operations can be moved much closer together. In a conventional, lot-size production environment, considerable space is needed to store the large buffers of inventory between machines and operations. Improved factory layouts, made possible by reducing the need to hold and move large quantities of inventory, reduce the need for space and indirectly improve quality by allowing all the operators who sequentially process a lot to be in close proximity to each other.

Traditionally, machines have been grouped by function so that all the grinding machines were in one location, all the drilling or milling machines in another location, all the extruding machines somewhere else. With such a functional layout, a part, in traversing its sequence of processing operations, traveled enormous distances as it moved from one section of the factory to another, usually detouring and stopping along the way in a storage area. With the improved layout made possible by JIT, discrete part production facilities become more focused and begin to resemble the efficient layouts and materials flows of continuous process operations. The average travel distance of parts (from incoming materials to finished goods shipment) has been reduced from several miles to one hundred yards or less. In one small project, a U.S. company cut lead time from thirty days to a few minutes, reduced work-in-process from forty pieces to one, and *cut travel distance from 2,000 feet to 18 inches*.[2]

Benefits from JIT

Successful adopters of JIT production have enjoyed tremendous savings. The most obvious saving arises from the much lower investment required to hold inventory. When inventory levels are reduced from three months to one month of sales (increasing inventory turns from 4x to 12x per year) financing costs are reduced by two-thirds. In fact, inventory turns can be increased to 30x or 60x once production problems, made visible by inventory reductions, are solved.

Beyond these obvious financing savings, companies also discovered large space savings. They found that up to 50% of factory space had previously been used to store in-process inventory. Having eliminated WIP, companies found another factory inside their old factory. Such savings permitted planned expansions to be curtailed, and previously dispersed operations could be consolidated inside a single location.

But even the carrying cost and floor space savings were smaller than the savings from improved JIT operations. As companies attempted to reduce inventories, many problems emerged in the factory that had formerly been hidden by inventory buffers: quality problems, bottlenecks, coordination problems, inadequate documentation, and supplier unreliability, among others. Without the discipline to achieve JIT operations, these problems would have remained unsolved. The rationalization of production processes, the elimination of waste, and the more visible display of production problems that were achieved under successful JIT operations led to great reductions in material losses and great improvement in overall factory productivity.[3] The enormous gains in productivity from successfully achieving JIT production led one electronics materials manager to claim that he expected to see two kinds of factories in the 1990s: JIT factories and closed factories.

---

[2] Ibid., p. 180.

[3] See Richard C. Walleigh, "What's Your Excuse for Not Using JIT?" *Harvard Business Review* (March–April 1986), pp. 38–54; Robert H. Hayes and Kim B. Clark, "Why Some Factories Are More Productive Than Others," *Harvard Business Review* (September–October 1986), pp. 66–73; and Robert H. Hayes and Kim B. Clark, "Exploring the Sources of Productivity Differences at the Factory Level," in *The Uneasy Alliance: Managing the Productivity-Technology Dilemma*, ed. K. B. Clark, R. H. Hayes, and C. Lorenz (Boston: Harvard Business School Press, 1985), Chap. 4, pp. 151–88.

As with the JIT environment, an immediate need is to deactivate some existing cost accounting measures if the new production technology is to be successful. Many companies in traditional manufacturing environments have devised informal rules to control the growth of overhead costs, such as by monitoring the ratio of indirect to direct workers. Such a measure reflects their view that useful work is done only by direct labor and that indirect workers and support staff are a necessary evil, but one that must be kept within bounds.

In a CIM environment, direct labor disappears and many "indirect" workers—product designers, software engineers, systems operators, and maintenance workers—are needed to design and control the flow of work through the automatic machines. Several companies have self-destructed their CIM installation when financial managers limited the hiring of key personnel because of concern with the rapid growth of the indirect to direct worker ratio. Clearly, financial rules of thumb, developed for traditional manufacturing environments, have to be examined to determine whether they are at all appropriate in a CIM environment.

In a CIM environment, a large fraction of costs will represent expenditures already made: for product design, prototyping, programming, process design, equipment acquisition, and the debugging of process and product design in the early production stages. For financial accounting purposes, many of these costs will have been expensed in the period incurred rather than traced to the period when production occurs. For internal purposes, companies have started to consider life-cycle costing to reflect better the economics of expenditures and receipts for CIM processes.

Life-cycle costing can already be found in military acquisition programs where project managers attempt to measure the total costs over a major system's life including design and development, acquisition, operation, maintenance, and service. For short life-cycle products to be run through a CIM facility, the initial costs would include those identified above: product design and development, process analysis, programming, and prototyping. Manufacturing costs would include materials acquisition and the conversion cost through the CIM equipment, most of which could be applied based on cycle time. Also traced to the product would be marketing, distribution, administrative, and after-sales service costs. In this way, the profitability of any given product or product line could be determined at the end of its economic life.

Many products will be characterized by large initial cash outlays followed by periods of large net cash receipts (if successful), where short-run variable costs are a small fraction of the selling price. In this environment, it will make sense to budget and accumulate expenditures, receipts, and ultimately profits for each product or project in the company. The exercise, however, of allocating front-end expenditures from one period to another in an attempt to compute a periodic profit figure will be more problematic. Thus, life-cycle costing will emphasize project accounting, not period accounting.

Target Costing

The target costing approach, a form of life-cycle costing, has recently received some attention. Marketing managers first estimate the performance characteristics and market price requirements in order to achieve a desired market share for a proposed product. A standard profit margin is then subtracted from the projected selling price to arrive at the target cost for the product. The product development team must then, through its product and process design decisions, attempt to reach the product's target cost.

This procedure is just the opposite of that followed by many companies today in which the product is designed with little regard either to the manufacturing process or to its long-run manufacturing cost. With this traditional procedure of first designing the product and then giving the design to process engineers and cost analysts, the product cost is developed by applying standard cost factors to the materials and processes specified for the design. Frequently, this cost may be well above that which can be sustained by market prices and the product is either aborted or, if marketed, fails to achieve desired profitability levels.

With the target cost approach, the new product team, consisting of product designers, purchasing specialists, and manufacturing and process people, works together to jointly determine product and process characteristics that permit the target cost to be achieved. The target cost approach is especially powerful to apply at the design stage, since decisions made at this stage have high leverage to affect long-run costs.

Figure 11–3 shows how the great majority of manufacturing costs become locked in early in the life cycle of the product. Once the product is released into production, it becomes much harder to achieve significant cost reductions. Figure 11–3 shows that the majority of costs become committed or locked in much earlier than the time at which the major cash expenditures are made.

Summary

The new manufacturing environment of Just-in-Time production and Computer-Integrated-Manufacturing will introduce major changes in companies' operations and sources of competitive advantage. Management accountants will need to stay abreast of the operating changes occurring in their organizations so that measurement systems can be devised that will be consistent with the company's strategy and operations. The gap

FIGURE 11–3
Pattern of Costs Committed and Costs Incurred Over Product Life Cycle

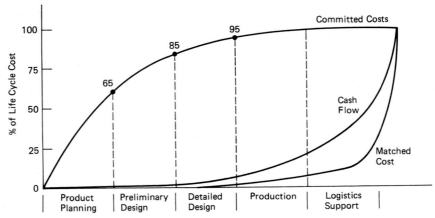

will widen between information produced for external financial statements and that required for internal management decisions and control. Much greater use will be made of a variety of operating measures for short-term feedback and evaluation. New ways to accumulate costs and apply them to responsibility centers and products will also evolve. While it is difficult to know just how this process will develop in the next decade or two, we can be confident that future management accounting systems will be very different from those that existed in organizations up through the 1980s.

PROBLEMS

11–1   General Electric—Thermocouple Manufacturing (A)

At exactly two o'clock on the afternoon of February 8, 1982, William P. (Bill) Draper, Manufacturing Manager of General Electric's Aerospace Instruments and Electrical Systems Department, Wilmington, Massachusetts, stepped into the conference room, motioned for quiet, and began to speak.

As you know, we're here to discuss the possibility of introducing a new system of production control, Toyota's "Just-In-Time" system, in our thermocouple product area. All of you, I hope, have reviewed the materials that I sent around last week, outlining the project and pro-

Copyright © 1983 by the President and Fellows of Harvard College. Harvard Business School case 9–684–040.

viding a brief description of how the system works in Japan. Since this is our first meeting, I'd like to spend the next few hours reviewing the major elements of "Just-In-Time" and considering how it might be applied here in Wilmington.

To help answer your questions, I've invited Roger Hyatt to join us at today's meeting. Roger is the president and founder of Production Systems, Inc., a consulting firm specializing in operations planning and control, as well as a leading expert on inventory management. He was one of the instructors leading the GE program I attended in Japan last fall. Feel free to speak openly in front of Roger; after two weeks in Japan as his bridge partner, I can vouch for his ability to keep confidential matters to himself.

I suppose some introductions are in order now. Working clockwise around the table, we have Sam Phillips, Manager of Production Planning; David Hartwell, Manager of Planning for the thermocouple area; Bob Stone, Production Control Supervisor for the third floor, which includes thermocouples; Eric Nelson, first-line supervisor in the thermocouple area; Steve Hansen, Advanced Manufacturing Systems; and Henry Malone, Manager of Shop Operations in the thermocouple area.

One final comment before I give Roger a chance to speak. You all know that inventory has been a perennial problem for us, and that something must be done to bring inventory levels down. That's the whole purpose of this project. My personal view, after visiting a number of Japanese factories, is that our goals are relatively modest. We're shooting for a reduction in the thermocouple area's inventory from the present level of $6.2 million to $2.1 million after three years, with a further reduction to $1.4 million or less after five years. Some of the Japanese companies we visited carried only six to eight days worth of inventory; many didn't even have stockrooms. I don't see why we can't do as well.

That's about it from my end. You all know that I believe in this project and think it can succeed. Roger, is there anything that you would like to add?

Roger Hyatt leaned back in his chair, looked slowly around the room, and addressed the group:

I'm sure that you've all read the materials that Bill sent around and have formed some opinion of the project. I'd like to hear what you think. Exactly what will it take to make the "Just-In-Time" system work here at Wilmington?

The GE Impact Program

Bill Draper and Roger Hyatt had first met at General Electric's Impact Program—the Manager of Manufacturing Course held in the fall of 1981. The program, staffed by a variety of consultants and educators specializing in manufacturing management, had been designed by General Electric to help the company improve the quality and productivity of its operations. Approximately twenty-five manufacturing executives attended the program each year. Their first four days were devoted to classroom work, including an overview of manufacturing strategy, a review of the major elements of operating systems (primarily production planning and material control, quality, processes and equipment, and workforce), and a contrast of U.S. and Japanese management systems. The remaining ten days of the program were spent in Japan, visiting three Japanese companies, analyzing their manufacturing and management practices, and discussing these findings as a group.

The participants then returned to the U.S. to begin applying what they had learned. After completing trip reports, each executive was expected to identify areas of opportunity within his or her own operation, and to propose a project embodying the principles and practices he or she had observed in Japan. All participants met again for a week to compare project proposals and strategies, and to receive updates on projects already initiated under the Impact Program. The group then disbanded, and each executive proceeded with his own project. If necessary, further assistance could be obtained from any of the program faculty.

It was after attending the Impact Program that Bill Draper had proposed a "Just-In-Time" system for the thermocouple area of General Electric's Aerospace Instruments and Electrical Systems Department.

The Thermocouple Product Area

Thermocouples, like thermometers, are used to measure temperature. They operate on a simple physical principle: when two dissimilar metals are joined at the ends and heat is applied, an electrical current is generated. If a gauge is then attached to the thermocouple, an extremely accurate temperature reading can be obtained.

Although they have a variety of applications, thermocouples are especially useful in aircraft engines, where accurate temperature readings are critical to safe and efficient operation. An aircraft engine thermocouple is generally roughly circular in shape, to conform to the interior dimensions of an engine, and consists of a number of probes joined to a main harness. These probes point toward the engine's exhaust gases; they, like all other segments of the harness, are constructed from swaged leads, which consist of rods containing two wires made of dissimilar metals, separated by magnesium oxide or some other insulator. Current is generated when heat from the engine's exhaust gases passes by the probes. Since the probes are attached, via a junction box, to a gauge in the plane's cockpit, the engine's temperature can be monitored continuously.

The thermocouple product area was one of five at the Aerospace Instruments and Electrical Systems Department in Wilmington. With 1981 sales of $21.5 million, it ranked second in total dollar volume. (See Exhibit

1 for a more complete profile of the thermocouple business.) Nearly thirty major types of thermocouples were produced by the area, and ninety different models. The simplest of these, the J-79 product line, was regarded as a likely candidate for any experiment with Just-in-Time techniques because it was relatively easy to manufacture, employed swaged leads that were less fragile than those used by other product lines, and enjoyed a comparatively stable business outlook.

EXHIBIT 1
General Electric—Thermocouple Manufacturing (A)
Thermocouple Business Profile, 1977–81
(millions of $)

	1977	*1978*	*1979*	*1980*	*1981*
Sales	$9.9	$12.3	$13.1	$20.8	$21.5
Cost of Sales					
Materials	2.5	3.0	3.1	5.1	5.6
Labor	1.0	1.3	1.8	2.8	2.2
Gross Profit	.2	.6	(1.2)	(.5)	.8
Inventories (12/31)	2.7	4.1	5.4	5.3	6.2

The Production Process for the J-79 Thermocouple

The J-79 thermocouple, like others manufactured at Wilmington, was composed of four subassemblies—probes, segments, resistors, and a connector. The connector was attached at one end, to plug into the engine; segments and probes then alternated around the main body of the thermocouple. Each probe contained two resistors. In total, the J-79 consisted of five segments, six probes, twelve resistors, and one connector.

The segments were built up from swaged leads. These were first cut to the proper length, and then passed twice through centerless grinding: once to reduce them to the proper diameter, and a second time to narrow their ends. The ends were then turned back to reveal the wires inside. After cleaning and annealing, the segments were "formed" (shaped), each in a slightly different pattern (i.e., there were five segments, and therefore, five shapes, per thermocouple). Finally, each segment was sandblasted and inspected. Many of these same steps were also followed in the manufacturing of connectors, another of the basic subassemblies.

Probes also began with swaged leads. These leads, however, were purchased pre-cut to the proper length. They then passed twice through centerless grinding, with both passes on the same machine. The initial setup of the grinder took between four and six hours; with a run time of 22 seconds per piece, this encouraged lot sizes of 1000 or more. The second pass through the grinder required another lengthy setup, and also involved a relatively brief run time. After cleaning and inspecting, a flange was welded to the end of the leads. The wires within the leads were then sandblasted, straightened, and separated. From this point on, it was necessary to keep the wires properly identified; each worker carried a small magnet to help determine which wires were positively and which were negatively charged. The probes were then formed and inspected, a protective casing (called the probe shield) was welded on and the weld inspected, and a box for holding the resistors was added. Additional cleaning and inspection followed, after which the probe assembly (now called a thermocouple box) was complete.

The simplest part of the production process was the making of resistors. Wire and a cement-like substance were combined in a mold, then baked for several hours. After inspection, the resistors were ready to be used.

Once these four subassemblies were complete, they were combined on a building board, which helped to insure that all pieces were welded in the correct order. In addition to welding, final assembly involved a number of forming operations, in which wires were combined and twisted together. These activities often alternated with welding. Welders were frequently idle while the formers were at work, and vice-versa. Various tests of resistance, voltage, and weld strength were performed next, a small piece of metal (called the stamp) was placed over the top of the probe box to protect the resistors, and the completed thermocouple was inspected a final time. It was then ready for shipment.

Workforce Issues

Most hourly workers were paid on an incentive wage system, based on piece rates that had not been reviewed for several years. Standards were tighter for some parts than for others. Because workers normally had considerable autonomy in the parts they chose to make, they often focused on those with the loosest standards, rather than on those that were in the greatest demand. The result was excess supplies of some parts and shortages of others. Probe assemblies, for example, which an experienced worker could make at 150% of standard, were at an inventory level estimated at six weeks usage under normal demand conditions. One plant employee, commenting on the problem, observed: "How can anyone keep them [the workers] from making whatever they want? All of the materials they need are right there on the floor. The supervisor would have to watch every move those guys made to keep them making the right parts. And the union certainly won't stand for such intervention all of a sudden." In fact, several managers had noted a strong correlation between the tightness of standards and the percentage of time that parts appeared on the critical list (indicating a parts shortage).

Welders, who were the most highly paid and most senior group of hourly workers, presented an additional problem. Several managers suspected that they were using the incentive system to their own advantage. Because the rate for reworking defective parts was higher than the rate for welding them in the first place, welders benefited from building in their own defects. As one manager noted: "Although the welding equipment that the welders have to work with isn't the greatest, I don't see how there could be a 22% defect rate without some help from them. But what can we do? No one has supervised those guys for years."

Order Entry, Purchasing, and Production Control

Orders were received from three groups: the military, GE's Aircraft Engine Group (AEG), which dealt with both military and commercial customers, and a distribution warehousing operation (DWO) that served as an interface between Wilmington and its customers. DWO received orders from the airlines, grouped them, and then requested the necessary thermocouples from Wilmington. It was concerned solely with commercial customers.

Commercial customers accounted for approximately 50% of thermocouple sales. Because they expected goods to be delivered exactly on the contract date, neither early deliveries nor delinquencies were acceptable. To increase the probability that contract dates would be met, the thermocouple manufacturing plan called for commercial orders to be completed approximately one month before the actual contract date. Delinquencies had declined in recent years, but continued to be a problem. (See Exhibit 2 for a summary of 1979–1981 delinquency statistics.)

EXHIBIT 2
General Electric—Thermocouple
Manufacturing (A)
Thermocouple Sales Delinquencies
(thousands of $)

	1979	1980	1981
January	$ 386	$845	$466
February	606	800	284
March	377	972	326
April	570	932	320
May	694	944	183
June	1043	909	195
July	1008	593	162
August	1382	558	212
September	1851	494	296
October	1640	396	287
November	1536	479	0
December	1142	341	341

Note: Delinquencies that have not been shipped by month end appear in the following month's total as well.

Military customers were willing to accept shipments at any time up to the due date. They also remitted advance payments based on Wilmington's investment in materials and labor. This gave the plant a bit more negotiating power than it had with commercial customers, who paid only after their goods were delivered. Military customers therefore allowed some flexibility in scheduling, which led to a smoothing of the manufacturing plan over time.

Manufacturing was not, however, permitted to build until a firm order was received. This kept inventories down because raw materials orders were placed only after thermocouple orders were confirmed. Until recently, DWO had been an exception to this rule. It had sometimes ordered from Wilmington on the basis of forecast, rather than confirmed, orders. DWO was now required to have an order in hand before contacting Wilmington, although cancellations remained an occasional problem.

Wilmington dealt primarily with sole-source suppliers. Many were located outside the Northeast; several considered Wilmington to be a very minor customer. However, 12 of the 21 items purchased from outside suppliers by the thermocouple manufacturing area were provided by GE's West Lynn plant, located in a nearby suburb.

West Lynn's quality and reliability, which had historically been high, were currently in decline. Rumors were circulating that the plant was soon to be closed. Wilmington management, however, did not feel that replacement suppliers should be approached until there was some official announcement about West Lynn's future.

Because production was planned on a monthly basis, workers could theoretically be building product up to four weeks ahead, adding that much more work-in-process inventory. If production were planned on a weekly basis, the problem would be greatly reduced. However, the production planning department was not optimistic about this approach. One manager commented: "Those guys can't even level a monthly schedule! How do they expect to level a weekly one?"

Wilmington's sister division, AEG, has been responsible for some of the volatility in scheduling. In the past, AEG had been unwilling to commit in advance to a preset schedule. It wanted to preserve its ability to respond to last minute orders. It was primarily these orders that caused the thermocouple schedule to be "nervous" and difficult to predict.

Inventory Management

Wilmington used a system called the Inventory Control Package (ICP) to manage inventories. ICP was a variant of MRP, in that it exploded backwards to determine raw materials needs. The system had been ordered from an outside consulting firm, which had not fully integrated it into Wilmington's operations. In-house systems people had therefore found it necessary to introduce modifications. Many of these changes were undocumented, and the people who had introduced them were no longer at Wilmington.

Because materials control was relatively loose once materials left the stockroom—Wilmington staff had nicknamed the shop floor "no man's land" because goods seemed to disappear there without a trace—it was difficult to know the accuracy of the inventory balances reported by the ICP. While the system was reinitialized every two months to clear old information from the computer, this process did not reflect goods already on the shop floor. Once these goods left the stockroom, there was no further accounting of them until the yearly physical inventory. For the J-79 thermocouple, inventory on the production floor was estimated at between $300,000 and $315,000, approximately 80 to 85% of the total inventory on hand for that particular product line.

Loss factors, representing the percentage of raw materials expected to end up as scrap, had not been reviewed for several years. These normally reflected either yield losses on the production floor or rejects from incoming inspection. In 1981, these losses totaled 6.3% of sales. However, certain items were being purchased in as much as double the actual quantity needed because the yield on their processes had been only 50% when loss factors were initially established. Over the years, many of these processes had been streamlined; yields had often improved dramatically, although loss factors had not been similarly adjusted.

The Meeting

Roger Hyatt glanced around the room as he waited for a response to his question. In the brief silence that followed, he added, "I'd like to walk out of this room with two things: a first cut at the problems that we're going to encounter when this program is implemented, and a reasonable action plan with responsibilities assigned to specific people. I'd also appreciate comments about what you perceive as being *good* about the plan."

Bill Draper spoke up immediately. "This plan is perfect for the thermocouple area. First, it is heavily process-oriented. That should make gains much easier to obtain. Second, thermocouple manufacturing is physically cut off from other areas, so it should be possible to isolate the working of the plan, as well as the results."

Nelson introduced the "people" aspect. "I don't see why it should be so natural to expect that our people will be willing to bust themselves for this plan. After all, what's in it for them? They get the same wage whether they do D− or A+ work. That would only change if we implemented an incentive system of some kind, and I think that would open a whole can of worms that we don't want to deal with right now. You all know that we promote on a seniority basis around here. Are we willing to jeopardize that system for potential improvements in one area?"

"Another thing that we need to deal with is whether workers will think that we'll begin laying them off as soon as productivity goes up. If the workers in the thermocouple area like you and believe that they'll keep their jobs even if productivity has improved, they *may* work with you. But, if they think that they are going to work themselves out of a job by improving the process, we're going to have some serious problems."

Draper replied, "We saw in Japan that financial incentives were not the primary motivation for working at a high level of quality. What could we do to make our workers want to do a better job? After all, most of what we've been hearing about Japan suggests that Japanese companies have been very successful in motivating American workers when they purchased factories here. Don't get me wrong. If an incentive system or profit-sharing system would help, I'd certainly consider it. On the other hand, we should remember that our workers know that there are problems in the thermocouple area, and that if things don't improve, we'd be forced to consider moving the area to another plant. We may have some unusual leverage as a result."

Hartwell joined the discussion at this point. "I agree with Bill that the people situation is manageable. I feel that the biggest problem will be with our vendors. It just doesn't make sense to talk about improving quality when our vendors are so unreliable. They neither produce good pieces nor deliver them on time."

"We have four major vendors: GE-West Lynn, Shelbyville, Owensboro, and ITT-Harper, as well as a number of small ones. Our best vendor is supposedly GE-West Lynn. Today they're having problems with the J-box, one of the most important parts we purchase. Just imagine what would happen if we were on a Just-In-Time system, and the J-box or some other vendor quality problem came up. With the inventory reductions that you're describing, we would have to shut down the line. Are we really willing to take such risks? AEG wouldn't be very happy with us if our delinquency rate went any higher.

"Talking about the Japanese and their great quality with so little inventory . . . do they have as much pressure to meet output goals as we do? Working in the shop, production comes first, with quality way behind. We would like quality to be better, but right now, output is the driver. Hell, even Bill, as excited as he is about inventory levels and as much as he wants to improve quality, knows that when it comes to the bottom line, you've got to meet the shipment schedule. In other words, our next promotion has a lot more to do with meeting shipments than with improving quality or reducing inventory."

Phillips interrupted: "Don't we share some of the blame? Don't we keep changing the schedule? We should establish and then stick to a six to eight month schedule, but we're willing to change at the drop of a hat."

Draper nodded, then added: "Let me give an example. AEG is in here now with an inquiry that would make us delinquent for the month of

January. Originally we were supposed to build 30 pieces. On January 7, they came in and told us to build 65 pieces in January and 50 a month in February, March, and April, rather than the 30 originally planned. They don't want anything in August, September, or October, but a lot more in November, then none in December because they don't want a high year-end inventory. That's the kind of schedule changes we deal with regularly. What's important is not that we get these occasionally, but that we get them on the average of one per week."

Hartwell observed: "We don't work with our vendors the way the Japanese do. Of coure, we have a very different situation. In Japan, vendors tend to be much smaller and more easily controlled by customers. Can you just see us trying to control West Lynn? They'd laugh in our faces! We can't be 5% of their business."

Stone added: "Most of our parts are sole-sourced. We need to develop second sources, but until then we can't force the vendors that we have to meet our needs. Nor should we forget how difficult and time-consuming it is to develop new sources. Besides, what assurance do we have that new vendors would be any more responsive to our needs? If we're a very small part of their business, why should we have any more leverage than we currently have? We might even make our first-source suppliers less concerned about our problems. With that little inventory, we're going to be very exposed."

Malone agreed: "Right now we have a thermocouple with an oddball part. The schedule for this thermocouple has been firm for the past 8 months. We're supposed to build 128 this month, but the vendor called last week and said that the entire batch of parts had to be scrapped. We won't get any for a month and a half. They simply don't feel any pressure to stand on their head to give us 128 oddball parts. They say, 'So what? We're late. Who is thermocouple any way? They buy 128 pieces every two years.' "

Roger Hyatt rejoined the discussion at this point: "We should probably spend some time discussing your production process. How much will the current process have to change to adapt to Just-In-Time?"

"In the future, people will have to be more versatile," said Malone. "Believe it or not, we've already started in that direction. We're now doing a lot more cross-training."

Draper observed: "In Japan, the most we saw were 6 labor grades, and they didn't even use the first one. We have 250–300 grades in this plant alone. In the thermocouple area, we have 12–18 grades, with hourly wages ranging from $8.60 to $10.62."

"We need to reduce set-up costs," said Malone. "That's the only way that we will be able to reduce our lot sizes. For example, one of our grinders requires 3 hours of set-up time for a typical run of 8 hours. We'll have to completely change our thinking in this area. Until now, we've always assumed that large lot sizes were the key to profitability."

"What kind of gains could be achieved if set-up times were reduced from 3 hours to 10 minutes?" asked Hyatt.

"It's impossible."

"Let's take an example to see if that's true. How long does it take you to change a flat tire on your car?"

"Fifteen minutes," replied Nelson.

"What if you were a racing car driver competing in the Indianapolis 500?"

"That's different. He has help. There it takes only about fifteen seconds."

"Then," continued Hyatt, "why couldn't you make similar improvements in manufacturing? Couldn't you set up a special team to do set-ups? Or break down the tasks and have some performed in advance?"

"It could be done in stamping," replied Nelson. "We would have to set up a special rate for the set-up team, but I guess that's not impossible."

Phillips added, "I hear that the workers in Japan do a lot of the thinking about reducing set-up times. Perhaps there's some way for us to get more input from our workers."

Draper noted: "In one plant we visited in Japan, there were 88 suggestions per employee per year, even though workers received only token payments for their contributions. Management tried to respond to all suggestions within a month. Those inputs from the workers can make a big difference."

"Let me introduce a new subject," suggested Hyatt. "Tell me about your reject rates."

Malone replied: "As you might expect, they vary by stage in the production process. In-process rejections, between subassembly and final assembly, run about 15%. At final inspection, the reject rate is 5%. In the field, the rate is less than 1%. That's not strictly accurate because we rework a lot before parts get to the in-process stage. At some early steps, our yield is only 60%. The major cause of this low yield is poor welds due to moisture."

Nelson disagreed: "No, the problem is in the cap. If you take ten caps, no two are the same. That's why there is an inconsistency in the way they weld. It's a vendor problem."

"What if," asked Hyatt, "we could get the yield losses at that operation down to 25%, at final inspection to 2%, and in the field to less than .5%? What would that mean?"

"Great savings! Productivity increases, better product, lower inventories," enthused Nelson. "I think that we should set some goals that will get us moving in that direction."

Malone interrupted: "I think that goals in those areas should be initiated by the quality control department. Quality hasn't yet given us any real targets to strive for."

"What kind of support are you going to need to make this project work?" asked Draper.

Malone replied: "We'll need engineering and quality control involvement. We'll also need a team dedicated solely to this project. That may be expensive, but I don't think that we can do this if we try to tackle it on a part-time basis. Most of us have had to cancel important meetings or else spend less time on the factory floor in order to be here today. Eric, for instance, was only able to spend two hours on the floor today, and he has 35 people. That will hurt his productivity by 2–3%."

Hyatt surveyed the group, then asked: "Are you all convinced that the project should move forward?"

Malone quickly replied: "I'm not."

"What will it take to sell you? You're the manager of the thermocouple department. It's not going to work if you're not sold. What about you, Eric? Are you on board?"

Nelson answered: "I'm sold. I want to give it a try. Of course, I have less to lose than Henry does. He's the manager. If this thing fails, he's going to be left holding the whole ball of wax. What's more, even if we do succeed in reducing inventory, the materials and inventory people will get all the credit. Henry and I will still be evaluated on whether the product gets out the door."

Malone added: "Don't get me wrong. I'm willing to try anything once. But I'm the one that has the most to lose here. I'm very open, I'm just not committed. I won't be a roadblock. But I don't have a Kanban stamped on my hand either."

Hyatt stood up to terminate the meeting. "I've asked some very tough questions today, and you've been honest and open in your responses. If this project is going to work, that honesty will have to continue. Part of your job will be to lower the walls that now exist between the various functions represented here. You'll need to encourage a lot more cooperation for the common good. Somehow, Bill will have to figure out a way to reward you for your performance. He'll do that. But if you continue to develop cooperation and trust, you have a great opportunity. You're trying to discover a new way to manage the business. It will no longer be an inventory problem, a quality problem, a shipment problem, but *our* problem. I'm very excited about the possibilities."

The group was silent for moment. Stone then observed: "One of the readings that Bill sent us contained a cartoon showing rocks that are exposed as the sea of inventory is lowered. The problem for us is that we don't want to know about the rocks."

"But," responded Hyatt, "you've told me about the rocks already. That's what we've been discussing for the last two hours."

Nelson chuckled. "We haven't told you about half of them! Come out on the floor with me and I'll show you what you're really in for!"

11–2   *General Electric—Thermocouple Manufacturing (B)*

The JIT Project

From its inception, the JIT project had been the responsibility of Sarah Miles, who reported directly to Bill Draper. Miles was a college-trained engineer, as well as a graduate of the two-year Manufacturing Manager Training Program (MMP) offered by GE. That program, which was designed to produce the company's next generation of middle managers, consisted of four six-month assignments in manufacturing. Typically, these were in quality assurance, first-line supervision, materials management, and manufacturing engineering.

Reflecting on the MMP, Miles singled out her exposure to manufacturing engineering and quality assurance as being especially valuable. She commented:

> The time I spent developing manufacturing methods and time standards was excellent training for my position as JIT coordinator. It really helped me to understand process planning, which was crucial in the early weeks of the JIT project. In addition, my exposure to quality assurance gave me much better insight into the ways that a process can be improved to increase the yield of good pieces.
>
> I saw myself as the original white knight, coming in to solve everybody's problems. The place was in such bad shape, with all kinds of delinquencies, and the inventory kept getting higher and higher. I really thought they were all sitting there waiting for me to come and make it go!

The JIT team's initial efforts focused on four major areas: process improvement, setup reduction, leveling the schedule, and overcoming worker and management resistance.

Process Improvement. Before introducing any changes in the layout or in production methods, the group spent several weeks developing a process flow diagram outlining the steps in thermocouple manufacturing. This not only increased their familiarity with the process, but also highlighted areas where materials movement could be smoothed and nonproductive time eliminated. For example, the process diagram showed that considerable time was wasted in final assembly because units were being passed back and forth between welders and formers. Each group

Copyright © 1985 by the President and Fellows of Harvard College. Harvard Business School case 9–685–002.

was forced to remain idle while the other completed its work. In addition, formers were idle during the first half hour of every shift while they waited for welders to complete their first pass on a unit. Once these inefficiencies were recognized, Miles was able to rewrite the methods for the affected operations, changing their sequence so that idle time was eliminated.

The process diagram was also used to rationalize the shop layout. A string chart was first created mapping out the path that work-in-process followed as it moved through the various stages of production; distances were then compiled to see how much walking operators had to do as they carried materials from one machine to the next. This information was used to reorganize the thermocouple area. Machines that were used in sequence were moved as close together as possible, equipment that had not been used for several years was removed from the shop floor, and additional tools were purchased so that each worker would have ready access to the required equipment at his or her work station, rather than having to walk periodically to the tool crib. The combined result of these efforts was a 22% reduction in the average distance walked per operator.

Setup Reduction. Three significant setups were involved in producing the J-79 thermocouple: those of the centerless grinder, the turnback machine, and the building board (die cart) used to hold pieces of the harness together during the welding stage of final assembly. The first two of these setups were completely eliminated by introducing additional equipment, while the third was significantly reduced by process redesign.

Centerless grinding, for example, typically involved setups of four to six hours. One machine was available. Since the process required two distinct operations, each with its own setup, only lot sizes of 1,000 or more were considered to be economical. By spending $28,400 to purchase a second centerless grinder, Miles was able to provide each operation with its own dedicated machine. Setups were completely eliminated, permitting an economic lot size of one unit. A similar approach was followed with the turnback machine. In that case, however, an idle old machine was discovered in another part of the factory, making the purchase of new equipment unnecessary.

The other major setup required for the J-79 was that of the building board, which was used to align segments properly before welding. The board required readjustment each time a new harness was welded, a process requiring approximately 1.5 hours. By creating a table with holes indicating where each part was to be placed—in essence, eliminating the need for operator judgment—the JIT team was able to reduce the required setup to 3 minutes.

Leveling the Schedule. A level (unvarying) build schedule was regarded as critical to smoothing the flow of production and moving toward more sophisticated JIT techniques. The build rate was set at 12 thermocouples per day, even though the line was capable of producing many more. The rationale for this decision was strictly pragmatic: since the J-79, as a military item, involved a fixed total production quantity, as soon as the number of items specified in the contract was completed, all workers on the project would have to be moved elsewhere. A build rate of 12 thermocouples per day was selected because it provided a reasonable production rate, yet did not "use up" the order too quickly.

This decision was closely tied to the development of standardized containers for controlling the amount of work-in-process. These were used primarily for subassemblies. For example, a styrofoam container was designed with room for exactly 6 probes. Since workers were not permitted to pile additional probes on top of these containers, they made it possible, in a matter of seconds, to see how much inventory was on the floor and to relate that quantity to the amount required by the daily build schedule. This had not been possible in the past, when large boxes, capable of holding as many as several dozen probes, had been used. Ron Byerly, the recently appointed first-line supervisor for the J-79 thermocouple, commented:

> One of the best things about JIT has been this "management by sight." It's so much easier to look at the new containers and know immediately what's out there: how much inventory is at each work station, and which places are having problems with either too much or too little material.

Overcoming Foremen Resistance. Foremen presented a difficult problem. They continued to be rated on their efficiency of labor utilization. Since efficiency was measured as the ratio of actual to standard labor hours worked, every time a foreman told one of his people to restrict output to the level mandated by JIT, he reduced his own rating. Joe Riscoe, the new manager of shop operations in the thermocouple area, commented:

> The impact of the efficiency rating system becomes clear once you recognize that during the last four months we had to shut down J-79 production 52 days out of 70—all because of vendor problems. You can imagine what that did to foremen's efficiency ratings. Either people believe that you'll ignore the big swings that result in declines in their ratings, or else they'll try almost anything to circumvent the JIT system.

Miles, for one, believed that the emphasis placed on efficiency ratings had encouraged foremen to attempt end-runs around JIT. As evidence, she cited the example of resistor assembly. Raw materials for resistors were the only ones left unmonitored on the shop floor; all others were kept in a locked storeroom and were released to the floor at weekly intervals. (An exception was made for resistors because they consisted primarily of wire and glue; the cost of keeping detailed accounts of these items would have greatly exceeded the value of the materials.) Because the foreman in charge of resistor assembly had ready access to these materials, and because he wished to maintain a high efficiency rating, he had instructed his people to make resistors every time they were without other work. Only when the J-79's inventory numbers rose steadily for two months in a row did Miles discover the problem. By then, $55,000 worth of resistors had been built (out of a total inventory on hand of $160,000). Moreover, demand for this type of resistor was expected to cease in December 1983, leaving $38,000 worth of obsolete parts. Miles found that the only way this behavior could be prevented was to keep all resistor materials under her desk, insisting that they be used only with her permission. Should resistors be made without consent, Bill Draper would be notified. Miles commented:

> One thing that the resistor incident taught me was the need for constant policing. As soon as my back was turned, someone was guaranteed to be trying to make something they shouldn't.
>
> On the other hand, I think worker resistance was less than it might otherwise have been because of rumors that GE was considering moving thermocouple production to another location. Without those rumors, the project would have been much harder to implement.

Ron Byerly added:

> At first, the workers were pretty nervous. They were sure that JIT was going to lead to a cut in pay, and they didn't like the idea of increased supervision. But after a couple of weeks, morale became very high. We made sure that the workers felt involved by having frequent meetings. In fact, during October, when things were really getting off the ground, we had meetings nearly every day. Every time there was going to be a change, we made a point of explaining it as far in advance as possible so that people could get used to the idea.

The Program Begins

After the initial groundwork, JIT was slated to begin operation on November 1, 1982. Shortly before that date, the project team discovered that a crucial part would be missing because of vendor problems. They decided to proceed anyway, even though this meant that the program would yield no final output on its very first day. In fact, nearly a week elapsed before any thermocouples were completed. Nevertheless, the discipline of the new build schedule remained in force, and workers were required to remain idle after they had completed the specified number of parts and subassemblies.

During the next two months, the program proceeded smoothly. The level build schedule was in place; the process flow had been rationalized; parts, subassemblies, and final goods were being built in small lots and stored in standardized containers; quality levels had been improved; and inventory levels were falling. By most accounts, the system was functioning effectively.

During the first six months of the JIT program, significant improvements were made in quality, productivity, and inventory levels. Defects, for example, had historically been a problem in two areas: segment welding and the welding of harnesses in final assembly. Defect rates in the former category were reduced from 59% to 2%; in the latter category, from 22% to 2%. These new levels were maintained over time.

Better documentation, in the form of defect summary sheets developed by the project team, was one stimulus for change. Previously, little systematic data had been collected on quality. Management had been unable to focus its efforts on those processes or people causing the most serious problems. This quickly changed once the data were in hand. For example, once segment welding was identified as a major source of defects, attention turned to the equipment employed in that stage of the process. Management discovered that the tooling employed had not been serviced for many years: there were several rough areas that left scratches on the segments, necessitating rework at another station. After the tooling was repaired and a regular maintenance schedule installed, defects dropped dramatically. Defects also fell at this stage because welders no longer had the incentive they previously did to produce errors that they could then repair at higher pay.

Productivity improved as well. Most gains were associated with the project team's early attempts at rationalizing the production process, which led to better material flows and reduced idle time. Because several critical setups were eliminated, effective capacity also increased.

The original motivation for JIT, however, was inventory reduction, and not productivity or quality improvement. Here, too, significant gains were made. Over a seven- to eight-month period, the J-79's overall inventory level was reduced by 19%. Other major savings were recorded early in the project. During September and October, for example, all excess material on the shop floor was returned to the stockroom. This produced a savings of $60,000 since this material would otherwise have been reordered (because all material not in the stockroom did not exist as far as Wilmington's inventory control system was concerned). Similarly, at the start of the project six weeks of probe assemblies were discovered on the shop floor, these being the parts with the loosest work standards. Workers were therefore not allowed to build probes for the next six weeks, eliminating the excess production that would otherwise have resulted.

Vendors remained a source of problems throughout the project. Shortages continued to occur on a regular basis. Only one vendor was induced to move to daily deliveries. In part, these problems could be traced to the shutdown of the West Lynn plant, which made supplying Wilmington that much more difficult. Members of the purchasing department also felt that because the JIT project was only one of a much larger set of responsibilities they faced, it deserved only limited attention.

While JIT had produced significant cost, quality, and productivity improvements, Miles felt that the project could have done even better if pressures to meet shipment goals had not intruded. On those occasions where other Wilmington divisions were having trouble meeting their output goals, the thermocouple area was sometimes pressured to increase its production, which could be sold to the military anytime. This made it difficult to maintain a level build schedule: in some weeks, as many as 24 thermocouples were being built each day, rather than the 12 that had originally been planned. The entire JIT work force was disrupted, interfering with efforts to smooth the production flow and reduce inventory.

11–3 The Ingersoll Milling Machine Company

> The challenge is not to remove all the people from the production floor. Our goal is to give skilled machinists the equipment and support they require to make them as productive as possible. The flexible machining system has allowed us to expand throughput dramatically. If we were still using isolated manual machines we would require 40 machines and 120 skilled machinists. The flexible machining system provides the same output using nine machines and 39 personnel. We could not have hired enough skilled machinists to operate conventional technology machines for the higher demand we are now experiencing.
> *George E. Frawley, Manager FMS.*

Introduction

The Ingersoll Milling Machine Company (IMM) manufactured about thirty large-scale custom-made metal cutting machines and machining systems for special applications per year.

The 1986 budget for IMM was approximately $100 million (Exhibit 1) with direct labor accounting for about 25% (Exhibit 2). This excluded the cost of materials purchased directly against a job.

The Flexible Machining System

When IMM decided to enter the FMS market, it chose a spectacular approach. It built its own FMS to manufacture a majority of the small parts (within a 40″ cube) required for the business. Construction of this FMS,

---

This case was prepared by Professors Robin Cooper and Robert S. Kaplan. Copyright © 1986 by the President and Fellows of Harvard College. Harvard Business School case 9–186–189.

EXHIBIT I
The Ingersoll Milling Machine Company
1986 Budget ($ thousands)

Direct Labor	$ 25,300
Indirect Labor (including supervision)	30,000
Fringe Benefits/Premium Pay	20,500
Operating Supplies	2,500
Tools, Jigs, and Fixtures	2,600
Purchasing Services (including legal, consulting, and auditing)	4,500
Travel	2,100
Communication	700
Miscellaneous Expenses, Net (warranty, freight, service)	2,700
Transfers (charges to affiliates)	(2,100)
Utilities	2,800
Depreciation, Insurance, Taxes	7,200
Maintenance	2,700
TOTAL	$101,500

EXHIBIT 2
The Ingersoll Mining Machine Company
1986 Budget
Analysis of Direct Labor Expenses by Function
($ thousands)

Engineering	6,700
N/C Programming	1,200
Fabrication	1,200
Light Shop (including FMS)	4,000
Heavy Shop	1,900
Assembly	8,000
Services (e.g. installation)	1,500
Paint Shop	500
Sheet Metal	300
	$25,300

which was expected to cost about $20 million, began in 1982, and by late 1984 the FMS was operational. Installation of all equipment was expected to be completed sometime in 1987 (see Exhibit 3).

The decision to become an FMS supplier was driven by several forces. First, the firm's leading edge strategy prompted it to master the technology of the "factory of the future." Second, the industry as a whole was slowly turning towards FMS technology and customers were beginning to request machines with FMS capability.

EXHIBIT 3
The Ingersoll Mining Machine Company
Press Release
Description of FMS

Twelve machining centers in a computer-integrated flexible manufacturing line will replace 40 stand-alone machines at The Ingersoll Milling Machine Company main plant in Rockford, Illinois.

With the third shift running unattended, there will be approximately 75% fewer operators than now required. However, this saving is incidental to the reduction in overhead costs that will be realized. Primary objectives of the installation are uninterrupted workflow, reduced inventories of work in progress, release of needed floor space and less manufacturing-support manhours. The investment is the latest step in what has been a long-continuing management program to stay cost-competitive internationally.

As part of Ingersoll's light machine shop, the automated system will process workpieces of 40-inch cube and less in the small lots peculiar to the company's special machinery business. History indicates that of 25,000 different parts to be produced annually, 70% will be in lots of one, and half will never be made again. The new FMS thus has been planned to provide unique flexibility and efficiency.

SYSTEM FEATURES

Centralized parts storage and setup will serve the workhandling system, with modular fixtures automatically drawn from high-rise storage. Automatic guided vehicles will transport palletized work to and from automatic pallet changers at each machine. Scheduling and monitoring of workflow will be computer-managed. Tool management will include monitoring according to normal life cycles and current condition, with automated replacement of worn and broken tools. Other features include an automated parts cleaning area and inspection of finished work by computer-directed coordinate measuring machines.

Because of the close tolerances specified for critical Ingersoll machine tool components, the production area will be temperature controlled. This will help assure uniformity of work quality attainable with nine Ingersoll/Bohle machining centers included in the system. These machines have inherent ability to perform full-horsepower milling and rough boring followed by finishing to jig-borer accuracy.

The new FMS is an integral part of Ingersoll's corporate-wide CIM system. The DEC/VAX system manager computer is in constant two-way communications with the corporate host computer, receiving new work assignments from the corporate planning and scheduling data base and feeding back lot-completion notices as parts exit the FMS headed for the assembly floor. The concept is a natural evolution of Ingersoll's award-winning CIM system into the CIFM (Computer Integrated Flexible Manufacturing) system of the future.

MACHINING CENTER CAPABILITIES

Ingersoll/Bohle machining centers selected for the line are 40-hp horizontal spindle models. Their design is particularly suitable for automatic around-the-clock operation with provision for periods of unmanned operation. Capabilities include:

- Fail-safe seating accuracy of pallets through sensing of foreign matter on pallet changer rest pads.
- Automatic release of spindle drive in event of overload.
- Automatic release of axis drives in event of a collision.
- Automatic changing of a servodriven boring/facing head with slide feed for taper turning, profiling and other complex operations.
- Air-jet cleaning of spindle and tool tapers during toolchange cycle.
- Diagnostic and maintenance alerts with pinpointing of problem locations.
- Hard-copy reporting to management of work interruptions and operator-initiated adjustments.

Direction of system planning has been the responsibility of manufacturing management with assistance from Ingersoll Engineers Incorporated, the company's independent consulting organization.

IMM decided to build an in-house FMS for several reinforcing reasons. First, management believed FMSs were cost justified. Second, they believed that IMM needed to demonstrate to potential customers the practicality and value of an FMS production process. Finally, they felt the best way for the firm to learn about the technology was first-hand.

A formal economic analysis to justify the IMM FMS was never undertaken. Management was convinced the firm had no choice. If it wanted to maintain a technological competitive edge, it had to become a leading supplier of FMSs. Despite this statement of faith and commitment, management believed the increased capacity, improved quality, reduced inventory, and savings in labor more than offset the high initial cost of the new productive facility.

The FMS, which was part of the light machining shop, produced about 25,000 different parts annually. The average batch size was under two, with 70% of the parts produced in batches of one. Because of the customized nature of each product, 50% of all parts manufactured will never be manufactured again. In 1985, the FMS was about 75% complete with five Bohle W2 horizontal and four Le Blond MC40 machining centers in place. The completed FMs was expected to contain twelve machines, six of each type and an automated materials handling system that would manage the part from cut-off to work-in-process. When fully operational, IMM planned to air condition the building. This would allow them to meet the extreme part accuracies required.

The Competitive Environment

In an industry known for being fragmented and undercapitalized, Ingersoll Milling Machine Company was virtually unique. Its stated objective was to remain at the cutting edge of production technology; every year, nearly all of its profits were reinvested in new equipment. While a typical competitor had one third of its machines over 20 years old, 80% of IMM's machinery had been purchased in the last five years. This practice was a consistent part of the firm's long-term strategy and management believed this strategy provided a substantial competitive edge.

The IMM salesforce worked with corporate customers to develop solutions to their machining problems. A customer proposal contained a description of the solution, the quoted price and an approximate delivery date. Preparing a proposal was a major undertaking. The engineering department scoped the job and estimated the cost to complete. The cost estimate was prepared using the firm's historical cost data base. While nearly every machine designed for a customer was unique, each contained a large number of common sub-assemblies. The actual cost of sub-assemblies manufactured for previous contracts was known fairly accurately and a skilled estimator could use these historic costs to develop an acceptable cost estimate for the cost of designing, building, and assembling most machines produced by the firm.

Manufacturing Process

When a proposal was accepted and the contract signed, the final delivery date was confirmed. As soon as possible after the contract was signed, the marketing department prepared a specification document describing the job, the intricacies involved and major unresolved items. After this document was completed, a transmittal meeting was held to discuss the specification document with representatives of the other functional areas.

The master scheduler determined two additional dates; the engineering date, when the design engineering was expected to be completed, and the machine work date, when manufacturing was expected to be finished. These two dates, along with the shipment date, defined the major milestones of the project. For a typical project, engineering was finished in 6 months, machine work completed by the 13th month, and the product shipped at the end of 18 months.

Engineering's first task was to design the machine. This task typically took three to four months. The first few weeks of the design process were considered the most critical; during that period the general design philosophy of the machine was identified and the overall level of profitability determined. Once the specifications were clear, the cost of the machine was re-estimated. This estimate, called the planned cost, was used to measure the performance of the project.

The completed machine design was transmitted to the purchasing department to initiate the procurement process. Procurement took about two months to complete. The lead times of the required parts were fed into the scheduling system to help plan the manufacturing sequences. Once finalized, the design drawings (completed on the firm's computer-aided design (CAD) system) and associated bill of materials were released to manufacturing.

Since all of the firm's major in-house production machines were numerically controlled, the routing sheets prepared by manufacturing engineering had to be converted into NC programs. The routing sheets defined the fixtures required, the orientation of the part in the fixtures and the operations to be undertaken. The NC programs were detailed machine instructions that enabled the firm's NC machines to machine the required parts. Programming typically took about two months. In 1985 the firm employed 60 NC programmers, of whom 27 were dedicated to programming for the FMS.

Production occurred in three major areas of the plant: in fabrication, steel plates were welded together to form weldments; in light machining, the smaller weldments and bar stock were machined; and in heavy machining, the larger weldments were machined. Total manufacturing time was typically seven months, split about evenly between fabrication and manufacturing (machining).

The final step, assembly, required about six months and was the most uncertain of the entire production process. An average machine contained several thousand machined parts and about four times as many purchased parts. Each of these parts had to be fitted together to produce a working machine. The assemblers were highly skilled workers. They often hand worked machined or purchased parts to make them fit together. If the parts were too far out of tolerance they were returned to the machining areas as rework.

On occasion, design problems did not become apparent until the assembly process. Engineers were then brought back into the process to redesign parts, culminating in an Engineering Notice of Correction (ENOC), which provided new specifications for a part or parts. Thus, a significant part of the workload in machining centers arose from the ENOCs, errors, and defective work which was not detected until the assembly process.

Rework was typically a rush job and had to be expedited. Management estimated that about 25% of the machining area's time was spent on such high priority rework and ENOCs.

FMS Production

To avoid work-in-process buildup, production in the FMS was not started until (1) NC programming was complete, (2) the bar stock was cut to size or the weldment manufactured, and (3) the appropriate tooling and fixtures became available.

Six tool setters (two on each shift) collected the tools identified by the NC program from inventory bins. After offsetting and gauging, the setters put the tools onto a special trolley. This trolley kept together all the tools required to machine a given part. This allowed the tools to be easily moved around the department while guaranteeing that they were available when the part was being machined.

Parts released for production were moved to the setup area where setup personnel placed the parts into fixtures. The fixtures were universal in design (i.e., not specially designed for the part), consisting of a part holder, such as a vise, and a pallet. To achieve the very high tolerances possible in the FMS (machining to accuracies of .00015 of an inch), the parts had to be held firmly in place. This required heavy part holders and pallets; for example, the pallets were steel and cast iron plates several inches thick.

An automatic guided vehicle (AGV) transported each part and its pallet between stations. When the central computer determined that an appropriate machine was available (i.e., that its input station would soon be empty) the AGV was sent to the setup area to pick up the part, move it to the available machine, and deposit it on the machine's input station.

The machine, when ready, moved the part from the input station onto the work station. A set of machining tasks that could be completed without repositioning the part was called an operation. A typical operation contained several transformation activities; for example, a part might be milled on two surfaces, have five holes drilled and three tapped. The ability to perform multiple operations for a given part on the same machine was one of the greatest benefits from using the FMS. With conventional technology, each operation (rough milling, drilling, smooth milling, boring) would be done on a different machine, requiring transport time, scheduling, and startup time for each processing stage. A preliminary study indicated that about 20 percent of machining time could be saved when parts were processed on the FMS rather than on conventional machines. When the operation was complete, the machine moved the part to the output stage. The AGV collected the part from the output stage and returned it to the setup area where it was removed from its fixture and, if finished, sent to assembly. Otherwise, the part was prepared for the next operation.

In September 1985, 27 operators were working in the FMS, one per machine per shift. While they did not perform the actual machining, the operators had specific tasks to complete. The operators were, in order of importance, expected to:

- Detect programming errors. If the program was incorrect, the operator was expected to intervene and stop the machine before any damage occurred.
- Manually alter the programmed speed if the part was being machined at an improper cutting speed. The firm had completed an analysis of operator interventions and determined that nearly all of the interventions were to reduce, not increase, the cutting speed. Management believed this occurred because the new machines cut at higher speed than the old NC machines and the operators had yet to become comfortable with these higher cutting speeds. Another problem was the failure of some operators to allow the FMS to work without intervening. Prior to the FMS the operators were rewarded for their skill in adjusting the cutting conditions to improve productivity. Some of the operators were finding it impossible not to try and "tweak" the system. In effect, they were not making the transition from machine operators to machine supervisors.
- Suggest improvement in the programming so that a library of efficient programs could be developed.
- Provide helpful suggestions about how to reduce the need for operator involvement or to improve the efficiency of the FMS. Examples of the types of suggestions received include: using three coolant streams aimed at different distances from the machine to guarantee that all tools, irrespective of length, received sufficient coolant automatically, and pointing out where common tools, rather than special tools, could be used to machine a part, thus reducing the cost and quantity of tools required.
- Undertake in-process gauging and adjust the cut to compensate for any tool wear.
- Insure that, when a large diameter long drill emerged from the other side of the part, the coolant, which was pumped through the tool to keep it cool, did not squirt on the floor. This had happened recently, and the coolant landed in the path of the AGV. The coolant was very slippery and caused the AGV to leave its path and crash into a wall.
- Deburr the machined parts while they were on the output stage waiting for the AGV to arrive. They were also expected to remove any metal tangled around the cutting tools. In the next twelve months the company expected to automate about 95% of all part and tool deburring.

The operators' responsibilities in the FMS were very different from what they were in the rest of the light machining shop. In particular the FMS operators spent more time watching and less time machining. The company was attempting to increase the operators' job content. The most significant change currently planned was to have them set up jobs at the setup station during the operating cycle of the machine. Thus, while one part was being machined, the operator would be setting up the next part.

Cost Accounting System

The cost accounting system at IMM captured the total cost of each finished product, including engineering, NC programming, machining, inspection, and assembly. The cost system was part of a company-wide central data base. The cost of each of thousands of machined parts within a finished product was collected. Management considered individual part costs to be valuable but overwhelming. Therefore, it was more useful to capture costs at a higher aggregate level than individual parts, such as by sub-assembly or by sub-shop order, depending on the needs.

Indirect costs in the engineering department were allocated to projects based on engineering direct labor dollars using an overhead rate of 175%. Roger Dougherty, IMM's controller, explained the rational for this procedure:

> Engineers cannot realistically assign their time to individual parts. They work on designing sub-assemblies and may be working on several parts at once. When [an engineer] changes the dimensions of one part it often affects several others. He cannot design each part on its own. For example, an engineer may use CAD libraries to create the subassembly on the screen and then make only slight adjustments in individual parts. He charges his time against the subassembly, not against each part.

NC programming charges were also accumulated at the sub-shop-order or subassembly level.

Machining costs, however, were traced to individual parts. In addition, manufacturing overhead was allocated to the manufactured parts based on direct labor dollars. Dougherty explained the rationale behind the more detailed part costing in manufacturing in contrast with the philosophy for costing engineering and NC programming:

> Part numbers are established to direct part movement through the shop. Because it is available, it is easy for an operator to measure the time spent working on individual parts. Therefore, we collect manufacturing time spent at the part level. This is quite different from Engineering, where it is unrealistic to capture part time.

Manufacturing costs were aggregated in several ways. First, for cost control purposes they were combined to give the cost of each sub shop order. These costs were measured against earlier estimates. In addition, estimators could use this information to develop bids for future machines.

The procedures used to collect direct labor and to allocate overhead costs were basically the same for all manufacturing cost centers. The setup person and machine operators entered the start and end times for each operation on their daily time cards and these times were used to assign labor costs to parts.

Overhead costs were allocated to parts based on the direct labor dollars charged to the part. There were 14 overhead pools representing the major manufacturing processes required to manufacture a machine, and an overhead rate had been calculated for each pool (Exhibit 4). The FMS was part of the machining centers. The *center's* overhead rate had dropped when the FMS was installed because the FMS had a much higher capacity rate than the older machines (Exhibit 5). This rate continued to drop as the firm gained experience and more parts were manufactured using the FMS. In 1986 it was expected to be even lower.

Prior to 1978, the manufacturing division used a single burden rate for the entire plant. The 250% rate was fixed for many years. Engineering (100%) and the service departments (65%) used different overhead burden rates for absorbing costs.

In 1978–79, a massive renovation started in the plant. Nearly $50 million of capital was invested during the next five years. This investment was directed disproportionately within the plant and within machine departments, and the use of a single plant-wide rate was no longer considered adequate. Initially, up to 40 different overhead rates were calculated, almost a separate rate for each cost center.

But the use of so many different overhead rates created new problems for cost estimators. In advance, the estimators did not know whether a particular sub-assembly would be machined on a manual or a NC machine. The actual job cost, however, was quite dependent on machine choice

EXHIBIT 4
The Ingersoll Milling Machine Company
Cost Pool Overhead Rates[a]

N-C Programming	350
Paint Shop	250
Fabrication and Sheet Metal	300
Heat Treat	550
Gear Cutting and Grinding	300
Machining (includes FMS)	500
Small Drilling and Boring	350
Lathe and Cutoff	400
Roll Grinder	350
Small Mills	250
Heavy Machine Shop	500
Assembly	200
Quality Control	300
Material (10% steel, 5% purchased parts)	7

[a] Allocated on direct labor dollars with the exception of Materials, which is allocated on the basis of material cost.

EXHIBIT 5

The Ingersoll Milling Machine Company

Machining Cost Pool: 1981–1986[a]

	Actual					Plan
	1981	*1982*	*1983*	*1984*	*1985*	*1986*
Direct Costs						
Direct labor	$112.5	$ 97.5	$112.5	$ 199.5	$ 681.0	$ 789.0
Helper labor	75.0	75.0	46.5	69.0	165.0	192.0
Helper overhead	112.5	112.5	69.0	103.5	249.0	286.5
Total Direct	300.0	285.0	228.0	372.0	1095.0	1267.0
Variable Overhead						
Indirect salaried	84.0	85.5	103.5	165.0	361.5	438.0
Overtime premium	12.0	10.5	6.0	30.0	118.5	102.0
Shift premium	43.5	49.5	45.0	66.0	177.0	183.0
Fringe benefits	79.5	87.0	85.5	144.0	385.5	450.0
Supplies	4.5	7.5	1.5	4.5	19.5	79.5
Tools, jigs, and fixtures	67.5	51.0	34.5	106.5	481.5	150.0
Maintenance	85.5	187.5	157.5	180.0	400.5	369.0
Other	4.5	7.5	6.0	19.5	84.0	81.0
Total Variable	381.0	486.0	439.5	715.5	2028.0	1852.5
Fixed Overhead						
Supervision	42.0	48.0	51.0	54.0	0.0	0.0
Utilities	7.5	7.5	6.0	15.0	36.0	39.0
Depreciation	292.5	141.0	115.5	283.5	499.5	792.0
Insurance	4.5	6.0	6.0	7.5	24.0	69.0
Total Fixed	346.5	202.5	178.5	360.0	559.5	900.0
Support departments	225.0	238.5	415.5	354.0	1027.5	1192.5
Helper Overhead	(112.5)	(112.5)	(69.0)	(103.5)	(249.0)	(286.5)
Total Overhead	840.0	814.5	964.5	1326.0	3366.0	3658.5
Full Absorption Rate (%)	747	835	857	665	494	464
Applied Rate	750	750	750	750	600	500

[a] This cost pool contains the costs associated with the FMS and two other stand-alone Bohle matching centers.

because of the different hourly rates between the two types of machines. Therefore, the cost system was changed to group machines into the same overhead pool if they performed essentially the same function, even if the machines were geographically dispersed about the factory. Roger Doughtery commented on this experience:

> We learned an important lesson. First, it was difficult for estimating departments to cope with overhead rates that try to cover every manufacturing situation. Estimating cannot predict which machines will be used to manufacture a given task. Secondly manufacturing management learned quickly that manual machines with lower overhead rates resulted in less costs while new technology with higher rates resulted in apparently higher cost. We did not want to offer incentives

to use manual machines, so we grouped similar manual and advanced machines together into a single pool.

By reducing the number of cost pools from 40 to 11, we maintained adequate accuracy for product costing while still not overloading the estimators.

This logic was applied when developing the overhead rate for the FMS. Instead of treating *it* as a separate cost pool, we group the new FMS with two older stand-alone machining centers.

In the next seven years two more cost pools, materials handling and quality control, were added. Dougherty noted:

Initially, we grouped all material overhead costs—inbound freight, purchasing, receiving, inventory control, and inventory adjustments—into one overhead category and allocated these costs to purchased materials using a single overhead rate of 6%. Recently, we decided to use separate rates for steel and for other purchased parts. Basically, the cost of freight and handling for steel was much higher than for all other purchased materials, and we wanted to trace these higher costs more accurately. Currently, the overhead rate is 10% for steel purchases and 5% on the price of all other purchased parts.

I suppose we could have added the freight cost to the purchase price of everything we order, but we prefer to keep freight costs in a separate category so that it becomes more visible and, we hope, more controllable.

Breaking out quality control costs was driven by another factor. We used to trace the direct labor cost of inspectors to individual parts, but we didn't bother with adding on any overhead costs to inspection labor since the amounts involved were trivial. Then we acquired our first Mauser, a machine which can measure with extreme accuracy the dimensions of an entire sub-assembly. It is a superb but expensive machine, and without any charge for its use, we soon found that engineers were directing that the more complex parts of products be built directly on the Mauser. While this permitted these parts to be assembled with fine accuracy, during the three months or so that the sub-assembly was being built, no one was able to inspect or test any other parts on the machine. Consequently, we introduced an overhead charge for Mauser machine time, and now it is used only as originally intended, for inspection of finished sub-assemblies.

Support department costs were allocated to the manufacturing cost centers on a number of different bases though direct labor hours was the predominant basis (Exhibit 6).

On the whole, management was satisfied with the cost accounting system and felt that it provided accurate cost data. There was a growing concern, however, about how well the system was reporting manufacturing costs for the FMS. This concern was reinforced by their belief that the

EXHIBIT 6
The Ingersoll Milling Machine Company
Allocation Bases for Support Department Costs

Direct Labor Hours

- Manufacturing Administration (all departments)
- Heavy Shop Administration (heavy machining, fabrication and paint departments)
- Customer Services Materials (all departments)
- Customer Service Operations (all departments)
- Facilities/Advanced Manufacturing Engineering (all departments)
- Product Manufacturing Engineering (all departments)
- Process Planning (heavy machining, light machining, fabrication)
- Manufacturing Engineering/Administration (50% NC, 50% in process planning)
- Shipping (all departments)
- Plant Facilities, Garage, and Grounds (all departments excluding NC programming)

Direct to Department

- Light Shop Administration
- Machine Shop Production Control (2/3 light machining shop, 1/3 heavy machining shop)
- Assembly Storeroom (assembly)
- Assembly Production Control (assembly)
- Machining Maintenance (10% paint, 4% fabrication, 50% light machining, 36% heavy machining)
- Burr Bench (50% light machining, 50% assembly)
- Assembly Administration (assembly)

Direct Labor Hours and Direct to Department

- Advanced Manufacturing Engineering (assembly 10%, rest to heavy machining, light machining, and fabrication using direct labor hours)

Material

- Manufacturing Operations—Material
- Receiving
- Steel Receiving
- Purchasing
- Inventory Control

---

amount of FMS manufacturing would increase across time until it amounted to about 50% of all light machining. Dougherty commented:

> We are rapidly reducing the amount of manufacturing direct labor in our product. FMS technology is part of a natural progression to substantially increase our productivity. As we develop FMS technology further we will continue to make progress. At some point we will be forced to move to some kind of machine hour or elapsed time system.

Other IMM personnel also expressed their belief that the FMS environment was sufficiently different from the other machining centers that new accounting measures would eventually be called for. For example, one of the project managers felt that direct labor hours were inappropriate for costing time in the FMS. He believed that a machine hour rate based on the actual time a part is on the machine makes more sense. He hedged his recommendation, however, with his concern about the impact of any new system on the pricing and bidding for new businesses. Bidding, pricing, and estimating were such important functions for the success of the business that any change in the existing system introduced "an element of risk that needed to be addressed."

Tom Linden, vice president for technology and one of the prime movers for promoting the FMS environment throughout IMM, believed that cost accounting could greatly expand its influence. By capturing more of the data after the NC program for a part was written, it would be possible to obtain an estimate for the amount of time implied by the program to drill a hole, mill a surface, grind an edge, etc. These estimates could serve as a standard against which actual machine operations could be compared.

11–4   *Tektronix: Portable Instruments Division (B)*

The existing cost system did not reflect the realities of our assembly-based production process. We only required about 4% labor to build the product and yet the cost accounting system was burdening on direct labor. There was a widespread belief that material usage was a cost driver and that the current system did not reflect that cost driver. Management was quite concerned that we did not have adequate product costs and did not know where to place our strategic emphasis.

Bruce Anderson, Division Controller

Introduction

In 1983, Joe Burger, Manufacturing Manager of the Portable Instruments Division (PID), initiated a series of radical changes in the 2400 series oscilloscope (scope) production process at PID. These changes were aimed at solving a number of managerial, technical and process related problems. They included consolidating production activities into one area, moving the support departments into the production area, moving the inventory of components into areas adjacent to each assembly operation, initiating

This case was prepared by Professors Robin Cooper and Professor Peter B. B. Turney. Copyright © 1988 by the President and Fellows of Harvard College. Harvard Business School case 9–188–143.

a JIT inventory pull system, using visual control in place of performance reports, implementing total quality control (TQC), and using people involvement (PI) to move responsibility for problem solving down to the line people.

Changing the Cost System

In 1985 management turned its attention to the design of the cost accounting systems. The first step was to assess the need for cost information. They identified three distinct uses of cost; special, management, and legal. Special costs were costs derived for situations, such as make versus buy decisions, where the average costs reported by the cost sysem were inadequate. Management costs were the costs reported by the product costing system. These costs were used in designing products and guiding cost reduction efforts. Legal costs were the costs used to value inventory for financial accounting purposes.

After these uses for costs information had been identified, the firm embarked upon a three year program to replace the existing accounting systems. The first change was the implementation of an integrated business system. This system tied together the information used by manufacturing, accounting and all other areas of the firm.

The second change was to simplify the accounting procedures. Reporting labor performance for each operation was abandoned, reducing the number of monthly labor transactions from 35,000 to less than a hundred. The number of inventory transactions was reduced by a similar extent, and the number of variances was reduced to three. This simplification freed up the time for a considerable portion of the accounting staff to work on the management cost system and special costing exercises.

The third change was the design of a new cost accounting system for the 2400 series line of scopes. Management believed that the existing cost system did not reflect the realities of the new production process. Direct labor accounted for only 4% of the manufacturing cost, yet the accounting system used direct labor as the exclusive basis for allocating overhead. The direct labor content of PID's products had been constantly decreasing over recent years, while overhead costs were increasing.

High overhead rates convinced engineers that the way to reduce overhead costs in products was to reduce labor. As a result, the focus of cost reduction programs had been the elimination of direct labor. Inevitably, since much of overhead was not driven by direct labor, this reduction did not have the desired effect, and overhead rates had continued to spiral upwards.

Given these facts, management was concerned that the product costs reported by the existing system were inaccurate, and were not helping them direct the strategic emphasis of the divisions. In 1985, they decided to create a special project team to redesign the cost system. The team initially consisted of Mike Wright, Financial Systems Application Manager, and Jeff Taylor, summer student intern. They were later joined by John Jonez, Manager of Cost Accounting.

Phase 1
Material Burdening

Bruce Anderson:

> The problem of the existing system was its inability to recognize the "true" cost of purchased parts. Therefore, it did not allow the engineer to understand the trade-off between parts proliferation and direct labor content. For example, we had hundreds of different resistors when a dozen would have sufficed. It was costing us money to maintain more and more active parts. Our objective was to reduce the number of vendors so that we could achieve JIT delivery and 100% quality. We believed this would increase our flexibility and reduce our overall costs. We were very worried about part number proliferation and felt that the material burdening system would help reduce it and keep it under control.

Jonez described his assignment to develop a new overhead allocation method:

> As a first step we established a set of characteristics to guide the new allocation for the new method. We decided that the method must be intuitively logical and easily understandable by management. In addition, it should allow a more accurate correlation of cost to products, thus providing better support for management decisions such as make versus buy decisions, product design decisions, product phase-out and start-up decisions, and strategic pricing decisions. Most important it must support the Just-in-Time manufacturing strategy of the Group. Finally, it needed to provide information that was accessible by decision makers.

The team recognized that the chosen allocation method had to be accepted and supported by management. The time was right for change because almost everybody believed that the current method of burdening was inequitable, and because accounting was convinced that the division's burdening method could be improved.

Initially, the team assumed that the new burdening method would be used for inventory valuation as well as for management purposes. This view was abandoned, however, when it was realized that the new burdening method might change the reported valuation of inventory. One concern was that this change might conflict with reporting consistency. PID also wanted to maintain the option of changing the burdening method for management purposes in the future without having to seek corporate accounting, auditing, and IRS approval. Another reason to keep legal costing separate from management costing was the desire to report full product costs. PID therefore adopted the idea of "management costs" that would use the new burdening method, and would coexist with the "financial costs" used for inventory valuation. One difference between the two systems was that more elements of costs were included in the new system. Purchasing costs, for example, were treated as a period cost in the old system, whereas the team preferred to include them in the product cost.

In its study, the team discovered that about 50% of overhead costs were related to materials (material overhead costs (MOH)). These costs included the costs of planning, procuring, inspecting, storing and distributing materials. It was felt that an allocation base should be selected that was relevant to these activities. The remaining 50% of overhead would, for the moment, continue to be allocated using direct labor.

After some preliminary analysis, three alternative allocation bases were identified:

1. Material dollars
2. Number of parts
3. Number of part numbers

Material dollars burdening calculated a MOH cost per dollar of material cost. For example, if the budgeted annual MOH was $8,200,000, and budgeted total material purchases was $70,000,000, then the material dollar overhead rate would be $.0117 of MOH per material dollar.

The second method calculated a single burden rate that was applied to each part specified in the bill of materials. If a bill specified 100 discrete parts, and the number used was 5 times each, the material overhead for the assembled item would be 500 multiplied by the rate per part.

The third method determined a different rate for each part depending on the volume of usage. If there were 6,000 part numbers, there would be 6,000 rates. Each rate was calculated using a two step procedure. The first step determined the standard burden cost for each part number. The second step divided the standard burden cost by the volume of each part number to obtain the cost per part for that part number. This calculation produced lower rates for high volume parts, and higher rates for low volume parts (Exhibit 1).

$$\text{Step 1:} \frac{\text{Material Overhead Cost (MOH)}}{\text{Number of active part numbers}}$$

$$= \text{Annual cost to carry a part number}$$

Step 2: $\dfrac{\text{Annual cost to carry a part number}}{\text{Annual usage of the part number}}$ = MOH rate for each part

EXHIBIT 1
Tektronix: Portable Instruments Division (B)
Number of Part Numbers
Overhead Cost Computation
(Illustrative Example)

Expenses in the MOH pool	= $5,500,000
Number of active part numbers	= 8,000
Annual cost to carry each part number	= $\dfrac{\$5,500,000}{8,000}$ = $687.50

– High usage part

Annual usage of example part number =	35,000 UNITS
MOH rate for example part number =	$\dfrac{\$687.50}{35,000}$ = $.02

– Low usage part

Annual usage of example part number =	350 UNITS
MOH rate for example part number =	$\dfrac{\$687.50}{350}$ = $2.00

In order to make a choice from among these three methods the team found it necessary to understand what costs should be included in MOH, to identify the factors that caused those costs, and to determine their relative materiality. Consultation with management permitted MOH to be broken into four distinct components:

1. Costs due to the value of parts.
2. Costs due to the absolute number of parts.
3. Costs due to the maintenance and handling of each different part number.
4. Costs due to each use of a different part number.

This breakdown showed that the costs incurred due to the frequency of the use of parts categories (2 and 4) were secondary to the cost of carrying each different part number (3). The costs due to the value of parts were similarly quite small.

The cost of carrying each different part number resulted from a number of activities that had to be carried out for each part number. These activities included planning, scheduling, negotiating with vendors, purchasing, receiving, handling, delivering, storing and paying for each part number. The more part numbers there were, the more these activities had to be performed.

Given these findings, the team concluded that the total MOH cost of the parts could reasonably be expected to decrease with the use of a smaller number of different part numbers. This cost reduction was the result of two factors. First, higher volume discounts could be achieved by replacing low volume unique parts with high volume common parts. Second, the total manufacturing overhead needed to support an operation with fewer unique part numbers would be less than the amount currently being incurred.

Upon reviewing these facts, management decided that the chosen allocation measure for MOH should focus on reducing overhead through the reduction of part numbers. They felt that method three, an allocation measure based on part numbers with a specific rate for each part number, best captured the relationship between material overhead and part numbers. Consequently, after the team made a series of presentations to management, the method received general acceptance.

During these presentations, a number of advantages were identified for adopting the part number method:

1. The part number method was the most accurate of the three methods because it reflected the differential consumption of materials-related activities by the products. An instrument that was designed with many unique components, for example, would be correctly given a cost penalty. The method would also avoid penalizing high volume products which, while they might contain a number of different parts, consumed relatively few material related activities per material number.

2. There would be an opportunity to provide engineers with a listing of all parts and the material overhead cost associated with each part. This information would be helpful in evaluations of the value of a new part versus using an existing common part, with a particular incentive to reduce the number of part numbers, and to increase the proportion of common parts used in the instruments. Such a listing did not currently exist, and engineers relied on their own judgment in making such evaluations.

The disadvantages of using the part number method were identified as follows:

1. Certain products might be allocated an excessive amount of overhead. The cost allocated to products with infrequent options, for example, might exceed the true cost of adding the options. Products that were being phased out, where little effort was being expended, might also be over-costed.

2. It was the most difficult of three methods to implement, and would require the most computer resources to maintain.

3. It was also the most complex method and probably the most difficult for management to understand. There was concern, for example, that management might draw the erroneous conclusion that the material overhead costs of $687.50 (Exhibit 1) were variable with each part number. Eliminating

EXHIBIT 2
Tektronix: Portable Instruments Division (B)
Product Cost Information Using Material Burdening Approach

Model	A	B	C	D	E	Total
Volume	3000	3000	750	400	300	7450
Selling Price	$3,590	$5,550	$7,150	$8,400	$9,200	$33,902,500
Costs:						
Material	$2,000	$2,400	$3,350	$4,100	$4,200	$18,612,500
Labor	250	260	320	380	390	2,039,000
LOH	300	360	250	500	540	2,529,500
MOH	150	160	320	650	700	1,640,000
Other	200	250	350	450	460	1,930,500
Total Cost	$2,900	$3,430	$4,590	$6,080	$6,290	$26,751,500
Gross Margin	$690	$2,120	$2,560	$2,320	$2,910	$12,151,000
Percent	19.22%	38.20%	35.80%	27.62%	31.63%	31.23%

one part number in the data base would not reduce total material overhead costs by this amount. Nor would the division save $2.00 in out-of-pocket costs using one less low volume part. Over time, however, and with a sufficient reduction in part numbers, the consumption of materials related activities and overhead cost would go down.

Given this perception, management had difficulty attaching any specific meaning to the $687.50 rate. It was merely an average calculation based on the current overhead cost structure and the current set of part numbers used by the division.

The MOH cost for each instrument was computed from the part numbers in the instrument's bill of materials. The rate for each part number was multiplied by the number of times that part was used in the instrument. The resulting cost was aggregated for all part numbers in the bill (Exhibit 2). Instruments with larger numbers of parts and/or a higher percent of unique parts carried a higher MOH cost.

The Expected Benefits

Since it was widely believed that the majority of material related manufacturing overhead costs resulted from having too many part numbers, management felt that it was important to have an allocation measure that was consistent with its desire to reduce the number of part numbers. While it was recognized that overall cost reduction would not be immediate, it was believed that the part number allocation method would increase the awareness of the costs associated with part number proliferation. This awareness would influence engineering decisions and result in real cost savings over time.

The belief that there was a strong relationship between cost and part number was supported by a number of factors. For example, as the number of part numbers was reduced, it was also likely that the number of vendors would be reduced. This would in turn reduce the demand for vendor-related activities. In addition, reducing the number of part numbers would increase the efficiency of JIT production.

The generation of more accurate product costs, as a result of using the new material burdening method, was expected to improve decisions by each of the functional users of product cost information. These users were design engineering, production management and marketing.

The new allocation method provided design engineering with the approximate incremental cost of adding an additional new part number to the active parts list. They would also have MOH calculations for each part. Such information would prove valuable for decisions such as whether to make or buy components, when to introduce or phase out products, and which products to produce when capacity was limited.

The new allocation approach would provide marketing with more accurate product cost information. Accurate product cost information was particularly critical for market segment strategies. It was also useful for strategic planning purposes, where product emphasis was influenced by expected profitability.

Phase 2
Cycle Time Burdening

Bruce Anderson:

> Cycle time became an issue as we began to drive inventory down. It became obvious in a return on assets environment that reducing cycle time and hence inventory takes the pressure off pricing. So we have a real push on reducing inventories and assets. Cycle time is a limit beyond which you cannot go however efficient you become. If a product is not designed for expeditious cycle time you cannot get away from processing time that is designed into the product. If you can't reduce processing time, you will always have more inventory in the system than desired.
>
> Cycle time burden, where longer cycle time products have higher reported costs, should cause an organization to focus on the reduction of the factors that cause cycle time to be long. Very low cycle times are beneficial because to get them everything has to be right: the people, the components and the purchased parts. To get to really low cycle time you have to be a world-class manufacturer.

After the material burdening system had been running successfully for over a year, management felt it was time to review the design of the product costing system. About half of the manufacturing overhead was still allocated using direct labor, and the principal concern at this time was to find an alternative allocation method for this large pool of cost.

A second special product costing study was conducted in the summer of 1987 to identify the allocation measure that would replace direct labor. At the time of the study PID allocated process related overhead—manufacturing overhead not allocated using material burdening—using frozen standard labor hours (FSH). Historically, it was believed that direct labor had been a critical manufacturing resource, and FSH had thus been a good indicator of effort. In the current manufacturing process, however, the direct labor content had shrunk to approximately 3.5% of total product cost. At this low level it was unlikely that direct labor was still a good indicator of effort.

Due to the introduction of JIT and the simplifications in the accounting measurements, it also became increasingly difficult to use FSH as a basis for allocating overhead. Since labor reporting had been discontinued, FSH were estimated for a product when it was introduced and remained constant over the life of that product, i.e., FSH were not updated for changes in the design of the product or the process. FSH represented an ideal quantity of direct labor, and did not reflect factors such as quality differences that would affect the amount of direct labor used by each product. Consequently, FSH failed to accurately measure the direct labor consumed by each product, and this inaccuracy increased across the life of the product.

The conclusion of the study team was that cycle time—the total time required to produce an instrument—was the preferred allocation measure. A report prepared upon completion of the product costing study summarized the appeal of cycle time:

> Cycle time costing is based on the theory that the cost of a product is related to the time required to produce it. Thus, attention will be focused on decreasing process time and WIP through increased manufacturing efficiency and quality. Cycle time costing should be implemented in the PID Division as an alternative to direct labor in allocating conversion costs. This measure is more relevant to the current manufacturing environment and is a more accurate reflector of cost.

Cycle time was defined as the total process (manufacturing) time required to produce an instrument. This was the elapsed time from the beginning of main board build to the end of packaging when the instrument was moved into the finished goods inventory (Exhibit 3). This time frame encompassed all the process related overhead that would be allocated using cycle time.

Process overhead included depreciation on equipment, indirect labor (including manufacturing managers, and manufacturing engineering ded-

EXHIBIT 3
Tektronix: Portable Instruments Division (B): Manufacturing Cycle Time

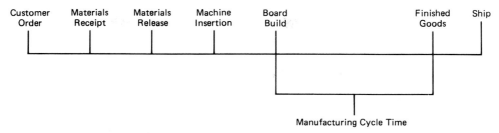

icated to process support), direct labor and payroll load, and property, maintenance, utilities and floor space associated with manufacturing. Process overhead was divided into several cost pools, one for each distinct manufacturing process or product line.

Cycle times were measured at PID by recording the time and date on a "cal" (calibration) card which accompanied the instrument through the manufacturing process. After being packaged, the time and date were again recorded. The cycle time was computed based on manufacturing hours per day (eight hours per shift) in each product line. Non-manufacturing time, such as weekends, was not included in cycle time. Cycle time was monitored over a number of days, and then an average was computed for each instrument type.

In the future, it is possible that cycle time would be measured automatically using bar coding. Bar coding provided an opportunity to record and track cycle time on a continuous basis. Product cost information calculated using bar codes would be more accurate because it would be based on the most recent cycle time information. In addition, manufacturing would be able to monitor cycle time more closely and get a better feel for the variability of the production process.

The cost of bar coding was quite low. Terminals and readers (wands) were already in place at the end of the process in finished goods, and additional hardware would only be required at the beginning of each line. Only one reader would be required for the 2400 series line, and the cost of programming to record the time and date automatically was low.

It was hoped that management would accept the cycle time concept. Interviews with management revealed a widespread belief that cost was related to the time required to produce an instrument. It was also felt that cycle time was closely related to the level of WIP inventory, quality, flexibility and customer service. These beliefs were reflected by the use of cycle time as a key measure of manufacturing performance.

The study team identified a number of advantages and disadvantages of using cycle time as an allocation measure:

1. Cycle time was a broader measure of cost consumption than FSH. FSH included only the time of touch labor, whereas cycle time also included machine time, and the time required for "non-value added" activities such as test time and queuing time. Cycle time was also up-dated every six months, and therefore would reflect changes in the manufacturing process and in the design of the product. FSH were set when a product was introduced and not changed over the life of the product.

2. Cycle time was thought to be a good indicator of cost and effort in PID's continuous process type manufacturing environment where relatively homogeneous products underwent similar steps in production. The study team confirmed this by studying the relationship between cycle time and the cost of each of the following constituents of process overhead:

   —*Indirect Labor*. Manufacturing managers and process engineers reported that they spent more time with products that had long cycle times.

   —*Payroll Load and Paid-not-worked*. Direct labor time was a component of cycle time, so it made sense to allocate labor-related overhead on the basis of cycle time.

   —*Depreciation*. The study showed that instruments with longer cycle time spent more time on depreciable equipment such as test equipment.

   —*Property, Maintenance, Utilities, Supplies*. An instrument with longer cycle time spent more time on the production floor. It was assumed that property, maintenance, utilities, and supplies were consumed proportionately to the time spent on the floor by the instrument.

   —*Direct Labor*. Direct labor was a component of cycle time, so cycle time was a good measure of the incurrence of this cost. Also, in JIT production, the line people performed tasks not traditionally included in direct labor, such as the rework of defective products, troubleshooting, and repairing equipment. Cycle time captured this non-traditional component of direct labor time.

The disadvantages of using cycle time were:

1. Cycle time (as defined) failed to capture direct labor time spent on a parallel process. In the presence of a parallel process, the cycle time measurement might fail to reflect all the resources consumed in the manufacturing process. Parallel processes, however, typically used little direct labor, space or other resources. They also improved the flexibility of production.

2. Cycle time was difficult to measure on low-volume products. There was considerable variability in cycle time from one instrument to another, so it was desirable to have a sufficient number of observations to calculate a reliable average cycle time. This issue would be less important, however, when bar coding was introduced.

3. The calculated cycle times (Exhibit 4) did not include time spent in the thermal environment chamber. It was felt that the thermal chamber was a necessary process to ensure quality. Including this time in cycle time might encourage managers to reduce the time spent in the cycle chamber, which would increase the risk of shipping defective unit to the customer. All instruments, however, were required to spend the same amount of time in

the thermal chamber, so the omission of chamber cycle time had no impact on the absolute time differences between product types.

EXHIBIT 4
Tektronix: Portable Instruments Division (B)
Average Cycle Times (Hrs)

Model	A	B	C	D	E	Total
CYCLE TIME HRS (AVG)	100	105	110	125	130	106

Computing Product Costs

The process overhead for each instrument was computed using the formula given in Exhibit 5. The calculation resulted in lower costs for instruments that had shorter cycle times. An analysis of these cycle times revealed that instruments with additional options, and instruments with quality problems, had higher cycle times.

EXHIBIT 5
Tektronix: Portable Instruments Division (B)
Overhead Cycle Time/Cost Computation

Cycle Time/Unit * Volume = Cycle Units
Product Line Conversion Cost
(Direct Labor Plus Conversion Overhead) $5,000,000

Product Line Cycle Units 975,000
$ Per Cycle Unit = $5,000,000/975,000 = $5.13

Expected Benefits

Other reasons were given to support the use of cycle time. These included:

- *Quality.* Cycle time included test, rework, troubleshooting, and repair time. Instruments with quality problems spent more time in each of these functions, so cycle time would capture quality-related cost differences between products. This was an important benefit because quality played an important role in the success of PID's products.
- *Capacity.* As cycle time was driven down, capacity increased. This reduced capacity cost, or made resources available for use elsewhere.
- *Work-in-Process.* WIP decreased as cycle time was reduced. Reduced WIP increased manufacturing efficiency and flexibility.

- *Manufacturing Complexity*. Instruments which required a more complex manufacturing process had longer cycle times. It was expected that a focus on cycle time would encourage design engineering to improve the manufacturability of products.
- *Mixed Model Lines*. It was believed that cycle time would encourage mixed model lines for similar products. Such product line flexibility was a lot less expensive than maintaining separate product lines for each product.

In late summer 1987, the team completed its project and presented its findings to management. Senior management now faced the decision whether to introduce cycle time costing.

Required:

1. Evaluate the part number burdening system adopted by PID. What are its strengths and weaknesses?
2. What are the strengths and weaknesses of the cycle-time burdening system?
3. Determine the impact on reported product costs of the part number and cycle-time burdening systems.

chapter 12

JUSTIFYING INVESTMENTS IN NEW TECHNOLOGY

Discounting procedures for evaluating investments in long-lived assets became widely adopted in corporations during the mid-1950s. Students today are trained extensively in these procedures in introductory cost and management accounting courses. Therefore, the mechanics of discounting techniques, especially net present value and internal rate of return calculations, should by now be familiar. With the increased availability of spreadsheets on personal computers, no technical barrier exists to the widespread use of discounting procedures for evaluating proposed investments.

But despite the extensive experience of many companies with the techniques and the theoretical training students receive in accounting and business programs, problems apparently still arise with the use and interpretation of discounted cash flow procedures.

Informed observers have expressed skepticism about whether discounted cash flow techniques can adequately evaluate important corporate investments. An award-winning article concluded that "the willingness of managers to view the future through the reversed telescope of discounted cash flow analysis is seriously shortchanging the futures of corporations."[1] A senior IBM executive, while acknowledging that "the commonly accepted Discounted Cash Flow (DCF) methodology is an excellent barometer for measuring capital alternatives," still was not convinced:

> Let's be more practical. DCF is not the only gospel. Many managers have become too absorbed with DCF to the extent that practical strategic directional considerations have been overlooked. DCF analysis tends to look at discrete investment opportunities, which are perhaps myopic when compared to the urgency of implementing integrated systems leading to vast productivity improvements.[2]

---

[1] Robert H. Hayes and David A. Garvin, "Managing as if Tomorrow Mattered," *Harvard Business Review* (May–June 1982), p. 72.

[2] John P. van Blois,"Economic Models: The Future of Robotic Justification," Technical Paper M583-318, Society of Manufacturing Engineers, (Dearborn, MI, 1983), p. 3.

In a Boston University Manufacturing Roundtable survey, 78% of the executives felt that

> most businesses in the U.S. will remain so tied to traditional quantitative investment criteria that they will be unable to properly evaluate the potential value of computer-aided manufacturing options.

A General Electric executive reviewed this evidence:

> Because business executives don't know how to run the numbers, companies are not acting decisively to put these technologies to work. We're not getting off the dime because we're not sure how to calculate what the return will be on investing that dime in manufacturing technologies.
>
> Urgently needed are new cost/benefit formulas and measurements, new manufacturing economics, if you will, that go beyond the usual return on investment (ROI) evaluations to take into account the total impact of automation on the business.[3]

Respondents to a study conducted by the Automation Forum listed financial justification as the number-one roadblock to the adoption of industrial automation in the United States:

> Unless accounting methods are developed that truly measure all of the benefits of industrial automation, the high initial costs associated with industrial automation projects will be a significant disincentive to the adoption of automation technology.[4]

Apparently, there is many a slip between the mechanical simplicity of discounting future cash flows and calculating rates of return, as taught in traditional accounting and finance courses, and the application of these procedures in the actual situations confronted by operating managers.

Is a New Theory Needed?

Such dissatisfaction and disillusionment are surprising to many students of DCF techniques. After all, the theory behind the use of discounting is simple and logical. The theory requires only that cash received in the future be valued lower than cash received or on hand today. Anyone who puts money in a savings or money market account, or who is paying off a mortgage or loan, understands all the theory required to recognize that

---

[3] Frank T. Curtin, "Planning & Justifying Factory Automation Systems," *Production Engineering* (May 1984).

[4] Sandra B. Dornan, "Justifying New Technologies," *Production* (July 1987), p. 50.

cash flows received or paid in the future are worth less than the same cash flows being received or paid today. No matter how glorious or exotic the new technology investment, it cannot overcome the logic that the dollar paid out today is worth more than receiving that same dollar back five or ten years from now. Discounting future cash flows provides the logic by which cash paid out and received in many different years can be made commensurate with each other so that all the cash flows can be summed together to provide an overall measure of investment worth.

Yet one cannot ignore the widespread skepticism about the application of the discounting logic. Our task is to recognize the nature of problems that have arisen in applying discounted cash flow analysis in complex, actual situations; problems that are not featured when the mechanics of discounting are presented to students in introductory textbooks and courses. Our study of the actual practices used by firms in applying discounting procedures to proposed capital investments reveals many flaws; but these are flaws in application, not in the underlying theory. Therefore, if students wish to apply DCF procedures in practice, they need to understand these flaws and how to overcome them. The flaws occur when managers

1. Require payback over arbitrarily short time periods
2. Use excessively high discount rates
3. Adjust inappropriately for risk
4. Compare new investments with unrealistic status quo alternatives
5. Emphasize incremental rather than global opportunities
6. Fail to recognize all the costs of the new investment
7. Ignore important benefits from the new investment

We will address each of these problems in turn.

Short Time Horizon

Many companies demand that investments, particularly new investments in untested process technologies, pay back their initial investment within a short time period, say two or three years. Various reasons have been offered to justify the use of short payback periods, including managerial distrust of the estimates of future cash flow savings and the need to stay liquid and self-financing in order to reduce the financial risk of the company. All of these are ad hoc explanations; none of them arises from the economics of discounted cash flow analysis. Certainly, if companies in the mining or timber industries demanded three-year payback periods, there would be little opportunity for such companies to grow or even survive.

Particularly for new investments in process technology such as Flexible Manufacturing Systems (FMS) or Computer-Integrated-Manufacturing

(CIM), arbitrarily short time horizons make it difficult to justify the extra investment required to achieve flexibility, especially when compared with the less-expensive alternative of hard-wired or dedicated automation. The benefits from flexibility arise chiefly from the ability of FMS and CIM to accommodate easily the variants of products and new generations of products that will be introduced in future years. The benefits from these variants and new products will arise several years in the future when, otherwise, major renovation or replacement of traditional automated machines would be required. To cut off the period when flexible automation would achieve its principal advantage over dedicated automation (such as specific purpose transfer or assembly lines) would make it impossible to justify the extra cost for the electronic controls, generalized fixturing, and automatic guided vehicles (AGVs) that provide the flexibility capability.

Nothing in the theory of discounted cash flow analysis justifies the use of arbitrarily short evaluation periods. In fact, quite the contrary. DCF analysis permits cash flows received many years in the future to be made comparable with cash flows received now or one year from now. Thus, the critics' complaints of short time horizons must be about the decision horizons of their senior managers, not of the analytic technique itself.

Excessively High Discount Rates

Perhaps the major pitfall to the successful application of DCF occurs when companies use discount rates in excess of 20% and 25% to evaluate proposed new investments. Use of an excessively high discount rate penalizes a long-lived investment just as much as the use of an arbitrarily short evaluation horizon. Because the discount rate compounds geometrically each time period, cash flows received five or more years in the future will be penalized severely in the analysis. For example, compare the difference in discount factors between a 12% rate and a 25% rate for years 5 and 10:

Year	Discount Factor at 12%	Discount Factor at 25%
5	0.567	0.328
10	0.322	0.107

Clearly, investments in long-lived technologies, such as FMS and CIM, will be severely penalized by excessively high interest rates.

Discounting future cash flows serves to repay investors for the lost opportunity to invest their cash while waiting for the returns from the investment project. Therefore, the discount rate should reflect the opportunity cost of capital for such investors—what they could otherwise be earning from investments of comparable risk. Extensive empirical and theoretical research in finance and economics during the past three decades has established useful guidelines for determining the opportunity cost of invested funds.

One can estimate the cost of equity capital in either of two ways: use the historical nominal return on corporate stocks of between 12% and 13% per year or use the real return (net of inflation) of about 8% to 9% and add the expected future inflation rate over the life of the project. Either method is reasonable and would be a dramatic improvement over the practice of some firms of using rates in excess of 20%.

The erroneous use of interest rates in excess of 20% for discounting future cash flows probably arises from several sources. Some firms derive their cost-of-equity capital from their accounting statements. It would not be unusual for organizations to have accounting returns on shareholder equity that exceeded 20%. But the accounting return-on-equity figure has many defects that make it a poor estimate of the rate of return the firm has been earning on its capital investments. Apart from leverage effects (we will discuss debt financing shortly), the return-on-equity figure is distorted by financial accounting depreciation conventions, by decisions on capitalization and expensing, and by use of leased assets (among other explanations). The impact of accounting conventions on the periodic return-on-investment figure will be examined subsequently in Chapter 15. For now, it is sufficient to note that it would be rare for a firm's return-on-equity ratio to be a good estimate of its rate of return from past investment.

A second error arises when managers use the discount rate to adjust for risk. With estimates of investment cost and future cash benefits already provided in the analysis, the discount rate becomes the only "free" parameter in the net present value analysis. Thus, it frequently serves not only to make future cash flows commensurate with present cash flows (its only real purpose) but also as a crude mechanism to adjust for risk. It is a crude mechanism because the geometric compounding of the interest rate over time implies that project risk must also be compounding geometrically, an assumption that is almost always wrong.

Much of the risk from new investment will probably be resolved early in the project's life. If there is uncertainty as to whether a new piece of equipment or a new technology will work, we will learn about this outcome in the first year or two. If there is uncertainty about demand for a new product, this too will undoubtedly become known relatively early. For example, when building a new shopping center or office complex, with a twenty- to thirty-year lease, the major uncertainty will be resolved when the project is built and occupancy and rental rates become established. There might be great risk about both occupancy and rental rates, but this is not a risk that is appropriately quantified by discounting thirty-year rentals at an interest rate that has been grossed up by ten or more percentage points.

As an extreme example, I might visit a race track where I expect to make lots of risky investments. The risk is real, but there is no interest rate for the time interval between when I place my bet and when the outcome from that action is revealed several minutes later that helps me decide whether or how much I should invest in each race. Except for a narrow definition of risk (to be discussed shortly), raising discount rates arbitrarily as an ad hoc adjustment for risk is a crude instrument and one that will systematically penalize long-lived investments.

A third error occurs when firms use nominal interest rates (such as the 12%–13% long-term return to equity holders) to discount future cash flows but make no adjustment for inflation in the cash flows themselves. Many firms project future cash flows using today's prices, wage rates, material costs, and energy prices. But if inflation is imbedded in the cost of capital estimates, such as by using the historical 13% return that reflects historical inflation experience of between 4% and 5%, then unit prices for output products and input resources should also incorporate expected future price increases. It is inconsistent to reflect expected inflation in the cost of capital used for the discount rate but to ignore price increases when projecting the future benefits from the proposed investment. An alternative possibility would retain the assumption of unchanging future unit prices but then use a real (not nominal) cost of equity capital of between 8% and 9%.

The analysis to this point has focused on the cost of capital for an all-equity-financed firm. Most companies finance some of their assets with long-term debt. The historical evidence from publicly traded high-grade corporate debt reveals that the cost of debt financing is well below the cost of equity capital. Long-term investment-grade corporate debt generally returns between 1% and 3% above the inflation rate. The return from smaller, riskier companies would have to be somewhat higher to compensate creditors for the higher risk that they were bearing.

The nominal interest paid on corporate debt is a tax-deductible expense for the corporation. Therefore, if the nominal cost of long-term debt is I% per year, the after-tax cost of debt capital to the company is $I * (1 - t)$, where t is the marginal corporate tax rate.

The overall cost of capital for the firm is a weighted average of its cost of equity and cost of debt capital. The weights should be the fraction of total market value represented by equity and debt capital, respectively. Many companies estimate their debt-equity ratios using book values from their accounting balance sheet; this is less desirable than the weights implied by the market values of equity and debt but may be an acceptable approximation if market values, particularly of privately held or off-balance sheet debt, are difficult to estimate.

When the 13% cost of equity capital is averaged with nominal after-tax debt costs in the 5% range, it is clear that the overall cost of capital for many firms will be in the single-digit range. This makes the use of discount rates in the 20 + % range even more indefensible. Thus, many of the objections raised by critics of DCF techniques, as quoted at the beginning of this chapter, may reflect nothing more than the frustration of attempting to push innovative projects through a corporate financial process that is systematically biased against investments in long-lived assets.

When a company has some debt in its capital structure, still another opportunity for error arises. Interest payments will appear as an expense in a company's income statement. When projecting the cash flows from an investment, companies frequently subtract a pro rata share of corporate interest expense from the cash flows of a project. This calculation is erroneous because the payment of interest (as well as dividends and capital gains to shareholders) is already included in the interest rate used to discount future cash flows. The cost of capital includes the ability to repay both interest and principal on any debt incurred for the project. Subtracting interest expense from a project's future cash flows will cause these payments to be counted twice (once in the numerator and once in the denominator) and will therefore cause the project to appear less attractive than it actually is.

Risk Adjustments

We have already expressed our skepticism about arbitrary escalation of interest rates in a misguided attempt to compensate for project risk. Both theory and evidence provide support for imbedding some adjustment for risk into the discount rate. But this risk adjustment arises from risk that is not diversifiable by investors. Pure uncertainty in outcomes does not require a risk adjustment if the uncertainty is not correlated with the uncertainties faced by other companies. The only risk for which investors, holding diversified portfolios, demand compensation is systematic risk— that risk which is not diversifiable across firms.

The systematic risk probably arises more from the nature of the firm's product markets than from uncertainties in its production processes. Therefore, this risk would be the same for both existing and proposed investments in process technology. The subject of measuring a company or division's systematic risk is complex and is discussed intensively in finance courses.[5] For our purposes, the contemporary conventional finance thinking leads us to use the division's "beta," as estimated from the Capital Asset Pricing Model, to adjust for risk. In practice, the beta adjustment could move the cost of equity capital up or down by several percentage points, depending on the typical business and financial risk of the division.

---

[5] Good treatments are available in Richard Brealey and Stewart Myers, *Principles of Corporate Finance*, 2nd ed. (New York: McGraw-Hill, 1984); and James Van Horne, *Financial Management and Policy*, 7th ed. (Englewood Cliffs, NJ: Prentice-Hall, 1986).

Adjusting for the systematic risk of shareholders through the use of the CAPM beta controls for one type of risk and avoids the distortions created by arbitrary escalations of the cost of capital. Nevertheless, managers still face risk that is specific to the project, and to their careers, anytime they undertake a major capital investment project. We have argued that increasing the discount rate is a poor method for controlling for this type of risk. Much better would be for managers to formulate different scenarios to represent the possible outcomes from a major investment.[6] Procedures for performing simulation analysis with Lotus spreadsheets on projected cash flows were presented in Chapter 2. Alternatively, managers could formulate most likely, optimistic, and pessimistic scenarios for the investment project. Returning to our example of constructing a shopping center or office complex, the three scenarios could correspond to normal occupancy and rental rates, full occupancy, and low occupancy. Under each alternative, the managers would estimate the investment cost and future cash flows that are consistent with the assumed scenario. The cost of capital would then be used to discount all future cash flows to the present—its intended and defensible purpose—with risk evaluation left to the manager after contemplating the distribution of net present values across the different scenarios.

Alternatives to New Investment

Any new investment is evaluated, either explicitly or implicitly, against an alternative of not undertaking the new investment. The desirability of the new investment depends critically on how this alternative is evaluated. Many companies use the present conditions, the status quo, as the baseline alternative. That is, they assume that present cash flows can be maintained with no investment in new technology. Thus, the proposed investment must be justified by improvements in future cash flows—lower labor, material, or energy costs for example—relative to the present situation. This situation is captured by the diagram in Figure 12–1, where the horizontal line represents the maintenance of present net cash flows into the future, and the small wedge above the line represents the cash flow improvements from undertaking the new investment. With this assumption, the area in the cash flow savings "wedge" may not be large enough to repay the initial investment in the new technology.

But the experience of many industries in Western countries has clearly shown that it is erroneous to assume a firm could maintain level cash

---

[6] See, for example, David B. Hertz, "Risk Analysis in Capital Budgeting," *Harvard Business Review* (January-February 1964), pp. 95–106; and "Investment Policies That Pay Off," *Harvard Business Review* (January-February 1968), pp. 96–108.

FIGURE 12–1
Comparing New with Existing Technology:
Extrapolating the Status Quo

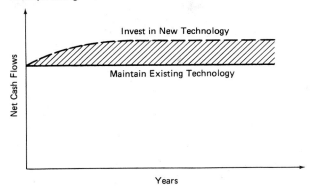

flows after rejecting new technology investment opportunities. For when a new process technology becomes available to one company, it will probably also be available to competitors. Even if existing competitors decide not to adopt the new process technology, a company overseas, such as in a newly industrializing country (NIC), could adopt the new technology when it built a new plant to produce competitive products. Therefore, the most likely alternative to adopting new process technology is to assume a declining cost and/or quality position relative to a leading-edge competitor. Once a firm has lost technological leadership, it will find it difficult to maintain present market share and gross margins. This will lead to declining cash flows in future years. And it is this pattern of declining cash flows—see Figure 12–2—that represents the most likely cash flow pattern for maintaining the status quo in rejecting the new technology option.

FIGURE 12–2
Comparing New with Existing Technology:
Recognizing Loss of Technology Leadership

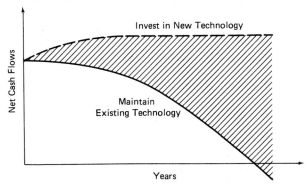

Once the process innovation "genie" is out of the bottle, it cannot be captured and corked up; it will flow to current or future competitors who will upset the existing market structure. Thus, the difference in cash flows between the new process investment and the status quo is the much larger area shown in Figure 12–2. Unfortunately, unlike our present cash flow position that we can estimate to considerable precision, we may not be sure how fast the curve in Figure 12–2 will decline in future years. Perhaps the experience of U.S. industries such as consumer electronics, steel, and machine tools can be studied to determine the rate of decline once technological leadership is lost to overseas competitors. It may be 5% per year; it may be 12% per year. Sensitivity analysis can be usefully applied to test how conclusions may vary with different decay rates. But we can be quite sure that assuming a zero rate of decay is precisely wrong.

Incremental vs. Global Analysis

An additional problem with current practice is its bias toward incremental rather than revolutionary projects. The capital approval process for many companies specifies different levels of authorization as a function of the size of the request.[7] Small investments, under $100,000 say, may need only the approval of the plant manager, whereas expenditures in excess of several million dollars may require board of directors' approval. This apparently sensible procedure, however, creates an incentive for managers to propose a sequence of small projects that fall just below the cutoff point where higher-level approval would be needed. Over time, a division may undertake lots of little investments, implementing minor changes in its basic facility, each one of which promises adequate savings in labor, material, or overhead costs or in higher revenues by relieving an existing production bottleneck. But collectively the factory become less efficient because of a less-than-optimal pattern of material flow. The factory may even be obsolete because of the outdated technology embedded in its core production equipment.

Each year, a division manager may propose and undertake a series of small improvements in the production process—to alleviate bottlenecks, to add capacity where needed, or to introduce islands of automation based on immediate and easily quantified benefits. Each of these projects, taken by itself, may have a positive net present value. By investing on a piecemeal basis, however, the division never gets the full benefit from a completely redesigned and reequipped plant that can exploit the latest or-

---

[7] Organizational and behavioral issues in the capital budgeting process are documented and discussed in Joseph L. Bower, *Managing the Resource Allocation Process: A Study of Corporate Planning and Investment* (Boston: Division of Research, Harvard Business School, 1970).

ganization and technology of manufacturing operations. At any point in time, there may be many of these annual, incremental projects scattered about from which the investment has yet to be recovered. Were the plant to be scrapped, the incremental investments made during the past several years would be proved incorrect.

One alternative to this piecemeal approach is to forecast the remaining technological life of the plant and then to enforce a policy of accepting no process improvments that will not be repaid within this period. At the end of the specified period, the old facility would be scrapped and replaced with a new one that incorporated the latest technology. Although none of the business-as-usual incremental investments might have been incorrect, the collection of incremental decisions could have a lower net present value than the alternative of deferring most investment during a terminal period, earning interest on the unexpended funds, and then replacing the plant. Again the failure to evaluate such a global investment is not a limitation of discounted cash flow analysis. It is a failure of not applying the analysis to all the relevant alternatives.

Front-End Investment Costs

Most investment proposals seriously underestimate the initial costs associated with installing new equipment, particularly equipment that embodies dramatically new technological features. In general, the hardware costs will be estimated well after obtaining quotes from vendors. But if the new equipment uses digital processors and controllers, considerable software development will also be required. Companies relatively unfamiliar with digital processing technology may overlook the extensive software investment required to make their new equipment operational and effective. Aggravating this tendency is the financial accounting requirement that in-house expenditures on software be expensed as incurred. Numerous instances could be cited where expensive new machines were never used to their capabilities because the projects were starved for software.

In addition to presenting a more realistic picture about the investment cost in the new technology, a behavioral reason exists for explicitly recognizing front-end software and programming costs. Many companies budget capital funds separately from operating expenditures. If front-end software and programming costs are not provided for in the capital budget, they will eventually have to be supplied from operating funds. As managers are pressed to meet short-term profit goals and budgets, it becomes seductive to reduce funding for "intangibles" such as software for new machines. The temptation exists to force the machines on-line prematurely, without sufficient software support, an action that will virtually guarantee the eventual failure of the new-process technology thrust.

A similar mistake is often made when organizations fail to budget funds to retrain and educate workers, supervisors, and managers in the new-process technology. We observed one automobile assembly plant where workers had been furloughed for the several months required to install electronically controlled welding, paint spray, and conveyor equipment. After all the hardware had been installed, the workers were called back and were instructed to start production on the new car line. This plant subsequently demonstrated the slowest ramp-up to capacity production in the company's history as workers struggled to learn, under severe production pressure, how to keep the radically new production equipment operating and how to trouble-shoot and repair it when it broke down (which was often). As the TV commercial reminds us, "You can pay now (in training and education); or you can pay later (in low production, frequent downtime, low morale, high turnover, and expensive repair costs)." Roger Smith, chairman of General Motors during the 1980s, learned that "spending money on new technology without adequate investment in training and educating our workers merely enables us to produce scrap faster." As with software and programming, the financial accounting requirement that training and education costs be expensed as incurred has prevented many companies from recognizing that such costs are investments, just as much as hardware costs, in the new technology process.

Recent studies have revealed a previously overlooked cost of new investment.[8] Studies of monthly productivity at the factory level found that productivity declines always follow the installation of new process equipment. The declines are significant (adding, on average, $0.37 of extra cost in the first year of operation for each $1.00 of new investment) and apparently increase with the increased novelty and complexity of the new equipment. Just how much of this productivity decline (which is eventually reversed and recovered in subsequent years) is due to inadequate preparation in the new operating and maintenance procedures required for the new equipment, and how much is inherent in adjusting to any new piece of equipment, is unclear at the present time.

Some companies rationalize away this initial productivity decline by labeling it as the learning or experience curve they expect from any new production process. They fail to realize that one way to enjoy a steep learning curve is to start out from a particularly ignorant (and expensive) initial point of operations. In any case, our exhibit of the future cash flows from new-process investment should probably show an initial cash flow decline to represent this disruption or learning effect.

The decline in productivity, whether caused by inadequate software

---

[8] Robert H. Hayes and Kim B. Clark, "Why Some Factories Are More Productive Than Others," *Harvard Business Review* (September–October 1986), pp. 68–69; and "Exploring the Sources of Productivity at the Factory Level," in *The Uneasy Alliance: Managing the Productivity-Technology Dilemma*, ed. K. Clark, R. Hayes and C. Lorenz (Boston: Harvard Business School Press, 1985), pp. 183–84.

funding, poor training and education, or just the normal shakedown associated with integrating complex new equipment into an ongoing production process, occurs at a particularly unfortunate time. Any time a major capital project has been authorized, particularly on a new technology process, one can be assured that headquarters will send out an internal audit team to check whether the promised productivity and operating savings are being achieved. And this audit will probably occur within six months of the receipt of the new equipment, just when the confusion and disruption are at their highest.

Senior financial and planning executives are aware that promised benefits from new technology investments are rarely achieved, particularly in early periods. If these executives see a new investment proposal that does not incorporate the additional front-end investments and costs that they know will eventually be required, they may take the expedient of raising the hurdle rate to compensate for such omissions. As we have already indicated, overly high discount rates take their toll on longer-term cash flows that have little to do with the near-term adjustment costs from new equipment. Both the authorization of funds for the "intangibles" of programming, education, and training and the analysis of investment projects will benefit from explicitly recognizing all required investment costs.

Measuring All the Benefits from the New Process

Traditional project evaluation procedures estimate future savings in material, labor, and energy because these inputs are generally measured and tracked well by the company's cost accounting system. Innovative process technologies, however, also provide benefits that are not measured by traditional cost accounting and project appraisal systems. These benefits include inventory reductions, improved quality, and reduced floor space requirements.

Reduced Inventory Levels

The process flexibility, more orderly product flow, higher quality, and better scheduling that successful adopters of flexible automation technology have enjoyed will drastically cut both work-in-process (WIP) and finished goods inventory levels. Inventory reductions of 75% to 90% have been reported by many companies.

Reductions in inventory levels represent a large cash inflow at the time when the new equipment becomes operational and the inventory can be reduced. Since the reduction usually occurs early in the project's life and thus is not discounted heavily, the cash flows from reduced inventory are especially valuable.

Consider a product line for which the anticipated monthly cost of sales is $500,000. Using existing equipment and technology, the producing division carries about three months of sales in inventory. After investing in flexible automation, the division heads find that reduced waste, scrap, and rework, greater predictability, and faster throughput permit a two-thirds reduction in average inventory levels. Pruning inventory from three months to one month of sales produces a cash inflow of $1 million. If sales increase 10% per year, the company will also enjoy increased cash flows from the inventory reductions in future years; if the cost of sales rises to $550,000 in the next year, a two-month reduction in inventory saves an additional $100,000 that year, $110,000 the year after, and $121,000 the year after that. Furthermore, there will be less obsolescence when new variants and models of products are introduced.

In addition to the obvious reduction in cash demands from holding less inventory, many overhead costs that are largely driven by holding, moving, scheduling, and inspecting inventory can also be reduced when inventory reductions are accomplished. The same studies cited earlier, which documented the decrease in productivity when new capital equipment is introduced, have found strong increases in productivity as inventory levels are reduced.[9] Thus, the initial productivity decline from introducing new equipment can be offset by the higher productivity arising from operating with much lower inventory levels. Also, with less inventory and with continual flow production of small lots rather than batch production of large lot sizes, the need for forklift trucks and drivers will be reduced, perhaps eliminated.

Less Floor Space

New-process technologies frequently enable the same job to be accomplished with far less floor space. Just eliminating inventory, which is stored on or about the floor in most factories, will free up large amounts of productive space. More efficient grouping of machines through better scheduling and coordination will produce significant floor space reductions. Companies have reported space savings of 50% to 70% after installing flexible manufacturing systems. Such space savings are real but are rarely measured by traditional financial and cost accounting systems. Most organizations have a continually increasing demand for space, if not for production then for engineering, support, and administrative personnel, so that any realized space saving represents a real cash benefit to the firm. The savings from reduced space requirements can be estimated either on

---

[9] Ibid.

an annual basis—using the square-foot rental cost for new space—or on a one-time basis, analogously to the computation of inventory reduction savings, based on new space construction cost.

Quality Improvements

Greatly improved quality represents a major source of tangible benefits from new technology investments. Automated process equipment, properly installed and operated, leads directly to more uniform production and, frequently, to an order-of-magnitude decline in scrap, rework, and waste. As production uniformity is increased, fewer inspection stations are required and the number of inspectors is reduced. Automatic gauging can eliminate virtually all manual inspection of parts; out-of-tolerance parts can also be detected immediately rather than waiting for an entire batch of products to be produced before the production problem is detected.

The opportunities for savings in quality can be estimated by first collecting information on how much the organization is currently spending on producing, repairing, and discarding poor-quality items. Some of these costs will appear in categories such as inspection, scrap, waste allowance, and rework cost. These categories will fail to capture all the cost of substandard quality production. Storing substandard items in the factory, moving them around, and rescheduling the production line to accommodate rework of faulty items all impose high costs on the organization. Typically, these costs are buried in overhead accounts and allocated to all production, both good and bad. The analysis should attempt to identify all the costs incurred to produce poor-quality items, including inspection, expediting, and rescheduling costs.

All these expenses provide the pool of current expenses that improved production processes can reduce. Once the size of this pool is known, we can estimate the benefits from new process technologies that offer the potential for 50% or higher reductions in the incidence of substandard quality production.

More-Accurate, Less-Precise Estimates Projected savings in inventory, floor space, and quality are frequently estimated from the experience of similar companies or divisions. These savings cannot be estimated to the four or five significant digits that are the customary precision from the firm's financial and cost accounting system. But many analysts err when they conservatively assume that difficult-to-estimate benefits must be zero. For purposes of financial justification, it will be sufficient to get the first and perhaps the second digit about right and to know how many zeros follow the first digit or two. It is better to be vaguely right than precisely wrong.

The Difficult-to-Quantify Benefits

New-process technologies, especially those that are information-intense, offer opportunities for radical changes in the way operations are performed. Some of these changes will be reflected in the substantial savings of inventory, space, and quality costs just described. But even beyond these tangible reductions in costs that we are currently incurring, the new-process technologies can provide dramatic improvements in flexibility, faster responses to market shifts, significant reductions in throughput and lead times, and opportunities to learn from and grow with technology advances.

These additional benefits are just as important, if not more so, than the inventory, space, and quality savings, but they are much harder to quantify. We may not be sure how many zeros should be in our benefits estimates (are they to be measured in thousands or millions?), much less which digit would be first. The difficulty arises in large part because the benefits represent revenue enhancements rather than cost savings. It is fairly easy to get a ballpark estimate for percentage reduction in costs already being incurred. For revenue enhancements from features not yet in place, it may be difficult to know which city you are in, much less the size of the ballpark in which you are playing. Let us proceed, however, by identifying the nature of these less-easily-quantified benefits and then suggest how to include them in the investment analysis.

Flexibility Computer-based process technologies provide unprecedented prospects for flexibility. Product specifications can be changed, process improvements implemented, schedule changes accommodated, and entirely new products and variants implemented on existing equipment with little disruption. Many advocates of Flexible Manufacturing Systems identify the potential for low-cost production of high-variety, low-volume products. Such a capability is considered an "Economy of Scope" that permits efficient manufacturing at much smaller scale than was heretofore possible.[10] Adoption of computer-based production processes has permitted some companies to produce efficiently in batch sizes of one.[11]

Even companies that have not yet achieved efficient high-variety production can still enjoy other flexibility benefits from Computer-Integrated-Manufacturing (CIM) technology. The reprogramming capabilities of CIM equipment permit these machines to serve as backups for each other. Some companies have dedicated FMS to a specific or narrow product line.

---

[10] Economies of scope from Computer-Integrated-Manufacturing are discussed in Joel D. Goldhar and Mariann Jelinek, "Plan for Economies of Scope," *Harvard Business Review* (November–December 1983), pp. 141–48; and Jelinek and Goldhar, "The Strategic Implications of the Factory of the Future," *Sloan Management Review*, (Summer 1984), pp. 29–37.

[11] "Allen-Bradley's Stark Vision," *New York Times* (October 6, 1986), pp. D1 and D8.

But each machine can still replace lost production—on a second- or third-shift basis—when a similar machine, normally focused on a different model or product, breaks down.

CIM machines can easily accommodate Engineering Change Orders (ECOs) and product redesigns. Thus, they provide considerable flexibility for product changes and introductions over time. In addition, if the mix of products demanded in the marketplace shifts, a CIM process can respond with no increase in costs. To cite one example, the flexible, programmed spot-welding robots in an automobile assembly plant easily accommodated a major shift in consumer preferences from the two-door to the four-door version of a given car model, whereas a nonprogrammable welding assembly line could not have adapted to this market shift.

Finally, the flexibility in CIM equipment gives it useful life beyond the life cycle of the product for which it was purchased. Thus, CIM machines provide many degrees of flexibility beyond those of dedicated special-purpose machines.

In the short run, CIM equipment may be performing the same functions as less-expensive, dedicated automation. In this case, the flexibility of CIM equipment is not being exploited, and it becomes difficult to justify the added expense of programmable controls and flexible material-handling equipment. It is only over time, with CIM's versatile backup capability and its ability to easily accommodate ECO's, product redesigns, and major product changes and innovations, that the payoffs from CIM flexibility will be realized.

Reduced Throughput and Lead Times Successful adopters of CIM technology have realized great reductions in throughput processing times. A Yamazaki factory in Japan and an Allen-Bradley plant in the United States have achieved processing times of one to two days for products that formerly took months to process. Other installations have reported throughput processing time savings ranging from a low of 50% up to 95%.

Some of the benefits from greatly reduced throughput times have already been incorporated into our estimate of cash savings from inventory reductions. But beyond these direct benefits, the ability to meet customer demands with much shorter lead times will provide major marketing advantages as well. Companies offering one- to two-week lead times when competitors are promising 60- to 90-day deliveries should be able to capture premium prices and higher market share.

Greatly shortened lead times will also permit companies to respond quickly to changes in market demand. If the marketing department detects a shift in customer preferences, the factory can respond quickly to product mix and design modifications. The company will beat technologically inferior companies to the market and will avoid the obsolescence of in-process and finished goods inventory that its competitors with two- and three-month lead times must absorb.

Organizational Learning Investing in new-process technologies permits the entire organization to learn about the capabilities of leading-edge production processes. Thus, many of the start-up costs could ultimately be shared by other projects that use similar technologies. Assigning all the front-end costs to the specific project being authorized will fail to recognize the eventual benefits to future projects.

A decision to acquire the new technology also gives the organization the opportunity to participate in future enhancements. Companies that invested in electronically controlled machine tools in the 1970s acquired a technology option, analogous to a stock option, in microprocessor and microcontroller technology advances. As the capabilities of integrated circuit chips improved by several orders of magnitude, these companies increased the machines' productivity by retrofitting the more-advanced electronic products. Companies that stayed with mechanical, manually operated machine tools failed to obtain an option in technology advances and hence could not benefit from the enormous performance-price improvements in electronic chips.

Some managers, in the face of rapid technology changes, feel that it is safer to defer investment and wait until the rate of change and technological advance has slowed down. These companies fail to realize how important the learning process is when shifting to an entirely new production technology. By waiting, they delay their learning process and eventually find themselves organizationally and technologically so far behind their competitors that they can never catch up. In effect, they have not acquired an option in technological advances.

Summary

At present, our experience with computer-based process technologies, such as CIM, are sufficiently limited that their benefits in flexibility, reduced throughput and lead time, organizational learning, and technology options are difficult to estimate. But although the benefits may be difficult to quantify, there is no reason to value them at zero when conducting a financial analysis. Zero is no less arbitrary than any other number, and we must avoid the trap of assigning zero value to benefits that we know exist but are difficult to quantify.

Apart from difficulties in measuring these benefits, we must also attempt to separate those features that have already been implicitly incorporated into the analysis from those that offer opportunities for radical improvements in future cash flows. We mentioned earlier that investing in state-of-the-art process technology would probably be required to maintain existing profit margins and market share relative to other adopting competitors; that the alternative which rejects the investment in new-process technology needs to be modeled as yielding declining cash flows in the future. Thus, some of the benefits from reduced throughput and lead times, more-reliable and higher-quality products, and a more-varied product line are required merely to maintain or slightly expand our current position relative to innovating competitors.

Strictly speaking, then, only the opportunities offered by the new equipment for order-of-magnitude breakthroughs in flexibility, reduced lead times, and consistent quality should be added to the analysis already performed. Of course, the option for technology advances and organizational learning remain as important additional benefits from the adoption decision.

The Bottom Line

One way to combine difficult-to-measure benefits with those more easily quantified is, first, to estimate the annual cash flows about which we have the greatest confidence. First we should estimate the relatively easily quantified annual cash flows: the cost of the new-process equipment and of introducing the new equipment (fixturing, materials handling, software, training, education, disruption), plus the benefits we expect to receive from labor, inventory, floor space, and quality savings. We can then perform a discounted cash flow analysis, using a sensible and defensible discount rate, considering relevant and realistic alternatives, and examining possible scenarios. Should the new technology investment show a positive net present value at this point, we can be comfortable with the acquisition decision, since the financial hurdle has been passed even without adding in some of the difficult-to-quantify benefits.

If the net present value, however, is negative, then it becomes necessary to estimate how much the annual cash flows must increase before the investment begins to look favorable. Suppose, for example, that an extra $100,000 per year over the life of the investment is sufficient for the project to have the desired return. Then management can decide whether it expects heightened flexibility, reduced throughput and lead times, organizational learning, and the technology option to be worth at least $100,000 per year. Would the company be willing to pay $100,000 annually to enjoy these benefits? If so, the project can be accepted with confidence. If, however, the additional cash flows needed to justify the investment turn out to be quite large—say, $3 million per year—management, while still valuing flexibility, short lead times, learning, and all those other good things, can still decide that they are not worth purchasing at $3 million per year. In this case, it is perfectly sensible to turn the investment down.

Rather than attempt to put a value on benefits that by their very nature are difficult to quantify, managers should reverse the process and estimate first how large these benefits must be in order to justify the proposed investment. Senior executives can be expected to judge that improved flexibility, rapid customer service, market adaptability, and options on new-process technology may be worth $300,000 to $500,000 per year but not, say, $1 million. In this final stage, we may be proceeding on faith, but at least our formal analysis has reduced the price that faith must pay.

PROBLEMS

12–1   Portsmouth Pottery Company

The Portsmouth Pottery Company (PPC) manufactures a line of pottery that is primarily related to the commemorative and tourist industries.

Sam Franklin, the production manager, is considering the possibility of purchasing a new kiln for the number 5 line. This line produces commemorative plaques. The kiln costs $700,000 and has a life of five years. PPC has a marginal tax rate of 35%. The tax depreciation schedule allows the following percentages of the cost of the kiln to be claimed during the kiln's life: Year 1, 16%; Year 2, 21%; Year 3, 21%; Year 4, 21%; and Year 5, 21%.

The new kiln would be used to replace an existing kiln, which has a useful life of five years. The existing kiln has been fully depreciated and has a salvage value of $25,000.

The new kiln promises annual cost savings of $100,000 in the production of the existing plaques. In addition, the size and operating attributes of the new kiln will allow PPC to begin producing a new line of mugs that could be printed with the customer's promotional message. The net income before taxes expected from this new line of business is $120,000 per year.

The salvage value of the new kiln would be $50,000 in five years. PPC is required to take any salvage value, in excess of the undepreciated historical cost of an asset, into income to be taxed at the normal rate.

PPC's required after-tax return on this type of investment is 14%.

Required:

1. Should the new kiln be purchased?
2. What is the rate of return on this investment?
3. What is the minimum level of total annual savings and new net income at which the new kiln is desirable?
4. What is the maximum purchase price of the new kiln at which this project is desirable?

12–2   MRC, Inc. (Consolidated)

In mid-1966, Archibald Brinton, President, and others of the top management of MRC, Inc. were considering a $25-million capital-budget proposal which would carry one of the company's divisions into the production of polyester fiber. Through its ARI division, the company was already heavily involved in the production of rayon fiber for tire cord; however, this market was rapidly shrinking because of the competitive inroads of nylon and polyester. An entry into polyester fiber might allow MRC to preserve its market position in tire cord and also move the company into the production of polyester fiber for other end uses.

Background, MRC, Inc.

Between 1961 and 1965, MRC had nearly tripled sales and earnings by implementing an active program of diversification by acquisition (Exhibit 1). During this period, acquisitions had been concluded at an average rate of one new company per year. Five of these transactions had been major. Ross Engineering had increased MRC sales in 1957 by $27 million. The purchase of Surface Combustion in 1959 had added about $38 million to annual sales. In 1961, American Rayon had boosted the company's growing sales volume by about $55 million. And the acquisition of Steel City Electric and National Castings in 1963 and 1965 had added about $16 million and $73 million, respectively, to annual sales.

In 1966, annual sales of MCR's 13 divisions were more than $340 million. No single division accounted for as much as 20% of total sales, but the largest five divisions contributed 70% of the total. The most important product lines in terms of sales were (1) industrial furnaces and heat-treating equipment; (2) parts used in the manufacture of railroad rolling stock and other foundry products; (3) rayon fiber for automobile tire cord and apparel fabrics; (4) auto, truck, and bus frames; and (5) power brake systems for autos, trucks, and buses.

All marketing, purchasing, manufacturing, R&D, personnel, and accounting were handled at the division level. Each division had its own general manager who reported directly to Brinton and was responsible for the growth and profitability of his division. Depending on the earnings and growth of his division, a division manager could get stock options and earn an annual bonus of up to 60% of his base salary. Divisional sales and earnings goals were formalized in an annual budget and in a rolling five-year plan; these were formulated by each general manager and submitted each November for review by Brinton and the corporate staff.

The corporate staff provided legal, administrative, and financial support to the divisions and handled external affairs, financing, and acqui-

Copyright © 1977 by the President and Fellows of Harvard College. Harvard Business School case 9–277–123.

EXHIBIT 1
MRC, Inc. (Consolidated)
Six-Year Summary of Financial Data
(Dollar figures in millions except per share data)

	1961	1962	1963	1964	1965	1966
Operations						
Sales						
Automotive and transportation	$ 57.8	$ 73.2	$ 80.9	$ 82.5	$ 94.2	$102.6
Capital goods	42.7	48.2	47.3	65.1	94.8	125.7
Buildings and construction	12.4	18.3	31.2	33.4	34.5	33.5
Railroad	—	—	—	—	39.6	42.7
Consumer goods	16.5	15.0	14.9	16.2	18.7	18.0
Aerospace and defense	8.3	11.6	15.7	13.9	14.3	21.6
Total	$137.6	$166.3	$190.1	$211.1	$296.1	$344.1
Net income	5.5	5.9	7.6	8.7	14.1	17.6
Earned on total capital	5.3%	6.3%	7.8%	9.1%	10.4%	12.1%
Earned on common equity	5.3	6.5	8.2	9.7	12.6	13.7
Common Stock						
Net income per share	$ 0.84	$ 0.97	$ 1.47	$ 1.82	$ 2.66	$ 3.33
Dividends per share	0.75	0.75	0.75	0.85	0.95	1.22
Market price	13–11	14–10	16–12	19–15	26–18	30–22
Dividend payout ratio	49%	45%	33%	31%	28%	31%
Average annual price-earnings ratio	15.1	11.3	10.5	10.3	8.2	7.9
Average annual dividend yield	5.8%	6.0%	4.9%	4.6%	4.4%	4.7%
Number of shareholders	13,125	12,165	11,750	12,725	12,750	15,150
Financial Position						
Working capital	$ 58.6	$ 47.4	$ 50.1	$ 49.3	$ 69.4	$ 70.2
Net property, plant and equipment	42.4	43.8	44.6	49.3	66.6	72.4
Long-term debt	—	—	—	13.5	9.0	7.9
Shareholders' equity	105.6	96.5	100.6	91.9	134.2	142.3
Additions to property, plant, and equipment	1.4	2.5	3.2	9.9	9.1	14.4
Number of employees	8,000	8,500	9,000	9,300	14,000	14,600

sitions as well. The staff, including corporate officers, numbered less than 60, of whom about half were secretarial and clerical.

Brinton felt that he exercised adequate control over the decentralized organization through his power to hire and fire at the division-manager level and, more important, through control of the elaborate capital-budgeting system (Appendix A).

Background, American Rayon, Inc.

In the spring of 1961, MRC had merged with ARI by an exchange of MRC common stock valued at $38.6 million. Almost all of ARI's sales consisted of rayon fiber; more than 60% of these sales consisted of rayon cord for use in the production of automobile tires. At the time of the merger, ARI was the third largest U.S. producer of rayon, had over $22 million of cash

EXHIBIT 2
MRC, Inc. (Consolidated)
Balance Sheet and Cash Flow Forecasts for American Rayon, Inc.
(millions of dollars)
At December 31, 1960

Assets		Liabilities & Net Worth	
Cash	$ 2.6	Accounts payable	$ 2.9
U.S. Government Securities	20.0	Accrued items	1.1
Accounts receivable	11.9		
Inventories	10.5		
Net plant	23.9		
Other	.3	Net worth	65.2
TOTAL	$69.2	TOTAL	69.2

	Pro Forma Cash Flow Forecasts						
	1961	1962	1963	1964	1965	1966	1967
Sales	$ 55	$ 55	$ 55	$ 52	$ 48	$ 43	$ 40
Net earnings	2.5	2.8	2.8	1.9	1.4	1.0	.4
Depreciation	3.0	3.0	3.0	3.0	3.0	3.0	3.0
Cash flow from operations	5.5	5.8	5.8	4.9	4.4	4.0	3.4

and marketable securities, was free of debt, and operated a modern central manufacturing facility (Exhibit 2). Furthermore, while the longer-term outlook for the rayon industry was grim, the near-term picture was appealing. It was estimated that ARI would be able to maintain current volume, prices, and margins through 1964, followed thereafter by annual sales declines of 10–15%. Capital spending needs under a gradual liquidation strategy would average no more than $300,000 annually. In view of MRC's need for finance to sustain its acquisition program, purchase of ARI by an exchange of shares had seemed attractive.

Efforts to Diversify ARI

From 1961 to 1966, ARI performed profitably, although the declining 1963–1966 trend was unsatisfactory:

Year	Sales Index of ARI Fibers Division	Pretax Profit as % of Sales
1961	100	6%
1962	100	8
1963	112	10
1964	115	9
1965	118	7
1966	124	4

The aggregate use of rayon in tire cord continued to decline during this period, and efforts were undertaken to reduce the division's dependence on the tire-cord market. In 1964, after the retirement of the original division manager, MRC invested $8 million in a facility to produce high-wet modulus rayon staple fiber, which was used principally in wearing apparel.[1] At the time this project was proposed by the new division manager, the selling price of the fiber was between 44¢ and 45¢ a pound. ARI management had felt that the price would decline to about 36¢ a pound within 5 years and stabilize there. At this reduced price level, the plant addition promised a 5-year payback and a healthy DCF–ROI.

According to Archibald Brinton:

ARI had process problems during the first year after the facility opened. These problems cut heavily into the division's profits. We also had some problem in getting the textile manufacturers to switch to our fiber. The textile people won't switch to the fiber of a new manufacturer until it's been thoroughly tested and evaluated. This testing is a costly and time-consuming process.

By the beginning of the second year after the plant was completed, the selling price of high-wet modulus rayon was down to 26¢ a pound.

Man-made fiber manufacture is a continuous process production operation. You run the plants 24 hours a day, 7 days a week. The production costs are such that you have to run at close to capacity to make any profit. If you cut back production very far, you might as well shut down entirely. We had a choice. If you cut production, your unit costs skyrocket; if you keep producing, your inventories skyrocket. With us it was a question of whether we might be better off shutting the plant down completely until prices firmed. We finally decided to keep it running and made staple fiber until it was coming out of our ears. Prices are firming now, but although we've had three price rises in the last 9 months, they are still not up to 36¢ a pound.

In 1966, ARI was still heavily dependent on rayon tire cord. During 1965, total industry production of rayon tire cord had amounted to 210-million pounds. This production was split among ARI (25%), American Viscose Corporation Division of FMC (30%), Beaunit Corporation (23%), and American Enka Corporation (23%).

---

[1] Staple fiber is "short length" fiber (approximately 1 to 1-½ inches) such as is found in cotton bolls.

Threats to the Tire-Cord Market

By 1966, the only real market remaining for rayon tire cord was the original-equipment tire market.[2] Of the 210-million pounds of rayon tire cord used for all classes of tires in 1965, about 150-million pounds went into the 50-million passenger car tires required by the original-equipment manufacturers (OEMs). The OEMs had purchased rayon-cord tires almost exclusively through 1965, but nylon started to break into this market when Chevrolet Division of General Motors Corporation indicated in 1966 that it would provide tires with nylon cord on the 1968 models. "The use of . . . nylon for Chevrolet production for this first year could mean a market of approximately 10,000,000 tires. . . ."[3]

If rayon cord were ultimately displaced from OEM passenger-car tires, the rayon industry stood to lose approximately 150-million pounds of its market. As this last market started to change, rayon producers would find it increasingly difficult to remain price-competitive with nylon.

> The nylon producers may be in a position . . . to further reduce the price of their material. However, the rayon producers most probably will not be in a position to do the same because of the decrease . . . in usage of their materials.[4]
>
> Du Pont recently pointed to acetate yarn as an example of a fiber having passed the low point in raw material price and already having capitalized fully on the lower cost attainable through very large scale of production. . . . This may also be the case for rayon staple fiber.[5]

The Rise of Polyester

While nylon was rapidly replacing rayon as the principal fiber in tire cord, a new fiber, polyester, was becoming important. Five-million pounds of this fiber had been used in 1963 by tire manufacturers, 19-million pounds was the estimated use in 1966, and a Goodyear spokesman predicted that over 100-million pounds would be used in tire cord by 1970.

Polyester was considered by some to be the "third generation" manmade fiber after rayon and nylon. The fiber had shown very rapid growth in recent years (Exhibit 3). After Du Pont's polyester patent had expired in July 1961, competition had rapidly appeared, prices had declined, and new markets had opened up to the fiber. Much of polyester's success up

---

[2] Original-equipment tires are purchased from tire manufacturers and placed on new cars by auto manufacturers.

[3] C. A. Litzler, "The Fluid Tire Cord Situation," *Modern Textiles Magazine*, September 1966, p. 22.

[4] C. A. Litzler, *Ibid.*

[5] National Advisory Commission on Food and Fiber, *Cotton and Other Fiber Problems and Policies in the United States*, Technical Papers, Vol. 2 (Washington, D.C., 1967), p. 43.

EXHIBIT 3
MRC, Inc. (Consolidated)
U.S. Fiber Consumption (in millions of pounds)
and Prices (in dollars per pound)

| | Natural Fibers | | | | Man-Made Fibers | | | | | |
| | Cotton | | Wool | | Rayon | | Nylon | | Polyester | |
Year	Pounds	Staple Price	Pounds	Staple Price	Pounds	Staple Price	Pounds	Staple Price	Pounds	Staple Price
1910	N.A.	$	N.A.	$	*	$		$		$
1930	2,617		263		119	.40				
1935	2,755		418		200	.31				
1940	3,959		408		300	.25	*			
1945	4,516	.39	645		420	.25	25			
1950	4,683	.57	635	1.41	650	.36	75	1.65	*	
1955	4,382	.39	414	1.08	966	.34	231	1.48	13	1.60
1956		.33		1.08	870	.32	246	1.30	20	1.35
1957		.36		1.22	836	.31	293	1.30	38	1.41
1958		.33		.90	750	.31	293	1.20	44	1.41
1959		.30		1.02	848	.33	356	1.06	79	1.36
1960	4,191	.31	411	1.07	716	.28	376	.92	110	1.36
1961		.31		1.03	797	.28	455	.92	112	1.24
1962	4,188	.30	429	1.09	884	.28	551	.92	162	1.14
1963	4,040	.29	412	1.18	960	.28	625	.92	223	1.14
1964	4,244	.29	357	1.28	975	.28	754	.92	274	.98
1965	4,477	.29	387	1.19	1,046	.28	861	.82	416	.84
1966	4,633 est.		370 est.		1,026 est.		978 est.		545 est.	

Fibers compete for shares of the total fiber market principally on the basis of relative prices and relative quality characteristics. Relative prices appear to have been an important consideration in the substitution of rayon for cotton in certain uses. The non-cellulose fibers offer serious price competition for apparel wool. However, price advantage has not accounted for the rapid increase in share of the fiber market gain by non-cellulose fibers, although sharply reduced prices in recent years have undoubtedly expanded their use.

Synthetic fibers yield a greater amount of fabric from a pound of fiber than does cotton, thus reducing the price of synthetic fiber per unit of product output. The equivalent net weight pounds of cotton staple for each pound of man-made fiber is (a) rayon staple fiber, 1.10, (b) nylon and polyester staple fiber, 1.37.

* Date of fiber introduction.

to 1966 was due to the enthusiasm that greeted the introduction of stay-press fabric in wearing apparel. In 1956, the total production of polyester fiber for all uses had been about 20-million pounds. By 1965, polyester output reached over 400-million pounds. Du Pont, the major producer of polyester fiber, accounted for well over half of U.S. production.

Alternative in the Face of Change

In mid-1966, the management of MRC was considering alternative courses of action with regard to the ARI division. The profits of this division were unsatisfactory in relation to the amount of capital required to support its operations. The market for ARI's major product line faced even greater near-term difficulty than in the past (owing to the Chevrolet decision); thus, MRC had to (1) continue realizing progressively less-satisfactory returns on the assets employed by ARI or (2) commit a substantial amount of new capital to production facilities for new fibers or (3) abandon certain areas of the rayon business.

Leaving the Market: Abandoning the rayon business entirely or in part presented a problem, since the physical plant of ARI was on the books of the company at a net book value of about $20 million. If this was sold substantially below book value, MRC would have to absorb a substantial nonrecurring loss on the sale, which would probably reduce the company's 1966 earnings per share below the level achieved in 1965. This loss would be nonrecurring; nonetheless, MRC management felt that investors might confuse it with a downturn in earnings from normal operations. The company was in the middle of its fifth consecutive year of earnings progress in 1966. Its stock price had moved up steadily since 1961 in response to these earnings gains, and management was reluctant to risk this share-price progress through investor misunderstanding.

Investing in New Fibers: Selling the ARI division was not a particularly attractive alternative; however, investing in facilities to produce newer fibers also raised some difficult problems. First, since nylon seemed to have already neared a peak in tire-cord use, an investment in a facility to produce this fiber would be practically obsolete by the time it was completed. On the other hand, polyester had not reached the level of acceptance in tire production which would justify the construction of a large new plant just to serve this segment of the polyester market. New fiber plants had to be large to be economically competitive (Exhibit 4). Economies of scale are clearly evident here, as they are in most chemical production processes. Similar production economies could be expected in polyester-fiber production. For this reason, if MRC went into the production of polyester tire cord, it would be necessary to produce polyester fiber for other uses as well. This would put the company into the textile-fiber business against firms such as Du Pont. Except for the venture into high-wet modulus rayon staple fiber in 1964, the company had had little contact with textile mills and had competed directly with large apparel fiber manufacturers such as Du Pont only to a limited extent.

EXHIBIT 4
MRC, Inc. (Consolidated)
Variation in Unit Cost of Production with Size of Plant

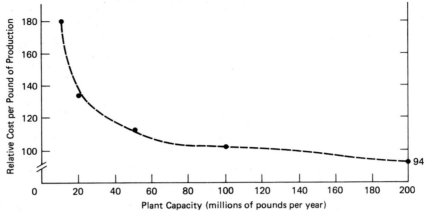

The Polyester Proposal

In mid-1966, the top management of MRC was considering a specific proposal that would carry the corporation into large-scale production of polyester fiber for tire cord and apparel fabrics. This proposal had been initiated by the ARI division general manager, John Wentworth, an experienced and highly-regarded young executive who had been lured away from Monsanto Company after MRC's experience with high-wet modulus rayon staple fiber.

From 1966 through 1971, the project would require an investment of $25.2 million. About $20.2 million of this amount would be used to construct a new plant for the production of polyester fiber; $5 million would be added to working capital to support the increased level of sales.

By 1969, the new facility would have given ARI the capacity to produce up to 50-million pounds a year of polyester fiber and resin. Ten-million pounds would go into tire cord, 30-million pounds would be marketed as staple fiber in competition with firms such as Du Pont, and 10-million pounds of resin chips would be sold to other polyester fabricators (Exhibit 5).

The Competitive Environment

During the months while MRC management was evaluating the new fiber project, the competitive situation in polyester was in considerable turmoil. In late March 1966, Du Pont announced that it would build a new polyester facility capable of producing 200-million pounds a year by the end of 1968.

EXHIBIT 5

MRC, Inc. (Consolidated)
Earnings and Cash Flow Forecasts for Polyester Project
(millions of dollars)

	1967	1968	1969	1970	1971–1980	1981
Sales	6.37	21.72	32.90	32.82	32.60	32.60
Cash costs (Note A)	6.23	14.44	20.80	20.80	20.80	20.80
Plant Start-Up Costs	.75	1.50	0	0	0	0
Special Marketing Costs	0	1.80	0	0	0	0
Depreciation Expense	.1	1.3	1.7	1.7	1.4	1.40
Profit Before Tax	-.70	2.68	10.40	10.32	10.40	10.40
Profit After Tax (Note B)	.55	1.74	5.30	5.16	5.20	5.20
Cash Flow from Operations	.65	3.04	7.00	6.86	6.60	6.60
Investment (Plant, Equip., Wkg. Cap.)	-14.90	-7.50	-2.00	-.80	0	0
Return of Wkg. Capital	0	0	0	0	0	5.00
Net Cash Flow	-14.25	-4.46	5.0	6.06	6.60	11.60

Internal Rate of Return = 26% – Payback Period = Year 6.

NOTES: A. Equals (38¢ × staple poundage + 43¢ × tire poundage + 21¢ × resin poundage + $3 million).

B. Includes investment-tax credit of $0.9, $0.4, and $0.1 million in 1967, 1968 and 1969.

	Assumed Volume (million lbs)					Assumed Price (¢/lb.)				
	1967	1968	1969	1970	1971–1980	1967	1968	1969	1970	1971–1980
Staple	0	18.8	30	30	30	78.5	72.5	70.5	70.5	70.5
Tire	7.5	10.0	10	10	10	85	80.9	79.5	79.5	79.5
Resin	0	0	10	10	10	38	38	38	37.2	35

The plant was to be twice the size of Du Pont's two other polyester plants. This facility, plus other announced additions at Du Pont's other polyester plants, would raise the company's capacity in polyester fiber from 240-million pounds a year in February 1966 (versus 456-million pounds for the industry at that date) to over 600-million pounds a year by the end of 1968 (Exhibit 6).

In April 1966, *Chemical Week* mentioned a number of other important competitive factors in the polyester situation:[6]

> Polyester sales in '65 increased 50% over '64 and '66 growth is projected for at least 35% to 500 million lbs. Demand got out of hand last year because a 14¢/lb. price decrease was coupled with an unexpectedly enthusiastic acceptance of polyester blends in durable-press apparel. . . .
>
> If all announced new capacity is built as scheduled, by the end of '68 U.S. production capability would be nearly 1.25 billion lbs./year. . . .
>
> With the Du Pont capacity disclosure, other polyester fiber producers theorize that marginal producers may scale down expansion plans and potential producers may think twice before entering the market. Intense competition in other fibers is in store as well.

The Point of Decision

It was in this environment that the management of MRC had to make its decision on the polyester-fiber proposal.

Appendix A: Capital Budgeting Procedures of MRC, Inc.

The formal capital budgeting procedures of MRC were outlined in a 49-page manual written for use at the divisional level and entitled "Expenditure Control Procedures." This document outlined (1) the classification scheme for types of funds requests, (2) the minimum levels of expenditure for which formal requests were required, (3) the maximum expenditure which could be authorized on the signature of corporate officers at various levels, (4) the format of the financial analysis required in a request for funds to carry out a project, and finally (5) the format of the report which followed the completion of the project and evaluated its success in terms of the original financial analysis outlined in (4).

---

[6] *Chemical Week*, April 2, 1966, p. 21.

EXHIBIT 6

MRC, Inc. (Consolidated)
Current and Planned Capacity of Polyester Fiber Competitors

	Polyester Capacity Feb. 1966 (millions of pounds)	Announced Expansion by End of 1968 (millions of pounds)	Number of Plants End of 1968	Other*** Fibers Manufactured	Total Sales Volume of Company in 1965 (millions)	Average Return on Total Capital (1961–1965)
Allied Chemical	-0-	?	?	N	$1,121	10%
American Enka	-0-	?	?	N, R	193	11
American Viscose (Div. FMC)	-0-	?	?	A, R		
Beaunit Fibers (Div. Beaunit Corp.)	-0-	?		R		
Chemstrand (Div. Monsanto)	20	40	1	N	1,468	9
Du Pont	240	360	3	A, N	3,020	19
Fiber Industries*	95	155	2	A, N, R	862	8
Firestone Tire & Rubber	-0-	?	?	N	1,610	9
Goodyear Tire & Rubber	60	40	1		2,226	10
Hercules	-0-	30	1		532	13
ARI Fibers (Division of MRC)	-0-	?	?	R		
Phoenix Works, Inc. (Sub. Bates Mfg. Co.)	-0-	25	1			
Tennessee Eastman Co. (Div. Eastman Kodak)	50	100	2	A		
U.S. Rubber Company	-0-	?	?			
Vectra Co.** (Div. Nat. Plastic Products)	-0-	?	?	N		
	465	750	11			

* Owned 62.5% by Celanese Corp. of America

** Jointly owned by Enjay Chemical Co. & J. P. Stevens & Co.

*** A = Acetate; N – Nylon; R = Rayon

503

Classification Scheme for Funds Requests

The manual defined two basic classes of projects: profit improvement and necessity. Profit improvement projects included:

a. Cost reduction projects.
b. Capacity expansion projects in existing product lines.
c. New product line introductions.

Necessity projects included:

All projects where profit improvement was not the basic purpose of the project, such as those for service facilities, plant security, improved working conditions, employee relations and welfare, pollution and contamination prevention, extensive repairs and replacements, profit maintenance, and services of outside research and consultant agencies. Expense projects of an unusual or extraordinary character included in this class were those expenses which did not lend themselves to inclusion in the operating budget and could normally be expected to occur less than once per year.

Minimum Amounts Subject to Formal Request

Not all divisional requests for funds required formal and specific economic justification. Obviously, normal operating expenditures for items such as raw materials and wages were managed completely at the level of the divisions. Capital expenditures and certain nonrecurring operating expenditures were subject to formal requests and specific economic justification if they exceeded certain minimum amount levels specified below.

Project Appropriation Requests shall be issued as follows:

1. Capital:
Projects with a unit cost equal to or more than the unit cost in the following schedule shall be covered by a Project Appropriation Request: items with lesser unit costs shall be expensed.

Land improvements and buildings	$1,000
Machinery and equipment	500
Tools, patterns, dies, and jigs	250
Office furniture and office machines	100

2. Expense:
Expenses of an unusual or extraordinary character which do not lend themselves to inclusion in the operating budget and could normally be expected to occur less than once per year shall be covered by a Project Appropriation Request.

The minimum amount at which a Project Appropriation Request for expense is required is $10,000.

Approval Limits of Corporate Officers

Officers at various management levels within MRC had the authority to approve a division's formal request for funds to carry out a project subject to the maximum limitations shown below.

Approvals:
Requests shall be processed from a lower approval level to a higher approval level in accordance with the chart below to secure the approving authorities' initials (and date approved) signifying approval. Lower approvals shall be completed in advance of submission to a higher level.

	Highest Approval Level Required
Expense projects:	
Minimum up to $10,000	Division manager
$10,000 up to $50,000	Corporate president
$50,000 and over	Board of directors
Capital projects:	
Minimum up to $5,000	Division manager
$5,000 up to $50,000	Corporate president
$50,000 and over	Board of directors

Expense and capital combinations:
Required approvals shall be the higher approval level required for either the capital or expense section in accordance with the above limits.

Project Appropriation Request

The formal financial analysis required in a request for funds was called a Project Appropriation Request (PAR). . . . The key output factors in the analysis (which included the amount of the total appropriation, the discounted cash flow rate of return on the investment, and the payback period) are summarized on the opening page . . . for easy reference.

The PAR originated at the divisional level and circulated to the officers whose signatures were necessary to authorize the expenditure. If the project was large enough to require the approval of an officer higher than the division manager, then five other men in the corporate financial group also reviewed the proposal. This group included the controller, the tax manager, the director of financial planning, the treasurer, and the vice president of finance. These men did not review very small projects, however, since capital items under $5,000 never reached the corporate office.

Division managers could authorize these small projects on their own signature.

Project Evaluation Report

On each PAR, the corporate controller had the option of indicating whether or not he desired a Project Evaluation Report (PER). When requested, the division manager submitted this report one year after the approved project was completed. The report indicated how well the project was performing in relation to its original cost, return on investment (ROI), and payback estimates.

Scrutinizing a PAR at the Presidential Level

In discussing capital budgeting at MRC, Brinton stated that the largest projects, involving more than $1 million, were almost always discussed informally between the president and the division manager at least a year before a formal PAR was submitted. He said:

> Let's look at a project involving a facilities expansion. The need for a new plant addition in most of our business areas doesn't sneak up on you. It can be foreseen at least a couple of years in advance. An enormous amount of work is involved in submitting a detailed economic proposal for something like a new plant. Architects have to draft plans, proposed sites have to be outlined, and construction lead times need to be established. No division manager would submit a complete request for a new facilities addition without first getting an informal green light that such a proposal could receive favorable attention. By the time a formal PAR is completed on a large plant addition, most of us are pretty well sold on the project.

In response to the question, "What are the most significant items that you look at when a new PAR lands on your desk?," Brinton replied:

> The size of the project is probably the first thing that I look at. Obviously, I won't spend much time on a $15,000 request for a new fork-lift truck from a division manager with an annual sales volume of $50 million.
>
> I'd next look at the type of project we're dealing with to get a feel for the degree of certainty in the rate of return calculation. I feel a whole lot more comfortable with a cost reduction project promising a 20% return than I would with a volume expansion project which promises the same rate of return. Cost reduction is usually an engineering problem. You know exactly how much a new machine will cost and you can be fairly certain about how many man-hours will be saved. On a volume expansion you're betting on a marketing estimate and maybe the date for getting a plant on stream. These are fairly uncertain variables.

On a new product appropriation, things get even worse. Here you're betting on both price and volume estimates, and supporting data can get awfully thin. Over all, I think our cost reduction projects have probably yielded higher returns and have been less risky than either plant expansion or new product proposals. They don't, of course, eat up anything like the amount of capital that the other two types of projects can require.

The third and perhaps most important item that I look for is the name of the division manager who sent the project up. We've got men at the top and at the bottom of the class just like any organization. If I get a project from a man who has been with the company for a few years, who has turned a division around, or shown that he has a better command of his business than anyone else in his industry, then I'll usually go with his judgment. If his business is going to pot, however, I may take a long hard look, challenge a lot of the assumptions, and ask for more justification.

Fourth, I look at the ROI figure. If the project is a large one, I have the finance people massage the numbers to see what happens to the ROI if some of the critical variables like volume, prices, and costs are varied. This is an area where knowing your division manager is enormously important. Some men, particularly those with a sales background, may be very optimistic on volume projections. In this kind of situation you feel more comfortable if you can knock the volume down 25% and still see a reasonable return.

I haven't established formal and inviolable hurdle rates which each and every project must clear. I want to avoid giving the division people an incentive to stretch their estimates on marginal projects or, alternatively, to build in fat cushions—insurance policies—on great projects. Still, I generally look for a minimum DCF–ROI of about 12% on cost reduction proposals, 15–16% on large volume-expansion projects and 18–20% or even more on new-product introductions. But these aren't magic numbers. Projects showing lower yields are sometimes accepted.

12–3   *Wilmington Tap and Die (Abridged)*

Len Green pulled on his coat and walked out the door of the Administration Building toward the loading dock of the adjacent factory. Four new automated Icahn thread grinding machines used in the production of taps had just been delivered and Len knew many of the managers would be gathering to see them. As he strolled toward the dock he couldn't help but remember taking this same walk seven months before in May 1978 when the first two Icahns had arrived. It had been his first day as plant manager of Wilmington Tap and Die (WTD).

This case was prepared by Research Associate Glenn Bingham under the supervision of Professor Robert S. Kaplan. Copyright © 1988 by the President and Fellows of Harvard College. Harvard Business School case 9–189–032.

WTD now had a total of seven Icahns (including this delivery and one prototype purchased in 1974). They had all been ordered by Len's predecessor as part of a manufacturing modernization program. The program called for the purchase of an additional 10 Icahns over a three-year period but Len had halted further purchases based on a September performance audit of the first three machines. The audit showed that the productivity and expenses associated with the Icahns had been much worse than expected. In addition sales of WTD taps for the first half of 1978 had been 20% below forecast. Len had to decide whether he should proceed with the purchase of the four Icahns planned for 1979.

Background of Wilmington Tap and Die

Wilmington Tap and Die was incorporated in 1912 after the merger of three machining firms. The three companies were located in the small industrial town of Wilmington and had started up based on an 1871 screw-cutting invention used to produce taps and dies. The company grew through a series of mergers and acquisitions in the 1920's, 1930s, and 1950s and added drill bits to the tools that it produced. Following a 1963 merger with the American Tool Corporation, WTD became one of the world's largest producers of threading and cutting tools. In 1971 the company was acquired by United Industries, a diversified manufacturer of electronic, aerospace, and industrial products.

United and WTD

WTD was a division in United's Industrial Products Group. WTD had sales of $18.5 million ($6 million from tap sales) in 1977 on total assets of $8.1 million. The division had been profitable even though sales had been stagnant for the past 4 years (see *Exhibit 1*). WTD had been acquired as part of United's strategy to purchase and rationalize high-quality manufacturing businesses with high engineering content. The merger with United had not caused many apparent changes in the management of WTD other than modifications made in the budgeting and accounting systems to conform with United's practices. The plant manager prior to Len Green had been with WTD for over 26 years. WTD operated autonomously except that the plant manager could not make any unbudgeted capital expenditures over $10,000 without approval from United superiors. Under United's capital budgeting process, expenditures over $1,000,000 required CEO approval, expenditures above $500,000 required sector approval and expenditures over $250,000 had to receive group-level approval. United normally applied a 20% ROI hurdle rate when evaluating capital expenditure requests.

EXHIBIT 1
Wilmington Tap and Die (Abridged)
Income Statement Summary
($ millions)

	1974	1975	1976	1977
Sales	18.3	17.6	17.6	18.5
Cost of Sales—Standard	10.2	9.7	10.0	10.2
Gross Margin	8.0	7.9	7.6	8.3
Variances	1.0	1.5	1.5	0.7
Actual Margin	7.0	6.4	6.1	7.6
SG&A	3.7	3.2	4.8	4.6
Profit Before Tax	3.4	3.3	1.3	3.0
Tax	1.6	1.5	0.6	1.4
Profit After Tax	1.8	1.7	0.7	1.6

Balance Sheet Summary
($ millions)

	1974	1975	1976	1977
Receivables	2.1	1.8	1.6	2.1
Inventories	4.8	3.7	3.6	4.3
Current Liabilities	−1.8	−1.2	−1.5	−1.4
PP&E	1.9	1.9	2.2	3.1
Total	7.0	6.2	5.9	8.1
ROI (Net Income/Net Assets)	25.6%	27.9%	11.9%	19.6%

Tap Production and Marketing

Taps are used to cut threads into a drilled hole. WTD, with a 9% share of market, was one of the largest producers of taps in the country (see *Exhibit 2*). It produced a full line of taps used in the automotive, hydraulic, construction, and machinery manufacturing industries. The company was known for its high-quality products and its sales support for distributors. WTD considered its strong distribution base as one of its principal strengths. WTD was especially strong among distributors that supplied the smaller end users.

WTD was considered one of the "traditional" manufacturers in the industry along with Greenfield, Winter Bros., Besley, Cleveland, Union Twist and some smaller operations. The "traditionals" generally represented the older companies (in business fifty years or more). Most were located in the Northeast (many near the Wilmington area), were unionized, and offered a full product line through a network of tool distributors.

The newer tap manufacturers ("independents") were mostly located in the South and generally had lower labor costs than the traditional firms.

EXHIBIT 2
Wilmington Tap and Die (Abridged)
Market Share of Tap Market

Greenfield	12%
Winter Brothers	10
Wilmington	9
Bendix	8
Cleveland	6
Brubaker	6
Regal Beloit	5
Vermont	4
Jarvis	4
Hanson-Whitney	4
Morse	4
Sossner	3
Reiff & Nestor	3
Bath	2
Hypro	1
Wood & Spencer	1
Detroit Tap	1
New England Tap	1
New York Twist	New
Other	16%

The independents had carved out part of the tap market by utilizing specialized marketing strategies. Low price was a key factor and quality was also important because long and consistent tool life expectancy enabled end users to reduce the expense and disruption caused by frequent tap changes. Companies such as Regal Beloit and Vermont competed by providing 24-hour (or less) delivery of taps that had to be custom produced. They were adept at producing small volumes that required frequent machine setups.

WTD anticipated that lower unit manufacturing costs when using the automated Icahn grinders would allow it to begin competing for the business of the large-volume, price-sensitive end users.

Thread Grinding Machines

Grinding the threads onto a tap blank was the last major step in the production process. It was also the most critical step from a cost and quality standpoint. Thread grinding was the most labor-intensive part of production and required the use of expensive machining equipment and skilled machinists. The quality of the tap was almost exclusively a function of how accurately the threads were ground. WTD used two types of grinding machines prior to purchasing the Icahns.

There were 16 Wilmington Automatic Mechanical Thread Grinders that produced sizes #6 MS to $\frac{1}{4}$" inclusive. These machines were designed and built by Wilmington engineers as hand machines in the 1930s and automated in the late 1950s. They operated by a single-rib (grinds one thread at a time), multipass grinding method that had remained essentially the same for twenty years. The age of these machines made it increasingly difficult to ensure quality output. Much of WTD's historical success was due to the high productivity of these machines when first developed and especially after their automation in the 1950s. Now, however, they were no longer as productive as the machines used by competitors.

The company also had eight Jones & Lamson Hydraulic Automatic Thread Grinders that manufactured tap sizes $\frac{5}{16}$" through $\frac{3}{8}$". These machines were purchased in the late 1960s when it became economically impractical to develop entirely new grinding equipment internally. The J&L grinders also operate using the single-rib, multipass grinding method. WTD had made several proprietary improvements to help increase the production efficiency of the J&Ls.

Icahn Grinding Machines

Shortly after the 1971 acquisition, United made a strategic commitment to maintain WTD's quality and leadership position in the industry. Most other tap producers were also using modified J&L grinders and any perceived quality gap was narrowing. Investment in the most modern equipment to improve manufacturing efficiency was considered an important part of WTD's future success. As a result WTD formed a manufacturing engineering team in early 1973 to rationalize the manufacturing process and investigate the latest alternative equipment available. The company discovered that no new thread-grinding technology had been developed so WTD began work with Icahn, a Swedish company, to design a fully automated multirib thread grinder. A prototype, known as the "yellow bird" (because of its yellow color), was purchased in 1975 and installed on an experimental basis in the Wilmington plant. The production experience with the yellow bird was encouraging. The machine was not only more efficient than other grinders but it produced a much higher quality tap. The principal quality advantage of the taps produced on the Icahn was a much longer life expectancy. This was apparently due to lower grinding temperatures which produced less metallurgical damage to the hardened steel used for the taps. WID engineers felt that over time several modifications could be made in-house to the Icahn machines to increase their efficiency and output quality beyond what had been achieved on the yellow bird prototype.

In January 1976 WTD prepared a capital budget request to purchase two Icahns as the initial phase of an overall plan to buy sixteen of the machines. The Icahns would enable WTD to phase out the eight J&L grinders by 1979 and would meet the needs for additional capacity based on the sales forecast through 1980. The request called for the expenditure of approximately $217,000 per machine (a total of nearly $3,500,000) and represented the largest equipment expenditure in WTD's history. The original request was sent back to WTD by the group executives who wanted a more thorough evaluation of the financial return that the investment would provide and a complete examination of alternatives open to WTD. A revised capital expenditure authorization request (known as a CEA) was submitted to United in 1977. Its principal justification was to maintain WTD's market share (see *Exhibit 3*) through the purchase of additional production equipment. The CEA explored several equipment alternatives. Two of these were:

1. Rebuild 16 WTD and 8 J&L Auto thread grinders. Total cost—$880,000.
2. Retire all thread grinders and purchase 16 Icahn Auto thread grinders. Total cost—$3,472,000.

EXHIBIT 3
Wilmington Tap and Die (Abridged)
Tap Market Outlook Without Investment
($000s)

	Present Outlook				
	1976	1977	1978	1979	1980
Total Market in Units	27,761	29,146	30,553	32,015	33,565
WTD Market Share	9.00%	9.00%	8.65%	8.31%	7.98%
WTD Sales (units)	2,498	2,623	2,643	2,660	2,678
WTD Price (average)	$2.51	$2.44	$2.42	$2.41	$2.39
WTD Sales	$6,280	$6,404	$6,404	$6,404	$6,404
Major Competitors' Market Shares;[a] (units)					
Greenfield	3,609	3,789	3,972	4,162	4,363
Winter Brothers	2,776	2,769	2,750	2,561	2,350
Bendix	2,221	2,405	2,597	2,881	3,189
Cleveland	1,943	2,113	2,291	2,561	3,021
All Other	14,714	15,447	16,300	17,190	17,963

Tap Market Outlook With Investment (000)

	1976	1977	1978	1979	1980
Total Market in Units	27,761	29,146	30,553	32,015	33,565
WTD Market Share	9.00%	9.00%	9.09%	9.15%	9.24%
WTD Sales (units)	2,498	2,623	2,779	2,929	3,102
WTD Price (average)	$2.51	$2.44	$2.42	$2.41	$2.39
WTD Sales	$6,280	$6,404	$6,724	$7,060	$7,413
Major Competitors' Market Share[a] (units)					
Greenfield	3,609	3,789	3,972	4,162	4,363
Winter Brothers	2,776	2,769	2,750	2,561	2,350
Bendix	2,221	2,405	2,597	2,881	3,189
Cleveland	1,943	2,113	2,291	2,561	3,021
All Other	14,714	15,447	16,165	16,921	17,540

[a] Assumes that competitors will not have similar new quality machinery.

The rebuilding or purchase of the various thread grinders would be spread over a five-year period (see *Exhibit 4*).

EXHIBIT 4
Wilmington Tap and Die (Abridged)
Production Machinery Schedule

	1977	1978	1978	1980	1981
Alternative #1					
WTD Grinders	14	14	14	14	16
J&L Grinders	7	7	7	7	8
Total	21	21	21	21	24
Alternative #2					
WTD Grinders	12	12	4	—	—
J&L Grinders	8	8	8	4	—
Icahn	—	6	10	14	16
Total	20	26	22	18	16

WTD estimated the costs under each alternative to determine the net cash flow of the projects (see Appendix A for detailed pro forma financial projections for the two alternatives). The capital expenditure request evaluated each alternative based on incremental cash flow as shown below:

	Alternatives	
	#1	#2
Cumulative Net Cash Flow ($000)	12,760	15,736
Present Value @ 20% ($000)	5,198	5,656
ROI	42.0%	43.6%

The CEA recommended that WTD pursue Alternative #2 and replace all existing equipment with the Icahn equipment. In late 1977, United approved the program to purchase 16 Icahns and authorized WTD to purchase 6 machines; 2 to be delivered immediately and 4 for delivery in 1978. It was also planned that 4 Icahns would be purchased each year in 1979 and 1980 and 2 machines would be added in 1981 to complete the program. Purchase of the final 10 machines would require final approval in each year conditional on the experience with the Icahns previously purchased.

Postaudit of the Icahns

In September 1978 an analyst from the group-level financial staff was sent to the Wilmington plant to audit the initial operating statistics for the Icahn equipment. At the time of the audit, the first two nonprototype Icahns had been operational for three months. The audit was conducted on the three Icahns at Wilmington in anticipation of the request to proceed with the planned purchase of four additional machines to be delivered in 1979 (the four machines delivered in December 1978 had already been ordered). The audit revealed three areas where the actual results differed substantially from the CEA projections as outlined below:

1. The strength of the Swedish kronor in foreign exchange markets had caused the price of an Icahn to rise more than 15% to approximately $250,000.
2. Sales and production of WTD taps were about 20% below the CEA projections in 1977. Unit sales were projected to be about 13% below in 1978 as noted below:

1977		1978	
CEA	Actual	CEA	Actual*
2,623	2,107	2,779	2,415

* 6 months actual, 6 months forecast.

While sales were below the CEA projections in both years the increase in sales from 1977 to 1978 was expected to be over 13%. This compared favorably with the 5% annual real growth forecast in the CEA.

The higher annual sales growth for Alternative 2 (5% vs. 2%) for WTD taps in the CEA was based on expected quality improvement in taps produced using the Icahn thread grinders. The postaudit revealed that while the quality had improved (initial tests showed a 20% increase in tap life), the WTD marketing group had not been able to capitalize on the improved quality. No effort had been made to publicize the improved Icahn taps because only a fraction of the WTD's total production was produced on the new equipment. This situation would continue for two or three more years until more of the Icahns were put into production.

3. The actual pieces produced per hour on the Icahns averaged about 10% below CEA projections and the operating costs associated with the machines were significantly higher than planned. The reduced output of the machine was caused by several problems:
   (a) The time required to change the grinding wheel had been omitted from the calculations of cycle times used in the CEA.
   (b) It was necessary to have the Icahn company build new work drivers (a mechanism that loads and aligns the tap into the machine) and install them for the machines to operate properly.
   (c) Maintenance technicians had difficulty in trouble-shooting the machines' programmable controls. The older thread grinders were operated strictly with mechanical controls. The yellow bird prototype incorporated hydraulic controls that were manually adjusted. But the two recently purchased Icahns had been improved with electronic computerized controls and the skills developed on

the old thread grinders were not applicable to the new machines. WTD had decided to retrain its machinists rather than to hire new personnel. A substantial training program using Icahn factory personnel was undertaken to train the operators and maintenance support. Video equipment had been ordered to help develop better training tools.

(d) Variations in the flute length of the tap blanks caused machine malfunctions. Unlike the other grinding machines, the Icahn's grinding stroke was a function of flute length as determined by a sensor on the machine.

(e) The CEA production figures were based on the production of regulars. In actual practice the Icahns were being used to produce some specials (custom-sized taps).

(f) CEA labor costs were based on the use of one operator per four machines. Since, at the time of the audit, WTD only had three machines there could only be three machines per operator.

The postaudit report was first sent to the auditor's superior at the group level. The group controller contacted Len Green and recommended that further Icahn purchases be stopped until a new CEA could be prepared using the actual data from the Icahns already in place. Len Green had already decided to halt further purchases of the Icahns when he received the memo from the group controller. He was concerned with the poor operating results of the Icahns but he was also worried that thread grinding equipment might soon be available from other manufacturers that would be even more efficient than the Icahn machines.

Postaudit Follow-Up

After the audit was conducted WTD recalculated the discounted cash flow rate of return of Alternative #2 using the actual performance at the time of the audit rather than the projections contained in the CEA. Just the effect of the external factors (lower sales and higher cost of the machines) reduced the return to 9%. The reduced productivity of the Icahns would have lowered the return even further but the exact level was not calculated because the accounting system was not structured to provide cost data on the Icahn machines alone.

There was considerable concern at WTD with these lower projections. The division had been averaging returns in excess of 20% in normal years and the compensation plan for the senior managers of WTD included bonuses, based on divisional ROI, which could amount to up to 30% of total compensation. Len Green asked his financial group to look closely at the figures to see whether the return from the Icahn investment could reasonably be expected to exceed the 20% hurdle rate.

Further tests were conducted to determine the actual piece rate output of the Icahns. The original CEA projected an average output of approximately 85 pieces per hour per machine. The actual output of the Icahns following the audit averaged 69 pieces per hour. Len Green felt that this would improve over time as WTD went further down the learning curve with the Icahn equipment but about half of the reduced output rate was due to wheel changing time that had been inadvertently left out of the original projections. Much of the lowered productivity was a result of the difficulty that had been experienced with the programmable controls.

In addition to the operating problems with the Icahns, Len Green had learned that his competitors, Bay State and Bendix, had ordered new Junker thread grinders and Greenfield was considering new Lindner grinders. He asked his manufacturing engineering manager to review the equipment from these German vendors. Preliminary indications were that the German equipment offered at best only marginal advantages over the Icahns so that the start-up costs associated with the alternative machines would not alone justify switching to them in the future. Len, however, was concerned that WTD would be known in the industry for its Icahn equipment because it was the only tap manufacturer that had purchased Icahns. This could be an advantage if the Icahns were acknowledged as "the" thread grinding technology. However, if the Icahn became outmoded it would be hard to overcome the stigma of being the only firm using Icahns when competitors were purchasing the newer Junker and Lindner grinders.

On a positive note, Len had just received a memorandum from the manager of product engineering who had been performing extensive tests on a random sample of taps produced by the three types of grinding machines now in use at Wilmington. The conclusions showed the taps produced on the Icahn grinders had longer life and higher resistance to breakage than taps produced on the older grinding equipment.

The most recent sales figures indicated that 1978 sales would be within 2% of original projections and sales were increasing at a faster rate than previously forecast. Len knew that he would have to proceed with the purchase of additional thread grinding equipment very soon if WTD were to have sufficient capacity to maintain or increase its share of market. He knew that it would be extremely difficult to gain approval for a new Icahn capital budget request based on recent operating data but he was convinced that the productivity of the Icahns would improve with experience. United's group management, however, had asked that any additional requests to purchase Icahns be based on actual production data of the Icahns already in use.

Required:

1. Evaluate the capital expenditure authorization request for the new machines.
2. How should Len Green evaluate the post-audit report?
3. What should Len Green do?

APPENDIX A: Wilmington Tap and Die (Abridged)
Financial Outlook Without Investment

ALTERNATIVE #1

Rebuild Present Machines—No Increase in Production

	1977	1978	1979	1980	1981	1982	1983	1984	1985	1986
1. Currency $U.S. Thousands Present Outlook (Up to 10 Years)										
2. Year	1977	1978	1979	1980	1981	1982	1983	1984	1985	1986
3. Sales	6404	6404	6404	6404	6404	6404	6404	6404	6404	6404
Cost of Sales:										
4. Labor	168	168	168	168	168	168	168	168	168	168
5. Material	312	312	312	312	312	312	312	312	312	312
6. Overhead (Excl. Depr.)	1557	1557	1557	1557	1557	1557	1557	1557	1557	1557
7.										
8.										
9.										
10.										
11.										
12.										
13.										
14.										
15. Interest	0	0	0	0	0	0	0	0	0	0
16. Depreciation	112	153	175	204	207	176	96	77	60	43
17. Div. Oper. Expense	1473	1473	1473	1473	1473	1473	1473	1473	1473	1473
18. Staff Allocations	218	218	218	218	218	218	218	218	218	218
19. AFC	96	96	96	96	96	96	96	96	96	96
20. Tax Rate	.50	.50	.50	.50	.50	.50	.50	.50	.50	.50
Assets & Liabilities:										
21. Inventory/Sales	.20	.20	.20	.20	.20	.20	.20	.20	.20	.20
22. Other WC/Sales	.17	.17	.17	.17	.17	.17	.17	.17	.17	.17
23. Gross Prop. Plt & Equip.	2225	—	—	—	—	—	—	—	—	—
24. Net Prop. Plt & Equip.	544	—	—	—	—	—	—	—	—	—
25. Other Assets	0	0	0	0	0	0	0	0	0	0
26. Capital Expenditures	220	220	220	220	220	220	220	220	220	220
27. Deferred Taxes	0	0	0	0	0	0	0	0	0	0
28. Investment Tax Credit	22	22	22	22	22	22	22	22	22	22
29. Other Tax Credits	0	0	0	0	0	0	0	0	0	0

APPENDIX A (continued): Financial Outlook with Investment

ALTERNATIVE #2
Retire Present Machines—Purchase 16 Icahns

	1977	1978	1979	1980	1981	1982	1983	1984	1985	1986
1. Currency $U.S. Thousands Present Outlook (Up to 10 Years)										
2. Year	1977	1978	1979	1980	1981	1982	1983	1984	1985	1986
3. Sales	6404	6724	7060	7413	7784	7784	7784	7784	7784	7784
Cost of Sales:										
4. Labor	167	154	148	148	152	152	152	152	152	152
5. Material	312	328	344	361	380	380	380	380	380	380
6. Overhead (Excl. Dept.)	1557	1440	1390	1390	1423	1423	1423	1423	1423	1423
7.										
8.										
9.										
10.										
11.										
12.										
13.										
14.										
15. Interest	0	0	0	0	0	0	0	0	0	0
16. Depreciation	134	261	399	518	566	513	409	341	273	204
17. Div. Oper. Expense	1473	1547	1624	1705	1790	1790	1790	1790	1790	1790
18. Staff Allocations	218	229	240	252	265	265	265	265	265	265
19. AFC	96	101	106	111	117	117	117	117	117	117
20. Tax Rate	.50	.50	.50	.50	.50	.50	.50	.50	.50	.50
Assets & Liabilities:										
21. Inventory/Sales	.20	.20	.20	.20	.20	.20	.20	.20	.20	.20
22. Other WC/Sales	.17	.17	.17	.17	.17	.17	.17	.17	.17	.17
23. Gross Prop. Plt & Equip.	2439	—	—	—	—	—	—	—	—	—
24. Net Prop. Plt & Equip.	824	—	—	—	—	—	—	—	—	—
25. Other Assets	0	0	0	0	0	0	0	0	0	0
26. Capital Expenditures	434	868	868	868	434	0	0	0	0	0
27. Deferred Taxes	0	0	0	0	0	0	0	0	0	0
28. Investment Tax Credit	43	87	87	87	43	0	0	0	0	0
29. Other Tax Credits	0	0	0	0	0	0	0	0	0	0

APPENDIX A (continued): Financial Study— Wilmington Icahn Project

The financial study was based upon the comparison of the production of high-speed ground threaded taps, sizes #6-32 through $\frac{3}{8}$"-24, under five different machine combinations involving three sales forecasts. Sales, production costs, and all other sales and/or production-oriented costs were determined on the basis of their relationship to production and sales levels for high-speed ground threaded taps as specified in the Wilmington marketing study.

I. Sales

Sales dollars (at net less returns and allowances, cash discounts, and freight-out) and sales/production in units are per the Wilmington Tap & Die (WTD) Marketing Department marketing study.

II. Material

Material dollar costs were developed using 1977 WTD standard material costs per 100 pieces and applying these costs against production levels as specified in the WTD marketing study.

III. Labor

Labor costs encompass all direct labor operations for the twelve sizes specified in the range of #6-32 through $\frac{3}{8}$"-24 at 1977 standard piece rates, adjusted for production levels per the WTD marketing study.

For direct labor operations other than thread grinding, a direct labor standard piece rate cost per 100 pieces for each of the twelve sizes of taps was applied against production for each size per the WTD marketing study to obtain piece rate direct labor for each size and for total production.

For the thread grinding operation, piece rate direct labor dollars per 100 pieces and direct labor man-hours per 100 pieces were obtained for each of the twelve sizes of taps from George Penrose, WTD standards department. Dollars per 100 pieces were divided by man-hours per 100 pieces to obtain direct labor piece rate dollars per man-hour for each of the twelve tap sizes. These twelve direct labor piece rate dollars per man-hour were then weighted by the percentage of units produced per each tap size to total units produced. A weighted average cost of $2.69 per man-hour was derived. This cost was then applied against direct labor man-hours for each alternative per the engineering man-hours loading schedule (see engineering summary) to obtain piece rate direct labor dollars for the thread grinding operation for each alternative.

IV. Overhead

Overhead was developed as a function of overhead rates and direct labor dollars. Overhead rates were developed on a plantwide basis taking into effect those changes in the overhead base caused by increased production of the twelve sizes of high-speed ground threaded taps. The overhead rates were then applied against direct labor piece rate dollars (see III. *Labor*) to derive the overhead applicable to the production of these taps. Overhead was computed *net* of depreciation (see *Property, Plant & Equipment—Depreciation*).

V. Property, Plant & Equipment

Gross and net property, plant, and equipment are composed of the cost of new or rebuilt machinery, depending upon the production alternative, and a portion of other WTD plant, property, and equipment applicable to the production of the twelve tap sizes.

A. The cost of sales applicable to the production of the twelve tap sizes represents 19.9% of total WTD cost of sales. This percentage was applied against the gross and net property, plant, and equipment (GPPE and NPPE, respectively) balances at 12/31/77 of WTD to obtain property balances applicable to the specified twelve tap sizes. The cost of capital additions (rebuilding and/or purchase costs) was added to this other WTD plant GPPE and NPPE to obtain the total balances of GPPE and NPPE for each of the two alternatives.

B. Depreciation for the other WTD plant, property, and equipment was obtained by applying the 19.9% rate against depreciation for 1977. The portion of depreciation obtained was applied on a straight-line basis until net book value for the related other property, plant, and equipment reached zero. Depreciation for the cost of rebuilding or purchasing of equipment was calculated on a double-declining balance/sum-of-the-year digits method over 9.5 years, as specified in Tax Bulletin No. 15, dated 11/11/74.

VI. Capital Expenditures

Capital expenditures were obtained for the two alternatives from the engineering study. Alternative #2, the purchase of 16 Icahns, makes an allowance for the disposal of the Model Fs in the form of offsetting the net book value of the Model Fs against the cost of the Icahns in the year of disposal, obtaining a "net" capital expenditure.

VII. Investment Tax Credit

Represents 10% of gross capital expenditures.

VIII. Other

The following expense ratios are based on historical data and were obtained from K.W. Stinger, controller, WTD.

A. *Percentage of Sales*:
    1. Division Operating Expense   23.0%
    2. Staff Allocations   3.4
    3. Allocated Finance Charge   1.5
B. *Tax Rate*:   50.0
C. *Other Ratios*:
    1. Inventory/Sales   20.0
    2. Other Working Capital/Sales   17.0

chapter 13

DECENTRALIZATION

Earlier chapters of this book focused on individual measurement issues: product-mix and profitability analysis, estimating the behavior of costs, pricing decisions, service department usage, joint-product analysis, and measures to promote improvements in quality, throughput, and acquisition and use of new technology. For each issue, we isolated the essential information required for the decision or analysis. This approach is helpful for understanding decision making in small relatively simple organizations and in decision-making units, such as departments or divisions, within large organizations.

In large multiproduct, multilocation, hierarchical entities, typical of our modern business enterprises, a broader set of information and measurement issues arises. Questions concerning who in the organization will have the authority and responsibility for making particular decisions and how such a decision maker will be evaluated and rewarded require answers from a broader perspective than we have taken in previous chapters. In this and the chapters that follow, we will introduce the notion of decentralized operations: the benefits, costs, and special problems that arise in the management and evaluation of decentralized organizational units.

A large corporation contains many diverse design, production, logistics, purchasing, financing, and marketing activities that interact with each other but may still be operated separately. The output products of one activity may be the inputs to another, making it important that the volume of these two activities (such as component production and assembly, or production and marketing) be balanced. Some commodities may have to be purchased from external vendors, stored at various sites, transported among and within plants, and assigned to the activities that use these commodities. Some activities produce finished goods that need to be transported, stored, and sold by the other activities. Coordination is needed not only at a single point in time but continually—over many time periods—as the diverse activities respond to changes in the marketplace.

In addition to the production and marketing activities of acquiring the inputs to the production process, performing the actual manufacture and assembly, and marketing the product to the customers, a whole range of support and service activities must be coordinated to supplement the production and marketing activities. Functions such as personnel, information systems, finance, legal, research and development, utilities, maintenance, and engineering must be made part of the firm's overall planning and control process.

One approach to managing the diverse and complex activities of a large organization has been to stress central control. With this view, organizations are characterized by vertical, hierarchical relations; control is exercised by orders from above and executed as specified by those below. Interacting activities are coordinated by plans set at higher levels. Accounting systems and periodic reports provide the central management with all the information needed to formulate plans and to detect any departures from centrally determined policies.

In practice, of course, no central management can possibly know everything about an organization's many activities. Therefore, central management cannot make all the decisions for lower-level managers. Many decisions must be made at the lower or local levels of any organization. The challenge in organizational and informational design is to balance the benefits and costs from decentralized decision making—benefits and costs that are a function of a firm's particular resources, constraints, and opportunities.

Alfred Chandler, in his landmark studies of the development of American industrial enterprises, has clearly articulated the demand for decentralized organizations:

> The lack of time, of information, and of psychological commitment to an overall entrepreneurial viewpoint were not necessarily serious handicaps if the company's basic activities remained stable, that is, if its sources of raw materials and supplies, its manufacturing technology, its markets, and the nature of its products and product lines stayed relatively unchanged. But when further expansion into new functions, into new geographical areas, or into new product lines greatly increased all types of administrative decisions, then the executives in the central office became overworked and their administrative performance less efficient. These increasing pressures, in turn, created the need for the building or adoption of the multidivisional structure with its general office and autonomous operating divisions.[1]

That a certain amount of decentralized decision making is necessary within a firm should not be surprising. A modern corporation, after all, is an economy in miniature (some of our largest corporations actually pro-

---

[1] Alfred D. Chandler, Jr., *Strategy and Structure: Chapters in the History of the Industrial Enterprise* (Cambridge, MA: M.I.T. Press, 1962), p. 297.

duce more goods and services than many economies around the world). A large corporation has internal capital and labor markets—or at least mechanisms for allocating capital and labor within the firm. It has unemployment problems, suffers from cyclic fluctuations, and must be concerned with its supply of money. The firm employs planners, forecasters, and stabilizers. The actions of one organizational unit can affect many other organizational units, so that externalities among organizational units are abundant.

Socialist economies, with central direction and resource allocation, tend to have ineffective production enterprises with insufficient incentives for response to consumer preferences and the continually changing demands of the marketplace. If information and computational complexities make it desirable to have decentralized resource allocation and decision making in an economy, then a certain degree of decentralization will also be desirable for large organizational units within an economy.

The problem is that prices, which play such a vital role in a capitalist economy, are not as readily available within the firm to guide local decision making. There are not enough economic agents within a firm to simulate a full market system. Moreover, because of the external owners' lack of information or inability to audit behavior, managers may be motivated to act in a way that promotes their own self-interest at the expense of the owners of the firm. Therefore, a firm uses a collection of nonmarket mechanisms (such as contracts, incentives, standards, penalties, and reporting) that facilitate resource allocation and decision making in the presence of information constraints that prevent markets from operating well. The focus of this and the next four chapters is to evaluate these nonmarket institutional arrangements within the firm.

Why Decentralize?

These introductory remarks provide some general motivation for the demand for decentralized decision making. Let us now look more closely at specific incentives for firms to decentralize.

The Environment of the Firm

Successful managers must continually track the key variables in their external environment so that the firm can act before external events overwhelm it. The need to constantly scan the environment has important implications for the internal organization of the firm.

Contingency theory, a popular organizational model, predicts that the complexity of a firm's environment will determine the complexity of the internal structure of the firm. Lawrence and Lorsch, after an extensive study, concluded that firms whose internal processes were consistent with external demands were more effective in dealing with their environment.[2] Complex and uncertain external environments demand that more resources be expended to monitor that environment and that more decision making will have to be decentralized within the firm to experts who can specialize in developing information about, and developing the expertise to deal with, the changes in the firm's environment. These local experts can then respond quickly and effectively to opportunities and changes.

In one of the most famous studies in the Organization Design literature, Burns and Stalker discovered a predictable relationship between the external environment and the management structure of the firms in their study.[3] Their results have been summarized as follows:

> When the external environment was stable, the internal organization was characterized by rules, procedures, and a clear hierarchy of authority. Organizations were formalized. They were also centralized, with most decisions made at the top. Burns and Stalker called this a "mechanistic" organization system.
>
> In rapidly changing environments, the internal organization was much looser, free flowing, and adaptive. Rules and regulations often were not written down, or if written down were ignored. People had to find their own way through the system to figure out what to do. The hierarchy of authority was not clear. Decision-making authority was decentralized. Burns and Stalker used the term "organic" to characterize this type of management structure.[4]

The results reported by Burns and Stalker are summarized in the following list:

Mechanistic Form	**Organistic Form**
1. Appropriate for stable conditions.	Appropriate for changing conditions.
2. Tasks are highly specialized and differentiated.	Tasks are shared jointly and on a cooperative basis.
3. Tasks and obligations are precisely defined.	Tasks evolve and are defined by the nature of the problem faced.
4. Control, authority, and the flow of information are hierarchical.	A network structure of control, authority, and information is used.

---

[2] Paul R. Lawrence and Jay W. Lorsch, *Organization and Environment* (Homewood, IL: Richard D. Irwin, 1969).

[3] T. Burns and G. M. Stalker, *The Management of Innovation* (London: Tavistock Publications, 1961).

[4] R. L. Daft, *Organization Theory and Design* (St. Paul, MN: West Publishing, 1983), p. 61.

Mechanistic Form	**Organistic Form**
5. Many operating rules and procedures, which are rigidly enforced.	The few rules that exist are commonly ignored.
6. The hierarchical structure of the organization is reinforced by locating knowledge and the control of tasks exclusively at the top of the hierarchy.	Knowledge and control are located where the decision is made in the network.
7. Communications are downward and vertical and consist mainly of rules, instructions, and decisions to implement.	Communications are lateral and consist primarily of sharing information and advice.

Information Specialization

Perhaps the strongest factor leading to decentralization is the difficulty, if not impossibility, of sharing all local information with the central management. Local managers, through observation and experience, develop expertise on such matters as local market opportunities, production possibilities and constraints, morale and capabilities of their labor force, and quality and reliability of local suppliers. It would be extremely difficult, costly, and time consuming for local managers to communicate all the relevant information they possess to a central management. Many of these observations would be difficult to quantify or even verbalize. Language limits people's ability to articulate their knowledge and intuition, whether using words, numbers, or graphics, in ways that will be understood by others. Managers will find, despite their best efforts, that their information is not sufficiently well formulated to communicate their intuition and judgment about relevant local information. Thus, an extremely important force toward decentralization is the desire to place decision making where the relevant information is acquired, stored, accessed, and processed.

Timeliness of Response

Decentralization also permits local managers to respond quickly when making and implementing decisions. By allowing some degree of local decision making, the decentralized unit can respond to unexpected conditions faster than if all actions had to be approved by a central management group. Centralized decision making introduces delays during (1) transmission of the decision-relevant information from the local to the central unit; (2) assembly of the relevant people in the central decision-making unit plus the time they require to assimilate information, deliberate, and reach a decision; and (3) transmission of the recommended decision from the central unit back to the local unit where it will be implemented. Ralph

Cordiner, one of the prime forces for decentralization during his tenure as president of General Electric during the 1950s, expressed this view well:

> Unless we could put the responsibility and authority for decision making closer in each case to the scene of the problem, where complete understanding and prompt action are possible, the Company would not be able to compete with the hundreds of nimble competitors who were, as they say, able to turn on a dime.[5]

Conservation of Central Management Time

Presumably, the time of the central management group is one of the firm's scarcest resources. The vast numbers of local decisions called for would overwhelm even the most talented, hard-working, and resourceful group of top executives. The law of comparative advantage operates within firms, as well as among firms. Even though, for any particular local decision, a top executive may make a somewhat better local decision (once all the relevant situation-specific factors are effectively communicated and explained) than the less-experienced or less-talented local manager, it is not necessarily optimal for the top executive to make all the local decisions. If the senior executives spend their scarce time making slightly superior day-to-day operating decisions, they may ignore the strategic decisions that in the intermediate to long run are more vital to the firm's success. Therefore, central management's attention should be committed to policy and strategic decisions and local managers should be allowed to make necessary operating decisions, consistent with the broader objectives established by top management.

Computational Complexity

Even if it were decided to centralize all decision making, it may not be possible to compute globally optimal decisions. With exceedingly complex operations characterized by extensive interactions and discontinuities in scale, it may be virtually impossible to solve reasonably sized resource allocation problems centrally. Limits exist to the complexity of problems that can be solved by human decision makers (a situation referred to as a bounded rationality), and even computer-based algorithms cannot optimize very large systems, especially systems with nonlinearities and discrete (integer) variables. When the environment is also characterized by uncertainty, the simplifications and heuristics required for centrally determined decisions could easily lead to decisions inferior to those that would be reached at decentralized levels. Again, the analogy between a

---

[5] Ralph J. Cordiner, *New Frontiers for Professional Managers* (New York: McGraw-Hill, 1956), pp. 45–46.

centralized firm and a socialist economy is instructive; socialist economies have found it impossible to make all major resource-allocation and production decisions centrally. Examples of these types of difficulties are the shortages and bottlenecks reflecting, perhaps among other things, the difficulty of coordination that must be faced in planned economies. In decentralized organizations, general directions and guidelines are provided to local plant managers, who still retain discretion for decisions on resource acquisition, product mix, and distribution. These decisions are guided by incentive plans and a limited use of the price system.

Training for Local Managers

If all significant decision making were done centrally, local managers would mainly be implementing the centrally determined plans. The managers would acquire experience in motivating employees and meeting production or distribution schedules but would not receive training in decision making. How, then, would the next generation of central management acquire the requisite experience to become good resource allocators and strategic decision makers? And on what evidence could we determine who, among the many local managers, would be best qualified for advancement to the higher decision-making levels? Some degree of local decision making is desirable to (1) provide training for future general managers and (2) indicate which managers seem best qualified for advancement to higher levels of decision making.

Motivation for Local Managers

Finally, good managers are ambitious and take pride in their work. If their role is restricted to carrying out instructions determined at higher levels, they may lose interest in their assignments and cease applying their talents to their assignment. The firm may also find it difficult to attract creative and energetic people to serve merely as decision implementors. Managers will become more motivated and interested in their assignments when they are permitted more discretion in performing their tasks. Allowing for decision making at a local level encourages managers to be more aggressive in their acquisition of local information, and more entrepreneurial and strategic in their actions. The challenge, of course, is to design incentive systems so that such aggressive, entrepreneurial, and strategic activities at a local level are consistent with overall corporate goals and objectives.

The arguments for decentralization seem compelling. The outcome or payoff of any reasonably sized organization depends on many interrelated decisions about decentralized or local activities. Different members in the organization have different bodies of knowledge and abilities to act. It is impossible for any individual or central group to possess all the relevant information, experience, time, and computational power to determine the detailed operating plans for the organization. Accepting this argument, however, still leaves us with the extremely difficult problem of how to decentralize decision making in practice. Present practice provides evidence on five types of decentralized organizational units. These units differ depending on the degree of authority and responsibility given to the local manager.

Organization of Decentralized Units

All units in an organization acquire inputs and produce outputs, either goods or services. Units differ, however, in the ease with which the outputs can be measured and in the discretion given to the local manager for acquiring inputs and choosing the type and mix of outputs. These considerations make different types of decentralized units appropriate depending on the difficulty of measuring outputs and the discretion or responsibility given to the local manager. We will briefly review five principal types:

1. Standard cost centers
2. Revenue centers
3. Discretionary expense centers
4. Profit centers
5. Investment centers

Profit centers and investment centers are treated in more depth in the subsequent two chapters.

Standard Cost Centers

Standard cost centers can be established whenever we can define and measure output well and can specify the amount of inputs required to produce each unit of output. Usually, we think of standard cost centers as arising in manufacturing operations where, for each type of output product, a standard amount and standard price of input materials, labor, energy, and support services can be specified. Standard cost centers, however, can be used for any repetitive operation for which we can measure the physical amount of output and specify a production function relating inputs to outputs. Thus, even in service industries such as fast-food franchises, banking, or health care, we can establish standard cost centers based on the number of hamburgers and milk shakes sold, on the number of checks processed, or on the number of patient tests or radiological procedures performed.

In general, managers of standard cost centers are not held responsible for variations in activity levels in their centers. They are held responsible for the efficiency with which they meet externally determined demands as long as the demands are within the capacity of the cost center. Efficiency is measured by the amount of inputs consumed in producing the demanded level of outputs. This implies that if a full-cost scheme is being used, the managers are not responsible for underabsorbed overhead due to volume variances. They are, however, responsible for controlling the discretionary fixed costs in the center.

Managers of standard cost centers do not determine the price of their outputs, so they are not responsible for revenue or profit. Nevertheless, if the output does not meet the specific quality standards or is not produced according to schedule, the actions of the cost center will adversely affect the performance of other units in the organization. Therefore, quality and timeliness standards must be specified for any standard cost center, and its manager must produce output according to these standards.

For a standard cost center, then, efficiency is evaluated by the measured relation between inputs and outputs, and effectiveness is evaluated by whether the center achieved the desired production schedule at specified levels of quality and timeliness.

Standard cost centers and the detailed analysis of variances from standards are discussed extensively in cost accounting textbooks, so that further discussion is not required here. For our purposes, standard cost centers will be useful when we can measure output objectively, including quality and timeliness as well as the quantity of physical units, and when we have a well-specified relationship between outputs and inputs. The product (or output) must be standard enough that the manufacturing unit need not make decisions on price, output quantity, or product mix; these decisions can be made centrally or delegated to a marketing unit. Also, decisions on plant equipment and technology for the standard cost center will usually be made centrally, not by the cost center manager. Perhaps the only variation of this simple model would be those firms that impute a capital charge for raw material and work-in-process inventory to encourage cost center managers to achieve production goals while attempting to reduce inventory quantities.

Revenue Centers

Revenue centers exist in order to organize marketing activites. Typically, a revenue center acquires finished goods from a manufacturing division and is responsible for selling and distributing these goods. If the revenue center has discretion for setting the selling price, then it can be made responsible for the gross revenues it generates. If pricing policy is determined outside the revenue center (say, at the corporate level), then the manager of the revenue center is held responsible for the physical volume and mix of sales. The profit and sales-mix variance analysis method described in Chapter 9 should prove useful in evaluating the performance of a revenue center. The decomposition of profit variance described in that chapter enables us to decompose a sales-activity variance into effects caused by changes in overall market size, market share, and product mix.

When a performance measure is chosen for a revenue center, some notion of the cost of each product should be included so that the center is motivated to maximize gross operating margins rather than just sales revenue. If evaluated solely on sales revenue, managers may be motivated to cut prices to increase total sales, spend excessive amounts on advertising and promotion, or promote low-profit products. Each of these actions could increase total sales revenue but decrease overall corporate profitability.

Discretionary Expense Centers

Discretionary expense centers are appropriate for units that produce outputs that are not measurable in financial terms or for units where no strong relation exists between resources expended (inputs) and results achieved (outputs). Examples of discretionary expense centers are general and administrative (G&A) departments (controller, industrial relations, human resources, accounting, legal), the research and development (R&D) departments, and some marketing activities such as advertising, promotion, and warehousing. The output of G&A departments is difficult to measure, whereas for R&D and marketing functions, often no strong relation exists between inputs and outputs. For the R&D and marketing functions, we can determine whether the responsible departments are being effective. That is, we can see whether they are meeting the company's goals in terms of new products and improved technologies (for R&D) and sales volume or market penetration (for marketing). Because of the weak relationship between inputs and outputs in these departments, however, we are unable to determine whether they are operating efficiently—that is, producing the actual amount of output with the minimally required inputs. For the G&A departments, it becomes even more difficult to measure output, so that neither effectiveness nor efficiency can be determined. Recent work, however, has shown some progress in obtaining quantitative measures of the output from corporate staff departments.[6]

Given the difficulty of measuring the efficiency of discretionary expense centers, a natural tendency may arise for their managers to desire a very high quality department even though a somewhat lower quality department would provide almost the same service at significantly lower

---

[6] See Dennis Loewe and H. Thomas Johnson, "How Weyerhaeuser Controls Corporate Overhead Costs," *Management Accounting* (August 1987).

costs. Accentuating this tendency, the white-collar professionals who typically staff these centers prefer to have the best people in their discipline associated with them so that they can take pride in the quality of their department. Thus, it becomes difficult for central management to determine appropriate budget, quality, and service levels for the firm's discretionary expense centers.

One solution is to look at industry practice to see whether the company's expenditures on a given function are in line with those of other companies. (A cynic could deride this guideline as the blind following the blind.) We frequently see a company's R&D budget, for example, expressed as a percentage of sales. Even though there is no plausible reason why a company's R&D expenditures should be causally related to its sales, such a percentage rule facilitates intercompany comparisons.

Basically, determining the budget for a discretionary expense center requires the judgment of informed professionals. The central management needs to trust and work closely with the managers of discretionary expense centers to determine the appropriate budget level. The managers of such centers are in the best position to predict the consequences of changing the budget by $+10\%$ or $+20\%$. After finding out which activities would be augmented or reduced by changes, central management could then decide on the budget and hence on the quality or intensity of effort for the next period. Discretionary expense centers are an excellent example of where great information asymmetry is most likely to exist between a local unit manager and central management.

Once the budget for a discretionary expense center has been determined, no great benefit can result from pressuring the local manager to bring actual costs in under budget. Having actual spending below budgeted levels is not necessarily favorable nor a sign of efficiency, unlike the situation in a standard cost center. In a standard cost center, we have good measures of output quantity and quality, so that producing a given amount of output for less than budgeted costs is a favorable indication. For a discretionary expense center, however, a favorable cost variance may only mean that the center has operated at a lower level of quality, service, or effectiveness than was intended when the budget was established. Typically, the control process for such expenses will involve ensuring that the quality and level of service of the center has been maintained. Similarly, cost overruns in a discretionary expense center may be caused by favorable circumstances, such as a new-product breakthrough that justifies higher development expenditures or an improved marketing climate in which increased advertising and distribution expenditures may yield great returns.

The existence of budgeted and actual expenses for discretionary expense centers may give an illusion of precision about their operations. But such data may yield little insight into whether the centers are operating effectively or efficiently. Ultimately, the control of discretionary expense centers requires the informed judgment of knowledgeable professionals on the level and quality of service the centers are producing.

Profit Centers

The three types of centers described above have limited decentralization of decisions. Managers of standard cost centers may acquire and manage inputs at their discretion, but the outputs from these centers are determined and distributed by other units. Revenue centers distribute and sell products but have no control over their manufacture. Discretionary expense centers must produce a service or staff function demanded by the rest of the organization.

A significant increase in managerial discretion occurs when managers of local units are given responsibility for both production and sales. In this situation, they can make decisions about which products to manufacture, how to produce them, the quality level, the price, and the selling and distribution system. The managers must make product-mix decisions and determine how production resources are to be allocated among the various products. They are then in a position to optimize the performance of their centers by making trade-offs among price, volume, quality, and costs.

If the managers do not have responsibility or authority for determining the level of investment in assets in their centers, then profit may be the single best performance measure for the center, although any profit figure may need to be supplemented with a variety of nonfinancial indicators of short-term performance (as discussed in Chapters 9–11 and subsequently in Chapter 14). Profit, properly measured, can provide a short-run indicator of how well managers are creating value from the resources at their disposal and the input factors they acquire. Units, where the managers have almost complete operational decision-making responsibility and are evaluated by a profit measure, are called **profit centers.** The importance of profit centers and the difficulties associated with measuring profit in them justify a separate discussion, which is presented in Chapter 14.

Investment Centers

When local managers have all the responsibilities described above for profit centers and also have responsibility and authority for working capital and physical assets, then a performance measure based on the level of physical and financial assets employed in the center is preferred. Investment centers are generalizations of profit centers in which profitability is related to the assets used to generate the profit. Return on investment (ROI) and residual income are typical investment-center performance measures; these measures are discussed in Chapter 15.

Developing a Performance Measure
for Decentralized Operating Units

Control rules, or principles, can be divided into two classes: operating rules and enforcement rules.[7] Operating rules tell people what to do, and enforcement rules specify the consequences to a decision maker of not following the operating rules.

In a simple firm or for observable tasks, the operating rules tell people specifically what they must do. The enforcement rules can then be related directly to the accomplishment of the task. For example, a clerk can be told (the operating rule) to order 2,000 units of some part. Subsequently, it is easy to observe whether this instruction has been carried out. The consequence (the enforcement rule) of not carrying out the instruction may be dismissal.

With decentralization, however, local decision makers who have specialized in the assigned task and concentrated on gathering information relevant to the task can often judge better than their superiors the best course of action. Thus, in decentralized organizations, operating rules seldom take the form of telling people exactly what they must do. Rather, the operating rules are stated in terms of the firm's objectives and people are told to do whatever must be done to best attain the goals of the firm. These types of operating rules require very different enforcement rules than those used when a specific directive is given. Enforcement rules must use an incentive scheme to provide the motivation for the decision maker to follow the operating rules. For example, the operating rule "Do whatever you need to do to maximize the profit of your division" may associate with it an enforcement rule that provides the decision maker with a share in reported division profits.

In each of the five types of decentralized centers, the centers' managers have discretion in selecting and implementing actions. To guide the managers' decisions and evaluate the performance of the managers and their centers, we require a performance measure. Specification of the local performance measure is perhaps the most difficult problem in decentralizing decision making and responsibility. Through this measure, the organization communicates how it wishes the local manager to behave and how this behavior will be judged and evaluated. Central management needs to determine rules, measures, and rewards for local decision making that are compatible with overall corporate goals. These guidelines and incentives must facilitate the coordination of individual or divisional goals with those of the overall corporation goals, and attempt to minimize informational gathering and processing costs as well as dysfunctional costs from local suboptimizing. Clearly, this is not an easy task. Perhaps the most thoughtful

---

[7] K. J. Arrow, "Control in Large Organizations," *Management Science* (April 1964), pp. 397–408.

and best articulated views on the challenges in organizing a decentralized firm have come from Alfred P. Sloan, who provided the organizational archetype for the multidivisional firm during his long tenure as president of General Motors. Sloan, and his brilliant chief financial executive, Donaldson Brown, described their views as "decentralized responsibility with centralized control":

> Good management rests on a reconciliation of centralization and decentralization, or "decentralization with coordinated control."
>
> Each of the conflicting elements brought together in this concept has its unique results in the operation of a business. From decentralization we get initiative, responsibility, development of personnel, decisions close to the fact, flexibility—in short, all the qualities necessary for an organization to adapt to new conditions. From coordination we get efficiencies and economies. It must be apparent that coordinated decentralization is not an easy concept to apply. There is no hard and fast rule for sorting out the various responsibilities and the best way to assign them. The balance which is struck between corporate and divisional responsibility varies according to what is being decided, the circumstances of the time, past experience, and the temperaments and skills of the executives involved.[8]

In a centralized decision-making environment, the local managers follow detailed operating rules that instruct them how to act. The decisions are determined centrally and implemented locally. Any failure to perform in a centralized system is relatively obvious because job descriptions and tasks are well specified.

In decentralized operations, the operating rules (the "centralized control" that guides the "decentralized responsibilities" of local managers) are much less specific; hence performance evaluation is more difficult. We can think of the operating rules as consisting of two parts: constraints and objectives. First, the bounds of permissive or admissible behavior are specified, and the action alternatives of the managers are limited; for example, illegal behavior is proscribed, and managers may be instructed to use certain suppliers, meet certain quality standards, meet the demands of particular customers, and refrain from disposing of certain assets.

Once their range of action alternatives is specified, the local managers must also be given a well-specified reward or incentive function that they are expected to maximize. Thus, managers may be instructed to maximize divisional income, return on investment, or residual income. Managers in a sales division may be instructed to maximize sales revenues, or managers in a production division to minimize costs when satisfying an externally derived demand for the product, including achieving stringent quality and

---

[8] Alfred P. Sloan, Jr., *My Years with General Motors* (New York: Doubleday, 1964), p. 429.

timeliness goals. The specification of the local reward or incentive function is both extremely important and extremely difficult. This function will be used to measure the local managers' performance. Therefore, they will probably act to improve this measure, perhaps at the expense of the goals of the corporation or other divisions. For example, the sales manager of a revenue center may try to increase total revenue rather than total contribution margin. The expectation that managers will attempt to improve their local measure to the exclusion of all other goals or measures is what makes the appropriate specification of a single local reward measure so difficult.

We must also be concerned with using financial measures of performance as the local reward measure. Many people are now questioning the appropriateness of assessing performance using a highly aggregate number such as net income. Instead these people advocate that the key success factors facing the firm be identified, that each organization unit participate in setting individual goals aimed at helping the firm achieve its critical success factors, and that performance be evaluated relative to achieving each of these goals. In this way, success factors are identified and communicated through the organization, and progress toward achieving each of these factors is monitored. The feeling is that this approach will allow the firm to be more responsive in identifying and responding to important changes in its environment. While General Electric and McDonald's were leaders in using these multiattribute measures of performance, the use of nonfinancial measures of performance such as market penetration, market share, material and labor yields, and parts per thousand (or million) error rates are becoming more common.

To gain a better understanding of the problem of specifying local performance measures, we analyze the dysfunctional aspects associated with developing a measure of performance for a decentralized operation.

Problems of Goal Congruence

The measure of performance of a decentralized unit is a new piece of information that must be developed by the firm. Recall, from the discussion in Chapter 1, that nonhierarchical firms may not need internal measures of efficiency and performance. They can assess their performance by measuring the difference in prices between buying and selling transactions conducted with economic agents external to the firm. More complex, decentralized firms must expend resources to acquire relevant data and to compute the performance measures for decentralized units that conduct many transactions within the firm.

The consequences of developing the local performance measure, though, go far beyond the cost of data acquisition and computation. Ideally, the local performance measure should be consistent with overall corporate goals. But it is just about impossible in complex and uncertain environments for any single performance measure to achieve perfect goal congruence between a decentralized unit and the overall corporation. The measure of performance tends to become an end in itself, more important than the economic performance that it attempts to represent. In a revenue center, for example, the sales force may be motivated to sell only high-priced items in an attempt to maximize revenues rather than contribution margin. Any single measure may be manipulated to benefit the decentralized unit at the expense of the corporation.

This fundamental problem arises because, unlike the situation in the physical sciences, the act of measurement in the social sciences and in management changes the event and the observer.[9] Measurement is neither neutral nor objective. The measure chosen for evaluating performance acquires value and importance by the fact of being selected for attention. People within the system change their behavior as a function of the measure chosen to summarize the economic performance of their organizational unit.

A second problem arises because most measures of performance are based on internal achievement rather than external opportunities. A unit may be perceived as having performed well because it exceeded last year's measure of performance or the budgeted measure. But the current good performance may have been caused by an unexpected expansion of demand in the industry, in which all the companies in the industry participated. When viewed against overall industry performance, the decentralized unit may not have maintained its market share or relative profitability. In this case, the performance will not look as favorable against an external reference base as it does against the more typically measured internal criterion. Senior managers of highly diversified corporations (conglomerates), however, may not be able to use such relative performance evaluations effectively because they possess less information about the market conditions of individual divisions than the managers of these divisions.

A third limitation on a single performance measure occurs when the future economic consequences from current activities are ignored. Typical performance measures focus on short-term operating results and ignore longer-term effects that are harder to measure. These longer-term effects usually arise from expenditures on intangibles—research and development, advertising and promotion, plant design, maintenance, human resource development, and quality control. Because the benefits from such expenditures on intangibles are difficult and subjective to measure, we tend to ignore such benefits and concentrate on aspects of performance

---

[9] Strictly speaking, the Heisenberg uncertainty principle establishes that even in the physical sciences the act of measurement affects the phenomenon being measured. But such effects show up at the subatomic level of observation and do not affect everyday measurement of speed, weight, and dimensions of physical objects.

that we can measure more easily. Managers will then have an incentive to spend less on intangibles and maintenance than would be desirable for long-term corporate goals. Such expenditures on intangibles reduce the current performance measure, while the adverse effects of neglecting them do not show up until later, perhaps much later when the current managers are in entirely different positions in the organization.

Similarly, many transactions in a period have characteristics and longer-term consequences that are difficult to measure objectively. The quality of the product, the morale of the employees, and the output of professional services (legal, R&D, controller's office), for example, are important characteristics that affect the long-term performance of the organizational unit but are not easily captured in a short-term performance measure. Undesirable consequences will occur if too much reliance is placed on a single measure of performance that ignores longer-term, less objectively measured consequences of current-period decisions.

Problems of Externalities

Interactions among organizational units introduce a second set of problems when local units focus narrowly on their individual performance measures. When such interactions exist, the actions of an individual unit affect not only its own measure of performance but also the measures of other units. For example, when goods or services are transferred from one unit to another, these goods or services are frequently priced in order to recognize revenue for the supplying unit and an input-factor cost to the purchasing unit. This **transfer-pricing** process is one of the most contentious activities in decentralized firms. We will examine the relevant issues surrounding transfer pricing in Chapter 14.

Even assuming that the transfer-pricing problem can be solved in a satisfactory manner, many problematic nonprice aspects are associated with transactions among organizational units. The quality of a product or service and the timeliness of the transfer will affect the operation of the unit receiving the good or service, but the financial impact of varying quality or delivery times will be difficult to quantify. In principle, a price system could be established as a function of delivery delay (or product quality), but such a system would be extremely complex. It would be difficult to develop and to maintain. It would also introduce uncertainty to both units about the price of the transfer, since some delay might be caused by random, unexpected factors. Both units might then change their operations to minimize the effect of this inherent uncertainty. This change in operation could reduce overall output, thereby affecting the firm adversely.

The performance of other decentralized units may also affect the performance measure of an individual unit. For example, the efficiency of a manufacturing plant may be affected by the quantity and timing of output demanded from it, which is determined in part by the activities of a sales division. Solely under conditions of certainty, it can be argued that the performance measure of the manufacturing plant should not be affected by the activities of the selling division; effects due to variations in activity level should be the responsibility of the sales division, not the manufacturing unit. But once we recognize conditions of uncertainty and private information, it is no longer obvious that the manufacturing plant's performance measure should be made independent of sales activity. We argued earlier that there are nonprice characteristics of transactions from one unit to another, especially quality and timeliness. Therefore, the performance of the manufacturing division could affect the performance of the sales division in ways that are difficult to capture in a price system (because of uncertainty, lack of observability, and so on). One remedy would be for part of the performance measure of the manufacturing division to depend on the level of sales. Such a measure would provide strong incentives for manufacturing and sales managers to coordinate their decisions. More generally, the performance measure of individual local units could include a component reflecting the performance of other organizational units and, perhaps, the overall corporation. This would provide an incentive for managers of individual units to cooperate, avoid unnecessary frictions, and emphasize a corporate rather than a local viewpoint when managing their operations. For example, Dent has described a company where product development managers were held responsible for the sales revenues of the products they developed, and sales managers were held responsible for the development costs of the products they sold.[10] We will return to the local versus corporate performance measurement debate when we discuss models of incentive contracts in Chapter 17.

Overconsumption of Perquisites

A further problem arises in decentralization if a local manager with discretionary spending authority consumes an excessive amount of perquisites. For example, the manager may decide to improve his local working environment by acquiring a large, expensively decorated office space, by hiring an unnecessarily large number of administrative assistants and support personnel, and by purchasing the latest and most elaborate office equipment. These expenditures will reduce the manager's performance measure, but the manager may prefer the direct consumption of these perquisites to the perhaps small increase in pecuniary compensation that could be earned by forgoing these expenditures.

---

[10] See Jeremy Dent, "Tension in the Design of Formal Control Systems: A Field Study in a Computer Company," in *Accounting & Management: Field Study Perspectives*, ed. William Bruns and Robert S. Kaplan (Boston: Harvard Business School Press, 1987), Chap. 5.

Also, some managers may engage in an activity called empire building, which attempts to increase the size of the organization they are managing. The nonpecuniary rewards from empire building include the increased power and prestige associated with managing a larger organization. These nonpecuniary factors can even become pecuniary if the managers' compensation or promotion probability is made an increasing function of the size of the units they are managing.

Summary

The complex environment in which business is conducted today makes it impossible for any but the smallest firm to be controlled centrally. Some degree of decentralization will be essential to capture the benefits from the specialized information and response flexibility of local managers. Decentralization also conserves the scarce time of the top executives and frees them from making complex, interdependent resource-allocation decisions. Providing local managers with discretion in managing their operations has the additional benefits of developing their capabilities as general managers and making their daily job more interesting.

Decentralization can take many forms. Repetitive processes producing well-specified and easily measured outputs can be managed as standard cost centers, where the manager must meet externally generated demands for products according to a cost-minimizing, efficient standard. Marketing departments can be organized as revenue centers with the objective of meeting targeted goals in sales revenue, market share, or contribution margin. Some functions for which the output is not easily measurable or where the outputs are not causally and deterministically related to the inputs expended cannot be controlled by the use of traditional techniques such as standard costs or budgets. These functions are usually organized as discretionary expense centers in which the level of expenditures and the number of personnel are determined by negotiation with the central management to determine appropriate levels of quality and service. Much greater decentralization can occur when an operating unit is given responsibility both for acquiring inputs and for selling or distributing its outputs. Such units can be organized as profit or investment centers.

While decentralization seems essential for organizing complex operations, it introduces many problems of its own. Local managers are evaluated with a performance measure that captures some but not all of the economic consequences of their decisions. Therefore, managers may engage in dysfunctional behavior, failing to internalize the effects of their decisions on other organizational units or on the future of the entire firm. Conflicts between decentralized units can arise over the transfer of goods.

All these problems are inherent costs of decentralization. We would prefer to have easy solutions to them, but the current state of the art does not provide any. The best we can do is to understand the costs as well as the benefits of decentralization, keeping alert to situations where narrow-minded local optimizing performance or misrepresentation of local information is significantly impairing the overall well-being of the firm. The challenge is to devise the right combination of delegation of effort and decision making, observation of effort, and reward or incentive schemes to balance the benefits and costs of decentralization. Such a balance requires the judgment and experience of the owners and senior managers of the organization.

PROBLEMS

13–1   Decentralizing Decision Making in a Large Organization

"We just could not react fast enough within the corporate structure," said Charles F. McErlean, Executive Vice-President and Chief Operating Officer of United Airlines.* Mr. McErlean was describing the motivation for decentralizing United Airlines' management structure. United, the largest airline in the U.S., had just split its route structure into three semiautonomous regions: Western, Central, and Eastern. The three regional divisions would compete with other airlines for passengers and with each other for earnings performance. In addition, 1,700 cost centers were identified and their individual managers made responsible for productivity and cost control.

Edward Carlson, the CEO of United Airlines, claimed "our people out in the field really know their own immediate operations so much better than we do at headquarters. We can provide over-all direction, but they can better make most of the routine decisions." These daily decisions included marketing programs, advertising levels and copy, service levels between cities in the region, type of in-flight meals served, and personnel staffing requirements.

The separation of United into three regional divisions created some surprises. The Central and Western regions discovered that their main competition came from other regional airlines (such as Continental and Western) rather than United's traditional transcontinental rivals American Airlines and TWA. Also, regional managers looked much harder at aircraft allocation decisions. The Denver regional manager revealed, "I wanted very much to put a 747 on the Denver-Hawaii trip but I knew there would be

---

* "How United Airlines Pulled Out of Its Dive," *Business Week* (June 29, 1974), pp. 66–70.

$350,000 in expenses for ground equipment charged to my income statement before the first planeload left. I decided to postpone a 747 flight for at least a year." Before the implementation of decentralized operations, the decision as to which routes would receive the latest aircraft were made centrally, based on proposals prepared and submitted by marketing managers around the country.

The new operating system was not without its costs. There was the expected confusion and disruption caused by an almost overnight switch from a highly centralized company, with nine executives making all important decisions, to a divisional and decentralized mode of operation. McErlean admitted, "It took a year for all the problems to work themselves out." The firm also greatly expanded its information and reporting system. The 1700 cost centers, which formerly operated with quarterly reports, had to institute a monthly reporting cycle and, in some cases, weekly or even daily summary of operations.

Required:

1. Comment, using the framework introduced in this chapter, on the motivation for decentralization at United Airlines. How would decentralization improve the performance and profitability of the airline? Is it possible to decentralize virtually all of the operating decisions for United Airlines?
2. What costs or difficulties were introduced by decentralizing decision making at United Airlines? Why was there an increase in the information collected and analyzed by United's managers?

13–2   *Emphasis on Short-Term Performance*

"A lot of what is preached at business schools today is absolute rot," claimed a New York financial consultant; ". . . Business schools teach that business is nothing but the numbers—and the numbers only for the next quarter."*

The overemphasis on short-term performance measures was echoed by other critics, "There has been too much emphasis on short-term profit, not enough on long-range planning, too much on financial maneuvering, not enough on the technology of producing goods; too much on readily available markets, not enough on international development."

One U.S. expert on productivity added, "Our managers still earn generally high marks for their skill in improving short-term efficiency, but their counterparts in Europe and Japan have started to question America's entrepreneurial imagination and willingness to make risky, long-term investments."

---

* "The Money Chase, *Time* (May 4, 1981), pp. 58–65.

Finally, even foreign executives criticized the U.S. system, "The misguided emphasis on short-term profit seems to blind U.S. managers to the need for more research and development; moreover, they appear unable to develop strategies for dealing with long-range problems of chronic inflation and soaring energy costs. Also the quality of U.S. manufactured goods is declining because managers have cared less about what they produce than about selling it."

Required:

1. Are business schools, in general, and cost accounting/management control courses, in particular, to blame for the alleged preoccupation of recent business school graduates with measurable short-term performance? What conditions provide the environment for short-term rather than long-term optimizing behavior?
2. What forces provide explanations for the accusations that U.S. managers are more concerned with short-term "safe" strategies rather than longer-term risky, entrepreneurial strategies?
3. What are the implications of these charges for the design of management control systems in decentralized organizations?

13–3   Cost and Profit Centers

Laitier S.A.

"It is terribly frustrating to be evaluated as a profit center when I do not have complete control over revenues," said Henri Goudal, Managing Director of Laitier S.A. "The Export Division is responsible for over 75 percent of our total sales. They determine the price, the destination and the quantity of most of the milk we sell. We have no direct authority over that department, yet we are held responsible when sales are poor. If they do not perform up to expectations, then we cannot meet the budgeted profit target for which we are held responsible by headquarters."

Company Background

Laitier S.A. was a Belgian-based subsidiary of Universal Brands, a widely diversified U.S. food manufacturer. Of Laitier's fiscal 1975 sales of 2,300 million Belgian francs, 2,140 million (93 percent) were milk products, 90 million (4 percent) were metal cans, and 70.0 million (3 percent) were pet food products. Laitier had two milk processing plants in Belgium, one making evaporated milk and the other condensed (sweetened) milk. These

This case was prepared by William A. Sahlman under the supervision of Professor M. Edgar Barrett. Copyright © 1975 by the President and Fellows of Harvard College. Harvard Business School case 9–176–118.

plants supplied products for export to more than 80 countries spread throughout Eastern Europe, Africa, the Pacific Basin and Central and South America. No milk products were sold within Belgium.

Laitier also had a can manufacturing plant in Belgium. Half of the output of that plant was used internally, and half was sold to outside customers, including Universal's German subsidiary. Finally, Laitier was in the process of introducing a line of Denmark-manufactured pet food products into the Belgian market.

Approximately 76 percent of Laitier's total milk production in terms of volume (72 percent of milk product revenues) was evaporated milk. The remaining 24 percent (28 percent) was condensed milk. Both products were sold to two different categories of outlets. The first category was foreign governments who purchased large quantities of milk for distribution to the poor. The second category for Laitier was the more traditional retail-oriented distribution network. That is, Laitier's products were sold to local distributing agents in each country who would in turn sell the milk to retail outlets.

Sales destined for retail distribution were handled by Universal's Export Division, a separate company from Laitier. Both companies were located in Brussels, Belgium. The Export Division was headed by a General Manager who reported directly to the Vice-President of Marketing at Universal Headquarters in Chicago. The General Manager of the Export Division had no formal reporting relationship with the Managing Director of Laitier, though it was necessary to coordinate the activities of the two groups. Well over 75 percent of Laitier's unit production (and of milk product revenues) was channelled through the Export Division. The Export Division also handled export sales for other European Universal subsidiaries.[1]

The remainder of Laitier's milk production was sold by an internal marketing group (See Exhibit 1). Generally, these sales were made directly to foreign governments which distributed the milk to the poor. This business was done on a bid basis, with Laitier submitting a bid directly to the foreign government, usually on a large quantity of milk. Laitier was also directly in charge of one or two markets in which the milk was intended for retail distribution. However, sales to these markets were small in relation to total sales.

The Production Process

The production process at Laitier was relatively simple. Laitier did not own any dairy farms. The company purchased milk from farmers in the area around the processing plant. There were no formal contracts between

---

[1] As a separate company, the Export Division was not actually required to handle the milk products of Laitier. They could handle the milk from whichever Universal subsidiary had the lowest overall cost and wished to sell through them.

EXHIBIT 1
Laitier S.A.

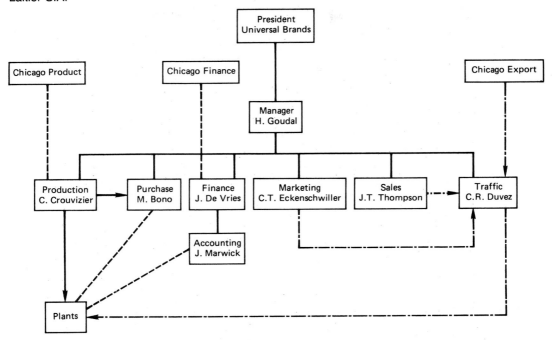

Laitier and the farmers, though the company had established a very strong, long-term relationship with its milk suppliers. As a result, Laitier felt that it had a moral if not a legal commitment to purchase all the milk produced by these farmers.

The raw milk was processed by Laitier at one of its two plants, one for evaporated milk and the other for condensed milk.[2] Within these two broad product categories, several variations were possible. Laitier had three standard levels of fat content milk, which it could produce according to market needs. Laitier could also produce several different standard sugar content levels in its condensed milk.

The processed milk was put into a number of standard containers. Laitier used six different sizes of tin cans and three different sizes of paper cartons. Beginning in 1972, Laitier produced its own cans, supplying ap-

---

[2] Laitier always had the option of turning the raw milk it purchased into a less processed product such as butter. Laitier might make this kind of intermediate conversion if it believed it had an excess supply of milk or could make larger profit in the butter than an evaporated or condensed milk.

proximately one-half its can needs from this source. Cartons were purchased from outside sources.

Because Laitier's products were sold in a very large number of countries, labelling created some difficulties. Laitier purchased labels from a local printer who could react quickly to their needs. Labels were printed directly on the cartons by the carton manufacturer, who also could provide the necessary flexibility to Laitier.

Once packaged, the milk was prepared for shipping by Laitier. Depending upon the final destination, the milk had different packaging requirements. Laitier was responsible for arranging for all transportation of its products, including those sold through the Export Division, to the port of final destination.

Raw Milk: Intervention Prices and Restitutions

Because raw milk was such an important cost component for Laitier, the process by which milk prices were set was of crucial importance. The price Laitier paid for raw milk was determined during periodic negotiations between all the milk users and the farmers in the region around each plant. The Belgium Government did not directly control raw milk prices. However, the European Economic Community did influence the level of prices through a system of EEC "intervention prices" for intermediate milk products (e.g., butter or powdered milk). Essentially, the EEC Agricultural Committee set a price for powdered milk, for example, which gave the farmer the option of selling his milk in unprocessed form or converting his raw milk to powdered milk and selling it directly to the EEC at the intervention price.[3,4] Because the farmer always had the option to sell to the EEC, he would not accept too low a price for his milk from processors like Laitier.

The system of intervention prices designed by the EEC was intended to maintain income stability for the farmers. However, the resulting raw milk prices were higher than those in New Zealand or in the United States, both of which were larger exporters of processed milk. In order to make EEC produced milk products competitive in the world market, the EEC had to subsidize exports through a system of restitutions. A restitution was a rebate given to processors like Laitier when they delivered their products outside the EEC. The level of restitutions was set by the EEC Agricultural Committee in Brussels and could amount to as much as one-third of the raw milk cost (See Exhibit 2). Even after restitutions, raw milk could represent as much as 50 percent of Laitier's manufacturing cost.

---

[3] Laitier also had the option of converting some of its raw milk supply into powdered milk, for example, if it believed this was a more profitable alternative than processing the milk.

[4] In the last few years, the EEC had accumulated a surplus supply of powdered milk amounting to 1 million tons. This milk was to be distributed as development aid.

EXHIBIT 2
Laitier S.A.

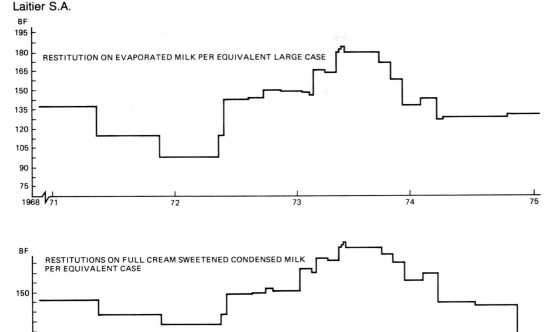

When the intervention price levels were changed, the restitutions generally were also changed. However, there was always considerable uncertainty about the extent to which higher raw milk costs would be offset by increased restitutions.

Because the levels of intervention prices and restitutions were sensitive political issues within the EEC, planning at companies like Laitier was very difficult. To facilitate planning for milk processors, the EEC allowed exporters to "pre-fix" a restitution for the next six months. To illustrate, Laitier could tell the EEC it intended to export a certain amount of evaporated milk in the next six months. The EEC would then guarantee a restitution for that period for that quantity of exports. Unfortunately, if the intervention price increased during the six months, then Laitier was faced with higher milk costs with no relief from an increased subsidy. Also, if Laitier did not export the quantity of milk products it originally estimated with the EEC, then it was penalized, and actually had to pay a fine to the

TABLE 1

Laitier S.A.—Belgium Monthly Export Cost Estimates[2]

Date: August 10, 1975	Local Currency—BFr.[3] Evaporated Milk—9.0% Butter Fat		Local Currency—BFr.[3] Condensed (Sweetened) Milk	
	Large Cases	Small Cases	8% Butter Fat	Skim
Line				
1. Cases Available August September October November				
2. Milk cost	427.50	354.82	364.52	213.14
2a. Sugar	—	—	146.61	144.45
3. Packaging Material	107.80	115.81	96.71	93.02
4. TOTAL MATERIAL COST	535.30	470.63	607.84	450.61
5. Miscellaneous[1]	27.41	24.95	36.65	30.65
6. Restitution	148.76	123.05	123.35	26.95
7. TOTAL OUT OF POCKET COST	413.95	372.53	521.14	454.31

[1] Fuel, power, freight and interest expense, among others.

[2] All figures have been disguised.

[3] At time of case, one U.S. dollar was equal to approximately 39 Belgian Francs.

EEC. Laitier, of course, always had the option of not pre-fixing the restitution if it believed that the intervention price would increase in the near future. The hope was that the restitution would also increase, thus protecting Laitier from the higher milk costs.

In order for Laitier to determine its restitution policy and its milk and other raw materials needs, it was very important to obtain accurate forecasts of milk product sales. As noted previously, Laitier depended on the Export Division for the sales of over 75 percent of its milk production. Thus, Laitier had to rely on sales estimates from the Export division to do its planning.

The process by which sales estimates were made at Laitier involved two iterative steps. First, Laitier provided unit manufacturing cost estimates to the Export Division. A distinction was made between fixed and variable costs in order to allow the marketing people to base their pricing decisions on the contribution margin of each product (See Table 1). The Traffic Department within Laitier also provided estimates of shipping costs to each of the export markets.[5] The Export Division then provided sales price

---

[5] Transportation costs could be as high as 30% of the cost of the finished product.

and volume estimates by product line for each market to Laitier. The process involved a certain degree of negotiation between the Export Division and Laitier, though it was difficult for Laitier to question the accuracy of the Export Division's forecasts.

The internal marketing group at Laitier also had to estimate sales of milk products generated internally. These estimates—when combined with those generated by the Export Division—formed the basis for production, purchasing and restitution policy at Laitier.

Budgeting and Performance Evaluation

The process of forecasting revenues, costs and therefore profits was formalized in Laitier's budgeting system. In August of each year, Laitier submitted to corporate headquarters a complete budget package for the next two fiscal years as well as a profit estimate for the third year.[6] The top management of Laitier made an oral presentation of Laitier's budget to Universal's management.[7] The final budget was arrived at through a process of negotiation between Laitier, the Export Division and Universal's management.

In addition to the initial budget, every month Laitier prepared a revised forecast of the current fiscal year. Every three months, a new budget for the current fiscal year was prepared. Finally, in February of each year, Laitier also submitted a revised budget for the next fiscal year (in addition to the revised budget for the rest of the current fiscal year).

These budgets formed the basis for performance evaluation of Laitier during the year. Universal required two different types of reports from Laitier. First, every month Laitier had to submit a brief (5–6 page) summary of its operations. Second, each quarter Laitier had to submit a series of reporting forms. The first group of forms showed the most recent budget (a complete income statement) for the next fiscal year, the revised forecast and the original budget for the current fiscal year, and the actual results for the previous fiscal year. These reports were also broken out by major product group. That is, detailed sales, costs and operating profit before tax estimates for such product groups as evaporated milk, condensed milk, pet food and cans would be shown (See Table 2).

A second series of forms showed the marketing expenses in aggregate and for each major product line. Marketing expenses included advertising, promotion, selling, distribution, commissions, and market research expenses. A third series of forms was devoted to non-operating income and expenses and to such miscellaneous items as tax computation, foreign exchange transactions and inventories.

---

[6] Laitier operated on an October 1 to September 30 fiscal year.

[7] Beginning in 1975, the Export Division manager was scheduled to be present at the budget presentation to Universal management.

TABLE 2
Laitier S.A. Statement of Profit and Loss[1]

		Fiscal 1976		Revised Fiscal 1975		Actual Fiscal 1974	
		PRODUCT—EVAPORATED EXPORT[2]					
1	Net Sales in Cases	2,422,000	Per Unit	2,262,060	Per Unit	2,006,973	Per Unit
2	Gross Sales Less Returns	1,666,505	688.07	1,453,312	642.49	1,170,161	583.04
3	Distribution Expenses	260,728	107.65	212,153	93.79	137,239	68.38
4	Trade Payments	7,823	3.23	6,628	2.93	9,272	4.62
5	Taxes and Duties						
6	Net Sales	1,397,954	577.19	1,234,531	545.77	1,023,650	510.04
7	Cost of Sales	1,258,471	519.60	1,084,742	479.55	971,158	483.89
8	Gross Profit	139,483	57.59	149,790	66.22	52,492	26.15
9	Selling Expenses	48,852	20.17	40,264	17.80	30,286	15.09
10	General Expenses	24,995	10.32	18,616	8.23	16,076	8.01
11	Operating Profit	65,636	27.10	90,910	40.19	6,130	32.96
		PRODUCT—CONDENSED EXPORT[2]					
12	Net Sales in Cases	452,300	Per Unit	511,792	Per Unit	482,804	Per Unit
13	Gross Sales Less Returns	380,340	841.46	381,701	745.51	328,025	679.14
14	Distribution Expenses	32,924	72.84	25,231	49.28	17,180	35.57
15	Trade Payments	556	1.23	394	0.77	816	1.69
16	Taxes and Duties						
17	Net Sales	346,860	767.39	356,076	695.46	310,029	641.88
18	Cost of Sales	324,441	717.79	331,791	648.03	278,338	576.27
19	Gross Profit	22,419	49.60	24,285	47.43	31,691	65.61
20	Selling Expenses	9,257	20.48	6,164	12.04	5,356	11.09
21	General Expenses	6,197	13.71	6,103	11.92	4,907	10.16
22	Operating Profit	6,965	15.41	12,018	24.49	21,428	44.36
		PRODUCT—EVAPORATED OWN TRADE[2]					
1	Net Sales in Cases	427,000	Per Unit	374,040	Per Unit	196,781	Per Unit
2	Gross Sales Less Returns	269,411	630.94	223,529	597.67	98,811	501.58
3	Distribution Expenses	26,961	63.14	23,270	62.22	4,399	22.33
4	Trade Payments	3,484	8.16	3,856	10.31	2,488	12.63
5	Taxes and Duties						
6	Net Sales	238,966	559.64	196,403	525.14	91,924	466.62
7	Cost of Sales	225,486	528.07	181,715	485.87	91,711	465.54
8	Gross Profit	13,480	31.57	14,688	39.27	213	1.08
9	Selling Expenses	2,434	5.70	1,952	5.22	1,062	5.39
10	General Expenses	4,274	10.01	3,403	9.10	1,426	7.24
11	Operating Profit	6,772	15.86	9,332	24.95	(2,275)	(11.55)

TABLE 2
Laitier S.A. Statement of Profit and Loss[1]   (continued)

		PRODUCT—CONDENSED OWN TRADE[2]				
12	*Net Sales in Cases*	*320,000 Per Unit*		*320,256 Per Unit*		*361,453 Per Unit*
13	Gross Sales Less Returns	279,910	874.72	240,486	751.52	255,844 708.71
14	Distribution Expenses	19,466	60.83	13,059	40.81	8,949 24.79
15	Trade Payments	1,331	4.16	2,557	7.99	2,170 6.01
16	Taxes and Duties					
17	Net Sales	259,113	809.73	224,870	702.72	244,725 677.91
18	Cost of Sales	230,877	721.49	210,678	658.37	213,647 591.82
19	Gross Profit	28,236	88.24	14,192	44.35	31,078 86.09
20	Selling Expenses	1,872	5.85	2,266	7.08	2,058 5.70
21	General Expenses	4,483	14.01	3,648	11.40	3,892 10.78
22	Operating Profit	21,881	68.38	8,278	25.87	25,128 69.61

[1] All figures in this Table have been disguised.

[2] "Export" sales were those handled directly by the Export Division. "Own Trade" sales were those handled by Laitier's marketing group.

A fourth series of forms was devoted to a detailed explanation of each item in the total company and individual product line profit and loss budgets. Laitier was required to make and analyze three comparisons. First, the most recent budget for the next fiscal year was compared to the revised budget for the current fiscal year. Each significant change from one year to the next had to be explained (See Table 3). The second required comparison was between the most recent revised budget for the current fiscal year and the original budget for the same year. Finally the most recent revised current year budget was compared with the actual prior year results.

A final series of reports was devoted to presenting and analyzing the most recent detailed manufacturing and packing cost budget for each product sold within each major product line. As with the profit and loss budgets, Laitier was required to make a series of comparisons of each significant cost item with prior budgets and with actual results from the previous year.

In summary, Laitier was responsible for preparing the initial budget and subsequent revisions thereof. The Export Division supplied volume and price estimates for each market it controlled, and Laitier did the same for its own markets. In addition, Laitier supplied all the transportation and production cost forecasts. Laitier was also responsible for preparing the reporting forms for submission to Universal. The comparative analysis required on those forms was done by Laitier. The Export Division was asked by Laitier to explain any significant volume or price variations from budget, and their explanations were included in Laitier's reporting forms.

Laitier was evaluated by Universal as a profit center, just as were each

TABLE 3
Laitier S.A. Profit & Loss Budget & Fiscal 1975 & 1976[1]
August 1st, 1975

Detailed P & L Budget Commentary
FISCAL 1976 VERSUS REVISED FISCAL 1975[2]
Evaporated (Exports)

Line No.

1   Fiscal 1976 shows a sales volume increase of 159,940 cases. Most significant changes:
     Decrease: Jamaica 117,000,Chad 34,000, Botswana 63,500
     Increase: Nigeria 257,000, Turkey 46,440, Okinawa 26,000, Angola 20,390, Rhodesia 24,610

2   Total *Gross Sales* per unit for fiscal 1976 is BFr. 45.58 higher, viz.
     Gross sales—Excl. restitutions
     (a result of increased selling prices) 67.38
     Export restitutions (reduced) (21.80)
     The calculations included the last known restitution rates and are those effective as from March 26, 1975.

3   *Distribution expenses* per unit for fiscal 1976 in BFr. 13.86 higher.
     This can be attributed to the ever increasing freight rates since October 1974.

Condensed (Exports)

12   Fiscal 1976 sales volume is 59,492 cases lower.
     Increase: Taiwan 68,241
     Decrease: Trinidad 98,133, Botswana 29,600

13   Total *Gross Sales* per unit for fiscal 1976 is BFr. 95.95 higher, viz.
     Gross sales (excl. restitutions)
     The calculations included the last known restitution rates and are those effective as from March 26, 1975.
     The apparently high increase of gross sales per unit in fiscal 1976 is mainly due to the impact of the Bangladesh tender (100,000) in fiscal 1975 at the low selling price $8.04 = BFr. 313.56
     When omitting such Bangladesh sales the increase per unit mainly caused by the fact that in fiscal 1975 the restitutions on the above mentioned Bangladesh sales were "pre-fixed" at a high rate of BFr. 199.60

14   *Distribution expenses* per unit for fiscal 1976 is BFr. 23.56 higher.
     When omitting the Bangladesh business (fob deliveries) the increase per unit for fiscal 1976 will only amount to BFr. 1.47
     Such a relatively minor increase in 1976 can be attributed to a higher incidence of fob shipments.

20   *Selling expenses* per unit for fiscal 1976 is BFr. 8.44 higher.
     The aparently lower expense per unit for fiscal 1975 is mainly caused by the impact of the Bangladesh sales at a low BFr. 1.85 commission per unit on 100,000 cases.
     When omitting the impact of the Bangladesh commissions the increase in selling expenses would be some BFr. 2.77 only and this can be explained by commissions on the higher average gross selling price per unit in fiscal 1976.

Evaporated—Own Trade

1   Sales volume in fiscal 1976 increased by 52,960 cases mainly due to:
     Increase: Bulgaria 10,760, Venezuela 69,000
     Decrease: Tunisia 26,800

TABLE 3 (continued)
Laitier S.A. Profit & Loss Budget & Fiscal 1975 & 1976[1]

2	Total *Gross Sales* per unit in fiscal 1976 is BFr. 33.27 higher, due to an increase in selling price per unit of BFr. 42.39 and a reduction in restitution rates of BFr. 9.12
	The calculations include the last known restitution rates and are those in effect from March 26, 1975.
	Condensed—Own Trade
12	*Sales volume* in fiscal 1976 decreased by 256 cases mainly due to increased sales to Venezuela of 13,100 cases and reduced sales to Bulgaria of 11,000 cases and to Angola of 1,744 cases.
13	Total *Gross Sales* per unit for fiscal 1976 is BFr. 123.20 higher due to increased unit selling prices by BFr. 141.99 and to reduced restitution rates by BFr. 18.79.
14	*Distribution expenses* increased by BFr. 20.02 per case in 1976 due to increased freight rates.

[1] All of the locations and figures in this Table have been disguised.

[2] Similar forms were also used to compare Revised 1975 with Actual 1974 and Revised 1975 with Original Budget 1975.

of Universal's other foreign subsidiaries. The Export Division was also treated by Universal as a profit center. Henri Goudal, Managing Director of Laitier, was evaluated by Universal on his performance relative to the budgets negotiated by Universal and Laitier. These budgets (and Laitier's reported results) covered the entire Laitier operation. Thus, the full financial impact of the sales handled for Laitier by the Export Division were included. The Export Division also received credit for these sales and their resultant contribution to profit.

The Informal Discussion

In early September 1975 Mr. Henri Goudal and the Finance Manager of Laitier, Mr. Jan de Vries, discussed Universal's performance evaluation of Laitier with the casewriters. The conversation began when a casewriter asked Mr. Goudal for his opinion about the treatment of Laitier as a profit center. The following is a paraphrased summary of that discussion.

Goudal: Conceptually, I believe treating a subsidiary as a profit center is a very useful way to motivate managers. The problem arises, however, that, as presently organized, Laitier is not completely in control of its profits. This makes it difficult to view us as one might view some other subsidiary. For example, the other Universal subsidiaries in Europe do the bulk of their business in their domestic markets. They only export what they cannot use domestically.

Unfortunately, Laitier has not been able to operate in the Belgian market, primarily because it is incredibly price competitive. We cannot make an adequate return on our investment by selling milk products domestically. As a result, we are very much dependent on the Export Division for our sales.

However, as I said before, I have no direct authority over that department. They are responsible only to the Vice-President of Marketing back in Chicago.

De Vries: I agree with Henri. In the processed milk business, the revenues are the crucial determinants of profitability. Many of our costs are either fixed or extremely difficult to control. For example, our labor costs are only controllable in the long-run. We cannot fire people as one can in the U.S.

We can only decrease our labor force through attrition, and even that is sometimes difficult. Also, because the union we deal with bargains at the national level with all milk processors, we have very little impact on the cost of labor.

Similarly, the cost of milk, which represents a very large proportion of our total manufacturing cost, cannot really be controlled by Laitier. The EEC basically determines our cost both by setting the intervention price and by fixing restitutions. All we can try to do is to predict EEC policy. We certainly cannot control it.

The point is that revenues are the primary factor in the profitability of our milk business. If revenues are bad, then so are our profits.

Casewriter: How does your relationship with the Export Division affect the budgeting process?

De Vries: We supply the Export Division with an estimate of our production and shipping costs. They, in turn, give us their volume and price forecasts. The problem is that it is very difficult for us to assess the reasonableness of their predictions. In the past, we have discovered that they have almost always been too optimistic. Our response to that problem has been to put reserves into our profit and loss forecast. If we didn't put in reserves, we would not be able to meet our profit target.

Goudal: One response on our part to the overall problem of not fully controlling our own destiny has been to try to exercise more control over our profits. Introducing the pet food line is an example. We wanted both to diversify away from milk products and to be solely responsible for one business venture. Our can plant provides the same diversification benefits and gives us a lower packaging cost in our milk business. We also make a very respectable profit on our external sales of cans. We have hired an extra marketing fellow here at Laitier to investigate other diversification possibilities.

13–4   *Empire Glass Company (A)*

In fall 1963 Peter Small of the Harvard Business School began to write case material on the budgetary control system of the Empire Glass Company, a manufacturing company with a number of plants located throughout Canada. In particular, Peter Small was interested in how James Walker, the corporate controller, saw the company's budgetary control system. Therefore, Small focused his research on the budgetary control system in relationship to the company's Glass Products Division. This division was responsible for manufacturing and selling glass food-and-beverage bottles.

Organization

Empire Glass company was a diversified company organized into several major product divisions, one of which was the Glass Products Division. Each division was headed by a vice president who reported directly to the company's executive vice president, Landon McGregor. (*Figure A* shows an organization chart of the company's top management group.) All of the corporate and divisional management groups were located in British City, Canada.

McGregor's corporate staff included three people in the financial area—the controller, the chief accountant, and the treasurer. The controller's department consisted of only two people—Walker and the assistant controller, Allen Newell. The market research and labor relations departments also reported in a staff capacity to McGregor.

All of the product divisions were organized along similar lines. Reporting to each product division vice president were several staff members in the customer service and product research areas. Reporting in a line capacity to each divisional vice president were also a general manager of manufacturing (responsible for all of the division's manufacturing activities) and a general manager of marketing (responsible for all of the division's marketing activities). Both of these executives were assisted by a small staff of specialists. *Figure B* presents an organization chart of the Glass Products Division's top management group. *Figure C* shows the typical organization structure of a plant within the Glass Products Division.

Products and Technology

The Glass Products Division operated a number of plants in Canada, producing glass food-and-beverage bottles. Of these products, food jars con-

This case was prepared by Assistant Professor David F. Hawkins. Copyright © 1964 by the President and Fellows of Harvard College. Harvard Business School case 9–109–043.

FIGURE A
Top Management Group

stituted the largest group. Milk bottles, as well as beer and soft drink bottles were also produced in large quantities. A great variety of shapes and sizes of containers for wines, liquors, drugs, cosmetics, and chemicals were produced in smaller quantities.

Most of the thousands of different products, varying in size, shape, color, and decoration, were produced to order. According to British City executives, the typical lead time between the customer's order and shipment from the plant was between two and three weeks during 1963.

The principal raw materials for container glass were sand, soda ash, and lime. The first step in the manufacturing process was to melt batches of these materials in furnaces or tanks. The molten mass was then passed into automatic or semiautomatic machines which filled molds with the molten glass and blew the glass into the desired shape. The "ware" then went through an automatic annealing oven or lehr where it was cooled slowly under carefully controlled conditions. If the glass was to be coated on the exterior to increase its resistance to abrasion and scratches, this coating—often a silicone film—was applied in the lehr. Any decorating (such as a trademark or other design) was then added, the product inspected again, and the finished goods packed in corrugated containers (or wooden cases for some bottles).

FIGURE B
Glass Products Division—Top Management and Staff

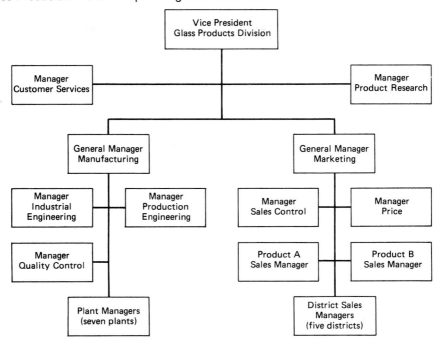

Quality inspection was critical in the manufacturing process. If the melt in the furnace was not completely free from bubbles and stones (unmelted ingredients or pieces of refractory material), or if the fabricating machinery was slightly out of adjustment, or molds were worn, the rejection rate was very high. Although a number of machines were used in the inspection process, including electric eyes, much of the inspection was still done visually.

While glass making was one of the oldest arts and bottles and jars had been machine-molded at relatively high speeds for over half a century, the Glass Products Division had spent substantial sums each year modernizing its equipment. These improvements had greatly increased the speed of operations and had reduced substantially the visual inspection and manual handling of glassware.

No hand blowing was done in the division's plants; contrary to the early days of the industry, most of the jobs were relatively unskilled, highly repetitive, and gave the worker little control over work methods or pace. The mold makers who made and repaired the molds, the machine repairers, and those who made the equipment setup changes between different products were considered to be the highest skilled classes of workers.

FIGURE C
Glass Products Division—Typical Plant Organization

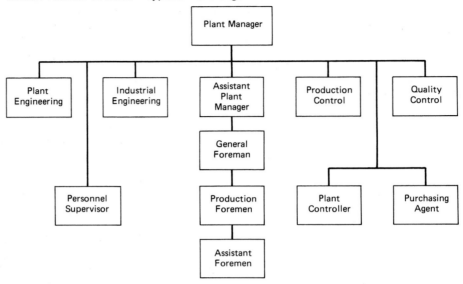

Wages were relatively high in the glass industry. The rumble of the machinery and the hiss of compressed air in the molding operation, however, plus the roar of fuel in the furnaces, made the plants extremely noisy. The great amount of heat given off by the furnaces and molten glass also made working conditions difficult. Production employees belonged to two national unions and for many years bargaining had been conducted on a national basis. Output standards were established for all jobs, but no bonus was paid to hourly plant workers for exceeding standard.

Marketing

Over the years, the sales of the Glass Products Division had grown at a slightly faster rate than had the total market for glass containers. Until the late 1950s, the division had charged a premium for most of its products, primarily because they were of better quality than competitive products. In later years, however, the quality of the competitive products had improved to the point where they matched the division's quality level. In the meantime, the division's competitors had retained their former price structure. Consequently, the Glass Products Division had been forced to lower its prices to meet its competitors' lower market prices. According to one division executive: "Currently, price competition is not severe, particularly among the two or three larger companies that dominate the glass bottle industry. Most of our competition is with respect to product quality and customer service. In fact, our biggest competitive threat is from containers other than glass."

Each of the division's various plants to some extent shipped its products throughout Canada, although transportation costs limited each plant's market primarily to its immediate vicinity. While some of the customers were large and bought in huge quantities, many were relatively small.

Budgetary Control System

In fall 1963 Peter Small interviewed James Walker, who had been the Empire Glass Company's controller for some 15 years. Excerpts from that interview are reproduced in the following sections.

Small: Mr. Walker, what is the overall function of your budgetary control system?

Walker: Well, Peter, to understand the role of the budgetary control systems you must first understand our management philosophy. Fundamentally, we have a divisional organization based on broad product categories. These divisional activities are coordinated by the company's executive vice president, with the head office group providing a policy and review function for the company's executive vice president.

Within the broad policy limits, we operate on a decentralized basis, with each of the decentralized divisions performing the full management job which normally would be inherent in any independent company. The only exception to this philosophy is that the head office group is solely responsible for the sources of funds and the labor relations with those bargaining units which cross division lines. Given this form of organization, the budget is the principal management tool used by head office to coordinate the efforts of the various segments of the company toward a common goal. Certainly, in our case, the budget is much more than a narrow statistical accounting device.

Sales Budget

Walker and Small discussed the preparation of the sales budget. This was the first step in the budget preparation procedure.

Walker: As early as May 15 of the year preceding the budget year, the top management of the company asks the various product division vice presidents to submit preliminary reports stating what they think their division's capital requirements and outlook in terms of sales and income will be during the next budget year. In addition, corporate top management also wants an expression of the division vice president's general feelings toward the trends in the particular items over the two years following the upcoming budget year. At this stage, head office is not interested in too much detail.

Small: Does the market research group get involved in these forecasts?

Walker: No. What we want is an interpretive statement about sales and income based on the operating executives' practical feel for the market. Since all divisions plan their capital requirements five years in advance and have made predictions of the forthcoming budget year's market when the budget estimates were prepared last year, these rough estimates of next year's conditions and requirements are far from wild guesses.

After the opinions of the divisional vice presidents are in, the market research staff goes to work. They develop a formal statement for the marketing climate in detail for the forthcoming budget year and in general terms for the subsequent two years.

Small: Putting together the sales forecast, then, is the first step in developing the budget?

Walker: Yes. This is an important first step since practically all of the forecasts or estimates used in planning either start with or depend in some way on a sales forecast.

The market research group begins by projecting such factors as: the general economic condition; growth of our various markets; weather conditions related to the end uses of our products; competitive effort; and labor disturbances.

Once these general factors have been assessed, a sales forecast for the company and each division is developed. Consideration is given to the relationship of the general economic climate to our customers' needs and Empire's share of each market. Also, basic assumptions as to price, weather conditions, and so forth, are developed and stated explicitly.

In sales forecasting, consideration is given also to the introduction of new products, gains or losses in particular accounts, forward buying, new manufacturing plants, and any changes in our definition of, say, gross sales.

The probable impact of information such as the following is also taken into account: industry growth trends, packaging trends, inventory carry-overs, and the development of alternative packages to or from glass.

This review of all the relevant factors is followed for each of our product lines, regardless of its size and importance. The completed forecasts of the market research group are then forwarded to the appropriate divisions for review, criticism, and adjustments.

Small: How would you summarize the role of the head office group in developing these sales forecasts?

Walker: Well, I suppose our primary goal is to assure uniformity between the divisions with respect to the basic assumptions on business conditions, pricing, and the treatment of possible emergencies. Also, we provide a yardstick so as to assure us that the company's overall sales forecast will be reasonable and obtainable.

Next, the product division top management goes back to its district sales managers. Each district sales manager is asked to tell his top management what he expects to do in the way of sales during the budget year. Head office and the divisional staffs will give the district sales managers as much guidance as they request, but it is the sole responsibility of each district sales manager to come up with his particular forecast.

After the district sales manager's forecasts are received by the divisional top management, the forecasts are consolidated and reviewed by the division's general manager of marketing. At this time the general manager of marketing may go back to the district sales managers and suggest they revise their budgets. For instance, a situation such as this might arise: We enjoy a very large share of the liquor market. In one year, however, it may be predicted on the basis of the consolidated district sales manager's estimates that we can look forward to a 20%–25% increase in sales.

Obviously, this is unreasonable. What has happened is this: Each district sales manager has been told by each of his liquor customers that they expect an increase in sales. When all these anticipated individual sales increases are summed, it looks like the market is going to grow considerably. However, this is not going to happen. What is going to occur is that company A will take sales from company B and company C will take sales from company D, and so forth.

Individually, the district sales managers know little of what's happening outside their territory. However, from the headquarters' point of view, we can ascertain the size of the whole market and the customer's probable relative market share. That's where the market research group's studies come in handy.

Let me emphasize, however, even in this case nothing is changed in the district sales manager's budget, unless the district manager agrees. Then, once the budget is approved, nobody is relieved of his responsibility without top management approval. Also, no arbitrary changes are made in the approved budgets without the concurrence of all the people responsible for the budget.

Small: At this point, have the plant managers—or the divisional general managers of manufacturing—been involved in the preparation of the sales budget?

Walker: Not in a formal way. Informally, of course, the plant managers know what's going on. For example, when a plant manager prepares his capital equipment investment program he is sure to talk to the district sales manager closest to his plant about the district's sales plans.

Next, we go through the same process at the division and headquarters levels. We keep on repeating the process until everybody agrees the sales budgets are sound. Then, each level of management takes responsibility for its particular portion of the budget. These sales budgets then become fixed objectives.

Small: Besides coming up with a realistic sales budget, what other objectives do the divisions have in mind when they review the sales forecasts?

Walker: I would say they have four general objectives in mind: First, a review of the division's competitive position, including plans for improving that position. Second, an evaluation of its efforts to gain either a larger share of the market or offset competitors' activities. Third, a consideration of the need to expand facilities to improve the division's products or introduce new products. Finally, a review and development of plans to improve product quality, delivery methods, and service.

Manufacturing Budgets

Walker and Small then turned their conversation to the preparation of the manufacturing budgets. According to Walker, each plant had a profit responsibility.

Small: When are the plant budgets prepared?

Walker: Once the vice presidents, executive vice president, and company president have given final approval to the sales budgets, we make a sales budget for each plant by breaking the division sales budget down according to the plants from which the finished goods will be shipped. These plant sales budgets are then further broken down on a monthly basis by price, volume, and end use. With this information available, the plants then budget their gross profit, fixed expenses, and income before taxes.

Small: How do you define gross profit and income?

Walker: Gross profit is the difference between gross sales, less discounts, and variable manufacturing costs—such as direct labor, direct material, and variable manufacturing overheads. Income is the difference between the gross profit and the fixed costs.

Small: Is the principal constraint within which the plants work the sales budget?

Walker: That's right. Given his sales budget, it is up to the plant manager to determine the fixed overhead and variable costs—at standard— that he will need to incur so as to meet the demands of the sales budget.
In some companies I know of, the head office gives each plant manager sales and income figures that the plant has to meet. We don't operate that way, however. We believe that type of directive misses the benefit of all the field experience of those at the district sales and plant levels. If we gave a profit figure to our plant managers to meet, how could we say it was their responsibility to meet it?
What we say to the plant managers is this: Assuming that you have to produce this much sales volume, how much do you expect to spend producing this volume? And what do you expect to spend for your programs allied to obtaining these current and future sales?

Small: Then the plant managers make their own plans?

Walker: Yes. In my opinion requiring the plant managers to make their own plans is one of the most valuable things associated with budget system. Each plant manager divides the preparation of the overall plant budget among his plant's various departments. First, the departments spell out the programs in terms of the physical requirements—such as tons of raw material—and then the plans are priced at standard cost.

Small: What items might some of these departmental budgets include?

Walker: Let me tell you about the phase of the budget preparation our industrial engineering people are responsible for. The plant industrial engineering department is assigned the responsibility for developing engineered cost standards and reduced costs. Consequently, the

phase of budget preparation covered by the industrial engineers includes budget standards of performance for each operation, cost
center, and department within the plant. This phase of the budget
also includes budget cost reductions, budgeted unfavorable variances
from standards, and certain budgeted programmed fixed costs in the
manufacturing area such as service labor. The industrial engineer
prepares this phase of the budget in conjunction with departmental
line supervision.

Small: Once the plant budgets are completed, are they sent directly to
the divisional top management?

Walker: No. Before each plant sends its budget into British City, a group
of us from head office goes out and visits each plant. For example,
in the case of the Glass Products Division, Allen [Newell, assistant
controller] and I, along with representatives of the Glass Products
division manufacturing staffs visit each of the division's plants.

Let me stress this point: We do not go on these trips to pass judgment
on the plant's proposed budget. Rather, we go with three purposes
in mind. First, we wish to acquaint ourselves with the thinking behind
the figures that each plant manager will send in to British City. This
is helpful because when we come to review these budgets with the
top management—that is, the management above our level—we will
have to answer questions about the budget, and we will know the
answers. Second, the review is a way of giving guidance to the plant
managers as to whether or not they are in line with what the company
needs to make in the way of profits.

Of course, when we make our field reviews we do not know what
each of the other plants is doing. Therefore, we explain to the plant
managers that, while their budget may look good now, when we put
all the plants together in a consolidated budget, the plant managers
may have to make some changes because the projected profit is not
high enough. When this happens we have to tell the plant managers
that it is not their programs that are unsound. The problem is that
the company cannot afford the programs.

I think it is very important that each plant manager has a chance to
tell his story. Also, it gives them the feeling that we at headquarters
are not living in an ivory tower.

Small: How long do these plant visits take?

Walker: They are spread over a three-week period and we spend an average
of half a day at each plant.

Small: I gather the role of the head office and divisional staff is to recommend, not decide. That's the plant manager's right.

Walker: Correct.

Small: Who on the plant staff attends these meetings?

Walker: The plant manager is free to bring in any of his supervisors he wishes. We asked him not to bring in anybody below the supervisory level. Then, of course, you get into organized labor.

Small: What do you do on these plant visits?

Walker: During the half-day we spend at each plant we discuss the budget primarily. However, if I have time, I like to wander through the plant and see how things are going. Also, I go over in great detail the property replacement and maintenance budget with the plant engineer.

Small: After you have completed the plant tours, do the plant budgets go to the respective division top management?

Walker: That's right. About September 1, the plant budgets come into British City and the accounting department consolidates them. Then the product division vice presidents review their respective divisional budgets to see if the division budget is reasonable in terms of what the vice president thinks the corporate top management wants. If he is not satisfied with the consolidated plant budgets, he will ask the various plants within the division to trim their budget figures. When the division vice presidents and the executive vice president are happy, they will send their budgets to the company president. He may accept the division budgets at this point. If he doesn't, he will specify the areas to be reexamined by division and, if necessary, plant management. The final budget is approved at our December board of directors' meeting.

Small: As I understand it, the district sales managers have a responsibility for sales.

Walker: Specifically volume, price, and sales mix.

Small: And the plant manager is responsible for manufacturing costs?

Walker: His primary responsibility extends to profits. The budgeted plant profit is the difference between the fixed sales dollar budget and the budgeted variable costs at standard and the fixed overhead budget.

EXHIBIT 3
Variance Analysis Sheet for Various Divisions and Plants

Line No.	Division or Plant	Budget Income	Gross Sales	Sales Price	Manufacturing Cost	Labor	Overtime	Employee Benefits	Outside Warehouse	Utilities	Overhaul and Repair	Depreciation, Rent, Insurance and Taxes	Controllable Plant Fixed Cost	Other Fixed Cost	Manufacturing Efficiency	Cost Reduction	Other Operating	Gains and Losses	Income From Seconds	Wage Changes	Price Changes	Division Expenses	Actual Income	Income Adjusted by Volume
1																								
2																								
3																								
4																								
5																								
6																								
7																								
8																								
9																								
10																								
11																								
12																								
13																								
14																								
15																								
16																								
17																								
18																								
19																								
20																								
21																								
22																								
23																								
24																								
25																								
26																								
27																								
28																								
29																								
30																								
31																								
32																								
33																								
34																								
35																								

Source: Company document

13–5 *Continental Can Company of Canada, Ltd. (B) (Abridged)*

By the fall of 1963 Continental Can Company of Canada had developed a sophisticated control system for use in its plants. This control system, begun in the years following World War II, stressed competition within the company as well as against other companies in the industry. Within its division at Continental, the can manufacturing plant at St. Laurent, Quebec, had become a preferred site for production management trainees as a result of its successful use of control systems. According to a division training executive, "The St. Laurent people look at the controls as tools. They show trainees that they really work. There are no secrets. Trainees can ask anyone anything, and the friendliness and company parties give them a feel for good employee relations."

The metal can industry was relatively stable, with little product differentiation. The St. Laurent plant to some extent shipped its products throughout Canada, although transportation costs limited its market primarily to eastern Canada. While some of the customers were large and bought in huge quantities (300–500 million cans), many were relatively small and purchased a more specialized product.

Plant Organization

Plant Management

Andrew Fox, plant manager at St. Laurent since 1961, had risen from an hourly worker through foreman up to plant manufacturing engineer in the maintenance of the business. He had developed an intimate first-hand knowledge of operations and was frequently seen around the plant.

Fox had no responsibility for sales or research and development activities. In fact, both Fox and the district sales manager in his area had separate executives to whom they reported in the division headquarters, and it was the superior of these executives who held bottom-level responsibility for sales and production combined.

Fox commented about the working relationships at the St. Laurent plant:

> You will see that frequently two managers with different job titles are assigned responsibility for the same task. [He implied that it was up to them to work out their own pattern of mutual support and cooperation.] However, I don't have to adhere strictly to the description. I may end up asking a lot more of the man at certain times and under

---

Copyright © 1977 by the President and Fellows of Harvard College. Harvard Business School case 9–478–017.

certain conditions than is ever put down on paper.

In effect, the staff runs the plant.[1] We delegate to the various staff department heads the authority to implement decisions within the framework of our budget planning. This method of handling responsibility means that staff members have to be prepared to substantiate their decisions. At the same time, it gives them a greater sense of participation in and responsibility for plant income. We endeavor to carry this principle into the operating and service departments. The foreman is given responsibility and encouraged to act as though he were operating a business of his own. He is held responsible for all results generated in his department and is fully aware of how any decisions of his affect plant income.

Our division personnel counsel and assist the plant staff and the plant staff counsel and assist the department foreman. Regular visits are made to the plant by our division manager and members of his staff. The principal contact is through the division manager of manufacturing and his staff, the manager of industrial engineering, the manager of production engineering, and the manager of quality control. [There was no division staff officer in production control.]

However, the onus is on the plant to request help or assistance of any kind. We can contact the many resources of Continental Can Company, usually on an informal basis. That is, we deal with other plant managers directly for information when manufacturing problems exist, without going through the division office.

Each member of the staff understands that we as a plant have committed ourselves through the budget to provide a stated amount of income, and, regardless of conditions which develop, this income figure must be maintained. If sales are off and a continuing trend is anticipated, we will reduce expenses wherever possible to retain income. Conversely, if we have a gain in sales volume, we look for the complete conversion of the extra sales at the profit-margin rate. However, this is not always possible, especially if the increase in sales comes at a peak time when facilities are already strained.

Fox was assisted by Robert Andrews, the assistant plant manager. Andrews, promoted from quality control manager in 1961, was responsible for all manufacturing operations within the plant. He appeared more reserved than Fox, talked intently, and smiled easily while working with the people that reported to him. Fifteen salaried supervisors reported to Andrews and helped him control the three-shift operation of the plant and its 500 hourly workers. (During peak periods in the summer, the plant employed as many as 800 people; most of the additional workers were the sons and daughters of plant employees.)

Andrews noted, "Our foremen have full responsibility for running their departments: quality, condition of equipment, employee relations,

---

[1] The personnel reporting directly to Fox. The organization chart was prominently displayed on the wall of the lobby (see *Exhibit 1*).

EXHIBIT 1
St. Laurent Plant Organization Chart, March 1, 1963

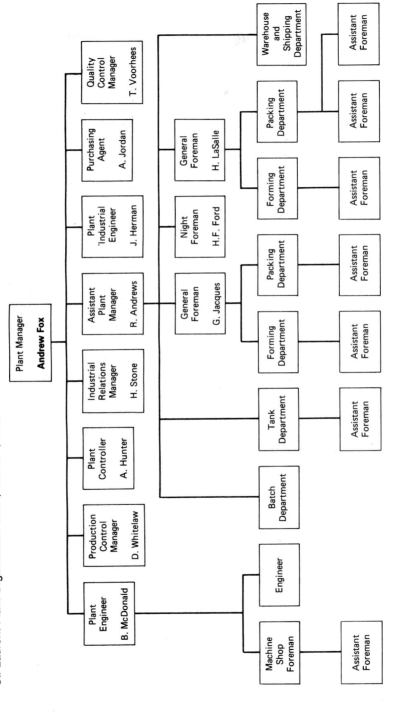

production according to schedule, control of inventory through accurate reporting of spoilage and production, and cost control. [The foreman] is just as accountable for those in his department as the plant manager is for the entire plant."

Production Control

D. Whitelaw, the production control manager, had worked all of his 18 years with Continental Can at the St. Laurent plant. He was responsible for planning and controlling plant inventories and production schedules to meet sales requirements consistent with efficient utilization of facilities, materials, and manpower. According to Whitelaw the main task of his job was "to try to achieve the maximum length of run without affecting service or exceeding inventory budgets."

Whitelaw was assisted by a scheduler for each major operating department and clerks to service the schedulers. The schedulers worked closely with the department foreman in the plant and were in frequent telephone contact with the sales offices. Whitelaw commented, "We in production control are the buffer between sales and operating people."

To facilitate their work, Whitelaw and Andrews headed biweekly production control meetings, each lasting about one hour. Fox, the plant manager, was a frequent observer, and the meetings were attended by the two general foremen. Each production foreman and the production control scheduler working for the department came into the meeting at a pre-arranged time; when their turn came they reported on operations and problems in their departments. Most of the questions as well as instructions given in the meeting came from Andrews and were seldom clearly addressed to either the foreman or scheduler. The questions were answered more frequently by the scheduler than the foreman; often a scheduler would supplement comments made by the foreman. Generally the schedulers were younger but spoke with more self-assurance than the foremen.

In these meetings there were frequent references to specific customers, their needs, complaints, and present attitudes toward Continental Can. Both Whitelaw and Andrews tended to put instructions and decisions in terms of what was required to satisfy some particular customer or group of customers.

A recent meeting involving a foreman, Maurice Pelletier, and the scheduler for his department, Dan Brown, is illustrative of the process. It was observed that while Dan presented the status report Maurice shook his head in disagreement without saying anything. Dan was discussing his plan to discontinue an order being processed on a certain line on Friday, then shift to another order, and finally return to the original order on Tuesday.

Andrews: I don't think your plan makes much sense. You go off on Friday and then on again Tuesday.

Pelletier: [*to Brown*] Is this all required before the end of the year? [*Asked with obvious negative emotions and then followed by comments by both Andrews and Whitelaw.*]

Brown: Mind you—I could call Sales again.

Whitelaw: I can see the point, Dan. It is sort of nonsensical to change back after so short a run.

Pelletier: This would mean our production would be reduced all week to around 300 instead of 350. You know it takes four hours to make the changeover.

Brown: But the order has been backed up.

Andrews: It is backed up only because their [Sales] demands are unreasonable.

Brown: They only asked us to do the best we can.

Andrews: They always do this. We should never have put this order on in the first place.

Pelletier: If you want to we could. . . . [*Makes a suggestion about how to handle the problem*]

Andrews: Productionwise, this is the best deal. [*Agreeing with Pelletier's plan*]

Brown: Let me look at it again.

Andrews: Productionwise, this is best; make the changeover on the weekend.

Whitelaw: [*Summarizes; then to Brown*] The whole argument is the lost production you would have.

Pelletier: It'll mean backing up the order only one day.

Andrews: [*After another matter in Maurice's department has been discussed and there is apparently nothing further, Andrews turns to Dan and smiles.*] It's been a pleasure, Dan. [*Dan then returns the smile weakly and gets up to leave, somewhat nervously.*]

As Whitelaw left the conference room after the meeting, he was heard to comment, "Danny got clobbered, as you could see. I used to stand up for him but he just doesn't come up here prepared. He should have the plans worked out with his foreman before they come up."

When discussing his job, Whitelaw frequently commented on how he thought a decision or problem would affect someone else in the plant:

> If all you had to do was manage the nuts and bolts of production scheduling and not worry about the customer or how people were going to react, this would be the easiest job in the whole plant. You could just sit down with a paper and pencil and lay it out the best way. But because the customer is so important and because you've got to look ahead to how people are going to react to a given kind of schedule, it makes the whole job tremendously complicated. It isn't easy!

Managerial Practices

Managing with Budgets

Management at the St. Laurent plant coordinated its activities through a number of informal, as well as scheduled, meetings. Impromptu meetings of two or more members of management were frequent, facilitated by the close proximity of their offices. Among the formal meetings the most important was the monthly discussion of performance against the budget. This meeting was attended by all of the management staff as well as production supervisors. Other regularly scheduled meetings included the production control meeting (twice weekly) and the plant cost reduction committee meetings.

In discussing the budget, Fox explained that the manufacturing plant was organized as a profit center. Plant income was determined by actual sales, not a transfer price. Consequently, income was adversely affected when either sales failed to come up to the forecast on which the budget was based or sales prices were reduced to meet competition. Fox explained that sales managers also have their incentives based on making or exceeding the budget and that their forecasts had tended to be quite accurate. Overoptimism of one group of products was usually offset by underestimation of sales on other products. However, because no adjustment was permitted in budgeted profit when sales income was below forecast, the fact that sales were running 3% below the level budgeted for 1963 was forcing the plant to reduce expenses substantially in order to equal or exceed the profit budgeted for the year.

When asked whether the budget was a straitjacket or if there were some accounts that left slack for reducing expenses if sales fell below forecast, Fox replied, "We never put anything in the budget that is unknown or guessed at. We have to be able to back up every single figure in the budget. We have to budget our costs at standard, assuming that we can operate at standard. We know we won't all the time. There will be errors and failures, but we are never allowed to budget for them." Hunter agreed with Fox, stating that "in this company there is very little opportunity to play footsy with the figures."

Fox conceded that there were some discretionary accounts, such as overtime and outside storage, that involved arguments with the division. For example, "I might ask for $140,000 for overtime. The division manager will say $130,000, so we compromise at $130,000." As far as cost-reduction projects are concerned, Fox added, "We budget for more than the expected savings. We might have $100,000 in specific projects and budget for $150,000."

Fox went on to note that equipment repairs and overhauls could be delayed to reduce expenses. But even the overhaul schedule was included as part of the budget, and any changes had to be approved at the division level.

Robert Andrews complained that the budget system didn't leave much room for imagination. He felt that overly optimistic sales estimates were caused by the salespeople's fear of sending a pessimistic estimate up to the division. These estimates, according to Andrews, were a major source of manufacturing inefficiency.

Asked whether he was concerned about increasing production volume, Andrews replied:

> We have standards. So long as we are meeting the standards we are meeting our costs and we do not worry about increasing production. We don't tell the foreman that he needs to get more goods out the door. We tell him to get rid of the red in his budget. I'm content with a 100% performance. I'd like 105%, but if we want more production it is up to IE [industrial engineering] to develop methods change.

Andrews talked about the necessary skills of a foreman:

> The foreman should be good at communications and the use of available control procedures. The foreman is expected to communicate effectively with all plant personnel, including staff heads. Our control procedures are easy to apply. In each department there is an engineered standard for each operation covering labor, materials, and spoilage. Without waiting for a formal statement from accounting, a foreman can analyze his performance in any area and take corrective action if necessary. Then he receives reports from accounting to assist him in maintaining tight cost control. One is a daily report which records labor and spoilage performance against standard. The monthly report provides a more detailed breakdown of labor costs, materials and supplies use, and spoilage. It also establishes the efficiency figure for the month. This report is discussed at a monthly meeting of all my supervisors. Generally the plant industrial engineer and a member of the accounting staff are present. Each foreman explains his variances from standard and submits a forecast for his next month's performance.

The Bonus Plan

Andrew Fox indicated that the budget was also used in rewarding employees. The incentive for managers was based on performance of the plant as compared to budget. According to Fox:

> The bonus is paid on the year's results. It is paid as a percentage of salary to all who are eligible—they are the ones on the organization chart [see *Exhibit 1*]. There are three parts to it—one part is based on plant income, one on standards improvement or cost cutting, and the third on operating performance. We can make up to 20% by beating our plant income target and 25% on cost reduction and operating efficiency together. But we have to make 90% of our budgeted income figure to participate in any bonus at all.
>
> I think we have the 25% on efficiency and cost reduction pretty well sewn up this year. If we go over our budgeted income, we can get almost 35% bonus.

In past years St. Laurent managers had made about 10% of their salaries from the bonus. The improved performance was the result of a change in the design of the bonus plan. Hunter explained the effect of the change:

> At one time the bonus plan was based on departmental results and efficiency. Under this there was a tendency for the departments to work at cross purposes, to compete rather than cooperate with each other. For the last seven or eight years the emphasis has been on the plant, not the department. The latest plan is geared not only to the attainment of budgeted cost goals but also to the attainment of budgeted income. This is consistent with the attention we are placing on sales. I think the company was disturbed by what they sensed was a belief that those at the plant level can't do much about sales. Now we are trying to get the idea across that if we make better cans and give better service, we will sell more.

Enforcing the Budget

By November 1963, sales for the year had fallen below expectations, and the management bonus was in jeopardy as a result.

One day in early November there was an unusual amount of activity in the accounting section. Fox came into the area frequently, and from time to time he and Hunter would huddle with one of the accountants over some figures. Hunter explained that the extra activity was in response to a report on the October results that had been issued about a week before.

Fox decided to schedule a joint meeting of the management staff and the line organization to go over the October results. This was a departure from the usual practice of having the groups in separate meetings. Prior to the meeting, Fox outlined what he hoped the meeting would accomplish:

> Those figures we got last week showed that some of the accounts did what they were expected to do, some did more, and some did a good deal less. The thing we have to do now is to kick those accounts in the pants that are not making the savings they planned to make. What we've been doing is raising the expected savings as the time gets shorter. It may be easy to save 10% on your budget when you've got six months; but with only six weeks, it is an entirely different matter. The thing to do now is to get everybody together and excited about the possibility of doing it. We know how it can be done. Those decisions have already been made. It's not unattainable, even though I realize we are asking an awful lot from these men. You see, we are in a position now where just a few thousand dollars one way or the other can make as much as 10% difference in the amount of bonus the men get. There is some real money on the line. It can come from either a sales increase or an expense decrease, but the big chunk has to come out of an expense decrease.

Fox did not feel there would be a conflict in the meeting about who is right and who is wrong:

> We never fight about the budget. It is simply a tool. All we want to know is what is going on. There are never any disagreements about the budget itself. Our purpose this afternoon is to pinpoint those areas where savings can be made, where there is a little bit of slack, and then get to work and pick up the slack.

Fox talked about his style in handling cost and people problems:

> When budgeted sales expenses get out of line, management automatically takes in other accounts to make up the losses. We'll give the department that has been losing money a certain period of time to make it up. Also, anytime anybody has a gain, I tell them I expect them to maintain that gain.
>
> The manager must make the final decisions and has to consider the overall relationships. But there are some things I can't delegate— relations with sales, for example. The manager, and not production control, must make the final decisions.
>
> Larry Adams, the sales manager in our district, feels that the budget gets in the way of the customer's needs. He thinks the budget dominates the thinking and actions around here. Maybe he's right. But I have to deal with the people and problems here.
>
> The manager must be close to his people. I take a daily tour of the plant and talk to the people by name. My practice as a manager is to follow a head-on approach. I don't write many memos. When I

have something to say I go tell the person or persons right away. That's why I'm holding a meeting this afternoon.

Bob Andrews commented on the methods used to pick up the projected savings:

When you have lost money in one sector you have to look around for something else that you can "milk" to make up the difference. But we don't ask for volunteers; we do the "milking." Those guys just have to do what we say. How much we can save pretty much depends on how hard the man in the corner office wants to push on the thing. I mean, if we really wanted to save money we probably could do it, but it would take a tremendous effort on everybody's part and Fox would really have to crack the whip.

Because of Fox's comments on relationships with Sales, Larry Adams, the district sales manager, was asked about his feelings on working with the production people at the St. Laurent plant:

The budget comes to dominate people's thinking and influence all their actions. I'm afraid even my salesmen have swallowed the production line whole. They can understand the budget so well they can't understand their customers. And the St. Laurent plant boys are getting more and more local in their thinking with this budget. They're not thinking about what the customer needs today or may need tomorrow; they just think about their goddamned budget.

   If the customer will not take account of your shortcomings, and if you can't take account of the customer's shortcomings, the two of you will eventually end up at each other's throats. That's what this budget system has built into it. Suppose, for example, you want to give a customer a break. Say he has originally planned for a two-week delivery date, but he phones you and says he really has problems and if you possibly could he would like about four days knocked off that delivery date. So I go trotting over to the plant, and I say, "Can we get it four days sooner?" Those guys go out of their minds, and they start hollering about the budget and how everything is planned just right and how I'm stirring them up. They get so steamed up I can't go running to them all the time but only when I really need something in the worst way. You can't let those plant guys see your strategy, you know. It is taking an awful lot out of a guy's life around here when he has to do everything by the numbers.

Special Budget Meeting

The meeting was held in the conference room at 4:00 P.M. Fox and Hunter sat at the far end of the table, facing the door, with an easel bearing a flip chart near them. The chart listed the projected savings in budgeted expenses for November and December, account by account. The group of about 30 arranged themselves at the table so that, with only a couple of exceptions, the management staff personnel and general foremen sat closest to Fox and Hunter, and the foremen and assistant foremen sat toward the foot of the table.

Fox opened the meeting and declared that performance against the budget for October would first be reviewed, followed by discussion of the November and December projections. He stated rather emphatically that he was "disappointed" in the October performance. Although money had been saved, it represented good performance in some areas but rather poor performance in others. The gains made in the areas where performance had been good must be maintained and the weak areas brought up, Fox declared.

He then turned the meeting over to Hunter, who reviewed the October results, reading from the report that everyone had in front of him. Where performance was not good, he called on the individual responsible for that area to explain. The typical explanation was that the original budgeted figure was unrealistic and that the actual amount expended was as low as it could possibly be under the circumstances. Fox frequently broke into the explanation with a comment like, "Well, that is not good enough," or, "Can you possibly do better for the rest of the year?" or, "I hope we have that straightened out now." When he sat down, the person giving the explanation was invariably thanked by Hunter.

Next, Hunter, followed by Whitelaw, commented on the sales outlook for the remainder of the year. They indicated that for two months, as a whole, sales were expected to be about on budget. After asking for questions and getting one from a foreman, Fox said, "Well now, are there any more questions? Ask them now if you have them. Everybody sees where we stand on the bonus, I assume. Right?"

Fox then referred to the chart on plant expense savings and began to discuss it, saying, "The problem now is time. We keep compressing the time and raising the gain [the projected savings for the year had been raised $32,000 above what had been projected in October]. You can only do that so long. Time is running out, fellows. We've got to get on the stick."

Several times Fox demanded better upward communication on problems as they came up. Referring to a specific example, he said, "This sort of thing is absolutely inexcusable. We've got to know ahead of time when these mix-ups are going to occur so that we can allow for and correct them."

As Hunter was covering manufacturing efficiency projections for November, he addressed Andrews: "Now we have come to you, Bob. I see you're getting a little bit more optimistic on what you think you can do."

Andrews replied:

Yes, the boss keeps telling me I'm just an old pessimist and I don't have any faith in my people. I'm still a pessimist, but we are doing tremendously. I think it's terrific, fellows [*pointing to a line graph*]. I don't know whether we can get off the top of this chart or not, but at the rate this actual performance line is climbing, we might make it. All I can say is, keep up the good work. . . .

I guess I'm an optimistic pessimist.

During the discussion of projected savings for December in the equipment maintenance account, Hunter asked, "Where in the world are you fellows going to save $8,000 more than you originally said you would save?" Jones responded:

I'd just like to say at this point to the group that it would be a big help if you guys would take it easy on your machines. That's where we are going to save an extra $8,000—simply by only coming down to fix the stuff that won't run. You're really going to have to make it go as best you can. That's the only way we can possibly save the kind of money we have to save. You have been going along pretty well, but all I've got to say is I hope you can keep it up and not push those machines too hard.

Although Jones spoke with sincerity, a number of foremen sitting near the door exchanged sly smiles and pokes in the ribs.

Fox concluded the meeting at about 5:30:

There are just a couple of things I want to say before we break up. First, we've got to stop making stupid errors in shipping. Joe [foreman of shipping], you've absolutely *got* to get after those people to straighten them out. Second, I think it should be clear, fellows, that we can't break any more promises. Sales is our bread and butter. If we don't get those orders out in time we'll have no one but ourselves to blame for missing our budget. So I just hope it is clear that production control is running the show for the rest of the year. Third, the big push is on *now*! We sit around here expecting these problems to solve themselves, but they don't! It ought to be clear to all of you that no problem gets solved until it's spotted. Damn it, I just don't want any more dewy-eyed estimates about performance for the rest of the year. If something is going sour we want to hear about it. And there's no reason for not hearing about it! [*Pounds the table, then voice falls and a smile begins to form*] It can mean a nice penny in your pocket if you can keep up the good work.

That's all I've got to say. Thank you very much.

The room cleared immediately, but Whitelaw lingered on. He reflected aloud on the meeting that had just ended:

I'm afraid that little bit of advice there at the end won't make a great deal of difference in the way things work out. You have to play off sales against production. It's built into the job. When I attend a meeting like that one and I see all those production people with their assistants and see the other staff managers with their assistants, and I hear fellows refer to corporate policy that dictates and supports their action at the plant level, I suddenly realize that I'm all alone up there. I can't sit down and fire off a letter to my boss at the division level like the rest of those guys can do. I haven't got any authority at all. It is all based strictly on my own guts and strength. Now Bob is a wonderful guy— I like him and I have a lot of respect for him—but it just so happens that 80% of the time he and I disagree. He knows it and I know it; I mean it's nothing we run away from, we just find ourselves on opposite sides of the question, and I'm dependent upon his tact and good judgment to keep from starting a war.

Boy, it can get you down—it really can after a while, and I've been at it for—God—twenty years. But in production control you've just got to accept it—you're an outcast. They tell you you're cold, that you're inhuman, that you're a bastard, that you don't care about anything except your schedule. And what are you going to say? You're just going to have to swallow it because basically you haven't got the authority to back up the things you know need to be done. Four nights out of five I am like this at the end of the day—just completely drained out— and it comes from having to fight my way through to try to get the plant running as smoothly as I can.

And Andrews up there in that meeting. He stands up with his chart and he compliments everybody about how well they are doing on efficiency. You know, he says, "Keep up the good work," and all that sort of stuff. I just sat there—shaking my head. I was so dazed, you know. I mean I just keep saying to myself, "What's he doing? What's he saying? What'so great about this?" You know, if I could have, I'd have stood up and I'd have said, "Somebody go down to my files in production control and pick out any five customer orders at random— and letters—and bring them back up here and read them—at random, pick any five." You know what they would show? Broken promises and missed delivery dates and slightly off-standard items we've been pushing out the door here. I mean, what is an efficient operation? Why the stress on operating efficiently? That's why I just couldn't figure out why in the world Andrews was getting as much mileage out of his efficiency performance as he was. Look at all the things we sacrifice to get that efficiency. But what could I do?

In early 1964 the report sent by Fox to division showed, despite the fact that sales had fallen about 3% below budget, that profits for 1963 had exceeded the amount budgeted and that operating efficiency and cost reduction had both exceeded the budget by a comfortable margin. This enabled the managers and supervisors at the St. Laurent plant to attain the salary bonuses for which they had been striving.

chapter 14

PROFIT CENTERS
AND TRANSFER PRICING

Profit is the most widely used measure of performance for a business firm. By evaluating the performance of decentralized units with a profit measure, senior managers hope to promote goal congruence between decentralized units and the firm.

Many definitions of a profit center have been proposed. At a purely descriptive level, one could define a profit center as any organizational unit for which some measure of profit is determined periodically.[1] But this definition fails to capture one of the major purposes behind the use of profit centers: to encourage local decision making and initiative. Merely measuring the profit generated by some organization unit does not make that unit autonomous or independent. For our purposes, then, a **profit center** is a unit for which the manager has the authority to make decisions on sources of supply and choice of markets. In general, a profit center should be selling a majority of its output to outside customers and should be free to choose the sources of supply for a majority of its materials, goods, and services. With this definition, it is unlikely that manufacturing or marketing divisions will be profit centers, even though many firms attempt to simulate local authority by assigning transfer prices to products transferred between manufacturing and sales divisions. This practice creates pseudo profit centers, since the company can now report a profit figure for these divisions even though they have limited authority for sourcing and pricing decisions.

Many managers of profit centers are evaluated not just on profit but on the level of profit related to the fixed investment for their units. In this case, we refer to the unit as an **investment center.** Return on investment and residual income are the most common performance measures used for investment centers. In this chapter, we will restrict our attention purely to profit measurement, deferring discussion of investment centers and their performance measures to Chapter 15. A profit center (as opposed to

---

[1] See Richard F. Vancil, *Decentralization: Managerial Ambiguity by Design* (Homewood, IL: Dow Jones-Irwin, 1978).

an investment center) is an appropriate structure for evaluating the performance of a unit manager if the quantity of plant and equipment is stable from year to year or is not controllable by the profit-center manager. For example, if all major capital-expenditure decisions are made at the top-management level, then the local profit-center manager is not controlling the level of investment and should not be held accountable for the past decisions on plant and equipment. Thus, the performance of the manager must be differentiated from the performance of the organization unit, especially when the best managers are assigned to problem or failing units in an attempt to revive those units.

Problems encountered in measuring profit include (1) choosing a profit index, including the allocation of costs and revenues to the center, and (2) pricing the transfer of goods between profit centers.

Choosing a Profit Index

Consider the following data from a division of the Easler Corporation:

Revenue from division sales	$15,000
Variable cost of goods sold and variable overhead	10,000
Fixed division overhead ($800 controllable, $1,200 noncontrollable)	2,000
Allocated G&A expense of corporation	1,000

We can construct a structured divisional income statement as follows:

	Revenues	$15,000
	Variable costs	10,000
(1)	Variable contribution margin	$ 5,000
	Controllable fixed costs	800
(2)	Controllable contribution	$ 4,200
	Noncontrollable fixed costs	1,200
(3)	Divisional contribution	$ 3,000
	Allocated corporate expenses	1,000
(4)	Divisional profit before taxes	$ 2,000

We have a choice of at least the four indicated measures to evaluate the division's performance.

Variable Contribution Margin

The division variable contribution margin of $5,000 may be important for understanding the short-run cost-volume-profit relationship within the division, but it is not useful for performance evaluation. The division manager has control over most of the fixed costs and has the option of trading off between fixed and variable costs. Therefore, the performance evaluation of the division manager should include, as a minimum, controllable fixed costs.

Controllable Contribution

The controllable contribution of $4,200 is the total division revenues less all costs that are (1) directly traceable to the division and (2) controllable by the division manager. This measure includes fixed costs that may arise from the use of indirect labor, indirect materials, and utilities. The division manager has the option of reducing these fixed costs, since they are fixed only with respect to changes in activity levels. They can be reduced if the division manager wishes to operate a "leaner" organization or reduce complexity and diversity in its product lines and marketing channels.

Controllable contribution is perhaps the best performance measure of division managers' performance, since it measures managers' ability to use effectively the resources under their control and authority. An important limitation of this measure is the difficulty of distinguishing between controllable and noncontrollable fixed costs. For example, depreciation, insurance, and property taxes on fixed assets would be controllable if division managers had the authority to dispose of these assets but would be noncontrollable if they did not have this discretion. Also salary levels of employees and supervisors may be set centrally, but division managers may choose how many workers and supervisors to employ at the division. In any event, controllable contribution ignores the long-run costs that can legitimately be assigned to a division and, therefore, some of the costs that a division imposes on the organization.

A trade-off exists between the need to evaluate managerial performance and the need to measure the economic contribution of the segment to the overall organization. Segment performance can be affected by market conditions beyond the manager's control. For example, a good segment performance can result from excellent market opportunities but weak managerial performance. On the other hand, a weak segment performance can result from terrible market conditions but excellent managerial performance. Any profit performance reported by a segment must be evaluated relative to the potential of that segment, perhaps as expressed in the annual budget for the segment. But the manager usually participates in the budget-setting process and may be motivated to misrepresent potential opportunities in order to avoid the imposition of high performance standards. Merchant has described how several companies resolve the conflict between controllability and responsibility in their decentralized units.[2]

---

[2] Kenneth A. Merchant, "How and Why Firms Disregard the Controllability Principle," in *Accounting & Management: Field Study Perspectives*, ed. William H. Bruns, Jr., and Robert S. Kaplan (Boston: Harvard Business School Press, 1987), Chap. 12, pp. 316–38.

Controllable contribution measures, to some extent, the performance of the division manager, unencumbered by costs that may have been committed by other managers. On the other hand, controllable contribution, by ignoring attributable, but noncontrollable (in the short run), fixed costs, provides an incomplete picture of the division's economic contribution to the organization.

Divisional Contribution

The divisional contribution of $3,000 represents the assessed contribution that the division is making to corporate profit and overhead. For the reasons mentioned above, it evaluates the performance of the division more than it does the performance of the division manager. Some of the division overhead, such as the costs of the fixed assets, may result from past investment decisions made by top management. Also, the salaries of the divisional executives may be set by central management. The divisional contribution is clearly an important figure for evaluating the division's profitability, but unless the division manager is given the authority to restructure the investments or key personnel of the division, these costs are not controllable and hence may not be relevant in evaluating the manager's performance.

Divisional Profit before Taxes

Many companies allocate all central general and administrative expenses to their divisions. The motivation, apparently, is to alert division managers to the level of these common costs and indicate that the company as a whole is not profitable unless the revenue-producing divisions generate enough contribution margin to cover a "fair share" of central G&A costs. While it is true that profits generated by divisions must exceed centrally incurred costs before the company is profitable, there seems to be little gain from including arbitrary allocations of these costs when evaluating the performance of a division or a division manager.

First, these costs may not be controllable at the divisional level. Therefore, an unfavorable profit variance caused by an unexpectedly large corporate expense allocation cannot be attributed to division managers who may have no control over expenditures on corporate staff functions.

Second, the basis for allocating corporate expenses to divisions is usually arbitrary, bearing no causal relation to the way in which divisional activities influence the level of these corporate expenses.[3] Common al-

---

[3] A notable exception to this practice is the careful, activity-based procedures used by Weyerhaeuser to charge out corporate expenses to divisions. See H. Thomas Johnson and Dennis Loewe, "How Weyerhaeuser Manages Corporate Overhead Costs," *Management Accounting* (August 1987), pp. 20–26.

location bases include percentage of sales, assets, or space occupied by each division. This procedure introduces an additional noncontrollable component to these allocated costs. For if the level of the allocation base (such as sales or assets) changes in other divisions, the percentage of costs allocated to a division will change even with no change in its own activity level. This effect is easily illustrated with an example.

Suppose $200,000 of corporate expenses will be allocated to three divisions proportional to their sales level as shown below:

	Expected Sales	Percentage	Allocated Expenses
Division 1	$2,000,000	40%	$ 80,000
Division 2	500,000	10	20,000
Division 3	2,500,000	50	100,000
	$5,000,000	100%	$200,000

If actual sales of Divisions 2 and 3 are below the anticipated levels, the actual allocation could be:

	Actual Sales	Percentage	Allocated Expenses
Division 1	$2,000,000	50.0%	$100,000
Division 2	300,000	7.5	15,000
Division 3	1,700,000	42.5	85,000
	$4,000,000	100%	$200,000

Division 1's actual sales equaled expected sales, and actual corporate expenses equaled the expected expenses of $200,000. Yet Division 1's share of corporate expenses increased from $80,000 to $100,000 because of the decline in sales of the other two divisions. Thus, under this scheme, Division 1 is being penalized for events outside its control (assuming that the activities of Division 1 did not contribute to the sales decline in the other two divisions).

If central management wishes to have divisions be profitable enough to cover not only their own operations but corporate expenses as well, it is probably better to establish a profit standard, well above breakeven, that the divisions are expected to achieve. The division managers can then concentrate on increasing revenues and reducing costs that are under their control and not be concerned with costs that they cannot control and that are allocated arbitrarily. Otherwise division managers may attempt to increase their reported profits by negotiation on allocation percentages rather than spending time creating real economic value within their operations.

Two counterarguments can be raised to the proposal that corporate expenses not be allocated to divisions. The first is that divisions should be charged for increments in central corporate expenses caused by divisional activities. These incremental expenses may not sum to total corporate expenses, so that an unallocated portion of expense could still remain. But, to the extent that expenses could be traced to divisional activities, the allocation would absorb part of these corporate expenses and would properly be allocated back as the costs of providing services to the divisions. These costs should be part of the controllable overhead costs of the divisions.

The second argument is that by allocating central overhead costs to divisions, the division managers are made more aware of these costs, so that they will exert pressure to keep down the costs of central staff departments. If the division managers are not made aware of these costs through some allocation process, they will not be as motivated to contain expansion of corporate staff functions. Thus, if central management is willing to let division managers participate in decisions on the levels of corporate staff activities, a case can be made for allocating these expenses back to the divisions.

Common Revenues

Occasionally a conflict may arise on the allocation of revenues between profit centers. This can occur if the sales force for one division promotes the sale of products made by other divisions when calling on customers. If a division receives no credit for selling the products of other divisions, little motivation exists for attempting to make such sales. A similar problem arises when branch banks are evaluated as profit centers. A customer may establish an account near her residence but conduct the majority of banking transactions with a branch near her place of work. Conflict between the branches could occur if all the revenues from the time and savings deposits were credited to the home branch and the costs of supplying banking services were charged to the branch near the business location.

In such instances, it seems reasonable to construct a fee schedule that will provide some compensation from the product division to a salesperson from another division who makes a sale (such as a finder's fee) and from the home bank to the service bank for providing services. Such arrangements are complicated, and they illustrate the problems that arise from decentralized profit-directed operations.

Transfer Pricing

We have already noted some of the difficulties that arise when decentralized organizational units have to interact with each other. Nowhere is there greater potential for conflict in such interactions than when goods produced in one unit are transferred to a second unit. If both units are organized as profit centers, a price must be placed on such transfers; this price represents a revenue to the producing division and a cost to the buying division. Therefore, the transfer price affects the profitability of both divisions, so that the managers of both divisions have a keen interest in how this price is determined.

Early applications of transfer pricing were designed to facilitate the evaluation of unit performance. Alfred Sloan and Donaldson Brown, the senior managers of General Motors in the 1920s, understood well the importance of transfer pricing in this role:

> The question of pricing product from one division to another is of great importance. Unless a true competitive situation is preserved, as to prices, there is no basis upon which the performance of the divisions can be measured. No division is required absolutely to purchase product from another division. In their interrelation they are encouraged to deal just as they would with outsiders. The independent purchaser buying products from any of our divisions is assured that prices to it are exactly in line with prices charged our own car divisions. Where there are no substantial sales outside, such as would establish a competitive basis, the buying division determines the competitive picture— at times partial requirements are actually purchased from outside sources so as to perfect the competitive situation.[4]

In a survey of transfer-pricing practice in large firms in Canada, 85% of the responding firms reported that they used transfer pricing. In the responding firms, the transfer price was determined by:

57%	cost
30%	market
7%	negotiated
6%	other

The rationales for using transfer pricing included:

47%	for profit evaluation
21%	for cost determination
23%	for control and accountability
9%	other

Transfer prices serve two roles, which, unfortunately, usually conflict. First, as prices, they guide local decision making; they help the producing division decide how much of the product to supply and the purchasing division decide how much to acquire. Second, the prices and subsequent profit measurement help the top management to evaluate the profit centers as separate entities. But a set of transfer prices providing motivations that produce maximum profits to the firm may cause one division to operate

---

[4] Donaldson Brown, "Centralized Control with Decentralized Responsibilities," Annual Convention Series No. 57 (American Management Association: New York, 1927), p. 8.

at a loss. For example, the transfer price that motivates the optimal short-run economic decision is short-run marginal cost. If the supplier has excess capacity, this cost will equal variable cost. The supplier will fail to cover any of its fixed costs and will therefore report a loss.

Conversely, a set of transfer prices that may be satisfactory for evaluating divisional performance may lead the divisions to make suboptimal decisions when viewed from an overall corporate perspective. If division managers are encouraged to maximize their individual divisional profits, they may take actions with respect to other division managers that cause overall corporate profits to decline. The conflict between decision making and evaluation of performance is the essence of the transfer-pricing conundrum. A further conflict occurs if managers emphasize short-term performance in their transfer-price negotiations at the expense of long-run profitability of their division and the firm (recall the discussion on short- versus long-run performance in Chapter 13).

Market Prices

Under a restrictive set of conditions, which are occasionally realized in practice, the choice of a transfer price is clear. If a highly competitive market for the intermediate product exists, then the market price (less certain adjustments) is recommended as the correct transfer price. The conditions of a highly competitive market imply that the producing division can sell as much of the product as it wishes to outside customers, and the purchasing division can acquire as much as it wishes from outside suppliers without affecting the price.

If the purchasing division cannot make a long-run profit at the outside market price (assuming that the market price is a reasonable approximation of the long-run price and not simply a short-run distress price), then the company is better off to not produce the product internally and go to the external market for its supply. Similarly, if the purchasing division cannot make a long-run profit when it must acquire the product at the external price, the division should cease acquiring and processing this product and should allow the producing division to sell all its output to the external market. With a competitive market for the intermediate product, the market price provides an excellent basis for allowing the decisions of the producing and purchasing divisions to be independent of each other.[5]

Some modifications to the pure market-price rule facilitate its use in practice. The company will usually benefit if the transaction occurs in-

---

[5] More formal arguments exist to establish the validity of the market price as an optimal transfer price under competitive conditions. See Jack Hirshleifer, "On the Economics of Transfer Pricing," *Journal of Business* (January 1956), pp. 172–84; and "Economics of the Divisionalized Firm," *Journal of Business* (April 1957), pp. 96–108; also Appendix A to Chapter 6 in David Solomons, *Divisional Performance: Measurement and Control* (Homewood, IL: Dow Jones-Irwin, 1965), pp. 167–71.

ternally rather than having a producing division sell a certain amount externally while the purchasing division is acquiring the same amount from its own outside suppliers. To encourage internal rather than external transfers, a discount from market price is offered to reflect savings on selling and collection expenses and the delivery, service, or warranty terms associated with external sales. This discount will encourage an internal transfer, all other factors being held equal.

Offsetting the desire to coordinate transactions within the firm is the frequent difficulty that division managers have in negotiating the terms of transfers with other divisions in the company. Hidden costs can arise if the buying division makes unreasonable delivery demands on the selling division (which may not be imposed on external suppliers) or when the selling division manager has concerns that any foul-up in product quality or delivery will become publicized throughout the organization, as expressed by the following complaint from the manager of a supplying division:

> It is more difficult to work inside than externally. In the smallest impasse, a person can go up the line. Nobody wants to have the boss coming and making accusations of not cooperating. It is always difficult, so you need a financial incentive or something else, such as recognition for being a good corporate citizen.

Sometimes the transaction must occur internally, rather than externally, to maintain product quality or product confidentiality requirements. In this case, the market price may be adjusted to reflect the extra cost required to meet a more stringent quality standard or special features available only from internal manufacture. The challenge is to keep an accumulation of such special charges from driving the price far above the prices of comparable products available externally. A profit-conscious manager of the purchasing division will usually provide the necessary discipline.

Additional problems arise from the conflict between short-run and long-run considerations. An external supplier may quote a low price in an attempt to buy into the business, with the expectation of raising prices later. The company ordinarily should not switch its source of supply from an internal division to an outside company unless it is confident that the outside company will maintain the quoted price for a substantial period. A similar conflict arises when the price for the intermediate product or service is quoted on both a long-term-contract and a spot-market basis. As more of these complicating factors intrude on the price-setting process, they begin to violate our basic assumption of a perfectly competitive market for the intermediate product. When the market is not perfectly competitive, as it usually is not for most manfuactured goods, the transfer-price problem becomes much more complicated.

As more of these complications intrude on the transfer-pricing mechanism, we get additional evidence of the difficulty of using market prices to coordinate transactions within the firm. If market prices existed that allowed optimal resource allocation and managerial evaluation decisions to be made within the firm, little reason would exist to keep the different divisions within a single corporate entity. The units could function as independent market entities, since no gain apparently arises from centralized control. Thus, an ability to decouple divisional operations through an extensive array of market-based transfer prices is inconsistent with any gains accruing from operating these divisions within a single corporate organization.[6]

The Case for Marginal-Cost Transfer Prices

Consider an extreme case in which no market exists for the intermediate product: all transfers must be made internally. To see the complex issues that arise in this situation, we look at an example.[7]

Division A of the Nicosia Corporation is the only producer of an intermediate product used by Division B for conversion into a salable final product. Division A has fixed costs of $500 per day. Its variable costs are $0.10 per unit. Division B incurs additional costs in converting the intermediate product into salable form. It can process up to 1,000 units per day at a fixed cost of $1,250 per day. Thereafter, it incurs costs of $0.25 per unit processed per day. Division B faces a nonlinear demand curve for the final product. Its revenue forecast as a function of the number of units sold per day is shown below.

Sales in Units	Net Revenue per Thousand Units
1,000	$1,750
2,000	1,350
3,000	1,100
4,000	925
5,000	800
6,000	666

Currently Division B is purchasing 2,000 units per day from A. Division A has computed that at this level of output, its fixed costs are $0.25 per unit and its variable costs are $0.10 per unit. Division A wants a markup over costs of $0.05 per unit and thereby establishes a price of $0.40 per unit for the intermediate product.

B's decision to acquire 2,000 units per day from A at this price of $0.40/unit is perfectly rational, as the analysis in Table 14–1 makes clear.

---

[6] See R. H. Coase, "The Nature of the Firm," *Economica* (November 1937).

[7] This example is adapted from David Solomons, *Divisional Performance: Measurement and Control* (Homewood, IL: Richard D. Irwin, 1965), pp. 167–71.

TABLE 14–1
Calculation of Division B Profit (Loss) at Various Output Levels

Division B's Output (Units) (1)	B's Own Processing Costs (2)	Cost of Product from A at $0.40 (3)	B's Total Costs (4) = (2) + (3)	B's Revenue per 1,000 Units (5)	B's Total Revenue (6) = (1) × (5) /1,000	B's Profit (Loss) (7) = (6) − (4)
1,000	$1,250	$ 400	$1,650	$1,750	1,750	$100
2,000	1,500	800	2,300	1,350	2,700	400
3,000	1,750	1,200	2,950	1,100	3,300	350
4,000	2,000	1,600	3,600	925	3,700	100
5,000	2,250	2,000	4,250	800	4,000	(250)
6,000	2,500	2,400	4,900	666	4,000	(900)

Division B's profit is maximized at $400 per day when it sets output at 2,000 units per day. Division A makes a profit of $100 per day at this output level (2,000 units at $0.40 less $500 fixed costs and $200 variable costs), so that the combined profits of the two divisions are $500 per day.

It may seem from this calculation that both divisions are operating reasonably well as decentralized profit centers. But this satisfaction is readily dispelled once we contemplate combining the two divisions and operating them to maximize total profits. In this case, the marginal and total revenue for the combined divisions are the same as before (columns 5 and 6 in Table 14–1), but the total costs are obtained from adding together the costs of Divisions A and B at each output level. This calculation is performed in Table 14–2.

We see that total profits for the combined divisions are maximized at an output level of 4,000 units. Doubling output from the current level of 2,000 units increases profits from $500 per day to $800 per day. Therefore, decentralization has caused these two divisions of the Nicosia Company to operate at too low an output level and to forgo $300 per day in profits.

In fact, the incorrect transfer price always leads to too little output being transferred between the two divisions. If the supplier sets the price, the price will exceed the optimal transfer price and the buyer will demand less than the optimal amount of the transferred commodity. Similarly, if the buyer sets the price, the price will be less than the optimal price and the supplier will be willing to supply less than the optimal quantity of the transferred product. In both cases, the amount of commodity produced and transferred is less than the optimal amount. In general, the nature of the suboptimization in the transfer-pricing problem is that less is produced and transferred than is optimal for overall firm profitability.

A natural question at this point is whether a transfer price exists that would motivate the two managers to reach the profit-maximizing solution of 4,000 units per day. Clearly, a transfer price of $0.40 was too high, since it led Division B to demand too little of the intermediate product from A. The general and theoretically correct answer to this transfer-pricing question is that the intermediate product should be transferred at the marginal cost of the producing division.[8] In this case, the marginal cost is the variable cost of $0.10 per unit. The proof that this transfer price motivates the correct economic solution is illustrated in Table 14–3. We see that with a transfer price of $0.10 per unit, B's profit is maximized at an output of 4,000 units, which we already know is the globally optimal solution.

This latest calculation vividly illustrates the conflicts between the role of a transfer price in motivating optimal local decision making and its role in evaluating divisional performance. The transfer price of $0.10 per unit

---

[8] Again, the proof of this proposition can be found in Hirshleifer, "On the Economics of Transfer Pricing," and "Economies of the Divisionalized Firm"; and in Appendix A to Chapter 6 of Solomons, *Divisional Performance*, 1965.

TABLE 14–2

Calculation of Combined Profit for Divisions A and B

Output (Units) (1)	Division A Costs (2)	Division B Costs (3)	Total Costs (4) = (2) + (3)	Total Revenues (5)	Profit (loss) (6) = (5) − (4)
1,000	$ 600	$1,250	$1,850	$1,750	$(100)
2,000	700	1,500	2,200	2,700	$ 500
3,000	800	1,750	2,550	3,300	750
4,000	900	2,000	2,900	3,700	800
5,000	1,000	2,250	3,250	4,000	750
6,000	1,100	2,500	3,600	4,000	400

TABLE 14-3

Calculation of Division B Profit at a Transfer Price of $0.10

Division B's Output (Units) (1)	B's Own Processing Costs (2)	Cost of Product from A at $0.10 (3)	B's Total Costs (4) = (2) + (3)	B's Total Revenues (5)	B's Profit (Loss) (6) = (5) − (4)
1,000	$1,250	$100	$1,350	$1,750	$ 400
2,000	1,500	200	1,700	2,700	1,000
3,000	1,750	300	2,050	3,300	1,250
4,000	2,000	400	2,400	3,700	1,300
5,000	2,250	500	2,750	4,000	1,250
6,000	2,500	600	3,100	4,000	900

that motivates the optimizing behavior causes Division A to show a loss of $500 (from its unrecovered fixed costs) while Division B shows a profit of $1,300. While this produces a combined profit of $800, the manager of Division A will not be happy with the allocation of this profit between the two divisions. On the other hand, without imposing a marginal-cost rule, Division A has quoted a "cost-plus" price of $0.40 per unit, leading to a suboptimizing output level of 2,000 units but a more equal sharing of the total profit of $500 between A ($100) and B ($400).

If this were the only product produced by A, then we could simply budget a $500 loss for A and direct it to transfer 4,000 units to B. But the transfer-price problem usually arises when only a few out of many products are involved in an internal transfer. In these cases, it is not convenient to budget losses and specify output for a few out of hundreds of different products and transactions. But if most of a producing division's output must be sold to other internal divisions, and little opportunity exists for a producing division to sell its output externally, then we should control the producing division as a standard cost center, pricing its output at standard cost and avoiding all these transfer-pricing problems.

We have now considered two polar cases: transfers in which a competitive market exists for the intermediate product, and transfers in which no market exists at all for the product. In the first case, the market price was the appropriate transfer price; in the second, the product's short-run marginal cost was the transfer price that motivated optimal decision making within the firm. Despite their apparent dissimilarities, both these prices are actually special cases of the general rule for determining an optimal transfer price.

The unifying theoretical concept for obtaining an appropriate transfer price is to recognize the opportunity cost to the company as a whole for making the transfer. For the Nicosia company, the opportunity cost is measured by what is forgone by the supplying division when it produces the last unit of the intermediate good and transfers it to the buying division. The only opportunity cost of a transfer from Division A (the supplying division) to Division B is the out-of-pocket variable cost of $0.10 per unit. This represents the incremental cost that Division A incurs for producing additional units of the intermediate product.

It may not be obvious how the opportunity-cost rule leads to transfers at market price when a competitive market exists for the intermediate product. But when a competitive market exists, the opportunity cost of the producing division (A) is no longer the out-of-pocket cost of production. The opportunity cost of an internal transfer is the loss of a potential sale to an external customer.

To see this, let us modify our example to allow for an outside market price of $0.40 per unit for the intermediate product. Is an internal transfer price of $0.10 still appropriate? At a transfer price of $0.40 per unit, we know that Division B will demand 2,000 units per day and earn a profit of $400. But Division A can now sell 4,000 units (say 2,000 units to B and 2,000 units externally) at a price of $0.40 per unit and earn $700 ($1,600 − $500 fixed costs − $400 variable costs) for a combined profit of $1,100 for the two divisions. Division A will actually attempt to produce and sell product until its incremental costs rise to the market price of $0.40 per unit. Thus, when a competitive market price exists, the opportunity cost of the transfer becomes the market price (less associated selling and distribution expenses), and this transfer price leads to a globally optimal solution, since either division can transact with external firms to sell excess production or acquire additional amounts of the intermediate product.

The Case against Marginal-Cost Transfers

The incremental-cost rule for internal transfers (when no intermediate market exists) may be theoretically desirable, but few companies follow this guideline. This suggests that the rule has defects that we have not made explicit. One problem, already mentioned, is that the supplying division will typically record a loss while large profits are allocated to the acquiring division selling the product in final form. In this case, we are forcing the supplying division to operate at a loss, thereby reducing its autonomy. If the transferred product represents a small fraction of the total output of the supplying division, this may be only a minor annoyance. If, however, the great majority of the supplying division's output must be transferred internally, and no external reference prices for these products exist, then it is a fiction to treat the supplying division as a profit center. The division should either be controlled as a standard cost center or be combined into a larger profit center with a division that processes the bulk of its output.

A second problem with incremental-cost transfers occurs if the marginal cost is not constant over the range of output. In this case, the supplying division must supply a marginal-cost schedule to the acquiring division. The situation becomes even more complicated if there is more than one purchasing division, so that the level of output is jointly determined by the separate decisions of each purchasing division. This would require an iterative solution as the supplying division varied its marginal cost according to the shifting demands of the purchasing divisions, or else a combined decision among all divisions involved. (This situation is illustrated in Problem 14–4 at the end of the chapter.)

The marginal-cost rule also starts to break down when the supplying division is operating near a capacity constraint. In this case, the proper economic transfer price shifts suddenly from the short-run marginal cost when operating below capacity to the long-run marginal cost (or profits forgone) when the supplying division can no longer meet all the demands for the product. When demand is at or above the capacity of the supplying division, incremental costs are well below the opportunity costs of production and provide poor guidance for resource-allocation decisions.

Marginal-cost transfer prices also provide an incentive for the manager of the supplying division to misrepresent the cost function of producing the intermediate product. If the transfer is to occur at marginal cost, and if the manager of the producing division is evaluated on the basis of the profits of this division, the manager can overstate the marginal cost of production and thereby obtain a higher transfer price. All the deterministic models used to demonstrate the optimality of the marginal-cost procedure assume that the cost function is known to all the organization participants or that the manager will truthfully report it when asked. But strong incentives exist for the manager to overstate the marginal-cost function, since this will increase the transfer price and thereby increase divisional profits.

In our two-division example of the Nicosia Company, the manager of Division A may claim that all costs are variable and that at the previous output level of 2,000 units the incremental costs are $0.35 per unit. (Recall that the actual costs of Division A at this output level are $700, of which $500 were fixed.) At this price, a computation similar to that performed in Table 14–1 reveals that Division B would earn maximum profits of $500 at a volume of either 2,000 units or 3,000 units. Assuming B decided to order 3,000 units, Division A would earn revenues of $1,050 and incur fixed costs of $500 and variable costs of $300, for a profit of $250. The manager of Division A is much happier at this transfer price of $0.35, since the division now shows a profit of $250 as opposed to the $400 loss reported at the marginal-cost transfer price of $0.10 per unit. The firm as a whole suffers, since it earns only $750 in profit per day ($250 for A, $500 for B) at an output level of 3,000 units as opposed to the maximum profit of $800 that could be earned at an output level of 4,000 units. Of course, the Division A manager may have to explain how a profit of $250 was earned when transfers were supposedly made at incremental cost. An appeal to cost-saving efficiencies or reduced incremental costs when increasing output from 2,000 to 3,000 units per day might serve to counter this accusation.

The incentive for misrepresenting local information was mentioned in Chapter 13. When managers are asked to provide information for decision making that will also be used to evaluate their performance, we should expect some strategic manipulation of information (lying). The distorted information will improve the local performance measure of the manager, but at the expense of overall firm profits.

In summary, then, marginal-cost transfers (1) conflict with the divisional autonomy of profit centers, (2) are difficult to implement if the marginal cost varies over the range of demanded output, especially if there is more than one purchasing division, (3) may be indeterminate as the supplying division reaches capacity, and (4) provide incentives for the supplying division to misrepresent its cost function.

Incremental Cost Plus Fixed Fee

One variation of the marginal-cost transfer-price scheme that has some desirable properties is to price all transfers at incremental (short-run marginal) cost but charge the purchasing division a fixed fee for the privilege of obtaining these transfers at incremental cost. Under this scheme, the purchasing division pays incremental cost for additional units, so that when it chooses an output level to maximize profits by equating marginal cost to marginal revenue, it is using the appropriate marginal costs of the producing division. The producing division has the opportunity to recover its fixed costs and earn a profit through the fixed fee charged each period. The fixed fee represents a reservation price that the purchasing division is paying for the privilege of acquiring the intermediate product at marginal cost.

The fixed fee plus marginal cost has some interesting control and motivational properties. Suppose the fixed fee assigned to each user is based on that user's planned (or long-run average) use of that facility. For example, if a division uses 20% of the average capacity, the division is assigned 20% of the fixed costs of the facility. The prepaid capacity would be reserved for the user paying for that capacity. This scheme has two desirable economic traits. First, in the short run, transfers will take place at short-run marginal cost, as economic theory dictates. Second, people will tend to be more honest in the capacity acquisition stage. If they overstate their expected requirements, perhaps to ensure adequate capacity for their own use, they will pay a higher fixed fee. If they understate their expected requirements, to avoid the fixed fee for capacity, they may not have sufficient capacity for their needs as capacity either is not acquired or is reserved for others who are paying the fixed fee for that capacity.

Suppose, however, that expectations are not realized. Then the approach may not be best for the firm overall. The capacity may no longer be assigned to the most profitable current uses. This problem can be overcome by allowing divisions to subcontract with each other so that a division, facing better opportunities, could rent the capacity previously reserved by another division.

This dual-price system is perfectly generalizable. For example, suppose an automobile dealership is choosing the level of its service operations. After negotiations with the new-car and used-car departments, a level of capacity is chosen. The plan is for the new-car operation to use 20% of capacity, the used-car department to use 30% of capacity, and the service department's own use (for outside customers) to consume 50% of capacity. Now suppose that the used-car operation falls upon hard times but must still pay its share of the fixed costs of the service department. This is proper, since otherwise these fixed costs would be reallocated to the other two departments; in effect, causing them to bear the costs of the used-car department's failure to use the capacity that it reserved. Therefore, this scheme is consistent with responsibility accounting.

In the limit, the fixed-fee plus variable-cost scheme will yield either a pure market or a pure cost-plus operation. For example, suppose the service department did no outside work. In this case, it would be responsible for none of its fixed costs and would become a pure cost center. Jobs would be priced at standard variable costs, and the only goal of the service department would be to provide quality service at below standard cost. On the other hand, suppose the service department did no internal work. Then it would be a pure profit center and all transfers would be at market prices. Therefore, this scheme blurs the distinction between pure cost and pure profit centers by operating over a continuum. Also, the scheme provides a justification for performing the buying and selling activities within the firm, since it uses a dual-price scheme for internal transfers that would be difficult to implement and enforce if the divisions did not operate under centralized control.

The approach of a budgeted fixed fee to cover period costs and provide a return to capital, plus an incremental cost based on marginal cost per unit for each unit transferred, is exactly analogous to the proposal made in Chapter 7 for charging for the cost of service departments. It leads to efficient resource allocation among divisions while still letting purchasing divisions see the full cost of obtaining goods or services from other divisions. If this is such a great scheme, why is it not widely used? We can only speculate that the need to account for usage and to acquire capacity on a planned and systematic basis may have prevented a more widespread use of this approach to transfer pricing.

Full Costs

Perhaps the most popular transfer price in practice is the full-cost pricing scheme. We have already seen, from the Nicosia Company example, that such a scheme distorts decision making. Nor does the full-cost pricing scheme seem to be a good guide for evaluating divisional performance. It provides the wrong incentives for the supplying division by allowing it to accumulate all costs and add markups to generate profits. Efficiency is certainly not rewarded nor inefficiency penalized on a full cost-plus transfer-pricing scheme.

As a simple illustration of the perverse effects of a full-cost transfer-pricing scheme, consider the practice of a large industrial company that allocates all corporate G&A expenses to its operating divisions and imposes a transfer price based on cost plus profit markup for all internal transfers. Assume it is manufacturing a product that must be processed through three divisions before final sale. The company allocates $12,000 of general and administrative expenses to the three divisions manufacturing this product. Transfers between each division are done at full cost plus 20% markup, which is also the procedure used to price the final product.

Suppose the G&A expenses are allocated equally to each division, $4,000 each. The first division takes the $4,000 allocation, marks it up by 20%, and transfers these costs to the second division (along with all other product-related costs). The second division now has not just its own $4,000 G&A expense allocation for the product but also the $4,800 from the first division ($4,000 + 20% markup). Division 2 takes the $8,800 G&A allocation, marks it up by 20%, and transfers a total of $10,560 to Division 3. The third division accumulates its own $4,000 allocation with the $10,560, adds the 20% markup to this sum of $14,560, and obtains a total of $17,472 of corporate G&A that must be added to the final price of the product. Thus, the $12,000 of G&A has been increased not by a standard 20% markup but by a 46% markup [(17,472 − 12,000)/12,000] because of the escalating effect as the product passes from one division to the next. When last heard from, the company was calling in a consultant to determine how competitors were able to price their products so much lower and why the company was steadily losing market share in its product lines. Poorly conceived transfer-pricing policies can be highly dysfunctional.

With all these problems, we must ask why the full-cost approach to transfer pricing is so widely practiced. We must distinguish between two situations.

Where an external market price exists, there appears to be little justification for the use of a cost-based approach to pricing. Where there is no external market price, a full-cost price may be used as a surrogate for the long-run marginal cost to the firm of manufacturing the product. This raises the question of why short-run cost is not used to price transfers as economic theory dictates. One executive observed:

> When we add a product to our product line, we expect to continue to offer it on a full-time basis. It is not practical to offer products only in the short-run when conditions seem right and then, in the longer-run, or periodically, say to our customers that we cannot produce this product this period because our costs are now too high.

This executive believes that irrespective of the short-run cost, product decisions reflect long-run commitments and should therefore be based on long-run cost that includes a fixed-cost component. Product decisions imply commitments to product continuity and the integrity of the product line and therefore provide a justification for full-cost pricing.[9] The discussion at the end of Chapter 6 on activity-based costing suggests how this method measures long-run variable cost and may therefore provide

---

[9] See Robin Cooper and Robert S. Kaplan, "How Cost Accounting Systematically Distorts Product Costs," in *Accounting & Management*, ed. Bruns and Kaplan, Chap. 8.

the right transfer price to reflect the costs of the long-run commitments made in capacity and product introduction decisions.

Dual-Rate Transfer Prices

In a dual-rate transfer-pricing scheme, the supplier receives the net realizable value (the market price less finishing costs) for the commodity that is transferred while the buyer pays the sum of any out-of-pocket and opportunity costs of producing the product. In this way, both the buyer and the seller are motivated to demand and supply the optimal amount of the quantity. The buyer pays opportunity cost, and the seller receives the net realizable value of what is produced. This scheme raises the issue of estimating opportunity costs, and as we discussed earlier, it can motivate suppliers to misrepresent their opportunity costs. Possibly because of these problems, the dual-pricing scheme is implemented in practice by substituting an allocation of fixed cost as an estimate of the opportunity cost; that is, the selling division receives its full cost in the transfer, but the buying division is charged only for the marginal cost.

At first glance, the dual-pricing scheme seems very attractive, but several companies that have tried it have eventually abandoned the practice.[10] Senior management objected to having the sum of divisional profits exceed overall corporate profits. In an extreme situation, buying and selling divisions could all show profits while the corporation as a whole is losing money. Thus, divisions would report profits at or above budget, only for large write-downs to occur, to eliminate the double-counting of profits among divisions, when the books were closed at the corporate level. One company president noted:

> Dual pricing sort of died of its own complexity and conflict. There were situations in which divisions could get something internally that didn't exactly fit their needs but went ahead and got it because actual full cost was so much less than market price.

The dual-price system encouraged divisions to shift more of their mix to internal sales and purchases at the highly favorable terms. Internal sales increased well beyond expected levels. When business was poor and the selling units could not meet their budget for external sales, they generated excessive internal sales. Similarly, since buying units received internal product at cost, they had little incentive to negotiate for more favorable prices from external or even internal suppliers. In general, neither division in a dual-pricing scheme has a high incentive to monitor the performance of the other division. Thus, the dual-pricing scheme, by lowering the in-

---

[10] Robert G. Eccles, "Control with Fairness in Transfer Pricing," *Harvard Business Review* (November–December 1983), pp. 153–54.

centives for buying and selling divisions to deal in the external market, could lower overall corporate profitability.

Negotiated Market-Based Price

Lacking a perfectly competitive market for the intermediate product and being aware of the limitations of cost-based pricing rules, perhaps the most practical method for establishing a transfer price is through negotiation between the managers of the two divisions. The negotiating process typically begins when the producing division provides a price quotation plus all relevant delivery conditions (timeliness, quality, and so on). The purchasing division may

1.   Accept the deal
2.   Bargain to obtain a lower price or better conditions
3.   Obtain outside bids and negotiate with external suppliers
4.   Reject the bid and either purchase outside or not purchase at all

In a different sequence, the purchasing division may make an offer to the producing division for a portion of its current output or an increment to current output. The producing division can then bargain with the purchasing division over terms, talk to its existing customers, or decide not to accept the purchasing division's offer.

In either case, a negotiated transfer price requires that the managers of both divisions be free to accept or reject a price at any stage of the negotiation. Otherwise we would have a dictated price rather than a negotiated price.

The conditions under which a negotiated transfer price will be successful include

1.   Some form of outside market for the intermediate product. This avoids a bilateral monopoly situation in which the final price could vary over too large a range, depending on the strength and skill of each negotiator.
2.   Sharing of all market information among the negotiators. This should enable the negotiated price to be close to the opportunity cost of one or preferably both divisions.
3.   Freedom to buy or sell outside. This provides the necessary discipline to the bargaining process.
4.   Support and occasional involvement of top management. The parties must be urged to settle most disputes by themselves, otherwise the benefits of decentralization will be lost. Top management must be available to mediate the occasional unresolvable dispute or to intervene when it sees that the bargaining process is clearly leading to suboptimal decisions. But such involvement must be done with restraint and tact if it is not to undermine the negotiating process.

A negotiated-price system has the following limitations:

1. It is time consuming for the managers involved.
2. It leads to conflict between divisions.
3. It makes the measurement of divisional profitability sensitive to the negotiating skills of managers.
4. It requires the time of top management to oversee the negotiating process and to mediate disputes.
5. It may lead to a suboptimal (too low) level of output if the negotiated price is above the opportunity cost of supplying the transferred goods.

The negotiated-price system depends also on the willingness of external suppliers or purchasers to supply legitimate bids to the company. If, each time these external bids are solicited, the transfer price is determined so that all transfers are eventually made internally, the external bidders will soon tire of participating in this exercise. Therefore, some amount of external purchase or sale should be a realistic expectation in order to keep the faith of these outside participants and thereby ensure a continuing source of legitimate external prices. Despite these limitations, however, a negotiated-transfer-price system seems to offer desirable mechanisms for permitting local managers to exploit the specialized information they possess about local opportunities.

Summary

We have covered much ground in our discussion of transfer pricing. We have obtained some results under fairly restrictive conditions, and we have discussed some pitfalls from using transfer prices inappropriately. We can summarize our current recommendations as follows:

1. Where a competitive market exists for the intermediate product, the market price, less selling, distribution, and collection expenses for outside customers, represents an excellent transfer price.
2. Where an outside market exists for the intermediate product but is not perfectly competitive, a negotiated-transfer-price system will probably work best, since the outside market price can serve as an approximation of the opportunity cost. At least occasional transactions with outside suppliers and customers must occur if both divisions are to have credibility in the negotiating process and if reliable quotes from external firms are to be obtained.
3. When no external market exists for the intermediate product, transfers should occur at the incremental cost of production. This will facilitate the decision making of the puchasing division. A periodic fixed fee should also be paid by the buying divisions to the producing divisions to enable the

producing divisions to recover budgeted fixed costs and the cost of invested capital. The fixed fee should allocate the fixed costs of the facility in proportion to each user's planned use of that facility. The fixed fee also forces the purchasing division to recognize the full cost of producing the intermediate product internally and provides a motivation for the producing divisions to cooperate in choosing the proper level of productive capacity to acquire.

4. We find it difficult to discover circumstances in which a transfer price based on fully allocated costs per unit (using present methods of allocation) or full cost plus markup has desirable properties. While the full-cost transfer price, as presently computed, has limited economic validity, it remains widely used. Perhaps an activity-based cost (see Chapter 6), which approximates long-run variable cost, provides the unifying concept that would enable a practical full-cost system to conform with economic theory.

Eccles, after an extensive field study of transfer-pricing practices, found it useful to link the transfer-pricing policy to two strategic decisions.[11]

Sourcing Decision

Some companies follow a deliberate strategy of vertical integration that mandates internal transfers between divisions. The vertical integration creates interdependencies among production, selling, and distribution profit centers, but the prices of the internal transfers are not factors in determining the sources of intermediate goods. When the firm has no explicit strategy of vertical integration, transfers are not mandatory and the price of the intermediate good determines whether a transfer is made internally or sold and sourced externally.

Pricing Decision

The pricing decision determines whether the intermediate good contains a margin for profit (or loss). A margin for profit (or loss) is included in the transfer price when the selling division is regarded as a profit center for the transferred product. Alternatively, the selling division could be viewed as a cost center for internal transfers, and a profit center only for products sold externally. In this case, the internal transfer could be made at some cost-based price, and all profits or losses for this product would be realized by the division making final sales to external customers.

With this classification scheme, Eccles found that companies without an explicit vertical integration strategy relied on negotiated transfer prices between buying and selling divisions. In general, the resulting transfer price included a margin for profit (or loss) for the selling division.

---

[11] See Eccles, "Control with Fairness in Transfer Pricing"; Eccles, "Analyzing Your Company's Transfer Pricing Practices," *Journal of Cost Management for the Manufacturing Industry* (Summer 1987), pp. 21–83; and Eccles, *The Transfer Pricing Problem: A Theory for Practice* (Lexington, MA: Lexington Books, 1985).

For firms following a vertical integration strategy, with mandated internal transfers of certain products between divisions, two possible transfer prices could occur. Market-based prices would be used when the selling division was to be viewed as a profit center for all its transactions. Full-cost, or occasionally dual-price, systems would be used when the selling division was treated as a cost center for internal transfers.

Other Measures of Performance

Apart from transfer-pricing policies, two additional problems remain with using profit as a measure of divisional or firm performance:

1. Profit provides only an aggregate indication of the firm's ability to achieve the goals that are crucial to its success. It provides no direct indication to the organization members of what they can do individually to improve the performance of the firm.

2. Profit has a short-run orientation and is therefore manipulatable. The manager can take steps to improve short-run performance at the expense of long-run profit considerations.

We have identified a number of problems with profit measurement, but probably the most serious concern with a narrowly focused attention on periodic profit reports is that managers will take actions that sacrifice long-term profitability to improve short-term reported profits, such as by lowering quality controls, inadequate maintenance, insufficient funding for R&D and employee training, and lack of attention to customer relations and employee morale.

To balance off an exclusive concentration on reported accounting profits, some companies have developed performance appraisal systems in which profitability is only one component. For example, a division manager may be given objectives to meet in human resources, distribution, technology, product quality, or new products, depending on which of these key areas are most crucial to the long-run success of the division and which are susceptible to the greatest improvement. The manager would then be evaluated on whether targeted objectives were achieved in these key areas.

At first glance, this seems like an intrusion into the decision-making authority of a division manager in a profit center, but it is not. Rather it represents a more accurate definition of the organization's goals and the factoring of those goals into the responsibilities of the individual decision makers in the firm. By discussing with each manager the specific goals that the manager is intended to achieve and the level of performance expected, the performance metric is much more clearly defined. Moreover, the intrusion may be necessary because of inadequate measurement of the long-term consequences of the manager's current actions. Because of limited observability of the division manager's actions and the cost of measuring the present value of all the relevant assets in a division (including customer goodwill, equipment availability and condition, quality of work force, product quality), it is likely that the best contract between the division manager and the corporation is a function of variables other than reported accounting profit. The focus on key areas with long-term benefit to the corporation may be seen as a means of ensuring that short-term profit maximizing is not the only objective of the division manager.

One computer company is experimenting with a twelve-point measurement system to provide feedback to manufacturing managers:

1. Problem-Free Installations (% of total)
2. System Reliability
3. Price of Nonconformance (a Cost of Quality measure)
4. Weekly Delivery Performance
5. Cycle Time
6. Supplier Relationships (from a survey of suppliers)
7. Customer Relationships (from a survey of customers)
8. Local Content Percentage (domestic vs. imported manufacturing costs)
9. New-Product Shipments (actual vs. promised delivery)
10. Process Yields (PPM)
11. Diversity of Employees (minorities, females, international)
12. Training

The performance measures from such a system would be reviewed by the manufacturing staff around the world and would also be shown quarterly to the executive committee and the board of directors to illustrate progress in the company's continuing improvement activities.

To implement such a plan, the key success factors of the firm must be identified and their implications broken down into what each segment of the business must accomplish. This results in setting goals, often stated in noneconomic terms such as yields, throughputs, service levels, and quality levels, that are negotiated between each segment manager and his or her superior. This process is intended to balance the needs of the corporation to achieve its key success factors and the capability of each segment to respond to these needs. By stating explicit performance-related goals rather than implicit economic (in terms of profit) goals, managers of each organization segment have a clear understanding of the objectives assigned to their units and how those objectives relate to common performance statistics within that unit. Moreover, by focusing on the primary factors of success rather than on a short-run estimate of realized success (reported profit), a clearer, more accurate, and more timely evaluation of performance can be provided.

PROBLEMS

14–1 Cost Allocations and Measurement of Division Profitability

The Young Corporation has three operating divisions. The managers of these divisions are evaluated on their divisional Net Income Before Taxes, a figure that includes an allocation of corporate overhead proportional to the sales of each division. The operating statement for the first quarter of 1990 appears below:

| | Division | | | |
	A	B	C	Total
Net sales (000)	$2,000	$1,200	$1,600	$4,800
Cost of sales	1,050	540	640	2,230
Division overhead	250	125	160	535
Division contribution	700	535	800	2,035
Corporate overhead	400	240	320	960
Net income before taxes	$ 300	$ 295	$ 480	$1,075

The manager of Division A is unhappy that his profitability is about the same as Division B's and much less than Division C's, even though his sales are much higher than either of these other two divisions. The manager knows that he is carrying one line of products with very low profitability. He was going to replace this line of business as soon as more profitable product opportunities became available but has retained it until now, since the line was still marginally profitable and used facilities that would otherwise be idle. The manager now realizes, however, that the sales from this product line are attracting a fair amount of corporate overhead because of the allocation procedure and maybe the line is already unprofitable for him.

This low margin line of products had the following characteristics for the quarter:

Net sales (000)	$800
Cost of sales	600
Escapable divisional overhead	100
Contribution	$100

Thus, the product line accounted for 40% of divisional sales but less than 15% of divisional profit.

Required:

1. Prepare the operating statement for the Young Corporation for the second quarter of 1990 assuming that sales and operating results are identical to the

first quarter except that the manager of Division A drops the low margin product line entirely from his product group. Is the Division A manager better off from this action? Is the Young Corporation better off from this action?

2. Suggest improvements to the Young Corporation's divisional reporting and evaluation system that will improve local incentives for decision making that is in the best interests of the firm.

14–2   Transfer Pricing Dispute*

A transportation equipment manufacturer is heavily decentralized. Each division head has full authority on all decisions regarding sales to internal or external customers. Division P has always acquired a certain equipment component from Division S. However, when informed that Division S was increasing its unit price to $220, Division P's management decided to purchase the component from outside suppliers at a price of $200.

Division S had recently acquired some specialized equipment that was used primarily to make this component. The manager cited the resulting high depreciation charges as the justification for the price boost. He asked the president of the company to instruct Division P to buy from S at the $220 price. He supplied the following:

P's annual purchases of component	2000 units
S's variable costs per unit	$ 190
S's fixed costs per unit	$ 20

Suppose there are no alternative uses of the S facilities.

Required:

1. Will the company as a whole benefit if P buys from the outside suppliers for $200 per unit?
2. Suppose the selling price of outsiders drops another $15 to $185. Should P purchase from outsiders?
3. Suppose (disregarding requirement 2) that S could modify the component at an additional variable cost of $10 per unit and sell the 2000 units to other customers for $225. Would the entire company then benefit if P purchased the 2000 components from outsiders at $200 per unit?
4. Suppose the internal facilities could be assigned to other production operations which would otherwise require additional annual outlays of $29,000. Should P purchase from outsiders at $200 per unit?

_____

* Problem adapted from one in Charles Horngren, *Cost Accounting*, 5th ed. (Englewood Cliffs, NJ: Prentice-Hall, 1982).

14–3   Effects of a Cost-Plus Transfer Price

The Conpont Corporation has decentralized its manufacturing and marketing activities. Each function is now organized as a profit center. The output of a manufacturing division is transferred to the marketing division at standard cost plus a 20% markup. For one of the company's largest volume products, the following flexible budget has been computed at typical output levels:

	Output (units)		
	40,000	50,000	60,000
Overhead			
Indirect materials	$ 80,000	$ 100,000	$ 120,000
Indirect labor	150,000	162,000	174,000
Equipment rentals + depreciation	200,000	200,000	250,000
Utilities, taxes, + misc.	140,000	145,000	150,000
Total overhead	$ 570,000	$ 607,000	$ 694,000
Direct materials	320,000	400,000	480,000
Direct labor	160,000	200,000	240,000
Total budgeted costs	$1,050,000	$1,207,000	$1,414,000

The standard cost per unit is calculated at an annual volume of 50,000 units, but the forecasted volume level for the next year is 45,000 units.

Required:

1. At what price is this product transferred from the manufacturing to the marketing division?
2. The marketing division has uncovered an opportunity to sell 15,000 additional units to a new customer at a price of $22 per unit. This is a special one-year contract that will not affect the pricing for current or potential customers. The manager of the marketing division has asked the manufacturing manager to supply these units at a transfer price of $20 per unit. The manufacturing manager has emphatically declined this offer, "How can I transfer these items below my cost? Not only will I not make my standard markup on each unit, I'll lose money on every item I produce at this transfer price. I'm willing to be reasonable since business is slower than usual, but this offer is ridiculous." Analyze the situation in an attempt to mediate this dispute.

14–4   Transfer Pricing in Imperfect Market:
One Supplying Division, Two Purchasing Divisions*

Division A produces a chemical Calmite, which is processed further and sold by two other divisions (B and C) of the company. Division A's nonlinear cost structure for producing Calmite follows:

---

* Problem adapted from example in Chapter 6 of Solomons, *Divisional Performance*, 1965.

Pounds of Calmite Produced	Division A's Total Cost
4,000	$2,000
5,000	2,100
6,000	2,250
7,000	2,425
8,000	2,625
9,000	2,925
10,000	3,325

For simplicity, you may assume that the marginal cost is constant between the production levels specified above.

Divisions B and C both face markets in which their output affects the selling price of their final product. The demand in these markets, plus the cost structure of the two finishing divisions, is summarized by the following tables showing each division's net revenues (total revenues less finishing costs in each division):

Division B

Pounds of Calmite Processed	Revenues—Net of Finishing Costs
1,000	$ 600
2,000	900
3,000	1,100
4,000	1,200

Division C

Pounds of Calmite Processed	Revenues—Net of Finishing Costs
2,000	$1,200
3,000	1,800
4,000	2,100
5,000	2,300
6,000	2,400

Required:

1. From the point of view of the firm, what is the optimal output of Calmite for Division A and how much of this should be transferred to Division B and Division C?

2. What transfer price will motivate Division A to produce this output and also motivate Divisions B and C to demand the appropriate quantities? How would you describe the rule used to generate this transfer price?

3. How would the above analysis be affected if Division A can also sell Calmite in an imperfect external market?
4. In practice, how could a firm determine and implement a transfer price that leads to optimal production and transfers in a situation with a supplying division, more than one purchasing division, and nonlinear cost and revenue functions, as described above?

14–5   Transfer Pricing with Imperfect Market for the Intermediate Product: The Linear Case

Penn Hills Computers manufactures small control units used in process control equipment. In the Manufacturing Division, two basic products are constructed: a Machine Control Unit (MCU) and a Process Control Unit (PCU). A Machine Control Unit can be either sold in an external market or transferred to the Assembly Division where it will be made part of a Precision Control Device that sells for $270. The Process Control Units are sold externally to other manufacturers at a price of $120 per unit. The firm has a contractual obligation to deliver at least 80 PCU's and can sell up to 120 more to its external customers at this price.

The Manufacturing Division has the following cost structure:

	MCU	PCU
Direct materials	$ 50	$ 20
Direct labor	40	20
Overhead	90	60
Total	$180	$100

Labor costs are $20 per hour and overhead is charged at $30/machine hour. The overhead charge includes an allocation of the Manufacturing Division's fixed overhead of $10,000 to the 1,000 hours of available machine time.

At present, the price of the MCU in the external market is $215, but this price had been below $200 recently. The internal price for transferring MCU's from the Manufacturing to the Assembly Division has been set at $198 based on a 10% markup over costs.

The cost structure for the Assembly Division for producing the Precision Control Device is:

Transfer price of MCU	$198
Direct materials	5
Direct labor	30
Overhead	30
	$263

The overhead rate is $20/Direct Labor Hour of which 50% is variable. The hourly labor cost in the Assembly Division is identical to the Manufacturing Division's, since they share the same labor pool.

At present, neither division manager is happy with the current transfer price. Walter Patterson, the Assembly Division manager, complains that at the $198 transfer price, he earns less than a 3% profit margin over costs, whereas the Manufacturing Division is allowed a 10% markup over costs. Linda Martin, the Manufacturing Division manager, however, is upset about the transfer price being well below the price at which she can sell the MCU's in the external market. At present, she is being asked to produce and transfer 240 MCUs to the Assembly Division. This doesn't leave much machine time to produce MCUs for the external market, especially when at least 80 PCUs must also be manufactured on the same equipment to meet already contracted sales.

At present the Manufacturing Division has been scheduled to produce 125 PCUs and 250 MCUs of which 240 MCUs are to be transferred internally and 10 will be sold externally. The budgeted profit for this plan is:

$$
\begin{array}{rcl}
125 \text{ PCUs @ } \$20 \ (\$120{-}100) &=& \$2{,}500 \\
240 \text{ MCUs @ } \$18 \ (\$198{-}180) &=& 4{,}320 \\
10 \text{ MCUs @ } \$35 \ (\$215{-}180) &=& \underline{\hspace{1em} 350} \\
\text{Total manufacturing division} & & \\
\quad \text{profit} & & \$7{,}170
\end{array}
$$

Linda Martin argues that she could increase her profits by selling all of her output externally and that it is silly for the firm to force internal transfers when there are more profitable external opportunities available.

Walter Patterson is upset about the proposed shift in Linda's sales plans. He reminds her that when the external price of the MCUs was below $200, she was glad to have a secure internal market for these units at the $198 transfer price. Walter continues, "One can hardly run a business on a sensible long-term basis if the supplying division shifts its output between internal and external customers based on short-term shifts in prices. How can I plan my production levels and schedule my labor force if there are dramatic swings in the output I am supposed to produce? Also, since I can hardly make money, even at the $198 transfer price, perhaps we should just stop making the PCU entirely."

Required:

1. Analyze the problems that have arisen from the transfer price of $198.
2. Given the current pricing structure, what production plan maximizes Linda Martin's profits in the Manufacturing Division?
3. Given the current pricing structure, what production plan maximizes the profits of Penn Hills Computer (the sum of the profits in the Manufacturing and Assembly Divisions)?

4. What transfer price will motivate the two divisional managers to seek the companywide profit-maximizing plan?
5. How does your answer to the above questions change if we introduce the additional information that no more than 1,000 Direct Labor Hours can be used by the two divisions, combined?

14–6 Shuman Automobiles Inc.

Clark Shuman, the part owner and manager of an automobile dealership, was nearing retirement, and wanted to begin relinquishing his personal control over the business's operations. (See Exhibit 1 for current financial statements.) The reputation he had established in the community led him to believe that the recent growth in his business would continue. His longstanding policy of emphasizing new car sales as the principal business of the dealership had paid off, in Shuman's opinion. This, combined with close attention to customer relations so that a substantial amount of repeat business was available, had increased the company's sales to a new high level. Therefore, he wanted to make organizational changes to cope with the new situation, especially given his desire to withdraw from any day-to-day managerial responsibilities. Shuman's three "silent partners" agreed to this decision.

Accordingly, Shuman divided up the business into three departments: new car sales, used car sales, and the service department (which was also responsible for selling parts and accessories). He then appointed three of his most trusted employees managers of the new departments: Jean Moyer, new car sales; Paul Fiedler, used car sales; and Nate Bianci, service department. All of these people had been with the dealership for several years.

Each of the managers was told to run his department as if it were an independent business. In order to give the new managers an incentive, their remuneration was to be calculated as a straight percentage of their department's gross profit.

Soon after taking over as manager of new car sales, Jean Moyer had to settle upon the amount to offer a particular customer who wanted to trade his old car as a part of the purchase price of a new one with a list price of $12,800. Before closing the sale, Moyer had to decide the amount he would offer the customer for the trade-in value of the old car. He knew that if no trade-in were involved, he would deduct about 15% from the list price of this model new car to be competitive with several other dealers in the area. However, he also wanted to make sure that he did not lose out on the sale by offering too low a trade-in allowance.

During his conversation with the customer, it had become apparent

Copyright © 1976 by the President and Fellows of Harvard College. Harvard Business School Case 9–177–033.

EXHIBIT 1
Shuman Automobiles Inc.
Income Statement for the Year Ended December 31

Sales of new cars			$7,643,746
Cost of new car sales*		$6,312,802	
Sales remuneration		324,744	6,637,546
			$1,006,200
Allowances on trade**			232,224
New cars gross profit			$ 773,976
Sales of used cars		$4,791,392	
Cost of used car sales*	$3,814,554		
Sales remuneration	183,308		
		3,997,862	
		$ 793,530	
Allowances on trade*		122,236	
Used cars gross profit			671,474
			$1,445,450
Service sales to customers		$ 695,022	
Cost of work*		513,968	
		$ 181,054	
Service work on reconditioning			
Charge	$ 473,160		
Cost*	488,624	(15,464)	
Service work gross profit			165,590
			$1,611,040
General and administrative expenses			983,420
INCOME BEFORE TAXES			$ 627,620

* These amounts include overhead assignable directly to the department, but exclude allocated general dealership overhead.

** Allowances on trade represent the excess of amounts allowed on cars taken in trade over their appraised value.

that the customer had an inflated view of the worth of his old car, a far from uncommon event. In this case, it probably meant that Moyer had to be prepared to make some sacrifices to close the sale. The new car had been in stock for some time, and the model was not selling very well, so he was rather anxious to make the sale if this could be done profitably.

In order to establish the trade-in value of the car, the used car manager, Fiedler, accompanied Moyer and the customer out to the parking lot to examine the car. In the course of his appraisal, Fiedler estimated the car would require reconditioning work costing about $700, after which the car would retail for about $3,700. On a wholesale basis, he could either buy or sell such a car, after reconditioning, for about $3,200. The wholesale price of a car was subject to much greater fluctuation than the retail price, depending on color, trim, model, etc. Fortunately, the car being traded in was a very popular shade. The retail automobile dealer's handbook of used car prices, the "Blue Book," gave a cash buying price range of $2,750 to

$2,930 for the trade-in model in good condition. This range represented the distribution of cash prices paid by automobile dealers for that model of car in the area in the past week. Fiedler estimated that he could get about $2,200 for the car "as-is" (that is, without any work being done to it) at next week's auction.

The new car department manager had the right to buy any trade-in at any price he thought appropriate, but then it was his responsibility to dispose of the car. He had the alternative of either trying to persuade the used car manager to take over the car and accepting the used car manager's appraisal price, or he himself could sell the car through wholesale channels or at auction. Whatever course Moyer adopted, it was his primary responsibility to make a profit for the dealership on the new cars he sold, without affecting his performance through excessive allowances on trade-ins. This primary goal, Moyer said, had to be "balanced against the need to satisfy the customers and move the new cars out of inventory—and there was only a narrow line between allowing enough on a used car and allowing too much."

After weighing all these factors, with particular emphasis on the personality of the customer, Moyer decided he would allow $4,270 for the used car, provided the customer agreed to pay the list price for the new car. After a certain amount of haggling, during which the customer came down from a higher figure and Moyer came up from a lower one, the $4,270, allowance was agreed upon. The necessary papers were signed, and the customer drove off.

Moyer returned to the office and explained the situation to Joanne Brunner, who had recently joined the dealership as accountant. After listening with interest to Moyer's explanation of the sale, Brunner set about recording the sale in the accounting records of the business. As soon as she saw the new car had been purchased from the manufacturer for $8,890, she was uncertain as to the value she should place on the trade-in vehicle. Since the new car's list price was $12,800 and it had cost $8,890, Brunner reasoned the gross margin on the new car sale was $3,910. Yet Moyer had allowed $4,270 for the old car, which needed $700 repairs and could be sold retail for $3,700 or wholesale for $3,200. Did this mean that the new car sale involved a loss? Brunner was not at all sure she knew the answer to this question. Also, she was uncertain about the value she should place on the used car for inventory valuation purposes. Brunner decided that she would put down a valuation of $4,270, and then await instructions from her superiors.

When Fiedler, manager of the used car department, found out what Brunner had done, he went to the office and stated forcefully that he would not accept $4,270 as the valuation of the used car. His comment went as follows:

"My used car department has to get rid of that used car, unless Jean (Moyer) agrees to take it over himself. I would certainly never have allowed the customer $4,270 for that old tub. I would never have given any more than $2,500, which is the wholesale price less the cost of repairs. My department has to make a profit too, you know. My own income is dependent on the gross profit I show on the sale of used cars, and I will not stand for having my income hurt because Jean is too generous towards his customers."

Brunner replied that she had not meant to cause trouble, but had simply recorded the car at what seemed to be its cost of acquisition, because she had been taught that this was the best accounting practice. Whatever response Fiedler was about to make to this comment was cut off by the arrival of Clark Shuman, the general manager, and Nate Bianci, the service department manager. Shuman picked up the phone and called Jean Moyer, asking him to come over right away.

"All right, Nate," said Shuman, "now that we are all here, would you tell them what you just told me?"

Bianci, who was obviously very worried, said: "Thanks Clark; the trouble is with this trade-in. Jean and Paul were right in thinking that the repairs they thought necessary would cost about $700. Unfortunately, they failed to notice that the rear axle is cracked, which will have to be replaced before we can sell the car. This will probably use up parts and labor costing about $530.

"Besides this," Bianci continued, "there is another thing which is bothering me a good deal more. Under the accounting system we've been using, I can't charge as much on an internal job as I would for the same job performed for an outside customer. As you can see from my department statement (Exhibit 2), I lost almost eight thousand bucks on internal work last year. On a reconditioning job like this which costs out at $1,230, I don't even break even. If I did work costing $1,230 for an outside customer, I would be able to charge him about $1,660 for the job. The Blue Book[1] gives a range of $1,620 to $1,700 for the work this car needs, and I have always aimed for about the middle of the Blue Book range. That would give my department a gross profit of $430, and my own income is based on that gross profit. Since it looks as if a high proportion of the work of my department is going to be the reconditioning of trade-ins for resale, I figure that I should be able to make the same charge for repairing a trade-in as I would get for an outside repair job."

Messrs. Fiedler and Moyer both started to talk at once at this point. Fiedler, the more forceful of the two, managed to edge out Moyer: "This axle business is unfortunate, all right; but it is very hard to spot a cracked axle. Nate is likely to be just as lucky the other way next time. He has to

---

[1] In addition to the Blue Book for used car prices, there was a Blue Book which gave the range of charges for various classes of repair work. Like the used car book, it was issued weekly, and was based on the actual charges made and reported by vehicle repair shops in the area.

EXHIBIT 2
Shuman Automobiles Inc.
Analysis of Service Department Expenses
for the Year Ended December 31

	Customer Jobs	Reconditioning Jobs	Total
Number of Jobs	2780	1051	3831
Direct labor	$213,860	$197,640	$ 411,500
Supplies	74,124	65,510	139,634
Department overhead (fixed)	63,116	52,134	115,250
	$351,100	$315,284	$ 666,384
Parts	162,868	173,340	336,208
	$513,968	$488,624	$1,002,592
Charges made for jobs to customers or other departments	695,022	473,160	1,168,182
Gross profit (loss)	$181,054	$ (15,464)	$ 165,590
General overhead proportion			114,160
Departmental profit for the year			$ 51,430

take the rough with the smooth. It is up to him to get the cars ready for me to sell."

Moyer, after agreeing that the failure to spot the axle was unfortunate, added: "This error is hardly my fault, however. Anyway, it is ridiculous that the service department should make a profit out of jobs it does for the rest of the dealership. The company can't make money when its left hand sells to its right."

At this point, Clark Shuman was getting a little confused about the situation. He thought there was a little truth in everything that had been said, but he was not sure how much. It was evident to him that some action was called for, both to sort out the present problem and to prevent its recurrence. He instructed Ms. Brunner, the accountant, to "work out how much we are really going to make on this whole deal," and then retired to his office to consider how best to get his managers to make a profit for the company.

A week after the events described above, Clark Shuman was still far from sure what action to take to motivate his managers to make a profit for the business. During the week, Bianci, the service manager, had reported to him that the repairs to the used car had cost $1,376, of which $640 represented the cost of those repairs which had been spotted at the time of purchase, and the remaining $736 was the cost of supplying and fitting a replacement for the cracked axle. To support his own case for a higher allowance on reconditioning jobs, Bianci had looked through the duplicate invoices over the last few months, and had found examples of similar (but not identical) work to that which had been done on the trade-in car. The amounts of these invoices averaged $1,610, which the customers had paid without question, and the average of the costs assigned to these jobs was $1,192. (General overhead was not assigned to individual jobs.) In addition, Bianci had obtained from Ms. Brunner, the accountant, the cost analysis shown in Exhibit 2. Bianci told Shuman that this was a fairly typical distribution of the service department expense.

Required:

1. Suppose the new car deal is consummated, with the repaired used car being retailed for $3,700, the repairs costing Shuman $1,376. Assume that all sales personnel are on salary (no commissions), and that departmental overheads are fixed. What is the dealership contribution on the total transaction (i.e., new and repaired-used cars sold)?

2. Assume each department (new, used, service) is treated as a profit center, as described in the case. Also assume in a–c that it is known with certainty *beforehand* that the repairs will cost $1,376.
    a. In *your* opinion, at what value should this trade-in (*un*repaired) be transferred from the new car department to the used car department? Why?
    b. In *your* opinion, how much should the service department be able to charge the used car department for the repairs on this trade-in car? Why?
    c. Given your responses to a and b, what will be each of the three departments' contributions on this deal?

3. Is there a strategy in this instance that would give the dealership more contribution than the one assumed above (i.e., repairing and retailing this trade-in used car)? Explain. In answering *this* question, assume the service department operates at capacity.

4. Do you feel the three profit center approach is appropriate for Shuman? If so, explain why, including an explanation of how this is better than other specific alternatives. If not, propose a better alternative and explain why it is better than three profit centers and any other alternatives you have considered.

14–7   *Transfer Pricing Among Related Businesses*

Kirkpatrick Associates, Incorporated*

Mr. Richard (Rick) Kirkpatrick, Sr. started Columbus Realty, Inc., a real estate firm, about 40 years ago. His personality and honesty made this undertaking a success. When his eldest son, John Kirkpatrick, graduated with an engineering degree, Kirkpatrick, Sr. incorporated K & S Construc-

---

* Copyright 1976 by Professor Felix P. Kollaritsch. Reproduced with permission.

tion Company and put John in charge. 40 percent of the stock was given to John, and 60 percent was deposited with Kirkpatrick Associates, Incorporated which Kirkpatrick, Sr. controlled, 100 percent. Having intimate knowledge of the housing market, Kirkpatrick, Sr. suggested, and John agreed, that the construction company should concentrate on custom designed and built houses in the price range of $100,000 to $200,000. John Kirkpatrick's technical knowledge and imagination made the construction company a success.

Kirkpatrick, Sr.'s second son, Court, received a degree in architecture but upon graduation was not ready to enter employment. Upon the suggestion of several friends and the family, Court Kirkpatrick continued with his education and pursued an M.B.A. degree. During this study, and because of a special project he was assigned, he became interested in the development of living complexes around shopping centers. In this project, both the living complex and the shopping center were designed with a continental motif. Further research convinced him that this project would not only be feasible, but also very profitable. He discussed his idea and all the information he had gathered with his father, who agreed that this kind of design seemed to be the upcoming style. Upon Court's graduation, the Columbus Rental Company was incorporated with the same stock arrangement as with the K & S Construction Company.

Court bought land and proceeded with the design and building of a shopping center and several apartment buildings around this shopping center. This undertaking was an instant success, too. The shopping center has an extraordinary 100 percent lease commitment, and some prospects on a waiting list. The apartments have an 85 percent occupancy rate. This complex has been and still is the "in thing" in this community. Mostly young upper middle class people are living there.

Up until several years ago, Court had to maintain a large maintenance crew whose task was to keep up both the shopping center and the apartment buildings. However, when the youngest of the children, Richard Kirkpatrick, Jr., graduated, this function was separated from his brother's company, and the Columbus Remodeling Company was incorporated. Stock arrangements were the same as for the other companies. Rick, Jr. was put in charge of this company. Over the years, the various family members have retired from active participation in the day-to-day activities of the companies. Each still sets overall policies and objectives for the entities, but leaves the daily operations to the general managers. Each general manager shares in the profit of his company. Although there still exists very close cooperation among these companies, they have grown to be rather independent of each other. If one inside company wants any service from the other, these services are priced the same as to outsiders. Managers of each feel they are competitive and offer the best service for the lowest cost. For instance, the Columbus Remodeling Company does all the maintenance for the Columbus Rental Company. However, to keep this contract, Columbus Remodeling must be competitive with other maintenance companies.

These arrangements have generally been successful although occasional complaints have been raised. Recently, however, the complaints have become more vocal. To some degree they were due to poor general economic conditions. Last year was a depression year and, although the Kirkpatrick complex fared better than the average real estate company, the general managers experienced a considerable cut in their profit participation, and are now very conscious of any dealing which would reduce their profits.

During the last year, the Kirkpatrick family came up with another innovation in the real estate business—the "house trade-in." The Construction Company will construct a house for a buyer with the understanding that his old residence be taken in as a trade, providing it is located in Columbus. In many instances, this practice would avoid downpayments for the buyer, as well as the inconveniences of selling the house.

The value of the trade-in is established by the real estate company and the Remodeling Company. The Remodeling Company will determine what should be done to the house and give an estimate for necessary repair work. The real estate company will make suggestions as to certain remodeling needs which make a house more valuable and salable. The Remodeling Company will also give firm estimates on these suggestions. The real estate company will then give the construction company a realistic market value of the house.

The value of the renovated house, less the renovation costs, is used internally by the construction company to determine its profit on a sale and trade-in. Externally, the construction company will quote the buyer the renovated house value as the trade-in value, but also will increase its normal price for a given house for the costs of the remodeling. The reason for this valuation is that the buyer may see the asking price for his old house in a sales advertisement and may feel cheated if the price is more than he received. Very likely, he may not be aware of the total renovation costs.

Until the house is sold, the construction company has title to the house. It is responsible for any house repairs and remodeling, and for any interest, taxes, insurance, or other costs. The real estate company will list and sell the house, collecting a 6 percent commission from the buyer. This plan has been successful and has made the name of Kirkpatrick a household word in the real estate business throughout the state. However, the plan is not without drawbacks. The following transaction is an example, and your advice is solicited.

The K & S Construction Company sold a newly constructed house to Mr. Baxter as follows:

Price of New House	$200,000
Trade-In from Old House	50,000
Cash (from mortgage)	$150,000
Value Received	
Cash	$150,000
Trade-In	40,000
Total	$190,000
Cost of Building New House	160,000
Profit	$ 30,000

The trade-in value was established as follows: the fair market value of the house, if fixed-up, was determined as $50,000 by the real estate company. The renovation needs were jointly determined by the manager of the real estate company and by the manager of the remodeling company. These needs were costed by the manager of the remodeling company as $10,000.

Two days after the deal was closed, a heavy rain occurred, and it was discovered that the roof must be replaced and the basement water-sealed. The costs for these repairs were established at $4,000 and $2,000.

The managers of the real estate and construction companies think that these repairs should be priced at $3,000 only, since the remodeling company has a 50 percent variable cost factor. The remodeling company's manager says that under no condition will he make the repairs for a price other than that quoted. He claims to have enough outside business to keep him occupied during the present high season. He might consider doing it for a somewhat lesser price during the off-season, which will begin in seven months. But his delay would mean not selling the house for at least a full year. Also, predictions for next year's prices for houses are impossible to make.

To complicate matters further, the manager of the rental company stated that he would like to acquire the house, since it is located within the general territorial boundaries which he would like, eventually, to incorporate. Furthermore, some of the people in the continental complex would prefer houses to apartments, if they were available. He is unwilling to pay more than $50,000 and the commission. He estimates rental income to be $500 per month, with an estimated 80 percent occupancy. Real estate taxes are $951 per year, maintenance is estimated to be about $500 per year, and allocated management expenses, $500 per year. Management expenses are fixed and would not change with the acquisition of this house. Income tax rate is 50 percent. Land value is estimated at $8,000. Life of the building is 30 years.

Required:

1. Determine the profit of the K & S Construction Company for this sale.
2. What should the charge be for fixing up the house?

3. Who should be charged with the fixing up costs? Why? Are there any changes in procedures you would suggest?
4. If the house is to be sold to outsiders, what alternatives are open to the company?
5. If the house is sold to the rental company, what is its price?
6. Should the house be rented or sold?

14–7 Chemical Bank: Allocation of Profits

In March 1983, Kenneth LaVine, senior vice president of Chemical Bank's Finance Division, was faced with a difficult problem: the profitability of Due Bills,[1] a lucrative product for the bank, had declined considerably. The retail branches had little incentive to sell the product actively since they received no credit for the revenues generated by Due Bills. The Treasury Group, however, which earned substantial profits on this product, felt strongly that Due Bills should be marketed aggressively. Since the Finance Division had the ultimate authority to legislate cost allocations and transfer prices, Ken had to decide what could be done to raise Due Bill volume and yet satisfy both divisions. He commented:

> This is one of those profit measurement conflicts that arise from time to time. We've got to iron out a solution which is fair to all the parties involved and, perhaps more important, which will cause the people involved to make the decisions that are in the bank's best interest.

Background of Chemical Bank

Chemical Bank, with 20,000 employees and $46.9 billion in assets, was the sixth largest U.S. commercial bank in 1983. As a major commercial bank, Chemical offered a broad range of financial services throughout the world.

In 1982, Chemical Bank reorganized into three major profit centers: Personal and Banking Services Group, World Banking Group, and Treasury Group. The three groups were further divided into divisions, most of which were also evaluated as profit centers. Four areas at Chemical were involved in the Due Bill controversy:

---

[1] Due Bills were receipts issued to customers that represented ownership in a security, in this case, Treasury Bills. They were issued to customers who had purchased Treasury Bills but did not need to hold the actual bills. The Due Bill promised that the bank would pay a specified rate of interest and upon maturity would remit principal and interest. (Further explanation of Due Bills is provided later in the case.)

This case was prepared by Carolyn M. Bitetti under the supervision of Professor Kenneth A. Merchant. Copyright © 1983 by the President and Fellows of Harvard College. Harvard Business School case 9–184–047.

1. Government trading segment of the *Treasury Group* which used Due Bills to generate revenue in the money markets.
2. *Metropolitan Division* of the Personal and Banking Services Group which sold Due Bills.
3. *Trust and Investment Division* of the Personal and Banking Services Group which administered Due Bills.
4. *Finance Division* which arbitrated the revenue and cost allocations of Due Bills.

Treasury Group

In 1983, Chemical Bank had a continual funding need of roughly $25 billion. The Treasury Group was responsible for raising these funds at the lowest possible cost. Treasury also managed the bond-trading, foreign exchange trading, bond investments and all other short-term money market activities.

Treasury was organized into four business segments, each a profit center: Government Trading, Money Market Trading, Municipal Trading and Foreign Exchange. Treasury Group's incentive system was very closely tied to profit performance. For each segment, a bonus pool was calculated as a fixed percentage (usually 10%–15%) of Net Earnings before Taxes, less direct and allocated expenses. This was then allocated among the traders and salespeople according to profits earned. The bonus opportunity for a trader could be as high as 200%–300% of salary and therefore represented an important part of the compensation package. Due Bills were handled by the Government Trading segment of Treasury and represented about 25% of its 1982 revenues and profits. Since Due Bills were a major contributor to the bonus pool, the government traders were very sensitive to any decline in the profitability of this product.

Metropolitan Division

The Metropolitan Division (Metro) included the retail branch network, VISA and MasterCard operations, and Chemical's consumer finance company. Metro provided services for individuals and small- and medium-sized New York businesses. One of Metro's strategic goals was to become a "one-stop" financial center for its customers. As part of this strategy, Metro priced deposit products very competitively and offered a broad range of financial products such as money market accounts and discount brokerage services.

Senior managers of Metropolitan were evaluated on a profit-center basis but the branch managers were rewarded on the basis of a goal system. The aim of the goal system was to evaluate branch managers on those factors which they could control. One bank manager explained the background of the goal system at Chemical Bank:

Back in 1976, when Bob Lipp[2] took over Metro, he moved from a bottom-line evaluation of the Metropolitan branch system to a goal system. A major source of revenue for the branch system is interest earned on demand deposit balances, but the amount of revenue they generate is uncontrollable. When interest rates were up, they got a big credit for it and when interest rates came down, their earnings came down. Bob said, "This is silly—let's focus on the controllables." So he set up the goal system and evaluated people on that basis—how well do they do against the goals that have been set.

Under the goal system, certain quantitative business objectives were established on a negotiated basis between the branch manager and senior Metro managers. Dick Orr, Chief Administrative Officer for Metro, commented on this process:

> The branch manager prepares budgeted objectives for his branch based on current performance, with an eye towards whether the market is growing or declining. This is reviewed by and negotiated with the district head who also understands the marketplace. All the branch objectives are then aggregated for Metro Division as a whole. If the aggregate is too low, we go back to the branches to renegotiate. It's really a very fair process and we achieve a strong commitment to the goals from the managers.

Each objective was assigned a certain number of points which could be earned by the branch manager when the objective was achieved. The maximum number of points that could be earned was 100 (see Exhibit 1). Three levels of goal difficulty were set for each objective:

1. *Budget* was the expected performance level. Half of the points assigned to each objective could be earned by achieving the budgeted level for that objective.
2. *Base Accountability Level (BAL)* was the minimum performance level that had to be attained for each objective before points could be earned. This was set at 10% below budget.
3. *Goal* was the target level for which the maximum possible points could be earned. This was set 10% above budget.

A portion of the maximum number of points set for each objective could be earned for performance levels between the BAL and the goal. The branch manager's aim was to earn as many points as possible towards the 100-point maximum. Bonuses and raises were 95% determined by performance under the goal system.

---

[2] As of 1983, Mr. Robert Lipp was senior executive vice president in charge of the Personal and Banking Services Group.

EXHIBIT 1
Chemical Bank: Allocation of Profits
Typical Point Assignment under Metropolitan
Division Goal System

Summary:

1.	Deposits	55 Points
2.	Loans	16 Points
3.	Revenues	10 Points
4.	Expenses	19 Points
		100 Points

Detailed Level:

1. *Deposits*

Business Deposits	25 Points
Personal Deposits	15 Points
Savings Accounts	5 Points
Other Time Accounts	10 Points
	55 Points

2. *Loans*

Installment Loans	7 Points
Revolving Credits	3 Points
Commercial Loans	6 Points
	16 Points

3. *Revenue*

Direct Fees	10 Points

4. *Expenses**   19 Points

* Includes only those expenses which are directly controllable at the branch level. Points are determined by comparing actual expenses to budgeted expenses.

Dick Orr commented on the effectiveness of the system:

The system really has teeth because it's so closely tied to financial rewards. In addition, there's a monthly rendering of the goal system so each branch manager sees where he stands versus all the other branches. There's a report listing the 10 branches which performed best under the goal system and the 10 worst. The branch managers of the 10 worst get a phone call from the Big Boss (head of Metro) at the end of the month. Believe me, it's a very powerful system.

The division head had the discretion to change the point weighting of each goal in order to tailor objectives to the geographic and economic environments faced by different branches. In 1983, the sale of Due Bills was not an objective under the goal system.

Trust and Investment Division

Like the Metropolitan Division, Trust and Investment (T&I) was a unit of the Personal and Banking Services Group. T&I provided money management services to a range of clients including individual and institutional clients. Its traditional function was as custodian or trustee and as general investment counselor. In addition, T&I offered international banking services such as the administration of investments in precious metals or foreign securities.

T&I was involved in the Due Bills controversy because it performed the administration functions. T&I set up the Due Bills accounts and provided the data processing services.

Finance Division

The Finance Division was the strategy and corporate planning arm of the bank. It had broad responsibilities for strategic planning, corporate finance and accounting and control.

Ken LaVine ran one of the four major parts of the Finance Division—Management Accounting and Taxes—which, among other things, managed bankwide profit planning and monitored management information such as organizational, product and customer profitability. Ken was responsible for resolving all transfer pricing issues and had ultimate decision-making authority in this area.

Explanation of Due Bills

A Due Bill was an acknowledgement that the bank had sold securities to a customer, that his account had been charged, and that, if requested, the securities would be delivered when they became available. The Due Bill also acknowledged that upon maturity Chemical would pay principal plus interest at a specified rate. Due Bills were issued to customers who had purchased Treasury Bills[3] through one of Chemical's branches, but who did not request actual possession of the T-Bill. The Federal Reserve Bank required that this transaction be collateralized with a similar security three days after the initial purchase.

The bank earned profits on Due Bills in three ways: a funding spread (net interest income), trading profits and fees.

1. *Net interest income* (NII) was earned when Treasury invested Due Bill funds to earn a higher rate than it had to pay the customer. The difference between

---

[3] *Treasury Bills* (commonly called "T-Bills") are short-term obligations of the United States government which are issued for three-month, six-month, or one-year periods.

the rate paid the customer and the rate earned on the investment was called a "spread" or net interest income.

To illustrate, assume a customer purchased a 30-day, $10,000 Treasury Bill with an interest rate of 8%. If the customer did not insist on receiving the actual T-Bill, he would be issued a Due Bill which stated that Chemical Bank owed him $10,000 at the end of 30 days, plus interest at 8%. Meanwhile, Treasury might invest those funds for 30 days at 9.5%, thus earning a 150 basis point spread (1% = 100 basis points). Rather than match the term of the investment with the term of the deposit, Treasury also had the option of investing the funds for a shorter or longer period than the term of the deposit. This was known as mismatching, and since it resulted in interest rate risk, it required skill on the part of the traders in anticipating interest rates and reacting quickly to any changes in the market. In 1982, Treasury's average funding spread on Due Bills was roughly 150–175 basis points.

2. *Trading Profits*: Since Due Bill transactions had to be collateralized after three days, Treasury held a pool of T-Bills in inventory for this purpose. This pool gave Treasury flexibility to trade (buy and sell) T-Bills in the secondary market thus earning a trading profit (for example, by selling a particular T-Bill for a slightly higher price than it paid for it). The trading operation also required skill since there was always the risk of losing money in a trade (i.e., selling a T-Bill for a lower price than was paid for it).

3. *Fees*: The customer was charged a $25 fee for each transaction.

Background of Controversy over Due Bills

The Due Bill issue first arose in early 1981. Metro Division had reviewed the profitability of Due Bills and calculated that they were losing $26.50 on a typical transaction (see Exhibit 2). This was because T&I was charging Metro for the cost of processing Due Bills but Metro was receiving no credit for Due Bill revenue. Dick Orr, chief administrator of Metropolitan Division, explained Metro's position:

> It was essentially a nuisance product for us. Selling a T-Bill required at least 20 minutes of branch personnel time—explaining the features of T-Bills versus other investments, obtaining recent interest rate quotes, filling out forms, notifying Treasury, etc. Branch personnel time is a scarce resource for us and here they were spending 20 minutes for a transaction for which Metro received *zero* credit.

Metro suggested that the transaction fee for Due Bills be increased with the additional fee allocated to Metro to cover the related expenses. Treasury, however, which was credited with all Due Bill revenue, was opposed to raising the $25 fee. In a memorandum written in February 1981, Bill Staples (Manager—Treasury Control) argued that for competitive reasons Chemical should not raise the fee:

EXHIBIT 2
Chemical Bank: Allocation of Profits
Metropolitan Division Analysis

DATE: January 12, 1982
  TO: J. R. Spressert (Vice President and Division Controller—Metro)
FROM: J. D. Furber (Metro Control Analyst)
  RE: Odd-Lot T-Bill Transactions

The Treasury Division performs the "trading" of all odd-lot (defined as securities under $100m) government securities within the bank. The actual purchase of the securities, however, is handled in the line areas of the bank, principally the Metropolitan Division branches, while Trust & Investment (T & I) handles the operational aspects. Metropolitan is the major contributor to the Treasury's odd-lot business, with a sampling in January 1981 indicating that the Metropolitan Division accounts for up to 85% of total odd-lot volume in the bank. It is largely due to our extensive branch system that Chemical Bank is the largest issuer of T-Bills of all the major NYC banks.

The following is a profit and loss analysis of a T-Bill sale in the branch system: Assume $10,000 principal—180 day maturity.

Revenues	*Metropolitan*	*T & I*	*Treasury*	*Total Bank*
NII—Due Bills	—	—	$54.00	$54.00[1]
Trading Profit	—	—	17.97	17.97[2]
Fee Revenue	—	—	25.00	25.00[3]
			$96.97	$96.97
Less				
Processing Expenses	$ 4.50[4]	$22.00[5]	$11.43[6]	$37.93
Allocation of T & I				
Expense to Metro	22.00	(22.00)	—	—
Pretax Profit (loss)	$(26.50)	—	$85.54	$59.04

In addition to absorbing our own direct expenses ($4.38/transaction) incurred in handling the T-Bill transaction, Metro is being charged for the operational expenses (22.00/transaction) of the T & I bank. Yet, *all* revenues from the odd-lot transactions are being credited to the Treasury Division alone. Thus, on the internal financial statements, Treasury's profits are somewhat overstated while Metro is bearing the bulk (70%) of the expenses associated with the transactions.

[1] The $54.00 is an estimate based on 1980 figures of net interest income earned per transaction.

[2] An estimate made by government traders of average profit achieved per trade in the secondary market.

[3] This is the $25.00 charged per transaction.

[4] Direct Metro processing, a handling expense calculated to be $4.50 per transaction.

[5] Calculations based on 1980 figures. A total T & I processing expense of $1,210,000 allocated over 55,000 Metro transactions ($1,210,000 ÷ 55,000 = 22.00).

[6] Estimates of Treasury's 1980 T-Bill expense associated with each transaction.

Note: Numbers are disguised.

Treasury feels that they have developed a strong customer base in the odd-lot market.[4] Even with this strong base, we believe that there is an untapped source of customers that we have not reached. If our fee is higher than competitive rates, we feel it would be extremely difficult to expand our existing customer base.

The memo went on to conclude:

The selling of odd-lot (Due Bill) transactions has been very profitable to Chemical Bank over the years. Treasury Group feels strongly that any increase in the fee at this time will have adverse effects on our bottom line. Additionally, we are making a reputation for the bank as a leader in the odd-lot market. If we were to increase our fee, customers may go to other commercial banks with the possibility that the entire account relationship will transfer. It is for the above reasons that Treasury Division feels that the bank should not increase the present fee of $25.

Treasury also steadfastly refused to give up any revenues to Metro. Petros Sabatacakis, senior vice president in Treasury, summarized their position:

The government traders in Treasury felt Metro's demands were unjustified. The traders felt they were the ones generating the revenue by playing the market. Besides, Metro was simply reacting to customers' requests for this product, they weren't actively pushing it. As far as the traders were concerned, they were doing Metro a favor by providing its customers with this service. So the traders were saying "Why should we share any revenue with Metro?" We were also taking a defensive approach. We were in a powerful position—receiving all of the revenues and incurring only relatively small direct expenses. Any change would be to our detriment.

Metro Division, however, was becoming increasingly impatient about Due Bills as reflected in an excerpt from a memo written by two Metro staff people in early 1982:

On December 31st, we received a phone call from a Metro Division head demanding to know why we in Metro weren't unilaterally increasing the T-Bill transaction fee. The activity was clogging his branches, his employees had a hard time in general getting through to Treasury, and Metropolitan was losing money on the transactions. Pressure is mounting within Metropolitan to do something about Treasury Bill transactions.

---

[4] The *odd-lot market* included all government securities transactions under $100,000.

December 1982

The issue remained unresolved through 1982, but the conflict came to a head towards year end. At that time, two events occurred which caused a decline in the total profits generated by Due Bills: a drop in interest rates and the advent of bank-offered money market accounts.

The decline in interest rates reduced Treasury's funding spread and trading profits from Due Bills. Lower interest rates also reduced the attractiveness of T-Bills as investments, and this negatively affected the volume of Due Bills sold.

The bank-offered money market accounts came into being because of a December 1982 mandate from the Depository Institutions Deregulation Committee of the United States Congress. Commercial banks could now offer interest-bearing money market accounts to their customers. The Metro Division saw this as an opportunity to attract deposits back into the banking system and to further its strategy of becoming a "one-stop" financial center. In an effort to capture a share of this market, Metro offered to pay branch officers an incentive of 10 basis points on all new deposits brought into the bank.[5] The proceeds of the new accounts, however, could not be from an existing Chemical checking or saving account; they had to come from another source, such as a Merrill Lynch account. Proceeds diverted from T-Bills (or Due Bills), even those purchased through Chemical, were also allowed under this scheme. Dick Orr commented on this move:

> In retrospect we should have checked with Treasury before we went ahead and offered that incentive. Treasury thought our action was outrageous, but we had little idea how profitable Due Bills were for them—in fact, Treasury was always complaining about how expensive it was for them to handle Due Bills. Anyway, we weren't expecting the negative reaction we got from them—they went bananas.

The Metro incentive system and the decline in interest rates combined caused Treasury's level of profits from Due Bills to drop—a fact which affected the government traders directly, given Treasury's incentive system. Petros Sabatacakis commented:

> The traders were putting pressure on me to get Metro to rectify the situation by raising the *volume* of Due Bills to compensate for the drop in profitability of each transaction. But what was Metro's incentive to sell the product? I knew we'd have to give something up if we wanted to get something in return.

---

[5] For example, a new $50,000 account would pay an incentive of $50 (.001 × 50,000 = $50).

Finance Division Review

In light of Metro's continuing complaints and Treasury's concern over their decline, the Finance Division undertook a detailed review of the situation. It quickly became clear that for the bank as a whole, Due Bills were very lucrative. According to Finance Division estimates, 1982 contribution from Due Bills was $9.9 million (see Exhibit 3 for Finance Group calculations). The Finance Division also determined that Due Bills were more profitable for the bank than the new Super-Saver (money market) accounts (see Exhibit 4), but because of the way profits were allocated, this same profit picture was not true for Metro.

EXHIBIT 3
Chemical Bank: Allocation of Profits
Finance Group Due Bill Contribution Analysis
(in millions)

	1982	Projected 1983
Revenues		
Net Interest Income	$ 7.5	$3.0–$5.0
Trading Profits	2.4	1.5
Fees	.5	.2
Balances[1]	.9	.2
Total Revenue	$11.2	$4.9–$6.9
Incremental Expenses (variable)		
Treasury	1.0	$.7
T & I Processing	.3	.2
Total Incremental Expenses	$ 1.3	$.9
Total Contribution	$ 9.9	$4.0–$6.0

[1] Additional balances were often gained because some customers prefunded their accounts before purchasing a T-Bill and/or did not withdraw the funds immediately upon maturity. Interest was earned on these balances.

Note: Numbers are disguised.

A memorandum written by a Finance Division analyst concluded that the main problem was that Metro had little incentive to sell Due Bills:

The absence of any incentive in the Metropolitan Division to stimulate T-Bill sales seems to result in counterproductive behavior. This is especially true when branch managers are motivated to offer instruments that may not be as profitable to the bank (e.g., money market accounts and savings certificates). Possible incentives include the following:

- Fee sharing on all *sales*—all or part of $25 fee.
- Fee sharing on *new* sales—all or part of $25 fee.
- Include Due Bills in Metro goal system.
- Others?

EXHIBIT 4
Chemical Bank: Allocation of Profits
Finance Group Analysis of Super-Saver Account and Treasury Bill Profitability

This compares the profit generated by a Super-Saver Account with a Due Bill transaction. The example assumes a $10,000 principal, a 180 day maturity, and a 13.25% interest rate.

	Super Saver	Due Bill
Interest Income	$725.00	$54.00
Trading Profit	—	17.97
Fee Revenue	—	25.00
Total Revenues	$725.00	$96.97
Interest Cost	$664.00	—
FDIC Assessment[1]	4.13	—
Processing Costs	10.60	31.11[2]
Total Costs	$678.73	$31.11
Pre-Tax Profit	$ 46.27[3]	$65.86

[1] Federal Deposit Insurance Corporation insurance was required for all Super Saver Accounts. FDIC charged a fee for this insurance.

[2] This differs slightly from the processing cost figures in Exhibit 2 due to a different allocation of indirect costs.

[3] This total was credited entirely to the Metropolitan Division.

NOTE: Numbers are disguised.

A second issue that was related to the Due Bill controversy was: Who should be performing the administrative duties associated with maintenance of Due Bill Accounts? The administrative functions included setting up the customer accounts, keeping track of the principal and interest payments, monitoring maturity schedules and performing other related functions. All these functions were being performed by T&I, but the Treasury Division maintained they could perform these functions at a considerably lower cost to the bank. For 1982, T&I charged Metro $1.3 million for processing costs, which included both fixed and variable costs as follows:

Variable processing costs	$ 290,000
Overhead	1,010,000
Total	$1,300,000

Treasury Division had the capability to perform the same processing functions as T&I, and the Finance Division learned that Treasury could process the existing volume of Due Bills for a variable cost of $90,000. This cost would be in addition to direct expenses of $1 million that Treasury was already incurring in connection with Due Bills (see Exhibit 3).

Due Bill Meeting

In order to get the Due Bills issue resolved as quickly as possible, Ken LaVine scheduled a meeting of the senior officials in all of the areas of the bank affected by the Due Bill controversy. The meeting was to be held on March 31, 1983.

Prior to the meeting, both Treasury and Metro suggested solutions to the problem. Treasury's recommendation was to share 50% of the $25 fee with Metro on all sales that exceeded the 1981 Average Due Bill Balance plus 10%. The rationale was that Metro should be rewarded only for bringing Due Bill volume above past levels.

Metro's recommendation (shown in Exhibit 5) involved sharing the

EXHIBIT 5
Chemical Bank: Allocation of Profits
Metro Recommendations for Solution

---

1. The fee for odd-lot Treasury Bill Transactions should be increased by at least $5.00. Our market research indicates attrition in transaction volume will be a minor risk.
2. Revenues associated with this product should be shared by the Treasury and Metropolitan Divisions. Since Metro has contact with 80% of T-Bill customers, perhaps revenue could be earned by Metro in terms of a finder's fee of $20 per transaction, which is sufficiently large to cover expenses incurred in processing purchases and to provide a margin of fee revenue to the Branch. Metro is the marketing and selling agent of this product, and, as such, should have an incentive for doing the job well. Further, under this scenario of "fee splitting," the T & I cost should be shared as well. A revised income statement on a single transaction with the fee set at $30 might look like this:

Revenues	Metro	T & I	Treasury	Total Chemical
NII	—	—	$ 54.00	$ 54.00
Trading Profit	—	—	17.97	17.97
Fee Revenue	20.00	—	10.00	30.00
Total	$20.00	—	$ 81.97	$101.97
Expenses				
Processing	$ 4.50	$22.00	$ 11.43	$ 37.93
Charge back	11.00	(22.00)	11.00	—
Total	$ 15.50	0	$ 22.43	$ 37.93
NEBT—Proposed	$ 4.50	0	$ 59.54	$ 64.04
—Current	(26.50)	0	$ 85.54	$ 59.04
Variance	$ 31.00	0	$(26.00)	$ 5.00

Based on Metro's 80% share of 78,000 transactions, the Division would expect to earn $280,800.

NOTE: Numbers are disguised.

fee (which would be raised to $30) *and* the cost of processing. But Metro was open to suggestions, as Dick Orr explained:

> We in Metro decided that being intransigent and refusing to sell T-Bills was not the best way to go. We made an effort to take a more positive approach to the whole thing. First of all, it is in the best interest of the bank to resolve the Due Bill issue. Second, we are working hard to develop a package of products that will make us a one-stop financial department store. With Treasury's products and our strong distribution system, it makes sense for us to develop a spirit of cooperation, and we hope to show that our branches could be used effectively to sell other Treasury products.

Ken LaVine hoped that getting the key people together would end the controversy. He explained:

> We have to get this issue resolved. The level of Due Bills has dropped sharply, and this is having an adverse effect on the bank's earnings. We need to find a solution on which all parties can agree and get it implemented as quickly as possible. I called the meeting because I think we can best resolve this issue by getting the senior personnel— the people who have the authority to make decisions—together in the same room. If I can't get agreement at the meeting, I may just have to make the decision myself.

14–9   *Transfer Pricing in a Multinational Corporation*

Del Norte Paper Company (A)

"If I had purchased the kraft linerboard for the African box sale from one of our mills, I would have paid $360 per ton, $140 per ton higher than the price I actually paid by purchasing the linerboard in the spot market," said Frank Duffy, Managing Director of Del Norte Paper's Italian subsidiary (DNP–Italia). "I can't possibly make a profit for Del Norte if I have to pay so much for my principal raw material."

Del Norte Paper Company was a large, fully-integrated paper manufacturer. 1974 sales were about $2.8 billion, making Del Norte Paper one of the 75 largest industrial companies in the United States. The company's product line ranged from raw pulp to a large variety of converted paper products, including corrugated boxes.

DNP–Italia purchased kraft linerboard from outside suppliers and converted it into corrugated boxes. These boxes were sold primarily within

This case was prepared by William Sahlman under the supervision of M. Edgar Barrett. Copyright © 1976 by the President and Fellows of Harvard College. Harvard Business School case 9–177–034.

Italy, though occasional sales were made outside of Italy. DNP–Italia had 6 plants, each of which represented a separate profit center.

The African Bid

In mid-1975, an African firm asked a number of paper companies to submit bids on a large quantity of corrugated boxes. In total, 22 companies submitted bids, including DNP–Italia and another Del Norte susidiary, DNP–Deutschland. The bids were said to have ranged from approximately $340 per ton to over $550 per ton, with most of them within 5 percent of $400 per ton. Del Norte–Italia won the contract by submitting the lowest bid from a firm viewed as being capable of meeting the customer's desired delivery and quality standards.

The price quoted by DNP–Italia had been substantially below that quoted by DNP–Deutschland. The primary difference between the two bids was the raw material (kraft linerboard) cost calculation embedded in each. DNP–Deutschland had formed its estimate using a per ton price for kraft linerboard of $360 while DNP–Italia had used $220. The $360/ton figure was the price (inclusive of freight) quoted for export by a Del Norte Paper mill located in the Eastern United States. The $220 figure was the price for kraft linerboard of comparable quality in the European "Spot" market.

There were basically two reasons why the Del Norte Paper mill price was so much higher than the European spot price. First, Del Norte Paper was a member of the Kraft Export Association (KEA), a group of kraft linerboard manufacturers which was responsible for setting and stabilizing linerboard prices for the export market. The Del Norte Paper Company mill could not, as a member of the KEA, offer a lower price to its own converting plant than to any other external customer.

The second reason for the large price differential was the extremely weak economic conditions present in mid-1975. The paper and container industries were suffering from a worldwide slump. As a result of this slump, many non–KEA producers of kraft linerboard were selling their product at very low prices. This was the exact opposite situation as had existed in 1973, a year in which there was a worldwide paper and container economic boom, when the spot price for kraft linerboard had actually exceeded by a small amount the KEA set price.

Del Norte's Transfer Pricing System

Prices on domestic (U.S.) intra-company sales of linerboard at Del Norte Paper were set at the "market" level. That is, the transfer price was the price at which the linerboard could be bought or sold in the market place. However, on international intra-company sales, the product price was set at a level determined by the Kraft Export Association. The KEA price could vary according to market conditions, but tended to fluctuate less than the so-called spot price. Officials of Del Norte Paper in San Francisco estimated that, even if all foreign subsidiary managers agreed to take all of the KEA priced, Del Norte Paper linerboard available, some 60 to 65% of their linerboard would have to come from other sources.[1]

When a Del Norte Paper converting plant located in the United States purchased its linerboard from a company mill, the profit made by the mill on the transaction was included as part of one of the reported profit figures of the converting plant. The method employed for allocating the profit was rather complex. At the time of preparing the annual budget, the converting plant made a commitment to purchase a specific amount of kraft linerboard from a specific mill. The income statement of the converting plant was then credited with the actual mill profit resulting from delivery of actual orders placed against the commitment.

The figure used for the "mill profit" was determined by taking the mill profit applicable to the specific shipment after a full allocation of both fixed and variable costs and amending it for two specific items. First, any manufacturing variances were added to or subtracted from the mill profit. Second, in the event that the converting plant did not take as much of the mill's production as expected, the proportional cost of the resulting mill down time was charged to the converting plant.

In Del Norte's international operations, the profit allocation process was similar. The foreign converting plant entered into a commitment for its U.S. produced requirements. The "mill profit," as defined above, was credited to the converting plant and its manager. However, in contrast to domestic operations, the set of financial statements in which this amount was credited was not made freely available to the foreign subsidiary's managing director and other management personnel. The reason for this was to maintain a legal, arms-length business relationship. Such statements of "integrated profit" were, however, available upon request to the managing director of each foreign subsidiary.

The African Sale

The bid submitted by DNP–Italia to the African customer was $400 per ton of corrugated boxes. DNP–Italia's direct costs (variable costs) were approximately $325 per ton of which 72% or $235[2] represented the cost of kraft linerboard.

The bid submitted by DNP–Deutschland was $550 per ton of cor-

---

[1] This 60 to 65 percent was basically in grade lines not produced by DNP mills in the United States. In addition, it generally consisted of lower quality material than was normally found in the American market.

[2] Editor's Note: This figure represents the linerboard cost per ton of corrugated box sold. The actual cost per ton of linerboard used was $220.

rugated boxes. DNP–Deutschland's direct costs on the transaction were approximately $460 of which $385 represented the cost of kraft linerboard.

The average Del Norte Paper mill had a direct cost per ton of linerboard of $190.[3] Thus, the contribution per ton at the mill was approximately $170, given the KEA selling prices of $360 per ton. The $170 contribution figure minus the actual freight costs from the U.S. to Germany (approximately $45 per ton) and the allocated overhead at the mill level would have been credited to the DNP–Deutschland converting mill had Germany won the contract.

An Informal Discussion

Late one afternoon in July 1975, Frank Duffy, Managing Director of DNP–Italia held a discussion with John Powell, General Manager—International Operations of Del Norte Paper's Container Division. The specific topic of the discussion was the African container sale, but the conversation also touched on the transfer pricing system used by Del Norte Paper.

Duffy: John, you know I would prefer to buy all my linerboard from a Del Norte Paper mill, but I just cannot compete if I have to pay $360 per ton. The price competition in the box market has been absolutely fierce this year. If I paid that much for linerboard, I would have to price my corrugated boxes below cost in order to win any contracts. If I am supposed to be a profit center, you can't expect me to report a loss on every sale I make—which is exactly what I would do using $360 per ton linerboard.

Powell: But you would get credited with the mill profit in the transaction—you wouldn't have to report a loss.

Duffy: Maybe on your books I wouldn't show a loss, but on my books I sure would. We never see that profit here in Italy. The transaction is noted in some secret little book back in San Francisco. How am I supposed to convince my plant managers and sales people they are being credited with the mill profit when they never see it?

Furthermore, from a financial point of view, the transfer pricing system doesn't make sense. Even if the mill profit were put directly into our profit and loss statement, our cash flow would not benefit. As you know, John, this is a completely self-financed operation in Italy. If I have to borrow more money than I need to, then I incur extra interest costs. There is no offsetting credit for these expenses.

---

[3] The direct cost figure of $190 per ton at the linerboard mill included the cost of raw wood going into the mill. Approximately 30% to 40% of the raw wood used by the mill was purchased from the Del Norte Paper Company Woodlands Division at a market determined transfer price.

Powell: I sympathize with you, Frank, but we also have a responsibility to keep our mills operating. Further, by not purchasing Del Norte Paper linerboard when times are bad, you run the risk of not being able to buy linerboard from our U.S. mills when there is a shortage like there was two years ago. As you know, we're moving increasingly toward long-term commitments for delivery by our kraft linerboard mills. You also don't help maintain the pricing stability we've been working so hard to establish through the KEA.

Duffy: I appreciate the problem, but I also have the responsibility to keep my plants running. Unlike the U.S., I can't fire any of my laborers in Italy—the unions just won't allow it. Any orders I can get to keep those laborers busy is pure contribution to me.

Powell: I still think you're making a mistake by not purchasing Del Norte Paper linerboard. However, we're not going to resolve the issue today. If it were not for this damn recession, the problem probably wouldn't even exist. If it's O.K. with you, Frank, I'd like to have a chance to give the problem some more thought.

Required:

Analyze the Del Norte transfer pricing situation.

14–10   *Wilkinson Transport (B)*

In December 1979, the managing director of Wilkinson Transport was considering a change in the organization. Wilkinson Transport was a wholly owned subsidiary of the Lex Service Group Limited. Lex was a diversified service company with 1979 sales of £500 million and profits of £22.8 million before taxes and £19.7 million after taxes. It was organized into seven business groups. Wilkinson Transport was one of the five subsidiaries included in the Transportation Business Group.

In general, Lex Service was highly decentralized. The top management of the business group participated in strategic planning; it reviewed and approved the annual budget. It reviewed accounting and budget performance reports each month. As long as Wilkinson was performing within expectations, top management did not involve itself in the day-to-day operations.

Copyright © 1980 by the President and Fellows of Harvard College. Harvard Business School case 9–181–056.

Operations

Collection and Delivery Operations

Wilkinson Transport was an express parcel company that collected and delivered parcels weighing between ten kilograms and one metric ton. It operated throughout the United Kingdom and in Ireland through an arrangement with an associated company located there. Wilkinson typically collected 58,000 parcels a day from 2,300 customers and delivered these parcels to 10,000 addresses, ranging from retail outlets to industrial users. The average consignment was 5.3 parcels weighing 80 kilograms.

Wilkinson operated 16 depots throughout the United Kingdom. Each depot was responsible for a geographic area. Daily, it collected parcels from the customers in its area and delivered parcels for the entire network to the consignees within its area.

Each morning vans from each depot delivered parcels to the consignees within its area, and then collected the consignments from its customers. The vans returned to the depot, were off-loaded, and the parcels consolidated for the depot located in the area to which the parcels were to be delivered. Thus, each day a depot would have 15 different consolidations for delivery to other depots, plus the retention of its own delivery traffic.

Trunking

Each consolidation was loaded into vans and, during the night, the vans delivered the parcels to the appropriate depot and collected the parcels for consignees within its area. This operation was known as "trunking." There were a variety of trunking configurations. For example, Depot A and Depot B vans would meet at an intermediate point and exchange loads. Or Depot A would do the entire trunking for Depot B by delivering to Depot B and picking up its own parcels. In some instances, a depot would not have enough activity to warrant direct shipments from all depots. In this case, Depot A might deliver to Depot B parcels for delivery by Depot C. The next day Depot B delivered the parcels to Depot C. This was called transshipment. About 80 percent of the trunking was made directly to the depot that was to deliver the parcels and about 20 percent were transshipped. The trunking configurations were determined periodically by a computer model that simulated the optimum trunking configuration based on the past six months' collections and delivery patterns.

The delivery schedule for a typical parcel was as follows:

Monday: The parcel was collected from the customer.
Monday night: The parcel was trunked to the depot that was to deliver it.

Tuesday: The parcel was unloaded and assigned to the appropriate route.
Tuesday night: The parcel was loaded onto a delivery van.
Wednesday: The parcel was delivered.

About 10 percent of deliveries were overnight shipments. In this case, parcels are placed onto the back of the appropriate van that evening, and removed immediately upon arrival at the delivery depot, and loaded onto delivery vehicles.

Marketing

The volume and quality of sales depended on three factors: service, price, and personal sales effort. Each is discussed below.

Service

The most important factor in retaining present customers was the reliability of the service provided. Also, to a considerable extent, the ability to obtain new customers was affected by the company's reputation for service. Service was measured by the speed and reliability of delivery, although other factors, for example, the ability to inform the customer quickly as to the status of a consignment or the prompt settlement of claims for lost or damaged goods, were also important.

Speed and reliability depended on:

1. the proper marking of the parcel and the correct information on the waybill;
2. the correct classification of the destination at the collection depot;
3. the correct classification of the route at the delivery depot;
4. the handling of parcels so as to minimize damage; and
5. the control of theft.

Price

The transport business was extremely competitive and price was an important factor in obtaining new customers and retaining present customers. Wilkinson published a price card that provided the prices for all of the usual types of deliveries. Prices were based on the weight of the consignment and the distance traveled. Discounts from the price card were made for special circumstances. For example, large customers were sometimes quoted a fixed price per kilogram delivered. Or, salespersons discounted the list price to take account of competition.

Salespersons

A third factor in selling the service was the personal contacts made by individual salespersons. Salespersons also handled complaints or contacted present customers to ascertain that the service was satisfactory.

Recent Developments

By July of 1980 Wilkinson Transport had largely completed a program of computerization and mechanization started two years previously. This part of the case describes these programs.

Wilkontrol

WILKONTROL was the name of the computer system that had been designed to:

1. keep track of consignments during the collection and delivery process; and
2. provide current operating data to management.

The WILKONTROL system was installed in 1979.

The Consignment Note

The consignment note was the main source of information in the WILKONTROL system. The consignment note was initially prepared at the collection point and contained all of the relevant information about the consignment; for example, the shipper's name and address, the consignee's name and address, and the number and weight of the packages in the consignment. The consignment note was prepared in duplicate and was numbered for identification. One copy of the consignment note remained with the consignment; the other copy was retained by the depot.

Keeping Track of Consignments

The information from the consignment notes was recorded in a central computer by clerks in the depot. From this information, the computer calculated additional data such as the revenue from the consignment.

When the consignment moved from the collecting depot to the delivery depot, this information was recorded into the computer. The information was continually updated as the consignment was moved through the system. Finally, after the consignment was delivered, the driver returned the receipted copy of the delivery manifest to the depot and the final delivery was recorded.

Throughout the system there were computer terminals with visual display devices that gave access to the information stored in the central computer. Thus, the status of any consignment could be ascertained within four seconds from any point within the system. The WILKONTROL system allowed management to identify quickly shipments that deviated from the standard pattern and to take appropriate corrective action.

Wilkinson was the only transport company in the United Kingdom that employed such a computer control system in 1980.

Operating Statistics

The WILKONTROL system made it possible to provide detailed operating statistics on a daily and weekly basis. For example, at 10 A.M. every morning, the following information about the previous day's operation was available by depot and, if desired, by route:

- Number of consignments
- Number of waybills
- Total weight
- Number of packages
- Total revenue

In short, it was possible on a daily basis to observe the "profile" of the business being done on the preceding day down to the smallest organization unit. This information was then summarized by week and month.

In addition to the profile information, the depot managers were provided daily or weekly with all information relevant to the effective operation of the system. Statistics on any deviations from standard were available. This information was also required by regional and headquarter executives.

Depot Mechanization

It was Wilkinson's plan to mechanize most depots by 1983. It was expected that mechanization would increase both the efficiency and the capacity of the depots. Also, since much of the labor would be machine-paced, better standards and performance measures against these standards would be possible.

The Hub

The Hub, a highly mechanized central depot, was built in Nuneaton, a town near Birmingham. It was designed to be fully operational in the latter part of 1980. The Hub would completely transform the trunking patterns.

When operational, *all* depots would send their collection to the Hub. There, the parcels would be sorted mechanically and trunked to the delivery depots. This had several important advantages.

First, the collecting depots would not be required to sort and consolidate the collected parcels except those that were to be delivered within their area. This increased the effective capacity of the depots.

Secondly, vans from both the depots and the Hub would move fully loaded because all collections and deliveries were made to the same location. Under the present system, each depot sent vans to fifteen other locations, many of them with less than a full load.

Third, it would be possible for all drivers to reach the Hub in eight hours. EEC regulations by 1981 would require that a driver work a maximum of eight hours. Under the present system, some locations required more than eight hours driving time to reach their destination.

Fourth, the Hub was designed to provide a highly mechanized, efficient method for handling parcels. It would be possible to exercise greater control over all of the aspects of parcel handling.

The Organization

Exhibit 1 is an organization chart of Wilkinson Transport as of July 1, 1980. There were five staff officers and three regional managers reporting to the managing director. The commercial manager was responsible for the rate structure, the settlement of claims, public relations and advertising. Other staff offices are self-explanatory.

The Region

Each region was a profit center. Four staff officers and the general managers of the depots reported to the regional manager.

The Depot

Each depot was also a profit center. The depot manager was responsible for operations, sales, accounting, and the repair shop. Although depot managers came from a variety of backgrounds, many had worked their way up from hourly employment. Each depot had its own accounting system, which collected from customers and paid suppliers. Throughout the system costs were recorded in the area where they were incurred and revenues were recorded in the area where they were received. Each month, the depot accounts were consolidated by the regional accounting staff and the regions were consolidated by the headquarters staff.

Purchasing was also done locally although some items were controlled through companywide contracts.

EXHIBIT 1
Wilkinson Transport (B): Current Organization

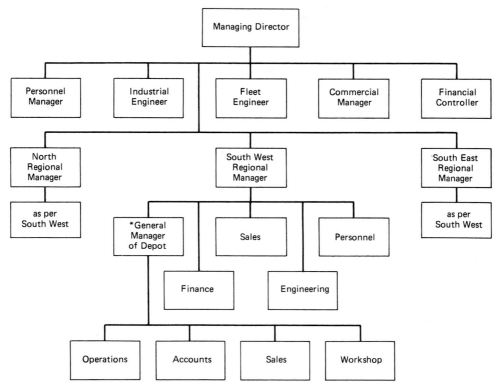

*N.B. Typical profit center consolidation at region.

The Financial Control System

The Lex organization exercised short-term control through an annual profit budget. Each year a budget was presented by Wilkinson's management to the management of the Transportation Business Group. The proposed budget was reviewed and either accepted or adjusted. The final version became the basis for the monthly reports that provided a comparison of the actual results with the budget on both a monthly and year-to-date basis. The report included the analyses of variances and explanations of the causes of the variances and the action being taken.

Within Wilkinson a similar type of control was used for each region and for each depot within the region. Each depot prepared a profit plan which was approved by the regional manager and each region prepared a regional profit plan that was approved by the managing director. Comparisons of actual performance to plan were made monthly by depot and consolidated by region. These reports included a great deal of operating statistics in addition to the financial comparisons.

In addition, there was a weekly information system that provided network profit contribution and efficiency indicators.

Transfer Pricing

Each depot typically performed two services for other depots and used similar services from other depots. The most important was to deliver parcels collected by other depots. Since the entire revenue was paid to the collecting depot, under a profit center system, part of this revenue must be reassigned to the delivering depot. Several methods of transfer pricing had been used. Currently, the intracompany charge made by the delivering depot to the collecting depot was a flat charge of £2.50 for each delivered consignment plus a variable charge of £10 per metric ton. This charge, on average, would compensate the delivery depot for its costs plus providing an allowance for profits.

The second service performed by one depot for the other was trunking, or delivering consignments between depots. This charge was £.40 a mile which also was sufficient to cover costs plus providing a profit.

Operating Control

Although the profit plan was an important tool for measuring managerial performance, management at all levels had access to detailed operating statistics daily and weekly. (These operating statistics were developed through the WILKONTROL system previously described.) For example, each week four pages of operating statistics were developed for each depot. One of the unique features of Wilkinson's measurement system was the amount of operating statistics that was available to management on a current basis.

Consideration of Change

In 1980, the managing director began to consider seriously whether the organization of Wilkinson Transport should be changed. In particular, he wondered whether the profit center system should be abandoned in favor of some other form of organization. Although he had always had some reservations about the profit center system, recent events had made it desirable to consider a change at this time. It seemed logical to him that if the organization were to be changed, it should be done in 1980.

The Strategic Plan

In 1979, Wilkinson Transport, together with the management of Lex, developed a new strategic plan. Among other things, the plan called for sales volume to be increased by 1985 to two and a half times the 1979 volume *at 1979 prices*. The managing director wondered whether volume increases of this magnitude could be accomplished with the present organization. Of principal concern was whether such a large increase in sales could be realized with a sales force that was decentralized into 16 separate depot organizations.

The Hub and Depot Mechanization

It is expected that the Hub would change significantly network operations and would result in a greater central control. In the same way, the mechanization of the depots would change the way that parcels were handled and, to some extent, would make central control easier. Although neither the Hub nor the depot mechanization would have an important direct impact on the profit center system, the managing director believed that these developments would have an impact on the timing of any organizational change. The operations of the depots would be changed considerably by these developments. It seemed to him that a change in organization, if one was to be made, would be more acceptable to those executives affected, if it were done coincidentally with the operating changes.

Concerns About the Profit Center System

Although the adoption of the 1979 strategic plan was the immediate cause for reconsidering the profit center form of organization, the top management of Wilkinson had experienced some concerns about the profit center system for some time. These concerns are described in this part of the case.

First, there was a question as to whether the depot manager controlled the critical elements of profit generation. For example, most of the delivery business was generated by other depots and most of the business generated by a depot was completed by other depots.

Second, there were questions as to whether excessive demands were being made on the depot manager. Was it not enough for the depot manager to be responsible only for operating the depot? Should not responsibility for sales, finance, and purchasing be assigned to functional experts? In fact, did the depot manager even have enough expertise in these areas?

Third, the profit center system tended to encourage depot managers to optimize depot profits at the expense of company profits. There was simply no incentive to sacrifice depot profits for the benefit of the company. For example, a depot manager could turn down (or, at least, not pursue aggressively) business that might benefit the company. If a depot was very busy, additional business might not be profitable to the collecting depot even though it might benefit the company. On the other hand, business that might be profitable to collect but marginal to deliver might be pursued aggressively. The problem was that the depot manager evaluated the desirability of business from the collection point of view only.

Finally, there was a question as to whether the transfer price system divided the revenue among contributing depots fairly. A related concern was whether the paper work required to implement the transfer price system was not only a waste of money but might even be producing misleading information.

Advantages of Profit Centers

In deciding upon any organizational changes, the managing director was well aware of the benefits that had accrued to the company because the profit center system *had* worked very well in the past. The depot general managers viewed themselves as managing their own business. Parcel collection and delivery was a geographic function and the depot general manager controlled all aspects within his area.

Three considerations were of particular importance in any change from the profit center system.

First, what would be the effect if responsibility for sales was taken from the depot manager? How would the trade-off between simply increasing the level of sales volume and increasing the quality of the sales be resolved? For example, additional business obtained from customers on established routes required almost no additional cost to collect; however, business in other locations might require considerable additional cost. If salespersons did not report to the depot manager, would they not be motivated to increase the level of sales regardless of location?

Second, the level of costs were to some extent a function of volume. The volume of activity, particularly of deliveries, was largely outside the control of the depot manager. Without the profit center system, how could the performance of a depot manager be measured?

Finally, the depot manager controlled the most important element of sales volume—service. Without profit centers, how would this be taken into consideration in the measurement system?

Required:

1. Should Wilkinson Transport change its organization? If so, how? If not, explain why the present system should not be changed.
2. How would you change the performance measurement system to accompany your revised organization? In particular, how would you evaluate depot managers to ensure goal congruence?
3. In order of potential severity, list the problems that you anticipate would occur in implementing your revised organization and measurement system. How would you handle these problems?

chapter 15

INVESTMENT CENTERS: RETURN ON INVESTMENT

Relating Profits to Assets Employed

Investment centers are decentralized units or divisions for which the manager has been given maximum discretion for making short-run operating decisions on product mix, pricing, and production methods as well as the level and type of assets to be used. Investment centers extend the profit-center concept by relating measured profits to the unit's assets or investment base. What we are calling an investment center is also referred to as a profit center by many companies, since a profitability measure is developed for the decentralized unit. We prefer to distinguish between the two terms so that we can talk about the particular problems in measuring profits that are common to both types of centers (see discussion in Chapter 14) separately from those that arise in measuring assets and relating profits to assets employed.

By relating a unit's profits to the assets employed, we attempt to determine whether the profits are generating a sufficiently high return on the capital invested in the unit. Capital always has alternative uses, so that we should evaluate whether the returns being earned on invested capital in a division exceed its cost (as measured by the return available from alternative uses). Most companies have elaborate systems for authorizing capital expenditures. Without some form of measurement of the ex post returns to capital, little incentive may exist for accurate estimates of future cash flows during the capital-budgeting process. Measuring returns on invested capital also focuses managers' attention on the levels of working capital—particularly accounts receivable and inventory—used by the decentralized unit.

A Historical Perspective

Despite the intuitive appeal of a measure that relates profits to employed assets, it was not until the early part of the twentieth century that the return-on-investment criterion was developed. Although business firms

657

used net earnings to measure performance long before 1900, earnings were measured relative to either sales revenue or the costs of operations. They were not measured relative to the organization's investment in productive assets.[1] The typical nineteenth-century owner-entrepreneur—whether of a textile mill, a railroad, a steel company, or a retail organization—had to concentrate on performing only a single type of economic activity efficiently. In the short run, the owner attempted to manage operating costs in this single activity. He did not have to choose among alternative types of activities in which to make investments. He only had to determine the appropriate scale of activity in his principal line of business. For this purpose, the operating ratio of costs to revenues or the return on sales apparently provided an adequate guide for investment profitability.

The DuPont Powder Company, formed in 1903 when a group of previously separate and independently managed enterprises were combined, had a new organizational challenge not faced by nineteenth-century organizations: to coordinate and allocate resources to the manufacturing, purchasing, and selling activities of units performing quite different activities. In making decisions on the allocation of investment funds, the founders of the DuPont Company declared that there

> be no expenditures for additions to the earning equipment if the same amount of money could be applied to some better purpose in another branch of the company's business.

The founders understood that

> a commodity requiring an inexpensive plant might, when sold only ten percent above its cost, show a higher rate of return on the investment than another commodity sold at double its cost, but manufactured in an expensive plant. The true test of whether the profit is too great or too small is the rate of return on the money invested in the business and not the percent of profit on the cost.[2]

To guide their investment decisions, the DuPont Company developed the return-on-investment (ROI) criterion, measured by net earnings (after depreciation but before deduction of interest on long-term debt) divided by net assets: total assets minus goodwill and other intangibles, current liabilities, and reserves for depreciation.

Donaldson Brown, the chief financial officer of DuPont (and subsequently at General Motors starting in the 1920s), greatly extended the value of the ROI measure by showing how it could be written as the product

---

[1] See the discussion in Chapter 2 of H. Thomas Johnson and Robert S. Kaplan, *Relevance Lost: The Rise and Fall of Management Accounting* (Boston: Harvard Business School Press, 1987).

[2] Quotations taken from original records at the DuPont Corporation as referenced in H. Thomas Johnson, "Management Accounting in an Early Integrated Industrial: E. I. duPont de Nemours Powder Company, 1903–1912," *Business History Review* (Summer 1975), pp. 187–88.

of two ratios commonly used in nineteenth-century organizations: the profit (*P*), or return-on-sales, measure and the turnover (*T*) ratio of sales to assets:

$$\text{ROI} = \frac{\text{Profit}}{\text{Sales}} * \frac{\text{Sales}}{\text{Assets}} = P * T$$

The *P* and *T* ratios could be decomposed, in turn, into their component parts, representing accounts from the income and expense statement or the balance sheet so that senior managers could understand how performance of individual activities contributed to the overall measure of organizational effectiveness. A copy of an actual chart describing operations for the year 1923 is shown in Exhibit 15–1.

Exhibit 15-1 shows how the overall ROI of 37.2% was earned by a return-on-sales profitability (*P*) percentage of 25.62% multiplied by a sales-to-investment turnover (*T*) ratio of 1.452. The *P* percentage is decomposed into its component income and expense accounts, and the *T* ratio is decomposed into the major balance sheet accounts as they relate to sales.

The early, vertically integrated and functionally organized DuPont Company used the ROI measure to guide investment decisions among individual segments, not to evaluate the performance of managers or divisions. The use of ROI to measure divisional and managerial performance arose in the 1920s when General Motors and DuPont reorganized into the multidivisional form where division managers were given much greater discretion for operating and investment decisions. The organizational and accounting innovations of DuPont and General Motors were subsequently adopted by most diversified U.S. corporations, especially in the post–World War II era, so that investment centers in general and the use of ROI in particular are now widespread in U.S. industry.

A Simple Example

The decomposition of the ROI calculation into the product of a profitability and a turnover ratio can be illustrated with the following numerical example. Consider the performance of a division during a consecutive three-quarter period:

Quarter	ROI	=	Profitability	×	Turnover
1	12.6%		17.1%		.736
2	13.4		20.2		.664
3	15.4		22.7		.679

At first glance, the operating performance seems excellent with a nice increase in ROI each quarter. The decomposition, however, reveals a sharp

EXHIBIT 15-1
Analysis of Return on Investment

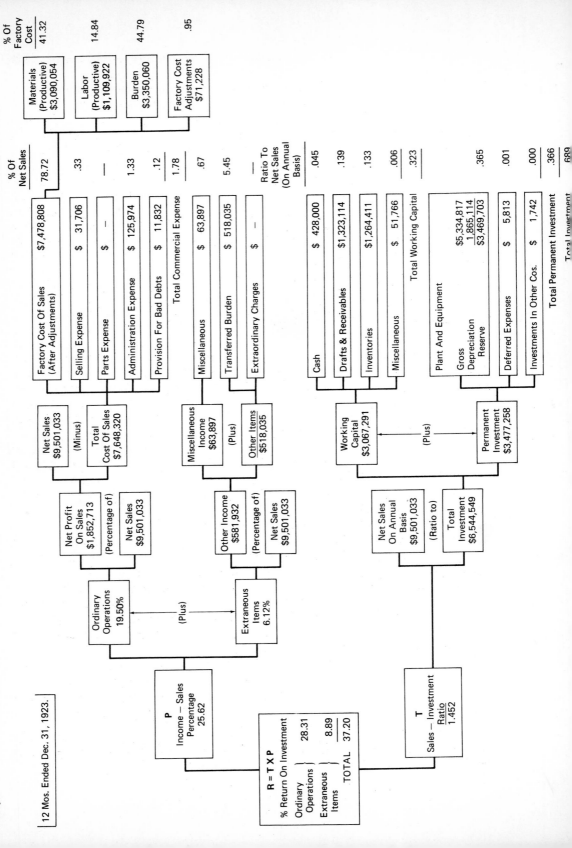

increase in profitability (return on sales) that overcomes a drop in asset turnover. Upon investigating the reasons for the increase in profitability and decrease in turnover, central management learned that the division manager had greatly increased production in quarters 2 and 3, with excess production accumulating as finished goods inventory. The much higher rates of production enabled period costs to be absorbed into inventory, allowing for a higher return on sales percentage on the goods actually sold. The buildup of inventory relative to sales was signaled by the decrease in the asset turnover ratio. Thus, by analyzing the contrary trends in profitability and turnover, central management was able to discover how the division manager had attempted to manipulate his performance evaluation.

The Matsushita Internal Capital System

Interestingly, a parallel and apparently independent development of the investment-center organizational form occurred during the 1930s in the Matsushita Corporation of Japan. The founder, Kohnosuke Matsushita, believed in "optimally scaled businesses." Concerned by health-imposed restrictions on his own ability to travel among all the new businesses of Matsushita, the founder understood that he could not manage a dynamic, growing company by himself. His management strategy was to select a suitable person for each business field and to delegate production and sales authority to that manager. The role of the president was to control division managers so that their actions would contribute to achieving organizational goals.[3]

K. Matsushita believed that each business must have independent, autonomous power in terms of funds and R&D ability. (Matsushita, unlike almost all other Japanese corporations, did not rely on debt to finance its operations.) Each business was to have a buffer of funds (and other corporate resources—including facilities, human resources, and technology) to adapt to change and continue to grow even under adverse economic conditions. Therefore, each division had to manage and rely on its own capital. Division managers were responsible for two principal tasks: *profit* management and *funds* management.

The company developed its own internal capital system for implementing decentralized funds management. A division's internal capital is the sum of its fixed assets and its working capital. Working capital is

---

[3] This discussion of the Matsushita history and control system was derived from Yasuhiro Monden, "Japanese Management Control Systems," in *Innovations in Management: The Japanese Corporation* ed. Monden *et al.* (Industrial Engineering and Management Press, Institute of Industrial Engineers, 1985), Chap. 4, pp. 41–58.

measured relative to a standard based on budgeted sales and production (see Exhibit 15–2). For example, the standard allowance for accounts receivable is computed from an estimated collection period, say 30 days, so that the allowance would be one month's worth of sales. Accounts payable is measured by assuming that the ratio of materials to total manufacturing costs is 50% and the turnover period is 35 days.

EXHIBIT 15–2
Structure of Standard Working Capital

Account Title		Computation Basis for Standards		Standard Amount (yen)	Ratio to Monthly Sales
		Basis	Computations		
Current Assets	Notes Receivable	Ratio of notes: 30% Sight of notes: 90 days	(Sales) $100 \times 30\% \times \frac{90 \text{ days}}{30 \text{ days}}$	90	Months 0.90
	Accounts Receivable	Turnover period: 30 days	(Sales) $100 \times 70\% \times \frac{30 \text{ days}}{30 \text{ days}}$	100	1.00
	Finished Products	Ratio of cost of sales: 70% Turnover period: 30 days	(Sales) $100 \times 70\% \times \frac{30 \text{ days}}{30 \text{ days}}$	70	0.70
	Work-in-Process	Ratio of manual cost: 70% Turnover period: 3 days	(Production) $100 \times 70\% \times \frac{3 \text{ days}}{30 \text{ days}}$	7	0.07
	Materials	Ratio of materials: 50% Turnover period: 15 days	(Production) $100 \times 50\% \times \frac{15}{30}$	25	0.25
	Other Current Assets	Sales amount: 3%	(Sales) $100 \times 3\%$	3	0.03
		sum: A		295	2.95
Current Liabilities	Notes Payable (materials)	Ratio of materials: 50% Ratio of notes: 10% Sight of notes: 90 days	(Production) $100 \times 50\% \times 10\% \times \frac{90}{30}$	15	0.15
	Accounts Payable	Ratio of materials: 50% Turnover period: 35 days	(Production) $100 \times 50\% \times \frac{35 \text{ days}}{30 \text{ days}}$	60	0.60
	Other Current Liabilities	Sales amount: 35%	(Production) $100 \times 35\%$	35	0.35
		sum: B		110	1.10
		Balance: A − B = Working Capital		185	1.85

The rules for the internal capital system are as follows:

1. Internal capital = Standard working capital + Fixed assets − Reserves.
2. Interest charged for internal capital = 1% per month, paid to central office each month.
3. Central office tax (to cover headquarter's expenses) = 3% of divisional sales, paid to central office each month. After deducting this payment, divisional *net profit* should equal 10% of sales (the target goal for *profit management*).
4. Dividends and tax equal to 60% of divisional profit are remitted to the central office in the following month. The remaining 40% of divisional profit is retained to support additional working capital and fixed investment.
5. If divisional funds fall short of required amounts, the division can borrow temporarily from the central office. If the division has excess cash, it can be deposited in the Matsushita Bank where it earns a competitive rate of interest.
6. When a division requires large funds for a major new investment, the proposal is submitted to the central office for approval and funding.

The evaluation of profit management performance is achieved by assigning its return on sales to one of four ranks:

- Rank A: Greater than 9%
- Rank B: Between 6% and 9%
- Rank C: Between 4% and 6%
- Rank D: Less than 4%

Any division manager receiving rank D for two consecutive years is transferred. Interest revenues are excluded from the return-on-sales calculation. Matsushita believes that profits should be earned from manufacturing high-quality goods at low cost, not from financial transactions.

A Technical Limitation

Despite the appeal of relating profits earned to assets employed, a number of technical problems exist with using the ROI criterion as the exclusive measure for evaluating division managers. Many of these problems have already been discussed in Chapters 13 and 14 where we pointed out that excessive focus on any single short-run measure, such as profits, can motivate undesirable actions by decentralized managers. But in addition to the problems introduced by the inadequacy of the profit measure to assess short-term performance, other problems arise when the profit measure is normalized by some measure of investment. Actions that increase the divisional ROI can make the corporation worse off and, conversely, actions that decrease divisional ROI may increase the economic wealth of the corporation.[4] Consider a division with assets of $90,000 and net income before taxes (NIBT) of $20,000. Its ROI will be measured at 22.2%:

$$\text{ROI} = \frac{\text{NIBT}}{\text{Assets}} = \frac{20,000}{90,000} = 0.222$$

Suppose the cost of capital for the division is 15% and a new opportunity appears that requires an investment of $15,000, yielding an annual profit improvement of $3,000 per year. The return from this new investment opportunity is 20%, which is well above the division's cost of capital. But the new ROI for the division, should the project be funded, would be

$$\text{ROI} = \frac{20,000 + 3,000}{90,000 + 15,000} = \frac{23,000}{105,000} = 0.219,$$

a decrease from the previous level of 22.2%. The ROI measure causes the division manager to be motivated to refuse this investment, since even though it returns in excess of the cost of capital (it generates $750 per year in additional profits after paying the investment financing cost of 15%), the project lowers the divisional ROI. If left uncorrected, this defect alone may cause ROI to be an inappropriate measure of divisional performance.

Problems arise when contemplating asset disposal as well. If the division has an asset carried at a $20,000 cost that earns $3,600 per year (an 18% return), the division can increase its ROI by disposing of the asset even though it is earning above the division's cost of capital. The division manager can perform the following calculation of the postdisposal ROI:

$$\text{ROI} = \frac{20,000 - 3,600}{90,000 - 20,000} = \frac{16,400}{70,000} = 0.234$$

A similar problem arises when two divisions with different investment bases are compared. For example, a second division with assets of $50,000 and net income of $12,500 will show an ROI of 25%. It might appear that the second division is more profitable, since its ROI of 25% exceeds the 22.2% ROI of the first division. But on closer inspection, we see that the first division has $40,000 more in assets, on which its incremental earnings are $7,500 (from $20,000 − $12,500). Therefore, its incremental ROI is 7,500/ 40,000, or 18.75%, well above the cost of capital of 15%. Hence, the first division is more profitable, after subtracting capital costs, than the second division.

The above problems are caused by evaluating divisional performance

---

[4] Technical limitations to the ROI measure have been pointed out in Chapter 5 of David Solomons, *Divisional Performance: Measurement and Control* (Homewood, IL: Richard D. Irwin, 1968); John Dearden, "The Case against ROI Control," *Harvard Business Review* (May–June 1969); and John Dearden, "Measuring Profit Center Managers," *Harvard Business Review* (September–October 1987).

by a ratio (ROI). Managers who wish to maximize a ratio can either increase the numerator (by earning more profits with existing assets) or decrease the denominator by shrinking the investment base and declining profitable new investment opportunities that can earn in excess of the divisional cost of capital but yield returns below the current average ROI of the division. In general, any project or asset whose return is below the average ROI of the division will be a candidate for disposal or will not be recommended for funding, since its inclusion in the investment base lowers the divisional ROI measure. Carrying this process to its logical but absurd limit, the division manager shrinks the investment base to the single project that earns the highest ROI but on an extremely low capital base.

Residual Income

The dysfunctional actions that accompany using a ratio to evaluate the performance of a manager or division can be eliminated by using the **residual income** approach. An explicit cost of capital is specified for the division and applied to the division's investment base to obtain a capital charge for the division. The residual income computation is identical to that used by the Matsushita Company. The capital charge is subtracted from net income before taxes, and the remainder is called the residual income—the income remaining after charging for the cost of capital. The residual income also corresponds closely to the economist's (but not the accountant's) measure of income.

Returning to the examples of the two divisions described above, the residual income (RI) calculation is presented in Exhibit 15–3.

EXHIBIT 15–3
Residual Income Calculation

	Division 1	Division 2
Invested capital	$90,000	$50,000
Net income before taxes	$20,000	$12,500
Capital charge (@15%)	13,500	7,500
Residual income	$ 6,500	$ 5,000

The residual income calculation in Exhibit 15–3 shows that Division 1 is indeed more profitable than Division 2, since its residual income is higher. The RI difference of $1,500 is precisely due to the return in excess of the cost of capital of 0.0375 (obtained from 0.1875 − 0.15) applied to the incremental investment of $40,000 [since 0.0375(40,000) = 1,500] in Division 1.

Also, if Division 1 takes its 20% project opportunity ($15,000 investment, $3,000 annual return), its RI will increase, whereas if it disposes of the $20,000 asset earning $3,600 per year, its RI will decrease (see Exhibit 15–4).

EXHIBIT 15–4
Options for Division 1

	Now	Option 1 (New $15,000 Investment)	Option 2 (Dispose of $20,000 asset)
Invested capital	$90,000	$105,000	$70,000
Net income before taxes	$20,000	$ 23,000	$16,400
Capital charge (@15%)	13,500	15,750	10,500
Residual income	$ 6,500	$ 7,250	$ 5,900

The RI measure will always increase when we add investments earning above the cost of capital or eliminate investments earning below the cost of capital. Therefore, it produces goal congruence between the evaluation of the division and the actions that maximize the economic wealth of the division and the firm. The firm will always prefer the division to have a higher rather than a lower residual income. In this regard, RI offers significant advantages over the ROI measure, since we have already found examples where actions that increased divisional ROI made the firm worse off. The RI measure is also more flexible, since a different percentage can be applied to investments of different risks. The cost of capital for divisions in different lines of business may differ, and even assets within the same division (contrast the risk of cash or accounts receivable with the risk of long-lived highly specialized fixed assets) may be in different risk classes. The RI evaluation allows managers to recognize different risk-adjusted capital costs that the ROI measure cannot.

Residual income is a less convenient measure than ROI, however, because it is an absolute number, not deflated by the size of the division. A large division will find it easier to earn a given amount of residual income than a small division. Consider two divisions, one with $1 million in assets and the other with $10 million in assets; both have a cost of capital of 15%. The first division may be highly profitable, with a 30% ROI earning $300,000 and an RI of $150,000, whereas the second division can earn an RI of $150,000 merely with a 16.5% ROI, generating Net Income Before Taxes and Capital Charge of $1,650,000. For this reason, companies using an RI measure will usually not simply direct managers to maximize residual income. Rather, they will set targeted or budgeted levels of RI, appropriate for the asset structure of each division, and evaluate division managers by whether they exceed or fall short of budgeted RI. An alternative procedure, of reporting residual income as a percentage of investment, reintroduces the problem with the ROI measure we attempted to avoid with the RI measure. It gives managers the opportunity to improve performance by reducing the denominator—not by increasing the numerator—of a ratio measure.

Despite the attractive features of the RI measure, several surveys and direct observations reveal that few companies have replaced the ROI measure with RI. Several companies may report an RI measure as a supplement to the ROI measure, but few rely on it entirely as a measure of investment-center performance. We can only speculate on the reasons for its lack of popularity:

1. The type of dysfunctional behavior we described may not be a real problem in practice.

2. The cost of capital for a correct residual income calculation requires that the cost of equity capital be explicitly recognized. If this capital cost is subtracted from divisions' net incomes, the combined total of divisional net income will not total the corporation's financial accounting net income, since the cost of equity capital is not considered an expense (or profit reduction) for financial accounting. Most companies want complete consistency between internal and external accounting numbers.

3. The extensive use of ROI by financial analysts causes senior company executives to motivate their division managers to make their ROI measure as large as possible.

4. Senior managers are unwilling to specify the company's or divisions' cost of capital, especially if they must make explicit calculations about appropriate risk adjustments for divisions or classes of assets.

5. Managers find a percentage measure of profitability, such as that obtained with ROI, more convenient when comparing a division's profitability with other financial measures, such as inflation rates, interest rates, and the profit rates of other divisions in the company or outside.

Interestingly, however, as we will see in Chapter 16, the bonus plans for senior executives are frequently based on a residual-income-type measure. In these plans, the bonus pool is defined as a percentage (say 10%) of net income in excess of a prespecified rate of return on invested capital.

The discussion so far has focused on properties that distinguish the ROI measure from the RI measure. Both measures, however, have additional significant problems that have deliberately been suppressed so far in our examples: measuring the investment and net income of a division, and interpreting the accounting ROI as if it were a surrogate for the cost of capital. Each of these issues requires greater elaboration in order to understand the properties of investment-center measures of performance.

EXHIBIT 15–5
Investment and Depreciation: 10% Annual Inflation

Age of Asset (Years) (1)	Asset Cost (2) = 30,000 × (1.1)⁴ ⁻ ⁽¹⁾	Annual Depreciation (3) = (2)/5	Net Book Value, End of Year 4 (4) = (2) − (1)(3)
0	$30{,}000 \ (1.1)^4$ = $ 43,923	$ 8,785	$ 43,923
1	$30{,}000 \ (1.1)^3$ = 39,930	7,986	31,944
2	$30{,}000 \ (1.1)^2$ = 36,300	7,260	21,780
3	$30{,}000 \ (1.1)^1$ = 33,000	6,600	13,200
4	$30{,}000$ = 30,000	6,000	6,000
	$183,153	$36,631	$116,847

distorted signals might delude corporate and division management into thinking that despite an inability to pass on cost increases to the marketplace, the division seems to be coping rather well during a difficult inflationary period.

Such reasoning, however, is fallacious. The apparent increases in net income, ROI, and RI are all caused by the failure to restate the assets' historical acquisition cost into units of current costs or current purchasing power. Were the inflation rate to cease suddenly at the end of Year 4 (a situation analogous to the precipitous drop in inflation rates in the United States and other countries in the early 1980s), the division would maintain its then current net operating cash flows, replace its older assets—one per year—at the most recent price ($43,923), and eventually see the consequences from its failure to keep net cash flows in line with the past inflation:

Investment[6]	$131,769
Net cash flows	$ 63,124
Depreciation[7]	43,923
Net income	$ 19,201
Capital charge (15%)	19,765
Residual income	$ (564)

$$\text{ROI} = \frac{19{,}201}{131{,}769} = 14.6\%$$

Net income has declined, the residual income is now negative, and the postinflation ROI of 14.6% is well below the preinflationary figure. The postinflation figures of both ROI and RI are now below the misleading high figures reported at the end of the inflation cycle when the firm had yet to replace its older assets. The effect is dramatic when inflation suddenly

---

[6] Investment, at (price-level adjusted) net book value, equals $43,923 × [1 + 4/5 + 3/5 + 2/5 + 1/5] = $131,769.

[7] From $8,784.60 × 5.

stops as in the above example. Were inflation to continue at its previous high rates, with the division's cash flows continuing to trail the inflation rate, it might continue to show satisfactory profits for a while but would find itself running out of cash to purchase new assets to replace the ones being retired.

The message from this example is simple and direct. During inflationary periods, the use of historical cost to compute depreciation expense and to measure the investment base causes net income, ROI, and RI to be deceptively high. During inflationary periods, divisions and companies find it easy to look highly profitable with these unadjusted measures. Worse, managers may be misled into thinking that asset returns are much better than they actually are. Reality sets in when the inflationary cycle is broken and assets have to be replaced at the now higher price level, but when price increases can no longer be sustained in the marketplace. Such distortions provide further motivation for firms to evaluate their progress by productivity measures (see discussion in Chapter 9) that are unaffected by relative price effects.

The failure to adjust for price-level changes affects not only the measurement of a single division over time but also the comparison among different divisions at the same point in time. Divisions with newer assets will tend to show lower ROI and RI measures than equally (or even less) profitable divisions whose assets were acquired at lower price levels. Unless some provision is made to neutralize such inflationary biases, managers will be reluctant to make new investments because of the negative impact on their ROI and RI. Conversely, managers will tend to delay the replacement of their low—(historical)—cost assets because of the misleading high ROI and RI apparently being earned on these assets.

Adjusting financial statements for the effects of inflation has been one of the most contentious accounting issues of the past two decades. Hundreds of books and articles have been written on the subject, mandatory external disclosure was implemented for several years and then rescinded in the United States, and many authoritative people still show confusion about the difference between movements in the general price level and changes in relative prices. Therefore, one can safely conclude that a consensus hardly exists on the subject. Even during the period when inflation adjustments had to be disclosed for external reporting purposes, so that the information was already being produced in virtually all large U.S. firms, only a handful—literally one handful—of companies opted to use inflation-adjusted statements for internal evaluation of divisions and their managers.[8]

---

[8] See Julie Hertenstein, "Management Control System Change: The Adoption of Inflation Accounting," in *Accounting & Management: Field Study Perspectives* ed. William H. Bruns, Jr., and Robert S. Kaplan (Boston: Harvard Business School Press, 1978); also J. Hertenstein, *FMC Corporation's Use of Current Cost Accounting* (Montvale, NJ: National Association of Accountants, 1988).

One final issue on this subject is the effect of inflation on the cost of capital. During a period of anticipated inflation, investors and creditors will demand a higher rate of return from their invested capital to compensate them for the lower purchasing power of the dollars or cruzeiros they will receive in the future. The nominal cost of capital, therefore, which is derived from data on market interest rates and expected rates of return on equity capital, is a function of anticipated inflation. Understanding the economics of adjusting assets for the effects of inflation and the cost of capital for changes in nominal interest rates and equity returns is not a trivial exercise. We present (without proof) the following advice to guide managers, students, and their teachers on this subject.[9]

We assumed a 15% cost of capital in our initial example when no inflation or price-level changes existed.[10] Then we assumed an environment with 10% annual inflation. Investors and creditors are not dummies. They are not going to leave their capital with companies during periods of inflation unless they are compensated, with higher expected returns, when they receive cash in future years. The exact relation between expected inflation and the cost of capital is not known precisely, but an excellent approximation is to assume that today's cost of capital equals the cost of capital in the absence of inflation (15% in our example) plus the expected inflation rate (10%) for a total of 25%. Many managers believe, however, that the 25% rate they would currently be observing in the marketplace provides the benchmark to evaluate their operations. But if inflation adjustments have already been made to asset values, it would be double counting to use the nominal 25% cost of capital. One should use the **real** rate of 15% as a benchmark in an ROI calculation or for calculating a capital charge in a residual income calculation after the assets' costs have been adjusted for the effects of inflation.

For example, suppose the nominal cash flows projected from a three-year project are:

Year	Cash Flow
1	10,600
2	11,236
3	11,910

These cash flows reflect an anticipated annual rate of inflation of 6%. The deflated cash flows (measured in current-year dollars) are:

---

[9] The arguments can be found in Franco Modigliani and R. Cohn, "Inflation, Rational Valuation and the Market," *Financial Analysts Journal* (March–April 1979), pp. 24–44; and Robert S. Kaplan, "Depreciation and Inflation," Harvard Business School Working Paper (December 1983).

[10] Fifteen percent was used for illustrative purposes only. As discussed in Chapter 12, the weighted-average real cost of capital for most organizations will be well under 10%.

Year	Cash Flow
1	10,000
2	10,000
3	10,000

and the present value of this three-year project, using a real interest rate of 10% per year, is $24,869.

Alternatively, we could use a nominal interest rate of

$$(1 + 0.10) * (1 + 0.06) - 1 = 16.6\%$$

to discount the nominal annual cash flows we first forecast:

Year	Cash Flow	Present Value @ 16.6%
1	10,600	9,091
2	11,236	8,265
3	11,910	7,513
Total		24,869

to get exactly the same answer.

Depreciation Method

The accounting rate of return obtained from an ROI calculation is frequently assumed to be an estimate of the division's economic rate of return on invested capital. Unfortunately, except in very special circumstances, the accounting ROI will not equal the underlying yield of the assets in the division. The difference between the asset's yield and its accounting ROI is easily illustrated by returning to our division with $90,000 in assets and annual net income of $20,000. While the accounting ROI equals 22.2%, each asset actually generates a return of about 20%. Exhibit 15–6 shows

EXHIBIT 15–6
Discounted Present Value of Cash Flows

Year	Cash Inflow	Present Value Factor at 20%	Discounted Cash Flow
1	$10,000	0.8333	$ 8,333.33
2	10,000	0.6944	6,944.44
3	10,000	0.5787	5,787.04
4	10,000	0.4823	4,822.53
5	10,000	0.4019	4,018.78
	$50,000	2.9906	$29,906.12

that the discounted present value, using an interest rate of 20%, of five annual cash flows of $10,000, is just short of the $30,000 initial investment.[11]

Even in this simple example, the accounting ROI of 22.2% does not equal the actual rate of return of slightly less than 20%. Therefore, we cannot infer the actual yield of assets in a division or company from the accounting ROI. The difference between these two measures arises from using a financial depreciation method—straight-line, in this case—that bears no relation to the periodic loss in present value of the asset. In order for the accounting ROI to equal the actual yield, a depreciation method derived from the decline in present value of the asset must be used.

The perverse incentives that are created by inappropriately using financial accounting depreciation methods for a managerial ROI calculation are also easy to demonstrate. Observe how the manager of our division can increase his ROI measure by working less hard, that is, by deciding to stop investing in a new asset each year to replace the five-year-old asset just scrapped (see Exhibit 15–7). The ROI steadily increases each year as the asset base shrinks, because the book value of the assets decreases faster than the net income falls. Note, however, that the manager of this division should hope for a promotion or transfer some time before the end of the fourth year after adopting this ROI-increasing policy. After that time, the division will be rather short of operating assets.

EXHIBIT 15–7
ROI by Years, No Asset Replacement, Straight-Line Depreciation

	Year				
	0	1	2	3	4
Net cash flow	50,000	40,000	30,000	20,000	10,000
Depreciation	30,000	24,000	18,000	12,000	6,000
Net income	20,000	16,000	12,000	8,000	4,000
Investment	90,000	60,000	36,000	18,000	6,000
ROI	22.2%	26.7%	33.3%	44.4%	66.7%

While we would not expect that many managers would manipulate their ROI measures so transparently, nevertheless the example serves to demonstrate how, on the margin, managers can improve their ROI measure by postponing new investment and continuing to operate with fully or nearly fully depreciated assets.[12] Conversely, we see that managers who

---

[11] The discounted present value would have been exactly $30,000 had we used an interest rate of 19.86% in the calculations.

[12] German companies commonly charge depreciation for assets still in use, based on their replacement value, even if the assets have been fully depreciated for financial and tax purposes.

invest in new equipment will show a lower ROI than their counterparts who operate with older equipment. The penalty arises not just from acquiring assets at the higher price level, as we discussed in the preceding section, but also because financial accounting depreciation methods artificially produce lower accounting ROIs in the initial years that an asset is placed into service.

Because of the bias against new investment when using straight-line depreciation and an ROI performance measure, several companies measure assets at their gross book value rather than net book value, a practice followed by the DuPont Corporation for many decades starting in the 1920s. When assets are measured at gross book value, the incentive to avoid investing in new assets is eliminated. In fact, a new incentive—to replace existing assets with new assets—is created, since the measured increase in investment is only the difference between the historical cost of the existing asset and the purchase cost of the new asset. This difference is well below the actual net outlay for the new asset, as measured by the purchase cost less trade-in or salvage value of the existing asset.

It is certainly possible to devise a depreciation schedule, based on the decline in present value of the asset each year, so that the accounting ROI will equal the economic rate of return of the asset. The economic or present value depreciation method can be derived directly from the cash flow schedule used to justify the acquisition of the asset.[13] But using the present value depreciation method would require that companies use a depreciation method for managerial accounting purposes completely different from the methods used for financial and tax accounting purposes. During the 1970s when inflation rates exceeded 10%, fewer than 1% of U.S. companies adjusted their accounting statements for inflation for internal purposes—even though data already existed from mandated supplementary disclosure. Therefore, we are not optimistic about managers' receptivity to implement an entirely new depreciation method for internal motivation and evaluation. Consequently, we will not burden readers with the derivation of economic depreciation methods.

The lack of interest in economic or present value depreciation methods for assets is curious, since the technology for performing such calculations is well known and, in fact, is already being used in financial statements, but to amortize liabilities, not to depreciate assets. The amortization of principal in a mortgage calculation, or the amortization of bond discounts and premiums, generates a nonlinear amortization schedule in order to maintain a constant yield-to-maturity of the liability. We are unsure why such a constant yield-to-maturity approach is easily accepted for liabilities but is considered unacceptable when one moves from the right-hand to the left-hand side of the balance sheet to amortize the

---

[13] Present value depreciation is discussed in John Dearden, "The Case against ROI Control," Solomons, *Divisional Performance*; and Robert S. Kaplan, "Depreciation and Inflation."

cost of asset acquisitions. Lacking such insight, we can only alert readers to the pitfalls lurking when using financial accounting depreciation methods for managerial accounting calculations but without offering much hope that the pitfalls will be eliminated by using more cash flow-based depreciation methods.

Capitalizing versus Expensing

For certain expenditures, especially on intangibles, discretion exists as to whether these expenditures should be expensed in the period in which they are incurred or should be capitalized and amortized over the future periods when their benefits are expected to be realized. The Financial Accounting Standards Board discourages the capitalization of most intangible expenditures (see, for example, Statement 2 on Research and Development Expenditures), but internal performance evaluation need not be bound by regulations established for external reporting. In a steady-state situation, where roughly equal expenditures on intangibles are made each year, net income is not affected, since the sum of amortization expenses of current and past expenditures will equal the current year's expenditures. But the failure to capitalize expenditures with expected future benefits will penalize earnings in the short run until the steady state is reached and will overstate the ROI and RI in the steady state, since the expenditures on intangibles will not be included in the measured investment base.

We can illustrate these distortions by allowing our five-asset division to engage in a promotional activity each year. This activity costs $3,000 but produces incremental cash flows of $1,000 for each of the next five years. (Note that this activity is analogous to purchasing an additional 10% of one of our basic assets.) If this expenditure is expensed, we will observe the following sequence of net-income measures:

			Year			
	0	1	2	3	4	5
Net cash flows	$47,000	$48,000	$49,000	$50,000	$51,000	$52,000
Depreciation	30,000	30,000	30,000	30,000	30,000	30,000
Net income	$17,000	$18,000	$19,000	$20,000	$21,000	$22,000

Initially, the $3,000 expenditure reduces net income with no compensating benefit. By Year 5, the annual $3,000 expenditure is more than offset by the five $1,000 increments in cash flows from the expenditures in the previous five years, and overall the net income has increased by $2,000 from these cumulative expenditures.

If the annual $3,000 expenditure had been capitalized and amortized over five years, the sequence of net-income figures would be:

			Year			
	0	*1*	*2*	*3*	*4*	*5*
Net cash flows	$50,000	$51,000	$52,000	$53,000	$54,000	$55,000
Depreciation and amortization	30,000	30,600	31,200	31,800	32,400	33,000
Net income	$20,000	$20,400	$20,800	$21,200	$21,600	$22,000

Thus, both methods eventually reach the same net-income figure in the steady state, but the capitalization/amortization alternative has a more gradual transition.

When used to evaluate investment-center performance, however, the two methods yield quite different measures. Under the expensing alternative, the ROI in Year 5 (at steady-state conditions) is

$$\frac{22,000}{90,000} = 24.4\%$$

and the RI is

$$22,000 - 13,500 = \$8,500$$

With the capitalization/amortization alternative, the investment base increases by $9,000 to $99,000, so that the ROI is $22,000/99,000 = 22.2\%$ and the RI is $22,000 - 14,850 = \$7,150$. The performance measures for the capitalization/amortization alternative are consistent with the measures we derived previously (ROI is the same, and the RI is 10% higher because of the effective 10% increase in our asset).

We conclude from this exercise that divisions that treat expenditures with future-period benefits as current-period expenses will

1. Show depressed profits until a steady-state level of such expenditures is reached, or any time an unusually large expenditure is made in a year
2. Report a higher ROI and RI than are actually being earned in the steady state because of the failure to properly classify such expenditures as investments

Divisions with a high proportion of expenditures on intangibles will therefore tend to show higher ROIs than, say, manufacturing divisions where most expenditures with future-period benefits tend to be tangible; one can see and touch what one acquired for these expenditures. This is why marketing divisions with heavy advertising and promotional expenditures, or divisions with large numbers of professional employees (whose human capital is not recorded on the balance sheet), will show unusually high ROI performance measures. These divisions are not as profitable as they appear. Their currently high profitability (as measured by ROI) occurs because profitability in earlier years was understated, as all expenditures on intangibles were expensed as incurred. In the current years, the firms are enjoying the benefits from these previous investments in intangibles, but the current benefits are not being related to the intangible investment base developed in previous years. Thus, these divisions' ROI appears to be higher because they have many assets that are not being counted as part of their investment base.

Identification of Assets in the Investment Base

Controllable versus Noncontrollable Investment

In determining which assets to include in a division's asset base, we must decide whether the primary purpose is to measure the performance of the division or that of the division manager. If the purpose is to evaluate the division manager, then only those assets that are directly traceable to the division and controlled by the division manager should be included in the asset base. Corporate assets used by the central administration or assets controlled at the central level, such as cash, are examples of assets that are unaffected by the actions of local managers and should be excluded from an evaluation of the division manager.

With this approach, the division manager would be held responsible for divisional property, plant and equipment, and inventories.[14] If the manager has control over sales terms and credit policy, then divisional receivables should also be included. This assumes that corporate records are kept so that the receivables traceable to each division's sales activities can be identified. Typically, cash will be controlled at the corporate level, but any cash balances held and managed at the divisional level could be included in the investment base. If the division manager can control the payment terms to suppliers, then accounts payable may be subtracted from the investment base. This will encourage the manager to seek out the most favorable credit terms for purchases.

We can refer to this narrowly defined investment as **controllable divisional investment.** These definitions, which exclude common corporate expenses, corporate investment, and, in general, expenses and assets not under the control of the division manager, attempt to base managerial performance measures on actions over which the manager has both responsibility and authority.

Central management, however, may also be interested in evaluating a division's economic performance and in comparing it with that of comparable firms in the same industry. For this situation, an evaluation based solely on controllable investment overstates the division's actual profit-

---

[14] Inventories should be valued at FIFO or average cost even when the company uses LIFO for financial and tax reporting. LIFO valuation would grossly underestimate the investment in inventories.

ability. The overstatement occurs because no division could operate without the services represented by corporate assets (such as buildings and furnishings for senior executives and corporate staff departments, and cash and marketable securities managed at the corporate level). Such assets will be included in the investment base of nondiversified firms in the same industry as the decentralized division, and the managers of the nondiversified firm will also attempt to earn a competitive return on these assets.

Therefore, many decentralized firms allocate investments in cash, marketable securities, and corporate assets to divisions when computing investment-center performance measures. As discussed elsewhere in this book, such allocations of noncontrollable investments will be mostly arbitrary, based on measures such as sales, square feet occupied, and personnel employed. Even though the division manager cannot be held responsible for the allocated values of such assets, their inclusion in the division's investment base serves to signal the division manager that, overall, investments in the division must earn somewhat above the cost of capital to provide a return on these common or corporate assets. This does not imply that the cost of capital be raised arbitrarily so that investments just returning the marginal cost of capital would be rejected. The hope is that enough investments are returning above the cost of capital to cover the investment in common assets.[15]

Some firms exclude idle assets from the division's investment base. Again, the critical question is one of controllability. If central management does not permit the division manager to dispose of idle or surplus assets, then these assets are not controllable at the divisional level and should not be included in the division's investment base. If the assets are thus excluded, then the central management should take possession of them and have the right to transfer them to other divisions where they may be needed. If the central management sees no other use for currently idle assets, then they can remain in the division's investment base and the decision whether to retain or dispose of them can be left at the local level.

Leased Assets

One ploy that a clever manager of an investment center might adopt is to lease assets instead of purchasing them. We have already noted the pervasive tendency for divisional accounting procedures to be driven by the procedures for external reporting. The limited capitalization of leases that existed before FAS 13, therefore, provided an incentive for managers to acquire assets through leases, since they would not appear in the division's investment base. The flexible conditions in FAS 13 (plus all subsequent modifications and interpretations) still enable managers to structure many

---

[15] A more extensive discussion of controllable versus noncontrollable assets in the investment base appears in Chapter 5 of Solomons, *Divisional Performance*, esp. pp. 129–31, 143–48.

leases so that the assets need not be capitalized for financial reporting purposes and hence will probably be excluded from the divisional investment base.

The incentive for leasing instead of purchasing assets can easily be illustrated in the context of our five-asset division. Suppose that, at the end of the year, instead of purchasing a new asset to replace the one just retired, the division manager finds a supplier willing to provide the asset on a five-year lease. The supplier has the same 15% cost of capital as the division and computes the equivalent annual lease payment using the five-year 15% annuity factor, 3.3522, as

$$\text{Annual lease payment} = \frac{\$30,000}{3.3522} = \$8,950$$

After one year with the leased asset, the division has the same physical assets and revenues but an extra cash expense of $8,950, a decrease in recorded investment of $30,000, and a decrease in (straight-line) depreciation expense of $6,000. The computation of the ROI and RI for the first several years is shown in Exhibit 15–8.

EXHIBIT 15–8
Effect of Substituting Leased Assets for Owned Assets

	Year			
	0	*1*	*2*	*3*
Investment	$90,000	$60,000	$36,000	$18,000
Net cash flows	$50,000	$41,050	$32,100	$23,150
Depreciation	30,000	24,000	18,000	12,000
Net income	$20,000	$17,050	$14,100	$11,150
Capital charge	13,500	9,000	5,400	2,700
Residual income	$ 6,500	$ 8,050	$ 8,700	$ 8,450
ROI	22.2%	28.4%	39.2%	61.9%

The ROI of the division increases dramatically as leased assets are substituted for purchased assets. Eventually, when all the assets are leased, the division will show an infinite ROI, since it will be earning net income of $5,250 with no recorded assets. The RI also increases initially but eventually declines. These fluctuations in ROI and RI are purely an artifact of excluding leased assets from the investment base. The size of the division and its profitability are identical to the situation in which all five assets were purchased and owned by the division. Regardless of what the company does for financial reporting purposes, there seems to be no reason for it to exclude leased assets from the divisional investment base. The exclusion provides an incentive for a division to substitute leased assets for purchased assets even when no apparent economic advantage exists for such a substitution; that is, the equivalent purchase price and cost of capital are identical in the two situations.

To remedy this condition, leased assets should be included in the investment base at their fair market value. If an independent estimate of the cost of the asset is not available, then the leased asset can be valued at the discounted present value of the lease payments, although this sounds simpler than it actually is. Considerable controversy still exists as to the appropriate discount rate for evaluating the leasing option. Tax effects that we are ignoring here become important.

Once on the books, the firm has two options on how to treat the annual lease payment. It would be incorrect to charge the full $8,950 lease payment as an expense of the period, since much of this payment represents a financing cost and financing costs are not charged to specific assets in an ROI or RI computation. We would be double-counting interest expense—once as a subtraction from operating cash flows and a second time as the capital charge in computing RI. This is the same reason why interest costs are not subtracted when performing a discounted cash flow analysis for evaluating a proposed capital acquisition. The preferable method would be to have the depreciation schedule follow the amortization of the debt as represented by the capitalized lease payments. The amortization and depreciation schedule appears below:

Year	Debt—Start of Year	Lease Payment	Effective Interest Expense	Debt Amortization (Depreciation Expense)
1	$30,000	$8,950	$4,500	$4,450
2	25,550	8,950	3,833	5,117
3	20,443	8,950	3,065	5,885
4	14,548	8,950	2,182	6,768
5	7,780	8,950	1,167	7,783[a]

[a] Rounding error caused by using annual lease payment of $8,950 instead of $8,949.50.

Only the depreciation expense, shown in the last column, would be charged as an expense to the division.

Most companies, however, will depreciate capitalized leased assets using the traditional straight-line method. In this case, the depreciation expense will be $6,000 per year (just as for owned assets), and the annual depreciation charge will have no particular relationship with the annual $8,950 lease payment. As we have already seen, the straight-line depreciation method distorts the ROI and RI computation, but at least the firm will be consistent in distorting owned and leased assets in the same manner.

Alternatives to ROI and RI

Because of the many difficulties that arise when using the ROI measure, some writers have advocated that the attempt to obtain a single summary measure of divisional performance be abandoned.[16] They recommend that profits and investments in fixed assets be controlled separately. Fixed assets would be controlled by capital-budgeting analysis procedures and post-investment audits. Profit performance of a division would be evaluated by comparing actual with budgeted profits for the period. Perhaps the only link between investment and profit performance would be to levy a capital charge (such as that computed in an RI calculation) on the net working capital of a division: accounts receivable plus inventory less accounts payable against the profits of the division. Such a charge would encourage division managers to conserve the working capital that is under their control and make the appropriate trade-off between higher levels of working capital and profits. Returning to the decentralization framework we established in Chapter 13, the division manager is presumed to have the best information about the appropriate levels of working capital and the trade-off among working capital, sales, and profits. Therefore, authority and responsibility for working capital can properly be assigned to the division manager.

This recommendation is consistent with a recent finding on the extensive use of the return-on-sales (ROS) measure in Japanese companies with a high degree of factory automation.[17] The reasons provided to explain the increasing popularity of the ROS measure include the following:

1. ROS can be calculated for individual products, an important consideration in an environment of high product variety.
2. It becomes virtually impossible to attribute an investment base to low-volume, high-variety products.
3. The ROS measure is easy to understand, both by workers and by management. It provides an excellent measure for the target-costing approach of many Japanese companies (see the discussion of target costing in Chapter 11).

Companies such as Toyota and Matsushita, which emphasize ROS at the individual product level, devise other measures to control investments in assets. For example, JIT methods are actively employed to reduce

---

[16] See, for example, John Dearden, "The Case against ROI Control," *Harvard Business Review* (May–June 1969), p. 134.

[17] Michiharu Sakurai and Philip Y. Huang, "Factory Automation and Its Impact on Management Control System: A Japanese Survey," *Journal of Business Research Institute* (Senshu University, No. 76, February 1988).

inventories, and appropriate physical measures are employed to track the level and reductions in inventory. Many companies have also adopted the Matsushita internal capital charge method (discussed earlier in this chapter) to supplement the ROS measure at the divisional level.

These recommendations bring us back to the derivation of the original DuPont formula. But rather than combine the profitability (ROS) measure and the turnover (T) measure into a single (ROI) measure, the companies prefer to manage each measure separately, especially to avoid the bias against investment in new technology (such as factory automation) created by unthinking and inappropriate use of the ROI measure.

Summary

Investment centers are decentralized units or divisions for which the manager has maximum discretion in determining not only the short-term operating decisions on product mix, pricing, and production methods but also the level and type of investment in the center. The accounting return on investment (ROI) is the most common measure used to evaluate investment-center performance, but this measure suffers from many defects. Managers, in attempting to maximize their ROI measure, have an incentive to reject investments that will earn below the division's average ROI but are still above the divisional cost of capital. This particular problem can be avoided by using the residual income (RI) measure, obtained by subtracting a capital charge for the average investment in the division from divisional net income.

Both measures, ROI and RI, are greatly distorted by failing to adjust assets and depreciation expense for price-level changes during and after inflationary periods. Financial depreciation methods, such as the straight-line and declining-balance methods, further distort the ROI and RI measures, biasing them downward for newly purchased assets and biasing them upward for older assets. A too-liberal expensing policy of investments in intangible assets and the exclusion of leased assets from the investment base also cause traditional investment-center performance measures to be overstated.

Because of the many problems associated with the use of a single measure, such as ROI, to motivate and evaluate the performance of decentralized divisions and managers, some companies are attempting to control profitability and asset turnover measures separately. Profit budgets and return-on-sales (ROS) measures are used to assess profitability, with additional measures and procedures used to monitor the investments in fixed assets and in working capital.

PROBLEMS

15–1   ROI and Divisional Performance

The Solomons Company uses ROI to measure the performance of its operating divisions. A summary of the annual reports from two divisions is shown below. The company's cost of capital is 12%.

	Division A	Division B
Capital invested	$2400	$4000
Net income	$ 480	$ 720
ROI	20%	18%

Required:

1. Which division is more profitable?
2. At what cost of capital would both divisions be considered equally profitable?
3. What performance measurement procedure would more clearly show the relative profitability of the two divisions?
4. Suppose the manager of Division A were offered a one-year project that would increase his investment base (for that year) by $1,000 and show a profit of $150. Would the manager accept this project if he were evaluated on his divisional ROI? Should he accept this project?

15–2   Evaluating Divisional Performance (CMA, adapted)

Darmen Corporation is one of the major producers of prefabricated houses in the home building industry. The corporation consists of two divisions:

1. Bell Division, which acquires the raw materials to manufacture the basic house components and assembles them into kits, and
2. the Cornish Division, which takes the kits and constructs the homes for final home buyers. The corporation is decentralized and the management of each division is measured by its income and return on investment.

Bell Division assembles seven separate house kits using raw materials purchased at the prevailing market prices. The seven kits are sold to Cornish for prices ranging from $45,000 to $98,000. The prices are set by corporate management of Darmen using prices paid by Cornish when it buys comparable units from outside sources. The smaller kits with the lower prices have become a larger portion of the units sold because the final house buyer is faced with prices which are increasing more rapidly than personal income. The kits are manufactured and assembled in a new plant just purchased by Bell this year. The division had been located in a leased plant for the past four years.

All kits are assembled upon receipt of an order from the Cornish Division. When the kit is completely assembled, it is loaded immediately on a Cornish truck. Thus, Bell Division has no finished goods inventory.

The Bell Division's accounts and reports are prepared on an actual cost basis. There is no budget and standards have not been developed for any product. A factory overhead rate is calculated at the beginning of each year. The rate is designed to charge all overhead to the product each year. Any under- or over-applied overhead is allocated to the cost of goods sold account and work in process inventories.

Bell Division's annual report is presented on the next page. This report forms the basis of the evaluation of the division and its management by the corporation management.

Additional information regarding corporate and division practices is as follows:

- The corporation office does all the personnel and accounting work for each division.
- The corporate personnel costs are allocated on the basis of number of employees in the division.
- The accounting costs are allocated to the division on the basis of total costs excluding corporate charges.
- The division administration costs are included in factory overhead.
- The financing charges include a corporate imputed interest charge on division assets and any divisional lease payments.
- The division investment for the return on investment calculation includes division inventory and plant and equipment at gross book value.

Required:

1. Discuss the value of the annual report presented for the Bell Division in evaluating the division and its management in terms of
   a. The accounting techniques employed in the measurement of division activities
   b. The manner of presentation
   c. The effectiveness with which it discloses differences and similarities between years
   Use the information in the problem to illustrate your discussion.
2. Present specific recommendations you would make to the management of Darmen Corporation which would improve its accounting and financial reporting system.

Bell Division
Performance Report
For the Year Ended December 31, 1990

	1990	1989	Increase or (decrease) from 1989 Amount	Percent Change
Summary data				
Net income ($000 omitted)	$ 34,222	$ 31,573	$ 2,649	8.4
Return on investment	37%	43 %	(6)%	(14.0)
Kits shipped (units)	2,000	2,100	(100)	(4.8)
Production data (in units)				
Kits started	2,400	1,600	800	50.0
Kits shipped	2,000	2,100	(100)	(4.8)
Kits in process at year-end	700	300	400	133.3
Increase (decrease) in kits in process at year end	400	(500)	—	—
Financial data $000 omitted)				
Sales	$138,000	$162,800	$(24,800)	(15.2)
Production costs of units sold				
Raw material	$ 32,000	$ 40,000	$ (8,000)	(20.0)
Labor	41,700	53,000	(11,300)	(21.3)
Factory overhead	29,000	37,000	(8,000)	(21.6)
Cost of units sold	$102,700	$130,000	$(27,300)	(21.0)
Other costs				
Corporate charges for				
Personnel services	$ 228	$ 210	$ 18	8.6
Accounting services	425	440	(15)	(3.4)
Financing costs	300	525	(225)	42.9
Total other costs	$ 953	$ 1,175	$ (222)	(18.9)
Adjustments to income				
Unreimbursed fire loss	—	$ 52	$ (52)	(100.0)
Raw material losses due to improper storage	$ 125	—	125	—
Total adjustments	$ 125	$ 52	$ 73	(140.0)
Total deductions	$103,778	$131,227	$(27,449)	(20.9)
Division income	$ 34,222	$ 31,573	$ 2,649	8.4
Division investment	$ 92,000	$ 73,000	$ 19,000	26.0
Return on investment	37%	43 %	(6)%	(14.0)

15–3   Effect of Depreciation on ROI Computations

The Streetorn Corporation is contemplating the purchase of a new piece of equipment. The equipment has an expected life of five years and is expected to produce the following after-tax cash flow savings for the following five years:

Year	After-Tax Cash Flow Savings
1	$50,000
2	46,000
3	42,000
4	36,000
5	30,000

The asset will cost $138,300 and thus has an after-tax yield of 16%, which is above the company's after-tax cost of capital of 15%. The declining pattern of annual cash flow savings is caused by higher maintenance costs as the equipment ages, as well as the reduction in tax benefits from use of the Sum-of-Years'-Digits Method for depreciation. For example, the gross cash flow savings in Year 3 (before depreciation and before taxes) is $51,560. The net after-tax cash flow savings is obtained by the following computation:

Gross cash flow savings	$51,560
Depreciation (138,300)(3/15)	27,660
Taxable income	23,900
Taxes (@ 40%)	9,560
Net income after taxes	14,340
+ Depreciation	27,660
After-tax cash flow savings	$42,000

Optional: Compute the Gross Cash Flow Savings for Years 1–5.

The president's bonus is based on the company's Return-on-Investment (Net Income After Taxes/Investment at Start-of-Year). The company prides itself on its conservative accounting policies and therefore uses the same depreciation method for financial reporting as it does for its tax return. The controller of Streetorn has prepared the following table to show the president the annual ROI from the new piece of equipment:

Year	(1) Book Value Start-of-Year	(2) Net Cash Flow After Taxes	(3) SYD Depreciation	(4) = (2) − (3) Net Income After Taxes	(5) = (4)/(1) ROI
1	$138,300	$50,000	$46,100	$ 3,900	2.8%
2	92,200	46,000	36,880	9,120	9.9%
3	55,320	42,000	27,660	14,340	25.9%
4	27,660	36,000	18,440	17,560	63.5%
5	9,220	30,000	9,220	20,780	225.4%
Average (5 years)	$ 64,540	$40,800	$27,660	$13,140	20.4%

The president is astonished by this table. He says, "Something's very wrong here. According to your cash-flow analysis, this piece of equipment has a 16 percent after-tax yield. Yet our financial statements show a different yield each year and the low ROI in the first two years is going to keep me out of bonus money. Sure the equipment shows a fantastic ROI in its last two years, but I may not be with the company by then. I need results right away, not four years from now!"

The controller decides that the trouble may be with the firm's conservative accounting practices. Perhaps, if the firm used straight-line depreciation for financial reporting, like most of the other firms in the industry, the numbers would look better. He proceeds to produce the following table:

Year	Book Value Start-of-Year	Net Cash Flow After Taxes	Straight-Line Depreciation	Net Income After Taxes	ROI
1	$138,300	$50,000	$27,660	$22,340	16.2%
2	110,640	46,000	27,660	18,340	16.6%
3	82,980	42,000	27,660	14,340	17.3%
4	55,320	36,000	27,660	8,340	15.1%
5	27,660	30,000	27,660	2,340	8.5%
Average	$ 82,980	$40,800	$27,660	$13,140	15.8%

The president is much happier with this presentation, especially since now the asset shows good returns in the earlier years. But he is still puzzled as to why an asset with a yield of 16% doesn't show a 16% ROI each year.

Required:

1. Verify that this piece of equipment does have a 16% yield.
2. Show, using the present value depreciation method, how the equipment can have a 16% ROI for each of the five years of the asset's life.
3. Why did the ROI using the straight-line depreciation method approximate the actual yield reasonably well (for at least the first four years of the asset's life)?

15–4   Effects of Inflation on ROI

The Carter Company uses the ROI criterion to evaluate the performance of its divisions. The company prides itself on the formal capital-budgeting procedures it uses for approving new investments, and the subsequent control procedures it has implemented to measure the performance of these new investments. Recently, however, the ROI measure has been producing performance statistics quite at variance with the criterion used to screen the investments. The company believes that recent high inflation rates may be contributing to the erratic performance evaluation measures.

The problem is well illustrated by comparing the performance of two divisions.

Division Y made a major investment ten years ago. This investment cost $3,000,000, had an expected life of fifteen years, and annual after-tax cash flows of $525,000. The rate of return of slightly more than 15% was above the Carter Company's cost of capital. During the past ten years, the price level had risen by 67%, and the after-tax cash flows from the investment had increased to an annual level of $800,000. The ROI for Division Y for the most recent year was computed as:

Investment book value (start-of-year)	$1,200,000
Investment book value (end-of-year)	1,000,000
Average investment	$1,100,000
Net cash flow	$ 800,000
Depreciation	200,000
Net income	$ 600,000
ROI—Division Y	54.5%

Division Z, in a different region than Division Y, made a major investment of a very similar type just two years ago. Because of the increase in construction and equipment costs, the investment now had cost $4,500,000. The expected life of this investment was ten years, and the annual after-tax cash flow was $900,000. This investment also had a yield slightly in excess of 15%, so that the performance measure of Division Z was expected to be similar to that of Division Y. In fact, Division Z's investment appeared to be much less profitable than Division Y's and did not even reach the expected 15% ROI cutoff figure. The most recent year's data show:

Investment book value (start-of-year)	$4,050,000
Investment book value (end-of-year)	3,600,000
Average investment	$3,825,000
Net cash flow	$1,000,000
Depreciation	450,000
Net income	$ 550,000
ROI—Division Z	14.4%

The price index was 120 ten years ago when Division Y's investment was made. Two years ago, when Division Z made its investment, the index was 180, and in the most recent year, for which the above data were prepared, the index averaged 200.

Required:

Analyze this situation explaining why two divisions with such similar investments (15% after-tax returns from the discounted cash flow analysis) are showing such disparate ROIs.

15–5   ROI and Leasing

The Malone Division of the Stoudt Corporation is organized as an investment center. Because of excellent operating results, the division manager, Terry Trocano, has been given considerable freedom in investment decisions. Terry knows that the top management of the Stoudt Corporation measures the performance of the operating divisions using an ROI criterion and that it is important for her to maintain a divisional ROI of 20% before taxes and 14% after taxes. Her annual bonus depends on achieving these targeted levels, and her compensation can increase considerably if she is able to obtain even higher ROIs.

Terry Trocano has just completed a five-year forecast of annual operating performance for the Malone Division. The best estimate is that the current net investment level of $20,000,000 will be maintained over this period (that is, new investment will about equal the depreciation charge each year) and that the Net Income Before Taxes will be $4,000,000 and Net Income After Taxes will be $2,800,000 each year.

While Terry is pleased that her forecasted results indicate that she will achieve both the before- and after-tax ROI targets, she is actively looking for projects that will enable her to exceed the targeted rates.

A new investment proposal has recently emerged that seems particularly promising. The project requires an initial investment of $15,000,000 and will generate annual before-tax cash flows of $6,000,000 for five years. The discounted cash flow analysis indicates that the project has a before-tax yield in excess of 28% and an after-tax yield of more than 19%. (The Stoudt Corporation has a marginal tax rate of 40% and uses sum-of-years'-digits depreciation for computing taxable income.) Since both of these yields are well in excess of the company's targeted ROI, the proposed project seems like an excellent investment.

Before making a final decision on the $15,000,000 investment, Terry has asked the division controller to forecast the first year's operating results for the Malone Division, including the income generated by the new project. She is surprised when she receives the following pro forma results:

Before-Tax Analysis (000)

	Net income from existing projects	$ 4,000
	Cash flow—new project	6,000
Less:	Depreciation (straight-line, 5-year life)	(3,000)
	Net income	$ 7,000
	Investment—Existing projects	$20,000
	—New project	15,000
	Total investment	$35,000
	ROI	20%

After-Tax Analysis (000)

Net income after taxes—existing projects	$ 2,800
Net income before tax—new project	3,000
Taxes on new project[a]	
(sum-of-years'-digits depreciation)	(400)
Net income after taxes	$ 5,400
Total investment	35,000
ROI	15.4%

[a] The company uses actual tax expense, based on the accelerated depreciation schedule, in allocating tax expense to divisions.

The project doesn't hurt the measured performance of the Malone Division, but it certainly doesn't show the large increase in divisional ROI that Terry had hoped for.

The controller proposes an alternative scheme for undertaking the investment. He has learned that another company is willing to acquire the buildings and equipment for the new project and lease these to the Malone Division at an annual rental payment of $5,200,000 for five years. The terms of the lease can be structured so that it is considered an operating lease and hence will not be capitalized on the Stoudt Corporation's financial statements. The controller has prepared the following pro forma analysis of the lease option.

Before-Tax Analysis (000)

Net income from existing projects	$ 4,000
Cash flow—new project	6,000
Less: Lease payment	(5,200)
Net income	$ 4,800
Investment—existing projects	20,000
ROI	24%

After-Tax Analysis (000)

Net income after taxes-existing projects	$ 2,800
Income from new project—net of lease	
payment	800
Taxes—new project	(320)
Net income after taxes	$ 3,280
Investment	20,000
ROI	16.4%

The lease option seems much more attractive to Terry Trocano, since it generates a significant increase in both before- and after-tax ROI for her division. She submits the proposed new project, with a recommendation to lease the new facilities, to the central administration staff expecting a routine approval for this attractive investment opportunity.

Required:

Assume that you are the newly hired assistant to the head of the corporate finance division and have been asked to review the project proposed from the Malone Division.

1. Verify that the proposed project will yield the forecasted returns (28 + % before tax, 19 + % after tax).
2. Compute the before- and after-tax ROI for the Malone Division for each of the next five years for both the purchase and the lease options. The investment base for each year is the book value (using straight-line depreciation) of investment at the start of the year.
3. At the company's after-tax cost of capital of 14%, is it better to purchase or lease the asset? (Assume that the company is not able to use the investment tax credit.)
4. Why does the leasing option generate higher ROI measures than the purchase option?
5. Suggest an alternative scheme that will reduce the incentive to lease rather than purchase assets. Demonstrate how your scheme will work were the Malone Division to enter into the five-year lease with annual payments of $5,200,000 per year.

15–6   Enager Industries, Inc.

"I don't get it. I've got a nifty new product proposal that can't help but make money, and top management turns thumbs down. No matter how we price this new item, we expect to make $130,000 on it pre-tax. That would contribute over ten cents per share to our earnings after taxes, which is more than the nine cent earnings-per-share increase in 1988 that the president made such a big thing about in the shareholders' annual report. It just doesn't make sense for the president to be touting e.p.s. while his subordinates are rejecting profitable projects like this one."

The frustrated speaker was Sarah McNeil, product development manager of the Consumer Products Division of Enager Industries, Inc. Enager was a relatively young company, which had grown rapidly to its 1988 sales level of over $74 million. (See Exhibits 1–3 for financial data for 1987 and 1988.)

Enager had three divisions, Consumer Products, Industrial Products, and Professional Services, each of which accounted for about one-third of Enager's total sales. Consumer Products, the oldest of the three divisions, designed, manufactured and marketed a line of houseware items, primarily for use in the kitchen. The Industrial Products division built one-of-a-kind

This case appears in Anthony and Reece, *Accounting: Text and Cases* 8th ed. (Homewood, IL: Irwin, 1988), and is reprinted here with permission of the case writer, Professor James S. Reece.

EXHIBIT 1
Enager Industries, Inc.
Income Statements for 1987 and 1988
(thousands of dollars, except earnings per share figures)

	Year Ended December 31	
	1987	*1988*
Sales	$70,731	$74,225
Cost of Goods Sold	54,109	56,257
Gross Margin	$16,622	$17,968
Other Expenses:		
Development	$ 4,032	$ 4,008
Selling and General	6,507	6,846
Interest	594	976
Total	$11,133	$11,830
Income before Taxes	$ 5,489	$ 6,138
Income Tax Expense	2,854	3,192
Net Income	$ 2,635	$ 2,946
Earnings per Share (500,000 and 550,000		
shares outstanding in 1987 and 1988 respectively)	$5.27	$5.36

machine tools to customer specifications; i.e., it was a large "job shop," with the typical job taking several months to complete. The Professional Services division, the newest of the three, had been added to Enager by acquiring a large firm which provided land planning, landscape architecture, structural architecture, and consulting engineering services. This division had grown rapidly, in part because of its capability to perform "environmental impact" studies, as required by law on many new land development projects.

    Because of the differing nature of their activities, each division was treated as an essentially independent company. There were only a few corporate-level managers and staff people, whose job was to coordinate the activities of the three divisions. One aspect of this coordination was that all new project proposals requiring investment in excess of $500,000 had to be reviewed by the corporate vice president of finance, Henry Hubbard. It was Hubbard who had recently rejected McNeil's new project proposal, the essentials of which are shown in Exhibit 4.

Performance Evaluation

Prior to 1987, each of the three Enager divisions had been treated as a profit center, with annual division profit budgets negotiated between the president and the respective division general managers. . . . At the urging of Henry Hubbard, Enager's president, Carl Randall, had decided to begin

EXHIBIT 2
Enager Industries, Inc.
Balance Sheets for 1987 and 1988
(thousands of dollars)

	As of December 31	
	1987	*1988*
Assets		
Cash and temporary investments	$ 1,404	$ 1,469
Accounts receivable	13,688	15,607
Inventories	22,162	25,467
Total Current Assets	$37,254	$42,543
Plant and Equipment:		
Original cost	$37,326	$45,736
Accumulated depreciation	12,691	15,979
Net	$24,635	$29,757
Investments and other assets	2,143	3,119
Total Assets	$64,032	$75,419
Liabilities and Owners' Equity		
Accounts payable	$ 9,720	$12,286
Taxes payable	1,210	1,045
Current portion of long-term debt	—	1,634
Total Current Liabilities	$10,930	$14,965
Deferred income taxes	559	985
Long-term debt	12,622	15,448
Total Liabilities	$24,111	$31,398
Common stock	$17,368	$19,512
Retained earnings	22,553	24,509
Total Owners' Equity	$39,921	$44,021
Total Liabilities and Owners' Equity	$64,032	$75,419

treating each division as an investment center, so as to be able to relate each division's profit to the assets the division used to generate its profits.

Starting in 1987, each division was measured based on its return on assets, which was defined to be the division's net income divided by its assets. Net income for a division was calculated by taking the division's "direct income before taxes," and then subtracting the division's share of corporate administrative expenses (allocated on the basis of divisional revenues) and its share of income tax expense (the tax rate applied to the division's "direct income before taxes" after subtraction of the allocated corporate administrative expenses). Although Hubbard realized there were other ways to define a division's income, he and the president preferred this method since "it made the sum of the [divisional] parts equal to the [corporate] whole."

EXHIBIT 3

Enager Industries, Inc.
Ratio Analysis for 1987 and 1988

	1987	1988
Net Income ÷ Sales	3.7%	4.0%
Gross Margin ÷ Sales	23.5%	24.2%
Development Expenses ÷ Sales	5.7%	5.4%
Selling and General ÷ Sales	9.2%	9.2%
Interest ÷ Sales	0.8%	1.3%
Asset Turnover[1]	1.10x	0.98x
Current Ratio	3.41	2.84
Quick Ratio	1.38	1.14
Days' Cash[1]	8.1	7.9
Days' Receivables[1]	70.6	76.7
Day's Inventories[1]	149.5	165.2
EBIT ÷ Assets[1]	9.5%	9.4%
Return on Invested Capital[1,2,3]	5.6%	5.6%
Return on Owners' Equity[1]	6.6%	6.7%
Net Income ÷ Assets[1,4]	4.1%	3.9%
Debt/Capitalization[1]	24.0%	28.0%

[1] Ratio based on year-end balance sheet amount, not annual average amount.

[2] Invested capital includes current portion of long-term debt.

[3] Adjusted for interest expense add-back.

[4] Not adjusted for add-back of interest; if adjusted, 1987 and 1988 ROA are 4.6% and 4.5%.

EXHIBIT 4

Enager Industries, Inc.
Financial Data from New Project Proposal

1. Projected Asset Investment:[1]

Cash	$ 50,000
Accounts receivable	150,000
Inventories	300,000
Plant and equipment[2]	500,000
Total	$1,000,000

2. Cost Data:

Variable cost per unit	$3.00
Differential fixed costs (per year)[3]	$ 170,000

3. Price/Market Estimates (per year):

Unit Price	Unit Sales	Breakeven Volume
$6.00	100,000 units	56,667 units
7.00	75,000	42,500
8.00	60,000	34,000

[1] Assumes 100,000 units' sales.

[2] Annual capacity of 120,000 units.

[3] Includes straight-line depreciation on new plant and equipment.

Similarly, Enager's total assets were subdivided among three divisions. Since each division operated in physically separate facilities, it was easy to attribute most assets, including receivables, to specific divisions. The corporate-office assets, including the centrally controlled cash account, were allocated to the divisions on the basis of divisional revenues. All fixed assets were recorded at their balance sheet values, i.e., original cost less accumulated straight-line depreciation. Thus the sum of the divisional assets was equal to the amount shown on the corporate balance sheet ($75,419,000 as of December 31, 1988).

In 1986, Enager had as its return on year-end assets (net income divided by total assets) a rate of 3.8%. According to Hubbard, this corresponded to a "gross return" in 1986 of 9.3%; he defined gross return as equal to earnings *before* interest *and* taxes ("EBIT") divided by assets. Hubbard felt that a company like Enager should have a gross (EBIT) return on assets of at least 12%, especially given the interest rates the corporation had had to pay on its recent borrowings. He therefore instructed each division manager that the division was to try to earn a gross return of 12% in 1987 and 1988. In order to help pull the return up to this level, Hubbard decided that new investment proposals would have to show a return of at least 15% in order to be approved.

1987–88 Results

Hubbard and Randall were moderately pleased with 1987's results. The year was a particularly difficult one for some of Enager's competitors, yet Enager had managed to increase its return on assets from 3.8% to 4.1%, and its gross return from 9.3% to 9.5%. The Professional Services Division easily exceeded the 12% gross return target; Consumer Products' gross return on assets was 8%; but Industrial Products' return was only 5.5%.

At the end of 1987, the president put pressure on the general manager of the Industrial Products division to improve its return on investment, suggesting that this division was not "carrying its share of the load." The division manager had bristled at this comment, saying the division could get a higher return "if we had a lot of old machines the way Consumer Products does." The president had responded that he did not understand the relevance of the division manager's remark, adding, "I don't see why the return on an old asset should be higher than that on a new asset, just because the old one cost less."

The 1988 results both disappointed and puzzled Carl Randall. Return on assets fell from 4.1% to 3.9%, and gross return dropped from 9.5% to 9.4%. At the same time, return on sales (net income divided by sales) rose from 3.7% to 4.0%, and return on owners' equity also increased, from 6.6% to 6.7%. These results prompted Randall to say the following to Hubbard:

"You know, Henry, I've been a marketer most of my career; but, until recently, I thought I understood the notion of return on investment. Now

I see in 1988 our profit margin was up and our earnings per share were up; yet two of your return on investment figures were down, one—return on invested capital—held constant, and return on owners' equity went up. I just don't understand these discrepancies.

"Moreover, there seems to be a lot more tension among our managers the last two years. The general manager of the Professional Services division seems to be doing a good job, and she's happy as a lark about the praise I've given her. But the general manager of Industrial Products looks daggers at me every time we meet. And last week, when I was eating lunch with the division manager at Consumer Products, the product development manager came over to our table and really burned my ears over a new product proposal of hers you rejected the other day.

"I'm wondering if I should follow up on the idea that Karen Kraus in Personnel brought back from that two-day organization development workshop she attended over at the university. She thinks we ought to have a one-day off-site 'retreat' of all the corporate and divisional managers to talk over this entire return-on-investment matter."

Required:

1. Why was McNeil's new product proposal rejected? Should it have been? Explain.
2. Evaluate the manner in which Randall and Hubbard have implemented their investment-center concept. What pitfalls did they apparently not anticipate?
3. What, if anything, should Randall do now with regard to his investment-center approach?

15–7 *The Inflation Accounting System*

AMERICAN STANDARD INC.

In the fall of 1981, Kenneth R. Todd, Jr., vice president and controller, was reviewing the inflation-adjusted accounting system that was used at American Standard. American Standard was committed to inflation-adjusted accounting as the primary measurement system for the company. Todd realized that this differed from the approach taken by most U.S. firms, which either provided inflation-adjusted accounting data to managers as supplementary information or did not provide these data at all, and even though American Standard had gone further than most firms in integrating inflation-adjusted accounting data into management systems, Todd was not satisfied with the company's accomplishments. In particular, he wondered whether it would be useful to restate prior years' current cost data

Julie H. Hertenstein, research assistant, prepared this case under the supervision of Professor William J. Burns, Jr. Copyright © 1983 by the President and Fellows of Harvard College. Harvard Business School case 9–183–169.

in constant dollars and whether changes should be made to the long-term incentive compensation plan.

American Standard's Business

American Standard was a major international manufacturing firm, with 1980 sales of $2,674 million (see Exhibits 1 and 2 for primary financial statements). The company manufactured products in 150 plants, which were located in 22 countries on five continents, and marketed these products in nearly every country in the world.

American Standard's products fell into four general categories: transportation products (braking systems for heavy trucks and systems for train monitoring and control); building products (plumbing fixtures and fittings); security and graphic products (bank safes, vaults, electronic alarms, bank

EXHIBIT 1

Statement of Income and Retained Earnings
($ thousands except per share amounts)

Year Ended December 31	1980	1979	1978
Sales	$2,673,589	$2,431,557	$2,110,860
Costs and expenses			
Cost of sales	2,039,715	1,849,217	1,597,343
Selling and administrative expenses	370,949	325,860	294,454
Net foreign exchange (gain) loss	(6,802)	10,219	12,906
Other (income) expense	(20,200)	(19,305)	(11,559)
Interest expense	32,679	33,057	28,791
	2,416,341	2,199,048	1,921,935
Income before taxes on income	257,248	232,509	188,925
Taxes on income	100,355	100,354	87,587
Net income	156,893	132,155	101,338
Retained earnings, beginning of year	419,009	334,157	265,238
Cash dividends:			
$4.75 convertible preference stock	—	(398)	(1,856)
Preferred stock	(105)	(111)	(116)
Common stock	(54,803)	(41,487)	(30,262)
Purchase of shares of stock in excess of par value	—	(5,307)	(185)
Retained earnings, end of year	$ 520,994	$ 419,009	$ 334,157
Average outstanding common shares and equivalents[a,b]	27,576,765	27,734,878	28,008,086
Net income per common share[b]	$5.69	$4.76	$3.61
Dividends per common share[b]	$2.00	$1.525	$1.175

[a] Per-share amounts are presented as though all the $4.75 cumulative convertible preference stock, series A, had been converted into common stock until its redemption effective April 3, 1979, and all relevant stock options had been exercised.

[b] Restated to reflect two-for-one split of the common stock in December 1980.

EXHIBIT 2
Balance Sheet ($ thousands)

At December 31	1980	1979	1978
Current assets			
Cash	$ 20,203	$ 42,028	$ 22,105
Certificates of deposit—1978 includes other			
marketable securities of $1,277	26,788	25,687	15,037
Accounts receivable, less allowance for doubt-			
ful accounts—1980, $17,230; 1979, $12,058;			
1978, $10,956	405,885	348,520	294,790
Inventories, at current cost	594,561	588,612	470,672
Less: LIFO reserve	212,662	192,545	148,510
Inventories, at LIFO cost	381,899	396,067	322,162
Future income tax benefits	49,183	45,457	40,618
Other current assets	66,533	17,123	13,263
Total current assets	950,491	874,882	707,975
Facilities, at cost			
Land	20,363	22,147	21,172
Buildings	272,207	262,094	243,068
Machinery and equipment	618,015	559,917	474,743
Improvements in progress	50,246	30,512	27,161
Gross facilities	960,831	874,670	766,144
Less: Accumulated depreciation	469,622	442,452	406,251
Net facilities	491,209	432,218	359,893
Other assets			
Investment in associated companies	31,599	31,130	31,103
Excess of cost over net assets of businesses			
purchased	70,316	71,475	71,475
Other	34,756	13,058	14,549
Total assets	$1,578,371	$1,422,763	$1,184,995
Current liabilities			
Loans payable to banks	$ 16,944	$ 34,593	$ 31,633
Commercial paper	—	21,236	—
Current maturities of long-term debt	13,585	14,803	16,777
Accounts payable	190,039	201,300	153,664
Accrued payrolls	115,743	99,350	82,005
Other accrued liabilities	130,327	104,978	96,242
Taxes on income	57,820	85,522	38,002
Total current liabilities	524,458	561,782	418,323
Long-term debt	279,982	193,466	198,568
Other credits			
Reserve for foreign pensions and termination			
indemnities	79,392	79,380	67,250
Deferred taxes on income	52,129	32,691	24,056
Minority interests in subsidiaries	6,363	6,289	9,679
Stockholders' equity			
7% preferred stock, 14,583 shares outstanding			
in 1980; 15,447 in 1979; and 16,617 in 1978	1,458	1,545	1,662
$4.75 cumulative convertible preference stock,			
337,762 shares outstanding in 1978	—	—	6,755
Common stock, 27,082,920 shares outstanding			
in 1980; 13,751,110 in 1979; and 13,029,172			
in 1978	27,083	13,751	65,146
Capital surplus	86,512	114,850	59,399
Retained earnings	520,994	419,009	334,157
Total stockholders' equity	636,047	549,155	467,119
Total liabilities and stockholders' equity	$1,578,371	$1,422,763	$1,184,995

checks, and business forms); and construction and mining equipment (off-highway, heavy construction trucks).

These businesses were managed through a decentralized management system, which was organized in a hierarchical structure that comprised global groups, groups, and companies and product lines (see Exhibit 3 for an organization chart). The many companies and product lines varied significantly in size, and a primary vehicle of communication among the diverse businesses within American Standard was the financial control system.

The Financial Control System

The overall corporate objective was to attain real, inflation-adjusted, rates of return on assets that were sufficient to finance the businesses (including growth) and to offer above-average, real returns to shareholders. The financial control system was designed to help achieve the corporate objectives. Todd explained its purpose as follows:

> A key assumption is that we're going to stay in these businesses. Therefore, American Standard has adopted the concept related to maintenance of productive capacity as the basic premise of its financial control system—in other words, staying in business. We define operating income as the funds left over and available for expansion of the business after maintaining the productive capacity of our unit and providing a minimum return to security holders.

To further the corporate goals, the financial control system had to encourage maximum asset utilization by managers and to provide them with the right tools for the best economic decisions. American Standard adopted an inflation-adjusted method of accounting to help accomplish these goals. The recent financial experiences of the firm were a significant factor in the decision to adopt this accounting method.

Top management traced the impetus for American Standard's use of an inflation-adjusted method of accounting back to the latter part of the 1960s. During that period American Standard aggressively expanded, with major acquisitions, such as Mosler Safe in 1967 and Westinghouse Air Brake Company (WABCO) in 1968, as well as numerous smaller acquisitions. From 1966 to 1969 the total assets of the company tripled; to finance this growth, American Standard borrowed heavily, significantly increasing its leverage.

EXHIBIT 3
Organization Chart

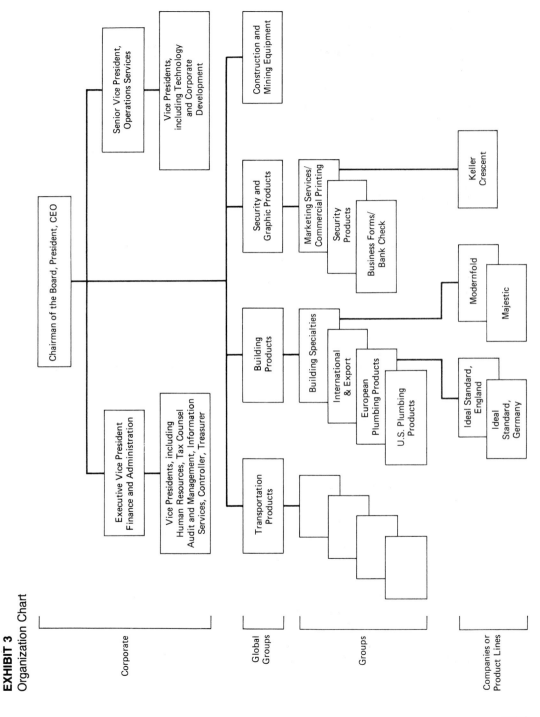

The recession of 1969–1970 kept American Standard from achieving the growth it had projected; and in 1970, as the seriousness of the situation became evident, the company began to retrench. It closed some plants and sold or phased out other operations. In 1971 William A. Marquard, who had previously been president of American Standard's subsidiary, the Mosler Safe Company, was named president and chief executive officer of American Standard, Inc. In the same year he announced to shareholders a program of asset redeployment, characterized by a philosophy of consolidation, that was in sharp contrast to the previous policy of rapid expansion. In 1971 American Standard took a writedown of $97 million (after a $25 million tax benefit) to provide for the costs to be incurred on sales or other dispositions of certain businesses and facilities; this resulted in a net loss for the year of $83.8 million. American Standard's executives thus began the steps necessary to turn the company around.

American Standard's executives were particularly aware of the need for information that reflected economic reality during this turn-around and realized that the management accounting system had to reflect their best understanding of economic reality. When American Standard's executives believed that external reporting requirements differed from economic reality, they were willing to modify their internal management accounting systems so that the data available to executives and their subordinates were as realistic as possible. Richard H. Francis, vice president and treasurer, provided an example that explained their willingness to diverge from the external reporting requirements.

> Past accounting practice did not require leased assets to be reported on the balance sheet, nor did it require the amount due to the lessor to be reported as a liability. But by following an accounting practice such as off-balance sheet leasing internally, you may forget what you were doing, or some managers may not have known. You could wind up misleading yourself, and that could cause problems.

This philosophy led to the eventual implementation of an inflation-adjusted accounting system. American Standard's managers generally agreed that the first steps toward inflation accounting occurred in the mid-1970s with the worldwide adoption of the LIFO method of accounting for cost of goods sold and inventory that led to a closer matching of the current cost of production with current revenues. In the fall of 1981 further modifications and extensions of the inflation accounting system were under consideration.

The Inflation-Adjusted Accounting System

American Standard's inflation-adjusted accounting system can best be understood by first considering the four basic accounting elements which differed from conventional historical cost accounting elements and then considering its two composite measures of performance, in which some or all of these four basic elements appear. The four basic elements are fixed assets, depreciation, inventories, and cost of goods sold, and the two composite measures are operating income and return on net assets (RONA).

Fixed Assets and Depreciation. Accounting for fixed assets was based on the estimated cost of replacing the assets. Replacement costs were computed by restating each asset, or category of assets, through the use of local, replacement-cost indices for each industry and country in which American Standard operated.

Exhibit 4-A illustrates the computation of replacement costs for the buildings in the Keller Crescent Company; first, the year of the acquisition of the existing buildings was determined, and then the replacement cost was calculated for each year's acquisitions. Local management selected various producer-price indices or construction-price indices that they considered to be representative of the particular assets.[1] These published indices were also acceptable for the required supplementary public reporting of inflation-adjusted data. Although this method did not incorporate technological change in the replacement cost, American Standard believed that the additional costs of a more elaborate method of calculating replacement cost would exceed the benefit to be gained, particularly since technologies were not changing rapidly in American Standard's industries. The published specific price indices were considered to be objective, and their use removed opportunities for optimism or manipulation to affect the data.

Under the basic purpose of the financial control system—to maintain productive capacity—depreciation was considered a provision for replacing productive assets used in the business; hence, depreciation was based on the replacement cost of the assets. Replacement depreciation was further based on management's realistic estimates of the economic lives of the assets involved (as shown in Exhibit 4-B). American Standard believed that to stay in business, the company should retain profits at a rate sufficient to have funds on hand for functionally replacing manufacturing equipment and facilities at the end of their useful lives. According to Todd:

> It does not matter that a replacement machine may have commensurate benefits in terms of lower production costs. Those reductions will take place after the investment has taken place. What is important is that

---

[1] Two examples of sources of such indices are the *Producer Prices and Price Indexes*, which is published by the U.S. Bureau of Labor Statistics and contains detailed categories, such as metal-cutting machine tools, metal-forming machine tools, and pumps and compressors, and *Construction Review*, which contains numerous composite construction-cost indices for commercial and factory buildings as well as indices for producers' prices of selected groups of materials and items used in construction.

EXHIBIT 4
Facility Analysis Keller Crescent 1981 Ongoing Assets; Buildings in U.S. Dollars

A. Calculation of Replacement Costs

Year of Acquisition	Ending Gross Facilities (historical cost)	Local Index		Ending Gross Facilities (replacement cost)[a]
		Year-end	Average	
1968	$1,343	1.0500	1.05	$3,594
1969	8	1.1300	1.09	21
1970	30	1.2000	1.165	72
1971	503	1.3100	1.255	1,126
1972	55	1.4200	1.365	113
1973	42	1.5300	1.475	80
1974	46	1.6900	1.61	80
1975	28	1.8600	1.775	44
1976	633	1.9700	1.915	929
1977	67	2.0700	2.02	93
1978	131	2.2700	2.17	170
1979	118	2.4700	2.37	140
1980	50	2.6500	2.56	55
1981	870	2.8100	2.73	895
Total	$3,924			$7,412

[a] Computation of Ending Gross Facilities (replacement cost):

$$\text{Ending Gross Facilities at Historical Cost} \times \frac{\text{Local Index} - \text{Year-End} - 1981}{\text{Local Index} - \text{Average} - \text{Year of Acquisition}}$$

B. Calculation of Replacement Depreciation

Total Ongoing Buildings (historical cost)	Amount	Life	Annual Depreciation	Average Life
Buildings	$2,501	40	$ 62.53	
Building Appurtenances	1,423	20	71.15	
Total Ongoing Buildings	$3,924		$133.68	29.354

Replacement Depreciation

Ending Gross facilities 12/31/81 (replacement cost)	Average Life	Total Depreciation (replacement cost)
$7,412	29.354	$252.5

a company retain from current operations sufficient funds to replace its fixed assets; charging income for realistic depreciation is how this is accomplished.

One indication of the extent to which the policy of replacement depreciation had been implemented was that a manager's operating income was charged replacement depreciation for all depreciable assets used, including those assets that had already been fully depreciated. Management reasoned that such assets were only considered fully depreciated because of a past error in estimating asset life, whereas, in fact, the manager was still using the assets, and therefore they ought to be providing a return. Further, charging depreciation on these assets might motivate managers to consider whether the assets should be disposed of; it would provide an incentive for managers at lower levels, who had the real knowledge of the assets' utilization and condition, to reevaluate the decision to keep the assets.

There were a few conditions, however, when replacement depreciation was not used; these occurred when an entire business was to be abandoned, or a unit's asset utilization was to be decreased substantially (and then only after concrete action had been taken to dispose of the assets). In these instances, two other changes occurred in the financial control system: first, the rate of historical cost depreciation was adjusted to reflect the remaining expected useful life, and second, any capital expenditures made in this business were expensed immediately.

The overall effect of using replacement costs as the basis for accounting for fixed assets and depreciation was significant; in 1981 these costs were each about 45% higher than they would have been under conventional historical cost accounting.

Inventory and Cost of Goods Sold. On the balance sheet, inventories were carried at current standard costs; each year, when the new current standard costs were determined, the inventory on the balance sheet was revalued to the new current standard cost. For example, if standard costs had increased by 10%, the inventory on the balance sheet would be revalued upward by 10%. This annual revaluation to current standards created an offsetting credit entry that was considered a corporate item and was not reflected in the operating income for the divisions.

American Standard determined the cost of goods sold by using current standard costs with immediate recognition of any variances from standard. It believed that this use of current standards, combined with any variance from standard that might have occurred during the period, provided an accurate estimate of the current cost of production.

The company also believed that the various historical cost methods of accounting for inventories and cost of goods sold did not match the current cost of production with current sales. Historical cost income included an element of "inventory profit," which arose from matching current revenues with the lower costs of production in earlier periods. American Standard believed that such paper inventory profits did not represent management performance, nor did they represent amounts that could be used by other divisions or distributed to security holders. The paper profits that resulted from higher inventory values had to be retained just to maintain the business at its current level; therefore, the company believed that it was beneficial for both executives and operating management to keep these paper profits out of the division's operating income.

Since American Standard had implemented LIFO for inventories and cost of goods sold, virtually no change to cost of goods sold was required to adjust for inflation. Since LIFO seriously understated the inventories on the balance sheet, however, the current cost of inventories ($551 million in 1981) represented a 61% increase above the conventional LIFO inventory cost of $342 million.

Operating Income. Operating income was the primary performance measurement at American Standard; it was calculated before the provision for taxes and contained provisions for three charges: replacement depreciation for pro-rata share of the productive capacity used, the current cost of inventory sold, and the minimum return required for security holders, known as the capital charge. (The capital charge is discussed in more detail below.) The following is a simplified statement of operating income:

> Revenues
> Less: Current cost of goods sold
>   Replacement depreciation
>   Other expenses
>   Capital charge
> _____
> Operating income (before tax)

Operating income was defined as the funds left over and available for expansion of the business, after maintenance of the productive capacity of the unit and after a minimum return to security holders had been provided. In other words, a unit at break-even had no funds left over for expanding its own business or for distributing to other units; break-even represented the minimal level of sustainable performance.

The *capital charge* represented (1) the recovery of corporate overhead not charged to the field and (2) the inflation-adjusted (or real) cost of capital for the corporation, including both debt and equity elements. In 1981 a capital charge rate of 12% was charged for use of the division's net assets (net assets are discussed below); since the cost of capital was stated in real terms, and hence would not vary with changes in the rate of inflation, American Standard's executives expected the capital charge to remain at 12% of net assets.

Net assets were defined as all assets of operations less current liabilities that were without financing cost; the assets of operations were those assets for which line managers were held responsible, such as inventories at current standard cost and fixed assets at replacement cost net of depreciation. Excluded were assets for which division managers were not held accountable, such as cash, marketable securities, and future income tax benefits; these were corporate responsibilities over which line managers had little, if any, influence. For example, American Standard had one central cash fund for all U.S. operations; it did not have separate cash funds managed by individual groups or companies.

In summary, net assets were defined as follows:

> Total inflation-adjusted assets
> Less: Cash
> Marketable securities
> Future income tax benefits
> Accounts payable and accrued liabilities
> _____
> Net Assets

Return on Net Assets (RONA). Whereas operating income was a stand-alone figure used to plan and control operations, RONA measured the long-term profitability of each operation. RONA was calculated as follows:

$$\text{RONA} = \frac{\text{Operating Income} + \text{Capital Charge}}{\text{Net Assets}}$$

American Standard believed that RONA could be directly related to the growth potential of a unit, and it developed a chart to illustrate this point (see *Figure A*). The chart contains two plotted lines: one shows the relationship of RONA to growth potential, assuming the dividend payout is 40% of inflation-adjusted earnings, and the other assumes a 50% dividend payout, given the assumptions in the footnotes. The chart demonstrates that a RONA of 20% will provide an 8% growth potential if the dividend payout is 40% and a 6% growth potential if the dividend payout is 50%.

Implementation

As previously mentioned, the inflation-adjusted accounting system was gradually implemented over an extended period. There were a number of reasons for this: the changes being implemented had to be explained

FIGURE A
Growth Potential

Growth potential is a function of:
• Rate of Return
—After-Tax Return on Assets (Debt + Equity)
• Dividends Paid
• Debt/Equity Ratio
• Interest Paid on Debt
Relationship of RONA to Growth Potential (with
a debt/equity ratio of 20/80)

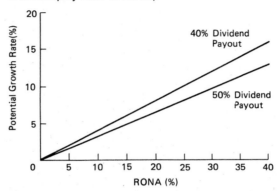

Note: Although RONA shown on this chart is a pretax
figure, in order to relate RONA to growth potential, it
was assumed that taxes paid would be 45% of operating income.

to a large number of people; operating groups provided suggestions for
improvement, which led to further changes, after initial elements of the
system had been implemented; and some of the concepts on which the
system was based continued to evolve as American Standard gained experience in using the system. For example, the capital charge, introduced
in the early 1970s, originally reflected actual interest expense; later, it
evolved into a "real cost of capital" concept (that is, inflation-free cost of
debt and equity). In 1981 the system reflected several important decisions
that had been made in the implementation process.

Gathering and Reporting Current Cost Information. The first decision
was to use the General Electric Information Services Company's worldwide time-sharing system to gather data and generate reports. As stated

previously, American Standard's companies were diverse in size, location, and nature of business. Using GE's time-sharing system, American Standard developed its own computer programs which gathered data from these diverse companies, performed financial calculations, and printed financial reports. This enabled local companies to enter data in local currencies at their own locations; for example, data on fixed assets included the acquisition date, historical cost, and the appropriate local, specific price indices. Local companies could print their own reports in local currency or U.S. dollars. Other programs consolidated data from the local companies; the consolidated data were accessible on the time-sharing system to the local companies' group and global group and to the corporate staff. Flexibility and simplicity were key objectives in designing this system, since it had to be used in the smallest to the largest companies, and in very different types of businesses. Todd reflected on the importance of this design:

> The time-sharing system gets the inflation adjustment down to the lowest levels of management. It provides the same data throughout the company and gives the plant manager the same vision as top management.

Primary Measurement System. A second important decision was that the inflation accounting system was to be the primary measurement system for the company; these measurements were incorporated into management systems such as budgeting and performance measurement. Historical cost data were still available and were frequently presented as supplementary information that enabled results to be reconciled with primary public financial statements; the emphasis, however, was on inflation-adjusted accounting results, as shown by the standard monthly performance reports in Exhibit 5.

Two points should be noted about these reports. First, since conventional historical cost depreciation is already incorporated in other items, the amount reported as *replacement depreciation* reflects the amount by which replacement depreciation exceeds conventional historical cost depreciation; e.g., if total replacement cost depreciation is $252 million, and historical cost depreciation is $134 million, then the amount reported on the line labeled "Replacement depreciation" will be $118 million.

The second point that should be noted about these reports is their computation of budgeted replacement depreciation, as appears in the middle column, labeled "Plan" (see Exhibit 5). When American Standard incorporated inflation-adjusted accounting into the budgeting system, it discovered an interesting problem. Budgets are forecasts or forward pro-

EXHIBIT 5
Standard Monthly Performance Report

					Statement of Income April 1982		Form No. 1 (Page 1) Date: 05/07/82 15:12 GMT	
	Month				*U.S. Dollar*		*Year to Date*	
Year	*Plan*	*Actual*			*000's Omitted*	*Actual*	*Plan*	*Last Year*
4646	4440	3798		5010	Orders received	17978	18949	21203
4725	5047	3478		5020	Order backlog	3478	5047	4725
4859	4590	3903		5030	Gross sales	17676	19584	20911
179	149	150		5040	Returns & allowances	632	634	703
					Net sales			
4584	4339	3675		5050	Customer	16813	18578	19869
96	102	78		5060	Intercompany	231	372	339
4680	4441	3753		5070	Total net sales	17044	18950	20208
					Cost of sales			
2836	2466	2147		5080	Standard cost	9883	10443	12274
352	612	480		5090	Std. cost variances	2060	2385	1512
204	232	182		5100	Distribution cost	846	941	879
0	0	10		5110	Exch. (g)l-oper trans	12	0	8
72	138	127		5120	Replacement deprec.	564	592	329
115	ι66	141		5130	Other costs	589	703	868
3579	3614	3087		5140	Total cost of sales	13954	15064	15870
1101	827	666		5150	Gross profit	3090	3886	4338
					Operating Expense			
135	140	103		5160	Administrative	440	521	518
296	286	255		5170	Selling	1027	1116	1160
103	113	128		5180	Advertising	459	454	433
0	0	0		5190	Research & development	0	0	0
534	539	486		5200	Total bef. allocation	1926	2091	2111
0	0	0		5210	Intragroup allocation	0	0	0
534	539	486		5220	Total oper. expense	1926	2091	2111
567	288	180		5230	Income bef. other items	1164	1795	2227
−5	−6	0		5240	Other oper. inc/exp	−12	−23	−79
−438	−448	−402		5250	Capital charge	−1629	−1746	−1817
124	−166	−222		5260	Operating income	−477	26	331
−74	71	84		5270	Other non-oper. inc/exp	−266	−199	−226
−510	−586	−529		5280	Reversal-line 5120 + 5250	−2193	−2338	−2146
708	349	223		5290	Pretax income	1982	2563	2703
368	180	116		5300	Taxes on income	1031	1330	1406
340	169	107		5310	Income bef. extr. items	951	1233	1297
0	0	0		5320	Extr. items-net (dr)cr	0	0	0
340	169	107		5330	Net income after extr.	951	1233	1297
					Percent to net sales			
39.4	44.5	42.8		5335	Std. gross margin	42.0	44.9	39.3
23.5	18.6	17.7		5340	Gross profit	18.1	20.5	21.5
11.4	12.1	12.9		5350	Operating expense	11.3	11.0	10.4
2.6	−3.7	−5.9		5360	Operating income	−2.8	0.1	1.6

EXHIBIT 5 (continued)

U.S. Dollar 000's Omitted	Actual	Last Forecast	Variance from L.F. Fav(Unfav) Due to: Perform.	Variance from L.F. Fav(Unfav) Due to: Currency	Plan	Variance from Plan Fav(Unfav) Due to: Perform.	Variance from Plan Fav(Unfav) Due to: Currency	Last Year
Financial Summary—Actual								
April 1982					*Date: 05/07/82*		*Form No: 13*	*15:12GMT*
Month								
Orders received— customer	3720	3980	−236	−24	4338	−318	−300	4550
Net sales	3753	4047	−271	−23	4441	−385	−303	4680
Gross profit	666	704	−35	−3	827	−107	−54	1101
% of sales	17.75	17.40			18.62			23.53
Operating expense	486	471	−19	4	539	14	39	534
% of sales	12.95	11.64			12.14			11.41
Operating income	−222	−181	−45	−4	−166	−74	18	124
% of sales	−5.92	−4.47			−3.74			2.65
Capital expenditures	42	81			151	108	1	73
Cash flow from operations	−631	−1403	862	−90	759	−1340	−50	−343
Replacement depreciation	127	128	0	1	138	0	11	72
Capital charge	−402	−414	9	3	−448	13	33	−438
Orders received— interco	78	68	10	0	102	−18	−6	96
Average employees— hourly	749	760			798			
Average employees— non-hourly	365	365			368			
Average employees— Total	1114	1125			1166			
Year to date								
Orders received— customer	17747	18007	−236	−24	18577	30	−860	20864
Orders backlog— customer	3478	3881	−461	58	5047	−1374	−195	4725
Net sales	17044	17338	−271	−23	18950	−1069	−837	20208
Gross profit	3090	3128	−35	−3	3886	−649	−147	4338
% of sales	18.13	18.04			20.51			21.47
Operating expense	1926	1911	−19	4	2091	71	94	2111
% of sales	11.30	11.02			11.03			10.45
Operating income	−477	−436	−45	4	26	−529	26	331
% of sales	−2.80	−2.51			0.14			1.64
Gross trade receivables	11262	11788	712	−186	12859	964	633	12910
Days sales in receivables	65	65			73			60

EXHIBIT 5 (continued)

	Financial Summary—Actual							
			April 1982				*Form No: 13*	
					Date: 05/07/82		*15:12GMT*	

| *U.S. Dollar* | | | *Variance from L.F. Fav(Unfav) Due to:* | | | *Variance from Plan Fav(Unfav) Due to:* | | |
| | | *Last* | | | | | | *Last* |
000's Omitted	*Actual*	*Forecast*	*Perform.*	*Currency*	*Plan*	*Perform.*	*Currency*	*Year*
Gross FIFO inventory	8863	8730	14	− 147	9224	− 137	498	9791
Inventory turnover	3.39	3.47			3.35			3.69
Payables & accruals	7084	6276	691	117	6788	693	− 397	7228
Net FIFO working								
capital	12992	13859	1083	− 216	14658	935	731	14870
Cents per net sales	26.28	27.87			28.55			26.58
Capital expenditures	140	179	42	− 3	590	442	8	355
Cash flow from								
operations	− 2897	− 3669			− 4059	873	289	1082
Net assets	41187	41412	906	− 681	44907	1403	2317	43107
R.O.N.A.	11.60	11.73			12.85			11.52
Replacement								
depreciation	564	565	0	1	592	0	28	329
Capital charge	− 1629	− 1641	9	3	− 1746	38	79	− 1817
Orders received—								
interco	231	221	10	0	372	− 129	− 12	339
Order backlog—interco	0	0	0	0	0	0	0	0
Average employees—								
hourly	756	756			797			
Average employees—								
nonhourly	376	376			368			
Average employees—								
Total	1132	1132			1165			

jections; that is, a manager preparing a budget for 1983 generally prepares it during 1982. At the time of preparation, however, the most recent specific price indices available reflect replacement costs as of the end of the prior year, e.g., 1981. The problem, then, was how to estimate a reasonable, budgeted, replacement depreciation. Since the replacement cost data available reflected the replacement costs as of the end of 1981, American Standard used the expected *general* rate of inflation for each country, from the end of 1981 through 1983, to estimate the 1983 replacement cost. Hence, for Keller Crescent's On-Going Buildings, which were originally presented in Exhibit 4, the budgeted additional replacement depreciation was calculated as shown in Exhibit 6. Accounting managers noted that there was some inaccuracy involved in using the expected general rate of inflation to forecast the replacement cost of specific assets in 1983, based on their

EXHIBIT 6
Budgeted Replacement Depreciation

Inflation Rates—Forecast			
1982	*1983*	*Half-Year 1983*	*End of 1981 through Mid-1983*
6.6%	5.0%	2.44%	1.066 × 1.0244 = 9.2%

Replacement Depreciation				
Ending Gross Facilities 12/31/81 (replacement cost)	*Ending Gross Facilities 12/31/81 (replacement cost— inflated by 9.2%)*	*Replacement Cost Depreciation*[a]	*Book Depreciation*	*Additional Replacement Depreciation*
$7,412	$8,094	$276	$107	$169

[a] Using average life of 29.354 years; see *Exhibit 4-B*.

known 1981 replacement costs. The complexity of the alternative, how-ever—estimating the expected changes in the price indices for each of the various groups of assets in each country—was unworkable; further, it might not necessarily be more accurate. By using the current cost of an asset as of the end of 1981, and restating it by the expected general rate of inflation in that country through the end of 1983, management felt that it had captured most of the expected current cost of that asset.

Applications

Managers at American Standard believed that inflation accounting was useful in various management applications, from strategic planning and resource allocation to performance measurement and to such operating decisions as pricing and the disposition of assets.

Strategic Planning and Resource Allocation. In the areas of strategic planning and resource allocation, there were two primary views on the usefulness of the inflation-adjusted accounting system; first, it provided the necessary information on real economic returns, and second, it satisfied the need for financial data that were comparable across diverse business units. These views appear in the statements of Kenneth R. Todd, Jr., vice president and controller, and Richard H. Francis, vice president and treas-urer, presented below. Todd was concerned about the deficiencies of measures based on acquisition costs:

Strategic decisions, resource allocation, these are the things corporate managers are supposed to worry about. But how do you know which businesses to be in or not? There's a big problem with comparability of different business units.

   The return on investment that a business is able to earn is one factor considered in allocating capital resources. A considerable amount of the difference in returns on book assets between units, when historical cost accounting is used, can just be a reflection of when a unit acquired its fixed assets. The unit that acquired its assets some time ago at deflated dollars in today's terms can look very good compared with a unit that acquired its fixed assets recently. It may be that the converse relation is actually true in terms of economic returns on new investments. The internal accounting system should have correct incentives for management to make economic capital investment decisions. New capital expenditures are evaluated using discounted cash flows incrementally, but overall profitability, RONA, of a unit, is a consideration in the capital investment decision.

Francis stressed that an accurate comparison of business performance was of paramount importance:

   An advantage to using inflation-adjusted accounting internally in a multiple business environment is that it puts the businesses on a common basis and allows for comparison.

   The inflation-adjusted accounting system is most helpful in giving senior managers, especially those who are in effect portfolio managers, another basis on which to assess the long-term viability of various businesses. It provides a more accurate assessment of the present, which is an important element in forming judgments about the future. It is also important in assessing a business over time—what has really been happening to the business? The issue is, *over time*, can you earn a sufficient rate of return to stay in business?

Performance Measurement. American Standard believed that the inflation-adjusted accounting system more accurately presented the performance of the operating managers. Todd commented:

   The financial control system must be designed to meet the essential roles of corporate management, which include the assessment of performance of operating units and operating management.

   Management must evaluate a unit's performance, both in comparison to its own goals and in comparison with other units in the corporation. Because of the differing impact of inflation on units, it becomes difficult to compare operations using just historical cost information. The conventional accounting definitions of "income" must be modified when trying to measure the operating units to assure fair comparisons between units and *not* to reward management for inflationary effects.

When inflation-adjusted operating income had been implemented, the operating income for most businesses was less than it had been on an historical cost basis; some businesses that had shown a profit on an historical cost basis had a loss on an inflation-adjusted basis. American Standard believed that "being in the red" would motivate and not discourage a manager. It believed this despite its managers' initial concern about whether an inflation-adjusted profit was achievable; in fact, many of those managers eventually improved earnings and earned an inflation-adjusted operating profit.

One operating manager stated:

> You're kidding yourself if you don't use replacement depreciation. It makes the profits look a lot less, but that's just what inflation is doing.

Francis commented:

> Most managers would say that they are simply conforming to a performance standard, not that they are taking special steps to beat inflation. But with this system, they know if they break even, they can fund their business and earn a fair return. Whether or not they fully understand inflation accounting, it's healthy to have a faith in the system, knowing that if you meet this standard, you are maintaining the business in an inflationary environment and earning a satisfactory return.

Operating income was also an important determinant of incentives under the short-term incentive compensation plan. The pool of funds available for distribution under the short-term incentive plan was largely determined by the company's overall operating-income performance. Individual incentive awards depended on various factors, but one that was considered to be very important was performance in meeting operating-income objectives.

Pricing. Many managers felt that the inflation-adjusted accounting data influenced pricing decisions. Todd believed that this was very positive:

> There are many factors influencing the pricing decision, but one key consideration is the cost of production. If the marketing department considers as cost the historic inventory cost, it can be deceived on the current profits generated from its pricing decisions. Operating management has to have an incentive to keep its pricing in line with current cost, and one incentive is to measure results using only the current cost of production.
>
> Business is becoming more competitive. There is not enough to go around. You are facing new competitors with very different cost structures or cost advantages. In order to be effective, you'd better have a good understanding of what your costs really are.

Francis added that inflation-adjusted accounting data may be useful even if prices cannot be raised·

> Some managers ask, particularly when confronting inflation-adjusted accounting for the first time, "Once I have all of this new information, can I do anything differently? In a market environment, will the market actually let me raise my prices?" This is a very real problem. Even with the information, you may not be able to raise prices. But you're better off knowing you have a problem and understanding the nature of the problem than not knowing it. There may be other opportunities to improve your profitability.

Roy Satchell, senior vice president, Security and Graphics Products, concurred:

> Prices are set by the market, but with the inflation-adjusted data, at least you know where you're at. The person doing the selling does not *want* to raise prices—that just makes the selling job more difficult. But with this system, you can't kid yourself.

Satchell believed that once results were adjusted for inflation, some managers found that they were not doing as well as they had previously thought, and this led to their being much more aggressive in pricing. He recalled the example of an American Standard subsidiary that participated in a market dominated by a large competitor. Facing increasing costs and low inflation-adjusted earnings, the American Standard subsidiary became more aggressive in its pricing strategy. Satchell felt that the availability of inflation-adjusted accounting data that quantified the magnitude and severity of the problem had encouraged managers to take actions that they otherwise might not have taken, or at least might not have taken so soon. In addition, Satchell stated that the data were used to clean up product lines and identify items that did not have a future.

Disposing of Assets. Todd believed that a lot of unutilized or underutilized assets had been disposed of; he felt that besides providing cash and freeing up space, this also encouraged managers to move to new technologies, since the managers were already being charged for the cost of "new" assets. Satchell concurred with this viewpoint.

> The system places a tremendous amount of heat on managing assets. There are situations I know about where managers in my group have fixed assets that are not fully utilized. Those managers are trying like heck to get them out, because the system hits them where it hurts.

A business manager echoed this view, stating that replacement depreciation was a consideration in his evaluation of old equipment in this business. He cited some 20-year-old equipment that had experienced a significant writeup when it was appraised; the equipment was only partially utilized, and the manager was currently evaluating whether or not it was worth retaining since it represented such a large expense.

Agendas for the Future

In Todd's opinion, the inflation-adjusted accounting system at American Standard was working well and was accepted by managers. A senior line executive agreed:

> It's the job of the operating manager to decide what to make and how to make it. They should not be left to their own devices to account for inflation and its implications for working capital, capital expenditures, and pricing. The operating manager may not know how to account for inflation, or may not be willing to spend the time.
>
> Given that American Standard has implemented inflation accounting, as a practical matter, it's impossible not to use the data. It's in all the reports; the inflation adjustments are already cranked in. One of the reasons American Standard is so successful during tough economic times is that these data are part of the management system; they are not outside the system. The inflation-adjusted accounting system provides a description that is directionally correct. It is not perfect; but it is better than assuming inflation is equal to zero.

Todd felt, however, that opportunities remained to further improve the system; one area was long-term incentive compensation. Although inflation-adjusted operating income was used in the measurement of short-term performance and the determination of short-term incentive compensation, the long-term incentive compensation plan had not yet been modified to incorporate inflation adjustments. As of the end of 1981 the eligible employees under the long-term plan were executive officers of the company and other key executives of the company or its subsidiaries. Cash awards were distributed after five-year periods, and they depended upon the performance of the company in meeting certain publicly reported, historical cost earnings objectives over the applicable period. Each objective related to a cumulative growth of earnings per share over an earnings base established by the board of directors. If the earnings objective was not reached, but cumulative earnings per share still exceeded the earnings base, the cash payment was proportionately less. No payments were made, however, unless cumulative earnings per share for the period exceeded the earnings base by an average of 5% (compounded annually) over the period. The amount of the individual's cash award was generally based on salary level.

Despite American Standard's commitment to the use of inflation-adjusted accounting, concerns arose regarding its application to the long-term incentive program. First, some managers wondered about how to set an appropriate target; they had very little inflation-adjusted data from prior years and, therefore, they did not have a track record that might suggest what would be a good return versus a poor one, and it would be very expensive to go back and produce such data for the years preceding American Standard's use of inflation-accounting data. Second, the managers did not have comparative data from other firms in their industries, and these data had been important in setting targets in the past. Finally, they were concerned about the experimental stage of the inflation-accounting rules for public reporting purposes. Under the current procedures of stating objectives according to publicly reported primary earnings per share, there was considerable stability in primary earnings per share calculations. Since the rules for inflation accounting were much less firm, however, and since companies were encouraged by Financial Accounting Standard No. 33 to experiment and discover better ways of preparing inflation-accounting data, the method of preparing the publicly reported, inflation-adjusted data might vary from year to year. Some members of the controller's department questioned whether changes in method alone might determine who received a bonus and who did not.

In addition, Todd was considering restating all prior years' accounting data on a constant dollar basis. Each year American Standard incorporated the effects of inflation in its financial statements, but when managers went to compare data for prior years, they felt that these data were not fully comparable since the dollar, the unit of measure, had changed in purchasing power. Some of the controller's staff believed that if managers were trying to use prior years' data as a benchmark to determine trends, then to the extent that the change in the data was a function of inflation, and not volume or real price changes, the managers might be misled. According to one employee:

> There are several different ways of assessing performance. One is, "What has growth been?" But with inflation, maybe there hasn't been any real growth at all. You could look at physical units, but it's hard to get your hands on physical units for a business which is not just in one product line. You can be misled as to which business in your portfolio you're the most excited about.

Another issue centered on whether any further changes to the system should be made at this time. Since the process of implementing the system had been an evolutionary one, managers had adapted to frequent changes over the years. This had resulted, at times, in the incomparability of prior years' data; that is, the data for the last year may not have been prepared on the same basis as the current year's data, and prior years' statements were not restated on the new basis. Were the benefits of the proposed changes sufficient to justify modifying the system again?

chapter 16

EXECUTIVE CONTRACTS AND BONUS PLANS

Compensation contracts, particularly incentive and bonus plans, provide important direction and motivation for corporate executives. One cannot talk about decentralization without an explicit treatment of how the top-division managers are rewarded (or penalized). Almost all highly decentralized firms have incentive compensation contracts for their top-management group (usually less than 1% of all employees) to encourage profit-maximizing decisions at the divisional and corporate levels and to stimulate individuals to higher levels of performance.

Executive compensation plans should

1. Be competitive to attract and retain high-quality managers
2. Communicate and reinforce the key priorities in the firm by tying bonuses to key indices of performance
3. Foster the development of a performance-oriented climate within the firm by rewarding good performance relative to potential[1]

Alfred Sloan was one of the most enthusiastic advocates of incentive compensation plans for top management. He instituted the General Motors bonus plan in 1918 to increase the commonality of interests between the senior managers and the stockholders of the firm.[2] Annual bonuses were awarded based on each manager's contribution to the overall success of the corporation. General Motors had decentralized its operating decisions, and before instituting the bonus plan, which focused attention and rewards on **corporate** performance, the key executives had little incentive to think of the overall welfare of the organization. Rather, they tended to focus narrowly on their own division's profitability, occasionally at the expense of the corporation's welfare. After the bonus plan was installed, the senior

---

[1] David Swinford, "Unbundling Divisional Management Incentives," *Management Review* (July 1987), pp. 35–37.

[2] The General Motors bonus plan is described in Chapter 22 of Alfred Sloan, *My Life with General Motors* (New York: Doubleday, 1964).

executives were more sensitive to how their individual efforts affected the welfare of the entire organization. Sloan noted that the plan was successful in molding top-level executives into a cooperative constructive group but without destroying individual ambition and initiative.

The General Motors bonus plan was structured so that rewards were increased more than proportionately to salary as executives were promoted to higher positions. Therefore, managers had a major incentive to become eligible for bonus awards and then to continue to perform in an outstanding fashion so that they could be promoted to even higher ranks. Apart from the direct financial reward from the plan, it seemed to provide an intangible incentive just by the recognition that the executive had made a significant personal contribution to the success of General Motors. One executive claimed that the ego satisfaction from receiving the award was prized just as much as the actual monetary compensation.

The enthusiasm of Alfred Sloan and the General Motors Corporation for executive incentive plans is now widespread. More than 90% of the top managers of decentralized profit centers in large corporations are eligible for an annual bonus. The median bonus is about 25% of annual salary.[3] The form of the bonus plan varies across corporations. Payments can be made in cash, in the stock of the company, in stock options, and, more recently, in performance shares, stock appreciation rights, or participating units. The bonus can be made contingent on corporate results (as in General Motors) or on divisional profits. It can be based on annual performance or on performance over a four- to six-year period. It can be paid out immediately, deferred, or spread over a three- to five-year period.

No single bonus incentive plan dominates all other plans for all companies. Incentive plans will vary as a function of the degree of decentralization, the time horizon for critical decisions of the firms, the degree of interaction among divisions, the amount of uncertainty faced by the firm, the nature of its business activities, and the structure of the industry. In addition, many plans, alleged to provide incentives to managers, have as their greatest benefit the reduction of taxes of the manager and the firm.[4] At present, both contemporary practice and the theory of incentive contracts are evolving rapidly. In this chapter, we will survey existing practice and comment on the properties, strengths, and weaknesses of different incentive schemes. In the next chapter, we will introduce the emerging literature in optimal contracting and describe some preliminary results for constructing optimal incentive contracts between owners and chief

---

[3] See, for example, the survey reported by J. Kamm in Section F, Part II, of Richard F. Vancil, *Deecentralization: Managerial Ambiguity by Design* (Homewood, IL: Dow Jones-Irwin, 1978).

[4] The tax consequences of different kinds of management compensation plans are analyzed in Merton H. Miller and Myron S. Scholes," Executive Compensation, Taxes and Incentives," in *Financial Economics: Essays in Honor of Paul Cootner*, ed. William F. Sharpe and Cathryn M. Cootner (Englewood Cliffs, NJ: Prentice-Hall, 1982).

executives, and between a central management group and its division executives.

Incentive Compensation and the Principal-Agent Relationship

Before starting our survey of incentive compensation arrangements, we must introduce the principal-agent paradigm.[5] Incentive compensation plans cannot be analyzed without some knowledge of the theory of agency relationships. An agency relationship exists whenever one party (the principal) hires another party (the agent) to perform some service; this service requires the principal to delegate some decision-making authority to the agent. For our purposes, two types of principal-agent relationships arise in management control systems. First, the firm's owners or shareholders, acting as the principal (perhaps through the board of directors), hire the chief executive officer (or, more broadly, the top-management group) to be their agent in managing the firm in their best interests. In the second principal-agent arrangement, the firm's top-management group acts as the principal and hires division managers as agents to manage the decentralized units of the organization.

The agency literature assumes that all individuals—principals and agents—care not only about financial compensation and wealth but also about perquisites of the job (such as attractive working conditions and flexibility in hours worked). The managers prefer leisure to hard or routine work.[6] Agents therefore require a specification of incentive, monitoring, and bonding relationships to minimize the net costs of the divergence of interests between them and the principal.

For example, the agency model argues that if the top executives of the company are compensated only by a straight salary, they may not be motivated to take actions that maximize the value of the firm to the shareholders. They will overconsume nonpecuniary items such as leisure, attractive working conditions, and company perquisites or will not invest sufficient time and effort to increase shareholder wealth. If the ownership group knew what actions were optimal for the firm and could costlessly observe the actions of the top managers, they could direct the managers to implement these optimal actions with the threat of withholding com-

---

[5] This literature was synthesized in Michael C. Jensen and William H. Meckling, "Theory of the Firm: Managerial Behavior, Agency Costs, and Capital Structure," *Journal of Financial Economics* (October 1976), pp. 305–60.

[6] The aversion to work may not be a realistic assumption for senior members of the organization. Usually these people have risen in the organization because of their demonstrated skills and their willingness to put extra effort into their work. For them, incremental monetary rewards may be secondary to the power and prestige that they attach to achieving senior positions in the organization.

pensation if these actions were not carried out effectively and efficiently. But because a dispersed ownership group will probably have inadequate information and will find monitoring costly, the owners are unlikely to either know what the optimal decisions should be or be able to direct and monitor the actions of the top executives. Therefore, to encourage the top executives to take actions that are in the firm's best interests, the owners introduce an incentive compensation plan that enables the top executives to share in the firm's increased wealth. These plans can take the form of stock options or bonuses based on reported performance.

Incentive compensation plans are designed to create a commonality of interest between the principal (owners) and the agents (managers). But because of differences in risk attitudes, the existence of private information (managers knowing more than the owners about the environment and their actions), and limited or costly observability, some divergence of interest will always exist between the principal and the agents. The principal attempts to limit divergence from his interests by establishing appropriate incentives for the agents and by incurring monitoring costs designed to limit actions that increase the agents' welfare at the expense of the principal. Audited financial statements are an excellent example of a costly monitor of managerial behavior. They generate an accountability report from the agent (managers) to the principal (shareholders and creditors). Even with costly incentive and monitoring arrangements, however, the agents' decisions will still diverge from those that would maximize the principal's welfare. For example, audited financial statements provide a less-than-complete summary of the manager's decisions and actions. This remaining divergence is referred to as the residual loss in the agency relationship. Thus, agency costs in the owner-manager relationship are the sum of the costs of the incentive compensation plan, the costs of monitoring the managers' actions, and the remaining costs of actions taken by managers that diverge from the preferences of the owners.

To see how agency costs affect the compensation managements of top executives, let us informally trace through a simple scenario. We have already noted that because of the private information of managers and costly observation of managers' actions, owners may provide an incentive compensation scheme for the top executives. One obvious incentive scheme is to provide managers with a stock option or stock bonus plan, since actions that the managers take to increase stock prices should benefit the owners in a direct and obvious manner. Although certainly popular, this incentive scheme is not used by all companies with publicly traded stock.

What factors limit the desirability of stock ownership plans for top executives? First, risk aversion problems arise. The highly paid top executives of the firm already have most of their wealth, in the form of human capital (measured by the discounted present value of their expected compensation), directly tied to the firm's well-being. If the firm were to do poorly, their managerial reputations would suffer, limiting their outside job offers and slowing the rate of compensation increases within the firm. If a significant part of managers' compensation were invested in shares of the firm's stock, the managers could suffer a significant decline in their financial wealth at the same time that bad outcomes were affecting their human-capital wealth.

To avoid this calamitous situation, the executives would tend to avoid risky investments and risky decisions, even those with high expected returns, since risk aversion causes them to value the potential gains far less than they fear the penalties from possible losses. Therefore, stock ownership by top executives reinforces risk-avoiding behavior—avoidance of risks that the owners would prefer the executives to take. The owners are less risk averse, since (1) their human capital may be independent of the firm's outcomes, and (2) they can diversify their wealth through ownership of many different firms. Firm managers already have more of their wealth (in the form of nondiversifiable and nontradeable human capital)[7] tied up in the firm than they would probably prefer. Additional stock ownership in the same firm increases their firm-specific risk even further. This problem was summarized by Michael Jensen:

> The problem we are stuck with is one of achieving the proper balance between linking managements' interests with stockholder interests by making them bear a lot of market risk, and at the same time, insulating them from some of that risk.[8]

A second problem with executive stock ownership arises from the lack of a direct causal relationship between executive actions and stock market performance. Many noncontrollable random events, such as general business conditions, governmental actions, unexpected material, energy, or labor shortages, and international developments, may overwhelm the best (or worst) efforts of management. If the stock price unexpectedly rises because of these noncontrollable events, the executives obtain a windfall gain at the expense of the original set of owners. Conversely, if the stock price plunges, the executives suffer a significant loss in expected income or wealth. The uncertainty of the stock market, therefore, introduces an additional component of noncontrollable risk into the executives' compensation schedule and does not provide reliable feedback on the quality of decisions and extent of effort exerted by these executives.

---

[7] Human capital cannot be easily traded because of laws against slavery as well as the moral hazard problem; once you sell shares in your human capital, you no longer capture the gains from hard work and good decision making. Nor do you suffer the losses from shirking or bad decision making. Therefore, were managers to sell rights to their human capital, they would have much lower incentives to work hard and to make good decisions.

[8] "A Roundtable Discussion of Management Compensation," *Midland Corporate Finance Journal* (Winter 1985).

In an attempt to obtain a performance measure more sensitive than stock prices to executive actions, owners may develop a measure based on an internal evaluation of the economic well-being of the firm. The stock market provides one estimate of the economic value of the firm's assets, but it has the problems described above. Appraising the value of the firm's assets provides another estimate, but this measure may be very costly to obtain each year and can be a source of controversy because of its subjectivity. An incentive contract could, however, be based on data that are already prepared and audited for external parties, namely, the historical-cost-based financial statements. Performance goals can be set based on earnings per share or return on shareholders' investment. These figures are more under management's control than stock prices and, at least in the long run, should correlate with the economic welfare of the firm. In fact, many incentive compensation plans do depend directly on earnings per share (EPS) and accounting return on equity (ROE).

The accounting-based measures for executive compensation, however, introduce problems of their own because of the imperfect association between accounting income and the economic well-being of the firm. Executives can take many actions that increase reported income—and hence increase their income from incentive compensation plans—but decrease the firm's value. For example, managers of U.S. corporations may choose to remain on FIFO for inventory valuation rather than switch to LIFO. For most companies, LIFO decreases the present value of cash paid in taxes (and therefore increases the present value of the cash flows to the firm) but reports lower income in the short run and hence lowers earnings-based performance measures.

Executives have many other opportunities to increase reported earnings via actions that do not benefit the firm and that may, in some cases, actually decrease the value of the firm. These actions include

1. Producing goods in excess of demand in order to absorb fixed costs into inventory and thereby increase reported income
2. Repurchasing debt or preferred stock selling at a discount
3. Switching to straight-line depreciation or the flow-through method for the investment credit for financial reporting
4. Purchasing other companies under terms that permit use of pooling-of-interests method
5. Selling off assets whose market value is well in excess of book value
6. Increasing the leverage of the firm by issuing debt and acquiring assets whose returns exceed the after-tax debt cost but are below the risk-adjusted cost of capital

Conversely, executives could decline investments that would increase the long-run value of the firm but penalize short-run earnings. For example, profitable capital investments with heavy initial start-up costs might not be undertaken, and research and development expenditures could be underfunded because of the longer-term risky nature of the rewards from such expenditures. Also factors such as new mandated accounting procedures that affect reported income will be viewed skeptically by executives rewarded under an earnings-based incentive scheme.

Thus, accounting-based performance measures may be preferable to stock incentives because they relate to activities that are more under the control of top executives. On the downside, however, such plans may be too controllable by executives who can manipulate the measures in ways that are detrimental to the owners. The board of directors must approve virtually all the actions that could increase an accounting-based performance measure without increasing the economic value of the firm, and the board can, in principle, play an important role in reducing the agency cost of the contractual relationship between owners and managers. For example, the board could define earnings for computation of executive bonuses to exclude expenditures on long-term intangibles (R&D, maintenance, quality control, personnel development) so that executives would not be motivated to underinvest in these important areas. Similarly, the board could undo accounting policies that increase reported income but do not benefit the company directly (holding gains reported under FIFO, flow-through of the investment tax credit, unadjusted historical cost, straight-line depreciation). In this way, more of the managers' reward would be related to actions that increase the long-run profitability of the firm. Such practices, while theoretically possible, do not seem common.[9] Apparently, directors are not comfortable rewarding managers on one income figure while reporting quite a different number to shareholders and creditors.

Having completed this introduction to agency cost in the contractual relationship between owners and managers, we can now present our survey of contemporary executive compensation schemes.

Role for Bonus and Incentive Contracts

A. Patton argues that the following conditions are ideal for the use of an incentive system:[10]

1. Profits are affected by numerous short-term decisions;[11]
2. The managers have the authority to make the decisions (this is most characteristic of decentralized firms organized on a product line basis);

---

[9] See the evidence in Paul Healy, Sok-Hyon Kang, and Krishna Palepu, "The Effect of Accounting Procedure Changes on CEO's Cash Salary and Bonus Compensation," *Journal of Accounting & Economics* (April 1987), pp. 7–34.

[10] "Why Incentive Plans Fail," *Harvard Business Review* (May–June 1972).

[11] For example, it would be of dubious value to implement an incentive system in a power utility that faced stable markets and a well-defined cost structure.

3. The control system is well defined and performance is evaluated on a systematic basis, either by comparison to a plan or by comparison to the performance of similar firms; and

4. The managers are expected to be entrepreneurial and ambitious.

On the other hand, Patton argues that firms with the following characteristics are poor candidates for the application of executive incentive plans:

1. Profits are most affected by a few long-term decisions;

2. The company is organized on a functional basis (say by marketing, production, accounting, and finance);

3. Budgets are difficult to develop, or data do not exist about competitors, to judge the adequacy of managerial performance; and

4. Decision making need not be rapid or responsive.

In the organization behavior literature, a line of research called **equity theory** appears to support the notion that individual performance-based compensation is both widely accepted and promoted in western cultures.[12] Leventhal, Michaels, and Sanford summarized the results of this theory, as of 1972:

> Equity theory . . . suggests that individuals are motivated to allocate rewards in accordance with recipients' inputs or work contributions. This assumption is supported by results from studies on reward allocation in task-oriented groups. When members [provide] equal inputs, an individual member usually attempts to bring about an equal division of reward between himself and his co-worker. . . . And when members of a group have unequal inputs, an individual member allocates rewards in accordance with perceived work contributions. . . . It has also been shown that allocators distribute rewards in accordance with work inputs when they themselves are not members of the group of recipients among whom the rewards are distributed.[13]

The tendency to allocate rewards based on performance is mitigated by many factors, including whether the person allocating the rewards must make the allocation decision public. In general, equity theory supports the contention that an individual's reward should reflect that person's contribution to the organization. On the other hand, Lawrence and Lorsch

---

[12] A formal statement of this theory, as well as some initial empirical evidence of its descriptive validity, can be found in J. S. Adams, "Toward an Understanding of Inequity," *Journal of Abnormal and Social Psychology* (1963), pp. 422–36; and J. S. Adams, "Inequity in Social Exchange," in *Advances in Experimental Psychology*, ed. L. Berkowitz (New York: Academic Press, 1965).

[13] G. S. Leventhal, J. W. Michaels, and C. Sanford, "Inequity and Interpersonal Conflict: Reward Allocation and Secrecy about Reward as Methods of Preventing Conflict," *Journal of Personality and Social Psychology* (1972), pp. 88–102.

argue that people who play an integrative role in organizations should be rewarded on the basis of overall performance.[14] Lawrence and Lorsch conclude that

> rewards systems . . . can help induce either the "you do your job, and I'll do mine" attitude or the "let's pull together" attitude. Each can be suitable under certain conditions. Reward systems should be designed with these conditions more clearly in mind.

This line of reasoning would imply that people at senior levels of the organization who perform integrative tasks should be rewarded on the basis of corporate performance, while people who are not engaged in integrative tasks should be rewarded on the basis of individual performance.

A published survey reported the distribution of the total compensation of senior executives in large corporations:

—Salary	46%
—Long-term incentives	28%
—Annual bonus	26%

Thus, 54% of the total compensation of the executives was performance related, and 52% of this performance-related compensation was in the form of long-term incentives. The article concluded that

> By limiting salary increases . . . and using long-term compensation as incentives, companies can more easily hold down the pay of poorer performers while rewarding corporate stars.
>
> At Xerox Corporation, for example, base salaries for comparable positions may vary by only 3% to 6% . . . but bonuses may increase this variation from base salary as much as 50%.[15]

Such plans put more of a person's compensation at risk and tie long-term compensation to the achievement of strategic goals. The bonus percentage in total compensation was highest in the energy and wholesale retail trade industries and lowest in the public utility and construction industries. This pattern is consistent with our prediction that the more volatile the industry, the greater the motivation potential for performance-based compensation schemes.

---

[14] Paul R. Lawrence and Jay W. Lorsch, *Organization and Environment* (Homewood, IL: Richard D. Irwin, 1969).

[15] Amanda Bennett, "Executives Will Gain Over Time as Lucrative Stock Plans Multiply," *Wall Street Journal* (April 10, 1987).

Types of Incentives

Executive compensation schemes can be characterized along several dimensions:

1. **Immediate versus long term**

   Awards can be immediate (usually in the form of cash or equity awards based on current performance) or long term (usually in the form of stock options whose value is tied to the long-run performance of the company's common equity).

2. **Cash versus equity**

   Awards can be in the form of cash or in the form of equity (shares, stock options, phantom shares, and performance shares). Although either cash or equity rewards can be tied to short-term or long-term performance, cash awards are usually tied to short-term profit performance, and equity awards are usually tied to long-term performance of the price of the firm's common equity.

3. **Monetary versus nonmonetary**

   Awards can be either cash or near-cash (equity) or perquisites and other nonmonetary entitlements. Perquisites take many forms. As reported by surveys of practice, the most common perquisites include vacation trips, executive parking privileges, the provision of a company car, life insurance, corporate loans at preferred rates of interest, club memberships, and specialized health care. In some cases, the perquisite is provided as a result of the position held. In other cases, the perquisite is awarded on the basis of an informal performance assessment. The granting of some perquisites, particularly vacation trips, may be tied directly to formal performance measurements, often in the form of a contest.

   The other nonmonetary awards include formal recognition in the form of a citation or a trophy, informal recognition in the form of social invitations from more-senior executives, and participation in personnel development programs that are reserved for executives being groomed for senior management. These awards are often based on informal performance assessments by superiors.

In this chapter, we concentrate on the cash and equity types of incentives. This does not imply that the perquisite and other nonmonetary forms are unimportant. Rather, it merely reflects the greater availability of information on cash and equity incentive plans.

Specific Forms Assumed by Monetary Compensation Plans

We consider the following forms of monetary compensation plans:[16]

---

[16] For an extended discussion of these alternative forms of compensation, as well as a collection of field studies illustrating the use of these plans, see Stephen A. Butler and Michael W. Maher, *Management Incentive Compensation Plans* (Montvale, NJ: National Association of Accountants, 1986).

1. Cash bonus or profit sharing and the stock bonus
2. Deferred compensation
3. Stock options
4. Performance shares or units
5. Stock appreciation rights

Cash or Stock Awards

Current bonuses, in either cash or stock, are awarded at the end of an accounting period. Corporate profit and individual performance are the most common bases used to determine the amounts of the bonuses. These awards reward executives for performance during the bonus period, which usually means annual performance. Therefore, these awards relate to short-run performance with the attendant danger of promoting a preoccupation with short-run results that are often detrimental to the long-run interests of the firm.

Typical formulas (to be discussed later in more detail) are a fixed percentage of corporate profits or a percentage of profits in excess of a specified return on stockholders' equity. Current bonuses are equivalent to salaries in their tax consequences to the firm and its executives. But bonuses may be cut or eliminated during a year of poor economic performance while salaries are rarely cut. A stock award creates a closer affinity of interests between the top-management group and the shareholders. A disadvantage is that the executive will need to find cash or financing to pay taxes on the stock award if the shares are not sold immediately. Also, significant stock ownership by managers may lead to risk-averse behavior, as mentioned in our principal-agent discussion.

Deferred Bonus and Compensation

Deferred compensation refers to any type of award, cash or stock, that is deferred until a future period. Deferred stock-compensation plans are often supplemented by restrictions that prevent the manager from selling the stock or that specify that the firm's contributions to the purchase price of the stock will not vest for some specified period of time, thus attempting to tie the manager to the firm.

In some companies, bonuses are not paid until the executive retires, so that the executive receives the income when in a lower tax bracket. As long as the deferred compensation is unfunded and based solely on the unsecured credit of the employer, current taxes can be avoided. The overall tax benefit of deferred compensation to the company and the executive combined is worthwhile only if the executive's original tax bracket on interest income exceeds the corporate tax rate.[17]

---

[17] See Miller and Scholes, "Executive Compensation."

Some plans defer the bonus over a period of three to five years after it is earned. Receipt is contingent on the employee's continuing to work for the company. Such plans are referred to as **golden handcuffs** because they make it very expensive for key executives to leave a company. These plans are especially useful in high-technology companies that attempt to minimize the loss of key executives to rivals.

Stock Options

A stock option gives executives the right to purchase company stock at a future date, at a price established when the option was granted (usually the current market price or 95% of the market price). With stock options, executives are presumed to attempt to influence long-term stock price performance rather than short-term profits. Of perhaps greater importance is that an option has no downside loss (since the executive does not actually own the stock) and unlimited upside potential. Therefore, executives may be encouraged to reduce the risk-averse behavior that would otherwise accompany their ownership of stock and to undertake riskier projects with higher payoffs.

Stock options have no apparent net tax advantage to the executive and the company. Therefore, incentive effects must explain their existence. But they have a disadvantage in that events not directly under managerial control may have a more significant impact on share prices.

Performance Shares

A performance share awards company stock (the share) for achieving a specified, usually long-term, performance target. The most common target is to achieve a growth in earnings per share over a three- to five-year period. A typical range for cumulative EPS growth is between 9% and 15% per year. Executives generally receive no additional reward for exceeding the EPS growth and may receive a fraction of the rewarded shares if the objectives are partially met. Performance share awards suffer from the same limitations as stock options: the imposition of risk on the manager and the influence of factors beyond the manager's control on the amount of the award. Performance shares also are subject to the problems of basing awards on accounting measures that may promote decisions that improve the measured accounting performance rather than necessarily improving the economic worth of the firm.

Performance share plans can be quite complex. For example, in one company that manufactured components used in the electronics industry:

1. Performance on six attributes of performance was measured. These attributes were (i) quality (measured by reported product failures), (ii) timeliness of production (measured by comparing scheduled completion times with ac-

tual completion times), (iii) cost control (measured by flexible budget variances), (iv) sales growth, (v) profitability (measured by reported corporate profits), and (vi) employee morale (measured by absenteeism).

2. Rewards were based on (a) the ability to meet annual targets and (b) the relative improvement of performance over a three-year period. Targets were set on the basis of discussions between subordinates and their superiors. Not only did these discussions relate to the choice of the standards but they also related to the appropriateness and controllability of the attributes being measured.

3. Rewards were made annually and based on performance over the previous three-year period.

Stock Appreciation Rights and Phantom Stock

Stock appreciation rights (SAR) are deferred cash payments based on the increase of the stock price from the time of award to the time of payment. SARs are frequently used in conjunction with stock option plans to provide a means for executives to purchase stock earned under stock option plans. Phantom stock plans are awards in units of number of shares of stock. After qualifying for receipt of the vested units, the executive receives in cash the number of units multiplied by the current market price of the stock. Both SARs and phantom stock are essentially deferred cash bonuses but with the value of the bonus a function of the future stock price. Thus, they have both the strengths and the weaknesses that result when compensation is a function of share price.

Participating Units

Participating unit plans are similar to SARs except that payment is keyed to operating results rather than stock price. Commonly used operating measures include pretax income, return on investment, sales and backlog, or a combination of these. The units awarded can vary continuously with the measure of operating results. Participating units are most useful for an organization with little or no publicly traded stock or for a specialized division whose fortunes are not closely linked to overall company results. Participating units permit the greatest flexibility in relating executive incentives to long-term performance measures internal to the organization. The measures are not affected by stock market fluctuations and therefore reduce some noncontrollable uncertainty in the executive's compensation function. The measures, however, suffer from a disadvantage because of the divergence of interests created between executives and shareholders. Participating unit plans require a careful and operational specification of the long-term operating results desired for the firm and the way in which incentive compensation will vary with partial or complete attainment of these operating results.

Evaluation of Accounting-Based Incentive Compensation Schemes

Within the broad framework of incentive schemes, ranging from the annual cash bonus to more recent and sophisticated schemes such as performance shares, many crucial design issues can determine whether the incentive plan provides the appropriate motivation at minimum cost to the firm's owners. The two most crucial questions are (1) how the total size of the bonus pool is determined each year and (2) how the bonus pool is allocated to the corporate and divisional executives.

Establishing the Size of the Bonus Pool

In choosing the magnitude of the bonus pool, compensation specialists must decide what items to exclude and what items to include in defining the pool. The ideal would be to have a performance measure defined for each individual that reflects that individual's personal contribution to the organization and makes allowances for the positive or negative factors in the environment that were beyond the executive's control and might affect the performance measure. Unfortunately, it is generally impossible to measure the contribution each individual makes to the organization, and it is equally difficult to make the performance measure totally independent of the factors over which the executive has no control. For example, how can one evaluate the contribution of an individual violinist to the overall sound and performance of a symphony orchestra? We must often use less than perfect motivational devices that sometimes reward or penalize managers for factors that were beyond their control and that reflect joint, rather than individual, contributions to the organization.

The simplest rule for determining the magnitude of executive bonuses is to compute the bonus pool as a fixed percentage of the profit earned by the organization. Some firms, however, determine the amount of the available bonus pool by performance relative to plan, irrespective of the absolute level of profits. The rationale for making awards, even at low or negative levels of corporate profits, is to retain executives in a severely depressed firm.

Profits, as a measure of performance, are closely related to the goals of the owners of the organization, are verified by an independent third party, and are well understood by the organization members. The most basic system defines the bonus pool as a percentage of reported profits, such as 15%. This rule, however, will award bonuses even with very low profits when the firm is earning a low return on invested capital. Variations on this basic system include a residual income concept wherein the bonus pool is only activated when the owners have received some predetermined return on investment (which raises the problem of defining the amount of the investment). In addition, maximum dollar limits, based on dividend payments, are often placed on the size of the bonus pool.

A fairly common procedure is to compute the bonus pool as a percentage of profits after a prespecified return on invested capital or shareholders' equity has been earned. For example, one firm described how the amount in its profit-sharing plan for officers and key personnel was determined each year:

> Under the present formula of the Plan, the company's consolidated net income after tax (adjusted) for any year must exceed 5% of the average amount of the consolidated book value of its capital stock before any amount becomes available for distribution to participants. Ten per cent of the excess of adjusted net income [is distributed, subject to the approval and discretion of outside members of the Board of Directors in cash and stock].

Another company's incentive plan for its key employees indicated:

> There shall be credited to the incentive fund an amount not to exceed 5% of the company's total income before any provision for incentive payments, interest, income taxes and extraordinary items, after deducting 13% of invested capital.

And Alfred Sloan's favorite, the General Motors bonus plan:

> The Corporation maintains a reserve for purpose of the Bonus Plan to which may be credited each year an amount which the independent public accountants of the corporation determine to be 8% of the net earnings which exceed 7% but not 15% of net capital, plus 5% of the net earnings which exceed 15% of net income, but not in excess of the amount paid out as dividends on the common stock during the year.

A variety of issues arise in these formulas. First is the definition of the investment base: shareholders' equity or invested capital (generally computed as shareholders' equity plus long-term debt). The use of shareholders' equity provides an incentive to increase leverage as long as the net cash flows from the asset acquired exceed the after-tax borrowing cost plus straight-line depreciation. By including long-term debt in the investment base, we eliminate the bias to increase debt. A more comprehensive approach might include all interest-bearing debt, short and long term, in invested capital.

A second problem arises if only shareholders' equity is used for computing bonus payments. Several years of losses may reduce the shareholders' equity to a low level and make future bonuses very easy to earn, even though total return on assets is still not at highly profitable levels.

As an aside, it is interesting to speculate whether one of the forces giving rise to occasional big baths in earnings is related to incentive compensation schemes. Under the big-bath approach, disappointing (or even negative) earnings cause the company managers to write off a variety of dubious assets on the balance sheet so that bad news in a single year can be concentrated (who cares how negative a price-earnings ratio gets?) to clean up the books for future profitability. Such an action becomes easy to explain if the managers reason:

1. With earnings this low, we're not going to earn a bonus this year anyway. Let's clean off these accruals so that we won't have to keep amortizing them against earnings in future years.

2. A good healthy loss reduces shareholders' equity and will make future bonuses a little easier to earn and a little larger.

A third and more serious problem with the use of shareholders' equity, either by itself or as part of total invested capital, is the failure to adjust for price-level changes. Shareholders' equity represents the capital contributed each year in the firm's history through retained earnings and sales of stock. This capital has been contributed at dramatically different price levels, yet it is added together as if it had all been contributed in the most recent year. For many companies, a simple price-level adjustment on shareholders' equity would probably completely eliminate what had been a lucrative bonus and incentive payment. The failure to restate shareholders' equity for price-level changes makes the bonus pool larger than it should be, if the goal is to reward the earning of income in excess of a specified return on invested capital.

A third method for establishing the bonus pool (in addition to a fixed percentage of profits or a percentage of income in excess of a specified return on invested capital) would base performance on profit improvement. With this procedure, bonuses would be awarded for annual increases in profits. Apart from increases in profits caused by accounting manipulations, as we discussed earlier in considering the principal-agent relationship, this procedure may reward or penalize executives for events beyond their control. General business conditions or specific industry factors could cause earnings to expand or contract for reasons not controllable by company executives. This could mean windfall gains or losses for these executives in their incentive plans.

The impact of noncontrollable factors could be reduced by comparing a company's performance with that of other firms in the same industry.[18] In this way, the executives of a company whose earnings increased 15% while the industry average earnings increased 25% would not be rewarded

---

[18] See Michael W. Maher, "The Use of Relative Performance Evaluation in Organizations," in *Accounting & Management: Field Study Perspectives* ed. William J. Bruns, Jr., and Robert S. Kaplan (Boston: Harvard Business School Press, 1987), Chap. 11, pp. 295–315.

for a good absolute but poor relative performance. The following excerpt from a *Wall Street Journal* article raises this point:

> All for one and one for all. That theme has traditionally determined how many executives receive incentive rewards. When the whole company does well, the executive does well; when the company flops, so does the incentive pay. But many companies are starting to break from that tradition. They are now tailoring incentive plans to the performance of an executive's division or business unit over a three to five year period. The goal is to motivate executives and to reward them more fairly when their unit performs well—regardless of corporate results.[19]

The article provides two quotations from directors of corporate compensation plans to reinforce the need to assess individual contributions as well as to identify the specific contributions expected from each business unit:

> "If you want incentive pay to change behavior, a manager has got to believe he has some control over what is being measured." John Hillers, Director of Corporate Compensation, Honeywell Inc.
>
> "[the divisional compensation plan] ties our compensation in with the business unit strategy and helps focus the executive on what is important for that unit." Wallace Nichols, Director of Compensation, Premark International Inc.

The article recognizes the problems created by basing rewards on local measures of performance, which include the following:

1. In firms with highly interrelated business units, many problems will arise from attempting to allocate joint revenues (the transfer-pricing problem) and joint costs. Moreover, in highly interrelated firms, a fiction may be created that the business units are separate economic units that can operate independently of each other. Measuring individual performance may create interdivisional competition and conflict that may discourage these business units from coordinating their activities.
2. Goal setting will be difficult due to the specialized nature of the tasks of each business unit as well as the need to understand the potential of each unit.
3. The use of long-term measures of performance would effectively end the practice of rotating managers among the various business units.

Awards based on overall corporate, rather than divisional, performance would seem to work best for dominant-product firms—that is, vertically integrated firms producing a single major product (such as

---

[19] "Firms Trim Annual Pay Increases and Focus on Long Term," *Wall Street Journal* (April 10, 1987), p. 25.

automobiles, tires, or steel) and where a high degree of interaction or co-ordination among divisions is required for the firm to function effectively. Awards based on divisional performance seem most appropriate when the firm is highly decentralized with little interaction among its divisions, which are organized as profit or investment centers. For example, firms that can be characterized as conglomerates, venture capitalists, or holding companies for diverse operating units can use incentive plans based primarily on divisional performance. For firms somewhere in the middle of the continuum between dominant-product and highly diversified firms, a combination of corporate and divisional performance may provide the right mixture of incentives for optimizing local performance while still looking out for overall corporate goals.

Finally, one can always attempt to evaluate managerial performance against a profit plan or budget and avoid all the problems that arise when using mechanical formulas for profitability. If the board of directors could obtain forecasts that truly represented what profits were achievable, given (1) anticipated business conditions, (2) high-quality managerial decision making, and (3) the best administrative efforts of the managers, then achievement of the profit plan would provide an excellent basis for incentive compensation. The problem, of course, with any incentive plan based on budgeted performance is to obtain information that is not biased or distorted in order to influence the ease of achieving the targeted plan. Budget-based incentive schemes suffer from the problem of strategic manipulation of information (see the discussion in Chapter 13), which makes it difficult to implement these plans in practice despite their many desirable properties.

Allocation of Bonus Pool to Managers

Once the size of the bonus pool is defined, the next issue is to determine how the bonus pool will be distributed to the members of the organization who are entitled to share in the bonus pool. The most basic distribution rule makes the share proportional to salary. In this system, a person's share equals the ratio of that person's salary to the total salaries of all the people entitled to share in the pool. Although this system is easy to implement, it is very crude. First, it assumes that a person's merit is proportional to that person's salary. This assumption is tenuous at best. Second, the scheme introduces a **free-rider** problem by providing bonuses for everyone who is entitled to share in the bonus pool, irrespective of whether that person did a good job or not. Some people may relax and rely on the hard work of others to provide a big bonus pool. The people who have relaxed then participate in the division of the pool along with the diligent workers. Carried to an extreme, the system falls apart as everyone shirks, waiting for someone else to do the hard work, and nothing gets done. That is why many companies base bonuses on individual performance, such as the performance of the manager's division. But recall Alfred P. Sloan's recommendation that basing rewards on individual performance inevitably causes managers to act in ways that are detrimental to the overall organization. Also, many Japanese companies reward group performance so that everyone takes responsibility for the successes and failures of the entire organization. These group reward systems must include some formal or informal monitoring mechanisms to mitigate the free-rider problem.

An alternative to basing the bonus pool distribution on salary is to award bonuses as a function of (1) the importance of the job that the person does and (2) the success that the person has in carrying out assigned tasks. This type of system requires that each individual's role in the organization be clearly defined and understood:

1. The content of a person's job is agreed to by both the person and the supervisor.
2. The individual develops performance targets for the job.
3. The individual and the superior discuss the performance targets and a target is agreed upon.
4. A control system is established to monitor progress toward achieving the target.
5. The superior and the subordinate meet at the end of the period to discuss the results and the relationship of the results to the target.

For example, the performance review system used by Lee Iacocca at Ford and Chrysler requires that, each quarter, superiors ask subordinates to specify their goals, priorities, and the manner in which they will seek their goals.

With this scheme, step 1 would be the point at which the importance of the job would be defined, and this would determine the potential bonus points that the individual could earn. Step 5 would determine whether all, some, or none of the potential bonus points defined in step 1 would be awarded. Although the approach seems sound, it appears to be seldom used. Perhaps the considerable effort required to operate, as well as maintain, the system makes it impractical.

In general, the bonus system will be more effective as an incentive and reward if the bonus allocation is reviewed by top management and the board of directors. This enables the bonus award to also be a function of longer-range, less-quantifiable performance criteria and thereby relieves the pressure on exclusive use of a short-term accounting-based measure of performance. The board of directors is in the best position to tie incentive payments to the establishment and implementation of plans for long-term profitability. Review by the board also permits an evaluation of relative performance, comparing results with industry performance, when awarding incentive payments.

Short versus Long-Term Performance Measures

A preoccupation with short-run performance may seriously damage the future potential of the firm. Classical examples of short-run suboptimization include curtailing discretionary cost expenditures, such as research and development, maintenance, and personnel development. A. Rappaport has pointed out the compensation plan astigmatism of most compensation plans.[20] Rappaport argues that incentive plans should be linked to the achievement of the long-run goals of the organization. Incentives should be paid for performance over several years rather than for just one year. Whether it is practical to devise incentive schemes that are tied to longer-run strategic factors, rather than shorter-run performance factors, is an open issue. Moreover, it may be difficult to measure an executive's performance over several years if the executive is constantly changing jobs within the company.

McDonald's attempts to evaluate its store managers on the basis of performance in the following areas:

- Product quality
- Service
- Cleanliness
- Sales volume
- Personnel training
- Cost control

The manager's performance on each of these factors is measured and is then evaluated relative to targets that have been set by the manager and the manager's supervisor. Obviously each of these factors will affect long-run profits. Evidently the senior management at McDonald's feels it important to evaluate these key success variables in the short run. Moreover, focusing on these key success factors, rather than short-run profits, identifies these factors as the key influences on long-run profitability.

Are Chief Executives Overpaid?

The following description commenting on the pay package offered to Steven Ross, the chief executive of Warner Communications, is typical of recent attacks on chief executive pay:

> The controversial agreement pays Ross a base salary of $800,000 plus $400,000 a year in deferred compensation. Ross, who owns less than 1% of Warner stock, also receives a bonus of 1% of Warner's net income

---

[20] "Executive Incentives vs. Corporate Growth," *Harvard Business Review* (July–August 1978).

each year (in 1986 Warner's net income was $186 million) and a long term bonus that pays him cash based on the movement of Warner stock and earnings.[21]

Determining the appropriate compensation for a chief executive is difficult for two reasons. First, the market of chief executives is thin, so that market prices for chief executives are not readily available. Second, chief executives possess a unique package of skills, intuition, and specialized information that is difficult to assess or verify. Moreover, these factors are likely to be industry specific. Therefore, the value of an executive's contribution may be difficult to assess outside that executive's industry. As a result, it is difficult to determine in any objective way whether an executive is overpaid.

One comment that is often made is, "Of course these people are not overpaid. Big rock stars, movie stars, and top athletes make as much, or more, than most chief executives." But justifying overcompensation of one professional by pointing to potential overcompensation of another professional is not a valid argument.

One approach to this question is to observe the forms that executive compensation takes. In one such study of seventy-three firms by Kevin Murphy:

> As measured by the rate of return on common stock, a strong, positive statistical relationship exists between executive pay and company performance . . . 50% of the chief executives in the 73 sample companies held more than $1.5 million in their companies' comon stock. . . . In general, securities markets react positively to the announcement of long-term executive compensation plans implying that these plans, at least as perceived by the capital markets, increase the wealth of the firm's shareholders.[22]

It is not possible from such a study to conclude that executives are not overpaid. We can say that these compensation schemes have a useful motivational property by tying the chief executive's compensation to the performance of the firm. The study does suggest that executive compensation packages do reflect performance and that executives are not carting away large wealth independently of performance. Other studies have reached the same general conclusion.[23] In commenting on the findings of

---

[21] Brian Dummaine, "Ross Gets a Few Dollars More," *Fortune* (April 13, 1987).

[22] Kevin J. Murphy, "Top Executives Are Worth Every Nickel They Get," *Harvard Business Review* (March-April 1986).

[23] Although a more recent study concludes that far too little of a CEO's compensation is tied to the performance of the firm; see Kevin Murphy and Michael C. Jensen, "Are Executive Compensation Contracts Structured Properly?" Harvard Business School Working Paper (1987).

two large studies[24] considering the effects of chief executive officers on the performance of their firms, R. Daft observed:

> A realistic interpretation of these findings is the conclusion that corporate performance is the result of many factors. General economic and industry conditions outside the control of the chief executive do affect sales and net earnings. However, outcomes under the control of executive strategy—such as net profit—are influenced by the chief executive because net profit is an outcome of strategic choices. The impact of chief executives on performance is also greater in smaller organizations and in organizations that serve ultimate customers directly. In these situations chief executives can formulate and implement strategy, and use symbolic action to affect the direction and the performance of the company.[25]

Summary

The use of executive incentive plans is widespread. Participation in these plans is usually limited to those employees whose activities have a significant effect on the performance of the firm.

The rewards provided by incentive plans are diverse and include cash, equity in the firm, perquisites, and intangible rewards. Of these rewards, cash, stock options, perquisites, and public recognition of outstanding performance appear to be the most commonly used.

Some people believe that individual performance should be evaluated relative to that person's tasks and assigned goals in the organization. In this approach, performance awards should be based on the individual's performance relative to plan, with due consideration of the factors over which the individual had no control and may have affected performance.

Others recommend that rewards should be based on group performance. The disadvantage of this perspective is that distinctive (good or bad) individual performance is not formally recognized and, if no effective group sanctions exist, may lead to individual shirking.

Many contemporary incentive schemes also focus exclusively on short-run financial performance. To offset the pursuit of short-run goals, it would be desirable to construct incentives so that executives are motivated to pursue long-run objectives or, alternatively, performance relative to the firm's key success variable.

Incentive plans provide strong motivation for the top corporate executives to perform well along specified measures of performance. For-

---

[24] Stanley Liberson and James F. O'Connor, "Leadership and Organizational Performance: A Study of Large Corporations," *American Sociological Review* (1972); and Nan Weiner and Thomas A. Mahoney, "A Model of Corporate Performance as a Function of Environmental, Organizational, and Leadership Influences," *Academy of Management Journal* (1981).

[25] Richard L. Daft, *Organization Theory and Design*, 2nd ed. (St. Paul, MN: West Publishing, 1986).

mula-based plans reduce uncertainty and ambiguity about how performance will be evaluated, but it can be difficult to devise mechanistic formulas that do not encourage dysfunctional behavior. Limitations of accounting-based formulas, such as the failure to control for changes in price levels, can lead to the awarding of large bonuses even when the firm is earning less than a competitive return on capital.

The board of directors, particularly an independent compensation committee consisting solely of outside directors, can play a vital role in offsetting these potential limitations. Such a committee could control for

1. Increases or decreases in profits caused by accounting conventions rather than operating performance
2. Increases in profits caused by the failure to adjust for price-level changes
3. Increases in profits not commensurate with performance of similar companies in the same industry
4. Increases in profits caused by concentration on short-term rather than long-term performance measures
5. Actions that maximize divisional performance measures at the expense of overall corporate welfare

PROBLEMS

16–1   Executive Compensation Plan

Fortune Magazine (July 27, 1981) reported on the new Chief Executive Officer of AM International (formerly Addressograph-Multigraph), Richard B. Black, characterizing him as a turnaround specialist. Black had recently announced huge write-offs, partly in connection with discontinued products. These had resulted in an $82.8 million loss on revenues of $206 million in the quarter ending April 30, 1981. The article stated that "Black [had] ample incentive to improve the bottom line. On top of a $300,000 annual paycheck, he gets a $1000 bonus for every penny increase in earnings per share up to $1, and more for every subsequent penny, up to a maximum of $550,000."

The *Wall Street Journal* (November 20, 1980) reported similarly on the value of compensation plans for chief executives:

> "Performance plans, which pay executives cash or stock bonuses based on a company's growth statistics, are increasingly replacing stock options as companies revamp their executive-incentive programs. Among the nation's largest 100 companies, 41 have adopted 'performance-share' or 'performance-unit' plans to reward executives for meeting growth targets up to six years away.
>
> Performance shares or units aren't tied to the stock market. Instead, success is measured by earnings per share, return on assets,

return on shareholders' equity, increases in capital spending, or some other measure. Some companies use a single guideline, others a combination.

Honeywell, for example uses growth in earnings per share as its performance guideline. The company has two overlapping four-year performance periods, one beginning in 1978 and the other in 1980. If the company achieves a cumulative average growth of 13 percent in annual earnings per share, executives will earn 100 percent of their performance shares. The maximum allowable is 130 percent, which would require a 17 percent growth rate; below 9 percent they get nothing."

Since Honeywell's earnings rose more than 50% in the first two years of the plan, executives were already starting to receive payments ($1.6 million in 1979 alone to 41 participating executives).

Champion International Corp. adopted a performance plan that compares the company's earnings per share growth with 15 competitors in the forest-products industry. If Champion's four-year EPS growth exceeds the industry average, twelve senior executives receive an award of 25% of their total regular bonuses during the four-year term.

Criticisms of performance shares also exist. Union Carbide scrapped its program because EPS growth was affected more by external events (such as inflation, energy price escalation, price controls) than by the actions of executives. Also, performance awards can sometimes prove embarrassing, as when the chairman of International Harvester was forgiven a $1.8 million loan because 1979 performance exceeded goals set in 1977, but the company then showed a large loss for fiscal year 1980.

Required:

Comment on the motivation for establishing incentive plans for the senior executives of large companies. What are the strengths and weaknesses of performance share plans, in general, and the specific plans described for AM International, Honeywell, and Champion International?

16–2 *Incentives and Decision Making*

Wilkinsburg Metal Works (WMW) specializes in custom metal work. For this reason the company uses many different types of machines which are repaired and replaced at regular intervals.

The factory manager, Ralph Smart, recently authorized the purchase from Grinding Machine Systems of a $1,000,000 automated grinding machine system. This system has just been installed. At the projected level of operations this machine is expected to last for ten years and have annual operating costs of $500,000. The machine is assumed to be worthless at the end of its life.

Ralph is concerned about a recent development. The Revolutionary Machine Corporation has just announced the availability of a new machine which performs the same tasks as the machine just installed in WMW. The new machine would cost $1,500,000, last for ten years and have annual operating costs of $200,000. This new machine has rendered WMW's current machine obsolete, and net of salvage, its current value is $200,000. The new machine would be worthless in ten years.

Ralph is currently paid a salary of $60,000 and receives a bonus of one half of one percent of corporate net income. Ralph estimates that he will remain with WMW for "about two more years." At that time he expects to achieve a promotion and raise by moving to another company.

In the questions that follow ignore income taxes and assume that the company's required return is 14%. The company uses the straight-line method to compute depreciation.

Required:

1. What is the best decision from the point of view of the company?
2. What is Ralph's preferred decision?
3. What motivation problems are caused by using short-run financial measures of performance as reward devices?
4. How might the inconsistencies raised in requirements 1 and 2 and the problems raised in 3 be mitigated?

16–3 McDonald's Corporation: Designing an Incentive System*

Designing an equitable compensation system is not an easy task for the top management of any company, as the attention the subject has received in these pages and elsewhere makes clear. But the difficulties of designing a compensation program for managers in a service business are particularly severe. When a company's product—be it flying lessons, cleaner offices, waffles, or Caribbean cruises—is manufactured and consumed almost simultaneously, there is no second chance to sell or perform.

Although bank tellers, chambermaids, and short-order cooks may have little in common, they are all at the forefront of their employers' public images. How they perceive and perform their jobs can promote or undermine the success of their organizations, and their proper and effective management keeps many a banker, innkeeper, and restaurateur on his toes.

The problems of motivation and reward in service-oriented companies are increasingly important as the provision of service assumes an

---

* Case originally prepared for classroom use by Charles Horngren based on W. E. Sasser and S. H. Pettway, "Case of Big Mac's Pay Plans," *Harvard Business Review* (July–August 1974) (reproduced with permission of *Harvard Business Review* and Charles Horngren).

ever-growing role in our economy. In this article we show how one such company—perhaps the world's largest and most successful food-service organization—is grappling with these problems and how other executives concerned with similar compensation issues view the plans the company has devised.

"We consider our first-line management to be the managers of our company-owned units," a senior executive of McDonald's Corporation told us. "And they do a tremendous job for us. Somehow we have to design a compensation system that will reward them for the hard work they do and still motivate them to continue putting in the extra effort that has made McDonald's a household name. We've tried various compensation programs, but none has proved to be totally successful."

The company's concern was not academic. At the time of the 1972 compensation system evaluation—the take-off point for this case— McDonald's and its subsidiaries operated, licensed, and serviced 2,127 fast-service restaurants throughout the United States and Canada, and a few in other countries. About 25 percent of the units were company owned and operated. (The ratio has now risen to about 30 percent.) By 1977, the company has estimated, the system will have some 4,000 units, and company-owned outlets will number more than 1,000.

The average volume of a company-owned unit in 1971 was $540,000. The company expected sales to rise to about $600,000 by the end of 1972.

Pervasive throughout McDonald's operations has been a success formula often stated by the founder, Chairman Ray Kroc: quality, service, and cleanliness ("QSC" in the corporate shorthand). Accordingly, McDonald's maintains a year-round training program at all levels of operations, such as at the world's only Hamburger University, at Elk Grove, Illinois. At this $2 million facility licensees as well as managers of company-owned restaurants must take an intensive course on McDonald's operational policies; refresher courses are also available. In 1973 some 1,200 persons were graduated from Hamburger U.

Below the managerial level, most jobs are quite simple and can be easily taught to new employees within hours, with the aid of operating manuals and in-store visual material supplied by the corporate training staff.

Initial Efforts

Between 1963 and 1972 McDonald's tried several compensation systems in an effort to encourage superior performance by managers of its company-owned outlets. But, as noted, none of the plans left front-line or top management entirely satisfied.

In 1963 a restaurant manager's bonus was merely a function of his sales increase over the previous year. The managers complained that volume frequently varied independently of their control, and so they jockeyed for assignments to units with the most potential for revenue growth. Equally detrimental to corporate health was the lack of recognition offered the cost-conscious manager. In 1964 the plan was abandoned.

For the next three years the company had no formal incentive system in effect and awarded bonuses purely on the basis of subjective evaluations. Many managers felt that their regional superiors were not adequately recognizing and rewarding their performance. In 1967 this informal plan was abandoned.

McDonald's then made its first attempt to provide a comprehensive and equitable compensation program. The company tied the base salaries of each unit's manager and first assistant manager to their ability to meet the QSC standards. It made the quarterly bonus payments depend on a profit contribution defined as "the difference between sales volume and those costs over which unit management normally exercises direct or indirect control through managerial judgment, decision, and action." The list of controllable costs on which unit management was being judged appeared to be reasonable and complete.

But the plan proved unpopular with those on the front line because it mainly rewarded high volume. Since a restaurant's profit contribution depended considerably more on increased revenues than on cost control, superior management and cost control did not always gain a commensurate bonus. The result was a wide disparity in bonuses; while the median was $2,000, they ranged from $700 to $8,000. In 1971 this plan was also abandoned.

The 1972 Plan

In the 1972 compensation package for line managers, McDonald's tried to satisfy the complaints and at the same time to maintain harmony between managerial incentives and corporate goals. The unit manager's annual compensation consisted of his base salary and a quarterly bonus that rewarded his ability to meet predetermined objectives in the areas of labor costs, food and paper costs, QSC, and volume projections.

1. *The fixed salary*: After surveying each market in which it owned restaurants, McDonald's established three salary ranges according to prevailing labor rates and other economic factors. Range I, the highest, usually applied to very large metropolitan areas; Range II applied to somewhat smaller areas where industrial and rural influences on the labor market were about equal; and Range III applied to small metropolitan markets with little industrial influence. In addition, annual merit increases were awarded within each range according to whether an employee was judged superior, satisfactory, or still in the new employee bracket. In 1972 the base salary schedule began at $6,800 for a trainee in Range III and rose to $15,000 for a consistently outstanding manager in Range I.

2.   *The bonus*: Meeting the optimum labor crew expenses—figured according to projected sales volume and labor crew needs for each month of the quarter—entitled the manager to a bonus of 5 percent of his base salary.

Together the area supervisor and the unit manager determined the food and paper cost objective based on current wholesale prices, product mix, and other operating factors peculiar to the unit. By meeting the objective to which he had agreed previously, the manager earned another 5 percent bonus.

An excerpt from the monthly management visitation report (on pages 748–49) by which each store's QSC was—and still is—rated. Based on the average score for the quarter, units were designated "A," "B," or "C." Managers of "A" stores received a bonus of 10 percent of base salary, "B" store managers 5 percent and "C" store managers no bonus.

In addition, the manager received a bonus of 2.5 percent of the increase over the previous year's sales, up to 10 percent of his base salary. If unit volume was significantly affected by operating circumstances beyond his control, the regional manager could grant him a semiannual payout of 5 percent of his base salary.

Therefore, the maximum annual incentive bonus to an "A" store manager who met all his objectives was 20 percent of his base salary plus an additional 10 percent of his salary because of the volume gain at his restaurant. (His first assistant was entitled to a bonus of approximately 60 percent as much.)

Bonuses for meeting cost objectives were paid quarterly; those for meeting QSC standards and volume increases were paid semiannually.

Still Another Try

While the 1972 compensation system eliminated many shortcomings of previous programs, unit managers now protested that it was much too complicated. Moreover, complaints about undue subjectivity and dependence on volume patterns were heard anew. McDonald's top management went back to the chalkboards and calculators and came up with four alternative plans.

Plan A: The unit manager's base salary would be determined initially according to the range system described earlier. Thereafter he would be rated monthly by the regional operations staff on six factors: quality, service, cleanliness, training ability, volume, and profit. Each factor would be rated 0 for unsatisfactory, 1 for satisfactory, and 2 for outstanding. A manager whose semiannual total is 12 would earn a bonus of 40 percent of his base salary for half a year, a score of 11 would warrant a 35 percent bonus, and so on. At the end of the year his two semiannual scores would be averaged and he would receive a salary increase of 12 percent for a score of 12, 11 percent for a score of 11, and so on, down to a point where the manager presumably would be encouraged to seek his fortune with a competitor.

Plan B: After receiving the base salary suggested by the range system in his first year as manager, the person would be placed on a draw against commission. The draw would be his salary as before; the commission would be a bonus of 10 percent of any sales gain plus 20 percent of the profit (provided that gross profit amounted to at least 10 percent of the gross take). For example, if sales increased by $50,000 this year to $550,000 and profit were 12 percent (or $66,000), the manager's total compensation package would be 10 percent × $50,000 plus 20 percent × $66,000 = $18,200.

A variation of this plan being considered would incorporate a sliding scale—that is, 10 percent of the sales increase at units with sales up to $500,000, plus 20 percent of the profit; 7 percent of the sales increase at units with sales up to $700,000, plus 17 percent of the profit; and 7 percent of the sales gain at units with sales exceeding $700,000, plus 15 percent of the profit.

Plan C: Similar to Plan B in its draw against commission, the so-called "supermanager" program would base total compensation solely on sales volume. For units having volumes of $500,000 and less, salaries were set at different levels—for example, $10,500 for unit sales of $300,000, $11,500 for sales of $400,000, and $12,500 for $500,000.

Any volume exceeding $500,000 would be multiplied by the factor of 2 percent and added to the base of $12,500. For example, the manager of a $750,000 unit would earn $12,500 plus $5,000. Managers of new stores and of stores considered to be in inferior locations would be paid at the $12,500 base rate for the first 12 months of their stay.

Plan D: Based on the size of the management team and the volume of the store, a predetermined lump sum would be allocated for management salaries. Individual performance as evaluated by the regional operations staff would determine the percentage of the total allocation to be received by each team member. The total amounts that would be available are shown in Table 1.

As this article was being written, McDonald's was still wrestling with these alternatives. A senior officer of the company summarized his feelings about the compensation dilemma in this way:

"When this company began, it was a fight for survival. Just meeting the payroll was an accomplishment. Later, as we became better known

MANAGEMENT VISITATION REPORT

Store Address: _____
                 NUMBER   STREET   CITY   STATE

This store is in the _____TV market. This report was completed by _____at ___
a.m./p.m. on _____197___ and the day of the week was _____. There were
          MONTH   DATE
_____cars on the lot, and _____customers in line waiting to be served and _____
persons seated in the dining area. The person totally in charge of the store during this visit is ___
and his title is _____. The manager of this store is _____;
the supervisor is _____; and the operator is _____. When
completed this report was reviewed with _____on _____.
                                                 DATE

SCORE: Outside (Sec. I) _____out of 30.   Inside (Sec. II) _____out of 35.
Food (Sec. IV) _____out of 35.   Overall _____out of 100
                  (MAXIMUM SCORE PER QUESTION IS 5.)

Question No.	SECTION I (Outside)	Item Score
1.	Is area within one block of the store free of all litter?	
2.	Are flags being displayed properly and are they in good condition? Are entrance and exit and road signs in excellent condition?	
3.	Are waste receptacles in an excellent state of repair and clean? Is trash being emptied as necessary?	
4.	Is the parking lot and landscaping as clean, litter-free, and well picked up as you could reasonably expect for this business period? Do these areas reflect an excellent maintenance program? Is traffic pattern well controlled?	
5.	Do the sidewalks surrounding the building and the exterior of the building reflect an excellent maintenance program? Were these areas being maintained properly during this visit?	
6.	Were all inside and outside lights which should have been on, on, and were windows clean?	
	SECTION TOTAL	

Question No.	SECTION II (Inside Store Pre-Purchase of Food)	Item Score
7.	Was the restroom properly maintained? Was the inside lobby and dining area properly maintained?	
8.	Does P. O. P. in the store present a unified theme?	
9.	Is menu board in excellent repair and clean? Are napkins and straws available near all registers?	
10.	Is the general appearance of all stations good? Is all stainless steel properly maintained?	
11.	Is there an adequate number of crew and management people working for this business period and are they positioned properly?	
12.	Are all crew members: wearing proper McDonald's uniforms, properly groomed, and does their general conduct present a good image?	
13.	Are all counter persons using the Six Step Method and does their serving time per customer meet McDonald's standards?	
	SECTION TOTAL	

Question No.	SECTION IV (After Food Order)	Item Score
14.	Was the sub total, tax, and total charged to you exactly correct and did you receive the correct change?	
15.	Was your order placed properly in the proper size bag, on the correct tray, and did the total packaging appear neat? Was the bag double folded?	
16.	Was the Production Caller controlling production properly?	
17.	Did sandwiches appear neat and do they reflect that the prescribed operational procedures were used when preparing the food?	
18.	Were all sandwiches hot and tasty?	
19.	Were your fries a full portion, hot, and did they meet finish fry standards?	
20.	Did all soft drinks, shakes, or coffee meet McDonald's standards?	
	SECTION TOTAL	

TABLE 1
Total Compensation Available by Unit According to Size of Management Team

Sales	2 Persons	3 Persons	4 Persons	5 Persons
$ 0– 300,000	$19,500	$28,500		
301,000– 400,000	20,000	30,000		
401,000– 500,000	22,500	32,500	$45,000	
501,000– 600,000		33,000	48,000	$60,000
601,000– 700,000		35,000	49,000	63,000
701,000– 800,000			52,000	64,000
801,000– 900,000			54,000	67,500
901,000–1,000,000			55,000	70,000

and began to grow, we could concentrate on perfecting our operations. We started the first comprehensive training program for fast-food service in the industry.

"Now is the first time we've been able to look carefully at an area that we really should have considered years ago—our compensation programs and how they affect our people. We know we have a real opportunity here but quite frankly we're not sure how to proceed. When you're growing internally at a 30 percent annual rate plus acquiring licenses, the issue of management training in the company stores becomes acute, particularly when so much training must be on the job.

"In short, we're faced with a situation where our unit managers are putting great pressure on us to simplify and improve their compensation system. At the same time we have to design a system somehow that's equitable across the board and encourages the manager to give close attention to training his subordinates."

Required:

1. What factors should *McDonald's* consider when designing a compensation plan for its first-line managers?
2. Assume you are a first-line manager. Outline your views on the 1972 plan and Plans A–D. Which plan would you prefer that *McDonald's* adopt and why?
3. Assume you are the senior officer charged with making recommendations on a compensation plan. Which plan would you recommend that *McDonald's* adopt and why?

16–4   Analog Devices, Inc. (A)

In reference to Analog Devices, Inc. (ADI) two bonus plans, one for management and one for technical personnel, Graham Sterling, Vice President, Strategic Planning stated the following:

This case was prepared by Assistant Professor Kenneth A. Merchant. Copyright © 1980 by the President and Fellows of Harvard College. Harvard Business School case 9–181–001.

The purposes of the Bonus Plans are first to communicate to the people that the company places a high value on concurrent growth and profitability and is willing to accept some trade-off between the two, undertaking at the Corporate level to balance the portfolio so that the total corporation enjoys self-funded growth. The second purpose is to carry out our objective of paying above-average compensation, some substantial fraction of which is conditional on company or group performance.

I do not like to refer to the plans as incentive plans. I visualize them as plans for communicating some important facts of life. The concept of rapid, self-funded growth has always been central to the corporate culture, because without rapid growth we could lose control of our markets, while without self-funding we might not long be viable as an independent owner-managed company. The bonus plans help us deliver this message and enable us to share the fruits of whatever success we accomplish as a total organization.

The Company

ADI was a medium-size semiconductor manufacturer with headquarters in Norwood, Massachusetts. Founded in 1965 with an initial capitalization of $100,000, the company had grown rapidly to a sales level of just over $100 million in fiscal year 1979 (ended November 3). Average annual growth from 1975 to 1979 was 35% (compared to an electronics industry growth rate over the prior decade of about 13%), and 1979 company sales were up nearly 50%.

ADI was primarily engaged in the design, manufacture and sales of precision electronic components and subsystems employed mostly in measurement and control applications. More than 90% of company sales were of components designed to acquire, condition and convert electrical analogs (voltage or current) or real world phenomena (temperature, pressure, flow, light, etc.). These components facilitate the recording, processing and display of the information content of these signals which is vital for managing a broad range of real world processes. These components are designed for incorporation in measurement and control instruments for markets such as avionics, industrial automation, and medical and scientific testing. ADI was the leading producer in this market segment.

ADI was able to compete with the giant semiconductor companies, such as Texas Instruments and National Semiconductor, which were able to generate high volume (and lower cost) because in this market segment, product design was more important than price. Customers were generally willing to pay premiums for components that would best solve their particular problems. The market was highly fragmented: ADI served over 6,000 active accounts. The company's strategy was to capitalize on and expand its market leadership positions and gradually to integrate vertically by combining its data acquisition components into higher level building blocks (subassemblies) and user-oriented, computer-based measurement systems.

ADI had two primary financial objectives: (1) growth of Sales at an average compound rate of 25% per year and (2) Pretax Return on average invested Capital of 19% per year. For internal control purposes, the 19% Return on Capital goal was translated to an equivalent 23% Operating Pretax Return on Assets (OPROA). Company financial models had shown that the 23% Operating Pretax Return would generate enough cash internally to support 25% annual growth and a modest cash dividend with a Debt/Equity ratio of not greater than 75%. The growth objective was considered to be a minimum goal, rather than a ceiling, so there was considerable emphasis on overachieving this goal, although it was realized that to be self-funding a higher growth rate would require some combination of higher Return on Capital, higher Debt/Equity ratio and lower cash dividend payout.

The company's growth was primarily internally generated. From time to time ADI would acquire a small company as an entree to a new product line, a new location or a new market, but these acquisitions were always small in proportion to the prior year's consolidated sales, so they served as bases for subsequent internal growth rather than as purchased expansions.

The rapid growth created the need for a substantial, continuous flow of innovative new products. Typically 80% of the company's sales had come from products introduced in the prior five years. This created a strong demand for capital and personnel. ADI, like all companies in the electronics industry, faced a critical shortage of technical personnel, both for professional functions such as engineering, marketing and manufacturing, and paraprofessional areas such as technicians and draftspeople.

The company's operations were organized into two main product groups—Instruments and Systems, and Semiconductors. Each of these groups was divided into product divisions which were organized functionally. A sales group sold the products of all divisions.

Financial plans were prepared quarterly with a four-quarter planning horizon. The intent of planning was bottom-up, although if the corporate consolidation of plans revealed inconsistencies or failed to meet the corporate objectives, the groups were asked to revise their plans. The November rolling plan, prepared in September and October, set the target for the following fiscal year (November–October).

The Parallel Ladder

To help conserve and develop the critical technical skills within the organization, ADI operated a Parallel Ladder organization structure that enabled technical employees to continue their career growth without the necessity of assuming line management responsibilities. The Parallel Ladder program provided technically-oriented individuals the opportunity for long-term career growth within his or her technical discipline and the rewards that are commensurate with those available to managers— increased compensation, status and recognition. By providing these rewards, the company hoped that technically competent personnel would not be tempted to leave their technical specialties for managerial positions when that choice was made for nothing more than a lack of alternatives for personal career growth.

The structure of ADI's Parallel Ladder is shown in Figure 1. It indicates the relationship between sample technical positions and those in the management hierarchy.

At the lower levels in the technical hierarchy, the emphasis was on individual contributions, perhaps as part of a technical team. At the Division Fellow level the emphasis was increasingly helping others, perhaps as a mentor helping to develop younger employees or as a consultant helping solve difficult technical problems. Corporate Fellows had demonstrated an ability to influence broad corporate objectives, strategies and policies and to help determine the future direction of corporate development.

Bonus Plans

ADI operated two bonus plans, both providing supplementary awards for specific performance in the form of a cash payment. The Management Bonus Plan was designed to reward all personnel with significant management responsibilities. The New Product Bonus Plan was designed for people on the technical ladder involved in developing new products and introducing them to the market.

The bonus awards were based on collective (corporate and/or group) achievement, not on individual performance. The bonuses of top-level managers, corporate fellows and corporate staff were based solely on corporate performance. Low-level managers and technical personnel were

FIGURE 1 Parallel Ladder

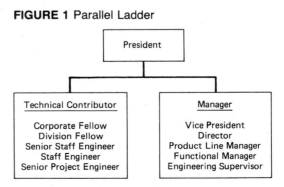

rewarded for the performance of their group (Instruments and Systems or Semiconductor). Upper-level managers and technical personnel in the groups received 50% of their bonus based on group performance and 50% on corporate performance, on the expectation that individually they could have a significant impact on corporate performance.

ADI established bonus plans to provide ADI employees with above-average compensation within an environment that encouraged concurrent achievement of personal and company goals. Graham Sterling explained:

> What we wanted was a wealth-sharing system which would make an objective determination of the incremental wealth available to be shared and would then share it among the people in an easily explainable and predictable manner. We felt that if we paid people well but made some of the pay conditional on company performance, they would better understand and have more concern for what we defined as "performance" and would cause the performance to stabilize at a higher level than would otherwise be the case. The plans were expected to promote a sense of teamwork rather than competition and encourage acceptance of trade-offs, where necessary, in the interests of the total corporation.
>
> Also, the company puts a high value on stability of operating margins. When a recession causes a drop in returns because fixed expenses and capacity are temporarily out of phase with demand, the compensation plan automatically cushions the operating margin, giving us the benefits of compensation cuts without the effort of negotiation and with minimum withdrawal pains. The opposite is true during boom periods, when the bonus plan triggers high rewards and moderates what would otherwise be unsustainably high margins.

A strict bonus formula was used to assure objectivity in the bonus allocation process. This was explained by a middle-manager bonus plan participant:

> We used to have individually calibrated bonuses here and the reason we're not doing that now, according to the general manager, is that it always ended up in a war. They only had so much money to divvy up, and individual managers had preferences for their people. For an outstanding performance it wasn't so bad, but as soon as you got away from there and started awarding to people who had done just a good job, not a terribly great job, then it got into a real shoving match. Given an ideal management committee where you didn't have some of the personalities involved (which is sort of an impossibility in this industry), I would recommend a more personalized plan based on your performance in that quarter and how you have met your objectives. But given the management here, we may be better off with our formula.

Despite use of the bonus formula, ADI management had the capability to recognize differences between people and to reward special accomplishments both within the rules of the bonus plans (e.g., assignment of level of participation) and outside the bonus plans (e.g., promotions, salary adjustments), so it was not seen as necessary or desirable to permit subjectivity in the calculation of the bonuses.

The General Bonus Formula

The general formula for both bonus plans was as follows:

$$B = S \times I \times F$$

where:

B = Amount of cash bonus (paid quarterly)
S = Individual's base pay (quarterly)
(I) = Individual Bonus Factor (described below)—varied with level in organization from 25% for top management to 10% for lower-level participants.
F = Bonus Payout Factor (described below)—derived from different performance-based functions, one for the Management Bonus Plan and one for the New Products Bonus Plan. Both were equal to 1.0 if plans were just achieved, and both were subject to a Maximum Personal Payout, an upper constraint, that varied by organization level.

Individual Bonus Factors (I) and Maximum Personal Payout

The plans were designed to offer rewards commensurate with risk. Since risk was higher for individuals in more responsible positions, the potential rewards were greater at higher organizational levels. This was accomplished by assigning Individual Bonus Factors and Maximum Personal Payouts, upper limits on the Bonus Payout Factor, that varied with level. These are shown in Exhibit 1. The maximum bonus for top executives was 100% of salary (4 times 25%) for outstanding performance in both ROA and growth, while the maximum for lower-level participants was 20% (2 times 10%).

EXHIBIT 1
Plan Differences at Different Organizational Levels

Organizational Position	Bonus Plan Assignment	Individual Bonus Factor (% of Salary)	Maximum Personal Payout
Officers, corporate staff	100% Corporate	10–25% (varies)	2.0–4.0x (varies)
General managers, senior operations managers, fellows	50% Corporate 50% Group	20%	3.0x
Division-level functional managers	50% Corporate 50% Group	15%	3.0x
Senior Staff Engineers	100% Group	15%	3.0x
Senior functional managers, senior project engineers	100% Group	15%	2.0x
Other designated line and staff managers and key engineers	100% Group	10%	2.0x

Bonus Payout Factor (F)—Management Bonus Plan

When the Management Bonus Plan was first instituted in 1975, the Bonus Payoff Factor was defined as a matrix function of the Average Rate of Growth of Sales and the Average Rate of Return on Assets. (Shown in Exhibit 2.) This operationalized the growth/profitability trade-off mentioned by Graham Sterling in the comment at the beginning of the case. Larry Sullivan, Senior Vice-President, Corporate Development and Finance, explained the rationale behind this two-dimensional performance measure:

> We at Analog Devices recognized several years ago the short comings of measuring corporate and divisional performance on short-term profit results such as net earnings and return on investment. In 1975 we developed an incentive bonus program for corporate and divisional management that is based on a trade-off between Return on Assets and long-term growth management. The concept behind this incentive program is that management must both do a good job of utilizing operating assets in the short term and make sound strategic investments for future growth and profitability.

Graham Sterling further explained the choice of two dimensions:

> Although in principle a Bonus formula could take any number of performance measures and compress them to a single Payoff Factor, it is neither necessary nor desirable to employ more than two measures. In the first place, over the long term, Rate of Growth and Rate of Return characterize the activity so thoroughly that very little if any new information can be brought in by adding a measure such as market

EXHIBIT 2

Corporate Bonus Matrix (Payout Factor as a Function of ROA and Sales Growth)

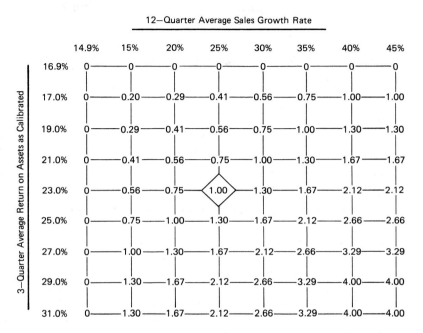

12–Quarter Average Sales Growth Rate

3–Quarter Average Return on Assets as Calibrated

	14.9%	15%	20%	25%	30%	35%	40%	45%
16.9%	0	0	0	0	0	0	0	0
17.0%	0	0.20	0.29	0.41	0.56	0.75	1.00	1.00
19.0%	0	0.29	0.41	0.56	0.75	1.00	1.30	1.30
21.0%	0	0.41	0.56	0.75	1.00	1.30	1.67	1.67
23.0%	0	0.56	0.75	1.00	1.30	1.67	2.12	2.12
25.0%	0	0.75	1.00	1.30	1.67	2.12	2.66	2.66
27.0%	0	1.00	1.30	1.67	2.12	2.66	3.29	3.29
29.0%	0	1.30	1.67	2.12	2.66	3.29	4.00	4.00
31.0%	0	1.30	1.67	2.12	2.66	3.29	4.00	4.00

penetration or customer service level. In the second place, having more than one or two performance measures might interfere with the desired concentration and encourage suboptimization.

A measure of return on assets was included in the summary performance measure to motivate managers to consider profitability and asset productivity in their decision-making and to encourage them to adjust expenses and production rates promptly as market conditions change. Return on assets was selected as an easily visualized internal measure that, unlike return on equity or capital, was independent of financing decisions. Return was defined as Operating Pretax Return so that managers were not held responsible for such corporate concerns as interest expenses and taxes. Operating Pretax Return on Assets (OPROA) was averaged over three quarters in the belief that for ADI it took about one quarter to detect a change in conditions, another quarter to implement corrective actions, and another quarter to see meaningful changes in results.

The sales growth dimension of the Summary performance measure was included because it was primarily a consequence of longer term strategic decisions. Management was encouraged to maintain expenditures intended to produce future growth rather than to compromise to accomplish short term profit objectives, and this suggested sales growth (in dollars) should be averaged over a long period. ADI defined this averaging period as 12 quarters (3 years) because the delay between initiation of new product development and significant contribution to sales from most investments was about three years. Although some investments might not have yielded returns in this period, longer horizons did not have much appeal as incentives for management performance because the career perspective of many executives in a single assignment did not extend beyond this time.

The Payoff Matrix was constructed so that the Bonus Payout Factor is equal to 1.0 when the corporate objectives of 23% ROA and 25% Growth were being achieved but not overachieved. The maximum Payout Factor possible was 4.0, at 29% ROA and 40% Growth, a level of performance considered outstanding, as established by assessing company capabilities and the performance of other companies in the industry. Lower limits were set so that no award was made if OPROA fell below 17% or Growth fell below 15%, performance levels considered poor.

The two performance elements, OPROA and sales growth, were weighted so that a 2% increase in OPROA performance was equivalent in payoff to a 5% increase in sales growth rate. This represented the feelings of management about the relative importance of these two areas to the future health of ADI. This weighting was held constant but could have been set differently to emphasize different business strategies.

The Matrix was constructed so that an improvement along either axis was rewarded, but the rewards increased most rapidly with progress along both axes simultaneously, i.e., along the diagonal of the Payoff Matrix. This was consistent with the corporate goals of rapid growth concurrently with Return on Assets high enough to assure self-funding. Corporate financial models showed that at the center point of the Matrix, defined as the intersection of 23% ROA and 25% Growth, the Company was self-funding with a 10% cash dividend payout rate and a Debt/Equity Ratio of 75%, and that movement in either direction along the diagonal connecting 23% ROA/25% Growth with 29% ROA/40% Growth preserved this self-fundability. Obviously, movement outward along this diagonal was very much desired. Progress horizontally through the matrix reduced or reversed the cash dividend payment ability and/or raised the Debt/Equity ratio, and since this was less desirable from the company standpoint, through the bonus plan it was made less rewarding to the participants. The cutoff limits at 29% ROA and 40% Growth reinforced the desire that improvement generally be along a diagonal.

A bonus plan *calibration factor* was used to adjust the center point of the bonus payout matrices to the performance level of the annual plan if planned performance, as accepted by top management, was below the timeless standard.

This was explained by Graham Sterling:

The justification for a Calibration Factor arose when the company's performance had not reached but was clearly trending toward the objectives established. At that time, we considered direction and velocity of progress as well as absolute performance in determining what Bonus Payoff Factor should result from attainment of the annual plan for the following year. In effect we said that if last year's results compared favorably to the prior year and to plan and if this year's plan showed significant improvement over last year's results, we might give these facts the weight of a few points of Return on Assets and incorporate this as a Calibration Factor in the numerator of the Payoff Function. At the outset of the year, a separate constant Calibration Factor was assigned to each quarter of the annual plan, so that the Planned Payoff Factor was at the desired level, contingent on accomplishment of the plan.

Since the standards for corporate consolidated performance were considered "timeless," the concept of a "calibration factor" at the Corporate level was something of a contradiction, and was being phased out. At the *Group* level, however, a Calibration Factor was always used to make the Planned Payoff Factor for each Group commensurate with the Planned Payoff Factor for the corporate consolidation, taking into account that Group's relative contribution to the corporate plan. The philosophy was that after a Group plan had been reviewed, iterated and finally accepted into the corporate consolidation, the managers responsible for executing the plan deserved essentially the same Planned Bonus Payoff Factors as the managers of the corporate consolidation and the other Groups. Thus, if a Group achieved its plan (without overachieving), the Group Bonus Payout Factor would be 1.0, regardless of how the actual performance compared with the corporation's long-term objectives.

A year or so after the start of the plan, the matrix function was replaced by an essentially equivalent algebraic formula. This simplification was desirable because use of the matrix required tedious double interpolation to determine the Bonus Payoff Factor for combinations of Growth and OPROA not explicitly defined on the matrix. The formula which most closely approximated the matrix for the Corporate Management Bonus Payout Factor was:

$$F_m = \left[\frac{OPROA + C + .4G}{P_s} \right]^{4.5}$$

where:

$$\begin{aligned}
F_m &= \text{Management Bonus Payout Factor} \\
OPROA &= \text{Operating Pretax Return on Average Assets (3-quarter average)} \\
C &= \text{Calibration factor} \\
G &= \text{Sales growth (12-quarter average)} \\
P_s &= \text{Performance standard}
\end{aligned}$$

EXHIBIT 3
Illustration of Quarterly Bonus Calculation—Corporate Management Bonus Plan

Assume the following facts for a hypothetical corporate staff manager:

a. he/she assigned 100% to corporate bonus plan
b. salary = $3000 per month
c. personal bonus factor = 15%
d. maximum personal payout = 3.0x
e. summary performance standard = 33%
f. 3-quarter average OPROA = 26%
g. 12-quarter average sales growth = 28%
h. calibration factor is zero

Bonus calculated as follows:

$$B = S \times I \times F$$

$$B = [\$3000/\text{month} \times 3 \text{ months}] \times .15 \times \left[\frac{26 + 0.4 \times 28}{33} \right]^{4.5}$$

$$B = 9000 \times .15 \times 1.714 = \$2315 \text{ cash bonus this quarter.}$$

Because of the maximum personal payout of 3.0x, the maximum quarterly bonus this manager could receive is $(9000 \times .15 \times 3) = \$4050$.

The performance standard (P_s) was timeless, fixed by the corporate long-range objectives. For the corporate plan, the performance standard was 33, calculated as the ROA goal (23%) plus 40% of the sales growth goal (25%). The effect of the exponent (4.5) was to impart the non-linearity present in the Matrix.

Exhibit 3 provides an illustration of a bonus calculation for a hypothetical manager, on the corporate staff, using the formula, with the assumption that the calibration factor was not used.

Bonus Payout Factor (F)—New Products Plan

The New Product Bonus Plan was designed in 1978 and patterned after the Management Bonus Plan, with analogous performance dimensions—growth in new product bookings and return on new product investment, weighted equally. The assumption was that a successful technical contributor innovated and would have to keep inventing more and more products.

Larry Sullivan explained:

> Since the development of the bonus program for managers and executives, we have come to realize that it is very important to plan and measure the results of investments in new products and reward the individuals that are involved in new product performance based on

those results. With new product activities in virtually any industry, there are three issues that are involved in success: (1) establishing objectives for new product efforts such that they directly support corporate growth and return on investment objectives, (2) selecting the right areas in which to invest in new products such that these investments generate high return on engineering, marketing and manufacturing start-up expenses, and (3) executing the investment decision rapidly. This is important as in a dynamic market, the company that gets the right product to the market first usually ends up with the largest market share and hence long-term profits.

To reflect these realities, we have established objectives for new product bookings as a percent of total bookings, the growth in new product bookings and the return we need to generate on new product investments. We have also devised the new product bonus system that pays off on the growth in new product orders from year to year and the return on investments made in new products.

In the New Products Plan, *Growth* was considered the short-term (i.e., highly responsive) performance measure. Growth was defined as a four-quarter average of the percent increase in total (corporate or group) new product bookings ($) in the quarter being measured over the same quarter a year ago. *New products* ranged from major strategic developments to minor modifications of existing products, anything for which a new product number was assigned. A product remained a new product for 15 months following the quarter in which it was introduced.

Return was conceptualized as a longer-term performance measure which put a high value on the volume and profitability of products released in the past three years. It was defined as the annualized value of the current quarter's marginal contribution from all new products (introduced in the past three years) divided by the development expense investment, engineering and marketing expense, needed to get the products to market (incurred in preceding four quarters). Marginal contribution was defined as revenue less manufacturing and selling costs, including variances (which could be significant during start-up).

The New Product Bonus Payout Factor formula was as follows:

$$F_{np} = \left[\frac{G_a + R_a}{G_s + R_s}\right]^2$$

where:

F_{np} = New Products Bonus Payout Factor

G_a = Growth in New Product Bookings (4-quarter average)

R_a = Return on Investment

G_s = Growth standard

R_s = ROI standard

EXHIBIT 4
Illustration of Quarterly Bonus Calculation—New Products Bonus Plan

Assume the following facts for a hypothetical project engineer:

a. he/she assigned 100% to group bonus plan
b. salary = $2000 per month
c. personal bonus factor = 10%
d. maximum personal payout = 2.0x
e. actual group new product growth = 50%
f. standard group new product growth = 40%
g. actual group new product ROI = 12%
h. standard group new product ROI = 15%

Bonus calculated as follows:

$$B = S \times I \times F$$

$$B = (\$2000 \times 3) \times .10 \times \left[\frac{50 + 12}{40 + 15}\right]^2$$

$$B = \$6000 \times .10 \times 1.27 = \$762 \text{ cash bonus this quarter.}$$

Because of the maximum personal payout of 2.0x, the maximum quarterly bonus this engineer could receive is $1200.

The performance standards were chosen as that level of performance necessary for the group to achieve the long-term corporate financial objectives. They were a function of such variables as asset intensity, growth rate, length of product life cycle and profitability.

Payoff constraints were again selected at both upper and lower levels. At the upper level neither G_a nor R_a were allowed to exceed twice their respective standards. At the lower level, no payoff was allowed if either performance measure fell below 50% of standard.

The exponent (2) was chosen so that the payoff factor equalled 4.0 when both growth and ROI performance were at or above 200% of standard.

Exhibit 4 provides an illustration of a bonus calculation for a hypothetical project engineer.

Required:

Evaluate the ADI bonus plans. How, if at all, would you modify the plans?

16–5   *Natomas North America (C)*
Management Incentive Bonus Plan

Natomas North America (NNA) was the Houston-based subsidiary of the Natomas Energy Company responsible for oil and gas operations in the U.S., Canada, and the Gulf of Mexico. In 1982, NNA owned interests in oil- and gas-producing properties in 14 states and 3 Canadian provinces.

NNA's major activity was exploration for and development of oil and gas reserves, both on-shore and off-shore. This involved analyzing potential drilling sites (performed by geologists and geophysicists), securing lease-hold interests in properties to be drilled (performed by landmen), and supervising the work of contract crews hired to drill the wells and produce the reserves discovered.

In 1981, NNA was decentralized into four regions—Northern, Central, Southern, and Canada—each headed by a regional general manager reporting directly to the senior vice president of operations. The objective in decentralizing was to increase sensitivity and awareness to local opportunities and concerns and to increase local initiative and accountability. The regional general managers, most of whom had a technical background, were responsible for all exploration, development and production activity in their region, but they worked closely with headquarters staff support personnel (e.g., geologists, geophysicists, engineering). At the same time, NNA sought to strengthen its domestic operations by greatly increasing the number of technical personnel in each region and at headquarters (Houston).

For management personnel, down to middle management levels, Natomas Company offered an annual incentive bonus, in addition to regular salary increases and a company thrift plan. This bonus plan was called *Management Incentive Bonus Plan* (MIBP).

Mick Seidl, president of Natomas North America (NNA), felt that the MIBP could be an important tool for communicating company expectations to individuals in key positions and for providing incentives for achievement, but he felt that significant changes were necessary in the way the plan was applied to NNA. He commented:

> What I wanted to do when I took over [January 1981] was to get in place a set of performance criteria that would govern the incentive compensation of the people who can, in fact, affect the company's financial success or failure. The incentive plan the company offered for management personnel was the MIBP, but that wasn't what I had in mind. The MIBP is based on net income alone, and this tends to

This case was prepared by Jeffrey M. Traynor, Research Assistant, and Assistant Professor Kenneth A. Merchant. Copyright © 1983 by the President and Fellows of Harvard College. Harvard Business School case 9–184–031.

screw up the incentives because there are all kinds of ways to maximize income which are not in the best interests of the shareholders. One obvious example is by deferring investments that won't pay off until future periods.

Description of the Management Incentive Bonus Plan

The objectives of the MIBP were:

- to attract and retain key personnel;
- to enable the company to maintain a competitive total compensation program;
- to provide levels of economic incentive that reflect the varying levels of impact incumbents have upon the company's direction and success;
- to stimulate performance which results in the attainment or surpassing of company goals and objectives.

The amount of the bonus depended on three factors:

1. *Natomas Company performance.* The corporatewide *target* bonus pool was the sum of the business units' target bonus pools (see #2 below). But the *actual* bonus pool was subject to how well consolidated Natomas earnings compared to budgeted earnings. Recent policy had been to limit the corporate budget pool to a maximum of 3–4% of consolidated earnings after taxes and dividends.

2. *Business unit (e.g., NNA) performance.* A target bonus pool was set for each business unit during the planning process by summing the "bonus opportunities" of all individual participants in that unit. Individuals' bonus opportunities ranged from 10% to 50% of base salary, with higher level personnel given the opportunity for larger bonuses. A business unit's actual earned share of its target bonus pool was determined at the end of the year depending on its profit performance compared to plan, according to the schedule shown in Figure 1. Total awards were, however, subject to the corporate constraints described in #1 above.

FIGURE 1

Percent of Profit Plan Objectives Achieved	Percent of Target Bonus Payable
Above 150	Up to 200
135–150	Up to 175
120–135	Up to 150
110–120	Up to 125
100–110	Up to 110
90–100	Up to 100
75– 90	Up to 75
Below 75	0

3. *Individual performance.* When the corporate and business unit factors were determined, a pool of bonus money was distributed to each business unit.

Business unit presidents then distributed their unit's bonus pool to their managers, after a review by headquarters. Company documentation of the MIBP suggested the following guidelines:

Performance Rating	Percent of Target Bonus Payable
Far exceeded goals	125–150
Generally exceeded goals	101–125
Generally achieved goals	90–100
Met some but not most goals	50– 89
Did not meet goals	0

The following caution was included in the documentation of the plan:

In making the decision about performance ratings for bonus payments, the rater should not eliminate judgment factors. To do so would make the performance review under the bonus plan purely mechanical, based solely on attainment of quantitative objectives. The range for each rating category allows the rater to make distinctions by taking into consideration less tangible behaviors which cannot always be measured quantitatively. The rater, moreover, may find that the above written performance ratings do not fit all situations. Then the rater's judgment must be applied. For instance, a participant could receive a grade below 90% when the rater believed the participant had "generally achieved goals" but did not exhibit other qualities expected of top managers such as the ability to plan properly, coordinate with others, lead and motivate subordinates, etc.

As a matter of practice, the business unit presidents did not apply the corporate guidelines strictly. For example, at NNA, a formal individual-level goal-setting and evaluation system was not in place, so Mick Seidl (NNA president) and the NNA vice presidents evaluated individuals' performances subjectively for the purpose of distributing the NNA bonus pool.

NNA Proposal for Change

Historically, evaluations of business units' performances had been based on only one criterion: full-cost-accounting[1] net income as compared to plan. But Mick did not think net income was the only measure on which to judge NNA's performance:

Top management of this corporation, like that in almost every publicly held corporation, faces intense pressure for increasing quarterly earnings. They're driven by it. I think that is crazy. It is nutty to expect quarterly earnings increases in businesses with long-lived assets, such as ours. We're investing in projects that will not pay off for years, and

---

[1] This was the method of oil and gas accounting Natomas had chosen for financial reporting purposes. The alternative was "successful efforts" accounting.

it doesn't make sense to respond to every perturbation in the economy by cutting back these investments just so we can show an earnings increase.

In July 1982, Mick proposed to Natomas management that a new set of business-unit performance criteria be used to determine NNA's annual earned bonus pool. These, and their suggested weights, were as follows:

	Weight
Net present value of new oil and gas reserves added during the year, compared to budget	45%
Earnings, compared to budget, taking into account controllable and uncontrollable factors	45%
Organizational development factors, defined as ability to set and achieve key management goals in a timely manner	10%

The *NPV-of-new-reserves-added* factor was included because reserves represented the company's major asset, and increases in this asset clearly represented successes. Finding reserves added shareholder value as the reserves could either be sold in the ground or developed and marketed at a later date. Mick considered the value of reserves added to be the primary measure of the success of NNA's exploration and development program. The reserves were necessary to ensure maintenance of NNA's earnings and growth.

Current *earnings* was a measure of how well NNA derived revenues and controlled costs. Mick included this measure for several reasons: (1) it measured aspects of performance not captured by the NPV-of-reserves-added measure, particularly cost control; (2) it was easy to apply because the measures were already a regular part of the organizational information system; and (3) managers were familiar with it.

He recognized that earnings had several significant limitations as a measure of performance, however. One limitation was that it did not recognize the longer term performance value of discovering new reserves. Another was that it could be distorted by uncontrollable factors, such as market price fluctuations and demand shocks (e.g., gas rationing), although he felt that variance analyses could be used to identify the amounts due to factors within and outside NNA managers' control.

The *organizational development* factors were measures of important managerial activities that would enhance company performance, particularly in ways that would provide longer term payoffs which would not be entirely captured by the accounting measures of performance. Examples were reducing personnel turnover, improving information systems, and improving purchasing procedures.

Mick felt that this combination of measures represented a clearer, more well-rounded picture of NNA's productive activity and better aligned bonus incentives with corporate goals. He explained:

> Use of net income alone in an incentive system tends to cause an overemphasis on the short term. In my view, the net present value of the reserves discovered is the single most important measure of our success. It's a tough concept to sell, however. Some of the people think it's nutty. They said: "Look at how you can manipulate those numbers." I replied: "Of course you can, but you can't manipulate NPV any more than you can manipulate many accounting numbers. As long as you can trace the assumptions and origins of the numbers, anyone can figure out if you're lying, cheating or stealing, by and large."

Management Bonuses in 1982

In 1982, management bonuses at Natomas were determined the same way as had been done in the past—by evaluating performance in terms of net income vs. budget for both Natomas Company and the business units. One process change was made: each business unit president had to submit a written assessment of his unit's results with his judgment as to the bonus pool award his unit had earned. Based on this analysis and input from the Executive Management Committee,[2] Dorman Commons (President of Natomas Company) would make the final 1982 bonus awards to the business units.

NNA Performance in 1982

The year 1982 was very painful for NNA. Net income was below budget by approximately $110 million. Of this total, $75 million was caused by a downward revision in estimates of NNA petroleum reserves thought to have been discovered in prior years and the impairment of Gulf of Mexico leases on which no reserves were discovered.

In January 1983, Mick Seidl sat down to prepare his recommendation to Mr. Commons about the 1982 NNA bonus pool. He explained:

> Overall we had a bad year, so I didn't go into this with the idea that we were going to be allocated a large bonus pool. But I felt that some parts of the organization had done very well and should be rewarded for their performance.
>
> My first task was to analyze our 1982 performance. I tried to separate out the uncontrollable factors and analyze the performance by region. Here is part of my analysis (shown in Exhibit 1). It shows that in total we did poorly in profit performance, and I couldn't attribute a significant percentage of the negative variance to uncontrollable factors. Further analysis showed this same general pattern for each of the regions.

---

[2] A formal committee of Natomas's senior management in San Francisco.

EXHIBIT 1

Income Variance Analysis
1982 Actual vs. 1982 Plan*
(000)

	1982 Actual	1982 Plan	Better (Worse)	Non-Controllable				Controllable				
				Price	G & A	Other	Total	Full Cost Rate	Production	G & A	Other	Total
Oil & Gas Sales	$115,500	$188,600	$(73,100)	$(14,900)	$—	$—	$(14,900)	$—	$(59,700)	$—	$1,500	$(58,200)
Expenses												
Lease Operating	$ 10,100	$ 8,700	$ (1,400)	—	—	$(3,400)	$ (3,400)	$ —	$ 1,500	$—	500	$ 2,000
General & Administrative	19,300	19,700	400	—	—	—	—	—	—	400	—	400
Depreciation	2,500	1,500	(1,000)	—	—	(1,000)	(1,000)	—	—	—	—	—
Full Cost Amortization	154,500	119,600	(34,900)	8,000	—	—	8,000	(75,100)	32,200	—	—	(42,900)
Total Expenses	$186,400	$149,500	$ (36,900)	$ 8,000	—	$(4,400)	$ 3,600	$(75,100)	$ 33,700	$400	500	$(40,500)
Net Income	$ (70,900)	$ 39,100	$(110,000)	$ (6,900)	—	$(4,400)	$(11,300)	$(75,100)	$(26,000)	$400	$2,000	$(98,700)

* All data are disguised.

But I knew that the Canadian region discovered a lot of oil in 1982; they found 3.4 million barrels more than was planned, and this is worth over $20 million to the company. This number dwarfs any controllable profit shortfall that might be attributed to them. Thus, I had to conclude that they did a good job in 1982. (This is a good example of why I think it is important to move to multiple criteria for evaluating performance in NNA, instead of relying strictly on net income.)

Based on these numbers, my recommendation was that the management personnel in the Canadian region should receive 100% of their target bonus and that no bonuses should be given to the rest of the managers in my organization.

Headquarters Response

Natomas Company also had a very disappointing year in 1982, due to a number of factors, including recession in the United States and worldwide, high interest rates, declining energy demand, lower oil prices and a major Indonesia settlement. Net income dropped from $233 million ($4.29 per share) in 1981 to $44 million ($.65 per share) in 1982. Many of these problems were recognized early in the year, and strong steps had been taken, including major cuts in expenses, capital expenditures and oil and gas exploration.

Because of these poor results, Mr. Commons decided that *no management bonuses would be paid in 1982*. He acknowledged that it was a difficult decision for him to make, but he concluded that before management received bonuses, the company on a consolidated basis should achieve a "reasonable level" of income (perhaps 25% of budget). He felt it would be difficult to justify to shareholders that bonuses were paid when corporate earnings were so bad that it was likely that dividends would have to be cut.[3]

Reactions by NNA Managers

Managers in NNA were understandably disturbed by the decision not to give bonuses, particularly those in Canada. Skip Jackson, one of the regional general managers of NNA Canada, commented:

> We had our best year ever in 1982. When we did not get a bonus, I felt cheated. In 1979 the reverse happened—the company did well, but we in Canada did not—and we didn't get any bonuses. I can understand that. But in 1982 this bonus system broke down, and it shouldn't have. In my view, the directors saved face because the company as a whole had a bad year; they could then tell the shareholders that no bonuses

---

[3] Quarterly dividends were cut in the first quarter of 1983 from $.35 to $.20 per share.

were paid. The whole idea of a bonus incentive scheme went out the window when that happened. They lost a lot of credibility with my staff who had worked very hard. I, and my staff, can only influence the results of my unit. This makes it a lot harder for me to keep the people in my unit motivated.

16–6 Wertheimer-Betz, A.G. Long-Term Incentive Plan

In February 1983, Wertheimer-Betz, A.G. (WB) instituted a long-term incentive plan in its U.S. subsidiary which provided cash awards for key managers whose business units were able to accomplish the targets set in their long-term strategic plans. Martin (Marty) Haynes (Senior VP–U.S. Finance and Administration) explained why the plan was established and what he saw as the major risk:

> The new long-term incentive plan is designed as an integral part of our compensation package, and we also hope it will have some positive motivational effects. In particular, we are hoping that it will reinforce the message that we are interested in managerial thinking that extends beyond just quarterly or annual earnings increases.
>
> I am worried, however, that the new plan won't accomplish what we want, and it may even be counter-productive. We are a highly decentralized firm, and the instructions we send to our division presidents about how they are to do strategic planning emphasize the fact that we want it to be a creative process. We say: "We want you to 'blue-sky' and theorize. You tell us, as an entrepreneur, where you want to take the business. Assume the money is there." But we haven't always been consistent. When the divisions come in with their plans, we are prone to say: "This is ridiculous. There's no way your business will quadruple in four years. Go back and be more realistic." And now we are saying that the managers' long-term compensation is based on the strategic planning numbers. We may be eliminating any chance of getting the blue-sky thinking the company wants and really does need.

The Company

WB was a large, privately held conglomerate based in Cologne, West Germany. The company consisted of a collection of manufacturing and service businesses in eight industry groups as varied as, for example, packaging products (e.g., glass containers), pumps, farm machinery, metal products, shipping, and information services. In 1982, consolidated sales totalled $1.6 billion.

This case was prepared by Assistant Professor Kenneth A. Merchant. Copyright © 1983 by the President and Fellows of Harvard College. Harvard Business School case 9–184–065.

WB was managed by a three-member Executive Committee consisting of the controlling stockholder and his representatives and a five-member Board of Management. Each Board of Management member had both line and staff responsibility; he was responsible for one or more of the eight industry groups and one or more staff functions. The industry groups were each run by a group president who was responsible for from three to seven product divisions. The divisions, of which there were a total of 44 in WB, were largely self-contained businesses which were organized on a functional basis.

Although WB had operating facilities in 14 countries, a significant proportion of the company's business was in the United States. In 1982, five of the eight industry groups and 19 of the 44 divisions were head-quartered in the United States, and the U.S. legal entity accounted for approximately 50% of the consolidated WB sales and 70% of the net income. Most of the U.S. operations had been part of a publicly held company that was acquired in 1976.

The Compensation Package

The compensation package for management personnel varied significantly by location. For personnel in the industry groups based in Cologne, compensation consisted almost entirely of salary. For managers in the U.S.-based groups, however, WB offered its management personnel a base salary that was competitive, but not on the high side, and relied on performance-based incentives to help retain its key personnel. The company offered two incentive plans which paid cash awards for business unit performance—a short-term plan and a long-term plan.

Short-Term Incentive Plan

The short-term incentive plan provided annual cash awards based on the level of return on investment (ROI) achieved by the profit center to which the individual was assigned (division or above). ROI was defined as pretax, preinterest operating income divided by book values of assets less current liabilities. About 150 managers were included in the short-term plan, including most managers down to one or two levels below division presidents.

As part of the operating planning process, the board of management member responsible for each division or group established a range of ROI performance that would qualify for the short-term incentive awards. Performance below the lower (threshold) level would qualify for no awards; in company terminology, the *payout factor* would be 0.0. Performance at the upper (maximum) level would qualify for twice the normal award (payout factor of 2.0), but no extra awards would be paid for ROI above

EXHIBIT 1
Typical Short-Term Payout Factor Range

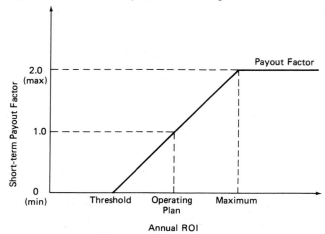

this level. The payout factor increased linearly with ROI between the threshold and maximum levels. The ROI target in the operating plan was generally near the middle of the range. This is illustrated in Exhibit 1.

At normal performance levels (payout factor of 1.0), the short-term incentive plan was designed to pay the following percentages of salary:

Organizational Level	Expected Payout (% of Salary)
Group President	65%
Division President	50
Functional Manager	35

The Long-Term Incentive Plan

The long-term incentive plan provided cash awards to approximately 60 high-level general and staff managers. Payouts were based on sales growth and ROI performance over a longer period, generally four years, again as compared to the targets established during the planning processes. Further details on the long-term incentive plan are provided later in the case.

The Weighting between the Elements of Compensation

The payouts were set to provide compensation in approximately the following proportions for a division president:

Salary	50%
Short-term incentive	25
Long-term incentive	25

For higher management (e.g., group presidents), salary was a lower proportion of total compensation, and for lower management it was a higher proportion.

History of Long-Term Incentives

WB's U.S. businesses had had a long-term management incentive plan since the early 1970s (before the acquisition by WB). Up until 1976, the long-term incentive plan was a performance share plan. Under this plan, participants, who included personnel down to division presidents and key staff personnel, were assigned a number of hypothetical shares of company stock and were paid biannually for growth in the value of the stock over the prior four-year period. Typical two-year awards were 100–150% of annual salary.

After WB acquired the public company, the performance share plan was continued, except that the payoffs had to be based on total corporate earnings instead of stock price because the shares were no longer publicly traded. The payouts were calculated with the assumption that the WB price-earnings ratio would be equal to, and remain equal to, that of the public company at the point in time when the shares ceased to be traded.

In 1980–81, however, the performance share plan fell on hard times. The worldwide shipping business collapsed, and business was so bad for WB's Shipping and Transport Services Group that the entire 1979 and 1981 share issues were wiped out, despite the fact the other groups were holding their own. This led WB management to replace the performance share plan with another form of long-term incentive plan. The new plan was announced in February 1983.

The New Long-Term Incentive Plan

The new long-term incentive plan was designed to:

1. Link motivation and rewards to the achievement of long-term strategic goals at the group and division levels.
2. Provide long-term incomes which, when combined with base salary, annual incentives, benefits and perquisites, would provide competitive total compensation opportunities required to attract and retain quality executives.

The following sections describe the details of the plan.

Participants and Payout Levels

Participants included the Group and Division managers and key headquarters staff managers. In addition, group managers could nominate other individuals for inclusion in the plan. These would be people who had made important contributions, who had significant responsibilities, and/ or who had high potential. These nominations were subject to the approval of the Compensation Committee of the Board of Directors. In 1983, the total number of participants in the plan was about 60 (2% of the exempt work force in the U.S.).

The payouts varied by level in the organization. The maximum payouts were as follows:

Organizational Level of Participant	Maximum Payout (%)
Group management	65
Division management/Headquarters staff	50
Functional management	35 or 25

Performance Measures

Payouts were based on: (1) real growth in sales, and (2) return on investment (ROI) in the business unit to which the individual was assigned over the performance cycle (generally four years). Real sales growth was measured on a cumulative, compound basis over the length of the performance cycle. The real growth was measured either in terms of numbers of units sold, where those numbers existed, or nominal dollars deflated by a price index which best reflected the price increases in the industry. ROI was averaged over the years in the performance cycle.

Payout Factors

The method of determining the long-term incentive payout factors was very similar to that used for determining the factor for the short-term awards. During the planning process, a payout range was established for each performance measure, and the extreme points on this range determined the line from which the payout factors would be calculated. (This was shown in Exhibit 1.)

In general, payout factors of 1.0 were promised if the sales growth and ROI targets in the strategic plan were achieved, but the responsible board of management member was allowed room for judgment. He could decide that the plan was either tough or easy and recommend to the Corporate Compensation Committee that the payout factor be skewed in one direction or another. Pam Widdett (Director–U.S. Personnel) explained:

> Assume a business unit planned a ROI of 20%. A normal payout range might be 14–26% because the threshold is generally set about 30%

EXHIBIT 2
Determining Long-Term Payout Factors—Example

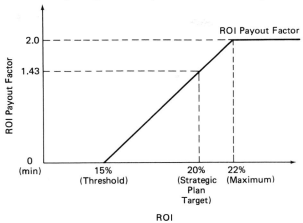

Formula: PF = 2/7 ROI - 30/7
At 20% ROI: PF = 1.43

below plan and the maximum is set about 30% above. But it is very rare that targets are set below 15%, which is what we assume as our cost of money (12%)[1] plus a 3% risk factor, so the range would probably be set at 15–26%.[2]

Further assume, however, that the responsible Board of Management member judged this plan to be optimistic or particularly challenging. He might then choose to skew the payout range downward, perhaps to 15–22%. He would be saying: "This is really a tough plan. If they make 20% ROI, I would be very pleased." Then if this unit actually achieved the 20% ROI, the payout factor would be approximately 1.4, or 70% of maximum.[3] (This example is shown in graphical form in Exhibit 2.) The opposite would also be true; if he thought the plan was conservative, the range might be set from 17–29%.

There are different ways to skin a cat. We could keep rejecting a plan because it's too loose, or too tough, or we can make this type of adjustment to the incentive plan to take care of the problem. We have been making the same kind of adjustments to the targets for the short-term incentive plan for years.

---

[1] The cost of money assumed for purposes of the long-term incentive plan could be changed annually. In 1983 it was set conservatively high. Marty Hayes estimated that in 1983 the company's marginal cost of capital was approximately $9\frac{1}{2}$%.

[2] For the sales growth measure, it was rare that the threshold was set below zero.

[3] The formula for the payout line would be PF = 2/7 ROI − 30/7; where PF is the payout factor and ROI is the ROI percentage.

The Award Calculation

The actual cash award was determined by multiplying the individual's award potential (i.e., assigned percentage of salary) by a weighted average of the payout factors achieved in sales growth and ROI. Exhibit 3 shows a sample calculation.

EXHIBIT 3
Long-Term Incentive Award—Sample calculation

Assume: Individual Assigned 100% to Business Unit with Performance Weighted 30% Sales Growth, 70% ROI. Award Potential: 50% of Salary = $40,000

Performance Factor	Target Award	Target	Maximum	Actual Achieved (Over 4 yr.)	Rating Achieved	Amount Payable
Sales growth	$12,000	2%	6%	4%	1.5	$18,000
ROI	$28,000	18%	23%	18%	1.0	28,000
						$46,000

The weighting between sales growth and ROI was set differently in different business units to reflect the relative importance of each, given the unit's business strategy. Growth-oriented units had a higher weighting on sales growth, while mature units had a higher weighting on ROI. For example, the following chart shows how the weightings were set for the rapidly growing Information Technology Group and the more stable Fluid Products Group:

Group	Sales Weighting	ROI Weighting
Information Technology	60%	40%
Fluid Products	30	70

One final feature was included in the award calculation. In the event that a unit's actual ROI was below the cost of money, penalties were assessed according to the following schedule:

Amount ROI Below Cost of Money	Reduction in Award
1 percentage point	25%
2 percentage points	50
3 percentage points	75
4 percentage points	100

It was expected that the assessment of penalties would be a rare occurrence.

Long-Term Incentives for Headquarters Personnel

For headquarters personnel (i.e., Board of Management, staff personnel), the long-term incentive awards were based on a payout factor calculated as follows:

- 90% was based on a simple average of the payout factors of the five groups, with no upper limit to the performance range considered.
- 10% was based on control of headquarters expense. Performance was rated at 1.0 at the budgeted level, 0.0 at 110% of budget, and 2.0 at 90% of budget.

Controllability Judgment Allowed

Provision was made for applying managerial judgment if it was felt that the actual performance as indicated by either measure was distorted by extraordinary circumstances. Marty Hayes explained why this after-the-fact judgment was allowed:

> We always have to keep in mind what we are trying to do—we are trying to motivate operating managers to make good business judgments. But uncontrollable factors can distort the measures so much that we can lose the motivational value.
>
> For example, one of our groups does a significant amount of business in Mexico. The Mexican devaluation has had a tremendous negative effect on that business, and if we didn't adjust the numbers, personnel in that division would lose the awards of several of four-year cycles in addition to their annual incentive. We're trying to be fair, and there are always going to be judgments that will have to be made.

Recommendations for judgments were to be made by the group president of the affected business unit to the Board of Management and the Compensation Committee.

Conclusion

Long-term incentive plans based on multiyear performance were a relatively recent development in the United States, and because the concept was new, WB management expected that the plan might have to be refined over time. Marty Hayes explained:

We had to do something. A high proportion of our compensation is based on incentives, and our package was not really competitive when the old performance share plan zeroed out.

But there are a number of unanswered questions, and we can't look elsewhere for answers because none of the companies that have implemented similar plans did it far enough back to have had executives go through a full cycle. Here are some of the questions in my mind:

- As I mentioned before, are we going to cause managers to become more conservative? Are we going to discourage really creative long-range thinking?

- Are we providing enough emphasis on the long range? There is still a tremendous proportion (30–40%) of compensation based on annual ROI performance.

- Are we providing too high a percentage of our management compensation on incentive pay? Some of our managers may have personally contracted for fixed payments (e.g., mortgage) at or close to the level of compensation they have come to expect. What if some of our businesses fall apart, for reasons that may or may not be under the manager's control? We might inadvertently cause some of our people to go into bankruptcy, and we can't allow that, can we?

- How do we encourage a manager to transfer from a healthy division to one that needs to be turned around? We have tried to get around this problem by offering a guarantee (good for two years only) that their long-term awards will be no less than what they would have been if they had stayed in the other division. Will that be enough?

- Do we have good control over our performance measures? We don't have an internal audit function, and the compensation of the most senior people who should be performing this control function is based on the same measures used to reward the managers. Is this a case of putting the "fox in the chickenhouse"? Do we have a significant risk of bias without the necessary controls?

As I say, I don't have the answers to these questions, as the plan has been in place less than one year. I expect we will be in the process of evaluating this plan for many years to come.

chapter 17

FORMAL MODELS IN BUDGETING AND INCENTIVE CONTRACTS

The Principal-Agent Paradigm Revisited: A Formal Approach

Contemporary research in organizational economics, finance, and accounting has explored how contracts can be constructed to motivate managers to act in the best interests of the company's owners. The research consists of formal economic and mathematical models of the behavior of individuals. The literature models the relationship between the owners, or principal, and their managers, or agents. Both principals and agents are assumed to be rational economic-maximizing individuals. They pursue their specified individual objectives within the organizational setting and the terms of the contractual relationship. Specifically, owners are interested solely in the expected monetary return that will be generated from their investments in the firm, and managers value both their **wealth** and their **leisure.**

The analysis assumes that managers prefer more wealth to less but that the marginal utility, or satisfaction, of wealth decreases as more wealth is accumulated. Therefore, managers display **risk aversion** leading them to value the outcomes from a risky investment as less than its expected, or actuarial, value. Owners, however, are assumed to be **risk neutral:** they value investments at their expected value.

For example, consider a large company. With shares widely dispersed among individual shareholders, who are also well diversified through investments in many other companies, we would expect that the individual shareholder would evaluate investments on an expected value (i.e., risk-neutral) basis. Individual managers, however, responsible for making large risky investments would be concerned about how negative outcomes would affect their compensation or opportunities for advancement. Because managers cannot diversify away from the consequences of bad outcomes, they are risk averse and may turn down risky projects that have positive expected values. The difference in risk attitude between managers and owners creates one source of conflict between the two groups.

779

Managers are also assumed to value their leisure. *Leisure* is defined as the opposite of the effort that increases the expected return to the firm. That is, managers who work hard sacrifice leisure in return for increasing the value of the firm. Leisure is treated as a generic concept that also represents the consumption, by the manager, of perquisites or benefits relating to the job. Examples of perquisites are company cars, lavish offices, first-class travel, and other nonmonetary benefits. Such perquisites divert the owners' capital away from productive investments in the firm and into the managers' consumption. Leisure could also represent time spent by senior managers on prestigious or personally remunerative external activities, such as boards of directors and trusteeships, which provide them with visibility and status but little in direct return to their companies.

Thus, owners hire managers (buy the managers' time) and also supply capital to the firm. Managers split their time between leisure and productive time, and deploy the owners' capital between productive investments and personal perquisites. The agency literature attempts to design incentives for managers so that excess consumption of leisure and perquisites is mitigated.

Note that we are not speaking of illegal theft as monitored by law-enforcement agents or auditors. We are concerned with a more subtle theft, of time (the manager does not work when or as hard as supposed to) and capital (the manager spends more money than necessary) to accomplish assigned managerial tasks.

Many readers of this agency paradigm state: "The agency literature involves fraud and theft. I believe that most people are honest. Therefore, the agency literature is cynical and irrelevant." But extensive evidence exists of efforts to monitor behavior and provide disincentives for engaging in effort diversion and time-theft.

A second common observation is: "Even if I grant that some people will shirk their assigned duties or will spend more money than they should on their personal consumption, I can always observe and discipline this behavior." **Monitoring** involves observing people to determine whether they have lived up to the provisions of a contract. If the job is well defined, monitoring is fairly easy. We can simply measure outputs. Like Frederick Taylor, we can assess the performance of a manual task by measuring the amount of work done or the amount of output created. However, if the job is more complicated, measuring output may not be realistic because of the possibility of many intervening variables between input and output.

Suppose we decided to assess the performance of a neurosurgeon by observing the patient six months after the operation. Consider the problems with a rule that assesses the neurosurgeon as having done a bad job if the patient dies or has suffered a disability as the result of the operation. For example, the outcome—patient disabled—could have occurred because the patient's condition was awful and it was only the surgeon's great skill that prevented death; or the unhappy outcome could have occurred because of a mild patient condition coupled with an incompetent surgeon. The intervening variable—the unobserved state of the environment (the patient's condition)—makes it difficult to infer inputs (the neurosurgeon's skill) from outputs (the patient's condition after the operation). Therefore, we have an outcome that is jointly determined by the manager (the surgeon) and the environment (the patient's condition at the time of the operation). Any given outcome can result from different combinations of the environment and the manager's skill and effort.

In general, inputs relate to the amount of effort and the quality of effort or skill. The agency literature has focused on the first aspect, namely, checking up on the withholding of effort. This withholding has been called **shirking.** Measurement, or monitoring, of inputs is introduced in order to verify that the conditions of the contract have been met: the manager has delivered the required amount of time and has not shirked.

It seems reasonable to conclude that the lack of time clocks for managers implies that shirking, at least overt shirking related to staying away from work, cannot be the crucial issue in manager-owner conflicts. The shirking, however, may be more subtle. Recall that we create decentralized organizations to allow managers the opportunity to specialize in terms of both action (the skill component) and information. Developing the market and technological information to accomplish these tasks successfully may require managers to leave their comfortable offices (and homes) to travel to diverse operating sites and to expend considerable amounts of their time in settings where they can accumulate relevant market, technological, and competitive information. In this case, shirking would involve not investing sufficient time and energy to develop the information required to be successful in the job and being prepared to alibi, should bad outcomes occur, that "I did my best—this bad outcome resulted from events beyond my control."

Owners must also be concerned with managers' skills. The difficulty of selecting managers with the appropriate skills for a required task is called the **adverse selection** problem. When a managerial contract is offered, it will only appeal to managers who have opportunities that are equal to or lower than the skill levels and compensation level envisioned in the contract of employment. Therefore, unless carefully designed, the contract will encourage people who are not qualified for the position to apply for the job. Once selected and installed in jobs, incumbent managers may not invest enough to keep their skills up to the level required for satisfactory job performance.

Because of the differences in information and skills between the owners and the manager, the owners can never be certain about how managerial effort and skill contributed to actual outcomes. This information difference, or **information asymmetry,** brought about by differences in skills, specialization, and the limited ability of owners to monitor the amount and quality of the manager's inputs, creates problems in contracting between owners and managers. The information asymmetry prevents the imposition of the obvious contract—namely, to pay the manager a wage and to verify that the manager's inputs were as specified in the contract of employment. It also creates a situation of **moral hazard** wherein the manager does not have to live up to the contractural terms.

Information asymmetry presents additional problems because the best information available for planning and control is in the hands of the controlled (the managers) and not in the hands of the controller (the owners). Moreover, managers are not motivated to disclose their private information for fear that it might be used against them. Managers' reluctance to disclose their specialized local information is called **information impactedness** and has led to interest in designing innovative schemes to encourage managers to reveal what they actually believe or know.

When inputs (managerial effort and ability) cannot be measured, the only variable available for constructing an incentive contract is the output, the consequences of managers' decisions, efforts, and skills. But this contract imposes undesirable risk on the manager. Managers invest effort (for which they have disutility, relative to leisure, by assumption) to improve the firm's return. The managers' increased efforts combine with factors outside the managers' control to determine the actual outcome. One can think of the manager's effort affecting the mean of the distribution that will generate the actual result, but not the actual realization from this distribution. A manager may think, "Wait a minute here. I might work hard (by sacrificing leisure) and then have all my hard work wiped out by something beyond my control like a general downturn in the economy or industry."

Therefore, managers face a gamble, or risk, when deciding whether to invest some of their leisure for a chance at increased outcomes (or, for that matter, by sacrificing perquisites for income-generating investments). In making this trade-off, managers will prefer a different allocation of effort or perquisite consumption than risk-neutral owners would select. The owners, because of their risk neutrality, should absorb all the risk in the firm. But by rewarding managers based on actual outcomes, owners end up imposing risk on risk-averse managers because the owners do not have the same information available to them as the managers. The contract is inefficient, since owners, willing to bear risk without cost, must provide additional compensation to managers to bear risk because of the owners' inability to observe the managers' information, actions, and abilities.

In designing an optimal incentive contract for the manager, we must make compromises between the desirability of having the owner bear all the risk in the firm and the necessity of imposing risk on the manager to minimize shirking and overconsumption of perquisites. For this reason, contracts requiring managers to bear risk are called **second-best** solutions to the incentive contracting, or motivation, problem. These contracts are second-best because an economic loss is created by the owners' inability to monitor inputs and thereby reward the managers who live up to the terms of the employment contract with a fixed (nonrisky) wage.

Any output (such as profit) that we can observe and that is correlated **in any way** with managerial effort can provide a useful basis for structuring incentives. Moreover, the more closely the outcome measure reflects (that is, is correlated with) the input of the manager, the more valuable the measure in an incentive contract.

Many variations have been created from this basic theme in the agency literature. First, to control for the adverse selection problem in hiring, we try to structure contracts that weed out people who are not qualified. As one example, research suggests offering salespeople contracts that provide high rewards for high sales achievement and low or no rewards for selling nothing. Such a contract would attract people who know (or believe) that they have strong selling skills and would help to eliminate unqualified applicants for a selling job. But by tying compensation solely to sales results achieved, we impose risk, created by factors beyond selling effort and ability, on the salesperson. Therefore, we have to offer a higher expected-cost contract to compensate the salesperson for absorbing this risk. Thus, we overcome the adverse selection problem but at the expense of having to offer additional expected compensation.

To avoid the imposition of risk on the manager, we might determine whether the outcome provides any indication of the manager's input. If the manager's input can be inferred exactly from the output, then a simple wage/penalty scheme can be used. For example, suppose that when a purchasing manager does not perform effectively, then one time in one hundred poor-quality materials are purchased. Moreover, the poor-quality materials can only be purchased when the purchasing manager is not doing the contracted job. The employment contract in this case is simple: the wage is paid unless poor-quality materials are purchased. If poor-quality materials are purchased, the manager is penalized, perhaps fired. If the penalty is large enough and can be enforced, shirking can be eliminated entirely.

These are the types of conclusions that have emerged from the agency literature. While the theory attempts to explain or predict contracts observed in practice, we must be cautious in interpreting the results literally. The conclusions have been derived from models with restrictive and perhaps unrealistic assumptions that are not likely to be met in practice. The literature's main contribution has been to provide us with a framework for thinking about incentive contracts and to point out relevant issues on risk sharing and observability that we might be less sensitive to without the formal analysis.

Problems of Obtaining Information for Standards and Budgets

Standards and budgets occupy a prominent place in the literature of cost accounting, management control, and organization theory. Standard-setting and budgeting activities are so pervasive in management teaching and practice that we tend to accept them without considering the fundamental forces that make these activities desirable. In an ideal world of certainty, costless information and observability, and unbounded computational capacity, a central decision maker can make globally optimal decisions and can direct subordinates (local managers) to implement centrally determined plans. In this setting, there would seem to be little role for budgets.

In the real world, however, local managers are given considerable degrees of decision-making authority. To motivate the managers to make decisions that are in the firm's best interests, profit-sharing incentive contracts may be instituted as described above, and in Chapter 16. But, as we have seen, simple profit-sharing contracts introduce uncertainty into the managers' compensation functions, and managers may take actions (such as lowering output levels) to compensate for this uncertainty. Such risk-avoiding behavior is not generally desirable for the firm as a whole or its stockholders. We must attempt to design the most efficient contracts to balance the conflicts between managers and owners.

Conflicts can arise in even simple situations. Consider a salesperson who is asked by the sales manager to provide an estimate of expected sales in the upcoming period. The estimate will be used to plan production and marketing efforts as well as to provide the basis for the compensation plan. More specifically, the salesperson is paid a base salary and a commission on sales in excess of a target amount. The sales manager will use the estimate of sales potential to set the target level of sales that the salesperson must attain before commissions are paid. In this situation, almost all salespersons tend to understate the assessed sales potential. The problem is not limited to sales. A production manager may understate the potential output from an assembly line so that, if something goes wrong, she will still have a good chance of attaining the production quota.

The misrepresentation of private information occurs because of two critical conditions: (1) the subordinate has information, by virtue of specialization, that the superior requires for planning purposes, and (2) the information is used both for planning and for control purposes. These problems are of such generality that the name **moral hazard** has been given to the situation where someone being controlled is motivated to misrepresent private information by the very nature of the control or evaluation system.[1] The condition for moral hazard arises whenever the manager's information or actions are not directly observable by the manager's superiors.

Moral hazard is not necessarily the consequence of a poorly designed control system. In fact, because of the specialization sought by decentralization, and the need for specialist information in control, moral hazard is almost guaranteed in a decentralized firm that attempts to assess individual contributions to the firm.

The existence of moral hazard creates the information impactedness situation, described earlier, where available, valuable information does not flow as required in the firm. As another example of information impactedness, consider a situation where a manager knows that he has made a bad decision but refuses to correct the situation because that would make the bad decision obvious to all. On the other hand, leaving the existing decision unchanged may cause damage to the firm but not harm the manager's reputation (or compensation), since no one else will recognize that a bad decision has been made.[2]

Information impactedness arises when local managers possess valuable, perhaps unique, information about their local environment but do not convey it truthfully. We are not suggesting that managers are evil or indifferent to the overall performance of the firm. We are suggesting that when managers are evaluated and promoted based on comparing their performance with a standard, we should not expect managers to act contrary to their own self-interest when asked to provide information on the appropriate level of the standard. Their self-interest may cause them to strategically manipulate their information and intentions. Because of inherent uncertainty and the costliness of observation, owners will rarely be able to detect whether an unexpected outcome was due to prior misrepresentation of information or an unusually good or bad outcome.

Information impactedness problems can be mitigated by basing rewards on companywide rather than individual performance. In this way, managers have more motivation to share information and cooperate. But, by basing managerial rewards on overall rather than individual performance, managers will not capture the full gains from their individual efforts, information acquisition, and decision making. As a consequence, they reduce their efforts along these dimensions. Many firms base rewards on individual performance. Apparently, the motivational benefits provided by measuring and rewarding individual behavior outweigh the potential costs of information impactedness and risk-avoiding behavior.

---

[1] In general, this literature assumes that people suffer no moral costs from lying. Even if people do suffer moral costs from lying, the substantive results of this literature are not changed.

[2] This phenomenon is known in bureaucratic circles as the CYA syndrome (referring to protecting one's rear from attack).

The Soviet Incentive Model

The central planners of the Soviet Union have devised and have apparently implemented a system of bonuses that rewards both accurate forecasts and outstanding performance.[3] Independently, an essentially identical scheme has been advocated for eliciting accurate forecasts in a sales organization and for a budget-forecasting system.[4] The proposed scheme provides penalties for managers who set output targets so low that the budget is easily achieved. Also, it attempts to provide an additional incentive for managers, after achieving the budgeted performance, to put out even more effort to exceed the budget. The scheme motivates people to disclose their information truthfully in the process of target setting and then, once the target is set, to work to achieve or better the target.

With the forecast incentive scheme, the top management establishes a basic bonus pool, B_0, and specifies three positive parameters: α, β, and γ. The manager first declares a targeted or budgeted output level y_h, which increases the bonus pool by the amount of βy_h. This factor provides the manager with an incentive to declare a higher, rather than a lower, budgeted output level. If the actual output level, y, exceeds the budgeted level, y_h, an additional bonus of $\alpha(y - y_h)$ is paid. This bonus component motivates the manager to exceed budgeted performance after the budgeted target has been established. But α is a set less than β, so that if output is going to be high, it is better to declare this in the budget than to realize it by exceeding the budget. If the actual output level, y, is less than budget, a penalty of $\gamma(y_h - y)$ is subtracted from the bonus. In this case, γ is set larger than β, so that the manager receives no benefit from inflating the budget, only to be disappointed later. In summary, the incentive properties of this mechanism require that $0 < \alpha < \beta < \gamma$.

Formally, if B is the actual bonus paid to the manager, the plan can be described by

$$B = \begin{cases} B_0 + \beta y_h + \alpha(y - y_h) & \text{if } y \geq y_h \\ B_0 + \beta y_h - \gamma(y_h - y) & \text{if } y < y_h \end{cases} \qquad (17\text{–}1)$$

---

[3] This system is described in Martin L. Weitzman, "The New Soviet Incentive Model," *Bell Journal of Economics* (Spring 1976), pp. 251–57. Extensions have appeared in Vinson Snowberger, "The New Soviet Incentive Model: Comment," *Bell Journal of Economics* (Autumn 1977), pp. 591–600; and Weitzman, "The 'Ratchet Principle' and Performance Incentives," *Bell Journal of Economics* (Spring 1980), pp. 302–308. Criticisms of the Soviet incentive system are presented in Martin Loeb and Wesley A. Magat, "Soviet Success Indicators and the Evaluation of Divisional Management," *Journal of Accounting Research* (Spring 1978), pp. 103–21.

[4] See Jacob Gonik, "Tie Salesmen's Bonuses to Their Forecasts," *Harvard Business Review* (May–June 1978); and Yuji Ijiri, J. C. Kinard, and F. B. Putney, "An Integrated Evaluation System for Budget Forecasting and Operating Performance with a Classified Budgeting Bibliography," *Journal of Accounting Research* (Spring 1968), pp. 1–28.

with $0 < \alpha < \beta < \gamma$. As an example of how this incentive scheme operates, Table 17–1 displays the bonus, B, as a function of y_h and y when $B_0 = 70$, $\alpha = 0.2$, $\beta = 0.3$, and $\gamma = 0.5$.

TABLE 17–1
Truth-Inducing Budget-Based Contract

$$B = \begin{cases} 70 + 0.3y_h + 0.2(y - y_h) & \text{for } y \geq y_h \\ 70 + 0.3y_h + 0.5(y_h - y) & \text{for } y < y_h \end{cases}$$

Actual Output, *y*	Budgeted Output, *y_h*							
	50	60	70	80	90	100	110	120
50	85	83	81	79	77	75	73	71
60	87	88	86	84	82	80	78	76
70	89	90	91	89	87	85	83	81
80	91	92	93	94	92	90	88	86
90	93	94	95	96	97	95	93	91
100	95	96	97	98	99	100	98	96
110	97	98	99	100	101	102	103	101
120	99	100	101	102	103	104	105	106

For any given value of actual output, y, in Table 17–1 (reading along a row), the highest bonus is achieved when the forecast y_h, equals y. That is, the largest bonuses appear along the main diagonal. If the manager knows for certain what the actual output will be, she can maximize her bonus by issuing a forecast equal to this actual amount. Any other forecast will decrease the bonus below the maximum achievable level. Looking down a column reveals that once a forecast y_h is issued, the manager will always prefer more output to less output. This provides an incentive for the manager to produce the maximum output regardless of the forecast. Also, the parameters have been established so that not achieving the forecasted output is penalized more heavily than output in excess of the forecast is rewarded. The key to obtaining all these desirable properties in the incentive scheme is to specify that $0 < \alpha < \beta < \gamma$. Soviet planners have developed a rule of thumb that β should be at least 30% larger than α and that γ should be at least 30% larger than β.

When we speak of exceeding the budget in this model, we introduce the prospect of uncertainty, which we have not formally developed. Uncertainty is important, since it introduces two dimensions that are not apparent in the certainty model: (1) the possibility of managerial risk aversion, which we will ignore for the moment, and (2) the need to further restrict the relationship among the model parameters. Note that this model really makes little sense without some form of uncertainty. If the controller knew that the manager knew, with certainty, what the result would be, the incentive scheme would simply be to penalize the manager heavily for not disclosing during the planning stage what turned out to have actually happened. Therefore, the certainty case is both trivial and unrealistic. Assume, therefore, that the manager does not know for sure what the outcome will be but does have beliefs about what will happen.

Using equation (17–1), and assuming that the manager can express her uncertainty about the outcome y in terms of a probability distribution, $f(y)$, we can construct the manager's expected return problem as choosing the communicated target y_h when the realized value of y is not known for sure. We can show that the manager's expected return is maximized under this scheme when the target communicated has the following property:

$$F(y_h) = \frac{\beta - \alpha}{\gamma - \alpha} \tag{17–2}$$

where the function F represents the cumulative distribution of the manager's assessed distribution for the outcome, y. Equation (17–2) states that the manager's targeted output is a function of the values of the parameters of the incentive model as well as her beliefs about the probabilistic nature of the outcome. If we want the mean of the manager's distribution of y communicated as y_h, then the parameters of the model will be chosen so that

$$0.5 = \frac{\beta - \alpha}{\gamma - \alpha}$$

or

$$\gamma = 2\beta - \alpha \tag{17–3}$$

This result imposes an additional constraint on the values of the model parameters.

To illustrate, return to the example in Table 17–1 and assume that the manager believes that actual output can assume any value on the interval 50 to 120, with all outcomes equally likely. In this case, the manager believes that the mean of the distribution of outcome is 85. With $\alpha = 0.2$, $\beta = 0.3$, and $\gamma = 0.5$, as in the previous example, the budgeted output, or target y_h, that will be communicated by the manager should satisfy:

$$F(y_h) = \frac{\beta - \alpha}{\gamma - \alpha} = \frac{.3 - .2}{.5 - .2} = \frac{1}{3}$$

That is, the manager chooses a budget target y_h with the property that the probability is one-third that the actual outcome will be less than, or equal to, the budget. In our numerical example, she will choose 73.33 as the budget [73.33 = 50 + 1/3*(120 − 50)]. If we had wanted the manager to communicate her expected value of output as y_h, we would have had to use the rule $\gamma = 2\beta - \alpha$ in equation (17–3) to set the parameters.

Suppose we use the Soviet rule of setting β 30% larger than α. Therefore, $\beta = 1.3\alpha$. Now using the $\gamma = 2\beta - \alpha$ rule, we have

$$\gamma = 2(1.3\alpha) - \alpha = 1.6\alpha$$

So, if we set $\alpha = .2$, we have $\beta = 1.3 * .2 = .26$ and $\gamma = 1.6 * .2 = .32$. Now,

$$F(y_h) = \frac{\beta - \alpha}{\gamma - \alpha} = \frac{.26 - .20}{.32 - .20} = \frac{.06}{.12} = 0.5$$

and the value of y_h that would be chosen is 85 [since $85 = 50 + 0.5*(120 - 50)$].

In summary, the bonus forecasting incentive system given by equations (17–1) and illustrated in Table 17–1 produces the desirable incentives of rewarding accurate forecasts and encouraging greater rather than lesser output. The parameters α, β, and γ can be set based on the relative values of accurate forecasts, the benefits of output in excess of the forecast, and the costs of not achieving the forecasted output level.

Limitations of the Truth-Inducing Budget Scheme

The forecasting incentive scheme provides an attractive but imperfect mechanism for eliciting realistic forecasts. It is a costly mechanism, since real resources (cash payments to managers) are being transferred on the basis of a forecast, y_h, rather than based on actual output, but it does serve to reward managers for information skill or knowledge (the forecast) as well as for performance (the outcome). The cost of operating this scheme seems necessary and even desirable if resource allocation and coordination decisions are to be based on budgeted output levels.

The scheme does have some other major limitations. First, multiperiod gaming effects exist that are not captured in the simple one-period incentive scheme. For example, the manager may believe that the bonus pool in the subsequent period will be a function of the budgeted and actual output levels in the current period—for example, $B_1 = B_0 + f(y_h, y)$. This ratchet effect is a well-known budgeting procedure, particularly in governmental organizations.[5] If the ratchet effect is a plausible assumption, the manager, when determining what the current forecast and actual output should be, will try to solve a multiperiod optimization problem,

---

[5] See Weitzman, "The 'Ratchet Principle.' "

based on expectations of how current forecasts and actual output will affect future bonus pools. If this occurs, the nice one-period properties described above (for example, optimal forecast equals expected output) will not be valid. To avoid these complications, the manager must be convinced that any current communication will not affect the setting of future standards or bonus pools. In the Soviet Union, standards are reset only every five years in an attempt to avoid the adverse consequences of the ratchet effect.

A second problem arises from risk aversion on the part of the manager in the presence of uncertainty, conditions not formally treated with our simple formulation. The piecewise linear-sharing rules, given by equations (17–1), will not yield the equation (17–2) result that we derived under conditions of risk neutrality. With risk aversion, the budget chosen by the manager will reflect, in addition to the parameters already discussed, the manager's attitude toward risk. In general, however, we would expect that if equation (17–3) were used to set the parameters of the incentive scheme, the manager would set a target such that the probability exceeds 0.50 and that the target would be achieved.

More important is the third limitation: If real resources are to be transferred among divisions (or among firms in the economy) based on the forecasts, an incentive still exists to misrepresent forecasts. When headquarters allocates resources to divisions based on forecasts, divisions may be motivated to conceal certain production or profit opportunities.[6]

The scheme is also a clumsy approach to incentive setting. Note in equation (17–1) that the central planner cannot control the amount of bonus that will be earned by the manager, since all the parameters of the bonus scheme must be set **before** the planned level of output is set by the manager. Any attempt to adjust the model parameters in response to the planned target set by the manager would eliminate the incentive properties of this model. Thus, despite the intuitive attraction of the proposed forecasting incentive scheme, implementation difficulties keep it from being a perfect solution to the problem of eliciting truthful forecasts from knowledgeable subordinates.

Truth-Inducing Schemes for Resource Allocation Decisions

Some research has been carried out to devise truth-inducing incentive mechanisms when two or more divisions are competing for common scarce resources (such as capital and computing facilities) of the firm. In this

---

[6] See Loeb and Magat, "Soviet Success Indicators"; and L. Peter Jennergren, "On the Design of Incentives in Business Firms—A Survey of Some Research," *Management Science* (February 1980), pp. 193–97.

situation, a central planner acquires a resource centrally (the motivation may be economies of scale in management and operation of the resource or a desire to tightly control the resource) and then allocates the capacity to the individual managers each period. To undertake the resource allocation, the central planner relies on forecasts, provided by the division managers, of the return that they can earn from using the centrally supplied resource. In a system where managers are rewarded on the basis of divisional profitability, the managers are motivated to overstate the return that the resource can provide in order to obtain as much of the centrally controlled resource as possible. Therefore, the objective is to find an alternative performance measure that will not provide an incentive to overstate the return from divisional use of the resource.

The Groves mechanism[7] to obtain truthful forecasts computes a performance measure for Division i based on the actual realized profits in Division i plus the forecasted profits of the other divisions at their actual allocated resource levels. We will not work through the proof, but it can be shown that if divisions attempt to maximize their Groves measures, then

1. Each division will attempt to maximize its actual profits, since the Groves measure is strictly increasing in the division's profits
2. Each division is best off sending an accurate forecast independent of what any other division sends or how it believes any other division is computing its forecast
3. Each division's performance measure will be independent of the realized (actual) profits or operating efficiency of the other divisions

Thus, this measure seems to have the desirable properties we would prefer to see in a performance measure. The Groves mechanism achieves its desirable properties by using a combination of realized division profits and a profit-sharing scheme based on expected corporate profits. The form of the incentive scheme is

$$\text{Reward} = a + k\,(Q + R)$$

where a is any constant, which can be construed as a wage; k is any constant (lying between 0 and 1), which can be construed as a profit share; Q is the **expected** profit of all the other divisions in the firm (given the final allocation of the centrally held resource); and R is the **realized** profit of the manager's division. Note that $Q + R$ equals the expected total

---

[7] This class of performance measures was derived by Theodore Groves, "Incentives in Teams," *Econometrica* (July 1973), pp. 617–31. It is also featured in Loeb and Magat, "Soviet Success Indicators"; and Groves and Loeb, "Incentives in a Divisionalized Firm," *Management Science* (March 1979), pp. 221–30.

corporate profits of all the divisions plus the variance of the manager's divisional profit.

If the division reward were based solely on realized division profits (R), each division manager would be motivated to distort the communicated information about the value of allocating the common resources to himself. The manager treats the allocated resource as a free good and wants to have as much of its capacity as he can. Eliminating this tendency is the portion (Q) of the reward function relating to corporate profitability. This term forces the manager to consider all uses of the centrally held resource and, in effect, charges the manager with the opportunity cost of the resource (reflecting its use in other divisions) when the resource is allocated to the manager's division. This term (Q) represents the sum of the profit expectations of all the other divisions conditioned on an optimal centrally determined resource-allocation decision and the prior information of the central agent. Because the reward function for each division represents overall corporate profits, the incentive for divisional honesty in communicating its opportunity set dominates the incentive for nontruthful reporting, and all divisions report truthfully. Finally, no division need be concerned, ex post, about efficiency or forecasting variances in other divisions, since such variances are allocated solely to the responsible division.

An element of noncontrollability still remains, since the evaluation of a division depends on forecasts produced by other divisions. But this interdependency seems inevitable because of the divisional competition for the common resource. The noncontrollable aspect may even be desirable in this setting, since it highlights the interdependence among the operating divisions and, therefore, the need for the divisions to work together for their overall benefit.

Unfortunately, the Groves scheme is cumbersome to implement in practice. It requires the managers' compensation to be a function of the Groves scheme measure. The parameters a and b of the Groves model must be specified before any type of communication takes place. Therefore, the resulting managerial compensation could be very large, insignificant, or even negative.[8]

A second shortcoming of the Groves scheme is the assumption that all managers are risk neutral. If any of the managers is risk averse or prefers leisure to working, the properties of the scheme are lost. For example, suppose a risk-neutral manager believes that another manager is highly risk averse. Because of the nature of the manager's risk aversion, that manager will request lower amounts of the centrally held resource than if he had been risk neutral. The risk-neutral manager in the second division, sensing this, will understate his opportunities to cause more of the centrally

---

[8] The properties of the Groves system are invariant under linear transformations. Deducting a constant or multiplying the Groves measure by a fraction does not change its properties.

held resource to be allocated to the first division in order to correct for that manager's risk aversion. When this starts to happen, the desirable properties of the Groves mechanism vanish as each manager second-guesses the decisions and actions of all the other managers.

The Role of Insurance

We have seen that uncertainty, in the form of noncontrollable random outcomes, makes it difficult to develop local performance measures for the managers of decentralized units. Uncertainty leads managers to engage in risk-avoiding behavior that may not be optimal for the overall firm. It also hinders contractual arrangements between units that interact with each other and leads to a demand for subjective information to develop budgets for performance appraisal.

An insightful reader may wonder whether some form of insurance contract cannot be developed to reduce the adverse effects of uncertainty. After all, on a personal level, we purchase insurance to limit the negative financial consequences from uncertain events such as death, illness, or accidents. Why cannot such arrangements be developed for commercial transactions within a firm? If local managers could purchase insurance to protect themselves (or their divisions) from the adverse consequences of uncertainty, deleterious risk-avoiding behavior could be eliminated.

Unfortunately, good reasons can be provided for why insurance against uncertain events is not readily available for local managers. Two factors, moral hazard and adverse selection, make it difficult to offer reasonably priced insurance in this situation. Moral hazard creates the problem of distinguishing between genuine risks (such as adverse outcomes caused by exogenous random events) and failures to take the best action to avoid the event being insured against. Once the insured manager is protected from the negative consequences of events such as sales declines, delivery delays, or uncertain product quality, the manager's incentive to exert a maximum effort to overcome normal commercial difficulties is greatly reduced. We do not want the managers, because they are insured against these events, to accept such commercial difficulties passively. We want them to do whatever they can to reach their sales targets, expedite deliveries, or improve the quality of their products.

Moral hazard arises in personal insurance when people with automobile insurance drive less carefully or when people with full medical insurance forego health-building activities or demand excessive amounts of medical care. Because of moral hazard, the insurer must insure not only against random factors causing losses but also against the expected reduction in effort to avoid the insured event by the insured.

Adverse selection problems also limit the role for insurance to reduce the consequences of uncertainty within the firm. In general, the insured knows its own risks better than the insurer. The insurer may set rates on an overall fair actuarial basis after observing many similar events. High-risk units will find it profitable to purchase this insurance while low-risk units will find the insurance too expensive. The actual experience for the insurer will therefore have a higher incidence of claims than had been expected when rates were initially set. When rates are raised to reflect the higher-than-expected losses, more lower-risk units will withdraw from the insurance contract. Thus, because of the inequality of information between the insured and the insurer, many units will have risks that are inadequately covered. Both moral hazard and adverse selection are caused by limited observability (or as we have called it earlier, private or asymmetric information).

Since limited observability will be characteristic of most activities within a firm, insurance arrangements are unlikely to be developed to eliminate the unfavorable consequences of uncertainty. Devices such as flexible budgets and annual budgeted performance can be viewed as limited forms of insurance to shield managers from some uncontrollable factors,[9] but a significant degree of uncertainty in evaluating managerial performance is unavoidable if incentives for excellent performance are to be part of the managers' compensation arrangement.

Summary

Many solutions have been proposed to determine optimal contracts between managers and their superiors in the presence of private (asymmetric) information and diverse risk attitudes. Agency theory attempts to design efficient and effective incentive schemes to motivate decentralized managers to act in the best interests of the owners. The optimal contracts under these conditions require that managers bear more risk, by sharing in the outcomes from their actions, than what would otherwise be required or desirable. Since risk-averse managers will have to be compensated for the risk bearing that has been imposed on them for motivational purposes, the owners of the firm suffer economic losses. Moreover, by putting managers in situations where they must bear risk, the managers may make decisions that reflect risk attitudes different from those of the owners and may be motivated to misrepresent their information they have about local markets, technologies, and opportunities.

---

[9] See Robert Simons, "Planning, Control, and Uncertainty: A Process View," in *Accounting & Management: Field Study Perspectives* ed. William J. Bruns and Robert S. Kaplan (Boston: Harvard Business School Press, 1987), Chap. 13, pp. 339–63.

PROBLEMS

17–1   *Effect of the Profit-Sharing Parameter on the Selection of a Risky Project**

Jane Atkins is choosing among three risky projects for the next year. The three opportunities are characterized by the following expected returns and variances:

Project	A	B	C
Expected Return	20	15	30
Variance of Return	8	5	20

Jane's annual compensation, w, consists of a fixed salary, a, plus a share of the return from the risky project. Formally this function is given by

$$w = a + b(y - 15)$$

where y is the return from the risky project, and b is a positive constant, less than 1, representing a share in the profit (or shortfall) in excess of the minimum desired return of 15.

Jane is risk averse and her preference for wealth can be characterized by a mean-variance utility function: $U(w) = E(w) - 2 \text{ Var } (w)$

Required:

1. Compute Jane's utility for the compensation from each of the three projects.
2. Central management prefers that Project A be selected and wants to set the parameters (a and b) of Jane's compensation function so that she will select this project. For what values of a and b will Project A be Jane's most preferred alternative?
3. Suppose Jane is compensated on a straight salary basis but wishes to make her decision as if she were the top management of the firm; that is, she acts as if $w = y$. Which project would she select and is this the project actually preferred by top management?

17–2   *Design of the Optimal Incentive Contract when Employee Is Work Averse*

Don Quack, the owner of North York Company, is pondering the employment contract currently in effect between himself and his sole employee, Arthur Milton.

---

* This example is adapted from Hiro Itami, "Evaluation Measures and Goal Congruence Under Uncertainty," *Journal of Accounting Research* (Spring 1975), pp. 73–96.

Arthur utilizes his unique engineering/craftsman/selling skills to manufacture the "Quacker," a novelty toy. This toy is the company's sole product. The firm's total output, X, is a function of Arthur's level of effort, a, and a combination of outside, uncertain events, θ, over which no one has any control $[X = X(a, \theta)]$.

Don and Arthur have studied the production function and found that it has the form:

$$X = a + \theta$$

where θ is thought to take on values lying between zero and b.

Don evaluates decisions on the basis of expected value and Arthur is admittedly effort averse. That is, Arthur suffers utility loss (or discomfort) when exerting effort.

This admission has prompted Don to offer Arthur a share in output "to motivate Art to provide higher effort." After a certain amount of haggling, Art has agreed to provide 100 units of effort in exchange for a salary of $1,000 and 10% of the value of the output.

The business is such that output, (X), is trivially and costlessly observed but neither θ nor a can be observed by Don at any cost. Although the matter has not been discussed, if Arthur is caught supplying less than 100 units of a he will face immediate dismissal from the firm. This will result in irreparable damage, so Art will avoid putting himself in danger of dismissal at any cost.

Required:

1. Do you think that this contract will achieve its intention of motivating "more effort" from Arthur? Consider both the situation when Arthur is risk neutral and risk averse. Can you think of a better contract?
2. How does the situation change if X is of the form $X = a\theta$?

17–3   *Effect of Observability on the Form of an Employment Contract*

Ralph Smart of Swissvale Investments is considering an investment in a farming venture in the country of Markovia.

The plan is to grow and harvest Gronk, a revolutionary natural food highly prized by distance runners for its sustenance attributes. The climatic conditions and soil of southwestern Markovia are unique and are the only known conditions under which Gronk can be produced.

Gronk-growing technology is well understood. Gronk production depends on weather conditions and the effort of the farmer in the growing season and hence is subject to uncertainty.

Markovia is a new and remote country which is virtually inaccessible to outsiders. Although Markovia has a well-established legal system, commercial development is backward.

Moral Hazard, a Markovian farmer and promoter, has invited Ralph and other investors to invest in Gronk farming. Moral would farm the Gronk and supervise the distribution of the proceeds to investors.

Ralph, and all other potential investors, are risk neutral. Moral is risk averse.

Required:

1. If no other information is available, what is Ralph's optimal course of action?
2. Suppose Ralph discovers that Markovia has a well-established and reputable public accounting profession. How, if at all, would this affect your response to requirement 1?
3. What further information, if any, might Ralph seek beyond the information that might be supplied by a public accountant?

17–4 Incentives for Distorting Information

Wren Jenner Construction specializes in remodeling existing buildings and constructing office buildings, private homes, and apartment buildings. For incentive purposes the company is organized on a profit-center basis with four profit-centers.

The critical resource of the firm is its carpenters. Since there is a shortage of carpenters in the area served by Wren Jenner, the company has a policy of hiring all carpenters at the corporate level and then assigning carpenters to one of the four profit-centers. The union rate for carpenters is $18.00 per hour, and at this price the managers of the four profit-centers have a joint demand for carpenters that is far in excess of the available supply.

Given this situation, the company is faced with the problem of how to ration the available supply of carpenters. The operation of each of the profit-centers is subject to some uncertainty so that ex-ante managerial claims regarding carpenter productivity are difficult to evaluate ex post. Consequently, the controller is reluctant to base allocations on a priori assertions by the divisional managers.

To simplify the discussion, assume there are two divisions. In Division 1, the return (p_1) received per carpenter hour (q_1) is

$$p_1 = 500 - .2q_1.$$

For Division 2, the return is

$$p_2 = 200 - .1q_2.$$

Suppose the controller successively announces prices and the division managers respond with demand at that price. The controller seeks to equate demand and the supply of carpenter hours which is 1,800. Divisions will be assessed a charge against profits which is equal to the bid amount. All managers are risk neutral.

Required:

1. Suppose both divisions respond honestly to the controller's price bids:
   a. What price will clear this market?
   b. How many carpenter hours will be allocated to each division?
   c. What will be the profit reported by each division?
2. Suppose the manager of Division 1 intends to respond honestly to the controller's bids. The manager of Division 2 knows this and also knows Division 1's return function.

   Show that there is an incentive for the manager of Division 2 to be dishonest. (HINT: How would managers behave to have a transfer price of $0?)
3. Can you suggest a method for solving the problem raised in requirement 2?
4. Under what circumstances will the solution proposed in requirement 3 not have the desired motivational consequences?

17–5   *Groves Mechanism*: Applications and Limitations

John Theodore, President of Garden Grove Nursery, plans the weekly operation of the firm. The crucial weekly operating decision is the allocation of the firm's ten gardeners to the firm's two operating divisions, *Commercial* and *Nursery*. No other gardeners are available.

The *Commercial* division solicits contracts for landscaping and garden maintenance. It is widely known that the return here is fixed and contracts reflect market conditions. Ralph Jones, the manager of this division, knows that this division can keep all ten of the firm's ten gardeners fully occupied at a net profit to the firm of $50 per gardener hour.

The *Nursery* division, John Theodore's original operation, consists of a greenhouse operation that grows plants and shrubs for the commercial market. The return here is uncertain and depends on volatile market conditions. Elmo Slack, the manager of this division, believes that, in the current market, the distribution of net profit per gardener hour is uniform over the interval $40 to $55. These beliefs are held privately by Elmo and are not known to the other members of the senior management team at Garden Grove.

Required:

Consider each question separately.

1. Suppose Elmo's compensation is a function of the reported weekly profits of the Nursery Division. Suppose further that John Theodore allocates gardeners to divisions on the basis of the expected returns estimated by the division

managers. If Elmo is an expected value decision-maker, show that this organization structure will motivate Elmo to lie about his division's expected return per gardener hour.

2. Suppose now that Elmo's compensation is a function of the reported weekly profits of Garden Grove Nursery. If Elmo is an expected value decision-maker, is there any motivation for Elmo to lie about his division's expected return per gardener hour? Explain the dysfunctional consequences of this reward mechanism if the divisional return can be influenced by managerial competence.

3. Supose John Theodore has decided to use the Groves mechanism to allocate the gardeners to the two divisions in his firm. For Garden Grove Nursery the Groves measure for the Nursery division would have the form

$$G_N = \pi_N^A(X_N) + \pi_C^F(X_C) - K_N$$

where $\pi_N^A(X_N)$ = actual weekly profits for the nursery division with X_N gardeners allocated to this division

$\pi_C^F(X_C)$ = forecasted weekly profits for the commercial division with X_C gardeners allocated to this division

K_N = a constant independent of the nursery division's forecasted or actual profits

How would use of the Groves measure improve the information elicited from Elmo Slack and the manager of the Commercial division?

4. Suppose further that Theodore wishes to make G_N relevant to Elmo by incorporating it into Elmo's compensation function. Elmo's compensation will be computed as

$$y_E = W_E + k\, G_N$$

where y_E = Elmo's total compensation

W_E = Elmo's fixed wage

k = a fixed positive constant

G_N = the Groves measure for the nursery division

Note that EG_N represents apart from the scalar K_N, *expected* corporate profits so that Elmo's expected return is a wage plus a share of expected corporate profits. Assume that Elmo could earn $550 per week in a comparable job outside the firm. Show that a compensation policy based on y_E is unlikely to be optimal. Is G_N a reasonable basis to use for compensating divisional managers?

5. Return to the original data of this problem but assume now that the net profit per gardener in the commercial division is only $47 per hour. Elmo has the same beliefs as before but is risk averse. Elmo's utility for his compensation (y_E) is given by

$$U(y_E) = -exp[-y_E/500]$$

where $y_E = \$500 + 0.1G_N$.

K_N is set equal to the profit of the firm if the nursery division received no gardeners; that is, $K_N = (\$47/\text{hour})(10 \text{ gardeners})(40 \text{ hours/week}) = 18{,}800$.

Suppose John Theodore is risk neutral. What is the optimal allocation of gardeners from John's point of view? Show that Elmo will lie about his beliefs in this case and that all gardeners will be allocated to the commercial division. What are the implications of this result?

6. Assume the same data as in requirement 5 with the following exception. Elmo's utility function is

$$U(y_E, X_N) = E(y_E) - 0.1X_N$$

where X_N is the number of gardeners assigned to the Nursery Division. In other words, Elmo is risk neutral but suffers a loss of well-being (or utility) when he is assigned workers to supervise.

Show that, in this case, Elmo will lie about his prospects and all gardeners will be assigned to the Commercial Division. What are the implications of this result?

17–6   The Effect of a Skill Parameter in Formulating an Incentive Plan

Outport Fishery Products is a large integrated fish-products company. The company operates its own fleet of fishing trawlers, whose catches are processed in one of the company's eleven processing plants. The final products are sold internationally under the company's brand name Bye-the-Sea.

Because of the demand for sea products and the limitations on the amount of fish that can be caught and processed, the company can sell as much fish as it can produce.

Many of the processing plants are located in depressed areas, and employment in the plants is highly valued. One of the most prestigious and skilled plant jobs is filleting, the process that separates the flesh of the fish from the bones. In filleting, the two fillets (one from each side) must be removed from the spine of the fish in whole pieces, since whole fillets command a large premium over broken pieces. Also, the cut separating the flesh from the bone should be deep enough that a minimal amount of flesh is left on the bone, yet shallow enough so that no bones remain in the fillet. Leaving flesh on the bone results in a loss of salable product. Leaving bones in the fillet requires indirect labor to remove the bones from the fillet. For this reason, the skill exercised in the filleting operation is a significant determinant of the value of the final product that is derived from a given catch (the others are the size of each fish and the specie of fish). Skilled filleters are highly paid.

Required:

How would you evaluate the performance of the filleters and how would you pay them?

17–7 *Setting the Parameters of the Soviet Incentive System*

In the Soviet Union factory, or enterprise, production is controlled by a central planning authority. In order to plan and coordinate aggregate production in the economy, the central planning authority requires forecasts from the enterprise managers about the production possibilities during the upcoming planning period. In the past, managers were rewarded on the basis of their ability to live up to production quotas that were, for the most part, based on the production forecasts of the managers themselves.

In response to evidence that enterprise managers build slack into forecasts of production possibilities, a new Soviet Incentive Plan was implemented. This plan provides a means of eliminating slack from forecasts by changing the basis of the rewards received by the enterprise managers.

The details of this plan were discussed in the chapter.

Required:

1. Explain why the ranking of the order of the three parameters of the Soviet Incentive model is important.
2. What relationship must exist among the three parameters of the incentive equation of the Soviet Incentive model in order to motivate the manager to set a planned target that equals the manager's expectation of the mean value of production?
3. In applying the scheme, the central planners have committed to changing the parameters of the incentive plan only every five years. Why is this characteristic important, and how would the properties of the incentive scheme be changed if the parameters of the incentive scheme were changed annually? What implications does this observation have for target setting in participative budgeting schemes in general?

The following question requires the use of differential calculus and a basic knowledge of the properties of utility theory.

4. Explain how the properties of the Soviet Incentive model would change if managers were risk averse.

17–8 *Incentive Considerations in Allocating a Scarce Resource*

The Fergus Electronics Corporation has 100 units of capacity available for production during the upcoming period. This capacity is to be distributed between the two major divisions in the company: the Military Products Division and the Computer Products Division.

The demand for the products of the two divisions is viewed as uncertain by the managers of each division. The nature of the demand facing either division is known only to the manager of that division.

The contribution margin provided by **each unit** of capacity allocated to the Military Products Division is $100,000, and the division manager believes that the potential demand for the products made by this productive capacity will require between 100 and 200 units of productive capacity; each value on this interval is equally likely.

The contribution margin provided by each unit of capacity assigned to the Computer Products Division is $150,000, and the division manager believes that the potential demand for the products made by this productive capacity will require between 0 and 100 units of productive capacity, with each value on this interval equally likely.

Because of the need for production line setups and tooling, once the capacity is assigned to one division during the production period, it cannot be transferred for the other division to use if the demand on the facility turns out to be less than the amount allocated. The managers of the two divisions have been asked to submit their requirements for use of the capacity during the upcoming period.

Required:

1. What level of capacity will be requested by each manager if the bonus of each manager is based solely on the manager's ability to meet the production plan for the allocated capacity? What is the expected contribution margin associated with this assignment of capacity?
2. What level of capacity will be requested by each manager if the bonus of each manager is based on the contribution margin generated by the capacity allocated to that manager's division and the managers are not assigned a charge for the capacity allocated to their respective divisions? What is the expected contribution margin associated with this assignment of capacity?
3. What level of capacity will be requested by each manager if each manager is rewarded on the basis of the contribution margin associated with the capacity that is earned by the company? What is the expected contribution margin associated with this assignment of capacity?
4. What do the results to requirements 1, 2, and 3 imply about the design of incentive schemes in decentralized organizations? Why might these results be misleading?

17–9   *The Revelation Principle in Budget Setting*

Bangor Electronics is a world class manufacturer of electronic components. Donna Wharton, the vice-president–controller of Bangor Electronics, is responsible for all aspects of budgeting and forecasting in the firm. She has become both disillusioned and dissatisfied with the traditional approach that Bangor Electronics has taken to budgeting. Donna summarized her concerns as follows:

> The traditional approach, where we set budget objectives and then evaluate performance relative to those objectives, is not working well. First, the budget is focusing attention on the wrong things. The managers are interested in making short-run profit as large as possible and are not doing things to improve long-run profitability. Second, I do not think that the model of evaluating performance on the basis of profits has the requisite variety to evaluate the jobs that the managers are doing. Their jobs are much more complicated than a simple profit measue implies, and we need a more accurate picture of how well they are doing. Finally, the existing system is motivating the managers to build slack into both their standards and performance targets so that they can make budget and earn bonuses. As a result, our forecasting system is unable to predict either sales levels or input usage accurately.

Donna went on to indicate that she was considering recommending to the senior management committee at Bangor Electronics that the current budgeting system be replaced with a new system employing participative budgeting techniques. Specifically, the new system would require that the objectives for each management job in the organization be defined relative to the organization's strategic goals by negotiations between the job's incumbent and the incumbent's supervisor. From these general objectives, specific performance objectives would be set for each job each year through negotiations between the incumbent and the incumbent's supervisor. The objectives would be multidimensional and would include performance objectives for all attributes of the job that are considered important.

The annual evaluation would reflect two dimensions of performance appraisal. First, the incumbent would be evaluated for innovation in developing ways of carrying out assigned responsibilities. Second, the incumbent's performance would be evaluated relative to the targets that were negotiated with the supervisor. Donna summarized her feelings as follows:

> The only thing that is holding me back is that I do not think that the proposed changes go far enough. The proposed system deals with the problem of inadequate performance measurement but still provides managers with incentives to understate their potential, since their performance will be evaluated relative to the targets that each manager

negotiates with his supervisor. Moreover, the planned system, like the old system, still has the aspect of checking up on people rather than relying on them to do their jobs. Perhaps we should go even further and implement the proposed system but only evaluate managers on their ability to be innovative in undertaking the tasks that they have been assigned. If they are not evaluated relative to the targets that they set jointly with their supervisors, they will be motivated not to understate their potential. The bottom line is that I think that we should get rid of the concept of standards altogether, irrespective of who sets the standards. As a result of eliminating the concept of standards, the budget will serve to communicate and coordinate rather than be a threat and a means of checking up on the managers.

Required:

Evaluate the initial proposal for the revision of the budgeting system as well as the proposal that would eliminate the use of standards.

17–10   *Individual Rewards versus Group Rewards*

Lake Erie Steel Products Limited is a large integrated steel-products firm producing a full line of steel products that are sold internationally.

The company is organized on a profit-center basis with the major primary profit centers being the coal mining operations, the iron ore mining operations, and the scrap steel operations. The major manufacturing profit centers are hot-rolled products, cold-rolled products, and shape products. The major finishing profit centers are fastener products, tube products, and specialty products.

The company has implemented a market-based transfer pricing system for every product that has a well-organized external market. This accounts for about 75% of the transfers that take place between the profit centers. The balance of transferred products are priced using a transfer price that consists of fixed fee plus standard variable cost.

The transfer-pricing system is used to evaluate profit-center performance along two dimensions. First, the profit center's controllable margin is used as an assessment of the performance of the manager. Second, the profit center's profit is used to evaluate the ongoing decision to continue the operations of the profit center or to abandon the profit center.

All the employees in the organization except the chairman, president, and vice-presidents participate in the corporate profit-sharing plan. (These individuals participate in a stock option plan instead.) The pool available for bonuses is based on corporate earnings and equals 10% of all corporate earnings in excess of the target level of earnings that is established for any particular year.

The performance of each profit center is evaluated, by the senior management committee, relative to its financial **and** operating goals. The overall performance of the profit center is rated as poor, acceptable, or outstanding. Performance values of 0, 0.25, and 1 are assigned to each of these qualitative ratings, respectively. Therefore, an overall profit center performance that is rated as acceptable is assigned a performance value of 0.25.

Next the individual performance of each employee is rated by the employee's supervisor. (In the case of the profit-center manager, the evaluation is done by the vice-president to whom the manager reports.) The employee's performance is evaluated relative to the objectives that the employee and his supervisor established for each job. There are, by design, exactly four attributes of each employee's job that are measured and evaluated. None of the four attributes is a financial measurement. The overall performance of the employee is rated as poor, acceptable, or outstanding and assigned the corresponding performance values of 0, 0.25, and 1.

The following sequence of calculations is then undertaken:

1. Sum the employee's profit-center performance rating and the individual's personal performance rating to determine the employee's aggregate performance measure.
2. Multiply each employee's aggregate performance measure by the employee's wages to determine the employee's weighted wages.
3. Sum the weighted wages of all the employees who are participants in the profit-sharing plan to compute a sum of weighted wages.
4. Divide the bonus pool available by the sum of weighted wages to determine the bonus per dollar of weighted wage.
5. Determine each employee's bonus by multiplying the employee's weighted wage by the bonus per dollar of weighted wage.

This calculation had resulted, on average, of bonuses of 18% of wages to be paid during the last five years.

Required:

Evaluate this incentive scheme discussing your impressions of its positive and negative aspects.

17–11   *Mitigating Factors in the Evaluation of Performance*

The Hogtown Mudcats, a professional baseball team, is located in Canada and plays in the Global Baseball League. The team is divided into three profit centers: operations, headed by the general manager of operations, which relates to the on-field activities and the scouting staff; marketing, headed by the general manager of marketing, which includes promotions, licensing and franchising of the team's trademark, and public relations; and administrative, headed by the general manager of administration, which includes all the administrative activities such as legal, accounting, negotiating leases, and payroll.

Typical of the industry, the general manager of operations is evaluated on the basis of the team's performance. The general manager of marketing is evaluated in terms of the revenues generated by the team. The general manager of administration is not subject to any specified performance measure but receives an overall evaluation from the team's president.

An important and serious issue facing the general manager of administration concerns salary arrangements for the players. By league decree, all the team players are to be paid in U.S. dollars. This represents a serious exchange rate exposure for the team, since most of the team's revenues are in Canadian dollars. During the past three years, the exchange rate has varied from $1US = $1.40CDN to $1US = $1.28CDN. The team payroll is about $25,000,000US annually.

At the beginning of each year, the annual payroll is projected in Canadian funds. The general manager of administration has been held responsible for any exchange rate fluctuations from the rate used to project the annual payroll. The general manager of administration has objected to this, saying, "Foreign currency speculation is not in my job description and, anyway, why should my evaluation be based on a risk that I cannot control?"

The team president responded: "This risk is a reality of life for our ball club and it must be managed and not ignored. We impose this risk on the general manager of administration for a purpose. It is his job to mitigate, or even take advantage of, the potential for exchange rate fluctuation."

Required:

Should the general manager of administration be responsible for managing the team's foreign currency exposure and, if so, how might this job be approached?

AUTHOR INDEX

SUBJECT INDEX

809